THE SUPR

This book presents a quantitative his_ ......utional law in the United
States and brings together humanistic and social-scientific approaches
to studying law. Using theoretical models of adjudication, Tom S. Clark
presents a statistical model of law and uses the model to document the
historical development of constitutional law. Using sophisticated statistical
methods and historical analysis of Court decisions, the author documents
how social and political forces shape the path of law. Spanning the history
of constitutional law since Reconstruction, this book illustrates the way in
which the law evolves with American life and argues that a social-scientific
approach to the history of law illuminates connections across disparate areas
of the law, connected by the social context in which the Constitution has
been interpreted.

Tom S. Clark is Charles Howard Candler Professor of Political Science at
Emory University. His research focuses on judicial decision-making and his
recent work has focused on the development of law. His first book, *The Limits
of Judicial Independence*, won the William Riker Award for the best book in
political economy from the American Political Science Association.

POLITICAL ECONOMY OF INSTITUTIONS AND DECISIONS

Series Editors

Jeffry Frieden, *Harvard University*
John Patty, *Emory University*
Elizabeth Maggie Penn, *Emory University*

Founding Editors

James E. Alt, *Harvard University*
Douglass C. North, *Washington University of St. Louis*

Other books in the series

(*continued after the Index*)

THE SUPREME COURT

An Analytic History of Constitutional Decision Making

TOM S. CLARK

Emory University, Atlanta

CAMBRIDGE
UNIVERSITY PRESS

CAMBRIDGE
UNIVERSITY PRESS

University Printing House, Cambridge CB2 8BS, United Kingdom

One Liberty Plaza, 20th Floor, New York, NY 10006, USA

477 Williamstown Road, Port Melbourne, VIC 3207, Australia

314–321, 3rd Floor, Plot 3, Splendor Forum, Jasola District Centre, New Delhi – 110025, India

79 Anson Road, #06-04/06, Singapore 079906

Cambridge University Press is part of the University of Cambridge.

It furthers the University's mission by disseminating knowledge in the pursuit of education, learning, and research at the highest international levels of excellence.

www.cambridge.org
Information on this title: www.cambridge.org/9781108422765
DOI: 10.1017/9781108525367

First published 2019

Printed and bound in Great Britain by Clays Ltd, Elcograf S.p.A.

A catalogue record for this publication is available from the British Library.

Library of Congress Cataloging-in-Publication Data
Names: Clark, Thomas S., 1980–, author.
Title: The Supreme Court : an analytic history of constitutional decision making / Tom S. Clark, Charles Howard Candler Professor, Department of Political Science, Emory University.
Description: New York : Cambridge University Press, 2019. |
Includes bibliographical references and index.
Identifiers: LCCN 2018040082 | ISBN 9781108422765 (hardback) |
ISBN 9781108436939 (pbk.)
Subjects: LCSH: United States. Supreme Court. | Constitutional law–United States–Decision making. | Judicial process–Social aspects–United States.
Classification: LCC KF8742.C53 2019 | DDC 347.73/2609–dc23
LC record available at https://lccn.loc.gov/2018040082

ISBN 978-1-108-42276-5 Hardback
ISBN 978-1-108-43693-9 Paperback

For Madeleine and Isabelle

Contents in Brief

Contents

Figures

Tables

Acknowledgments

Scholarly work is often lonely but never an individual pursuit, and so it is important that the first step in a book is to thank those to whom one is indebted. Unfortunately, if I were to adequately thank those who made this book possible, I would run out of time and space before getting to the first chapter. However, I will try, humbly, to acknowledge those who have taught, guided, and encouraged me along the way.

The first and most obvious thanks goes to my co-author, Ben Lauderdale. Just over a decade ago, we were office neighbors, and at that point we began what turned out to be a twisting intellectual journey. Ben taught me a lot about measurement theory and was a driving force behind many of the innovations we proposed. This book represents a culmination in the broader substantive points I'd hoped to make through the collaborations we shared. Without his support, this would not have been possible.

The second person I want to thank is Barry Weingast. Barry told me, in a rather matter-of-fact way, to write this book. We sat down to dinner, Barry ordered a pretty good bottle of Gigondas and said, "Wouldn't it be interesting if constitutional law could be described with a small handful of dimensions? I'll bet it can, and you should write a book about it." That was years ago now, but the seed he planted was certainly the origin of this book. I take all of the blame for what you are about to read, but I credit him with the genesis.

Third, I must thank Chuck Cameron. Since I was just a young graduate student, Chuck has been a consistent, thoughtful, engaged, and curious advisor. He helped me think through the right way to write this book and read, at his usual level of impressive depth, many drafts. Whether he was calling me on Skype from Tokyo or meeting me in New York, Chuck has been supportive of this project and helpful in its development since the very beginning. During a year in Princeton, he encouraged me to make progress but also made me pace myself with his cooking, wine, and scotch. I am fortunate to have him as a friend, mentor, and teacher, and anyone else would be lucky to have such a stand-up scholar in their corner.

I also owe a debt of gratitude to The Center for the Study of Democratic Politics (CSDP) at Princeton. I was on leave from Emory during the 2015-2016 academic year, and they offered me a wonderful position as a visiting scholar. This was a "coming home" of sorts, as CSDP was the place where I worked in graduate school and where Ben and I began that collaboration years ago. Markus Prior, who was directing CSDP, helped create the kind of nurturing intellectual space that can only help one's creativity and productivity. The other fellows at CSDP that year, Vin Arceneaux, Rachel Stein, and Chloe, Bakalar provided intellectual stimulation, warm comradery, and a small degree of liver damage. Of course, Michele Epstein made it all possible. There are not enough words to say about her helpfulness, thoughtfulness, support, and friendship.

The Institute for Advanced Study in Toulouse also provided a vibrant, welcoming, and productive place for me to work on this book during the summer of 2016. After finishing my year at Princeton, I of course found myself with the need for more time to sit and keep pushing at it until my return to regular life at Emory. I had the great opportunity to find such a welcoming and comfortable place.

My colleagues back home at Emory have been indispensable. From the beginning, Jeff Staton and Adam Glynn have served as the kind of sounding boards that make academics a great career. Jeff, in particular, dealt with the brunt of the lows and suffered dealing with me during the highs. He's the sort of colleague anyone would want to have and one of the most supportive friends I could hope for. Adam is an incredibly curious, insightful, sharp, and friendly person. He has taught me much and provided invaluable feedback that shaped this project in important ways. Greg Martin posed good questions from the beginning and helped me think through some complicated points. Tom Walker and Micheal Giles offered intellectual guidance and insight as only they can provide. The rest of the department has similarly helped me think through the scope of this project and has tolerated my inattention to other obligations as I have worked through this project. The administration at Emory provided me with a sabbatical year at Princeton, which was essential for my ability to write this book. Rob O'Reilly, the genius who works at the library, helped me locate data I never could have imagined existed and reaffirmed his place as one of the most helpful people at the University.

Outside of Emory, others have been especially supportive. Ken Benoit made much of this work more efficient and powerful – he did not just write software, though – he talked me through a number of issues related to text analysis and helped me make judgment calls in which I can be confident. Jeff Jenkins was very supportive and helpful as I began to dig into the world of quantitative history.

As the project neared completion, Lewis Kornhauser organized a conference at which I was treated to a day of thoughtful feedback from some of the smartest people you can encounter: Deborah Beim, Ryan Bubb, Chuck Cameron, John Ferejohn, Sandy Gordon, Dan Huselbosch, John Kastellec, Dimitri Landa, Jeff Lax, Anna Harvey, Deborah Malamud, Howard Rosenthal, Pasquale Pasquino, and Melissa Schwartzberg all provided their precious time and invaluable feedback and guidance. They all saw the strengths and kindly pointed out the weaknesses. Again, I take the blame for the remaining limitations and credit these kind and smart people with getting the book where it is today.

I like to save the best for last, and for me, that's my family. Foremost, my wife, Leigh Anne, who has made not just this book, but my entire career, possible. Her patience can only be described as saintly and seemingly limitless. When I had a sabbatical year, she and my daughters tolerated me going to Princeton during some of these weeks. When we went on vacations, they tolerated me having my nose in a laptop. When I was frustrated and burned out, they made me laugh and offered to help. My daughters, Madeleine and Isabelle, to whom I dedicate the book, create the kinds of distractions I need. Isabelle is always asking if she can press some buttons on the computer. (It doesn't seem to matter how I respond, though.) Madeleine has sat next to me while doing her own writing. What better way is there to write a book than with those two at your side?

I

The History of Constitutional Law: Inside and Outside

This is a book about the way social conditions affect the path of constitutional law. In particular, my goal is to document the relationship between various political, cultural, and social phenomena and the way the Supreme Court decides constitutional questions. That evidence will help us understand when, how, and why political, cultural, and social events shape the content of American constitutional law.

At its core, this book argues for a middle ground between two intellectual traditions in the study of Supreme Court decision making. Political scientists often reduce legal decision making into the kind of unidimensional, partisan cleavage that characterizes legislative policy making. Lawyers and legal academics, on the other hand, typically organize constitutional law into doctrines focused on the legal analysis or procedures that guide judicial decision making. I argue that constitutional decision making is more complex than a simple, traditional left-right political cleavage, but neither is it a collection of substantive doctrines that can only (or best) be understood through the perspective of legal argumentation and the substantive problems that arise in the law. Rather, because constitutional law is a form of higher-order politics, the terms of debates in constitutional cases before the Court are different from other kinds of political debates.

What I argue is that constitutional decision making is best characterized by a small handful of political cleavages that correspond to substantive elements of constitutional politics. That is, judges' views on how to resolve constitutional disputes are multidimensional. I show in this book that while there are systematic, consistent, political patterns in how judges decide constitutional cases, the substantive and legal context in which a case is framed matters for how the judges decide these questions. One way in which social conditions influence the path of constitutional law is through the role they play in shaping the nature of the cases that come before the courts. For example, when crime rates increase, criminals and law enforcement officials behave differently, giving rise to new kinds of disputes and constitutional questions. Moreover, as I document in this book, social, political, and cultural events shape not just what kinds of cases judges decide but also the context in which they decide those cases and, thereby, the political cleavages that characterize constitutional decision making.

By approaching the history of constitutional decision making as I do, one can uncover historical patterns and empirical phenomena that do not emerge from more traditional historical analyses. For example, I show substantively nuanced but systematic patterns in Supreme Court justices' preferences across seemingly unrelated areas of the law. By combining historical and substantive richness with rigorous social-scientific methods of analysis, I suggest a middle ground between historical description and parsimonious explanation. In addition, the analytic techniques I employ facilitate the construction of counter-factual examples on which claims about causal factors in historical events necessarily must rely.

To illustrate how this process plays out, consider a salient yet instructive example.

1.1   A MOTIVATING EXAMPLE

Perhaps one of the most widely discussed events in the history of American constitutional law is Justice Owen Roberts' decision to vote to uphold a Washington State minimum wage law in 1937. The justices were closely divided, splitting 5-4 in favor of the legislation. However, what made the decision notable was that a year earlier, the same justices had voted, again 5-4, to *strike down* a New York minimum wage law. In the short period of time between those two cases, Justice Roberts had seemingly changed his mind about the constitutionality of state-enacted minimum wage laws. Why the sudden change of opinion? Why, in the context of Progressive efforts to regulate the economy and recovery from the Great Depression, had he changed his opinion about such an important constitutional matter?

Among social scientists and many legal academics, a popular account, which has been called the *externalist* account, attributes Justice Roberts' change in vote to the politics of the time. In November 1936, after the Court had invalidated the New York law, New Deal Democrats won a landslide election. Following that election, in February 1937, President Roosevelt announced the so-called "Court-packing plan," which was a legislative proposal that would allow the president to appoint additional justices to the Supreme Court. The legislation's purported goal was to alleviate workload pressure the justices faced. According to Roosevelt, the justices faced large caseloads, and the aging of some of the older justices made it difficult for them to keep up with their work. (The justices denied this allegation in testimony to Congress.)

However, despite the public presentation, most politicians and the media perceived the legislation's true aim to be more political. The true motivation for the legislation was to dilute the votes of those justices who opposed federal economic regulation and recovery efforts. Specifically, there were four justices, known pejoratively as the "Four Horsemen," who had either ideological or doctrinal opposition to the New Deal Democrats' legislative agenda. By giving Roosevelt the power to appoint additional justices, who would surely be more supportive of his agenda, the legislation would nullify their ability to invalidate New Deal legislation.

Just weeks later, the Court announced its decision upholding the Washington State law. The sequencing of these events led contemporary observers and scholars during the decades since, to attribute Justice Roberts' switch in vote to a political calculation that if the Court continued to block progressive economic legislation, a constitutional crisis could erupt as the Democrats would use control of the government to undermine judicial power altogether. Subsequently dubbed the "switch in time that saved nine," Justice Roberts' change in opinion has emerged as a quintessential example of strategic calculation at the Court in anticipation of the broader political climate in which the justices operate. That is, the events of 1937 are seen, in this view, as an example of how constitutional law can be driven by politics and inter-institutional dynamics.

However, this account has been challenged by some who favor an account of Justice Roberts' change in opinion that is driven more by forces internal to the law. In this view, which has been called the *internalist* account, the difference between Justice Roberts' vote in 1936 and his vote in 1937 is time and the corresponding evolution in doctrine that was taking place. Constitutional law had been evolving during the early decades of the twentieth century and, in this view, by the time the Washington State law made it to the Court, the doctrinal connections among related areas of law had been made in such a way as to establish the foundations for permitting states to regulate wages (for a canonical discussion of these developments in constitutional law, see Cushman 1998).

What is more, not only do these internally based accounts document a clear pattern in the steady progression of doctrine, they also make note of historical facts that undermine the plausibility of the more political story. Specifically, Cushman (1998, 18) points out that Justice Roberts' vote could not be attributed to a reaction to the Court-packing plan, because he actually cast his vote in December 1936. The Court-packing plan had been held in close confidence by Roosevelt and his advisors, and it was not possible that Roberts was aware of the proposal. Thus, in the internal account's view, there are both reasons to see the change in Justice Roberts' vote as a part of a doctrinal process that had been taking place for a number of years and reasons to doubt the external account's emphasis on strategic political calculation in response to the Court-packing plan.

Of course, it is possible that Roberts was sensitive to the broader climate, including the Democrats' electoral victory in November 1936 and the great deal of criticism of the Court that had been taking place during the election year (see, for example Clark 2011). Despite that possibility, one thing is clear, the notion that Roberts' vote can be understood as a calculation in direct response to the Court-packing plan.

In this book, I provide an approach to the history of constitutional law that yields a new understanding of the switch in time as well as broad, more regular patterns in the evolution of law. As I show in the following chapters, the path of American constitutional law can be understood as a process whereby social conditions shape how cases are presented to the Court and, in turn, the dimension of conflict along which the justices divide.

I show, for example, that the change in Justice Roberts' vote in the minimum wage laws can be explained by a shift in how the question was presented to and framed by the justices. In 1936, the justices viewed the question more as a matter of the appropriate policies to deal with the on-going crisis that began with the Great Depression, voting along a dimension that corresponded to the justices' tastes for government authority in economic regulation. However, by 1937, a conscious decision was made by the lawyers litigating the case to recast the question as a matter of the appropriate degree of deference to states in matters of such regulation. Indeed, the Court's opinions in the later case reflect this shift. And, I show later that Justice Roberts' vote reflects a broader, systematic pattern in which Justice Roberts was more likely to side with the progressive members of the Court in cases that were dominantly about matters of federalism.

In this book, I argue that in order to understand the path of constitutional law through American history, we must examine broad, systematic forces that come from outside of the Court and the ways in which they shape the internal dynamics among the justices themselves. Regarding the switch-in-time example, then, the model of constitutional law development I adopt is one of a middle ground between the externalist and internalist accounts. In my view, the switch can be understood as part of an internal evolution, but that internal evolution itself was fueled by forces from outside of the Court. Social conditions met with clever lawyering to provide Justice Roberts both the will and the way to revisit his earlier stance on the matter of state minimum wage laws.

The question remains, how typical are examples such as this? How precisely do external social conditions systematically interact with internal decision making to shape law? How can we document such patterns?

I.2   A MODEL OF LEGAL DEVELOPMENT

These questions raise a set of challenges that I hope to address here. The first question goes to the heart of my over arching goal: how do we approach history from a social-scientific, quantitative, analytic, historical perspective? One claim I make is that inference from empirical observation – historical or otherwise – must be grounded in a theory of the underlying process. Biologists often make inferences about the purpose of an animal's attributes or behavior that are valid because they share an underlying theory of evolution. Social scientists, in contrast to natural scientists, are less likely to share a theory of human behavior that can be used to interpret choices we observe individuals make. It is therefore incumbent upon the analyst to specify how a process is purported to operate before evaluating what patterns in the data mean. This is no less true of studies of the law than any other area of social science.

To document the path of constitutional law and its interaction with internal and external social and political forces, I adopt a fairly simple but straight-forward model of the judicial process.[1] I focus the US Supreme Court, but the essential process I outline here applies to any court that might be engaged in law development, such as state courts of last resort or the US courts of appeal. There are five elements to this model. First, social conditions give rise to disputes that generate cases. Those cases are of a limited set of types. Second, a case's type determines what kind of preference cleavage it creates among judges. Third, I argue that judicial preferences are multidimensional, and judges may line up differently in any given case, according to which dimensions are activated by the case. Fourth, the location of the median justice determines which disposition the Court chooses for each case (i.e., which litigant wins). Fifth, after

---

[1] I use the term model here in an informal sense. While throughout the book I rely on formalized models of various aspects of the judicial process, my overarching perspective is less formal and instead simply meant to outline the broad structure I use to evaluate and describe the path of constitutional law.

deciding on a disposition, the justices engage in collegial interaction to determine the content of the various opinions that will be written.

The factors that influence the path of constitutional law, given this model of judicial decision making, vary along two dimensions of interest here. The first concerns the nature of the causal force. At its crux, the challenge facing social-scientific history is about the balance between understanding general patterns that in the long run describe society versus a commitment to understanding the uniqueness of particular events. Often, this is framed as a tension between structure and agency (or contingency). Structure refers to the broad forces that push behavior into a common pattern, whereas agency refers to the particular features of individual actors and time-specific context that ultimately determine one's choices when structure is (as it usually is) not completely determinant.

The reason this distinction is particularly relevant for social-scientific history is that by its very nature, historical inquiry seeks to understand how events that take place over time relate to one another. When we consider the history of the law, on one hand, there is good reason to believe large structural forces have significant consequences for the development of law over time. The procedures by which courts resolve individual cases are generally constant, or at least well understood by the individuals within those institutions, and so create substantial incentives for litigants who bring cases (e.g., Baird 2004), judges who select which cases to resolve (e.g., Callander and Clark 2017; Beim, Clark, and Patty 2017), and how rules are built over time (e.g., Gennaioli and Shleifer 2007; Lax 2007; Kornhauser 1992a). At the same time, particular events taking place both at the courts and beyond can have dramatic effects on the creation of consequential precedents. Consider the "separate but equal" doctrine articulated in *Plessy* v. *Ferguson* or the wide discretion given to Congress to regulate commerce after the constitutional confrontation between FDR and the Supreme Court during the New Deal era. Obviously, those examples are historically salient and highly dependent upon particular contingencies and conditions when they took place. Thus, the question becomes, how does one develop a historical account of the development of constitutional law that is both grounded in rigorous theory about the effects of institutions and politics – i.e., that is grounded in general first principles – while also accounting for the most significant and substantively important events in the course of legal development?

A number of examples from other contexts provide some guidance. For example, Greif's (2006) study of the emergence of institutions for trade in the Medieval era suggests that one way of understanding seemingly unique, consequential events is as the culmination of processes that take place slowly over time under the force of structural factors. Greif shows how economic behavior among traders created incentives for them to build institutions that could facilitate cooperation. Greif's account places specific contingencies – the technological and economic conditions at the time – at the center of the causal path driving the establishment of new institutions. Those institutions would then subsequently have powerful systematic influences on commerce and trading behavior. In other words, specific contingencies can be accounted for as part of a systematic theory when that theory accounts for the ways in which structural incentives can recursively reinforce (or undermine) themselves, ultimately leading to periods of stability or seemingly abrupt changes (e.g., Pierson 2000; Page et al. 2006; Weingast 2005). The role for each of these types of considerations depends, seemingly obviously, on the goals of the historical analysis.

The second dimension of factors that shape constitutional law is the locus of analytic attention. One class of theories of constitutional decision making emphasize *internal* politics. That is, the primary driving force behind judicial decisions and the content of constitutional law is located within the judiciary itself. The justices' own ideological and legal views, the decision-making institutions, existing doctrine, and the like constitute the best perspective for understanding why the courts shape constitutional law as they do. Some work in both traditional behavioral and institutional as well as doctrinal perspectives on constitutional law emphasizes these internal forces. One of the most successful theories of judicial decision making, the Attitudinal Model (Segal and Spaeth 2002), specifically emphasizes judicial attitudes over forces external to the courts. Many legal histories emphasize the path of doctrine and interpretation within the courts.

Another class of theories, however, places the locus of analytic attention outside of the courts. Constitutional litigation is driven in this view by the emergence of conflicts or disputes from real-world interactions among people. That litigation forms the basis for the cases that the courts confront and therefore sets the agenda for constitutional decision making. In conjunction with electoral politics, which influence the individual justices who serve on the courts, the content of the legislation they interpret, and the institutional incentives the justices face, those social conditions also shape the ways in which the justices approach cases and the decisions they make. These approaches have much in common with sociological and functionalist theories, which emphasize the influence of social and political forces (e.g., Horwitz 1992).

Putting together these two dimensions of historical analyses – the nature and locus of influences on the law – we can summarize the various

Table 1.1. *Examples of factors influencing constitutional law.*

		Nature	
		Structural	Contingent
Locus	Internal	*Judicial Institutions* Collegial courts with majority rule	*Judicial Behavior* Individual preferences
	External	*Social Structure* Separation of powers	*Social Conditions* Electoral politics

Each cell shows examples of factors influencing constitutional decision making, according to their locus (interval v. external) and nature (structural v. contingent).

approaches to constitutional history as follows. One class of explanations for the path of constitutional law is *Judicial Institutions*. This class of explanation focuses on structural factors located within the courts. These factors include the rule that American law-making courts, such as the Supreme Court, are collegial (i.e., composed of multiple judges) and decide cases by majority rule. Another class of explanations, which we might call *Judicial Behavior*, focuses on contingent factors located within the courts. These factors include many of the causal explanations that occupy much of the research on judicial decision making, such as the profile of preferences among the justices who serve on the Supreme Court at any given time. I label the third class of explanations *Social Conditions*, which focuses on particular contingencies outside of the courts at any given point in time. For example, the electoral environment and economic conditions, which affect the cases that come to the courts, are typical examples of causal factors that drive the path of constitutional law from this perspective. Finally, *Social Structure* explanations focus on structural, institutional forces that exist beyond the courts. Theories of the separation of powers, which emphasize institutional checks and balances or federalism, focus on the effects of the constitutional structure and elite-level politics on how judges resolve constitutional cases. Table 1.1 summarizes these types of explanations and provides examples of the types of factors that influence constitutional law from the perspective of each.

Returning, then, to my five-step model of constitutional decision making, we can consider the stages at which we expect different theoretical approaches to judicial politics to affect the path of constitutional law. Structural-internal forces will be likely to affect the collective decision making among the justices at the Court. Contingent-internal forces will be likely to affect how individual justices view particular cases – i.e., the extent to which the preference cleavage activated by a case matters for how the justices' align themselves when voting. Structural-external forces will be likely to affect how litigants, lawyers, and other branches of government interact with the Court. Contingent-external forces will be likely to affect the kinds of cases and disputes that make their way to the Court. Of course, there will be ways in which multiple kinds of forces influence various aspects of the judicial process, but this rough organization imposes modest structure on how we should interpret various empirical patterns in constitutional decision making.

1.3 EXPLANATION OR DESCRIPTION?

I wrote above that articulating a model of the judicial process is the first challenge to addressing questions about how the law systematically evolves with social conditions. A second challenge – indeed, perhaps one more daunting – requires me to adopt a perspective on what the historical record *can* tell us about the role social conditions play in shaping the law. Contemporary political science has witnessed renewed attention being paid to the validity of our claims about causal relationships among potential influences. In light of that revolution, I must be clear about what in my analysis I intend to be explanatory (and, therefore causal in nature) and what I intend to be merely descriptive. Both description and explanation have important roles in documenting the history of constitutional law, but their utility depends in part on drawing crisp lines between which is which.

My goal is to strike something of a middle ground. Part of the challenge is that a sixth element of the model of judicial decision making I lay out above is that judicial opinions subsequently affect the way in which people behave and the kinds of disputes that arise in society. With that step, we necessarily have a circular path whereby, roughly speaking, judicial decisions affect social conditions, which affect judicial decisions.[2] That circularity is going to pose a significant challenge to studying the effects of either judicial decisions or social conditions. As a consequence, much of what I am able to accomplish in this book is descriptive in nature. I will show systematic patterns in how judges decide cases and how social conditions are related to those decisions.

---

[2] Along with two co-authors, I have argued that the decision to step in and resolve a legal question itself can be influenced by the justices' expectations about how the Court's decision will influence future litigation (Beim, Clark, and Patty 2017).

However, as we will see, historical accidents and careful empirical designs can occasionally allow some insight into the question, how much are social forces affecting the path of law? For example, during the late nineteenth century, the Second Industrial Revolution contributed to a significant change in the American economy. Large corporations emerged that reached across wide geographical areas, crossing state boundaries. Middle management emerged as a common form of industrial organization. In turn, new types of commercial conflicts arose, and the federal government's role in economic regulation took on a qualitatively different form. While the unification of the national economy was affected by the structure and content of American law at the time, there were certainly effects that were attributable to the exogenous changes in technology, such as the development of railroads. Similarly, the human rights atrocities of the mid-twentieth century had an effect on how the justices evaluated constitutional questions, as did the rise of terrorism in the early twenty-first century. In subsequent chapters, I exploit these and other events to show how constitutional law is shaped by social conditions more systematically.

The consequence is that the analyses in this book, taken together, illustrate the connections among political and social forces and the path of constitutional law. Taken together, I believe they jointly provide evidence for my claim that constitutional law must be understood as a product of the history of American society but also illustrate empirical patterns for which no existing theory of law-making can fully account. Therein lies the goal of my analytic-historical approach. It is neither fully analytic nor fully historical but rather a blend of two intellectual traditions that can provide new fodder for students of law in myriad disciplines.

1.4   THE SCOPE OF THIS PROJECT

My goal is to document the way in which social and political forces, both inside and outside of the Court, are related to and affect the path of constitutional law. This is an admittedly ambitious objective, and I hope to make a meaningful contribution to how scholars understand the body of constitutional law. As such, I study a variety of institutional features of the Supreme Court, focusing typically on the preferences of the justices who serve on the Supreme Court, the relationship between the Court and other branches of government, and the Court's internal procedures.

As the above description of my model of the judicial process makes clear, though, I do not have a particular model of the *content* of the opinions the justices produce. In subsequent chapters, I often focus on the relative conservatism or liberalism of the median justice as a proxy for the policy content of the Court's opinions. Of course, I do not mean to endorse the claim that the median justice controls the content of the Court's constitutional doctrine.

Rather, I focus on the median justice because a broad class of theoretical models implicates the median justice. For example, some models predict the median justice controls the content of all Court opinions, because competing factions on either side will vie for the median's support. Other classes of model suggest that opinion content is a function of the preferences of those justices voting in the majority, and the median justice's relative conservatism or liberalism is a reasonable proxy for the ideological orientation of the voting blocs on any given Court. Independent of precisely *which* model of opinion writing one subscribes to, the location of the median justice is a rough proxy for the center of power on the Court and, therefore, the nature of the Court's doctrine over time.

Beyond the internal processes at the Court, I also study a broad range of social phenomena, including economic factors, sociological events, and politics. In this way, the analytic history of constitutional decision making I present has implications for an age-old debate about the meaning of the Constitution. Is constitutional law simply a conservative force that restrains the ability of political majorities to change the rules that govern us? Is the Constitution a binding contract under which the views of the Founders dictate the resolution to the most pressing problems facing contemporary America? Or, instead, is the Constitution a living document that grows with and responds to the nature of American society?

However, while the kinds of analyses I offer are connected to those larger debates in the scholarly literature, it is beyond the scope of this project to speak directly to that line of inquiry, which is primarily normative in nature. Rather, I anticipate that the history I document provides additional empirical fodder for the normative debate about the proper way to apply the Constitution to modern disputes.

1.5 A ROADMAP TO THE BOOK

In the remainder of this book, I lay out an analytic history of constitutional decision making that builds from the considerations I have described here. Chapter 2 describes four main intellectual traditions in the study of constitutional law —doctrinal approaches that are dominant in the legal academy, behavioral approaches most common in political science, political development approaches most common in history, and institutional approaches most common in economics and political economy. The chapter then describes a theoretically grounded empirical approach to studying microprocesses of judicial decision making and macropatterns in constitutional law and identifies the particular features of law and constitutional decision making we need to analyze.

Chapter 3 introduces the statistical model I use through the rest of the book to analyze patterns in constitutional decision making. The model was first developed and published with my co-author Ben Lauderdale and is designed to uncover the dimensionality of judicial preferences (Lauderdale and Clark 2014). Standard models of political preferences typically summarize voting behavior by political actors – legislators, judges, etc. – and seek to recover a latent dimension of ideology. I show how those models relate to theoretical models of judicial behavior, most notably the case-space model (e.g., Cameron 1993; Kornhauser 1992*b*; Lax 2011), and describe the logic and formal definition of the model I use here. To preview, the model assumes that the dimensions of a decision can best be estimated using the text of judicial opinions and that the votes reveal the preference ordering along the relevant dimensions. At various points, the chapter has technical content, though I strive to make the presentation accessible to the non-technical reader. The chapter concludes with a discussion of the various quantities of interest we can derive from the model for the purposes of the analytic history.

Chapter 4 introduces the data to be used in estimating the model described in Chapter 3. There are three components. First, the chapter describes the set of cases that comprise the body of constitutional law. I rely on the Congressional Research Service's ("CRS") report, *The Constitution of the United States of America: Analysis and Interpretation* (Thomas 2014), which is a comprehensive treatment of all case law interpreting the Constitution, updated regularly by the CRS. Second, the chapter describes the justices who participated in constitutional interpretation and the votes they cast in those cases. To identify these data, I rely on the Supreme Court Database (Spaeth et al. 2015), which is the bedrock of contemporary quantitative empirical research on Supreme Court decisions. Only recently has this database been backdated from the 1940s back through the Founding. Third, the chapter describes the opinions written in the constitutional law cases – the distribution of types of opinions across cases and over time, as well as the basic content, length, and other relevant details. Taken together, these data represent the first aggregate, quantitative evaluation of the major patterns in constitutional case law over such a long period of time.

Chapter 5 begins the analytic component of the project, applying the statistical model described in Chapter 3 to the data described in Chapter 4. The chapter reports a number of findings that guide the remainder of the book. First, the analysis of voting patterns in constitutional law cases suggests there are roughly six distinct ideological preference dimensions. Importantly, these are distinct from particular substantive provisions in the Constitution but instead represent preference dimensions onto which substantive legal questions are mapped in any given context. Moreover, as we will see, any given legal policy question can be mapped onto multiple preference dimensions at the same time, and that mapping can change over time, as legal questions activate different political cleavages. Roughly, though, the ideological preference dimensions can be labeled. They are: Judicial Power, Economics and Business, Central Authority, Balance of Power, Crime and Punishment, and Individual and Civil Rights. Finally, the chapter evaluates important aspects of these topics and preference dimensions, showing how the preference alignment among the justices varies across topics at any given point in time and how changes in the Court's composition – through departures and nominations – affects different preference dimensions differently.

Chapters 6 and 7 take the aggregate patterns and description of constitutional decision making and use them to interpret the content of constitutional law since Reconstruction. Chapter 6 examines the period from Reconstruction through to 1937, and Chapter 7 examines the late-1930s through to 2012. This division of time is practical. In order to organize the historical content, it is best to divide constitutional history into discrete periods where important events trigger what are essentially structural breaks in the politics of constitutional decision making. Importantly, I do not go in search of "critical junctures" but rather trace the evolution of constitutional politics from Reconstruction, when the Constitution was radically reformed through the New Deal, to when the Constitution – specifically judicial interpretation of the Constitution – was again dramatically reformed.

The historical analysis uncovers a number of features in the development of constitutional law. First, we see that up through the Second Industrial Revolution, most constitutional questions were mapped onto a preference dimension that is characterized by preferences over judicial power. This represents the historical legacy of constitutional doctrine from the Founding through to the Civil War. However, as the economy unified, large corporations came into existence and the nature of commerce – both what commerce was and its role in American society – changed dramatically. The Court began, then, to interpret questions of commercial activity in light of an orthogonal preference dimension, and the precedents it established would affect the way in which it confronted new questions about the relationship between the national and state governments, especially during the Roaring Twenties and the Great Depression.

Following the collapse of the economy in 1929 and the New Deal Democrats' efforts, led by President Roosevelt, to strengthen national (and executive) power, the Court found itself confronted with a new host of questions that organized interests framed to implicate alternative preference dimensions. The nature of constitutional law changed dramatically in light of those policy debates and the constitutional litigation to which they gave rise. Through the remainder of the Twentieth Century, then, the Court began to sort cases into multiple preference dimensions, most notably distinguishing between the way it approaches the growing role of criminal law in constitutional law from regulation of non-criminal activity. As we see in Chapter 7, one of the major struggles among the Court, the national and state governments, and organized interests was whether and how to characterize individual behavior as implicating criminal, as opposed to civil, rights.

Finally in Chapter 8, I take a step back from the details that occupy Chapters 5 through 7. I return to the broader goal of the project to lay the foundations for an analytic history of constitutional decision making. I offer some thoughts about what the exercise here demonstrates about how we can study the myriad forces that shape political decision making, and I reflect on the integration of micropolitics with macropatterns in history. I show how the simultaneous consideration of external and internal forces on constitutional law allows for a richer and deeper understanding of both the how and why behind the path of constitutional law. My goal in this chapter is not to offer a final word on how constitutional decision making has played out in American history but rather to call for a sustained analytic treatment of American constitutional history. Or, at least I hope to do so.

2

Modeling Constitutional Doctrine

How the Constitution works, how political and legal actors have interpreted it and applied it, and what constitutional law means for democratic performance are questions that run deep in the study of politics. What is the relationship between constitutional law and what we might think of as more conventional politics? And, how does the politics of constitutional law making play out through the dynamics of governance? How does law shape, if at all, the types of questions and battles that play out in the application of law? *How do social and political movements shape constitutional decision making? How do the Court's internal politics shape constitutional decision making? How do those internal and external forces interact?* In this chapter, I briefly survey a small number of intellectual traditions concerned with constitutional law, drawing from each distinct lessons for how we approach the politics of judicial decision making. I then describe the approach to constitutional law that motivates the analysis in this book – conceiving of politics as a force that maps legal questions and disputes into a manageable number of cleavages or conflicts. With that description in hand, I review the features of law that are relevant for my approach, drawing our insights from the main intellectual traditions for studying law and describe the ways in which scholars have attempted to empirically measure those features of law.

2.1 STUDYING CONSTITUTIONAL LAW: APPROACHES AND BARRIERS

The origins of the study of constitutional law lie deep in the history of government. At least as far back as Medieval England, legal theorists were contemplating the limits of government authority. Those legal theorists in the sixteenth and seventeenth century – among whom Edward Coke is one of the most famous – asserted there exists a higher law that trumps otherwise legitimate acts of government (e.g., Corwin 1929). Through that era, lawyers, judges, and scholars began to develop principles of limited governmental power that would form the basis for modern constitutional theory and the method of constitutional inquiry. Perhaps most notable among the intellectual thrusts of time was a sustained commitment to developing a coherent and complete doctrine of the *king's prerogative* (e.g., Goebel 1938). Central to this intellectual development was the idea that there exists a point of reference – a body of higher, natural law that can be interpreted in the context of individual disputes. As legal theory shifted away from natural law and more towards man-made law that can serve as higher law, the lack of a single constitutional document in England led to the development of a body of constitutional law based on history and case law. Thus, the method of common law reasoning and adjudication emerged.

In the United States, the subject of this book, the Constitution is the formal higher law, serving as the bedrock of our principles of legislating and litigating under the limited powers of the state. However, at the time of the Founding, judges and lawyers had only their experience with the English system of law and their knowledge of other systems through history. As a consequence, their methods of reasoning needed to come into line with the form of government based on a single written constitutional document. The result was a steadily developing constitutional theory and body of law that has been studied from a variety of intellectual perspectives and traditions that have changed over time. Here, I briefly describe four dominant approaches to studying constitutional law before turning to the theoretical orientation to constitutional law I develop.

Of course, there are many intellectual traditions to studying law, in disciplines as diverse as philosophy, political science, sociology, anthropology, history, and, of course, traditional vocational legal training. Among these traditions, we also find different intellectual commitments and goals. Here, my goal is to analyze constitutional law as a positive matter, rather than a normative one. That is, whereas important and consequential analyses have been motivated to explain what the law *should* be, given some social welfare objectives, our focus here is on the analysis of what the law is, how it works, and how judges decide cases. Obviously, the normative analyses are of great importance, but it is only with an understanding of law as a positive phenomenon can we begin to make normative prescriptions. It is my goal to contribute to that positive inquiry.

2.1.1 *The US Constitution, Its Elements, and Judicial Interpretation*

The traditional method to studying, teaching, and categorizing constitutional law derives directly from the intellectual legal traditions of the Middle Ages. Scholars, judges, and lawyers read the law, read cases decided under the law, and decipher principles that emerge from and unite the history of constitutional questions – and answers. In other words, this approach to studying constitutional law might be thought of as doctrinal and is the main method of studying law, including constitutional law, taught in law schools.

Indeed, if you ask people where you could learn about constitutional law, I expect many, if not most, would say, "law school." And, in fact, law schools are the primary place where you can study law, and the study of constitutional law has a place of particular importance in modern legal training. Part of the standard curriculum in law school, "con law" touches on most of the substantive and political problems that first attract students' attention. When taught to undergraduate students (usually, in political science departments), constitutional law ranges from topics such as civil liberties and civil rights to substantive due process, to modern privacy law, to procedural due process, and beyond. In law schools, constitutional law curricula place more emphasis on the organization of government, the distribution of powers across the branches, and federalism. In these traditions, constitutional law is studied from a doctrinal perspective. The question asked in most analyses is: what does the Constitution say about a given dispute, and how has it been interpreted in other contexts by previous courts?

As indicated, past cases are of central importance, primarily for their interpretations of the Constitution. What did a past court say the Fourth Amendment means in that past case? How relevant is that interpretation for the current case? The dominant method of legal reasoning involves analogizing from past cases, applying the interpretations, principles, or rules from those cases to the new ones (e.g., Levi 1949). Of course, not all cases are equally relevant for a new case. Which ones are? The answer under this approach is usually to divide the Constitution up into its constituent parts and begin there.

Modern constitutional law textbooks are traditionally organized around thematic topics of case law arising under the Constitution. In the ninth edition of a famed constitutional law casebook, published in 1970, Gunther (1970, xviii) observes there are essentially three ways of organizing a casebook on constitutional law: topically, historically and chronologically, or methodologically. Gunther, as most other authors, opts for a topical organization, dividing constitutional law into the following main sections: (1) the Nature and Sources of Supreme Court Authority, (2) the Structure of Government, and (3) Individual Rights. The goal for this approach is to understand how particular parts of the Constitution have been interpreted. The specific policy questions or political conflicts that relate to them are of second order. As contrasted with the other approaches to studying constitutional decision making, which we encounter next, political and policy questions are second-order concerns in these case books. The same political or policy fight might appear in multiple parts of the analysis. The goal is not to understand the history of politics and its effect on constitutional law but instead the history of a particular constitutional provision or doctrine.

The traditional, doctrinal approach to constitutional law is both long-lived and intellectually powerful for a number of reasons. Foremost is the richness of what we can learn from studying individual questions that arise and the legal context in which they are adjudicated. Further, the doctrinal approach mirrors the approach lawyers traditionally take to resolve a case – suggesting at the very least the importance for doctrinal analysis in the vocational training that takes place in a law school. When presented with a client's case, a lawyer must ask him- or herself what the rule or principle is that will be used to resolve the case, and what that rule or principle says about the client's position. In the absence of other things, such as who the judges are or what the broader political circumstances might be, doctrinal analysis seems a powerful predictor of how legal questions will be resolved. Finally, doctrinal analysis places an emphasis on what the text of the Constitution (or other legal materials) says. If a case is about a First Amendment claim, then why should we ask ourselves about bigger political problems or cleavages, when we can look to the First Amendment itself, and its associated doctrines, to infer what the law says about a case? In sum, the doctrinal approach shows us that how a case is framed, as well as what the legal and substantive issues in a case are, is crucial for understanding what judges do.

The doctrinal approach places great analytic effort on aggregate, temporal patterns in the law. In this way, traditional doctrinal approaches have elements of the institutional and behavioral approaches to legal development and innovation – it pays close attention to individual choices, though textual and doctrinal forces, rather than institutional and behavioral ones, are the driving incentive. At the same time, the traditional doctrinal approach also provides much of what externally oriented theories see as important. The role of social dispute and changing economic and political challenges gives rise to the problems the Court confronts in its decision making, but those forces are not considered influential for the choices judges make. However, at the same time, this approach often foregoes a focus on systematic microfoundations, instead setting out to provide relatively complete, but often *ad hoc*, accounts of individual decisions in the context of describing their place in the broader, aggregate doctrine. Thus, whereas the doctrinal approach provides considerable insight in terms of placing rich, case-specific context into a macro-level perspective on doctrine, it sacrifices what we can learn about general microfoundations and therefore the link between institutional and legal structures and the development of law.

2.1.2 *Political Science Approaches to Constitutional Law*

While the legal academy has developed a thorough and widely followed approach to studying constitutional law and conflicts, the other discipline that most often addresses constitutional law and theory – political science – has proceeded down a distinctly different path. There is, to be sure, a long tradition in the discipline that looks much like the traditional doctrinal approach to law. Political scientists in the tradition of Edward Corwin, C. Herman Pritchett, and Walter Murphy, among others, have studied constitutional law with an eye towards the politics of doctrine.

This line of research tends to be more explicitly positivist – interested in how the law works and how to describe the relevant elements and contours – rather than normative – interested in comparing the law to ideal criteria. Moreover, whereas the doctrinal approach places macro-level patterns at the center of its analytic goals, political scientists tend to be mostly concerned with micro-level patterns in behavior. That is, the political science of constitutional law is mostly about what choices individual judges make in cases and what the law is, rather than long-run doctrinal patterns and what the law ought to be. To the extent this work has a normative and historical component, normative questions typically serve as reasons for the positivist inquiry – only by understanding how laws and institutions work can we make prescriptions about how to change or improve the condition of government.

Beginning with the empiricists of the early- and mid-twentieth century, and continuing into contemporary literature on judicial politics, these scholars have been motivated by an interest in understanding the causal factors that drive judicial choice and in particular have focused on how judges vote. That focus, while often criticized in the legal academy, is not without merit. Indeed, some might argue, building from the central insights of the legal realists that the law is nothing more than what judges do (Holmes 1897), the empirical social science side of the law has narrowed in on the study of what factors explain who wins and who loses.

As contrasted with the traditional doctrinal approaches to studying judicial decision making, which tend to focus on the uniqueness of each case, the social-scientific approach is primarily concerned with identifying behavioral regularities. A hallmark characteristic of this line of research is a concern with elements of judicial choice that are objectively observable, quantifiable, and lend themselves to systematic analysis. The legal realist movement inspired scholars such as Pritchett (1948) and Schubert (1958) to begin to collect data on voting patterns by judges in an effort that would ultimately demonstrate judges vote in predictable, consistent ways, characterized, in part, by "voting blocs." At the same time, psychological research into human behavior was very much in vogue, and political scientists took much of their theoretical and empirical perspective from that discipline.

The goal shifted, by the mid-twentieth century, from characterizing voting blocs to *explaining* voting blocs. The dominant characteristic that described the voting blocs during this era was an ideological dimension – conservatives tended to vote together, while liberals tended to vote together. Moreover, that the primary dimension that discriminates between voting blocs seemed to be politics – as commonly understood by political scientists – paved the way for a fundamental rethinking of judicial decision making, and the study of law more generally. The culmination of that line of thought was the Attitudinal Model, which conceived of judges as characterized by a latent ideological orientation which was activated by case stimuli and explained their voting patterns (Segal and Spaeth 1993, 2002).

The parsimony of the Attitudinal Model dovetailed nicely with its contemporaries in other subfields of the discipline, as scholars of Congress and mass voting alike were settling on simple, parsimonious, and unidimensional models of politics (e.g., Campbell et al. 1966; Poole and Rosenthal 1997).[1] Indeed, empirical scholarship has often argued that a simple undimensional model of judicial preferences is sufficient to understand most meaningful variation in judges' voting patterns – or, at least, the votes of justices on the US Supreme Court.

As the behavioral approach to studying judicial decision making developed, the distinction between constitutional cases and other cases was not lost, even if the theoretical models were, in principle, general. However, whereas legal approaches to judicial decision making often emphasize the *substantive* distinctions between constitutional law and "ordinary" law, behavioral social science tends to focus on the political differences. The most salient distinction on which scholars focused was the political distinction between a statutory case and a constitutional one. Constitutional decisions are more difficult for other branches of

---

[1] Importantly, the Attitudinal Model is not in-and-of-itself a unidimensional model, and its foremost proponent has in fact argued that judicial decision making is potentially high-dimensional (Spaeth and Peterson 1971). However, in practice, the Attitudinal Model is very often thought of as a unidimesional model, and it is empirically operationalized as a unidimensional model.

government to contend with, whereas the separation of powers in the US provides legislatures and executives with more tools to use to respond to non-constitutional decisions. While substantive differences remain, though, the focus on the micro-level political calculus underlying justices' constitutional decisions teaches us a great deal about individual decisions, judges' decision calculus, and the way in which institutional structures interact with judicial goals. At the same time, in a way that mirrors the doctrinal approach, and continuing the theme laid out in the preceding chapter, the benefit of that attention to micro-level details comes at the expense of a broader, systemic perspective on judges, courts, and law. Missing from this approach to studying constitutional decision making is any significant role for the broader social and political context in which law develops through history.

Two more recent intellectual traditions have been motivated by the goal to negotiate this trade-off. The first, the political development tradition, places an emphasis on law and macropatterns over politics and microfoundations, whereas the latter, case-space modeling, places an emphasis on politics and microfoundations over law and macropatterns. However, both represent fundamental shifts towards a perspective in which law plays a more integrated, and substantively consequential, role in political theories of judicial decision making.

2.1.3 *Political Development and the Law*

The approach known as "American Political Development" represents an effort to bridge the intellectual divide between doctrine-oriented approaches to the law and politically oriented approaches to judicial decision making. Scholarship in this vein has grown in recent decades into a full-blown research program that advertises itself as being concerned with both how the political context in which law is made shapes the content of law and therefore also with the temporal, sequential elements of constitutional law (e.g., Novkov 2015). This research tradition makes an important advance that underlies much of the conceptual claim I make here – law and politics go hand-in-hand, and understanding doctrine, law, and judicial decision making requires one to consider the political context from which legal disputes arise and in which they are resolved (e.g., Gillman, Graber and Whittington 2012a,b).

In many ways, political development approaches to constitutional law represent an effort to bring some of the fundamental lessons of twentieth-century political science to bear on the historical approaches in political science dominant in the nineteenth-century. Where they depart from traditional constitutional history and doctrinal analysis, though,

[handwritten marginalia: APD emphasis! Political context in which laws are made and interpreted]

is in the emphasis placed on the political context in which law is made. Thus, as Novkov (2015, 820) observes, "[t]he distinction between APD [American political development] and constitutional history is probably more one of emphasis than kind." However, even while political development approaches may resemble history in its substantive interest and methodology, the implications for more social-scientific approaches to the law – and the approach I advance in this book in particular – are crucial and immediate. Namely, political development approaches to constitutional law demonstrate the inextricable connection between law and politics and the way in which politics can shape and structure legal arguments, developments, and conclusions.

As an example, consider one study Novkov engages. Brandwein's (2011) analysis of the Supreme Court's jurisprudence concerning civil rights and the Civil War Amendments during the late nineteenth century shows one way in which politics, law, and society interact iteratively over time. During the 1880s, the Supreme Court, led by Chief Justice Morrison Waite, developed the principle of "state neglect." That jurisprudence held that "the federal government could prosecute private violations of rights when states failed to do so. The state's inaction itself meant that the private offense was committed under the color of law or custom" (Benedict 2011, 117). However, the Waite Court generally adopted a fairly circumscribed view of the extent of the federal government's power under state neglect, limiting the power to only those situations where an individual was being deprived of a right explicitly granted by the Constitution. As the Court turned more conservative during the 1890s, the Fuller Court whittled away at the state neglect principle, as judges, historians, and politicians jointly worked to rewrite the history of Reconstruction. Simply put, history shows that how an issue is handled at one point in time – the development of state neglect by the Waite Court – shapes politics and policies as the issue continues to evolve – as the Fuller Court worked with the state neglect principle to undermine the Fourteenth Amendment's practical "teeth."

Brandwein's analysis, and other important work in the political development tradition, shows how law and politics go hand-in-hand. The legal infrastructure (for example, the content of the Constitution) shapes how political conflicts play out, what policies are pursued, and, consequently, how the law continues to develop (see also Graber 2006). Thus, the political development approach to constitutional law goes a long way to linking law with politics and thereby macropatterns with microfoundations. However, as the discussion here shows, what is often missing are explicit microfoundations that can explain both stability and change at the same time. In addition, the perspective's emphasis on law over politics tends to encourage the induction of microfoundations from macropatterns, rather than the other way around. By turning the model of inference around, the political development approach makes it more difficult to make general claims about institutional, systemic factors and causal relationships between individual choices and legal and social outcomes.

2.1.4 Case-Space Modeling of the Law

At the same time as the political development tradition was growing, there were other developments in political science and economics that also sought to bring law back into the picture. The case-space model is a theoretical framework tailor-made for the judicial environment and is designed to capture all elements of the judicial process. Traditionally, models used to study judicial decision making were imported directly from the political science of legislative behavior. Judges were imagined as having ideal points in a policy space – spatial points representing their most favored policies – and cases presented opportunities to bargain over policies in that space. In none of these models were cases, legal rules, and judgments explicitly included as elements of the model. In a seminal paper, Kornhauser (1992b) objects to that modeling approach and proposes the case-space framework, which has been extended and elaborated on in various contexts ever since (e.g., Cameron 1993; Cameron, Segal, and Songer 2000; Lax 2007; Lax and Cameron 2007; Kastellec 2007; Gennaioli and Shleifer 2007; Lax 2011; Carrubba and Clark 2012; Clark and Carrubba 2012; Lax 2012; Beim, Hirsch and Kastellec 2014; Callander and Clark 2017).

The basic insight Kornhauser makes is that cases are the central unit of judicial decision making but play no role in the legislative models imported to the judicial context. Moreover, and crucially, judicial decisions almost always consist of two related elements – judges vote on dispositions, and they draft opinions. This is especially so in the context of peak appellate courts, such as the US Supreme Court, which serve as the focus for most scholarship. The case-space model resolves these intellectual tensions in the theoretical scholarship by proposing a space of "cases," rather than policies; judicial actions as the resolution of those cases, including both the articulation of a rule or principle and also the resolution of the case into a judgment; and judicial preferences as ideal resolutions of all possible cases. In this way, just as political development scholars sought to bring politics law back into the historical and legal perspectives on judicial decision making, case-space theorists sought to bring law back into the political perspective on judicial decision making.

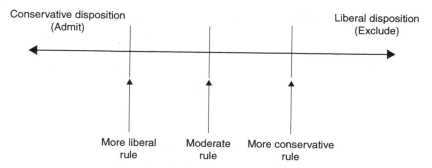

Figure 2.1. *Example of case-space model with one-dimensional search-and-seizure cases.*

Points in the theoretical space represent cases, where their particular locations represent "bundles of facts." For example, the most commonly used illustration is search-and-seizure law, where a unidimensional space might represent all cases as entailing more or less intrusive searches, as in Figure 2.1. Here, cases further to the right entail very intrusive searches, whereas cases to the left entail less intrusive searches. What judges do in this model is resolve cases that come before them into discrete, mutually exclusive categories – permissible searches and impermissible searches. Judicial preferences in this model are not ideal policies, but instead ideal partitionings that divide the case space into preferred judgments for all cases. To continue the search-and-seizure example, a judge's preferences in Figure 2.1 can be represented as a point below which the judge prefers all searches to be permissible and above which the judge prefers all searches to be impermissible.

Thus, the central contribution of the unidimensional case-space model can be seen in the intellectual coherence it imposes on our thinking about the relationships among cases, dispositions, opinions, and judicial preferences. However, when we extend the framework to a multidimensional setting, we uncover a variety of even richer findings. Most important among these, Lax (2007) shows that bargaining and opinion writing in a multidimensional case space are not subject to the typical social choice pathologies that plague standard policy-space models. The critical reason why is that for any given point in the case space – i.e., any possible case – the judges are not bargaining over multiple possible policies, but rather are bargaining over a dichotomous choice (guilty/innocent, liable/not liable, reverse/affirm, etc.). Thus, there is only a single choice for any given case and therefore no risk of cycling through myriad alternatives. What is more, the crucial observation Lax makes is that while judges might in principle cycle over what the ideal partitioning of the case space is, because their ultimate choice is dichotomous, and because judges decide each case separably, what emerges is an implicit rule, constructed piecemeal over the case space, that is not vulnerable to the typical cycling that takes place in multidimensional policy choices.

The upshot of the move to case-space modeling is that we have a rigorous theoretical framework that provides analytic clarity about the central elements of judicial decision making, as distinct from non-judicial policy making. The modeling structure can be used to derive predictions about all elements of judicial choice, including case dispositions (and the related votes that have served as the basis for most empirical work), opinion content (including both individual cases and legal content that spans multiple cases), the clarity, complexity, or breadth of legal rules, the factual relationship among cases heard by courts, and the strategic incentives facing courts in relationship to each other, among other things. However, and perhaps most important, the case-space model also provides guidance for bridging the gap between substantive depth, theoretical rigor, and empirical tractability, as we see next. What is more difficult, though, is using the framework to capture the macropatterns and temporal dynamics that give meaning to the microprocesses we study. Whereas case-space modeling originally developed in the context of thinking about path-dependence in legal development (e.g., Kornhauser 1992*a*), the articulation of coherent, micro-founded theories of dynamic processes has proven elusive.[2]

2.1.5 A Scholarly Divide

The four areas of research in constitutional law – (1) doctrinal, historical studies, (2) empirical analysis and description, (3) political development histories of law and politics, and (4) theoretical models of institutional incentives – have common goals: to understand the process that leads to the development of constitutional law and the decisions and choices made by judges. However, the foci in these intellectual traditions are different (as we have seen) and often so different as to render difficult a combining of their respective analytic strengths. One of the goals in this book is to bring together these different perspectives in pursuit of an analytic perspective that allows us to more effectively address the driving questions about how judicial institutions operate and function in a democratic system. To develop an analytically rich history of constitutional decision making, we will need to bring together the strengths of these diverse

---

[2] Notable examples do exist, but they often must sacrifice analytic attention to parts of the judicial process we often think fundamental to the politics of law making (e.g., Callander and Clark 2017; Fox and Vanberg 2014; Baker and Mezetti 2012; Bueno de Mesquita and Stephenson 2002).

intellectual traditions. However, in the existing literature, there are often cited at least two barriers to collaboration that contribute to the scholarly divide over the analysis of judicial decision making.

BARRIER 1: LAW V. POLITICS. The first barrier to integrating the various intellectual traditions concerns the different philosophical approaches the traditions have regarding what are the primary strategic and political tensions and sources of conflict. In traditional legal studies, conflict emerges over how to implement the law, what the law itself says, and how to craft legal doctrine that will achieve judicial goals (e.g., possibly political goals, possibly some objective notion of justice). In traditional empirical social science studies, the tension is over politics – different judges have different world views and value systems, and the struggle for power over political outcomes (e.g., case resolution) is a political one in which judicial institutions shape the structure of interaction among judges. In both political development and case-space approaches, the tension among judges is something of a hybrid. In those perspectives, judges' preferences over how to resolve cases form the basis of conflict; however, their interactions are shaped by a combination of formal institutions and the content of the law.

Indeed, one of the defining questions underlying the bulk of social-scientific research on judicial decision making is whether law acts as a *constraint* on judicial choices. Few, if any, doubt that the law leaves to judges some degree of discretion in many circumstances, but the issue here is whether the law constrains that discretion. Many of the most influential works in judicial politics explicitly conceive of law as some force that acts against politics, as some motivation that is in tension with political goals. By conceiving of law as a goal in and of itself, scholars have created a barrier to studying law and politics as distinct components of a single political-legal model.

The key to moving past this barrier is recognizing an important fact about the judicial process. *Law is not a constraint on politics. Rather, law is an element of the judicial process; it is the medium with which judges work.* As Posner (2008, 9) puts it, "'Law' in a judicial setting is simply the material, in the broadest sense, out of which judges fashion their decisions." Politics, by contrast, is a set of strategic incentives and goals the judges pursue when they work with the law. Law, then, is no more a constraint on politics than clay is a constraint on pottery; it defines what is possible and how one can create the end goal. Lax's (2007) analysis, which I described above, makes plain how this approach to thinking about law changes the nature of our analytic focus in studying political conflict. Rather than developing theories and empirical studies of law versus politics, we can bridge the divide by developing theoretical and empirical models of law *and* politics.

We need, then, an approach to law and politics that builds from the insights that underlie contemporary approaches such as political development and case-space modeling. Only by re-conceiving the relationship between law and politics can we begin to think about what it means for judges to want to build law through their cases or appreciate the political and institutional tensions inherent in the effort to build "workable" doctrine. *More crucially, when we think of law and politics as two components of the judicial process, we can begin to identify the ways in which judicial processes interact with political and social forces outside of the courts as well as institutional and behavioral forces within the courts. Law and politics together allow us to consider both structural determinants of constitutional decision making as well as historical contingencies that matter in particular cases.* Thus, in this sense, the barrier imposed by competing disciplinary perspectives on law and politics runs very deep in the challenges facing contemporary studies of judicial law making.

BARRIER 2: EMPIRICS V. THEORY. A second barrier to integration of the various intellectual traditions in the study of law and politics is a common one in social science – how best to marry theory with empirical analysis. Indeed, in many ways, the case-space modeling approach to studying judicial politics was born of criticisms that legal scholars leveled against empiricists grounded in the observation that the things empiricists could measure and study did not mesh with the theoretical mechanisms at work in the law. Case-space modeling hopes, at its core, to provide a scientific framework for evaluating legal decision making. Thus, the incorporation of the distinct elements of the judicial process. However, case-space modeling often runs into a brick wall when confronted with measurement limitations. Fully 17 years after Kornhauser's seminal paper, Knight (2009, 1538) observed, "To my knowledge there have not been any serious efforts to translate the results of the case-space analyses into an empirically meaningful research agenda." That observation seems a damning critique of the scientific merit of case-space modeling.

Unfortunately, Knight's criticism may have been a bit overstated. Cameron, Segal, and Songer (2000), for example, develop a canonical model of case selection by the Supreme Court in which the justices strategically select cases from the lower courts in an effort to induce compliance by lower court judges who may have preferences that conflict with those of the Supreme Court justices. Their theoretical model is a case-space model, and the empirical design they adopt derives directly from that theoretical apparatus. In the nearly two decades since, their theoretical model has informed scores of empirical studies, though many have, admittedly, had to rely on designs that indirectly measure case-space concepts (for just a few examples, see, Spriggs and Hansford 2001; Hettinger, Lindquist and Martinek 2004; Giles, Walker and Zorn 2006; Schanzenbach and Tiller 2006; Scott 2006; Daughety and Reinganum 2006; Kastellec 2007; Jacobi and Tiller 2007; Giles et al. 2007; Clark 2009*b*).

However, almost at the same time as Knight made his observation, a series of papers were published that sought to empirically measure the theoretical concepts at play in case-space models. Scholars began to collect more extensive data about the legal concepts and authorities cited in opinions, for example which precedents are cited (e.g., Fowler et al. 2007; Fowler and Jeon 2008), the legislative history invoked (Brudney and Ditslear 2008), and what opinions say about the authorities they cite (Clark and Lauderdale 2010). Moreover, scholars around the same time began to explore the use of text analysis to measure the similarity – generally, in an ideological sense – among opinions (e.g., McGuire and Vanberg 2005).

Of course, the progress made does not mean there do not remain significant barriers in the empirical operationalization of case-space modeling. Some of the most compelling and innovative applications of theoretical modeling of the law contemplate concepts such as the vagueness of a judicial opinion (e.g., Staton and Vanberg 2008), the breadth of a judicial rule (e.g., Fox and Vanberg 2014; Clark 2016), and the complexity of a doctrine (e.g., Gennaioli and Shleifer 2007; Callander and Clark 2017). Burgeoning relationships between political science and computational linguistics, for example, suggest the potential to overcome the challenge of empirically measuring these theoretical concepts, paving the way for a new, powerful generation of research in the law (e.g., van Deemter 2010). And, the effort to draw into our theoretical apparatus richer notions of the law than ideologically driven voting promises to enrich the types of questions and problems the research can address.

Similarly, the political development tradition to studying the path of law confronts limitations in its ability to describe the mechanisms by which institutions work. The goal of political development research is typically to not distill general, systematic features of an institutional framework or political organization. Rather, the goal is to fully understand the determinants of a particular outcome. But, that often leads the analyst away from general features of a situation towards particularities. The problem then is that the framework developed in any given setting does not easily generalize beyond that setting and so lacks predictive power. When a model of historical examples cannot predict – indeed, is not intended to predict – one must question whether the model is one of institutional causes and effects or instead a careful account of history.

It is from this vantage point that we now move onto the perspective on constitutional law and politics that motivates this book. In particular, the bridging of empirics and theory as we will see in subsequent chapters points directly to how we can study relatively vague concepts like judicial learning or the relationship between doctrines and outcomes. Given the nature of these phenomena, which make the central objects of interest inherently unobservable, the connection between theory and empirics is of particular importance in order that we can draw meaningful inferences from the things we can observe in the world.

2.2 THE THEORY OF LATENT POLITICAL DIMENSIONS

These scholarly divides pose challenges but also offer a way forward for an analytic-historical approach to constitutional decision making. My goal is to rely on the power of these various intellectual traditions in order to document the path of constitutional law as it has evolved with American society. Each of the approaches I have described speaks in part to the driving questions about law, judicial institutions, and governance that motivate the study of judicial politics. How do major societal and political events, demands and needs shape the path of constitutional law? How do judicial institutions and the individuals who serve on the courts shape constitutional law? How do those external and internal forces interact with each other? How do the structural and contingent aspects of those forces interact with each other?

I propose a way of unifying the various theoretical and empirical agendas and focusing on the nexus of microfoundations and macropatterns. To do so, I recast law as a series of political dimensions. Law, in this view, is a matter of central import, because it defines the problems and policies with which political actors work. Politics is important, because it defines the organization of legal substance. Thus, we can think of the law as the method by which judges make policy and politics as the goals that structure legal decision making. Taking this analytic perspective allows us to focus on the process by which micro-founded individual choices aggregate over time into a pattern of legal development.

2.2.1 *Politics as an Organization of the Law*

To integrate the analytic value of both internal and external forces on the development of constitutional law, I argue that we should think about politics as a force that organizes the law. To better develop an

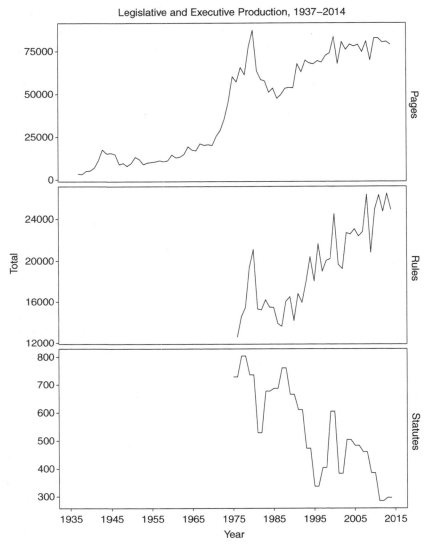

Figure 2.2. *Total Statutes Enacted, Federal Rules Published, and Pages Published in the Federal Register, 1937–2014.*

intuition for this idea, let us consider what a law is. This is not a straight-forward matter. Law exists in many forms – statutes, regulations, case law, etc. Indeed, simply trying to assess how many laws there are poses considerable conceptual challenges. However, we might begin by considering the bottom panel in Figure 2.2, which depicts the total number of statutes enacted during each Congress over time. Some statutes simply reauthorize old laws, and some repeal old laws – obviously, these two kinds of statutes do not create new law. However, the number of statutes enacted does at least serve as a proxy for the number, or variety of statutory topics on which Congress legislates. As the figure shows, during any given Congress (two-year period), the federal government enacts between 300 and 700 statutes – roughly one every 1–2 days! Even during the recent Congresses that have not produced much enacted legislation, they are still enacting almost 300 statutes.

We see a similarly striking level of activity when we consider agency rule-making. In the center panel of Figure 2.2, we see the total number of agency rules published each year (these are final rules only, not including proposed rules), and the top panel shows the total number of pages published each year in the federal register. (The federal register is an official journal in which the government prints rules and public notices.) In the 1980s, at least 15,000 final rules were published in most years, while today roughly 25,000 rules are published each year. Simply put, a lot of law making takes place every year, in all departments of government.

Certainly, one would not claim that there are 25,000, or even 800 or 300, unique political issues in the law. For example US Code Title 29, which concerns Labor, has 3,058 distinct sections, organized into 31 Chapters. Chapter 15 is titled Occupational Safety and Health and has 28 sections, while Chapter 16 is titled Vocational Rehabilitation and Other Rehabilitation Services and has 97 sections. Certainly these two subjects of legislation – occupational safety and vocational rehabilitation – touch on similar substantive problems and therefore likely stimulate similar political reactions. Indeed, one might think there are natural ways to group entire Titles of the US Code together into substantively connected "blocs" of legislation, and that intuition surely extends beyond the US Code to the myriad forms of law that exist.

Another question naturally arises from the intuition that many substantive issues in the law group together. Why do they group together naturally, and what makes us have that intuition? One answer, which has its roots in perhaps the most comprehensive and consequential study of American politics during the past century is that everything in politics is linked to a single, common underlying dimension of political conflict. Poole and Rosenthal's (1997) claim that American politics can best be described as a dominantly unidimensional phenomenon (described in Chapter 1) suggests that politics organizes all substantive policy issues into a single dimension of conflict. We all align along that dimension, and so all political issues are really a matter of debating the same political conflict, just in a different context.

If the politics of law making are in fact unidimensional, then the only difficulty is in establishing how forward-thinking judges today anticipate what future judges, legislators, executives, bureaucrats, public citizens, and so forth will want to do along that given political dimension. But, if the politics of law making is more complicated, then the incentives created for individual choices by temporal considerations become more complicated. In other words, it is the complexity of micro-level politics that makes it difficult to link them with macropatterns. However, structural factors, such as the language of the law or the Constitution, can shape how a case or dispute implicates different *preference dimensions*. To the extent that judges at any given time have different preferences across those dimensions, the particular coalitions that will constitute a decision-making majority is contingent upon the case's relationship to the preference dimensions in the law.

Further, social and political events will jointly influence that process. Electoral politics are often driven by major events and factors outside of the courts' control. Economic crises, war, social angst, and the like can have dramatic consequences of political control of the government. In turn, political control of the government shapes the kinds of policies and laws that are adopted, the nature of constitutional disputes and questions that arise, as well as who are the individuals who serve on the Court and resolve those disputes. Thus, the structuring of constitutional and legal questions is a function of external politics. And, of course, judges are free to conceive of new or recurring political and legal questions as they see fit, arguing among themselves about what the relevant dimensions of a problem are in any given case. Thus, the politics of constitutional law are shaped by internal politics. And, as we will see below, a clever political agent might try to strategically manipulate the way in which a policy question relates to competing preference dimensions in the law.

Returning to our example from the US Code, one is unlikely to think that all of the subjects regulated in the US Code are manifestations of the same political conflict. For example, what would it mean for Food and Drugs (Title 21), Education (Title 20), Labor (Title 29), Bankruptcy (Title 11), and Copyrights (Title 17) to always divide Americans similarly? Recall our discussion of the Attitudinal Model, which posits that judges line up neatly on a single dimension and cases serve as stimuli to which they respond. That dimension corresponds to a propensity to vote "liberally" in any given case. In this context, we would be assuming that all Americans line up on a single left-right dimension corresponding to a propensity to have a liberal policy preference on all issues, and a given policy question simply divides people differently, but with a consistent ordering on all issues. In other words, the context of a policy question is not particularly important for knowing who is to the right of whom. If, however, individuals shift their relative conservatism across policy issues, then the simple unidimensional model of politics misses a systematic element of the political process. Critically, the substantive and political relationships among issues and cleavages will affect, among other things, the way in which individual decisions play out in society and government, how the political agenda develops, and, consequently, the individual choices law makers confront.[3]

The concern that politics does not neatly organize all substantive issues into a single dimension of conflict has particular import in the context of the law for a variety of reasons. Law touches on many substantive areas of governance, and constitutional law, in particular, touches on virtually all of the deepest aspects of governmental power over and regulation of life. In order to systematically and transparently interpret the Constitution when implicated in a case, the Supreme Court has articulated a series of *doctrines*. A doctrine is a "rule, principle, or tenet of the law" that is established through judicial decisions.[4] *As such, a doctrine can span across multiple substantive questions or areas of the law.* For example, the *political question* doctrine is a rule that the federal courts will not answer questions that are political in nature. Another example is the doctrine of *promissory estoppel*, which is the principle that one cannot undo a promise made to another once the promissee has done something relying on the promise. These doctrines are often articulated piecemeal, through a series of related cases, as the doctrines grow through interpretation in new and different disputes. Judicial doctrines, then, represent rules and principles that give life to the Constitution's broad promises and purposes, and they arise out of political, and other, conflicts that come to the courts.

The use of doctrines in constitutional interpretation is a symptom of an underlying feature of the law – there are common ways of tackling disparate substantive issues. In other words, doctrine is used, in part, to map substantive issues in the law onto political cleavages of conflict. By focusing on both social and political forces that shape law as well as behavioral and institutional factors, we are led to see doctrine as emerging as a product of the interaction between context-specific contingencies

---

[3] There is, moreover, evidence that American politicians do not exhibit the kind of straight party-line voting that characterizes parliamentary democracies (Ansolabehere, Snyder Jr and Stewart III 2001). Further, popular discussion of "mavericks" in the legislative arena find support in systematic analysis of roll-call voting (e.g., Lauderdale 2010), suggesting there is nothing inherent in the organization of politics into a single dimension.

[4] While formal definitions of the concept vary source-to-source, this definition is broadly consistent with a variety of well-regarded legal dictionaries, such as *Merriam Webster's Dictionary of Law*.

– the social conditions that give rise to the problem being resolved and the individuals who themselves make the decisions – as well as structural factors – the law, the institutions of judicial decision making, and the organization of governance. This is how conceiving of politics as organizing law moves us towards an analytic historical model. *Structure and contingency exist both inside and outside of the Court, and it is when these forces come together that we see how a legal question relates to the politics of the time. The politics shape what will be decided and how it will be resolved.*

2.2.2 *Microfoundations and Macropatterns*

As I discussed in Chapter 1, making sense of how these different kinds of factors interact to shape the course of development of constitutional law requires microtheories of judicial choice. Microfoundations to a theory specify how specific choices, conditions, and structures interact with each other to produce outcomes. As we also saw in Chapter 1, a complete causal chain avoids temporal gaps in the logical chain from cause to consequence.

Specifying a complete, micro-founded theory of the development of constitutional law is not likely to be a fruitful endeavor. The range of factors and complexities is so broad that any comprehensive model would prove intractable. However, there are a number of microtheories that complement each other and, in conjunction, yield insights about macropatterns in the history of constitutional decision making. Let us consider two classes of theories in particular. The first class of theories concerns the structure of collegial decision making on a court. These theories focus on the politics of collective choice and the features of judicial decisions that distinguish them from other types of political choice, such as legislative decision making. The second class of theories concerns the social and political factors that bring questions and issues before the courts. These theories focus on the role of law in society, how judicial institutions create incentives for potential litigants, and the role of courts in the broader political-institutional setting of government.

Microtheories of collegial politics The literature on judicial decision making does not lack for theories of collegial interactions. I consider first the case-space model of collegial politics, because it implicates the greatest variety of internal factors that are relevant for the politics of interest. Indeed, the premise underlying the case-space model is one in which judges have different preferences on different dimensions of a given case. Any given case may activate some of those dimensions relatively

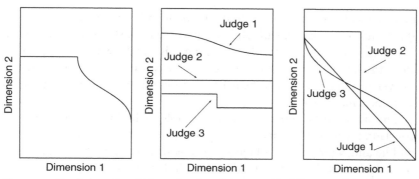

Figure 2.3. *Depiction of multidimensional case spaces, with different political cleavages.* The left panel illustrates an example of a single judge's preferences in a two-dimensional case space. The center and right panels illustrate a potential configuration of preferences among three judges who have different ways of partitioning the case space.

more or less. In other words, political disagreements – cleavages – among judges structure the legal questions relevant for a case.

Consider Figure 2.3, which depicts several different types of political preferences by judges in a case space. This figure is adapted from the figures Lax (2007) employs to illustrate multidimensional rule-making in a case space. Each panel shows a different possible judge's preferences about how to dispose of cases in the case space. For the sake of abstractness, we assume cases that fall below a judge's preference line are those in which she prefers to reverse (the lower court) and those above a judge's preference line are those in which she prefers to affirm (the lower court). Consider first the left-most panel. This panel illustrates the scenario where a single judge decides a case. (Or, more generally, we might think of this situation as one where all judges agree completely, and therefore collegial interactions are not consequential.)

The cases to the left are ones where dimension 1 – e.g., political liberty – is not considerably implicated. Where a case falls on that dimension is not especially relevant for a wide range of cases; all that matters is where the cases fall on dimension 2 – e.g., intergovernmental relations. However, moving to the right, we encounter a set of cases where both dimensions are relevant for how a court evaluates the disposition. Thus, in this example, we see politics structuring the legal evaluation and resolution of each case. There are many cases, namely, those to the left in the figure, where the first dimension is irrelevant, and so resolution of the case turns entirely on where it is situated on the second dimension. When judges confront a case under this preference profile, the doctrine they develop will depend in part on where the case is located in both dimensions. This might give rise to the potential that judges engage in

heresthetical maneuvering – what we might call "judicial heresthetics."[5]
If a strategically thoughtful judge wanted to establish a simple precedent
that relies on a single consideration, then she might want to hear a case
from the left-side of the case space or at least one from a region where
the vertical dimension is sufficient to distinguish the case from all similar
cases that might arise.

The situation becomes even more complex when we consider a court
consisting of multiple judges, who might have conflicting preferences. The
middle and right panels in Figure 2.3 illustrate two possible examples of
such situations. Here, we see that each judge's preferred partitioning is
relatively flat. In other words, what the judges think about dimension 1 is
relatively inconsequential for how they think about resolving most cases,
and instead where a case falls on dimension 2 is almost all that matters
for each judge individually. Importantly, for any given case that Judge
2 thinks should be reversed, Judge 1 agrees with her; for any case that
Judge 2 thinks should be affirmed, Judge 3 agrees with her. And, any time
that Judges 1 and 3 agree, so too does Judge 2. In other words, Judge 2
will always be in the majority, and how a case will be resolved depends
simply on how a case is framed *relative to Judge 2's preferences across the
dimensions*. The ability to manipulate the way a case will be resolved, or
the rule that will be adopted, then, is somewhat limited.

Consider, though, the right-hand panel in Figure 2.3; in this configuration of preferences, which judge is pivotal depends on where a case is
along both dimensions. At the far left of the Figure, Judge 1 is pivotal;
Judges 1 and 3 agree on all cases above Judge 1's ideal partition, whereas
Judges 1 and 2 agree on all cases below Judge 1's ideal partition. However,
as we move to the right, there is a point where Judge 3 becomes relatively
less sensitive to the second dimension, and her ideal partitioning crosses
that of Judge 1. At that point, Judge 3 becomes pivotal. Moving further
to the right, though, because Judge 2's ideal partition drops sharply along
Dimension 2, Judge 1 becomes pivotal again. However, because of the
way Judges 2 and 3 react to the second dimension, the voting coalition is
the opposite of what it was at the far left end of the space. Here, at each
end of Dimension 1, with whom Judge 1 sides can depend on the case.
Further to the right, those coalitions flip, so that Judges 1 and 2 agree
on all cases *below* Judge 1's ideal partition, and Judges 1 and 3 agree on
all cases *above* Judge 1's ideal partition. Finally, as we move further to
the right, Judge 2 and then Judge 3 become pivotal. What this example

---

[5] The phrase "judicial heresthetics" was coined informally by Charles Cameron who,
seemingly, first thought that Riker's (1982) notion of heresthetics could play out in
the framing of legal questions before the courts.

illustrates is that because of the different ways individual judges might balance competing preference dimensions, who is pivotal and what kind of voting coalition one can assemble can depend on how a case is situated along the dimensions of the case space.

What is more, as these figures suggest, a case's location will not just determine which judge will be pivotal, but it can also influence the rule a group of judges will adopt. Different configurations of judges might employ different rules, depending on where the case is located in the case space. They might choose a rule that emphasizes only a single dimension, or they might choose one that implicates multiple dimensions. As this process plays out over time, through a sequence of cases, judges will have to work to connect those rules and develop a sensible one that covers the entire case space.

The sensitivity of the voting coalitions and the legal rules a court would adopt to a case's location in the case space opens the door to the possibility of heresthetical maneuvering. By emphasizing a given dimension of the case space, a strategic litigant might be able to situate a case in a region of the case space that is more likely to yield the desired outcome. Organized interests setting out to build doctrine will have incentives to pick cases that present factual and legal questions that will divide the justices as they want or induce them to apply a legal rule that reflects the organized interest's goals.

Of course, in practice, as we will see in Chapters 6 and 7, when a case presents a question that implicates multiple preference dimensions, there is often a choice – sometimes on the part of the justices, sometimes on the part of the litigants – about which dimensions to consider or base an opinion along. In the spirit of Lax's (2007) notion of the implicit median rule, one can imagine that what a court is doing in any given case is constructing a tiny portion of the implicit median rule when it decides any given case. The voting coalition and the opinion it produces can focus on a single aspect of the case – such as being too far left or right or too high or low in Figure 2.3. For example, in Callander and Clark (2017), each case establishes only a doctrine about the very particular facts of the case, communicating where the case is relative to the threshold between dispositions, but that information can be communicated by emphasizing distance from the threshold along one or both dimensions, as a judge sees fit.

More generally, we might imagine each of the dimensions represents a collection of substantive issues in the law. For example, suppose there are a set of issues that are connected generally on the subject of "political liberty," such as voting rights, freedom of speech, and possibly public education regulation. We might also imagine a different dimension of politics onto which other issues map, such as "intergovernmental relations," which could include federalism, administrative delegation, electoral law, etc. For some cases, a single dimension, such as political liberty, might be all that matters. For others, judges might refer to their broad views on political liberty while also relying on their views about intergovernmental relations. Without losing too much of the theoretical crispness and clarity of the case-space model, we might then want to reinterpret the dimensions not as single fact dimensions but rather as projections onto a substantive consideration from multiple facts related to each other in the political-legal constellation.

Moving beyond a static case-space model in multiple dimensions, a number of microtheories of the judicial process consider what happens as case resolution takes place over time, through a series of cases. There are several components of the judicial process that play out in individual decisions made in sequence. First, judges need to learn about how the legal rules they adopt play out in practice in the world. Because judges make decisions in the context of discrete, real-world cases, part of the function they serve is crafting legal rules that yield the desired outcomes. But, because the world is a complex, and complicated, environment, it is hard to foresee exactly how a given rule will function in the rich contexts to which it will be applied going forward. Theoretical work on experimentation and learning by the courts illustrates that how a judge can use individual cases to work their way through a complicated doctrinal environment. Judges use their decisions to communicate how a new case relates to existing precedent and provide guidance to future courts looking to apply a line of precedent to myriad future problems (e.g., Bueno de Mesquita and Stephenson 2002; Ellison and Holden 2014; Callander and Clark 2017). To the extent politics organizes law into a number of preference dimensions, working through the case space, as in Figure 2.3, judges can discover what kinds of rules best relate the dimensions of a problem to the outcomes they want to see take place.

Indeed, a second strand of literature concerned with judicial learning specifically considers the world where judges do not know what rule they prefer. In these models, judges use the litigation process to generate arguments and proposed legal rules and to observe how those rules and arguments play out in practice – for example, by allowing a legal question to "percolate" in the lower courts (e.g., Baker and Mezetti 2012; Iaryczower and Shum 2012; Clark and Kastellec 2013; Beim 2017; Beim, Clark, and Patty 2017). What these theories tell us is that the selection of cases, in sequence over time, is driven by microprocesses involving judges' efforts to learn about the law and how it relates to the real world as well as the collegial interactions that are driven by potential ideological disagreements about how best to resolve disputes.

Importantly, these models of judges deciding individual cases one-at-a-time illustrate how microtheories of the judicial process can orient an analytic approach to the history of constitutional decision making. When we study constitutional decision making, the inferences we can draw from statistical patterns in justices' choices and the cases they hear depend on what they are trying to accomplish at the moments of their choices. What is more, the microtheories of judicial decision making point us to see what kinds of patterns we should look for and where, empirically, those patterns are likely to appear. Further, as we will see in Chapter 8, understanding what these patterns mean for judicial performance and democratic health in the United States will require careful theoretical interpretation.

Microtheories of context. In addition to theories of judicial decision making within the Court, there are a host of microtheories about how context from outside of the Court influences the content of constitutional law. Scholars have studied two aspects of the external environment in particular. The first is what we might think of as the elite-level institutional context. "Separation-of-powers models," for example, are concerned with how institutional checks and balances create constraints on courts' discretion when deciding cases. Typically, these models are static, in the sense that they imagine a single, rather simple interaction between Congress and the Supreme Court. The second is what we might think of as the mass-level legal context. These studies, often historically oriented, are typically concerned with litigation, social actors, and the broader legal institutional environment, outside of the courts.

Separation-of-powers models typically capture a sequence of institutions with different kinds of authority deciding on a single policy. For example, a typical model may consider a Court reviewing and interpreting a law, making a decision that is to be implemented by an administrative agency and then potentially revised by legislation from Congress (there are many variants of such models, but see generally Ferejohn and Shipan 1990; Gely and Spiller 1990; Eskridge 1991; Clinton 1994; Knight and Epstein 1996; Rogers 2001; Vanberg 2005; Rogers and Vanberg 2007; Staton and Vanberg 2008; Staton 2010; Clark 2011). The key factor these models isolate is the cross-checking vetoes that various institutions can exercise against each other. For example, in statutory interpretation cases, Congress has wide discretion to simply rewrite a law that the courts have interpreted in a way that conflicts with congressional preferences, will, intent, etc. Administrative agencies and other actors responsible for implementing court decisions typically have wide discretion in how they carry out those decisions. Typically, these models have somewhat less bite for understanding constitutional decision making, because it is usually assumed that courts have, and others will defer to, the final word in constitutional interpretation. Though, as has been noted in myriad studies, constitutional decisions are frequently met with resistance, especially in Congress (e.g., Meernik and Ignagni 1997; Blackstone 2013; Devins and Fisher 2015), and there is evidence that the Supreme Court does respond to others' concerns about its use of judicial review (for a review of the relevant literature, and an example, see Clark 2011).

The key theoretical result from these studies is that having the ability to review another institution's choices can create incentives for the reviewed institution to exercise restraint. In particular, if the Court anticipates that Congress will rewrite a statute if the Court interprets it as it sees fit, then perhaps it will accommodate congressional preferences in its interpretation of the statute in order to mollify enough legislators that a majority will not be willing to rewrite the statute. One way this might play out is that the Court might give more on one dimension while taking more on another. If the policy space is multidimensional, then the Court might be able to find a way to cut up the majority coalition along the multiple dimensions and induce gridlock.

One puzzle these models point to is, why do other institutions, such as the Congress or the President, defer to the judicial claim to finality in constitutional interpretation? One of the founding debates in the United States was about who, if anyone, ought to have the final say on questions of what the Constitution means. Thomas Jefferson, notably, made strong arguments that his own capacity to interpret the Constitution was no less than that of the courts. And, the Civil War was in large part driven by a conflict about the competing claims by the state and federal governments to constitutional interpretation. However, today it is widely accepted that the Supreme Court's interpretation of the Constitution is authoritative and final, even if we do not understand exactly how the agreement is sustained. (Of course, there are often notable examples of challenges to the Supreme Court's authority and the finality of its decisions (e.g., Clark 2011), of which recent efforts to evade the Supreme Court's support for same-sex marriage is but one example.)

In fact, that insight in particular gives rise to the kinds of issues that drive the mass-level approaches to judicial context. Scholars working in the law and society tradition, for example, emphasize the social and electoral forces that shape constitutional (and other legal) decision making. In his famous account of implementation of judicial decisions, Rosenberg (1991) illustrates how major social change such as the integration of public schools was not achieved once the Supreme Court ordered an end to racial segregation in *Brown* v. *Board of Education* but rather after social demand for integration grew and electoral politics shifted, giving rise to efforts by Presidents Kennedy and Johnson to pass civil rights legislation. In general, Rosenberg claims, courts can only bring about social change when others in politics and society also desire the change to happen – for example, the courts can partner, in effect, with legislators who can pass legislation, executives who can use enforcement powers, or the private world and market forces. Rosenberg's conclusion that courts are not effective agents for social change unless they can marshal the support of other segments of society, while still really focused on elite-level interactions, sets into motion a complicated line of thought about the way society uses the law – especially, constitutional law – to change the world.

One of the primary concerns of these studies is the process by which individuals who have legal claims (constitutional or otherwise) get to court. These studies are consequential for our analytic history of constitutional decision making, because they go to the heart of the selection process that translates the set of constitutional questions or disputes in the world into the issues on which the Supreme Court ultimately decides. Epp's (1998) study of legal support structures shows there is considerable variation around the world in the extent to which people have access to the resources they need to bring rights claims to the courts, and later studies show how variation in the availability of motivated, resourced lawyers can explain varying patterns of bureaucratic reform and legal change (e.g., Epp 2010; Wahlbeck 1997; Galanter 1974).

Much of this line of thought derives from Galanter's (1974) observation that not all litigants are created equal; some are "repeat players" who appear before the courts often and develop expertise in achieving their policy goals, whereas others are "one-shotters" who are unlikely to appear before the courts often.[6] Galanter points out that the differences between these types of litigants create several advantages for repeat players. For example, repeat players are incentivized to conceive of any given case as just one of a routine set of disputes and can "play the odds," benefit from economies of scale in preparing for litigation, develop relationships with judges, and use reputation as a commitment device to aid in bargaining (Galanter 1974, 98–100). In addition, interests in society differ with respect to their access to resources that can give them

---

[6] Galanter conceives of the difference as a matter of degree rather than a sharp dichotomy, and that the repeat player and one-shotter are simply "ideal types" of litigants.

access to government. One of the consequences, Galanter notes, is that litigants with less access to resources – the "have-nots" – will be less likely to be able to use traditional pathways to legal change, such as by lobbying for legislation or administrative action. Thus, these interests in society are relatively more likely to use the litigation process to change legal rules. However, the litigants who will be best-positioned to make use of litigation to pursue rule changes will be repeat players, rather than one-shotters.

An integral part of the history of constitutional law, then, is the interaction between the distribution of resources in society, organization of interests, and macro-level patterns in the economy and electoral politics. Demand for legal change or constitutional protections rises out of political movements, economic conditions, and other contingencies. However, from whom those demands come can determine the extent to which they make their way into court and ultimately affect constitutional law. Poorly organized or resourced interests are less likely to be able to make their way through the litigation process and bring about major legal change. This is even more so the case when the social troubles that give rise to the demand do not affect masses of individuals in transparent ways and therefore create a rather diffuse class of aggrieved individuals.

As we will see in Chapters 6 and 7, the role of advocating for marginalized or unorganized interests has been filled at various times by special groups that organize for the purpose of becoming repeat players who advocate for their constituents through litigation (among other methods). The National Association for the Advancement of Colored People (NAACP) formed in 1909 to protect individual rights, particularly for racial minorities. The American Civil Liberties Union (ACLU) formed in 1920 to advocate for civil liberties protections. Each of these groups made litigation a high priority early on, recognizing the relative accessibility of change in the law through the courts. Clearly, their emergence was driven by social and political conditions during the early twentieth century, and their efforts have had considerable influence on American constitutional law. Thus, a further component of the contextual microtheories that are relevant for understanding constitutional decision making is the method by which special interests organize in response to societal demands for legal remedies to problems. As civil rights progress made during Reconstruction was rolled back during the late nineteenth century, African-Americans developed a need to organize and pursue their rights, in part through litigation, and the answer was the establishment of the National Association for the Advancement of Colored People (NAACP). As the fear of communism grew during and after World War I, politicians responded with efforts to curb free speech, and the

American Civil Liberties Association (ACLU) emerged as an institutional organization to solve that problem. Because those groups have been so influential in constitutional law, theories of their emergence – including the social and political conditions that bring about their existence – as well as theories of their litigation strategies can account for changing patterns in the issues and questions that give rise to constitutional precedents and developments in the law.

Importantly, as the theoretical dimensionality of a policy space increases, these dynamics are further complicated. The more dimensions there are to a problem, the more "lines of attack" there are on a given case. There are more ways of distinguishing a new case from a past one (e.g., Gennaioli and Shleifer 2007), as the number of "similar but different" cases increases. This more complicated fact-space means that organized interests – potentially focused on a single dimension of a subset of the dimensions – face problems coordinating with each other and competing interests have a greater number of opportunities to challenge each other. Moreover, the task of constructing a policy that consistently handles cases and pleases all of the relevant interests becomes far more challenging.

Taking the insights from the literature on both separation of powers and social change to the analytic history of constitutional decision making, there are a number of instructive lessons. The first is that the political-institutional setting in which the Court finds itself can have important implications for the direction of constitutional law. Judges craft legal rules in order to produce real-world outcomes when the law is applied. How elected officials will implement a decision therefore can shape what type of rule the judges will select. Second, the consequences of the application of their rules can create significant feedback, driving social organization, political and legal responses, and other related developments. The contextual microtheories, therefore, make clear that in order to interpret aggregate patterns of decisions we must incorporate information about the context in which the individual decisions were made as well as the contextual developments that unfold in between those individual decisions.

2.2.3 From Microtheories to Political Cleavages and Macropatterns

The microtheories of judicial decision making we have seen here, as well as others I have not covered, illustrate the complexities involved with interpreting aggregate patterns of constitutional decision making. Microtheories illustrate how aggregate patterns are driven by the inter-actions among structural factors and time-specific contingencies – both internal and external to the Court. They also shed light on the logic of understanding politics as an organizing principle of law. If constitutional law is an extremely low-dimensional, perhaps single-dimensional, political space, then judicial heresthetics, social organizations, and inter-institutional conflicts have different implications for judicial choice than in a world where constitutional politics are higher dimensional. For example, when we think about law from the perspective of political cleavages, we begin to see a way to approach the nexus of microfoundations and macropatterns in the law. The legal rules depicted in the panels in Figure 2.3 are built through the resolution of individual cases. So, the way to resolve any given case at any given point in time may be relatively straight-forward, but difficult problems arise when we start thinking about how those well-understood decision processes play out in sequence over time. As we can see in Figure 2.3, the greater judges disagree – i.e., the more polarized the judges' preferences about how to partition the case space – the more room there is for cases to arise that divide the judges differently. It is also the case that there is a greater chance for cases to arise where, under the existing precedent, some group of judges is displeased with how those cases are resolved. Thus, the dimensionality of the constitutional-political space interacts with the preferences of the particular justices on the Court at a given point in time as well as with the structure of existing precedent and law.

The question remains, how many dimensions best describe the legal landscape, and what is the right balance of parsimony and substantive nuance? The answer to this question, as we will see, lies in better bringing our theoretical knowledge to bear on our empirical methods and making better use of the variety of information we have at hand about judicial decision making. On one hand, standard political science accounts of politics that envision a very low-dimensional model – typically, all debates are projected onto a single underlying dimension – mask important nuances in the way law and courts work. Doctrinal models, by contrast, often lack parsimony and overstate the degree of complexity in judicial decision making. The claim here is that there is a middle ground in which politics projects the high-dimensional doctrinal model into a more manageable, but still substantively meaningful, space of a small number of political-legal dimensions.

It is instructive to contrast this view of law and doctrine to the more traditional approaches, especially the political development tradition. There, as we saw above, law is thought to be a force that shapes politics – especially, constitutional law is thought to shape constitutional politics. The politics of judicial decision making, in particular, are structured by the content and text of the constitution, laws, doctrines, and so forth. The view I propose here is one in which we consider the flip side of that argument, where politics, and political cleavages and battles, shape the content of the law. The issues considered, the resolutions reached, the rules judges develop and apply are themselves shaped by the larger political cleavages that characterize political decision making. Importantly, this perspective explicitly embraces the notion that law does not operate as a constraint on politics but instead that, as noted above, law is the medium with which judges work, while politics is the motivation that gives rise to their goals.

Put perhaps most simply, by joining the microfoundations of judicial choice with an interest in the macropatterns of legal development, a focus on how politics organizes legal disputes provides some traction on a very complicated process. We can more effectively understand how decisions that take place at different points in time relate to each other through the common or disparate political dimensions at play. More specifically, orienting analysis of constitutional law around the political cleavages that characterize the judiciary provides a powerful way to study how judges perceive the stakes of a given case, how they perceive the ways in which various cases link to each other to build a body of doctrine, and how they interpret broader political and social developments as they relate to their cases. The more general point is that the macropatterns in doctrinal development can be understood best in light of micro-level theories of judicial decision making and the political cleavages that organize the conflicts among judges, politicians, and the public.

2.3 CONCLUSION

The study of constitutional law has a rich, long history in academic scholarship. Various intellectual traditions focus on particular aspects of constitutional law, ranging from humanistic, historical accounts of the development of law to social-scientific studies systematic features of judicial decision making. As these lines of study have evolved, they have brought about a stark contrast between "law" and "politics." Today, powerful theoretical models are being developed that help reconcile that tension, providing analytic leverage over the relationship between law and politics. I argue that a fruitful avenue for understanding the development involves using the various intellectual approaches in conjunction to study the various forces that drive the development of constitutional law. Specifically, these complementary approaches to constitutional law best illuminate the model of judicial decision making that I described in Chapter 1 when taken in conjunction.

In the next chapter, I present an empirical model that I use through the rest of the book to document the path of constitutional decision making.

I show in that chapter how the model can be derived from the case-space model and as a consequence how we can interpret the empirical quantities in light of the theoretical models of the judicial process I have outlined here. The model is useful for both estimating specific quantities of interest that drive case-space models of judicial decision making as well as for studying macropatterns from groups of cases decided across long periods of time. Such an analysis facilitates the application of various intellectual traditions to a single analytic history of constitutional decision making.

A significant challenge one must confront in bringing these various intellectual traditions together concerns how to integrate competing, or even just complementary, theoretical perspectives that begin from inconsistent first principles. For example, political development approaches to constitutional decision making typically have the goal of explaining the forces and factors responsible for a particular outcome in a particular case. Behavioral models, as well as case-space models, typically have microfoundations at the level of the individual case but are designed to explain aggregate, macropatterns, rather than any given case. As I have argued here, the objective of an analytic history of constitutional decision making is not to start with a single, unified model of constitutional law to be articulated and evaluated; rather the goal is to provide a rich account of constitutional decision making that makes use of the various models of constitutional law as appropriate. Thus, in the remaining pages of this book, I borrow extensively from the various intellectual traditions outlined here and rely at different points on different models to different extents. The unifying theme is an effort to describe aggregate patterns in constitutional decision making by reference to microtheories of politics inside and outside of the Supreme Court.

3

An Empirical Model of Constitutional Decision Making

In this chapter, I turn from the theory of studying constitutional law as a set of political cleavages to an empirical approach for measuring and describing constitutional law from our theoretical perspective. The key obstacle to address is that the theoretical apparatus developed in the preceding chapter posits an abstract set of political dimensions that do not exist in the legal world but are instead useful constructs for summarizing the law. How do we empirically measure and represent the political cleavages that motivate our theories of decision making? One approach, which motivates the empirical strategy in this chapter, relies on things we *can* see and measure to represent the abstract, latent concepts. In the world of statistics – especially in statistical social science – there is a long tradition of using mathematical models to tease out the common underlying patterns in things we see in the world in order to estimate those unobserved, latent patterns or ideas. Many of the empirical tools I rely on here are derived from or are similar to models that researchers in education have developed in order to translate students' answers to questions on tests into summaries of latent characteristics. The SAT, for example, measures college applicants' aptitude for math, reading comprehension, and writing, using test-takers' answers to questions that rely on that aptitude.

In what follows, I describe a series of models that can be used to estimate ideological preference dimensions in constitutional jurisprudence. The model is the product of collaboration with my co-author, Ben Lauderdale, and comes from a series of related publications we wrote together. The goal is not to lay out a single, unified, comprehensive model of "the law" – such a model would be too complex and cumbersome to be analytically useful. Models must, by necessity, focus on select elements of the subject being studied. Instead, in this chapter, I present a single empirical model that can be used to study a variety of the elements of

judicial decision making that can shed light on the theoretical approaches
I have considered. As we will see below, the model not only delivers
on the theoretical, and conceptual, concerns raised in previous chapters,
but in doing so also overcomes many limitations confronted in previous
attempts to empirically model the law.

As I present the model, I offer both its general intuition as well as
formalizations of the model. Where it makes sense to do so, I reserve
technical details for the appendix, though there are several points at
which more formal presentations warrant inclusion in the main body
of the chapter. At each point, however, I strive to convey the logic and
method in broadly accessible language to facilitate comprehension by the
non-technical reader.

The chapter proceeds in two steps. First, I describe an approach to
modeling the dimensions of the law and judicial preferences across those
different dimensions. The approach I advance begins from the premise
that the best way to empirically study judicial voting and the law will
both relate to the theory of judicial voting and law we saw in the previous
chapter (especially the case-space model) and make use of information
contained in data as appropriately as possible. Second, I describe an
approach to modeling the content of what judges do in their opinions,
specifically focusing on the evolution of an area of law through a series
of cases (i.e., how new cases logically build on old ones) while also
investigating the content of that doctrine (i.e., how liberal or conservative
are the judicial rules). Third, I describe how we can relate the empirical
tool to theoretical models and develop an analytic history.

3.1 MODELING JUDICIAL TOPICS AND VOTING

A defining characteristic of my empirical approach is that I set out to use
various kinds of data in conjunction with each other in order to extract
the information that each kind of data best captures. Typically, in most
empirical studies in political science – and related social sciences – we
start with a theoretical concept and then ask what data best measure
that concept. The twist, then, is to start with the data we have and
ask what we can learn from them and then to ask what we can learn
by using various kinds of data in conjunction with each other. This
approach is particularly promising in the context of trying to measure
judicial preferences across different dimensions of the law. Traditionally,
as in most measurement exercises in politics, one takes the judges' votes
as the clearest manifestation of what judges think about any given case,
and then use the patterns in those votes to infer not just how the judges
align relative to each other, but also the dimensionality of their political

disagreements. This last part is where things become complicated. To see why, consider an analogous example – educational testing.

The SAT or GRE generally measure scholastic aptitude on two dimensions – verbal skills and quantitative reasoning. However, those tests do not combine every question together and then try to estimate two dimensions of aptitude. Trying to do so means we would be trying to learn more from the data – test-takers' answers – than is practical. We would be trying to learn both the test-taker's aptitude and what the question is measuring. In the most trivial illustration of why, consider a single question that a test-taker answered correctly. One possibility is that the question was a question about verbal aptitude, and so the correct answer contributes to a higher estimate of the test-taker's verbal aptitude score. Alternatively, the question might be about quantitative aptitude, and so the question contributes to the test-taker's quantitative aptitude score. How can the mathematical equation know which it is?

One approach might be to have the test-taker answer many questions in the hope that we could uncover a common pattern among quantitative questions and verbal questions. But, that may be asking a lot of our estimation methods, in part because it would rely on making (potentially strong) assumptions about the relationships among quantitative and verbal aptitudes. Suppose a student answers exactly half of the questions correctly. We might conclude all of the incorrect answers were on the verbal section, all of the correct ones on the quantitative section, and therefore that the student has high quantitative aptitude and low verbal aptitude. Alternatively, we might conclude that the questions are evenly mixed across the two dimensions and so the student has moderate aptitude on both dimensions. How could we know? The problem is that we are still trying to learn two different things from the answer to each question: the student's aptitude and what the question itself is measuring (i.e., quantitative or verbal aptitude). However, responses to the questions are most informative about aptitude; there is other, better information regarding what the question is measuring. We ought not to use the answers to determine what the question was about. Instead, the answer, from the perspective of educational testing, is that the test-writers *know* which questions are verbal aptitude questions and which questions are quantitative aptitude questions. So, they divide the questions into two separate tests and then simply scale each of the aptitudes separately. In other words, there is, in fact, better information than the answers to tell you what the questions are measuring – the content of the questions themselves.

This basic principle carries over to the context of measuring political ideology. Unfortunately, judges do not neatly divide their decisions into separate categories, such as "cases about individual liberty" and "cases about constitutional limits on delegation" and so forth. Indeed, in some sense doing so would artificially divide up cases more so than they truly are. Many – possibly most or all – cases touch on issues that activate multiple political dimensions judicial ideology. As we will see in Chapter 5, many cases reach across what one might suspect to be very disparate political consideration. However, that does not mean that we cannot determine which cases associate more or less with other cases. The key is to use auxiliary information about the substantive connections among cases.

The particular structure of political voting, in which votes are not clearly (or easily) divisible into discrete dimensions, thus poses a problem for the standard toolkit social scientists use to measure political preferences. In the context of the US Supreme Court, as an example, multiple scholars have attempted to develop ideal point models that extend the baseline framework commonly used to multiple dimensions. Below, I discuss some of the technical aspects of these studies, but the crucial point to observe here is that the challenges of inferring multiple dimensions of political conflict from nine yes/no votes per case mean that scholars have traditionally had to rely on the models themselves, rather than the richness of the data they study. The goal here is to develop a statistical model that is minimally restrictive and instead relies on the richest kinds of data we can.

3.2 A MODEL OF JUDICIAL VOTING

The case-space model of judicial behavior has many attractive properties; however, it is not clear how to relate vote-based estimates of judicial preferences to the theoretical representation of preferences employed in case-space modeling. One of the most widely used models for estimating preferences from voting is the item-response theory ("IRT") model. I describe the model in technical detail below, but briefly, the IRT model is a model that measures individuals' propensity to vote the same way, and that propensity is then typically interpreted to be a measure of latent ideology. The IRT model is one of justices picking which litigant they are closer to, but in a case-space model of judicial voting, preferences are thresholds separating cases into case dispositions. The distinction is consequential, because, as we will see shortly, the derivation of the IRT model from a theory of legislative voting is what gives the quantities a theoretical interpretation. However, because the theoretical model of legislative voting is qualitatively different from the theoretical model of judicial voting, we lose the interpretation that comes from an IRT model applied in a legislative setting. It turns out, though, that one can derive the IRT model from the case-space model itself. First, however, it is useful to provide a more thorough background of the development and application of IRT models in traditional political settings.

3.2.1 Derivations of Statistical Models of Voting

In Chapter 2 I described the case-space model of judicial decision making. This model posits cases as the analytic unit and judicial preferences as thresholds. In a unidimensional model, these thresholds are simply points that divide the space into two outcomes. In a two-dimensional model, the thresholds are lines that partition the space, and in higher-dimensional models, they are (hyper)planes. How does one relate the theoretical concepts in the case-space model of judicial decision making to traditional estimators of judicial preferences? To answer this question, let us first begin with a brief overview of a simple version of standard approaches (Martin and Quinn 2002; Bailey 2007; Clark and Lauderdale 2010; Lauderdale and Clark 2014), which is to employ an item-response model (Jackman 2001) to model judicial votes. The application of this model to the judicial context was most effectively developed and implemented by Martin and Quinn (2002), who proposed a dynamic version of the model in which individual justices' ideal points could vary over time. Their paper is among the most widely cited in the field and remains to this day a mainstay of empirical research on judicial behavior.

The traditional derivation of ideal point models. As noted above, the item-response model of ideal point estimation is usually grounded in a theoretical model of voting. Of course, there are many behavioral models of voting that yield observationally equivalent predictions about the choices individuals will make. Therefore, the fact that a statistical model can be derived from a given behavioral model does not ensure that we can discriminate among competing theories (e.g., Bateman, Clinton, and Lapinksi 2016). Nevertheless, given many theories of voting behavior, scholars often assume a random-utility model of voting, in which voters have an ideal point in a (usually) unidimensional policy space. Voters are confronted with a choice between two options. (Typically, one option is the status quo, and the other is an alternative, the proposal being considered.) Several possible versions of this model have been proposed, one of which is advanced by Clinton, Jackman and Rivers (2004). In their formalization, voters receive utility equal to the (negative of the) quadratic distance between their ideal points and the option for which they vote – i.e., either the status quo or the alternative proposal – plus a random error associated with each vote.[1] The random error means that

---

[1] Another model assumes Gaussian, rather than quadratic, utility losses (Poole and Rosenthal 1997).

there might be something about any given vote that makes a voter like one proposal better than the other, independent of the options' locations in the policy dimension. The model simply assumes those differences are random relative to the policy element of the choice.

Consider a vote, c, between two options. (Typically, j is used as a subscript to denote votes. In what follows, when we move this model into the judicial voting context, judges will be voting on cases, and so I used c to ease interpretation of notation later.) Clinton et al. (among others) assume that the alternative proposal is given by ζ_c, which is a point in the policy space, and so voting "Yea" (in favor of the alternative) yields utility $U_i(\zeta_c) = -\|\theta_i - \zeta_c\|^2 + \eta_{ic}$ for voter i. (The notation $\|\cdot\|$ indicates the Euclidean distance.) The status quo is given by ψ_c, also a point in the policy space, and so the utility for voter i for voting "Nay" is given by $U_i(\psi_c) = -\|\theta_i - \psi_c\|^2 + \nu_{ic}$. In other words, a voter's utility depends only on the proximity of the policy options to her ideal point and a random (i.e., orthogonal) component. We therefore can express the probability that voter i votes "Yea" as the probability that $U_i(\zeta_c)$ is greater than $U_i(\psi_c)$. The random elements of the utility – the stochastic things associated with each vote – are what make it a question of probability. If there were no random elements, then the ideological distance would completely determine the voting behavior.

Clinton et al. show how one can algebraically rearrange those two utility functions to give rise to the item-response model itself. I reproduce their arithmetic and derivation in the appendix to this chapter. However, the crucial point is that the simplest version of the item-response model, which assumes all individuals have constant ideal points, is given as follows. Let $y_{ic} =$ Yea if $y_{ic}^* \geq 0$, and $y_{ic} =$ Nay if $y_{ic}^* < 0$, where y_{ic}^* is the difference in utility between voting Yea and voting Nay. That is, voter i votes Yea on vote j if the latent utility associated with the Yea vote is positive and votes Nay otherwise. Then, the random utility model implies

$$y_{ic}^* \sim \mathcal{N}\left(\beta_c\theta_i - \alpha_c, \sigma_y^2\right) \qquad (3.1)$$

The random elements of the voters' utilities are captured by the parameter σ_y^2, which can be estimated or assumed fixed.[2] Typically, we assume that α_c is an unknown parameter to be estimated and that it can take on any value in a given range. A standard approach is to assume it is normally

---

[2] In principle, one can assume anything about the distribution of the error terms. A common alternative to the model described here is to assume that the errors in the random utility voting model underlying this estimator follow an extreme value distribution and therefore that the link function is the logistic distribution rather than the normal.

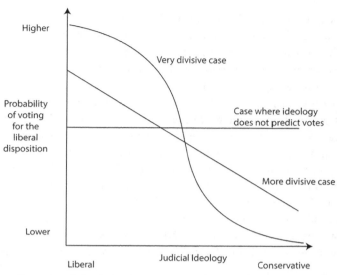

Figure 3.1. *Examples of discrimination parameters for cases that are more or less divisive on ideological grounds.*

distributed with mean zero. Formally, we usually assume $\alpha_c \sim \mathcal{N}(0, \sigma_\alpha^2)$, where we set σ_α^2 to be very large. This permits the voting data to be relatively unconstrained in how much they can influence our estimate of α_c. The α parameters are commonly called *difficulty* parameters. This label derives from the item-response model's use in educational studies – such as SAT or GRE settings – in which the dependent variable, Y, indicates whether a test-taker gets each question correct. The more difficult a question, the less likely a student with any given aptitude is to get any particular question correct. In the setting of ideal point estimation, the difficulty parameters capture, instead, how likely a justice is, *ceteris paribus* to vote with the majority. That is, some cases are those such that relatively many judges (i.e., liberals and conservatives alike) are going to agree, compared with other cases that are more divisive. In the language of the case-space model, these are cases where the case location is relatively extreme compared with the distribution of judges' thresholds.

The β_c parameters, by contrast, are often called the *discrimination* parameters. These parameters measure how much case c *discriminates* among judges of different ideological orientations. Consider Figure 3.1: the different lines show different discrimination parameters. The flat line is one where a judge's ideal point does not predict whether she will vote with the majority in a given case; the increasingly steeper lines show cases where the ideological dimension more sharply divides judges along the ideological dimension. In educational settings, we generally assume that β is positive. We know what a correct decision is, and so we assume that the higher a test-taker is on the latent dimension (θ), the more likely she is to answer the question correctly. Therefore, we assume that β_c can take on any positive value and typically assign very diffuse priors to β_c with support only on positive values. However, in the context of ideal point estimation, especially when scaling legislators using roll calls or judges using case disposition votes, we cannot make such an assumption. The reason is, we do not know whether being higher on the latent dimension makes you *more* or *less* likely to vote Yea. That depends, obviously, on whether the proposal is to move policy in a conservative or a liberal direction, for example. As contrasted with the educational setting, we cannot easily know which outcome is more liberal or more conservative. Thus, we instead assume that β_c is distributed similarly to α_c – it can be positive *or* negative. Typically we assume $\beta_c \sim \mathcal{N}\left(0, \sigma_\beta^2\right)$, where, as above, we set σ_β^2 very large.

An important consequence of this difference between roll call ideal point estimation and educational scaling is that there are two ideal points that are equally likely for every judge or legislator (e.g., Rivers 2003). Suppose we estimate that Justice Scalia has an ideal point of +2. We could instead estimate that his ideal point is −2 by simply flipping the signs on all of the difficulty (α_c) and discrimination (β_c) parameters and flip everyone's ideal point sign. In this situation, the posterior estimates of ideal points, difficulty, and discrimination parameters are said to be bimodal, because they place equal likelihood on each value and its negative for each case and justice. As a consequence, the model is unidentified up to a polar rotation, a problem that is well understood in the statistical and applied literatures (e.g., Jackman 2001; Rivers 2003). Recall our educational testing example. Suppose each question only had two answers – a correct and an incorrect answer – and we did not know which answer was the correct answer for each question; instead all we could know is that students who picked one answer on the test tended to group together with students who pick common answers across all questions. We could not know, then, which positions for the test-takers – higher or lower on our scale – are associated with higher or lower aptitude. In educational testing, this would be a major problem.

In the political context, there are several ways of dealing with this technical incompleteness in the model (for a thorough treatment, see Rivers 2003), but one way that is commonly adopted is to simply accept the bimodal posterior estimates and to select the posterior estimates that place individuals we strongly believe to be conservative at the positive end and individuals we strongly believe to be liberal at the negative end (e.g., the model where Scalia is at $+2$ instead of -2 and Thurgood Marshall is at -2 instead of $+2$). Other approaches include fixing the ideal point for two justices, rather than estimating them – e.g., assuming Marshall is at -2 and Scalia is at $+2$. This has the consequence of fixing the scale itself so that a 4-unit difference on the dimension is defined to be the difference between Scalia and Marshall (e.g., Martin and Quinn 2002). In a multidimensional setting, this approach is at best difficult and potentially impossible, because we need to select distances between two actors that we believe are comparable across all of the dimensions. Selecting a distance of, for example, four units in a single dimension simply sets an arbitrary scale to that dimension. However, once the scale is fixed, it is no longer arbitrary, and we need to make comparable assumptions along all of the other dimensions.

Of course, one could, in principle, make a decision about which case outcome is conservative and which is liberal. One might use, for example, exogenous coding of which litigant represents the liberal orientation in a case (e.g., Spaeth et al. 2015). This approach is not common, however, and there are likely several reasons why. First, it would require collecting additional information for each case; the votes would not be sufficient, but rather we would also need to know the "polarity" for each case. Collecting that information would require the development of extensive coding rules that would hopefully be reliable and valid. As we saw in the previous chapter, there have been various attempts to code this information directly, most notably in the Supreme Court Database. However, as we also saw in that chapter, it can be very difficult to develop coding rules that do not allow discretion to creep into the coding in undesirable ways.

However, there exists a second, more philosophical reason to not fix the polarity of each vote *a priori*. Namely, given there are sufficient votes cast by each justice, there should be enough information in the voting data to tell us how the two possible dispositions in each case (reverse v. affirm) align across all of the cases (see Tahk 2015, for a discussion). That is, we should "let the data speak for themselves." Consider an example. In one case, a labor union is the petitioner and is asking the Court to find that the employer discriminated against female employees who became pregnant by not accommodating them in the workplace with alternative work duties. One might reasonably conclude that the labor union was on the "liberal side" in that case. However, we might imagine many details about the union, the case, the employer, and the law that could change our interpretation of what constitutes the "liberal" side. The philosophical point that we should let the data speak for themselves holds that if the model is flexible enough (as it is), then we should not impose strong assumptions about the polarity of each case but instead estimate the polarity by looking at which justices vote for the labor union. If the justices vote as the model predicts – if they divide along a latent political dimension – then voting patterns will reveal which cases present a "liberal" petitioner and which present a "conservative" petitioner. We will be able to know this because the justices who commonly vote together in other cases will, theoretically, also vote together in this case.

A case-space derivation of the ideal point model. Returning to our motivation, a major question implicated by the traditional derivation of the item response theory model concerns how one theoretically interprets the various quantities in the model. The random utility model of voting is one of voters choosing between two alternatives as a function of their relative distances in some ideological space to the voter. However, the case-space model of judicial voting and conventional understanding of what judges do does not proceed from such a theory of judicial voting. A judge may see a litigant as being very near to her own ideal point, in terms of the litigants' world view, desired outcomes, or actions, etc., but nevertheless to have taken an action that is beyond what the judge sees as acceptable. The judge may therefore be compelled to vote for a "more distant" litigant. In this sense, then, the judge is not selecting between some status quo and alternative proposal on the grounds of which is more attractive. Instead, the judge is deciding whether the case presents a factual scenario that exceeds the judge's ideal threshold of what is acceptable. Notably, this element of the decision-making process is fundamentally different than the idea that there may exist random factors associated with different votes that are orthogonal to the spatial element of the vote.

Does this imply, then, that the item-response model of judicial voting is a lost cause from a theoretical perspective? How do we interpret the estimated ideal points? What does the difficulty parameter represent? Are the myriad studies developing or making use of ideal point models of judicial voting fundamentally, theoretically, and fatally flawed? The answer is *no*. It turns out one can derive the same estimator from the case-space model of judicial voting and that such a derivation provides us with a theoretically grounded interpretation of the model's parameters.

In principle, the item-response theory model can be derived from any voting model in which there is a latent dimension along which individuals are located and there is a threshold in that dimension that neatly divides them into voting blocks. To see how the item-response theory model can be interpreted from a case-space perspective, consider the following model. Let each case j have a location in a unidimensional case space, where each case's location is denoted x_c. Similarly, let each judge i have an ideal threshold θ_i, such that the judge prefers to vote for the plaintiff, denoted Π_c, if $x_c \geq \theta_i$ – that is, if the case presents a factual scenario exceeding the judge's threshold, then the judge prefers to vote for the plaintiff. Otherwise, we say the judge prefers to vote for the defendant, denoted Δ_c. In particular, assume that the utility for judge i from voting for the plaintiff is given by

$$U_i(\Pi_c) = \beta_c(\theta_i - x_c) + v_{ic} \tag{3.2}$$

where v_{ic} is a random error associated with the case. That is, as in the random utility voting model typically used, we here assume some random element that is not related to the case's location relative to the justice's ideal point. Notice, this utility function simply assumes that the utility a judge gets from her vote is a function of how much of a "close call" the case is, as well as a random component. Cases that present factual scenarios relatively close to the judge's threshold do not have much consequence for the judge's utility. Getting a "close call" case wrong is less painful than getting an obvious, "easy" case wrong. The further away a case is from the judge's threshold, the stronger the judge's distaste for casting a vote inconsistent with her own opinion. Now, further assume a parallel utility function characterizes the judge's utility from voting for the defendant in case j:

$$U_i(\Delta_c) = \beta_j(x_c - \theta_i) + \eta_{ic} \tag{3.3}$$

where, as v_{ic}, η_{ic} is a random component.

Following these assumptions about the judge's utility function, the relative attractiveness of voting for the plaintiff is given by

$$y_{ic}^* = U_i(\Pi_c) - U_i(\Delta_c) \tag{3.4}$$

Now, let $y_{ic} = 1$ if we observe judge i voting for the plaintiff in case c, and $y_{ic} = 0$ if we observe judge i voting for the defendant in case c. Our model of judicial voting implies

$$y_{ic} = \begin{cases} 1 \Longleftrightarrow y_{ic}^* > 0 \\ 0 \Longleftrightarrow y_{ic}^* \leq 0 \end{cases} \tag{3.5}$$

Substituting in the expressions of $U_i(\Pi_c)$ and $U_i(\Delta_c)$, we have

$$y_{ic}^* = \beta_c(\theta_i - x_c) - \beta_c(x_c - \theta_i) + v_{ic} - \eta_{ic} \tag{3.6}$$

which can be rewritten as

$$y_{ic}^* = 2\beta_c\theta_i - 2\beta_c x_c + e_{ic} \tag{3.7}$$

where $e_{ic} = v_{ic} - \eta_{ic}$. It we divide through by 2 and let $\alpha_{ic} = \beta_c x_c$, then we can rewrite the equation as

$$y_{ic}^* = \beta_c \theta_i - \alpha_c + e_{ic} \qquad (3.8)$$

If we assume simply that the errors – η_{ic} and v_{ic} – have a joint normal distribution with $\mathbb{E}[v_{ic}] = \mathbb{E}[\eta_{ic}]$ and $\text{Var}(v_{ic} - \eta_{ic}) = \sigma_y^2$, we have

$$y_{ic}^* \sim \mathcal{N}\left(\beta_c \theta_i - \alpha_c, \sigma_y^2\right) \qquad (3.9)$$

where judge i votes for the plaintiff if $y_{ic}^* \geq 0$ and for the defendant otherwise. Notice this is identical to Equation (3.1). Thus, we have derived the item-response theory model from an alternative voting model – one grounded in a theoretical model of judicial decision making rather than legislative voting.

Moreover, our derivation allows us to theoretically interpret each of the various parameters in the model. For example, we now know that θ represents the dimension of thresholds in a case-space model. We also know that $x_c = \frac{\alpha_c}{\beta_c}$, so that dividing each case's difficulty parameter by its discrimination parameter yields the case location itself. In fact, in any model, the point of indifference between voting choices is given by $\frac{\alpha_c}{\beta_c}$. In the case-space model, the case location is the point of indifference; in policy space models, the point of indifference is the midpoint between two policy choices.

This last part is particularly important. *The item-response model of judicial votes yields a valid empirical representation of the theoretical elements of the case-space model: both the judges' thresholds and the case locations.* As I alluded to in the previous chapter, the inability to simultaneously measure these features of the model have given rise to deep challenges to the practical utility of the model in empirically driven social science of law and courts (Knight 2009).

Being able to theoretically interpret the quantities we estimate from the IRT model of voting, in the context of a case-space model, provides considerable new empirical leverage to a line of research that has had trouble going from theoretical models to empirical research. The derivation here shows us that we can not just estimate judges' ideal points but that their estimated ideal points have a direct interpretation as thresholds in a fact space. That is, rather than interpret ideal points as latent preferences for voting for one litigant or another, as we might under the traditional random utility voting model that motivates the IRT estimator, we can now interpret ideal points as thresholds in fact space. This helps shift our focus from dispositional voting as the central interest to doctrinal or legal preferences. Moreover, we can also now estimate case locations, given our knowledge of how the difficulty and discrimination parameters relate to each other in terms of the fact space. Because the case-space model puts cases in a position of central analytic importance, the absence of them from past measurement strategies has presented a conundrum to scholars seeking to empirically operationalize these theoretical models.

These features of the model provide particularly powerful tools for analytic history. We can use the IRT model of judicial voting to study both aggregate patterns – where the justices stand relative to each other – as well as particular examples – using the case parameters in a theoretically structured way. As Knight (2009) has pointed out, one of the limitations of the case-space model as an analytic tool is that it has been difficult to translate the model into an empirical research agenda. In Chapter 2, we saw how the model can be used to help identify the causal mechanisms that play out at the micro-level when we interpret aggregate historical patterns. The discussion here shows how we can use the model in conjunction with empirical models to evaluate voting patterns in light of those microtheories. Indeed, I think that this observation moves us further in the spirit of Knight's concern that the case-space model be put to empirical use, as the relationship between the quantities of interest from the empirical model and the theoretical framework allows us to use those microtheories to interpret macropatterns in constitutional decision making. These two tasks, taken together, provide the foundation for an analytic history of constitutional decision making.

Limitations to estimating and interpreting the model. Of course, simply because the case-space model allows us to theoretically interpret the IRT model parameters does not mean that the IRT model itself does not still present challenges – conceptual as well as practical. First, as we will see in Chapter 4, most cases are decided by a unanimous vote. When a vote is unanimous, we cannot infer from the votes anything about the justices' ordering relative to each other or about the case-specific parameters (the difficulty and discrimination parameters). Therefore, in those cases, the voting data do not yield any information about the case location, and so the locations of all unanimous cases will be driven entirely by our assumptions about the distribution of case parameters.

What is more, the case-space interpretation of the IRT model does not resolve the identification problem we saw above. The IRT model is still unidentified up to a polar rotation about 0, unless we want to make assumptions about which justices have ideal points above or below 0 or about the cardinal distance between two justices (e.g., Rivers 2003). Thus, we cannot use the model to orient the case-space model. However, as we also saw above, there is a sufficient number of approaches to resolving this difficulty.

Third, changing docket/issues could make over-time comparisons hard. As with all models of voting, we must make some assumptions about how the difficulty and discrimination parameters relate to each other over time, as well as how individual voters' ideal points change (if at all) over time. Most models, including the one here, assume that there is a common distribution of difficulty and discrimination parameters at all points in time. That is, the extent to which the cases the justices decide divides them along ideological grounds is not systematically changing over time. However, to the extent the preference dimensions activated by a case are associated with the divisiveness of the case, the model I present below should be able to incorporate at least part of any systematic variation over time. Further, I assume that justices' ideal points are constant over time. This decision is made both for reasons of technical tractability but also because of past work in which we show that most variation in justices' voting is due to differences in their preferences across substantive areas of the law, rather than temporal variation (Lauderdale and Clark 2012). Thus, while not a perfect solution, the combination of the substantive information from the opinions with the voting data can mitigate some of these challenges.

In sum, the case-space model provides a useful analytic tool for interpreting the empirical technology captured by the IRT model. However, the theoretical framework is not a silver bullet of sorts. Theory can guide us to appropriate and powerful applications of the empirical technology, but it cannot make the empirical model do things the model is not designed to do. As we move forward and apply the IRT model to present an analytic history of constitutional decision making, the nexus between theory and empirics will be of central import, and theory will help keep these caveats, as well as others, in focus.

3.2.2 *Extending the Model to Multiple Dimensions*

The spatial voting approach to modeling political preferences provides a powerful technique for the statistical analysis of political behavior. What is more, scholars have long argued that politics can neatly, parsimoniously, and effectively be described as a very low-dimensional endeavor. We saw as much in Chapter 2. However, we also saw there that there are important political phenomena that we miss with a unidimensional perspective on politics, and even the most staunch proponents of a low-dimensional model of politics concede that, at least at times, additional dimensions (usually only a second) can be critical for

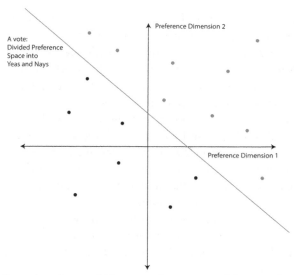

Figure 3.2. *Example of a multidimensional voting model.* The figure depicts a two-dimensional space with voters' preferences shown as coordinates in each dimension (points). The grey diagonal line shows a vote, which separates voters into Yeas and Nays. In the random utility version of the model some voters may be on one side of the line but nevertheless vote the other way, if the random factor associated with that vote sufficiently moves her toward the alternative vote.

understanding politics (Poole and Rosenthal 1997). What is more, in the context of judicial decision making, issues are often deeply intertwined, and there exists great potential for cross-cutting cleavages in judicial voting. Indeed, as described in Chapters 1 and 2, the potential for judges to have preferences on orthogonal dimensions, rather than simply projecting all issues into a single dimension of conflict, is part of the root cause dividing different intellectual approaches to the law.

In this spirit, scholars have advanced a series of multidimensional ideal point models. At their core, though, most derive from a simple extension of the standard IRT model of spatial voting (e.g., Equation (3.1)) to a k-dimensional latent space. Jackman (2001) most effectively describes the model.[3] The key intuition behind the k-dimensional model is that voters' ideal points are now points in a multidimensional space, rather than points on a line. Votes manifest as (hyper-)planes that cut through the multidimensional space, dividing voters into "Yeas" and "Nays." Figure 3.2 shows a simple example of one such model with only

---

[3] Jackman's particular focus is on estimation of the model and how Bayesian methods of estimation facilitate estimation of the model's parameters.

two dimensions. The left-right axis shows one dimension of political preferences; the vertical dimension shows another. Each of the points shows one voter, depicted as a pair of coordinates – an ideal point on each dimension. Votes, in this example, are lines, which divide all voters into "Yea" voters and "Nay" voters, subject to discrepancies due to the random elements of the voter's utility from each vote. In this figure, we show each voter's ideal point, but the model includes, as does the unidimensional model, a random element associated with each vote that can push voters above or below the vote-specific cutting line. The model assumes that they vote consistently with their ideal points *on average*. A three-dimensional version of the model would entail a three-dimensional policy space, and votes would be planes dividing the space into Yeas and Nays. And so forth, for higher-dimensional spaces.

While not necessarily trivial, robust derivations of the multidimensional model have been offered in a variety of contexts. Formally, the model is given by

$$y_{ic}^* \sim \mathcal{N}\left(\alpha_c + \sum_{d=1}^{D} \beta_{cd}\theta_{id}, \sigma_\theta^2\right) \qquad (3.10)$$

where we typically assume $\sigma_\theta^2 = 1$ in order to identify the scale of the model.

Just as in the standard unidimensional IRT model, we need to estimate a difficulty parameter – the model intercept – discrimination parameters, and ideal points. However, now we do not estimate a single slope for the discrimination parameter but instead a k-dimensional (hyper-)plane, and we do not estimate a single parameter for each ideal point but instead a k-dimensional vector of coordinates that describes each voter's ideal point as a point in the k-dimensional space.

These differences between the unidimensional and multidimensional models raise a number of important considerations – some technical, others qualitative. I set aside the technical considerations, except for one. Notice that as the number of dimensions grows, it has a multiplicative effect on the number of parameters we must estimate for each vote. Whereas in the standard IRT model, we must estimate 2 case-specific parameters – the difficulty and discrimination parameters – in a 3-dimensional model, we must estimate four case-specific parameters – the difficulty parameter and all three dimensions of the hyperplane that describe the vote. Clearly, as the number of dimensions increases but the number of voters stays constant, the quality of our information about each of these parameters deteriorates. In the worst-case scenario, we will have a small voting chamber – say, for example, a court with nine justices on it – and we will simply be unable to estimate all of the model parameters because of, in essence, a lack of degrees of freedom. What is more, we are also estimating three coordinates for each voter, and so we will need more votes to be able to estimate each voter's ideal point than if we were only estimating one coordinate for each vote (i.e., a unidimensional ideal point).

Turning to the qualitative considerations, I focus on one in particular. Recall the multidimensional case-space model of judicial decision making. Judges' preferences are represented there as hyperplanes cutting through a space of cases, dividing the *case* into "Yeas" and "Nays." This is exactly the opposite of what the multidimensional ideal point model estimates, which conceives of voters as points in a space and votes (cases) dividing them into "Yeas" and "Nays." We are again confronted with the inferential problem we had with the unidimensional model – how do we map the estimates from the model onto our theories of judicial behavior? How do we interpret the model parameters? Is there a way of deriving the multidimensional estimator from a case-space model of voting, as we saw above?

Jackman (2001) makes an observation that suggests a way forward. Jackman shows we can interpret the multidimensional discrimination parameters as factor loadings, telling us which votes load onto which dimensions. That is, for any given alignment of preferences, the magnitude of the discrimination parameter along any particular dimension reveals the extent to which that case divides the voters (i.e., justices). As a given case is more or less divisive along any particular dimension, we might think that the dimension is more or less relevant for how the justices perceive the case. Jackman's interpretation provides an insight that can help move us forward, past the challenges of estimating multidimensional ideal points at the Supreme Court. If we could marshal some additional information, beyond the voting, to inform our beliefs about the relevance of each dimension, we could at least partially estimate the discrimination parameters from that alternative information. That is the notion that drives the model Lauderdale and I develop and which I describe here. Our idea is to use voting data to estimate preference orderings and use alternative, auxiliary data to estimate the loadings onto each of the dimensions. While many possible such sources might present themselves, we propose to use the text from the opinions themselves to estimate the loadings onto each of the dimensions.

3.3 A MODEL OF CASE TOPICS

As described in Chapter 2, one of the challenges to interpreting the political cleavages we find when we summarize votes with ideal point models is interpretation. The dimensions are, by construction, whatever dimension best explains variation in voting. When we go from a unidimensional model to a multidimensional model, the dimensions are (1) whichever explains the most variation in voting, followed by (2) whichever explains the most variation among what is not explained by the first, and so forth. Interpreting these dimensions is usually *post hoc* and inductive. For example, in Poole and Rosenthal's (1997) study of congressional roll-call voting, they find that at distinct periods in time, voting in Congress is two-dimensional. The substantive interpretation of that second dimension, though, is something they can only interpret after finding a second dimension is useful for describing voting and then investigating the substantive context to infer what that second preference dimension must have captured.

Related to the problem of interpretation, one of the most significant problems with extending ideal point models to multiple dimensions is that we do not necessarily know which dimension is activating the judges' preferences in any given case. To see how this difficulty arises, recall our analogy from educational testing. There, we saw that if we cannot neatly divide judicial decisions *ex ante* into discrete "bins" of cases, as educational testers do, we may nevertheless hope to use auxiliary information to measure how likely two cases are to be tapping into the same dimension of political ideology. Lauderdale and Clark (2014) argue that statistical models of the language in written opinions can be useful for this purpose.

As contrasted with the statistical models of voting, models of speech (or, language more generally) are not as closely associated with theoretical choice models (cf., Kim, Londregan, and Ratkovic 2015). Political scientists have worked extensively on argumentation, persuasion, and communication (some examples include Popkin 1994; Ansolabehere and Iyengar 1995; Knight and Johnson 1997; Gutmann and Thompson 2009) but have not developed formal models of the linguistic choices that our data on language enable us to study. That is, whereas the statistical models of voting surveyed in the previous section derive from theoretical models of spatial politics, the statistical models of language most commonly used derive from computational models, sometimes with linguistic foundations. This discrepancy presents a conceptual challenge to using the language of judicial opinions in conjunction with voting patterns to statistically describe the dimensions of constitutional law, at least in a theoretically interpretable way.

One approach is to build an original theoretical model of opinion writing in the judiciary, akin to Kim, Londregan, and Ratkovic's (2015) approach to modeling legislative speech-making. A challenge to such an approach, however, is that the politics underlying judicial opinion writing are complex and subject to intense theoretical debate (see Clark and Lauderdale 2010, for an overview). Moreover, building any such model into the measurement strategy itself would undermine the utility of this exercise for future applications that seek to evaluate theories of opinion writing or to describe empirical regularities in need of theorizing. Indeed, this latter concern – the ability to identify empirical patterns that highlight limitations in theoretical models – is one of the primary goals of the current research. What is more, compared with more typically political speech – e.g., speeches, patty manifestos, etc. – legal documents such as judicial opinions use a very constrained and specialized language. The subject matter of a case largely determines the vocabulary used in those documents. In political documents and speech, on the other hand, there exists an entire industry and practice associated with the creation of political terms and the development of a vocabulary to encapsulate the ideas underlying a political movement (e.g., Noel 2013). Of course, the generation of legal ideas and arguments is a central part of intellectual legal movements (e.g., Teles 2008), but there is a considerable difference in the magnitude of vocabulary creativity in the two settings. The key point this claim suggests is that variation in the language of judicial opinions is primarily due to variation in the topics judges consider, rather than the ideological content of their doctrine. Thus, they can be used as an auxiliary measure of how a case loads onto the different preference dimensions, given an appropriate model.

To model the dimensions of political ideology that a case activates, I employ a "topic model" from the science of natural language processing. Topic models are statistical models of language that posit a number of "topics" in the set of documents and then estimate which topic each document is about. There are many possible topic models, but the one I employ is known as latent Dirichlet allocation (LDA) (Blei, Ng and Jordan 2003). Following Blei et al., LDA has a simple structure. The model takes the *word* as the basic unit of data. Formally, words are assumed to come from a vocabulary, which is a set of discrete *terms*. A *document* is then a collection (really a sequence) of K words, denoted $\mathbf{w} = (w_1, w_2, \ldots w_K)$. A collection of M documents is called a *corpus* and is denoted $\mathbf{D} = \{\mathbf{w}_1, \mathbf{w}_2, \ldots \mathbf{w}_M\}$. Here, the corpus is the set of all decisions in constitutional cases between 1877 and 2014. Each document is all of the opinions in a given case, which consist of a sequence of words, one after the other.

The model itself then assumes the words that appear in each document are generated as follows. For each document, we first choose a length (i.e., the number of words) as $K \sim \text{Poisson}(\xi)$. That is, the number of words in each document is a Poisson random variable drawn from some latent distribution. Critically, the model assumes the length of the document is

Table 3.1. *Summary of notation and terminology used in the LDA model.*

Notation/Term	Definition
Corpus	A set of documents
Document	A vector of words
Word	A random variable that is realized as a term
M	The number of documents in a corpus
K	A random variable giving the number of words in a document
T	The number of topics in the corpus
ω_d	A Dirichlet-distributed random variable giving the distribution of topics in document d
z_k	A random variable giving the realized topic for word k
τ	The probability that a word takes on a given term, conditional on the realized topic for the word

independent of all of the other data-generating variables; in particular, the topic mixture does not affect how long a document is. Then, for each document, a distribution of topics in the document is drawn as a Dirichlet random variable.[4] Formally, we denote ω the topic mixture in each document and assume $\omega \sim \text{Dir}(\alpha)$. Next, we draw a topic for each word from the distribution of topics in the document from the (Dirichlet) topic mixture in the document. Formally, we draw $z_k \sim \text{Multinomial}(\omega)$ for each of the K words – z_k is the realized topic for each word. Finally, we assume that for each topic, there is a probability distribution across all of the terms in the vocabulary, so that conditional on the topic, there is some probability that any given term will be selected. That is, given the topic we randomly drew for each word, z_k, which term the word takes on is randomly selected. We draw the term itself from the distribution of terms for the drawn topic. Formally, we assume $p(w_n|z_k, \tau)$ is a probability distribution across all terms in the vocabulary where the probability of a term appearing in a document depends on the document's topic mixture, and where z_k is the topic drawn from the topic mixture for word k. We assume that there are T topics in the corpus, and that τ is a $T \times V$ matrix with $\tau_{t,j} = p(w^j = 1|z^t = 1)$. In other words, each cell of matrix τ gives the probability that the word in the column is selected conditional on the topic in the row. We then assume that each word w_n is drawn from p. Table 3.1 summarizes the terminology and notation used in this model.

---

4 A Dirichlet distribution is a distribution of T random variables that can take on any value between 0 and 1 and together sum to 1. It is a multivariate generalization of the Beta distribution.

The critical thing we want to estimate from this model, for our purposes here, is the topic mixture in the documents, ω. Each ω_d is a vector with T elements – the assumed number of topics. So, for each document, we obtain an estimate of how much the document's words come from each of the T topics.

It is important to highlight a number of features of this model and what they imply for how we are treating judicial opinions. First, the model is a so-called "bag of words" model, which treats a document as having only a set of words; there is no structure or formal relationship among the words, other than the common latent topic distribution in the document. Thus, we are not seeking to derive information about the document via the structure or organization of the words. Rather, we simply assume that each word, essentially independently, provides information about what the document's topic is. Second, we are assuming that the primary determinant of which term from the vocabulary appears at each word is primarily a function of the latent distribution of topics in the document. This is not to say there are not other determinants, simply that any other factors are orthogonal to the effect of the latent topics on the words. Moreover, what we are assuming about the process by which the particular term from the vocabulary at each word is selected is stark – conditional on the topic for that word, which term from the vocabulary appears is random.

The LDA model is fairly minimalist and does not require the analyst to make too many assumptions about the structure of the topics. However, one choice that is of particular import is the number of topics that should exist in the data. Recall that the goal of the LDA model is to sort documents into topics, associating the distribution of term frequencies with the topics. However, that goal presupposes we know how many topics we think there are. How best to choose the number of topics to fit the data, then? In computational linguistics applications, how to best select the number of topics for a model such as LDA is a matter of controversy and considerable research effort. A common approach is to choose a number of topics that minimizes perplexity or the point at which further increases in the topic number has a diminished effect on perplexity. A related approach is to consider a large set of possible topic numbers and choose the number of topics that yields the highest log likelihood. A more subjective approach that can augment the use of statistical fit criteria is to evaluate the content of the estimated topics to assess their substantive meaningfulness. In the next section, I describe an approach to selecting the number of topics that is oriented around the goal of our application here – to estimate the extent to which each vote loads onto the difference preference dimensions.

3.4 A UNIFIED MODEL

With statistical representations of judges' preferences and what their preferences are over, we are prepared to combine these models into a unified
model of judicial preferences. The model I employ here was first developed
by Ben Lauderdale and me to study how judicial preferences vary across
substantive areas of the law (Lauderdale and Clark 2014). The key insight
derives directly from the guiding principle behind this book – we should
make use of as many of the available analytic tools as makes sense, using
each in the most appropriate way. The model assumes that votes are very
good at telling us how judges line up relative to each other, and the text
of their opinions is very good at telling us what they are lining up.

The intuition behind the model is straight-forward. As we saw above,
one issue with scaling judges in a multidimensional space is that we
do not know which votes are more or less about which dimensions. In
particular, as the number of dimensions increases, so too does the number
of discrimination parameters. Recall, Jackman (2001) shows us these
parameters can be interpreted as factor loadings. The model I describe
here looks to an alternative set of data – the text – to aid us in estimating
the factor loadings. So, we take from the text information about which
cases are about which dimensions and *assume* that the voting behavior
reflects the dimensions revealed by the text. In particular, we measure the
distribution of topics in each document with our estimate from LDA of
the probability that each case is about each topic. This is a particularly
strong assumption. The model assumes that there is an exact equivalence
between the proportion of the text coming from each topic – how the LDA
model estimates the assignment probability for each case – and the relative
weight of the justices' preferences each dimension on the justices' votes.

Formally, we estimate a vector, λ_c, of length D, for each case,
which gives the assignment probability for each topic for case c,
where D is the assumed number of topics in the texts. Notice that
using the LDA-estimated assignment probabilities means that each
element of λ_c is weakly between 0 and 1 – i.e., $0 \leq \lambda_{c,d} \leq 1$, for all
dimensions d. Further, notice that $\sum_{d=1}^{D} \lambda_{cd} = 1$. Next, we modify the
standard multidimensional IRT model. Instead of estimating a matrix
of ideal points and discrimination parameters, we now estimate a *single*
discrimination parameter and create a case-specific ideal point that is a
weighted sum of the justices' topic-specific ideal points, where the weights
are taken directly from the text – namely, using λ_c.

Thus, we can rewrite Equation (3.10) as follows:

$$y_{ic}^* \sim \mathcal{N}\left(\alpha_c + \sum_{d=1}^{D} \beta_c \lambda_{cd} \theta_{id}, \sigma_\theta^2\right) \qquad (3.11)$$

Table 3.2. *Summary of notation used in LDA+IRT ideal point model.*

Notation	Definition
θ_{id}	Justice i's ideal point on dimension d
λ_{cd}	The extent to which case c loads onto dimension d
α_c	The difficulty parameter for case c
β_c	The discrimination parameter for case c

Moreover, we can further write the model by combining the case-specific weights and topic-specific ideal points:

$$y_{ic}^* \sim \mathcal{N}\left(\alpha_c + \beta_c\theta_{ic}, \sigma_\theta^2\right) \qquad (3.12)$$

where

$$\theta_{ic} \equiv \sum_{d=1}^{D} \lambda_{cd}\theta_{id} \qquad (3.13)$$

Notice that Equation (3.12) is identical to Equation (3.1) and therefore avoids the identification and estimation problems associated with the standard multidimensional ideal-point model (e.g., Equation (3.10)). Finally, as with the models described above, we assume throughout that $\sigma_\theta^2 = 1$ in order to identify the scale of the model. Table 3.2 summarizes the notation used in this model.

The consequence is, we are estimating *case-specific* ideal points for each justice – θ_{ic} – by assuming that each justice has a single, constant ideal point on each of the D topics and that each case presents some weighting of the different topics. We therefore can estimate how the justices line up relative to each other in particular cases. Those kinds of estimates will facilitate the analytic history of constitutional decision making by allowing us to investigate both aggregate patterns over time as well as to examine particular historical examples of interest. This model, then, captures the basic notion and insight described above that cases are not neatly binned into discrete, unrelated issue areas but instead often touch on multiple topics and activate multiple dimensions of political ideology. These are, then, the *preference dimensions* we seek to study.

Model flexibility. As I have described it to this point, and as Lauderdale and I do in the original publication of this model, we estimate λ_c via the text of the opinions, assuming the extent to which an opinion is about a given topic is proportional to the extent to which that topic's political cleavage drives the justices' voting. However, the model we develop is itself much more general, as the matrix of case loadings onto each dimension, λ_c could be estimated in any way that satisfies the assumption that the loadings are proportional to the relevance of the political cleavages. So, one might employ manual coding of the cases into topics, relying on expert judgments about what issues or preference dimensions are at stake. One readily available source of such data is the Supreme Court Database's Issue or Issue Area variable (discussed in Chapter 4). However, since those data generally only assign a case to a single issue, those data in particular do not allow us to study the political dimensions of constitutional law together. (Notably, the topics one recovers from the application of LDA to Supreme Court opinions tend to be highly correlated with the Supreme Court Database Issue Area variable (e.g., Lauderdale and Clark 2014; Rice 2017). I explore that relationship in Chapter 5.)

Importantly, one of the intellectual strengths of the model I employ here is that it permits cases to involve a mixture of issues, which reflects the nature of real-world legal questions. A first principle behind the historical analysis in this book is that while constitutional questions may involve a limited number of legal and policy issues, the substantive context of any given case can implicate multiple preference dimensions. The model of voting patterns is designed to measure justices' locations along those preference dimensions, and so we do not want to employ a measure of the relationship of a case to those dimensions that needlessly constrains which or how many preference dimensions a case may activate.

An alternative approach might be to use richer measures of case topics, such as Westlaw KeyNotes. KeyNotes are a proprietary system developed by Westlaw for tagging legal documents – namely, court opinions – for the legal topics present in each case. According to Westlaw's website, "The American system of law is broken down into Major Topics – there are more than 400 topics, such as Civil Rights, Pretrial Procedure, and Treaties" and those topics are then subdivided into multiple levels of a categorical hierarchy, with roughly 100,000 narrow concepts at the bottom level.[5] Importantly, there appears to be no limit to the number of topics to which a case can be assigned, and so one might use the proportion of the narrowest concepts from each of the main 400 topics as a metric of the case's distribution across the substantive dimensions. Unfortunately, though, the Westlaw data are proprietary and therefore not available to be used and shared in this kind of scientific undertaking. More important, though, is that the Westlaw method still imposes a constraint that the identification and content of the topics remains fixed, according to Westlaw's decisions about what the relevant topics are. The method we develop, and I use here, allows us infer what are the relevant

5 https://lawschool.westlaw.com/marketing/display/RE/24.

cleavages that characterize voting on the Court. To see why that is, it is instructive to examine how we estimate the model itself.

Estimating the model. There are two considerations that bear on how we can interpret the model, once estimated. First, how many topics ought one to assume exist in the data? As noted, when simply trying to fit the topic model to text, there are a number of approaches and diagnostic techniques for selecting the number of topics. However, here the goal is not to find the number of topics that best describes Supreme Court opinions. Rather, the goal is to find the number of preference dimensions that best characterizes the voting behavior of the justices. Thus, in order to select the number of topics, I estimate the model using a variety of numbers of topics and, for each version, examine how well the model fits the voting data. There are several possible metrics one might use to measure the fit to the voting data, but I rely on the Deviance Information Criterion ("DIC") (Spiegelhalter et al. 2002). The DIC is a measure of fit that accounts for model flexibility, similar to the more familiar Akaike information criterion ("AIC") and Bayesian information criterion ("BIC").

Second, in standard scaling models, unanimous votes do not provide any information, because the lack of division among the justices means we cannot learn anything from a unanimous vote about how the justices line up relative to each other. Thus, the only information that contributes to an estimated ideal point comes from non-unanimous votes. If we believe, for some reason, that unanimous cases are systematically different – specifically, that the justices' ideal points are different and differently ordered – then we will want to incorporate that information into our interpretation of the ideal points. Typically, one does not include unanimous cases in the data used to estimate ideal point models simply because they cannot provide information about the ideal points but do require one to estimate the case parameters. Here, I include unanimous decisions because the opinion content in those cases provides information about the distribution of topics on the Court's docket and the similarity among cases. The unanimous cases, in other words, do not convey information about the justices' orderings relative to each other, conditional on the mix of topics in the case, but they do contribute information to the estimate of the distribution of topics across all cases. When interpreting the ideal point estimates, though, one still needs to recognize the assumption that the justices' orderings relative to each other are not systematically different in unanimous cases compared to non-unanimous cases.

Constraining and interpreting the model. Related to the method of estimating the model, there is an important question that must be addressed concerning the ability to statistically identify the dimensions and preference orderings in the model. Specifically, we must contend with the possibility that in any given case, each judge decides on her own onto which preference dimension to map the legal question the justices confront. If that occurs, then it raises a host of questions about what the preference dimensions mean, what it means for the judges to vote on the case, and how we interpret the varying preference orderings. However, there are a number of reasons to believe the distribution of topics in any given case, and therefore its loading onto the preference dimensions, is fairly constrained and exogenously set.

For example, when a case is brought to the Supreme Court, the litigants offer briefs, which frame the policy and legal question before the Court. The litigants' choices about how to frame a case are shaped by at least three considerations. First, the real world nature of a case goes a long way to setting up the relevant dimensions for a case. Cases involve events that took place and conflict between parties over the resolution to a problem that ensued. That dispute between the parties itself is the core issue the Court must resolve. Second, there is a practice in the courts that issues or questions that were not raised during the lower court proceedings cannot become the substance of subsequent appeals. If the parties failed to raise an issue, they cannot bring to the Supreme Court a question that the lower courts never resolved. There are good reasons for that practice, the main one of which (from my perspective) is that the Supreme Court relies on the record from the courts below to inform the justices about the issues and relevant considerations in any given case. In fact, when the justices accept a case for review, they typically instruct the parties exactly what questions they want framed and briefed. Certainly, what the Court is trying to do is to focus the case so that when deciding among themselves how to resolve the case, the justices will not simply cycle around through the preference dimensions, leaving the vote and resolution potentially indeterminate.

Of course, it need not be the case that the topic distribution is completely exogenous to the voting and politicking on the Court in any given case. It surely is not. However, what I am assuming is that within meaningful boundaries, the set of preference dimensions that may be involved is limited. A case not involving any kind of business law, property rights, interstate commerce, or similar substantive problem will not be decided along a preference dimension primarily about economic regulation. Similarly, a case involving a conviction for drug trafficking will not be able to completely avoid preferences related to criminal procedure. In the context of the Supreme Court, and my application here, I assume that because litigation is zero-sum, any preference dimension that is relevant for conceiving of a legal problem will be raised by some member of the Court. Related, any litigating lawyer will have a strategic incentive to shape a case in the best possible light for her client. This means that all potentially relevant dimensions of a problem will be raised (as well as perhaps some irrelevant dimensions). Thus, I use in my analyses all of the opinions written in every case (for more detail, see Chapter 4) – all majority, plurality, per curium, concurring, and dissenting opinions. The assumption I make then is simply that the distribution of topics across the opinions within a case represents the extent to which the justices *collectively* perceive each preference dimension to be relevant.

Quantities of interest. Estimating the LDA+IRT model yields a number of quantities that are relevant for various aspects of the analytic history. Most directly, the model yields estimates of each justice's ideal point in each of the dimensions. It is important to emphasize what that ideal point represents, theoretically. As we saw above, in a single dimension, the ideal point is the case-space threshold that indicates the point at which a judge's preferred disposition switches. Thus, the ideal point in any preference dimension corresponds to the judge's ideal threshold among the cases that map *entirely onto that single preference dimension*. If a case implicates multiple preference dimensions – and the claim here is that most do – then a judge's threshold is given by a combination of her ideal points along each of the relevant preference dimensions. In particular, a judge's preferences in any given case are a weighted average of her ideal point across all dimensions, with the weights being given by how much the case loads onto each dimension, as determined by the LDA component of the model. We can use these data, then, to study a number of features of the history of constitutional decision making. How do judges' preferences shift across cases dealing with similar legal provisions as the context of the cases differentially activates the various preference dimensions? How correlated are the justices preferences across the distinct preference dimensions, and which justices vary a lot across the topics? How do the politics of coalition building change as cases shift across the preference dimensions?

Thus, a second quantity of interest that emerges naturally from the model is the distribution of case topics. For any given case, these data tell us how much the case loads onto each preference dimension. During a period of time – for example, a Term of the Court – the data tell us how much the Court's docket concentrated on each of the preference dimensions. And, over time these data can show how the Court's docket shifts, allowing analysis of the ways in which the docket is affected by social and political events outside of the Court. What is more, in conjunction with other forms of data – such as common measures of the policy areas in which the Court works – we can use these data to study how the preference dimensions relate to the subject matter before the Court. How do certain substantive policy issues relate to specific preference dimensions? When do we observe a shift in how the Court maps policy questions onto preference dimensions? As we will see, for example, the Court's shift in its approach to economic regulation during the late 1930s was manifested by a change in the way the Court mapped issues of regulation onto the preexisting preference dimensions.

Related, we can also estimate the location of each case on the Court's docket, by constructing a case-specific preference dimension (using the loadings we estimate from the LDA component) and identifying the indifference point along that dimension. As we saw above, the point of indifference between each disposition corresponds theoretically to the case location in the case-space model. Using case locations, we can study notable historical examples to assess the politics of case selection, voting, and opinion writing, among other things. Moreover, we can use the macropatterns in case locations to study how the politics of law making play out over time (e.g., Baird 2007).

Beyond these features we can study with the estimates that come directly from the model, there are several other features we can study. For example, we can study the distribution of preferences on the Court at at given time, across the preference dimensions. This can entail calculating the median justice, whose vote is crucially pivotal, along each of the preference dimensions, or the degree of preference polarization on each of the preference dimensions. Knowing where the pivotal justices is, as well as how polarized or unified the justices are on each dimension, can be useful for understanding the politics of constitutional decision making, by providing leverage on the kinds of cases where the Court is favorably disposed to a given kind of outcome. We can also identify the kinds of cases where disagreement is sharpest and therefore the justices will have a relatively harder time assembling an opinion-writing coalition.

In what follows, I turn to the data we will use to estimate the LDA+IRT model and generate these, and other, quantities of interest. In the subsequent chapters, I use the model to study the history of constitutional decision making. We will see in that application how these quantities facilitate an analytic perspective on both aggregate historical patterns as well as important particular examples.

3.5 CONCLUSION

The analytic history goals I set out in Chapter 1 entail three tasks – theoretically grounded exploratory data analysis, the identification of macropatterns in constitutional decision making along with the isolation of specific cases of illustrative use, and the interpretation of those cases and macropatterns in light of microtheories of the judicial process. Doing so requires the application of an empirical tool that can be directly related to theoretical models. The LDA+IRT model I have described in this chapter, which was developed elsewhere with my co-author (Lauderdale and Clark 2014), provides just that tool. I have shown how the model can be derived directly from the case-space model, which enables me to, in subsequent chapters, directly relate the quantities I estimate from the model to existing microtheories of judicial decision making.

Turning to the next chapters, I put this model to use. The next two chapters present the data that I use to estimate the model, and the following chapter summarizes the broad aggregate patterns and estimates from the model. However, as we will see, those macropatterns only tell one part of the story – they describe the forest, so to speak. The structure of the individual trees still remains to be seen, and that subject will occupy the subsequent chapters. In both types of analysis, though, I interpret the history of constitutional decision making through the lens of the LDA+IRT model. The model provides structure to the politics of judicial decision making that allow me to relate both the macropatterns and the micropatterns to political theories.

It is important to underscore, though, exactly how the model provides that structure and what that means for subsequent data analysis. The dimensions this model recovers are the dimensions that *best fit the voting data*. In other words, they are defined by the justices' voting patterns. To the extent the justices line up consistently in most cases, the model will find fewer dimensions than when the justices vary in their voting patterns across cases. However, because that is the extent to which the dimensions are defined, they are not necessarily related to substantive legal provisions in the Constitution or any other source of law. Thus, a crucial distinction for which this model provides analytic leverage is between the legal substance of a case – is the case raising a First Amendment challenge to a prior restraint law, is it alleging a violation of Congress' power to regulate interstate commerce, etc. – and the ideological preference dimension to which the legal question is mapped. We might imagine, for example, that sometimes First Amendment cases activate one preference dimension – for example, preferences about federalism – whereas other times they might activate alternative preferences – for example, preference about civil liberties. This need not be true, but the model allows it to be so. In Chapter 5, we will see that in fact, the preference dimensions are orthogonal to the legal context of a case. Instead, the dimensions capture a more political and ideological notion of preferences.

Myriad studies have demonstrated how the item-response theory model can be derived from a random utility voting model – most notably, Clinton, Jackman and Rivers (2004). Here, I reproduce the arithmetic underlying the derivation.

Let there be two policy choices, ξ_c and ψ_c. Assume that ξ_c is the proposal for which a "Yea" vote counts, and ψ_c is the status quo, for which a "Nay" vote counts. Further, assume there are $j = 1, \ldots, J$ voters, each of whom has an ideal point, θ_j in Euclidean space, and who also has quadratic spatial preferences over outcomes, subject to a random error term (this allows for the possibility of errors in voting, idiosyncratic or valence features orthogonal to voting, etc.). Therefore, denote voter j's utility from voting for option ξ_c

$$U_j(\xi_c) = - \| \theta_j - \xi_c \|^2 - \eta_{jc} \qquad (3.14)$$

and denote voter j's utility from voting for the option ψ_c

$$U_j(\psi_c) = - \| \theta_j - \psi_c \|^2 - \nu_{jc} \qquad (3.15)$$

Where η_{jc} and ν_{jc} are random error terms. Assume a theory in which voters seek to maximize their utility. Further assume that η_{jc} and ν_{jc} have a joint normal distribution where $\mathbb{E}[\eta_{jc}] = \mathbb{E}[\nu_{jc}] = 0$ and $var(\eta_{jc} - \nu_{jc}) = \sigma_c^2$. It therefore follows that the probability of a "Yea" vote is given as follows:

$$\Pr(y_{jc} = 1) = \Pr\left(U_j(\xi_c) > U_j(\psi_c)\right) \qquad (3.16)$$
$$= \Pr\left(\nu_{jc} - \eta_{jc} < \| \theta_j - \psi_c \|^2 - \| \theta_j - \xi_c \|^2\right)$$
$$= \Pr\left(\nu_{jc} - \eta_{jc} < 2(\xi_c - \psi_c)'\theta_j + \psi_c'\psi_c - \xi_c'\xi_c\right)$$
$$= \Phi\left(\beta_c'\theta_j - \alpha_c\right) \qquad (3.17)$$

where $\beta_c = 2(\xi_c - \psi_c)/\sigma_c^2$, $\alpha_c = (\psi_c'\psi_c - \xi_c'\xi_c)/\sigma_c^2$, and $\Phi(\cdot)$ is the cumulative standard normal distribution function.

The representation given by Equation (3.17) is the item-response theory model.

4

The Cases, Votes, and Opinions

In this chapter, I present the data I use throughout the remainder of the book to study the development of constitutional law. The model I described in the previous chapter anticipated these data, and here I show the procedures I have used to collect the data and describe the major patterns in the raw data. In some instances, the data collected here are not original to this study and have been described extensively elsewhere. In those situations, I present only limited discussion of the data, focusing on the patterns most relevant for the analyses in this book. However, in other instances, the data reported here have not previously been described in the aggregate. In those situations, I present a more extended discussion of the data.

I divide the description of the data into three sections. First, I describe the universe of cases that constitute the body of constitutional law. In Chapter 1, we saw the general distribution of these cases over time, but here I provide a more substantive discussion of these cases. Second, I present data on the justices included in these cases and their voting patterns. Third, I describe the opinions written in the constitutional law cases over time. Several notable patterns in the data emerge. Among them are four worth highlighting at the outset. First, constitutional law has focused differentially across the various provisions of the Constitution. There are some highly litigated provisions. The Fourteenth Amendment stands out as a very central component to constitutional law, underscoring its transformative importance in American history. Second, as others have documented more generally, among the constitutional cases, we see an increase in the rate at which justices issue dissenting opinions after roughly 1940. At the same time, the real shift was an increase in dissenting among less important cases, whereas there has been, historically, a fairly constant level of dissent in landmark cases. Third, the rise of the Court's discretion over its docket, especially with the massive expansion of its certiorari jurisdiction in 1926, is not noticeably associated with a change in the Court's constitutional docket – either in terms of the rate at which it focuses on constitutional law, the subjects of its constitutional decision making, or the politics of voting in constitutional law cases. Fourth, there is a major shift in the Court's constitutional decision making in the post-World War II era, as the Court began to focus more heavily on constitutional issues. As we will see in Chapters 6 and 7, this is largely due to the incorporation of the Bill of Rights and the expansion of federal constitutional law into policy realms previously not seen as implicating the Constitution. However, before turning in the following chapters to an analytic approach to the history of constitutional decision making, I first describe here the data themselves and the raw patterns that emerge from a high-level survey.

4.1 THE CONSTITUTIONAL CASES

The first step in describing constitutional law is to compile a list of what cases "count" as constitutional cases. Combing through the tens of thousands of cases decided by the Supreme Court and evaluating which ones contribute to constitutional law and which ones do not poses a significant logistical challenge, as well as a challenge in terms of the validity and reliability of those coding decisions. How does one systematically determine what makes a case count as part of the body of constitutional law? Fortunately, as described in Chapter 1, Congress undertook an effort to do this during the early twentieth century, led by Edward Corwin, the giant of public law scholarship and professor at Princeton. Since then, the Congressional Research Service has kept up with Corwin's initial effort and regularly published updates to its important publication, *The United States Constitution: Analysis and Interpretation*. Indeed, that document's primary function is to compile an authoritative interpretation and analysis of constitutional case law. While the source of this document, the Congressional Research Service ("CRS"), does not in and of itself guarantee the validity or reliability of the coding decisions, it has a particular benefit in that it compiles the list of decisions that Congress believes have interpreted the Constitution. Critically, because of the CRS's mission to serve as a nonpartisan legislative research institution, there are fewer concerns about strategic omission of decisions on political grounds.

Included with that document is a table of cases that are included in the analysis – it is these cases that constitute the body of US constitutional law. In Chapter 1, we saw the number of cases appearing on that list over time, and one thing that became apparent was that the engine of

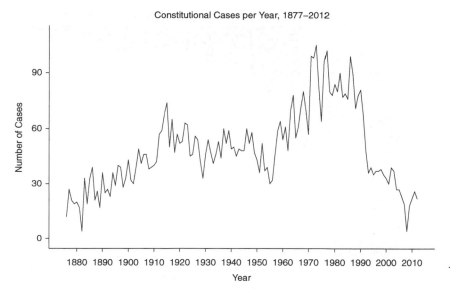

Figure 4.1. *Number of constitutional law cases over time, 1877–2012.*

constitutional law really started revving after Reconstruction, at about 1877. These cases are listed in the Appendix. Between 1877 and 2012, the US Supreme Court decided 6,654 cases in constitutional law, roughly 49 per year. However, those cases are not evenly distributed across history, as we see in Figure 4.1, which shows the number of constitutional law cases each year. The number of constitutional law cases decided by the Court each year increased steadily from 1877 through the early 1980s, but it has begun to wane ever since. Indeed, this is a pattern consistent with the Court's overall decision making, as the number of total cases decided by the Court dropped steadily throughout that period as well.

Figure 4.2 shows the distribution of cases across the various parts of the Constitution they interpret. The CRS report discusses each section, or what I call provision, of the Constitution separately, giving an analysis of the various ways in which the provision has been interpreted over time. Here, I show the count of the number of cases mentioned in the section for each provision. I count the number of cases in each provision by referencing the list of cases included in the CRS report, which contains an index linking cases to pages in the document. For each case in the data, I cross-reference the pages to which it is indexed and the report's table of contents. (The exact numbers here are subject to some random measurement error, as I matched cases by automated parsing of the

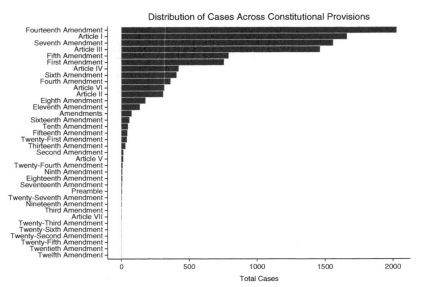

Figure 4.2. *Case referenced by constitutional provision in the United States Constitution: Analysis and Interpretation, 2014 edition.* Counts are derived by linking page numbers in index of cases cited to the table of contents. Some cases included in the cases cited index are not specifically cited in the document's discussion of the Constitution and are only listed in other references, such as the list of laws held unconstitutional. Other cases are mentioned in multiple sections of the constitutional analysis.

table of cases; in a handful of instances, formatting errors and other typographical issues created problems. I have corrected manually each instance of which I am aware.)

The "gorillas" of constitutional law, as characterized by these data, are the Fourteenth Amendment (due process, equal protection, citizenship), Article I (Congress and its power), the Seventh Amendment (trial by jury), and Article III (the judiciary and its power). That the Fourteenth Amendment has been so extensively interpreted through judicial decisions comes at little surprise. The Amendment has served in many ways as a foundation for the federal government's powers, the balance of powers between the federal and state levels, and the interpretation of individual rights, ever since its enactment in the wake of the Civil War. In many ways, the Fourteenth Amendment represents a fundamental reinterpretation of the constitutional order, representing a codification of the political repercussions of the Civil War (e.g., Ackerman 1991). For example, one of the primary questions about the Fourteenth Amendment during the mid-twentieth century, which was resolved (at least, partially) through myriad judicial decisions, is whether the Amendment "incorporates" the Bill of Rights. Incorporation is the idea that the prohibitions on government power provided in the Bill of Rights apply to the states as well as to the federal government. (The Bill of Rights only prohibits the federal government from violating the various rights it sets out to protect.) Related, the Fourteenth Amendment has been used as a constitutional basis for the articulation of various "unenumerated rights" – freedoms that are not specifically granted in the Constitution but understood, via the Amendment, to be implied by the spirit of the Constitution.

The other three provisions that are the most represented in the body of constitutional law cases are similarly central to the powers, structure, and boundaries of the federal government. Article I is the source of Congress' powers, including the extensively litigated "enumerated" powers, which are the specific powers granted to the national legislature, as well as the other grants of authority that have been more-or-less expansively interpreted over time. As I describe in greater detail in the next chapter, the interpretation of congressional power was one of the two components of constitutional law during the antebellum years and continues to be a touchstone of constitutional law today. Indeed, congressional authority to enact legislation – and the specific grants of and restrictions on power – constitute in many ways the essence of our national government. The Seventh Amendment, which provides for the right to trial by jury, was the subject of extensive federal litigation, especially during the early twentieth century, as the Constitution was used to bring states' criminal procedures into line and especially to fight against Jim Crow racism, which often manifested in biased criminal procedures. However, even before that, as the Congressional Research Service report reveals, the Supreme Court began resolving questions about law and equity in the early nineteenth century, which often implicated questions about the nature of a trial by jury (e.g., Thomas 2014, 1548–57).

However, as we see in Figure 4.3, the Court has expended greater effort in different substantive areas of the law at different times. This figure shows the frequency of cases cited in the CRS report's discussion of each provision of the Constitution (setting aside provisions that do not have any associated case law in the CRS report). Here, I identify each case listed in the CRS report (Thomas 2014), and the page numbers identified in the Table of Cases (the list discussed above) and cross-reference the identified pages in that index against the document's Table of Contents. Many cases (most notably, Seventh Amendment cases) are not discussed anywhere in the document's substantive discussion of the Constitution but are only mentioned in the list of cases overturning laws (federal or state). A number of patterns emerge quickly.

First, prior to the Civil War, there was almost no interpretation of the amendments. (Of course, the Thirteenth and subsequent amendments

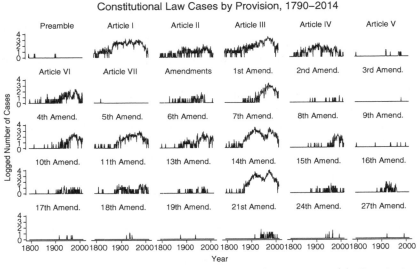

Figure 4.3. *Number of cases each year referencing each of 30 provisions of the Constitution.* Counts are calculated by identifying each case listed in the table of cases in the CRS Report (Thomas 2014) and cross-referencing the pages identified for each case against the report's table of contents.

were not enacted until after the War.) Aside from a few cases that interpreted various components of the Bill of Rights, the bulk of constitutional interpretation during the antebellum period concerned Article I (congressional power), Article II (executive power), and Article III (judicial power). There was also a fair amount of interpretation of Article IV of the Constitution, which governs the relationships among the states. Not surprisingly, these cases peaked during the mid-1800s. However, in the wake of Reconstruction, and most significantly beginning in the early twentieth century, the Court turned its constitutional docket to the amendments, most prominently the Fourteenth, Seventh, and First Amendments.

More generally, we see here the bulk of cases cited as interpreting the Constitution, have implicated a relatively constrained set of constitutional provisions – Articles I, II, III, and IV, and the First, Fourth, Fifth, Sixth, Seventh, and Fourteenth Amendments. The Sixth Amendment has also been extensively interpreted, especially during the second half of the twentieth century. Many other provisions have been interpreted by the Supreme Court in only extremely limited instances. Most notably, only a single case, from 1820, has interpreted Article VII, which is the article of the Constitution that provides for its ratification procedure. The CRS Report (Thomas 2014, 1043) notes, "In *Owings* v. *Speed* the question at issue was whether the Constitution operated upon an act of Virginia passed in 1788. The Court held it did not..."

It is also instructive to note that many of the trends and major shifts we see in Figure 4.3 correspond to important political and societal events. For example, in the years leading up to the Civil War, there is notable jump in the amount of cases before the Supreme Court involving Article IV of the Constitution, which governs relations among the states and established the supremacy of the Constitution, during the three decades preceding the Civil War. Much of that litigation concerned the states' ability to tax federal government entities or employees. We also see in the wake of the Civil War a rapid increase in the Court's interpretation of other key provisions of the Constitution, such as Article I (outlining congressional power).

Towards the end of the Nineteenth Century, during the Second Industrial Revolution, there is similarly an increase in the role of Article III, which outlines judicial power; the Fifth and Fourteenth Amendments, which provide the legal basis for due process and equal protection; and the Eleventh Amendment, which provides for states' sovereign immunity. It is not coincidental that this area of the law was being developed as the railroads expanded and facilitated both an integration of the economy and the growth of large corporations, the rise of middle management, and the development of difficult working conditions and weak positions for laborers.

Then later during the mid-to-late-twentieth century, in the wake of the federal government's consolidation of power over economic matters during the New Deal, and the rise of the civil rights movement as well as the war on crime, we see an explosion in the Court's interpretation of the civil liberties amendments (for example, the First and Fourth) as well as of the amendments dealing with criminal defendants and punishment (for example, the Sixth, Seventh, Eighth, and Fourteenth). What is more, throughout the entire period, from the Civil War on, there is a steady increase in the role of Article III, the basis of judicial power, in the Court's constitutional jurisprudence.

In the next chapter, I analyze these data more systematically, in conjunction with the justices' votes on constitutional cases, to discover how the politics of the Court link together these various substantive issues. For now, it is instructive to note that different constitutional provisions have been more or less extensively interpreted by the Court at different periods in time. Some of that variation appears to be linked to obvious, structural factors (amendments passed later in history naturally are not part of the body of constitutional law beforehand). Other variation seems to be driven more by endogenous forces in the evolution of constitutional law – for example, the steady growth in the Court's interpretation of Article III.

4.2 THE JUSTICES AND THEIR VOTES

Collecting data on the justices' votes is relatively straight-forward. As discussed in Chapter 2, one of the main motivations for political scientists' historical focus on judicial votes is the objectivity, simplicity, and easy quantification of voting data. All one needs to do is read each case and record, as the justices do themselves when they meet to discuss cases, which justices vote to reverse the lower court's decision and which justices vote to affirm the lower court's decision. Of course, there are examples where the voting is not so simple, as in cases where the Supreme Court resolves multiple questions, and so any given justice may vote to affirm the lower court's decision in part and reverse the lower court's decision in part. However, for the most part, the voting patterns are easily discerned.

Moreover, extensive databases have been built with voting data. Most notably, the Supreme Court Database (Spaeth et al. 2015) includes a record of every justice's vote in every case it covers, and I rely on those data. Table A.1 in the appendix to this chapter lists each of the justices that voted in at least one of the constitutional law cases between 1877 and 2012. The table shows the justice, his or her start date on the Court and the date he or she ended service on the Court (unless still serving), as well as the total number of votes cast by the justice, the number of those votes that were with the Court majority, and rate of dissenting. A few patterns emerge that bear mentioning. First, as the number of constitutional cases decided rose over time, so too did the length of time justices served and, consequently, the number of votes justices cast, on average, grew even faster. Second, consistent with well-documented patterns in Supreme Court decision making (e.g., Walker, Epstein, and Dixon 1988), the justices serving before World War II dissented at much lower rates than do the justices appointed since Franklin Roosevelt became president. This is an important point that will be particularly important when we interpret voting patterns in the next chapter. Before roughly 1937, the justices who served on the Court typically dissented in fewer than 10% of the constitutional cases in which they voted. Beginning with the appointment of Hugo Black in 1937, justices on the Court dissent more typically in roughly 20% of the cases in which they vote.

Indeed, that pattern is borne out even more clearly when we consider the average size of majorities in constitutional law cases over time. Figure 4.4 shows the number of justices in each case majority, from 1877

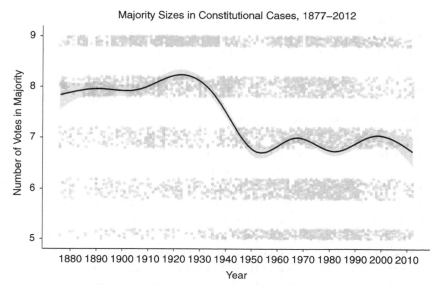

Figure 4.4. *Sizes of majorities in constitutional cases, 1877–2010.* The figure shows each constitutional law case decided by the Supreme Court and its year of decision and majority coalition size. The line is a nonlinear scatterplot smoother. (Sources: Congressional Research Service and Supreme Court Database.)

through 2012. We see here that before 1940, the average constitutional law case had roughly eight justices in the majority, though the average majority size has dropped since by almost a whole justice. In other words, the average majority size in constitutional law cases has declined by about 1 justice. More important, though, is the overall distribution of majority sizes. The grey points in Figure 4.4 show each case, and we see here that before 1940 there were very few cases with only five, six, or even seven justices in the majority. However, ever since, there are consistently many cases with majorities smaller than eight justices in size.

Why the sudden breakdown in the norm of unanimity on the Court? A number of possible reasons have been proposed or are at least suggested by the extant literature on Supreme Court justice voting. We might group these possible explanations into three categories – legal, behavioral, and structural. Among the legal explanations are claims that the New Deal era constituted a sort of unofficial constitutional amendment, as the national government's powers were fundamentally reinterpreted through the Court's decisions and a changing public understanding of what the national government could regulate in wake of the integrated economy (e.g., Ackerman 1998; Cushman 1998). One might infer that the resulting constitutional developments, never having been enshrined in formal amendments, left the door open to greater flexibility in judicial interpretation and, therefore, great room for disagreement and a concomitant drop in unanimity rates. Further, the changes in the Court's interpretation of the Constitution's grant of power to the national government meant that the government's power and breadth would grow, bringing into the Court's purview a greater range of substantive questions and debates than it had previously encountered.

Among the behavioral explanations, we might consider analyses that focus on the changing nature of the types of judges who served on the Court. Beginning most especially after the Judges' Bill of 1925, when the justices gained virtually complete control over the content of their docket, and when former President Taft led the Court, as the Chief Justice, into the public eye, the prominence of being a justice on the Court increased to an extent that rendered the job virtually unrecognizable from perspective of those who served on the Court a century earlier. At the same time, the great conflicts between the Court and the elected branches (and states) during the first three decades of the twentieth century fundamentally changed the nature of the Supreme Court appointment process. During the first roughly 120-130 years of its existence, nominees to the Supreme Court were generally skilled lawyers with political connections who accepted the post but did not necessarily perceive the Court as the pinnacle of one's career. (Indeed, one of George Washington's nominees to the Supreme Court refused to serve.[1]) Franklin Roosevelt, perhaps most prominently, set out to remake the Supreme Court with his nominees, choosing individuals with strong personalities and constitutional philosophies that would not hinder his political agenda, as the more conservative Court had done during the 1930s (e.g., Feldman 2010).

Thus, perhaps a second account – not necessarily incompatible with the first – for the increasing rate of dissent during World War II is that the justices who took the bench during and after the New Deal were qualitatively different in temperament, world views, and the way they approached the job of judging on the Supreme Court. Perhaps the most well-known account is offered by Walker, Epstein, and Dixon (1988), who argue that the demise of the norm of unanimity may have been influenced by all of these kinds of developments but that a single behavioral factor – namely, the leadership style of Chief Justice Harlan Fiske Stone – was most important. What is more, as they point out, the associate justices serving during the 1940s were, compared with their predecessors, young and inexperienced, suggesting that they may not

---

[1] Though, this was most likely due to ill health.

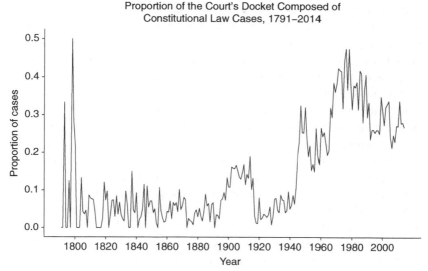

Figure 4.5. *Proportion of the Court's docket composed on constitutional law cases, 1791–2014.* For each year, I calculate the proportion of cases that are coded in the Supreme Court Database as resting primarily on the Constitution or a Constitutional Amendment from among all of the cases decided that year. (Source: Supreme Court Database.)

have fully internalized the norms of consensus that had characterized the Court up to that period. Moreover, contra Feldman's account of the FDR justices as "scorpions in a bottle," Epstein et al. argue they were relatively ideologically unified and therefore not necessarily prone to disagreement.

A third account, which we can think of as more structural, concerns the nature of the Court's work itself. As noted, the Judges' Bill of 1925 gave the Supreme Court near complete discretion over which cases it hears. As a consequence, the Supreme Court might have been able to shift its attention to more complicated, legally interesting, and therefore potentially divisive issues. This possibility is in part corroborated by Figure 4.5, which shows the proportion of the Court's docket composed of constitutional law cases each year. (Here, I rely on the Supreme Court Database's indication of whether the primary law at issue in each case was the Constitution or a Constitutional Amendment.) The data indicate that other than a short uptick in the Constitution's representation on the Court's docket at the beginning of the 1900s, the docket consisted of a relatively constant and low proportion of constitutional law cases until the mid-1940s, when constitutional law more than doubled, to a level that has since been sustained. This suggests a fundamental shift in the nature of the Court's work right around the time we see a rise in the rate of disagreement among the justices. Of course, as Epstein et al. note, there is not a sharp jump in the rate of dissent immediately following the Judges' Bill (enacted in 1925, first affecting the Court's discretionary docket in 1927). Similarly, as we see in Figure 4.5, there was not a sharp jump in constitutional law cases during that period, either. (If anything, the Court backed away from what had been a growing constitutional docket beforehand.)

Of course, all of these possibilities may be taking place at the same time, and it is beyond the scope of work here to lay out a comprehensive account for what appears to be a significant, structural break in the Court's voting patterns during the 1940s. But I do want to account for these patterns and provide some analytic context for the changing rate of disagreement. A final observation, though, that sheds some light on what was taking place in the Court during the twentieth century emerges when we consider so-called "landmark" cases distinctly from non-landmark cases. Several organizations – journalistic, scholarly, and others – regularly assemble lists of which Supreme Court cases constitute "landmark" decisions. Here, I use the Legal Information Institute's list of landmark decisions to identify which cases constitute landmark decisions, though the results are qualitatively similar when we consider alternative lists, such as the *Oxford Guide to Supreme Court Decisions* (Hall 1999).

Figure 4.6 replicates Figure 4.4, separating cases by whether they are landmark decisions. A striking pattern emerges. Whereas there has been a slow, though monotonic, decrease in majority coalition sizes since Reconstruction, there is no obvious change in the rate of that decline or anything else resembling a structural break around 1940. There does seem to be an increase in that over-time trend around the mid-1960s. However, when we consider the non-landmark cases, we find a pattern that looks essentially identical to the pattern in the aggregate data. In other words, the landmark decisions do not exhibit the same major break during Chief Justice Stone's tenure that the cases writ large exhibit. Many possible explanations for this difference might be possible, and as we investigate the politics of judicial coalitions in Chapters 6 and 7, we will consider this pattern again.

4.3   THE OPINIONS

Figure 4.7 shows the number of opinions written per case, among the constitutional law cases, during each year from 1877 through 2012. The data here recover the well-documented rise of the rate of dissenting by Supreme Court justices after the New Deal, most prominently documented in Walker, Epstein, and Dixon (1988). There are a few important, and notable, trends that emerge here. First, we see a relatively low number of opinions – roughly 1.5 per case – up until World War

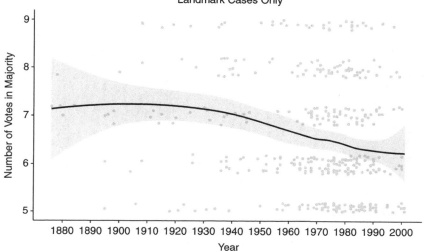

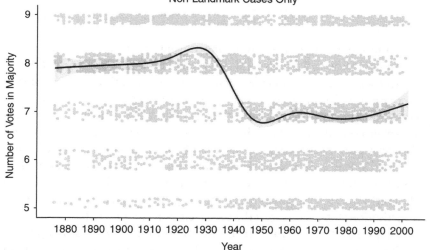

Figure 4.6. *Majority coalition sizes in Supreme Court constitutional law cases, 1877–2002, separated into landmark and non-landmark cases.* The figure shows each constitutional law case decided by the Supreme Court and its year of decision and majority coalition size. The lines are nonlinear scatterplot smoothers. The top panel shows only landmark cases; the bottom panel shows only non-landmark cases. (Sources: Congressional Research Service and Supreme Court Database.)

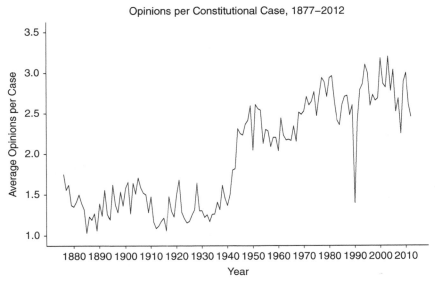

Figure 4.7. *Total number of opinions written per case in constitutional law cases, 1877–2010.* (Source: Justia.us.)

II, with a particular drop occurring during the second decade of the twentieth century. We then see a sharp increase following World War II – up to roughly 2.5 opinions per case – and a slower, though fairly steady increase in the number of opinions per case ever since. In recent years, constitutional cases have averaged nearly three opinions per case! When taken in conjunction with Figure 4.4, this suggests a striking pattern. As the Court began making more and more constitutional decisions, the fractiousness of those decisions increased. Majority sizes decreased, and the number of opinions written in cases increased. However, during the early years of the twentieth century, the Court has made fewer constitutional decisions, but the divisiveness has remained.

Figure 4.8(B) shows the distribution of how long the majority opinions in these cases are. (For purposes of analytic clarity, I set aside the less than 1% of the opinions that are perfunctory, brief statements (less than 50 words in length)). The distribution is exponential – it is skewed to the right, as is typical of length measurements. The median opinion is 3,258 words long, but there is a long right tail, so the mean opinion length is 4,051. The shortest opinion (among those longer than 50 words) is just 70 words, and the longest is 69,640 words. Figure 4.8(B) shows the distribution of word counts for all types of opinions – majority opinions, concurring opinions, dissenting opinions, and opinions concurring and

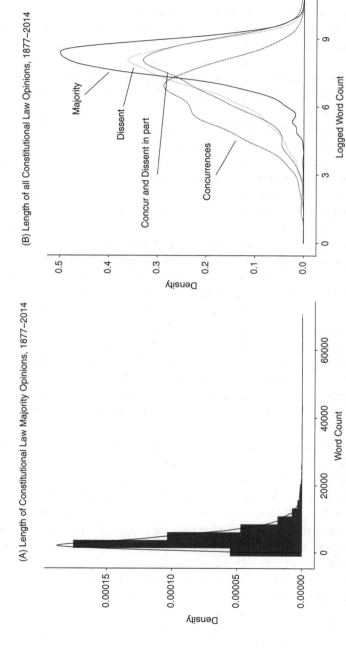

Figure 4.8. *Distribution of opinion lengths in constitutional law cases, 1877–2014*. The left-hand panel shows the distribution of word counts in all majority opinions. The right-hand panel shows the distribution, on a log scale, of opinion lengths in all types of opinions – majority opinions, concurring opinions, dissenting opinions, and opinions concurring and dissenting in part.

dissenting in part. This figure transforms the word counts to the log scale to ease comparison.

The patterns here are intuitive, yet instructive. The typical dissenting opinion is similar in length to the typical majority opinion, though there is a thicker left tail indicating dissenting opinions are more likely to be shorter than are majority opinions. The same is true of opinions that concur in part and dissent in part. However, concurring opinions are typically much shorter than are majority opinions. Presumably, this is because dissenting opinions disagree with the majority opinion and therefore need to set out an entirely different rationale. Concurring opinions are frequently what are known as "regular concurrences," which means the justice writing the opinion agrees in large part with the majority opinion but has some separate thoughts to share. Thus, these opinions need to make fewer points and can be much shorter than dissenting opinions or majority opinions, which by their nature must present relatively comprehensive accounts of the case.

Turning to Figure 4.9, we see how the lengths of these opinions has changed over time. This figure indicates the length of majority opinions has remained relatively stable over time, especially as compared to the change in majority sizes. The only possible pattern is what seems to be a very slight increase in the length of majority opinions since 1975, though that increase does not seem to be very different in magnitude than other historical fluctuations in opinion length. And, critically, as Figure 4.10, any such changes are not due to variation in the docket size. Here, we see the total amount written in all majority opinions each year against the total number of cases decided. A striking linear pattern emerges – as the Court hears more cases, the justices write more. In other words, it is not as though they account for an increased number of cases by writing shorter opinions.

In sum, the patterns in the constitutional law opinions are the following. Around the same time as the norm of unanimity was breaking down after the New Deal era, the number of opinions written per case increased, fairly naturally, but there was little effect on the amount that the justices write. Majority opinions have been of a fairly consistent length over time and are similar to most other types of opinions, except for concurrences which are typically shorter than majority opinions. However, what remains to be seen is how these patterns reflect changing politics and conflicts among the justices in the process of constitutional decision making. In the next chapter, when we begin to apply the statistical models described in Chapter 3, we will see how the political cleavages among the justices changes over time as a function of forces both internal and external to the Court itself.

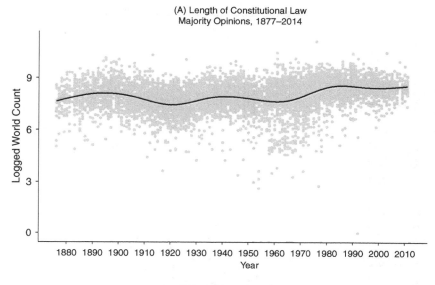

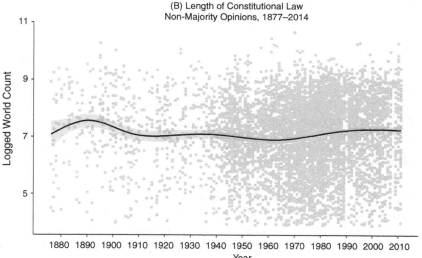

Figure 4.9. *Length of constitutional law opinions over time, 1877–2014.* The top panel shows the length of each majority opinion over time. The bottom panel shows the length of each non-majority opinion – majority opinions, concurring opinions, dissenting opinions, and opinions concurring and dissenting in part – over time.

4.4 CONCLUSION

Constitutional decision making took on a markedly different nature after the Civil War, compared to the antebellum period. The rate at which the Supreme Court engaged in constitutional interpretation increased

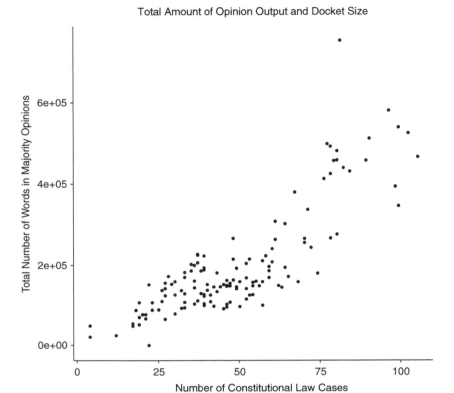

Figure 4.10. *Total number of words in all majority opinions in all cases each year, against the total number of constitutional law cases, 1877–2012.* Each point represents one year and gives the total number of words written in all majority opinions and the total number of constitutional law cases heard that year.

markedly, especially after Reconstruction. Later, especially during the early twentieth century, there was another major shift in constitutional decision making at the Supreme Court, as the justices became more willing to write separate opinions, and the provisions of the Constitution that were implicated in constitutional decisions shifted. For example, once the Fourteenth Amendment was enacted, it became a major fixture in constitutional decision making, and it was often interpreted in cases involving economic regulation, early civil rights cases, and the extent of judicial power. By the mid-twentieth century, however, the Court's constitutional attention had shifted away from economic regulation to other areas of individual liberty. In this era, the Court began to interpret the Fourteenth Amendment in conjunction with the Bill of Rights. In Chapters 6 and 7, we will see how this process played out, from the perspective of analytic history.

At the same time as the constitutional provisions the Court interpreted changed, and as the justices became more willing to write separately, the Court also became more focused on constitutional decision making. Especially before the Court gained near complete control over its docket, constitutional cases comprised a relatively small proportion of the Court's docket. Constitutional questions surged in the late-nineteenth century, as the country's legal system sought to handle problems associated with the unified economy that came with industrialization. However, it was not until the mid-twentieth century, when the Bill of Rights became a more central component of constitutional law that we saw a structural shift in the extent to which the Court focused much more extensively on constitutional law, to the exclusion of other areas of judicial decision making. As we will see in Chapter 7, this change has much to do with the proliferation of substantive policy matters that came to have constitutional implications.

At the same time as these changes were taking place, a number of things remained constant. We do not see a major change in the length of Court opinions, or the number of opinions written in cases – other than the increase associated with more dissenting after 1940. Typically, majority opinions and dissenting opinions are of roughly comparable length, whereas concurring opinions tend to be shorter on average. This pattern makes sense, as concurring opinions often are statements "in addition to" the majority opinion or an opportunity for a justice to register disagreement with a portion of the majority opinion. In any event, that the nature of opinion writing has remained stable over the period I study here will be useful when we want to examine the forces behind changing substantive and voting patterns among the justices, a subject to which I turn to in the next chapter.

Table A.1. *Summary of justices and their votes in constitutional law cases, 1877–2012.*

Justice	Start of Service	End of Service	Total Votes	Majority Votes	Dissent Rate
Nathan Clifford	January 21, 1858	July 25, 1881	82	77	6%
Noah Swayne	January 27, 1862	January 24, 1881	92	88	4%
Samuel Miller	July 21, 1862	October 13, 1890	335	318	5%
David Davis	October 17, 1862	March 04, 1877	7	7	0%
Stephen Field	May 20, 1863	December 01, 1897	549	501	9%
William Strong	March 14, 1870	December 14, 1880	88	78	11%
Joseph Bradley	March 21, 1870	January 22, 1892	367	347	5%
Ward Hunt	January 09, 1873	January 27, 1882	69	66	4%
Morrison Waite	March 04, 1874	March 23, 1888	263	249	5%
John Harlan	December 10, 1877	October 14, 1911	1043	919	12%
William Woods	January 05, 1881	May 14, 1887	142	140	1%
Stanley Matthews	May 17, 1881	March 22, 1889	182	180	1%
Horace Gray	January 09, 1882	September 15, 1902	603	565	6%
Samuel Blatchford	April 03, 1882	July 07, 1893	299	299	0%
Lucius Lamar	January 18, 1888	January 23, 1893	126	122	3%
Melville Fuller	October 08, 1888	July 04, 1910	764	709	7%
David Brewer	January 06, 1890	March 28, 1910	724	652	10%
Henry Brown	January 05, 1891	May 28, 1906	538	505	6%
George Shiras	October 10, 1892	February 23, 1903	356	337	5%
Howell Jackson	March 04, 1893	August 08, 1895	46	41	11%
Edward White	March 12, 1894	May 19, 1921	1226	1149	6%
Rufus Peckham	January 06, 1896	October 24, 1909	527	478	9%
Joseph McKenna	January 26, 1898	January 05, 1925	1294	1219	6%
Oliver Holmes	August 11, 1902	January 12, 1932	1460	1342	8%
William Day	March 02, 1903	November 13, 1922	947	924	2%

Name					
William Moody	December 17, 1906	November 20, 1910	112	108	4%
Horace Lurton	January 03, 1910	July 12, 1914	211	203	4%
Charles Hughes	October 10, 1910	June 10, 1916	343	331	3%
Willis Van Devanter	January 03, 1911	June 02, 1937	1385	1323	4%
Joseph Lamar	January 03, 1911	January 02, 1916	271	260	4%
Mahlon Pitney	March 18, 1912	December 31, 1922	610	569	7%
James McReynolds	October 12, 1914	January 31, 1941	1327	1170	12%
Louis Brandeis	June 05, 1916	February 13, 1939	1123	985	12%
John Clarke	October 09, 1916	September 18, 1922	323	283	12%
William Taft	July 11, 1921	February 03, 1930	413	406	2%
George Sutherland	October 02, 1922	January 17, 1938	738	697	6%
Pierce Butler	January 02, 1923	November 16, 1939	814	740	9%
Edward Sanford	February 19, 1923	March 08, 1930	335	329	2%
Harlan Stone	March 02, 1925	April 22, 1946	1000	900	10%
Charles Hughes	February 24, 1930	July 01, 1941	562	536	5%
Owen Roberts	June 02, 1930	July 31, 1945	715	638	11%
Benjamin Cardozo	March 14, 1932	July 09, 1938	279	245	12%
Hugo Black	August 19, 1937	September 17, 1971	1798	1390	23%
Stanley Reed	January 31, 1938	February 25, 1957	854	737	14%
Felix Frankfurter	January 30, 1939	August 28, 1962	1081	881	19%
William Douglas	April 17, 1939	November 12, 1975	2014	1451	28%
Francis Murphy	February 05, 1940	July 19, 1949	472	390	17%
James Byrnes	July 08, 1941	October 03, 1942	52	49	6%
Robert Jackson	July 11, 1941	October 09, 1954	527	421	20%
Wiley Rutledge	February 15, 1943	September 10, 1949	330	265	20%
Harold Burton	October 01, 1945	October 13, 1958	581	460	21%
Fred Vinson	June 24, 1946	September 08, 1953	323	280	13%

(continued)

Table A.1. (continued)

Justice	Start of Service	End of Service	Total Votes	Majority Votes	Dissent Rate
Tom Clark	August 24, 1949	June 12, 1967	863	726	16%
Sherman Minton	October 12, 1949	October 15, 1956	254	207	19%
Earl Warren	October 05, 1953	June 23, 1969	859	737	14%
John Harlan	March 28, 1955	September 23, 1971	946	691	27%
William Brennan	October 16, 1956	July 20, 1990	2493	1792	28%
Charles Whittaker	March 25, 1957	March 31, 1962	262	213	19%
Potter Stewart	October 14, 1958	July 03, 1981	1670	1375	18%
Byron White	April 16, 1962	June 28, 1993	2355	2019	14%
Arthur Goldberg	October 01, 1962	July 25, 1965	185	169	9%
Abe Fortas	October 04, 1965	May 14, 1969	226	194	14%
Thurgood Marshall	October 02, 1967	October 01, 1991	1892	1246	34%
Warren Burger	June 23, 1969	September 26, 1986	1426	1208	15%
Harry Blackmun	June 09, 1970	August 03, 1994	1860	1506	19%
Lewis Powell	January 07, 1972	June 26, 1987	1282	1135	11%
William Rehnquist	January 07, 1972	September 03, 2005	2106	1626	23%
John Stevens	December 19, 1975	June 29, 2010	1841	1306	29%
Sandra O'Connor	September 25, 1981	January 31, 2006	1299	1102	15%
Antonin Scalia	September 26, 1986		1015	801	21%
Anthony Kennedy	February 18, 1988		895	808	10%
David Souter	October 09, 1990	June 29, 2009	623	489	22%
Clarence Thomas	October 23, 1991		635	490	23%
Ruth Ginsburg	August 10, 1993		552	405	27%
Stephen Breyer	August 03, 1994		512	391	24%
John Roberts	September 29, 2005		133	111	17%
Samuel Alito	January 31, 2006		124	98	21%
Sonia Sotomayor	August 08, 2009		71	53	25%
Elena Kagan	August 07, 2010		37	29	22%

5

Patterns in Constitutional Law

In this chapter, I turn to an analysis of the political cleavages and dimensions of constitutional law. The questions we confront are: (1) how many political dimensions are there to constitutional law since 1877; (2) what substantive issues link together along those dimensions; (3) how do those answers differ using the tools and data described in previous chapters, as opposed to more traditional approaches; and (4) what are the basic contours of constitutional law and politics in American history? With those issues resolved in this chapter, the subsequent chapters in this book turn to analytic-historical questions about how the puzzles outlined in Chapter 1 drive the aggregate patterns we encounter here. To preview briefly, we will see shortly that American constitutional law can neatly be summarized with six political dimensions. Before the mid-twentieth century, though, there tended to be only a single dimension or two that best characterized judicial voting at any period in time. In more recent decades, though, we have witnessed the emergence of a more complex, multidimensional constitutional politics.

5.1 THE TOPICS OF CONSTITUTIONAL LAW

To estimate the topics and dimensions of constitutional law, we turn to the model described in Chapter 3 and the data described in Chapter 4. In particular, I estimate the joint LDA + IRT model, using the text of Supreme Court opinions to determine the extent to which a case maps onto each dimension, and then scale the justices' voting accordingly. For each case, I include the full text of all of the opinions produced in each case. So, for example, a case without any separate opinions relies only on the text of the majority opinion, whereas a deeply fractured decision will include the majority (or plurality) opinion as well as all concurring or dissenting opinions. Typically, when we estimate ideal point models, we do not include unanimous decisions, because there is no information to be gained about the justices' relative alignment. However, in this setting, I still include unanimous decisions, because while they do not provide information about the alignment, they do provide information about the distribution of topics the Court confronts at any given time.

The results I report here are based on 20,000-iteration simulations of the model, after discarding a 20,000-iteration burn-in period. Diagnostic evidence, such as traceplots, suggest good convergence within the burn-in period. I also note that I have experimented with estimating the model using particular subsets of the data – such as only non-unanimous decisions, only decisions after the 1925 (when the Court's docket became almost entirely discretionary), only decisions after 1937, etc. Below I provide some comparisons between those results and the ones I emphasize here. However, for now I note that there are no significant differences at any given period between any of those subsets and the results from the full data.

5.1.1 *Selecting Dimensionality*

As I described in Chapter 3, one primary question we must address in estimating the ideal point model is how many dimensions we want to *assume* there are. As I described in that chapter, when one wants to characterize the cleavages of voting, rather than simply the number of topics that best explain word usage in the opinions, the most sensible approach is to select the number of dimensions that best explains variation in voting patterns. In order to do this, I have fit the entire model 20 different times, using every number of dimensions from 1 through 20. While, in theory, we could consider dimensionality higher than 20, as we will see shortly, there is strong evidence that higher dimensionality would not be fruitful for explaining the law. Further, as Lauderdale and Clark (2014) show, the entire body of judge-made law is best characterized by roughly 20 dimensions or so, and here we are only considering a small subset of that law – constitutional cases.

Figure 5.1 shows the Deviance Information Criterion (DIC) (Spiegelhalter et al. 2002) for the IRT component of the model, using each different number of topics. The DIC is a measure of model fit, which is especially useful in the context of Bayesian modeling. The DIC is similar to more familiar metrics of model fit, such as the AIC or BIC. Lower values of the DIC indicate a better fit to the data.[1] There is no

---

[1] Also, like the AIC, but unlike the BIC, the DIC includes a penalty for model complexity.

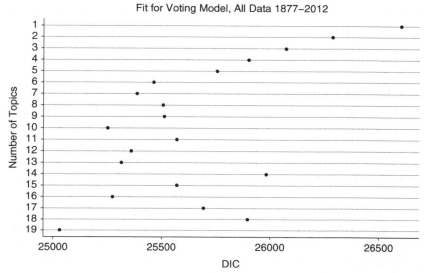

Figure 5.1. *Fit for voting component in LDA+IRT model using different numbers of topics in constitutional law cases, 1877–2005.* The figure shows the deviance information criterion (DIC) for the IRT component of the model for numbers of topics ranging from 1 through 20. A lower DIC implies a better fit to the voting patterns.

hard-and-fast rule about what kind of decrease in the DIC statistic from one model to the next is a substantively meaningful improvement, a difference of at least 10 in the DIC serves as a useful rule of thumb for considering two different models.

As we can see in the figure, moving from one dimension to two dimensions results in a dramatic decrease in the DIC. The two-dimensional model fits the voting data much better than does the one-dimensional model. And, this is not simply because by allowing two dimensions we simply permit the model to account for more variation in voting. As we see, moving down the figure (increasing the number of dimensions), we reach a point, around six dimensions, where adding more dimensions begins to produce a worse fit to the data. The reason is that the marginal predictive power of the additional dimensions is outweighed by the complexity of the model. Conceptually, this is analogous to the more common notion of "overfitting" in statistics – the model stops being about general patterns subject to some noise and instead about perfectly predicting each observation (here, all votes).

One way in which one assesses confidence in the selected number of dimensions, then, is to inspect the substantive content of the topics recovered from the model using different numbers of topics. In this case, a substantive evaluation reveals that after roughly six topics, further differentiation only splits up substantively coherent topics without providing much more in the way of statistical fit or interpretation. Table 5.1 shows the three words most strongly associated with each topic, for the version of the model using each of two through 13 topics. (I omit higher numbers of topics to make the table more legible.) While certainly not the only way to evaluate the model, this is a common diagnostic approach, which I describe below. The crucial point here is simply that the patterns make sense; as we increase the number of topics, we further distinguish the data into substantively coherent topics. After roughly six topics, the differences become less meaningful. Instead, the model starts breaking substantively coherent topics into distinct blocks, such as the division of the topic associated with judicial power into different preference dimensions concerned with the same substantive matter. Combined with the better statistical fit to the voting data we find with six topics, this suggests the political preference space for constitutional decision making is best described with the six-dimensional model.

That constitutional law can neatly be summarized with six political dimensions onto which the various legal questions map makes sense in light of the institutional, legal, and political theories of judicial decision making we encountered in Chapter 2. The political nature of Supreme Court decision making – in particular, the wide degree of discretion justices have in resolving constitutional questions, the collegial environment in which the justices work, and the policy-making nature of their decisions – raise the typical kinds of dilemmas that we encounter commonly in political and social choice settings. Thus, we see here evidence that politics, in the sense of distinct cleavages over distributional outcomes, organize the law by linking substantive issues together and mapping them onto those underlying cleavages. Throughout the remainder of this book, I show how these six ideological preference dimensions relate to the substantive content – often dynamically – through the history of constitutional decision making.

5.1.2 The Dimensions

What are these ideological preference dimensions along which constitutional law is organized? Unfortunately, the LDA model does not "spit out" a label for each of the topics. Instead, it is up to the investigator to examine the topics and make a determination of whether (1) they make sense, substantively, and (2) what their substantive meaning is. An extremely common approach to determining the substantive meaning of the topics is to identify the words most strongly associated with each topic – that is, the words that have the most predictive power that an opinion

Table 5.1. Top words associated with each topic for varying numbers of topics.

state act tax	court footnot state					
footnot court district	state tax act	court trial juri				
state court jurisdict	tax compani state	footnot school district	trial juri court			
commerc interst tax	feder footnot court	trial juri court	school public elect	state properti court		
state courts law	tax commerc interst	water land indian	feder footnot court	trial juri court	school elect speech	
school speech public	juri trial sentenc	properti compani state	employe employ labor	tax commerc interst	court feder jurisdict	unit congress state

(continued)

Table 5.1. (continued)

school speech public	search polic offic	feder footnot court	trial juri court	properti court state	tax commerc interst	unit state congress	water land indian					
indian alien militari	trial juri court	water river navig	footnot court feder	child parent medic	tax bank taxat	school elect public	state law court	commerc interst commiss				
compani railroad water	patent broadcast copyright	footnot employe district	commerc price interst	unit state congress	court jurisdict suit	search polic warrant	juri trial sentenc	school religi child	tax corpor properti			
alien militari foreign	school elect vote	search offic polic	tax bank taxat	state law court	speech child public	footnot court feder	trial juri court	land indian water	commerc interst commiss	patent vessel maritim		
state law court	vessel damag maritim	trial court juri	speech patent public	indian unit alien	footnot court feder	elect vote district	search warrant offic	land water river	tax commerc interst	sentenc death prison	school religi child	
search polic warrant	tax commerc interst	prison inmat parol	elect vote district	indian tribe reserv	footnot court feder	militari alien presid	state law court	school religi child	speech public broadcast	water navig vessel	patent price liquor	trial juri court

Each row shows a distinct estimation of the LDA+IRT model, with the number of assumed topics varying from two through 13. In each column, I show the top three words associated with each of the assumed number of topics for that estimation.

Table 5.2. *Top words associated with each of six constitutional law topics, 1877–2005.*

Judicial Power	Economics and Business	Central Authority	Balance of Power	Crime and Punishment	Individual and Civil Rights
state	tax	water	feder	trial	school
court	commerc	land	footnot	juri	elect
law	interst	indian	court	court	speech
act	busi	patent	congress	sentenc	public
properti	rate	river	act	crimin	district
case	state	navig	employe	convict	polit
power	commiss	tribe	u.s.c	petition	religi
unit	sale	vessel	state	evid	educ
plaintiff	compani	reserv	employ	defend	vote
judgment	regul	maritim	action	search	candid
statut	incom	admiralti	labor	crime	children
constitut	price	tribal	respond	counsel	child
jurisdict	transport	owner	jurisdict	offens	footnot
contract	gas	ship	union	wit	interest
question	carrier	copyright	law	case	protect
made	railroad	fish	petition	judg	parent
suit	taxat	take	claim	punish	racial
bank	oper	invent	agenc	arrest	amend
author	product	project	district	prison	student
page	manufactur	compens	administr	state	court

Words are the words most strongly associated with each of the six topics selected from estimating a six-topic LDA+IRT model on all constitutional law cases, from 1877 through 2005. The order of the topics is arbitrary, but words are listed in order of the strength of their association with each topic.

is associated with each of the six topics. Table 5.2 shows the top ten words most strongly associated with each of the six topics. The topics themselves are listed in no particular order. For each topic, I assign a substantive label. These labels are completely subjective and are my own labels. They do not correspond to legal provisions or areas of the law. Rather, they are impressionistic, based on the terms that are associated with the topics. Readers are free to substitute any alternative label one might want. I employ them here simply as a more efficient, shorthand way of referring to the topics.

The first topic is what I refer to as "Judicial Power." The Judicial Power topic involves cases that present issues about what kinds of questions the courts have the authority to resolve, what kinds of remedies are at the Court's disposal, and more generally how the courts operate and exercise jurisdiction. A typical case that is largely about this topic is *Cole* v.

Cunningham, 133 U.S. 107 (1890). That case dealt with whether a court in one state could enjoin creditors of an insolvent party from pursuing the insolvent debtor in another state's courts once the first state had already begun dividing up the debtor's assets. The Supreme Court concluded that it does not violate the Full Faith and Credit Clause of the Constitution for the first state court to stop the debtors from going to another state's courts. Other typical cases include *Smith* v. *Reeves*, 178 U.S. 436 (1900), which held that a state cannot be sued without its consent; and *Harris* v. *Balk*, 198 U.S. 215 (1905), which involved a complicated jurisdictional question. In that case, Harris owed money to Balk, and Balk owed money to a third person, named Epstein. Harris and Balk lived in North Carolina, but Epstein lived in Maryland; when Harris traveled to Maryland, Epstein maneuvered to bring a suit against Harris to take over his debt to Balk in order to help settle Balk's to Epstein. The Supreme Court concluded that the Maryland courts could exercise that jurisdiction over Harris.[2]

The second topic, "Economics and Business," concerns questions of interstate commerce, national regulation of the economy, and relations between business and labor. Typical of this topic are classical cases on interstate commerce, concerning, among other things, whether a state can tax a business's profits that derive from interstate commerce (*Matson Navigation Co.* v. *State Board of Equalization*, 297 U.S. 441 (1936)), whether energy produced on one state and sold in another is interstate commerce (e.g., *Public Utilities Comm'n* v. *Attleboro Steam Co.*, 273 U.S. 83 (1927), *Illinois Nat. Gas Co.* v. *Central Illinois P.S.C.*, 314 U.S. 498 (1942)), or the regulation of shipping rates by the Interstate Commerce Commission (*Chicago, M. & St.P. Ry. Co.* v. *Public Util. Comm'n*, 274 U.S. 344 (1927)), among other topics.

The third topic is what I refer to as "Central Authority." This topic touches on a number of issues related to the national government's enumerated powers. A typical case associated with this topic is *United States* v. *Utah*, 283 U.S. 64 (1931), which dealt with whether a river is subject to federal (as opposed to state) jurisdiction when parts of the river are not navigable and the navigable sections lie wholly within a single state's boundaries.

The fourth topic, "Balance of Power," deals with the negotiation of authority between the national and state governments. A typical case here is *Yellow Freight Syst.* v. *Donnelly*, 494 U.S. 820 (1990), which held that claims made under Title VII of the Civil Rights Act could be brought in state courts – that they did not have to be in federal courts – and reaffirmed the principle that state courts are "presumptively competent,

---

[2] The case was overruled in 1977 in *Shaffer* v. *Heitner*.

to adjudicate claims arising under [federal law]" (494 U.S., at 823). Other cases very typically involve questions about whether a state can serve a function in place of the national government or when the national government can preclude state action.

The fifth topic is what I refer to as "Crime and Punishment" and touches on a variety of issues related to crime, law enforcement, and criminal procedure. Typical cases in this topic include *Parker* v. *Randolph*, 442 U.S. 62 (1979), which considered whether a confession by a co-defendant could be used as evidence against other co-defendants if the confessing defendant does not take the stand and so cannot be cross-examined; and *Clemons* v. *Mississippi*, 494 U.S. 738 (1990), which deal with how judges instruct jurors in a capital case and when errors in a judge's instructions to a jury necessarily require a new sentencing.

The final topic, "Individual and Civil Rights," touches on a variety of issues that typically interest political studies of the Court, especially – though by no means exclusively – during the latter half of the twentieth century. Cases that are most typical here span a variety of issues, such as the entanglement of public facilities and education with religion (e.g., *Good News Club* v. *Milford Central School*, 533 U.S. 98 (2001), *Widmar* v. *Vincent*, 454 U.S. 263 (1981)), electoral and political campaigning processes (e.g., *Storer* v. *Brown*, 415 U.S. 724 (1974)), race relations and integration (e.g., *Monroe* v. *Board of Comm'rs of City of Jackson*, 391 U.S. 450 (1968)), electoral redistricting (e.g., *Gaffney* v. *Cummings*, 412 U.S. 735 (1973)), privacy and reproductive rights (e.g., *Akron* v. *Akron Ctr. for Reprod. Health*, 462 U.S. 416 (1983)), and myriad other issues.

Figure 5.2 shows the distribution of each topic's representation on the Court's docket over time. In particular, for each Term of the Court, I calculate the average proportion of each case represented by each topic. The plots show, for each topic, the average proportion for that topic among the Court's cases, and the lines are locally weighted regression estimates (lowess smoothers). The grey and white regions represent different Chief Justice regimes. A number of important patterns emerge. First, we see, in general, that most of the topics are most prevalent at a given point in time – no topic composes a consistent portion of the Court's constitutional docket. However, one consistent pattern is that the *Central Authority* topic, which deals with congressional power over maritime regulation, Indian affairs, and other enumerated powers, commands a low, but steady amount of the Court's constitutional docket.

Second, there is something of a natural progression in the substantive content of the Court's constitutional docket. During the earliest years covered here, the docket was mostly comprised by cases implicating

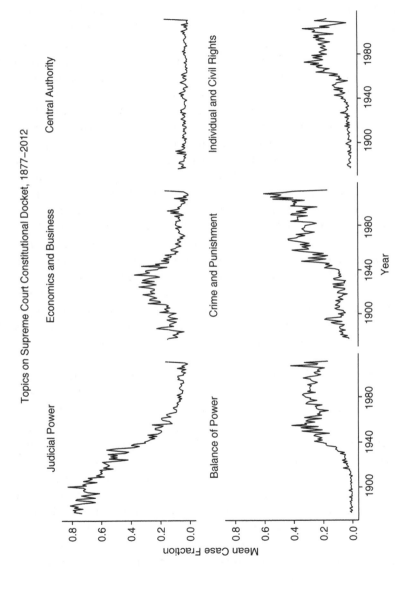

Figure 5.2. *Representation of each of the six topics of constitutional law on the Court's docket each year, 1877–2012.* Each panel shows one topic. For each term, I calculate the mean assignment probability for each topic across all cases. The black lines show nonlinear (loess) smoothers of those fractions over time.

judicial power. However, during the late nineteenth century, as the Second Industrial Revolution was causing a unification of the national economy, the role of interstate commerce and federalism quickly began to occupy a greater share of the Court's time. As we will see below, the Court's constitutional docket during the late nineteenth century was largely shaped by social and technological developments driving much of the political and legal discourse in the United States. The expansion of the railroads after the Civil War, which accompanied the Second Industrial Revolution, facilitated a rapid transition in the national economy away from more locally based agrarian production to a consolidated economy of manufacturing. The integration of relatively rapid transport, with the manufacturing economy and means of communication that accompanied those developments, radically transformed what kinds of activities were taking place in the context of interstate commerce. Consider larger social developments taking place at the time, memorialized in cultural landmarks, such as Upton Sinclair's *The Jungle*, which depicted the horrifying conditions in which many laborers worked. This changing economy brought the national government into a greater role policing the economy. It also caused the Court to have to adjudicate new questions about the national government's power, especially in light of the Civil War Amendments, which in some important ways restructured the balance of power between the national and state governments, reflecting the larger political conclusions of the Civil War.

By the mid-twentieth century, though, the Court had turned its attention away from questions about economic regulation and focused more on questions about criminal law, and later on civil liberties issues, especially after the civil rights movement accelerated during the 1950s and 1960s. One may suspect some of these patterns are attributable to major structural changes in the Court's institutions and the national politics surrounding constitutional interpretation. For example, one may suspect that the turn away from questions of judicial power is driven by the expansion of certiorari in 1925 – the mechanism by which the Supreme Court exercises discretion over its docket. Another possibility is that the transformation the country underwent in the wake of the Great Depression and FDR's New Deal legislative agenda, as well as larger social movements that took root in the wake of World War II, fundamentally altered the role of the federal government. Questions of humanity, morality, and justice that were forced onto the Western political agenda during that period certainly influenced the kinds of legal questions that arose and made their way into constitutional jurisprudence (e.g., Klarman 2004). This is in many senses consistent with Ackerman's (1998) claim that the New Deal era constituted an informal period of constitutional amendment. In Chapters 6 and 7, I unpack these patterns in greater detail and offer a historical analysis of the patterns of stability and change in the Court's constitutional docket.

While we may be able to make sense of the recovered topics *ex post*, how confident are we that the statistical model actually *fits* the data? As we saw above, the six topics chosen here best fit the voting cleavages, but it remains to be seen how these topics relate to the cases themselves. Let us begin with Figure 5.3, which shows the distribution of posterior assignment probabilities. This figure shows, for each case, how much it loads onto each of the six topics. These distributions reveal there is a large mass at 0 for each of the topics. That demonstrates that a large proportion of cases has zero probability of being associated with that topic. This makes intuitive sense. If the groups are substantively meaningful and distinct, most cases should not be associated with a large number but rather a small number of topics.

For two preference dimensions – Judicial Power and Crime and Punishment – we see there are some cases that load very heavily onto just that one topic. Setting aside the masses at 0, the most common assignment probabilities are either 0.1 or 1.0. That is, for those two preference dimensions, a case is most likely to be almost entirely about the topic or to have a small fraction of the opinion related to the topic. So, those cases that load onto either Judicial Power or Crime and Punishment are most likely to load either entirely or only marginally onto the topic. By contrast, the other four topics – Central Authority, Balance of Power, Economics and Business, and Individual and Civil Rights – have a distinct distribution where the most common values are lower. In other words, the rarest case, involving one of those topics, is the case that is essentially entirely about the single topic. Rather, if a case involves one of those dimensions, it almost surely involves a mix of topics.[3]

To understand the relationships among the topics as they appear in the opinions, consider Figure 5.4. Here, I subset the cases by topic, taking only cases that have at least a 40% probability of being assigned to each topic. (95% of all cases have at least a 40% probability of being assigned to at least some topic.) Then, for each topic, I show the posterior assignment probabilities for all other topics, among those cases. So, for example, in the top-center panel, we see cases that are at least 40% about Economics and Business. Each row shows those cases' posterior assignment probabilities for the other five topics. In this panel, we see that Economics and Business cases are most likely to also involve

---

3 In the appendix to this chapter, along with diagnostic results, I show the distribution of maximum assignment probabilities among all cases.

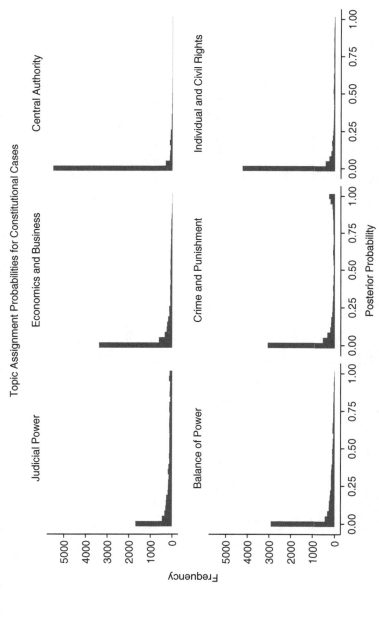

Figure 5.3. *Distribution of posterior assignment probabilities for each of the six topics.* Each panel shows the distribution of posterior assignment probabilities among all constitutional law cases, for the given topic.

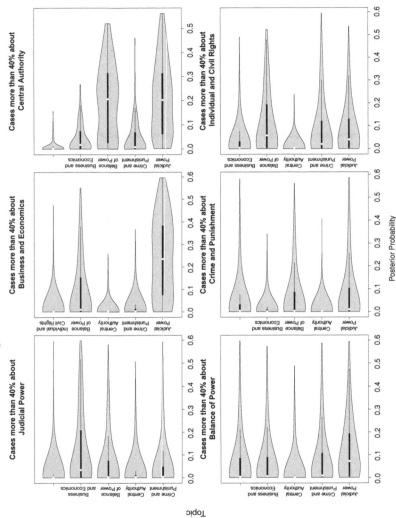

Figure 5.4. *Distribution of posterior assignment probabilities conditional on at least 40% assignment probability for each other topic.* Each panel subsets all cases to those with at least a 40% posterior probability of being assigned to that topic and shows the distribution of posterior assignment probabilities to each of the other five topics.

questions about Judicial Power and Balance of Power, and least likely to involve questions about Central Authority and Crime and Punishment. Indeed, for most of the preference dimensions, Judicial Power is a very common topic to be associated as a secondary topic. In other words, no matter which dimension a case primarily taps onto, most cases implicate a distinct dimension about the power of the courts as well. The justices of the Supreme Court are often making decisions where the political cleavage involves some aspect of the power of the courts to resolve the dispute with which they are confronted.

Taken together, the panels in Figure 5.4 present an instructive lesson about how substantive topics hang together in the Court's constitutional jurisprudence. Consider the Individual and Civil Rights and Crime and Punishment panels. As we noted, civil liberties cases are disproportionately associated with criminal law and civil rights issues. However, when considering criminal procedure cases, one finds that they are much more evenly distributed across the other five topics, and that political rights is actually one of the smallest intersections for criminal procedure. Individual freedom, judicial power, and federalism are much more likely topics to appear in a criminal procedure case. In general, we see here that certain topics (for example, Individual and Civil Rights and Balance of Power) appear in a mixture of other types of cases whereas other topics (such as Judicial Power and Economics and Business) tend to be associated with a smaller number of complementary issues in their respective cases.

Returning to the question whether these patterns recovered ex post actually fit the data as we understand them, these patterns suggest a sensible underlying structure to constitutional law. There are a handful of distinct ideological cleavages, but most cases implicate more than just one of those dimensions. Instead, because cases arise in the real world, they come to the Court entangling multiple preference dimensions. What is more, any given policy question might activate different ideological dimensions, depending on the particular context of the case. Federal regulation of the medical industry, for example, activates competing ideological dimensions when it arises in the context of abortion than when it arises in the context of health insurance.

On this latter point, in particular, it is also instructive to consider how the topics recovered from the voting patterns and text compare to other substantive typologies of cases that are oriented around policy dimensions, rather than preference dimensions. Perhaps most well known is the "issue area" categorization in the Supreme Court Database (Spaeth et al. 2015). The issue area typology divides all cases into one of 13

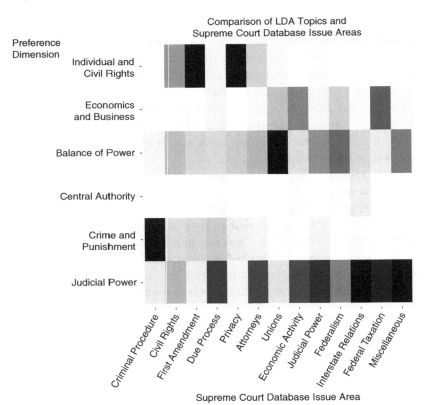

Figure 5.5. *Distribution of posterior assignment probabilities conditional on at least 50% assignment probability for each other topic.* Each panel subsets all cases to those with at least a 50%.

broad issue areas.[4] Specifically, cases are assigned to one of the following issue areas: criminal procedure, civil rights, First Amendment, due process, privacy, attorneys, unions, economic activity, judicial power, federalism, interstate relation, federal taxation, and miscellaneous.[5] Some of those issue areas are defined to include smaller classes of cases and are associated with specific types of litigants (for example, attorneys or unions) whereas others encompass large, diverse areas of law (for example, criminal procedure or civil rights). How do the political dimensions uncovered by the LDA+IRT analysis relate to these categories of cases? Figure 5.5 shows a heat map comparing cases' assignments to

---

4 Technically, a case may be assigned to two issue areas, but there is an exceptionally strong preference for assigning a case to only a single issue area.
5 A fourteenth issue area exists, private law, which is a very small group of cases and irrelevant for the study of constitutional law.

these issue areas with their assignment probabilities for each of the six topics. Each cell in this matrix is shaded according to the strength of the association between the two categorizations. Darker colors indicate that cases assigned to the issue area indicated in the column have higher, on average, posterior probabilities of being on the topic indicated in the row.

A number of patterns emerge quickly. The first is that none of the issue areas maps cleanly and entirely onto one of the six political dimensions recovered from the voting patterns and opinion texts. In other words, the cases grouped together in these issue areas combine substantive topics that activate different political cleavages on the Court. However, some of the issue areas are more politically complex than others. In particular, criminal procedure, privacy, unions, and interstate relations are each strongly associated with a single topic. Unsurprisingly, the criminal procedure issue area is strongly associated with what I have labeled the Crime and Punishment topic from the LDA analysis. There is some association with what I have labeled the Individual and Civil Rights topic as a secondary political topic. The interstate relations issue area is very strongly associated with the Judicial Power topic, with the interstate commerce topic being a secondary topic for those cases. Finally, the privacy and unions issue areas are very strongly associated with the individual freedom topic. The privacy issue area is often associated with political rights and criminal procedure as secondary topics, and the unions issue area is associated with Economics and Business topic secondarily.

The cases in the other issue areas, by contrast, are more spread out across the six political dimensions. Many issue areas are strongly associated with the Individual and Civil Rights dimension, suggesting that dimension captures substantive issues that are diverse and cross across many areas of the law. Consider, though, the Economics and Business topic. This political topic, a unique dimension of political conflict on the Court, brings together cases from due process, economic activity, federalism, interstate relations, and federal taxation. In other words, what these data suggest is that the justices have mapped these diverse legal issues onto a common dimension of political conflict. Similarly, we see that the Crime and Punishment topic brings together cases involving not just criminal procedure but also civil rights, the First Amendment, due process, and judicial power, among others. Indeed, this may not be too surprising. There are common issues that can be at stake in cases ranging across these varied legal areas. However, it is surprising from the perspective of traditional political science perspectives, which claim that nearly all political questions can be nearly summarized with a single dimension of conflict. Moreover, what these examples we see in Figure 5.5

indicate is that within any given area of the law – the First Amendment, due process, etc. – myriad dimensions of preference conflict may arise. This should not necessarily be surprising, though, crucially, it is different from standard accounts of judicial decision making, such as the doctrinal and behavioral approaches surveyed in Chapter 2. In the final section of this chapter, I turn to these patterns in greater detail.

Understanding how these topics group together is important for at least two types of inferences we will want to draw. First, in the next section, I consider the justices' preferences across the different topics, and, second, I then later turn to a substantive account of the evolution of substantive questions through the Court's constitutional cases. With respect to the former, understanding what it means to be "liberal" on, for example, federalism requires one to know what a federalism case is like – really, what the range of typical federalism cases encompasses. With respect to the latter, we will see below that various issues wax and wane in their political prominence, often in part to social forces outside the Court's control. Understanding how issues link together in the Court's constitutional jurisprudence will be important to recognizing the symbiotic process by which judge-made law and social development take place. Social conditions and political events outside of the Court can markedly shape the ways in which policy questions are linked together (or separated from each other) in the context of the law. At the same time, how judges resolve disputes typically has implications for what subsequent problems or questions emerge both in the law and as matters of policy more generally. In other words, an analytic history of constitutional decision making requires careful attention to the relationships among policy and legal questions, potentially crossing what might seem like natural categorizations.

5.2 THE PREFERENCE DIMENSIONS OF CONSTITUTIONAL LAW

As we saw in Chapter 2, the dimensions described here are defined by the cleavages that characterize judicial voting patterns. The dimensions tell us what the substance of those cleavages is, but what we have not yet seen is what the politics of those cleavages is. We turn now to that question.

5.2.1 *The Justices and their Preferences*

Figure 5.6 shows the estimated ideal point of every justice, along each of the six dimensions. The justices are ranked in order of their "average" ideal point, where the average is taken by weighting their ideal points

Estimated Ideal Points in each Topic

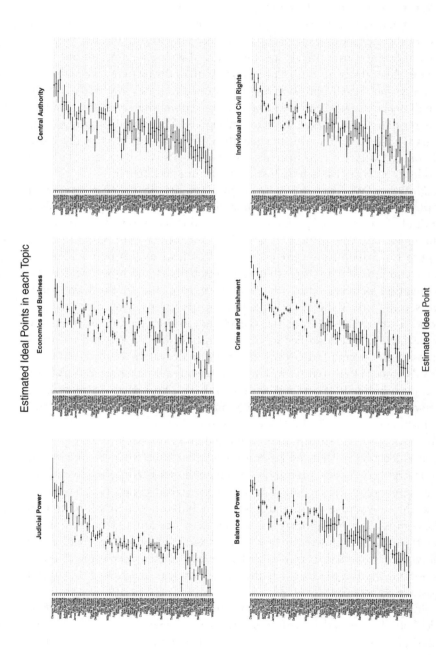

Figure 5.6. *Estimated ideal points for all justices, in each of the six dimensions.* Positions to the right are more "conservative" ideal points. Justices are ordered by average conservatism. Points show posterior means, and the horizontal bars show 95% highest density credible intervals.

across all of the topics, proportional to the topic's representation on the Court's docket during the entire period. A number of patterns stand out. First, whereas a justice's average liberalism is a fairly good predictor of where she falls along each of the preference dimensions, in each topic we see important, substantively meaningful, and widespread deviations from average liberalism. Second, it appears that all of the justices serving before roughly the Great Depression are all grouped together at the left ends of the dimensions, whereas all of the justices serving thereafter are grouped together at the right ends of the dimensions. This seems puzzling, as it is hard to believe that late nineteenth century justices were really more liberal on issues of civil liberties and civil rights, for example, than are modern-day justices such as Justices Ginsburg and Breyer.

However, whereas the justices' ideal points do shift around from topic-to-topic, this does not mean there are, practically speaking, multiple dimensions of preferences that produce consequentially different alignments of the justices. One way to consider this question is in Figure 5.7, which shows the correlations of justice ideal points between each combination of topics. In the top half of the plot, we see the correlation between ideal points in each pair, and in the lower half, we see the raw data underlying those correlations. The first thing to notice is that there is a positive correlation in each pair. (This is true by construction. As I described in Chapter 3, I assume a positive correlation across dimensions.) Justices who are more conservative on any given topic are also more likely to be more conservative on each other topic. However, the magnitude of those correlations varies. The lowest correlation is between justices preferences on Economics and Business and Crime and Punishment (0.56). The highest correlation is between justices preferences on Crime and Punishment and Individual and Civil Rights (0.89).

It is instructive that the highest correlation is between the Individual and Civil Rights and Crime and Punishment dimensions. These two topics are dominant in the modern Court's docket (recall Figure 5.2). These are also the substantive issues that attract the bulk of scholarly attention in the context of contemporary social science, which argues that the politics on the Court is inherently low-dimensional. However, as Figure 5.7 shows, even in that example, and certainly in the other topic pairs, it is not uncommon to observe many, considerable outliers from the overall positive correlation.

It is useful to consider a few examples of justices who vary in their ideal points across the ideological preference dimensions. Justice Tom C. Clark, for example, exhibits a fair amount of variation that is consistent with expectations, given his background characteristics. On the topic of Economics and Business, for example, he was relatively to the left.

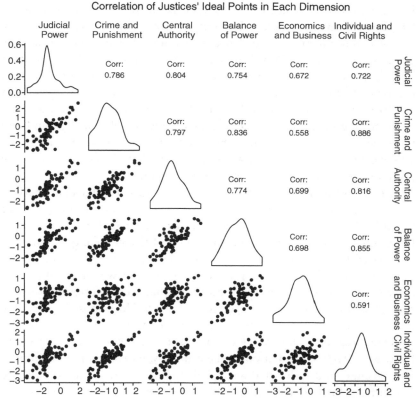

Figure 5.7. *Correlations of justices' ideal points in each combination of topics.* The lower half of the figure shows each justice's ideal point in the topic noted on the row against his or her ideal point in the topic noted in the column. The upper half of the figure reports the correlations for each pair of ideal points. The diagonal shows the distribution of ideal points for that topic.

Clark had served in the FDR administration, working in the Department of Justice Antitrust Division (ultimately being the Assistant Attorney General for Antitrust). However, he also served in the Criminal Division of the Department of Justice (DOJ), and we see that on Crime and Punishment, Clark was much further to the right than on Economics and Business. Indeed, Clark's preference profile is something that has been well-documented and makes sense in light of his role as a Southern Democrat who was part of the New Deal era (e.g., Gronlund 2010).

Another instructive example is to compare Justices Lewis F. Powell and Stephen Breyer. On Crime and Punishment, Powell and Breyer's ideal points are indistinguishable. And, indeed, they both have reputations as ideological moderates on issues of criminal punishment and procedure.

However, on the Balance of Power dimension, Breyer is far to Powell's left. Powell was a moderate Republican from Virginia who had fairly strong commitments to state sovereignty and had experience in state government. Notably, Powell was chair of the state board of education during the years when Virginia was working to evade integration in the wake of *Brown* v. *Board of Education*. Breyer is a Democrat from California who worked in the Antitrust Division of the DOJ and was a law professor with expertise in administrative law. Powell's background and life experiences likely influenced him to be skeptical of federal authority, whereas Breyer's background was one that would influence one to see the positive effects of a strong national government.

A final example to consider here involves Justice John Paul Stevens. Stevens was nominally an independent, was nominated by President Gerald Ford (a Republican) but consistently voted with his more liberal contemporaries, especially during Chief Justice Rehnquist's tenure. Compared to his relative moderate liberalism in general, Stevens' ideal point on the Judicial Power preference dimension was markedly more conservative. Stevens often took positions that were cautious about the role of courts in overseeing policy decisions. He opposed aggressive judicial oversight of legislative choices. However, Stevens typically endorsed relatively liberal views on issues involving civil rights and liberties, as well as regulation of the economy, and so on the Economics and Business and Individual and Civil Rights preference dimensions he is relatively further to the left. Thus, in cases where questions of civil liberties and judicial oversight came together, Stevens would often adopt a cautious doctrinal orientation that pursued a decidedly liberal objective without claiming an overly broad role for the courts.

A final note about the individual justices' estimated preferences. In each dimension, Justice William O. Douglas is estimated to be to the very far, extreme left. He is, in some sense, "off the scale." This finding is consistent with other ideal point estimation exercises (e.g., Martin and Quinn 2002; Bailey 2007) that find Douglas to be consistently far off to the left. In the figures here, his ideal points are not pictured in order to avoid distorting the scale. Moving forward through the rest of this book, the individual justices' preferences and differences across the topics will return again as an important component of the "internal politics" aspect of constitutional doctrine.

The significance of the justices' varying preference orderings across the topics is made all the clearer when we consider Figure 5.8, which shows the location of the median justice during each year for each topic. (I calculate the year median using the justices serving on the October Term beginning the preceding year; where more than nine justices serve

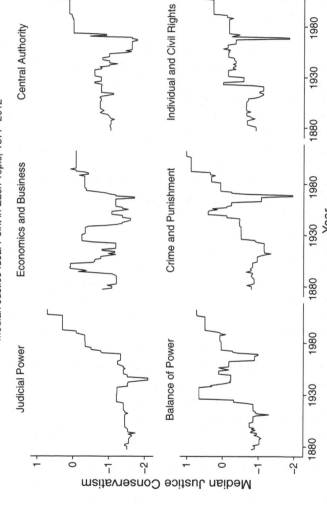

Figure 5.8. *Location of median justice in each ideological preference dimension, 1877–2012.* For each year, I calculate the median of all justices voting on any case during that year. In years where there is an even number of justices participating, the median is the midpoint between the two middle justices.

in a given Term, I use all justices serving during the Term.) A handful of preliminary patterns emerge that bear discussion. First, the overall trend, though it is by no means uniform across the six dimensions, is that the Court moved to the political left during the mid-twentieth century, relative to where it was during the late nineteenth and early twentieth centuries. Then, beginning in the late-1960s, coinciding with the replacement of Chief Justice Warren with Chief Justice Burger, the Court began a general move to the right, which was more prominent in a few dimensions than in others.

What we also see in Figure 5.8 is that the moves in the Court's relative conservatism over time occurred at different rates and at different specific points in time across the six dimensions. For example the conservative shift in the Court's preferences on the Economics and Business dimension preceded its conservative shift on federalism. Similarly, its liberal shift during the mid-twentieth century seems to have begun with a change in its preferences on Central Authority before its shift on Crime and Punishment. These types of patterns provide insight into how appointments to the Court are more complicated than simple "move-the-median" politics (e.g., Krehbiel 2007; Cameron and Kastellec 2016), as judges can affect policy issues as they map differentially onto competing preference dimensions (e.g., Lauderdale and Clark 2012).

Let us briefly consider a few of the key shifts in these patterns. First, consider Melville Fuller's Chief Justiceship, which extended from 1888–1910 and coincided with a number of important developments in the consolidating economy. During the last decade of the nineteenth century, the Court moved dramatically to the right on the Economics and Business preference dimension and then swung back to the left in the first decade of the twentieth century. The consequence was a Court that was for a period resistant to federal regulation of the economy and then became more accepting of regulation. In part, this was driven by the justices who served on the Court. Fuller had been Stephen Douglas' presidential campaign manager in 1860. Douglas was a fierce advocate for popular sovereignty, and Fuller shared his view of a limited role for the national government. In addition, Fuller was from Chicago, where he built his law practice, and as a consequence, was intimately familiar with, and opinionated about, railroads and their role in the modern economy. Fuller was joined on the Court by Justices LQC Lamar and Edward White, who were both Southern Democrats who were active during the Civil War and supported Secession. Other justices who joined the Court during this period include George Shiras, who was a Republican from Pennsylvania but was far from a progressive, providing a pivotal vote to strike down the national income tax in *Pollock* v. *Farmers' Loan & Trust Co.* as well as siding with the majority in the notorious case of *Plessy* v. *Ferguson*. However, by the end of Fuller's chief justiceship, Teddy Roosevelt had made a number of important appointments to the Court, which moved the Court back towards a more skeptical perspective on industry. (In Chapter 6, I examine this case in greater detail.)

Another example of an important shift in the Court occurs during Chief Justice Earl Warren's tenure during the late 1950s and 1960s. Here we see a steady shift to the left on cases that activate the justices preferences on the Crime and Punishment dimension, as Warren is joined by Justices William Brennan, a staunch opponent of the death penalty; Potter Stewart, a fierce advocate for a strong interpretation of the Fourth Amendment; and Byron White, who argued against excessive sentences for criminal convictions. At the same time, whereas the Court was moving steadily towards a more progressive criminal law jurisprudence, its efforts to move political and individual liberty to the left were less successful until later in Warren's tenure, when Justices Frankfurter and Clark, who held rather constrained views of what kinds of actions the government could take to enforce political and civil rights (Frankfurter's role in the ACLU notwithstanding), left and were replaced with Justices Goldberg (then, Fortas) and Marshall.

Importantly, it is not just the case that the relative conservatism of the median justice changes different across the different preference dimensions over time. This would be somewhat less interesting if a single justice were the median across all of the preference dimensions at any given point in time. Instead, though, what we find is that the justices line up sufficiently differently so that who is the median justice really does depend on what preference dimensions are activated by a case. Figure 5.9 shows the number of individual justices who are the median across the six preference dimensions each term from 1877 through 2012. Typically, there are 3-4 median justices in a term, though there have been terms where there is a unique median for each dimension, and in some years, especially recently, there have been only about two distinct medians. As we will see below, as cases combine the different preference dimensions, the consequence is considerable variation in whose vote is pivotal in any given case.

Of course, the median justice is just one metric of where the Court stands on the various ideological preference dimensions, and it is a metric that masks important dynamics. As I described in previous chapters, most of the theories of opinion writing at the Supreme Court contemplate the median justice *in conjunction with the preferences of the other justices.* Thus, another feature we may wish to consider is how closely aligned all of the various justices are to each other or how spread out they

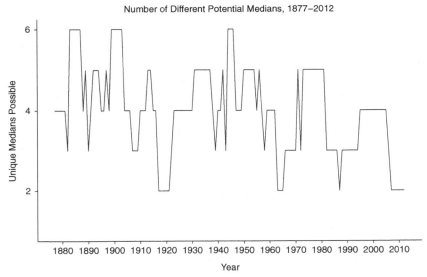

Figure 5.9. *Number of unique median justices by term, 1877–2012*. Figure shows the number of unique individuals who are the median justice across the six preference dimensions each term.

are across the preference dimension. To do this, I consider a measure of how polarized the justices are on each of the preference dimensions each year. In previous work (Clark 2009a), I employed a model of polarization developed by Esteban and Ray (1994) to measure income polarization. The basic intuition is straight-forward. Common measures, such as the Gini index, calculate how far each individual is from each other individual. The model Esteban and Ray propose derives directly from a series of axioms about what factors are related to polarization – most importantly homogeneity within groups and heterogeneity among groups. The main innovation over the Gini index is that the model includes that information but goes further to allow for one to have an affinity for others close by. "Thus, a justice may feel polarized from those who are unlike her but may also feel close to her ideological allies" (Clark 2009a, 148).

Figure 5.10 shows this metric of polarization on each of the ideological preference dimensions, from 1877 through 2012. (I exclude Justice Douglas from these calculations, because his ideal point is consistently estimated as very extreme and therefore distorts the scale during his tenure.) A number of very striking patterns emerge. First, the trends in polarization – towards more-or-less polarized Courts – is inconsistent across the ideological preference dimensions. For example, as the

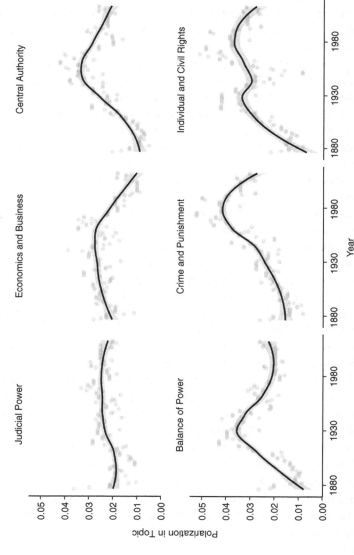

Figure 5.10. *Polarization of ideal points in each ideological preference dimension, 1877–2012.* For each year, I calculate the level of ideal point polarization (Esteban and Ray 1994; Clark 2009a) among all justices serving during that year. William O. Douglas is excluded from all calculations.

median's location on Balance of Power became first more liberal and then again more conservative during the twentieth century, the level of polarization on that dimension steadily decreased up until the 1980s. This indicates that while the Court was moving around from right to left back to the right, the justices were closing in on each other. It was only during the late part of the century, under Chief Justice Rehnquist, that the latest move in a conservative direction began to increase polarization on Balance of Power.

An entirely different pattern emerges when we consider Crime and Punishment, though. Here, the median justice moved steadily to the right during the first half of the twentieth century until a very sharp and abrupt swing to the left under Chief Justice Warren, followed by an even more dramatic swing back to the right under Chief Justices Burger and Rehnquist. However, from the beginning of the period studied here up until the 1980s, polarization on the Crime and Punishment dimension steadily increased. Since then, though, polarization has begun to decrease, owing mostly to the departure of liberal justices appointed by mid-century Democratic presidents and their replacement by conservative Republican presidents and moderate nominees by President Clinton. Thus, despite similar back-and-forth patterns in these two topics, the Court has seen preference polarization decline in one topic but increase in another.

Still other topics exhibit more complex patterns in preference polarization. An interesting comparison involves the Central Authority and Individual and Civil Rights topics. Along the National Power dimension, while the median did not change much up through the mid-twentieth century, polarization of preferences on that dimension increased steadily until the middle of Chief Justice Warren's tenure and has been declining somewhat since. The peak of polarization coincides with a temporary liberal shift to the left by the median during the Warren Court, but a subsequent and more dramatic shift to the right has led to a lowering of preference polarization. In the Individual and Political Freedom dimension, though, a slow drift to the right, aside from a very abrupt, but substantively consequential jump to the left during the Warren Court, has accompanied a somewhat erratic pattern in polarization. Polarization on that dimension increased markedly between 1880 and 1930 but then began to decline for the next 20 years as President Roosevelt and his successors appointed justices who were like-minded on this preference dimension. However, the Republican presidents, beginning with Richard Nixon, steadily introduced more varied justices to this dimension, and polarization rose sharply during the 1960s and 1970s. All of this took place, though, without very much movement in the center of the Court, as measured by the median's ideal point.

Finally, let us consider the two remaining preference dimensions – Judicial Power and Economics and Business. As we saw in Figure 5.8, the median did not move much on Judicial Power until roughly 1970, whereas the median on Economics and Business bounced around a great deal. However, on both topics, polarization remained somewhat constant during this period. Since 1970, though, the median on Judicial Power has moved steadily to the right, whereas the median on Economics and Business has remained somewhat constant. Polarization, though, has not changed much on Judicial Power, whereas it has decreased on Economics and Business. This indicates that during the first 100 years studied here, the preference profile – both its location and the distribution of preferences – remained roughly constant on Judicial Power, but the justices have shifted in unison during the last few decades to the right. On Economics and Business, the preference profile has bounced around in terms of its location – from the left to the right and back and then again to the right and back and then once more to the right. However, despite that movement, polarization remained relatively constant until this final move to the right the entire Court seems to have coalesced around the modern conservative Economics and Business preference.

The balance of preferences on the Court only addresses one aspect of what was taking place – changes inside the Court – and ignores the larger societal and political factors that affected the Court's jurisprudence. However, it is important to bear in mind that the internal politics of the Court – and, crucially the differences in the patterns of alignment across these topics – is essential for understanding the microprocesses that play out as the Court decides individual cases over time. In Chapters 6 and 7, I offer a richer account of the evolution of issues and ideological cleavages on the Court show how those forces – those inside as well as those outside the Court – work together to shape the content of law.

CONCERNING THE COMPARABILITY OF DIMENSIONS. A final note about interpreting the estimates we recover from the LDA + IRT model concerns how we can compare the different dimensions. The first thing to observe is that at the very least, the rank orderings of the justices is well-identified. To the extent we are statistically confident that one justice is to the left of another, we can be confident in the rank ordering. The more complicated question concerns the cardinality of the estimates – how do we know whether a given difference between two justices' ideal points is comparable to the difference between another two justices' ideal points? Perhaps more crucial, to what extent can we be confident that a given distance in one dimension is comparable to the same distance in another dimension? Relying on the cardinality of estimates from a voting model is always a delicate matter (e.g., Ho and Quinn 2010), but here we have a particularly challenging task. By assumption, the error distributions across the different dimensions are the same, and the discrimination and case parameters are assumed to come from a constant distribution, independent of the topic distribution. These assumptions help constrain the dimensions but do not guarantee that they will be cardinally comparable. Moreover, as I discussed in Chapter 3, it is difficult, if not impossible, to use substantive knowledge to make assumptions about how far apart any pair of justices ought to be along multiple dimensions.

However, one thing we can do to assess whether the distances are comparable across dimensions is to evaluate whether the mixture of topics in a case predicts the distribution of ideal points. One way to to do this is to examine the case-specific discrimination parameters. If an increase in a topic's representation in a case predicts an increase in the case's discrimination parameter, it implies that in that topic, the justices' ideal points are closer together. I estimate a linear regression model in which the dependent variable is the absolute value of each case's discrimination parameter (β_c), and the independent variables are the posterior estimates of each topic's representation in the case (the λ_c vector). Formally, I estimate the model

$$|\beta_c| = \gamma_1 \text{Judicial Power}_c + \gamma_2 \text{Economics and Business}_c \qquad (5.1)$$
$$+ \gamma_3 \text{Central Authority}_c$$
$$+ \gamma_4 \text{Balance of Power}_c + \gamma_5 \text{Crime and Punishment}_c$$
$$+ \gamma_6 \text{Individual and Civil Rights}_c + \varepsilon_c$$

Table 5.3 summarizes the results of this regression. What we see here is that each of the coefficients is roughly 1.5, varying between 1.31 and 1.68. These values suggest substantively little variation in the discrimination parameters can be explained by variation in the topic distribution. The standard deviation of all values of λ_c is 0.26, and the standard deviation of $|\hat{\beta}_c|$ is 0.87. Thus, the most that a standard deviation change in topic distributions can possibly explain is 0.11 standard deviation change in the discrimination parameter. These findings suggest, then, that the cardinality of the various ideological preference dimensions is comparable.

5.2.2 The Cases and Cleavages

As we saw in Chapter 3, we can use the case parameters from the IRT+LDA model to examine the nature of the cases the Court decides at any given time. One of the useful quantities that we can interpret theoretically from the LDA+IRT model is that indifference point, which

Table 5.3. *Relationship between topic distribution and discrimination parameters.*

	$\hat{\gamma}$
Judicial Power	1.68 (0.03)
Economics and Business	1.40 (0.04)
Central Authority	1.55 (0.13)
Balance of Power	1.31 (0.04)
Crime and Punishment	1.52 (0.03)
Individual and Civil Right	1.54 (0.04)
N	6651
R^2	0.75

Entries are linear regression coefficients, with standard errors in parentheses.

is the point in the preference space that separates the justices who prefer to vote with the majority from those who prefer to vote with the minority. In a case-space model, as we saw in Chapter 3, this quantity corresponds to a case's location in the fact space. Recall, in the case-space model, justices' ideal points correspond to thresholds in a latent ordering of cases such that a justice prefers one case disposition for all cases to one side of that threshold and another disposition for cases to the other side of that threshold.

Figure 5.11 shows the estimated case location for each case decided between 1877 and 2012. Recall that a case location is defined as the case-specific intercept, divided by the case-specific slope, from the voting model. Thus, there is only a single case location, and the relevance of a justice's ideal point on each preference dimension is determined by the weight of that dimension as estimated from the topic model component of the model. Cases further to the right are cases such that more justices would be to the left of the case and therefore prefer a "liberal" disposition; cases further to the left are cases such that more justices would be to the right of the case and therefore prefer a "conservative" disposition. All else equal, then, the more extreme a case location, the larger we should expect the majority in a given case, and the further to the right a case, the more likely we should expect the justices to endorse a liberal outcome.

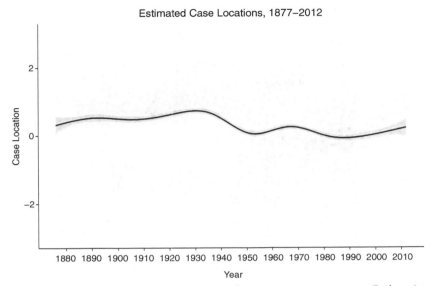

Estimated Case Locations, 1877–2012

Figure 5.11. *Location of cases in latent preference space, 1877–2012.* Each point corresponds to the point of indifference in the latent policy space for each vote taken by the justices. Each case has only a single location, which is constant across the six dimensions and is defined as the case-specific intercept, divided by the case-specific slope. The definition of the indifference points as case locations derives from the case-space model described in Chapter 3.

Two features of the pattern in these data bear noting. First, there do not appear any exceptionally dramatic swings in the case locations at given periods. As the mixture of topics over time has changed, the cases have been fairly consistently coming from the middle of the policy space. To a certain extent, though, this pattern is driven by the statistical model's assumption that cases come, throughout the period, from a common prior distribution of potential cases. Second, to the extent there are trends, they are generally consistent with broad historical impressions of the Court. Cases drift to the right, during the early twentieth century, as the Court becomes more liberal, and they have drifted back to the left, as the Court has become more conservative over the past 40 years. Moving forward, these data will be important for interpreting the pattern of cases that underlies the development of constitutional doctrine on the Supreme Court.

What is perhaps most striking is that there does not seem to be a systematic shift in these data occurring around 1925, when the Supreme Court began to exercise a great deal of control over its docket. One might have expected that before the Court had discretion about which cases to hear, we would have observed more extreme case locations – cases where the justices were in greater agreement about how to resolve a case and where the fact patterns were so extreme as to be not useful for developing doctrine. This, however, is not what we observe. If anything, the spread of case locations seems to grow during the mid-twentieth century, suggesting more extreme factual patterns are being considered between 1925 and 1980 than before or after. Why might this be?

One account comes from the theoretical models described in Chapter 1. There, we saw that to make law and influence doctrine, a justice needs to both (1) win the dispositional vote, and (2) craft an opinion that his or her colleagues will join. In an era where the Court controls its docket, control over which cases to decide might help with these objectives, but theoretical models of decision making might suggest some counter-intuitive ways in which that takes place. More extreme case locations make it easier to assemble a winning coalition, by definition. In addition, more extreme case locations might make it easier to convince one's colleagues of the propriety of a doctrinal stance or change in the law. Of course, the location of the case itself only tells part of the story, and to see how those theoretical mechanisms might work, we need to consider how the case locations relate to the way a case is actually resolved.

As I mentioned above, conservative dispositions result from cases that are relatively further to the left (putting more justices to the right of the case), and liberal dispositions result from cases that are relatively further to the right (putting more justices to the left of the case). In Figure 5.12, I divided the data in Figure 5.11 according to the nature of the case disposition. I rely on the Supreme Court Database (Spaeth et al. 2015) for these data, which provide a valuable metric of whether a case endorses a politically liberal or a politically conservative outcome.[6]

Consider first the top panel, which shows all cases where the Court ultimately made a liberal disposition. Here we see that from 1877 through roughly 1940, cases that resulted in a liberal disposition came increasingly from the right, meaning that liberal outcomes increasingly involved coalitions that included more politically moderate justices. Notably, this coincides with the Court's move to the right on Balance of Power, Crime and Punishment and, aside from the decade between 1900 and 1910, Economics and Business. In other words, as the Court became more conservative during this era, the cases that could possibly lead to a liberal outcome were ones that necessarily included more moderate justices. This suggests that more extreme factual scenarios were needed to get a

---

[6] Of course, these data have been criticized as being sometimes biased in favor of finding dispositions that correspond to preconceived notions of the justices' liberalism or conservatism (e.g., Harvey and Woodruff 2013).

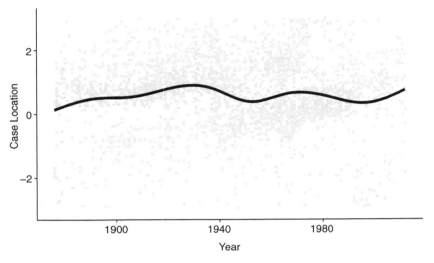

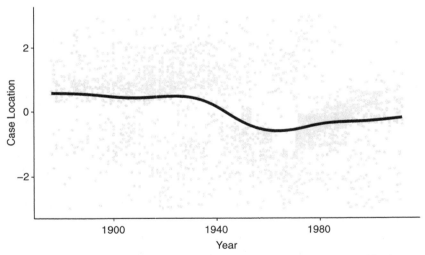

Figure 5.12. *Location of cases in latent preference space, 1877–2012, separated by the case disposition direction in the Supreme Court Database.* The upper panel shows only cases where the nature of the disposition in the case is coded in the Supreme Court Database as liberal, and the lower panel shows only cases where the nature of the disposition in the case is coded in the Supreme Court Database as conservative. Each point corresponds to the point of indifference in the latent policy space for each vote taken by the justices. Each case has only a single location, which is constant across the six dimensions and is defined as the case-specific intercept, divided by the case-specific slope. The definition of the indifference points as case locations derives from the case-space model described in Chapter 3.

liberal outcome during this period. Meanwhile, in the bottom panel, we do not see such movement among cases with conservative dispositions. Rather, those cases were rather consistent across time, suggesting that conservative outcomes did not necessarily need different kinds of factual patterns to occur.

After 1937, a very different pattern emerges. There is a sharp change in the case locations among those cases that were resolved in a conservative direction. These cases moved dramatically to the left. In other words, in order to get a conservative disposition once FDR began appointing liberal justices to the Court, a case would have to divide the justices such that more moderates would prefer the conservative outcome. There is also a slight, though less pronounced and sustained, shift among the liberal disposition outcomes, indicating that the Warren Court was able to take cases that were further to the left and therefore had majorities of increasingly homogenous liberal voting blocs.

However, ever since, these trends have flipped somewhat, starting with the nomination of Chief Justice Burger to the Court; for the most part, cases with conservative and liberal dispositions have been trending to the right, suggesting more moderate liberal majorities and more extreme conservative majorities. Notably, this coincides with a rightward shift and increasing polarization on the major preference dimensions of the era – Crime and Punishment and Individual and Civil Rights (recall Figures 5.8 and 5.10).

It is also instructive to consider the patterns we see here in conjunction with the increased rate of dissent we saw in Figure 4.4 in Chapter 4. Those data showed the well-documented pattern of a sharp drop in the rate of unanimity in the Court's decisions during the 1940s (e.g., Walker, Epstein, and Dixon 1988). When that major change takes place, we do not see a corresponding shift in the case locations. This reinforces the claim that the breakdown in consensus on the Court was not driven by a change in the nature of the cases the justices were deciding. That is, if the justices suddenly started in the 1940s hearing cases that were more divisive, we would expect the estimated case locations to be more concentrated within the range of the justices ideal points – this would mean that justices more often find themselves preferring alternative dispositions. To the contrary, it does not appear there was a systematic change in the case locations after the point where dissenting becomes more common.

Returning to the implications of case locations for the development of law, these patterns bring our question into focus. When the justices are more conservative on the major issues of the day – for example, Crime and Punishment since 1970 – in order to shape the content of the doctrine, they need both winning disposition coalitions and cases that will enable to the writing of more conservative opinions. By 1980, the Supreme Court's conservative dispositions are coming increasingly from the left end of the fact space, facilitating larger majorities of justices and raising questions and issues that enable the establishment of precedent that pushes the law to the left. In the next chapter, we will see this particular example in greater depth, but for now the point to take away is that the patterns in case locations make intuitive sense in light of the micropolitics that underlie law making through individual case resolution.

5.3   LEGAL ISSUES AND POLITICAL CLEAVAGES

The patterns uncovered here – the preference dimensions that make up constitutional decision making and their substantive meanings, the justices' locations along those preference dimensions, and the representation of those dimensions on the Court's constitutional docket – yield a series of lessons about how the Court has built constitutional law since Reconstruction. These lessons are best understood in light of the theoretical models of judicial decision and law making outlined in Chapter 1 and the historical material to which I turn to in the next chapter.

5.3.1 Interpreting Preference Dimensions

Let us consider, though, how to interpret these aggregate patterns in light of the microprocesses that constitute the actual choices the justices make. First, in order to decide cases and make law, Supreme Court justices must build voting coalitions. In an oft-cited example, Justice Brennan was famous for telling his law clerks that the most important law at the Supreme Court was the number five. "Five votes. Five votes can do anything around here" he instructed them every year (Hentoff 1990, 60). What Brennan is saying is that a majority of the justices can always have their way, and a not-so-subtle implication is that if one wants to get anything done, one needs to build a political coalition. At the same time, it is often argued that the Supreme Court is relatively passive in that, unlike a legislature, the justices must wait until cases are brought to them for resolution (for an overview and analysis, see Perry 1991). Taken together, those two observations about how the courts work suggest some consequential ramifications of the patterns uncovered here.

As we saw in Figure 5.2, which preference dimensions are more or less prominent in the justices' decision making at different points in time has changed in large part as a function of societal demands and the broader political context. Theories of innovation, politics, and law making that place a strong emphasis on society's role in shaping the law suggest a perspective on constitutional law that suggests those trends are driven by forces outside of the Court's control, shaped largely by exogenous forces. Society demands regulation of industry in the early 1900s, and the Court responds by intervening. Institutional and behavioral theories, by contrast, provide an internal perspective, whereby what the Court decides to address, and how it makes its decisions are shaped by the views, goals, and preferences of the individuals who sit on the Court at any given point in time. How those internal and external forces interact is the subject of the more substantive discussion in the next chapter. However, what the statistical results here show is that the different preference profiles across the various preference dimensions that characterize constitutional decision making can sharply influence the Court's ability to respond to the political and social context that brings cases to the Court.

The patterns in both the ideological orientation on the Court (for example, Figure 5.8) and the preference diversity among the justices on the Court at any given time (for example, Figure 5.10) interact with the incentives facing the justices as they resolve distinct cases. As Justice Brennan points out, one needs a coalition of at least five justices to win a case and write an opinion establishing precedent. The logic of bargaining and negotiation among the justices suggests, for example, that more diverse coalitions will have greater difficulty building and maintaining coalitions than will more homogenous groups of justices (e.g., Lax and Cameron 2007; Carrubba et al. 2012; Cameron and Kornhauser N.d.). In addition, political conflict can condition the nature of the law judges make by creating incentives for judges to make rules that are more or less flexible as to accommodate the justices' more-or-less diverse viewpoints (e.g., Staton and Vanberg 2008; Lax 2012). Of course, the data I have shown here do not demonstrate those patterns hold; that is the subject of Chapters 6 and 7. What we do see, though, is that there is considerable variation in the extent to which conditions are hospitable to major constitutional law making. When there is a change in the Court's ideological preferences that accompanies a reduction in ideological polarization – for example, in the Balance of Power dimension during the Rehnquist Court – we should expect to see significant changes in the law. By contrast, when there is little change in the median's preferences but an increase in polarization among the justices – for example, in the Individual and Civil Rights dimension during the Fuller and White Courts – we should not expect the justices to be capable of significantly altering the law. As we will see in the subsequent chapters, these types of patterns are largely born out in both the qualitative and quantitative patterns in the history.

A second microprocess that is useful for interpreting these patterns concerns the process of law making itself. As I have noted, the resolution of individual cases by the Court is only one part of the story. Law is developed incrementally through the creation of a line of precedents that link to each other sequentially over time. Elements of a given legal doctrine or policy are fleshed out in discrete cases. Because, as we have seen, the hospitableness for legal innovation waxes and wanes over time, the politics of decision making in a single case interact with the temporal, incremental nature of legal innovation to shape the rate and scope of legal development. Seen from this perspective, starts-and-stops in the extent to which the Supreme Court responds to societal demands or changing external politics can be conditioned by the political conditions, cleavages, and conflicts that exist inside the Court. In Chapters 6 and 7, I turn to those questions directly. In addition, these data allow us to ask how the internal politics of the Court relate to the Court's role in broader American politics and constitutional law, a question to which I also turn to in the coming chapters.

Consider, for example, the conservative legal movement that began in earnest during the last third of the twentieth century (e.g., Teles 2008). Conservatives in American society sought to pursue a number of policy objectives, largely in reaction to social progressivism from the 1960s and 1970s. However, their ability to use the courts for their policy objectives was initially stymied by the lack of a deep conservative legal "bench," so to speak. Conservative interests organized and began to cultivate like-minded lawyers, founding organizations in law schools such as The Federalist Society, and used political opportunities like the presidencies of Richard Nixon and Ronald Reagan to staff the courts with conservative jurists. In this sense, the internal politics of the courts, and particularly of the Supreme Court, were shaped by the external politics of social demands for conservative policies, and thereby created a hospitable environment for development of conservative doctrine in areas of criminal law, individual freedom, and, later, political participation.

As the analysis in this chapter illustrates, there were differential patterns of changing internal politics during the period from 1960 through 2012 across the different preference dimensions, which was driven by the effects of electoral politics on composition of the courts. What we will see in the next chapter is that as the elected politicians were able to shift the Court's profile across the different preference dimensions, the activists responded by bringing their claims to the courts when the conditions for specific questions were right, and the Court, in turn, was able to move the law when the majority was best positioned to make effective precedent.

5.3.2 *The Dimension We Do Not Find*

It also bears discussing one substantive dimension of the law one might reasonably have expected to emerge as a distinct preference dimension. One of the most prominent cleavages in American politics concerns race. Racial attitudes touch on myriad substantive policy matters, and at times racial preferences have emerged as a cleavage that cuts across standard political preferences in American politics more broadly (see, e.g., Poole and Rosenthal 1997). However, the analysis in this chapter suggests that in the context of constitutional decision making, there is not a distinct preference dimension corresponding to racial views. Rather, constitutional questions involving race map onto one of the distinct six preference dimensions. As we will see in the remaining chapters, these cases are typically decided along the lines of the justices' views about Individual and Civil Rights. However, at times we will also see that race-based cases are decided more in line with the justices' views about Crime and Punishment or the Balance of power.

Importantly, though, this does *not* mean that the justices do not see cases involving a racial component differently than they see other cases. Rather, what this means is that the preference ordering of the justices in race-based cases is not distinct from the preference ordering in some other cases, and so racial cases do not emerge as their own distinct political cleavage in the context of constitutional decision making. A case with a racial component may implicate the cut-point, in terms of the case-space model. That is, a justice who might find a governmental practice acceptable when there are no racial implications may be less likely to find it acceptable when it does have racial implications. However, that phenomenon is a matter of the case location, rather than of the ordering of the justices on the matter of whether it is an acceptable practice.

In sum, the pervasiveness of race as a political issue in America has had profound consequences for the path of constitutional law. However, what the analysis in this chapter indicates is that it has not had those consequences because it *systematically* causes a different ordering of the justices than do other types of cases. Instead, as we will see, race often drives the framing of a case and, therefore, the mix of preference dimensions that a case activates. Moreover, racial conflict in the US has shaped the kinds of legal questions that are asked, the sequence of problems that come to the courts, and the social conditions in which the justices' decisions are made and subsequently implemented. It is therefore not possible to understand the path of American constitutional law without appreciating the consequences of racial conflict, it is just not by way of emerging as its own distinct cleavage.

5.4 CONCLUSION

The analysis of constitutional decision making at the US Supreme Court since 1877, using the LDA+IRT model, suggests that constitutional decision making can be summarized in roughly six preference dimensions. That is, six is the number of preference dimensions that best characterizes the voting cleavages in the Court. The topic model component of the model facilitates substantive interpretation of those dimensions by reference to the words that are most closely associated with each topic. In the analysis here, those six topics include "judicial power," "economics and business," "central authority," "balance of power," "crime and punishment," and "individual and civil rights." It is important to remember, though, those labels are simply my own interpretation of the substantive content of the cases that map onto each preference dimension. There is nothing in the model that specifically requires legally similar cases to map onto the same preference dimension. In fact, one thing the preliminary analysis here reveals is that cases implicating similar legal questions can map onto different preference dimensions. What remains to be seen, and what I consider in the next two chapters, is how and when legally similar cases are decided along different preference dimensions. As one might expect, a component of the answer is the broader policy context in which the case is brought – what are the political implications of the legal issue at hand?

That the justices' preferences are multidimensional in constitutional cases points to a number of features that can give rise to interesting and consequential politics in constitutional decision making. As we have seen, the preference profile among the justices varies across the different topics. The relative conservatism of the median justice depends on the topic one considers, and, further, the degree of ideological polarization among the justices depends on the dimension. More importantly, as we will see in the next two chapters, *who* is the median justice in any given case can depend on which preference dimension is activated by the case. This corroborates previous findings that there is not one median justice but rather a number of potential medians (e.g., Lauderdale and Clark 2012, 2014). That different voting coalitions can emerge when cases are mapped onto different preference dimensions suggests opportunities for strategic issue framing in the process of litigation. Indeed, taken in conjunction with the observation that similar legal questions can be linked to different preference dimensions by the context in which they arise points directly to one mechanism by which social events and particular historical contingencies can interact with the structural, institutional forces within the Court that drive decision making as well as with the structure of policy-driven litigation.

What is more, the history of constitutional decision making covered here is marked by a telling pattern in the prevalence of the preference dimensions in the justices' voting. During the earliest years, the justices decided almost all cases by reference to the judicial power preference dimension – all legal questions were decided by the preferences that characterize the justices' views on the courts' role in governance. By the turn of the century, however, the justices were more nuanced in how they resolved constitutional questions, with a distinct "economics and business" preference dimension characterizing their voting patterns, in conjunction with the primary "judicial power" preference dimension. By the mid-twentieth century, however, the justices' voting was more complex, involving at least three distinct preference dimensions rather consistently. Part of the goal of the remaining chapters is to examine why the justices' approach to constitutional decision making became more nuanced as well as to show that the evolution of the Court's constitutional docket is part of a larger account of American political and social history. The patterns described here are neither strictly exogenous factors driving constitutional law nor simply the direct product of an evolution in the law being shaped outside of the justices' views themselves. Rather, as we will see, the patterns here are part of a symbiotic, back-and-forth process of constitutional development that has been unfolding since at least the Civil War.

In the following chapters, I turn to an analysis of the history underlying these developments, and to do so I rely on the empirical evidence reported here, a variety of microtheories of the judicial process, and qualitative, historical accounts of exemplary or noteworthy decisions in constitutional law. We will see how social developments, such as industrialization, World War II, and the late twentieth-century technology boom interacted with electoral politics to shape the kinds of questions that arose in constitutional law and the way politicians and judges resolved those cases. The story that emerges is one in which constitutional law structures social and political interactions that in turn give rise to new questions and problems begging for new constitutional interpretations. Individual decisions made by judges in one given context have long-run ripple effects that spread across legal, policy, and social cleavages. Aggregate historical patterns go hand-in-hand with small-scale decisions that are made at the micro level. Structural forces interact with peculiar contingencies to shape the path of American constitutional law. To see this, we now turn to an historical evaluation of constitutional decision making.

In this appendix, I present some diagnostic evidence to evaluate the fit of the LDA+IRT model. First, in Figure 5.13, I show traceplots for the case parameters for a sample of 100 cases. The left-hand side shows traceplots for the difficulty parameter (α), and the right-hand side shows traceplots for the discrimination parameter (β). In each plot, I show the sequence of draws from the posterior distribution for each case separately. Figure 5.14 shows traceplots for each of the justices' ideal points in each of the six dimensions. (There is a separate plot for each dimension.) Each justice is shown with a separate line. Together, these plots suggest the model converges well during the burn-in period.

In addition, in Figure 5.15, I show the distribution of the *maximum* assignment probability for each case in the LDA step of the model. That is, for each case, I identify the highest posterior assignment probability, across all six topics. This figure shows the distribution of those maximums. As one can readily see, most cases have a maximum assignment probability of greater than 50%, indicating that most cases are mostly about a single topic. Indeed, roughly 80% of the cases have a greater than 50% posterior assignment probability for a single topic. However, there is a group of cases that are more mixed in their distributions across the topics. At the far left of the figure, we see a small group of cases that have a maximum assignment probability of 16.6%,

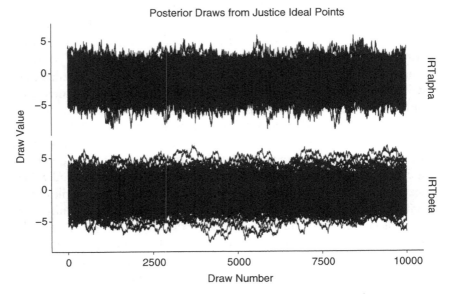

Figure 5.13. *Traceplots for each case parameter for a random sample of 100 cases.*

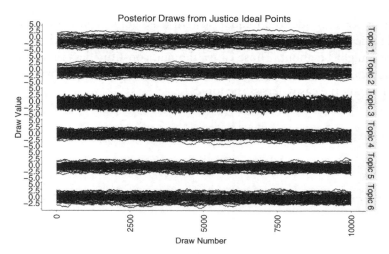

Figure 5.14. *Traceplots for each justice in each of the six dimensions.*

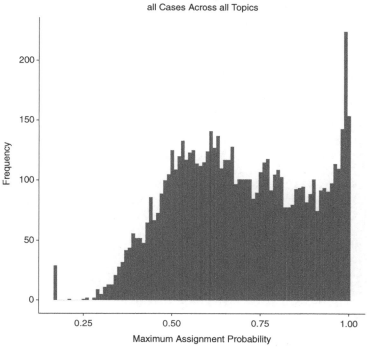

Figure 5.15. *Distribution of maximum posterior assignment probabilities for all cases.* For each case, we calculate the highest posterior assignment probability for any of the six topics. If a case has a 100% assignment probability for one topic, then it takes the value of 100%. If a case has equal assignment probability for all topics, then it's assignment probability is the lowest possible for all topics – 17%. This figure shows the distribution of the maximum for each case.

which corresponds to an equal posterior assignment probability across all topics. In other words, the LDA model cannot assess which topics the cases might be about. Those cases, though, constitute less than 0.1% of all cases. This figure suggests, then, that the LDA model performs well in separating the cases across the topics.

6

From Civil War to Regulation and Federal Power

The preceding chapter provided a systematic overview of the evolution of ideological cleavages on the Court and their relationships to the substantive problems the Court has confronted through its history in constitutional jurisprudence. The goal there was not to provide a historical account but rather to describe some of the trends and patterns. In this chapter, we begin a deeper investigation of those patterns, with a focus on the analytic history. I seek to show both the "inside" and the "outside" of constitutional history – what changes are attributable to the institutions and individuals on the Court, and what changes are attributable to social and political forces operating outside of the judiciary.

This chapter focuses on the development of constitutional law from Reconstruction through World War II. The next chapter takes up constitutional law in the post-war era. As we see below, constitutional law after the Civil War confronted two significant questions. The first was how to negotiate the new constitutional order that had been ushered in with the conclusion of the war and Reconstruction. At the time of the war, existing doctrines about the scope of government power were developed in a context of cautious balance between the states and national government and were not evidently well-suited to the new challenges the system would face after the war. Moreover, the justices who served on the Court were not necessarily predisposed to expand national power any more than they had to.

The second issue constitutional law confronted was more externally oriented, driven by the Second Industrial Revolution. Technological advances led to the unification of the economy and the rise of large corporations. Those new corporate behemoths brought about new industrial organization of the workplace, prominently giving rise to middle management and simultaneously leading to challenging and often dangerous workplace conditions. The changing nature of the economy led to political conflict over regulation. Progressives emerged as proponents of strong national government power and regulation of the economy. At the same time, conservative Republicans also set out to strengthen the role of the federal system in order to protect corporate interests from electoral politics in the states (e.g., Gillman 2002). These political policy objectives clashed with existing due process doctrine, and during the first three decades of the twentieth century constitutional law oscillated between conservative and progressive approaches to due process and protection of industry from regulation by the national government. At the same time, immigration, global conflict, and the rise of socialism in Eastern Europe (as well as in America) engendered class and ethnic conflict, which ultimately implicated the Supreme Court's due process doctrine as well. A second line of jurisprudence developed around regulation not just of the economy but of individuals in contexts outside of the workplace. By the end of the third decade of the twentieth century, the Great Depression led to a major shift in political control of the government and renewed regulatory zeal. A well-documented conflict between the elected branches and the Supreme Court ensued, culminating in a fundamental shift in constitutional law.

In this chapter, I show how the statistical analysis of the political dimensions of law shine new light onto these historical developments. By considering the aggregate patterns of politics and law in light of microtheories of judges and their decisions, the chapter helps us understand how forces both internal and external to the Court influenced the move in constitutional law from a focus on the distinction between *who* can regulate activity – economic or otherwise – to a distinction between *which* activities can be regulated. This transformation entailed a shift first from a presumption against national regulatory authority towards a presumption of national authority, and second from a presumption that constitutional protections were designed to limit the government to a presumption that constitutional protections were designed to protect the individual. This latter transition was especially important for interpreting the authority to regulate the economy as well as the Constitution's civil liberties protections.

This chapter proceeds as follows. I begin by first providing some discussion of the history of constitutional law before the analyses that occupy this book. The function is to lay the intellectual groundwork for what follows. Namely, I show how constitutional interpretation before the Civil War was primarily shaped by external forces – namely the tension between state and national power and the delicate arrangement that held the union together. I then describe the era of constitutional law from Reconstruction through the World War I, examining how industrialization and electoral politics brought together a new host of regulatory issues that the Court had not seen before with a Court wrestling with ideological conflicts driven by the electoral politics of the turn of the century and the split of the Republican Party between conservatives and progressives. Next, I show the final transition from conservatism and laissez-faire economics following World War I to the liberal takeover of first electoral and then constitutional politics in the wake of the Great Depression. One key factor in this period is the conflict between (1) regulatory zeal developed during the war and the possibilities that had been realized in the wartime economy, and (2) conservative control of the national government during the 1920s. Another key factor is growing class conflict associated with the struggle between labor and business as well as the rise of socialism. Those developments complicated the nature of economic regulation and also engendered xenophobic, ethnic, and political fear that helped shift government power towards social control. The era ends with an unofficial rewriting of the Constitution and a marked shift in the political perspective through which the Court would interpret constitutional questions.

6.1 CONSTITUTIONAL LAW BEFORE THE CIVIL WAR

The statistical analysis I presented in Chapter 5 does not include data from the period before Reconstruction. There are a number of reasons for this, the primary one being that the Civil War marked a major structural break in the constitutional order, and the Civil War Amendments themselves fundamentally altered the basic structure of American federalism. As Novak (1996, 235-40) argues, the political changes that took place during and immediately after the Civil War gave rise to competing goals – the centralization of power and the increasing individualization of Americans – that was resolved through the development of extensive constitutional law. In fact, as we saw in Chapters 1 and 4, there were very few cases of constitutional law during this time period, which precludes meaningful statistical analysis. However, we do have a great deal of information about what the Supreme Court was doing during that period and what kinds of political cleavages characterized the judicial politics of constitutional law before the Civil War, and that information helps construct a useful baseline context from which we can consider the internal and external forces shaping constitutional law since Reconstruction. To do so, it is instructive to consider histories of constitutional law written before and shortly after that war.

In these histories we find a not surprising, but consistent, theme. The major constitutional question before the Civil War centered on whether the law could trump political will. That is, does the Constitution impose limits on the will of the people? As Pound (1905) succinctly describes, the evolution of the common law took distinct paths in England and the US. The English interpretation was that Parliament had ultimate authority, meaning that the only way to overcome an Act of Parliament thought to be contrary to the limits on government authority would be through the political process or popular revolt. In the United States, by contrast, it was settled during the nineteenth century that congressional authority could be limited by judicial interpretations of the Constitution. However, that arrangement was not universally shared during the first few decades of the Republic, and its resolution is the focus of much pre-Civil War constitutional jurisprudence. In fact, perhaps the most powerful idea in American constitutional thought in the wake of the American Revolution, lasting through the Civil War, was the notion of popular sovereignty and the struggle to give meaning to the belief that the new government was founded on the idea that the people were the ones with the power to rule (e.g., Fritz 2007). In other words, how could the institutions of government be employed in such a way that empowered them enough to be effective but retained meaningful limits on their powers and the sovereignty of the people?

The power of the courts, especially with respect to constitutional interpretation, was often a subject of intense debate, frequently reignited by new political conflicts. Indeed, the development of the power of judicial review has been extensively studied in the literature on constitutional history (e.g., Friedman 2002a). Notable political confrontations marked the first decades of the nineteenth century. Serious arguments were made that courts did not have the jurisdiction to declare Acts of Congress unconstitutional and that the Constitution should "be amended to provide a special tribunal for the determination of questions as to the authority of Congress and of the several states under the constitution" (Pound 1905, 341). The tension over the limits of congressional power vis-à-vis the states engendered a number of noteworthy conflicts culminating in landmark Supreme Court cases. In *Martin v. Hunter's Lessee*, the Supreme Court concluded that it could review state court decisions that rely on federal law. However, at the same time, Justice Story, in interpreting the Constitution, points out that the only powers the national government could claim are those that are explicitly granted in the document. In *McCulloch v. Maryland*, the Court held that the states could not interfere with congressional power, as in this case where Congress had claimed an implied power to establish a national bank. In *Gibbons v. Ogden*, the Supreme Court held that the power to regulate interstate commerce means that Congress could regulate navigation in rivers even if they were wholly within a state's jurisdiction.

Each of these decisions contributed, along with others, to incrementally build the federal government's power, both expanding the interpretation of congressional authority and asserting the Court's role in arbitrating questions of constitutional interpretation. In fact, that basic move – the Court claiming authority but using the authority claimed to make a decision that Congress supports – is part of the logic of how the Court has built its power, ever since the famed decision in *Marbury v. Madison* (e.g., Clinton 1994; Knight and Epstein 1996; Carrubba 2009). Moreover, in the particular context of the United States national government before the Civil War, an especially strong principle that guided constitutional thought was that the federal government was explicitly one of delegated powers, and so any strength the government was to claim had to come from a careful interpretation of the Constitution's grants of authority.

At the same time as the Court was establishing its power to interpret the Constitution and expansively reading congressional authority, it was developing a very important rule of constitutional construction. "The restrictions imposed upon government by the Constitution and its amendments are to be understood as restrictions only upon the government of the Union, except where the States are expressly mentioned" (Cooley 1898, 18). In other words, before the Civil War, the Constitution's restrictions on State power were broadly understood to be just those things the Constitution specifically forbade the states from doing. There was great focus on the states' ability to engage in foreign affairs, print money, emit bills of credit, pass bills of attainder and ex post facto laws, regulate contracts, or grant titles of nobility (for a discussion just before the Civil War, see Duer 1956). Indeed, those restrictions are specifically spelled out in Article I, Section 10 of the Constitution. This principle of constitutional construction would serve throughout the period, and the Civil War, to create a tension between the states and the national government. In large part reflecting the commitment to popular sovereignty that underlay the American Revolution and the constitutional politics of the pre-Civil War era, the Constitution was construed so as to impose as few limits on the states as possible. Most notable was the question whether the Bill of Rights would apply to the states, a question that was a political issue from the very beginning. As the CRS report on constitutional interpretation points out (Thomas 2014, 1051):

One of the amendments which the Senate refused to accept – declared by Madison to be "the most valuable of the whole list" – read: "The equal rights of conscience, the freedom of speech or of the press, and the right of trial by jury in criminal cases shall not be infringed by any State." In spite of this rejection, the contention that the Bill of Rights – or at least the first eight – was applicable to the States was repeatedly pressed upon the Supreme Court. By a long series of decisions, beginning with the opinion of Chief Justice Marshall in *Barron v. Baltimore*, the argument was consistently rejected. Nevertheless, the enduring vitality of natural law concepts encouraged renewed appeals for judicial protection through application of the Bill of Rights.

Indeed, as Chief Justice Marshall argues in *Barron*, "The Constitution was ordained and established by the people of the United States for themselves, for their own government, and not for the government of the individual States…The powers they conferred on this government were to be exercised by itself, and the limitations on power, if expressed in general terms, are naturally, and we think necessarily, applicable to the government created by the instrument." That claim is particularly revealing, as it demonstrates the tension inherent in the Constitution's origins – to enable the central government without limiting the states.

The tension that was being built by the Court's navigation of federalism during the first five decades of the nineteenth century came to a head when the Court decided the case *Dred Scott v. Sandford*, 60 U.S. 393 (1857). In that case, which has been well recounted and examined elsewhere (e.g., Fehrenbacher 2001; Graber 2006), Dred Scott, who was a slave, sued for his freedom, claiming that under the Missouri Compromise, he was in effect freed when his owners took him into Illinois and the Louisiana Territory and hired out his labor. The Supreme Court, which was at the time comprised of a majority of Southerners, decided the case against Scott, invalidating the Missouri Compromise in the course of making its decision. In the majority opinion, Chief Justice Taney wrote that African-Americans could never be citizens under the Constitution and that the federal government could not prohibit slavery in the territories. Many observers credit the *Dred Scott* decision as making the Civil War all but inevitable (for an instructive discussion, see McPherson 1988, 170-189).

The constitutional politics that led to *Dred Scott* and other notable antebellum conflicts reflect both the internal and external forces on the Court. However, they also created a tension that was deeply sewn into the law and would ultimately only be decided through a fundamental rethinking of the compact among the states. On one hand, constitutional jurisprudence increasingly built up the national government's powers, expansively reading the Constitution's grants of authority to Congress and the role of the federal courts in negotiating questions about the limits on government power. On the other hand, the principles of constitutional construction it used to achieve those goals entrenched very constricted limits on state power, setting up a conflict over which – the federal or state governments – actually had supremacy. Thinking first about the external forces on the Court, the federal government was busy establishing itself and its authority and did not have much precedent to guide it and help navigate the complexities of federalism. The basic intuitions that had guided the constitutional framers about the best way to balance authority between national and state government were abstract ideas that, once put into practice, gave rise to a host of practical questions. Who has the final say when interpreting the Constitution? Under what conditions are state or federal judges superior to the other? Could the states impose taxes on the national government? And so forth. These and related questions were of paramount importance for the entire system. The first problems that had to be resolved concerned, in essence, what the federal system would look like in practice. Indeed, in deciding any given case, a critical tension facing the Court would have been about the political and practical need to enable the federal government to govern. During the first few decades of the nineteenth century, the failure of the Articles of Confederation loomed large, and it was widely accepted and understood that the failure was attributable to the weakness of the national government and its consequent inability to carry out the basic functions that were the purpose of having a union to begin with (for contemporary observations, see Sergeant 1832; Story 1833; Adams 1839). However, the principle of popular sovereignty that guided American constitutional ethos in the aftermath of the Revolution, and the political realities that induced what were essentially logrolls among the states (consider the various compromises built directly into the Constitution) meant that any step towards increasing national power could come at the expense of state power and threaten the mutual independence that enabled the states to cooperate in the first place.

Complicating matters was the Supreme Court's perceived lack of power and authority during the first years of the Constitution. The Court had extremely limited jurisdiction, and there remained real questions about the scope of its power. (We will see more on this below.) Wary of pushing too hard lest it undermine the growth of national institutional power and its own institutional capacity, the Court increasingly engaged itself with constitutional decision making throughout the antebellum years. While it did not frequently use its power to thwart majority-enacted laws, it did use its power to review laws at a much greater rate than is often acknowledged in historical accounts (see, for example Clark and Whittington N.d.). Similarly, lest it risk open defiance by the states, the Court would have faced a strong incentive to read the Constitution in such a way as to impose as few limits on state authority as possible. The lessons from the Court's interpretation of the Bill of Rights during the antebellum period are consistent with the Court having pursued this strategy. Moreover, notable instances in which the Court did support Constitutional limits on state power, such as in *McCulloch v. Maryland*, were often marked by heated debate and argument that the national political institutions were betraying fundamental principles of the system (e.g., Taylor 1920).

At the same time, there were several important internal dynamics that are relevant for understanding why the justices seemingly knowingly built into constitutional law an irreconcilable tension. Nominations to the Supreme Court during the nineteenth century were often made to ensure regional diversity among the membership (in large part reflecting the external forces shaping constitutional politics at the time). This meant that in order to make decisions that were not deeply divisive and established coherent precedent, the justices would often decide cases in a very minimalist way. However, the problems they confronted were significant and required the establishment of fundamental principles of constitutional law. It is hard not to emphasize, then, the role that Chief Justice John Marshall played in laying the foundation of constitutional law. A champion of judicial and national power, having led the push for ratification of the Constitution in Virginia and represented Virginia in the US House of Representatives as a Federalist, he came to the chief justiceship in 1801 during an era where there were legitimate questions about the importance, power, and authority of the Court. Marshall presided over a number of important developments. He famously ended the practice of seriatim opinion writing (whereby each justice wrote his own opinion in each case) and began a practice of issuing a single majority opinion in each case. Marshall led the Court in its famous confrontation with President Thomas Jefferson in *Marbury v. Madison* and wrote majority opinions in important cases such as *McCulloch v. Maryland*, *Gibbons v. Ogden*, *Worcester v. Georgia*, and others that had very deep implications for the power of the national government and the role of the Court in interpreting the Constitution.

When Marshall died in 1835, after having been Chief Justice for more than 34 years, he was replaced by Roger Taney, a Jacksonian Democrat from Maryland who was a slave owner and strong supporter of states' rights. Taney had served in the Jackson administration as Attorney General and Secretary of the Treasury and was closely involved in the fight against the Bank of the United States (a conflict that would be a watershed moment in Jacksonian political philosophy). Taney was unlikely to represent a continuation of the legal and constitutional theory that guided Marshall. Moreover, accompanying Taney's appointment as Chief Justice, a number of consequential appointments were made during the 1830s. Bushrod Washington, a Federalist from Virginia, was replaced by Henry Baldwin, a Democrat from Pennsylvania. Gabriel Duval, a Federalist from Maryland, was replaced by Philip Barbour, a Democrat from Virginia. William Johnson, a Republican from South Carolina, was replaced by James Wayne, a Democrat from Georgia. Robert Trimble, a Republican from Kentucky, was replaced by John McLean, a Democrat from Ohio. And, in 1837, a new seat on the Court was created, and the first justice appointed to it was John Caltron, a Democrat from Tennessee. In short, during the 1830s, the Court went from being a bastion of judicial and national power led by Marshall and a strong bloc of Federalists and Republicans to a bench led by Taney and other Southern Democrats, who were skeptical of the national government and supportive of slavery and states' rights. This transformation would set the stage for a Court that would either have to reinterpret the constitutional principles developed under Marshall or more directly confront the tension between state and federal power that characterized the existing jurisprudence.

Thus, seen in this perspective, the *Dred Scott* decision can be understood as the product of a growing political tension in the country that interacted with rapidly changing internal politics on the Court and a lightning-rod policy question that the Court was all-too-ready to dive into. The result was war. Popular commentators at the time of the Civil War saw slavery and the constitutional tension between state and federal power as the central political issue, they appreciated that the root cause itself was a fundamental tension in the Constitution between state and national power and predicted the conclusion of the war would necessitate a fundamental rethinking of the Constitution (e.g., Phillips and Graham 1862). In particular, as Stephens (1868, 10) notes, in the immediate aftermath of the Civil War,

That the War had its origin in *opposing principles*, which, in their action upon the *conduct of men*, produced the ultimate collision of arms, may be assumed as an unquestionable fact...[The opposing principles] lay in the organic Structure of the Government of the States. The conflict in principle arose from different and opposing ideas as to the nature of what is known as the General Government. The contest was between those who held it to be strictly Federal in its character, and those who maintained that it was thoroughly National. It was a strife between the principles of Federation, on the one side, and Centralism, or Consolidation, on the other.

In response to this sentiment, we find in treatises on constitutional law written shortly after the Civil War that constitutional debates were often focused on the resolution of fundamental questions of authority of the national government over the states.

Thus, during Reconstruction, the addition of the Civil War Amendments accompanied a fundamental rethinking of the constitutional order. Obviously, the need to rearrange the balance of powers in the Constitution was made apparent by the Civil War and the Union victory. However, the way in which that rethinking took place cannot be understood outside of the larger context of the politics of the time as well as the evolving political and social movements. Indeed, whereas the Civil War might not have arisen without the deep, structural tension built into the Constitution, the way in which the Civil War Amendments were drafted and interpreted during their early years was endogenous to the political processes that had been playing out since the Founding. In particular, because slavery had become *the* question at the heart of the structural battles over governmental power, the abolitionists plated a particularly important role in setting an agenda for the post-War rethinking and rewriting of the Constitution. Indeed, the Fourteenth Amendment was heavily influenced by abolitionists who were able to exert great political influence after the War (e.g., Graham 1950; TenBroek 1965). Of course, revisionist accounts of the period suggest the politics of the time were not as monolithic as one might presume, and that there remained a great tension over how much authority to retain in the states, which can be seen in the various ways in which civil rights legislation allocated enforcement authority between the national and state courts (for a brief discussion of the revisionist accounts, see Kaczorowski 1987).

Much of that history can be seen in the constitutional history of the final decades of the nineteenth century, which were described in 1898 as "little more than a commentary on the Fourteenth Amendment, which indeed nationalized the whole sphere of civil liberty" (Guthrie 1898, 1–2). Thus, we now turn to an analysis of the development of constitutional law after the Civil War, taking as our starting place the idea that in the wake of Reconstruction we found a new Constitution, radically transformed by the Civil War Amendments, and the Fourteenth Amendment in particular, during which the major political cleavages had shifted away from a focus on the relative importance of the national government to a question of how the newly empowered federal government would use its powers.

6.2 *POST-BELLUM* POLITICS AND THE SHRINKING WORLD

Understanding how constitutional law developed from roughly the end of Reconstruction through the Great Depression requires us to focus on at least three distinct features of the world in which the Supreme Court found itself. First, the legal infrastructure the Court had built since the Founding was oriented around a careful balancing effort between national and state power. The Court's previous interpretations of the Constitution were designed to build national strength in light of the specific grants of authority found in the document, while emphasizing the states' sovereignty. The Civil War, and in particular the Fourteenth Amendment passed during Reconstruction, fundamentally altered the Constitution's balance of national against state power. However, its language was also so broad and vague that the Court would be forced to interpret the Amendment while trying not to completely upend the legal order that it had established during the preceding 70 years. In large part, the language reflected the political climate in which the Amendment was written in the wake of the war, with the national government having triumphed over the states, and the secessionists in a weak political posture. *Thus, a crucial challenge the Court faced during the late nineteenth century was how to incorporate the new Constitutional provisions and the political climate that was set up by the end of the War with existing law to maintain workable, sensible doctrine.*

Second, the end of the Civil War coincided with the Second Industrial Revolution. The railroads had expanded rapidly during the early- and mid-nineteenth century, and during the subsequent decades industrialization transformed the economy from a local, agrarian-based one to a unified, manufacturing-heavy economy (see, for example, McPherson 1988). The consequences for the Court were twofold. First, an entirely new set of challenges emerged in society, for which legal resolutions were sought. The unification of the economy gave rise to the creating of large companies. Middle management was borne at first in the context of railroads, where management became difficult because of the geographic diffuseness of the business model itself. Large manufacturing jobs entailed forms of workplace difficulties, discrimination, and abuse that had not been contemplated under the existing legal doctrine. Second, because of the nature of the expanding economy – a manufacturing-based economy run by large corporations – commerce shifted from a primarily local enterprise to one that increasingly crossed jurisdiction and state boundaries, implicating the national government's role in regulating interstate commerce on a scale the Founders had not foreseen. *Thus, a second challenge the Court faced was how to interpret a constitutional order that was established when the current nature of social, economic, and political conditions was unimaginable.*

Third, the Court was emerging from a period in which politics had been highly polarized – the Civil War had quite literally divided the country – and Reconstruction had led to a period where new justices came to the Court, often individuals who had not long before been at extreme odds with each other. Working together meant these individuals needed to find a common ground from which they could interpret the Constitution. As we saw in Chapter 5 and will consider in greater detail in this chapter, the internal politics on the Court during this era were, consequently, at times volatile and at others more stable. Indeed, the shifting internal politics at the Court in many ways reflected the larger social and political developments taking place throughout the country. The politics of decision making in the various periods of transition would be more complicated than during periods of stability. And, as we will see, the choices and decisions made early on would shape how the Court would later handle dramatic shifts on the Court. *Thus, a third challenge the Court faced during this era involved negotiating internal political dynamics that were interacting with the two other challenges – the Court's changing role in governance and the new legal, political, and social problems the justices were asked to resolve.*

6.2.1 Macropatterns of Industrialization in Constitutional Law

In Chapter 1, I emphasized the value in not just incorporating the "inside" and the "outside" of the history of constitutional law but also linking those factors to theoretical microfoundations. Let us consider a few of the patterns we saw in Chapter 5 in light of the historical record and the microprocesses that were playing out at the time. I then turn to a deeper examination of several substantive examples from the era to illustrate the theoretical mechanisms at work.

The first thing to consider is how the aggregate patterns in cases coming to the courts reflected specific social developments taking place in the country. During Reconstruction, efforts were made in the political world to advance an early view of civil rights. To the extent the courts found themselves involved, it was often to interpret the new constitutional amendments – especially the equal protection and due process clauses of the Fourteenth Amendment. (Recall Figure 4.3 in Chapter 4, which showed that the Fourteenth Amendment was a frequent subject of constitutional interpretation by the Supreme Court immediately after its enactment.) While those early cases involved legal questions about the relationship between the national and state governments and the national government's power in light of the constitutional revisions following the War, the various types of problems presented to the Court often tapped into disparate preference dimensions. Most commonly, the Court resolved these cases by mapping questions about equal protection and due process onto the Judicial Power preference dimension. Changes in the substantive questions the Court confronted implicate both external and internal forces on the path of constitutional law.

THE COURT AND ITS POLITICAL ENVIRONMENT.   To understand why the Court would have interpreted so many different policy and legal questions as implicating the Judicial Power preference dimension, it is useful to consider a class of theoretical arguments about the separation of powers. The country was still reeling from the Civil War, for which many contemporaries laid a considerable amount of blame at the feet of the Court (see, for example Wilson 1878, 9). Moreover, in his first inaugural address, Abraham Lincoln had specifically called out the Court for its decision in *Dred Scott v. Sandford*, arguing that the Court could not possibly be the final arbiter of questions of constitutional interpretation. He wrote,

[T]he candid citizen must confess that if the policy of the Government upon vital questions affecting the whole people is to be irrevocably fixed by decisions of the Supreme Court, the instant they are made in ordinary litigation between parties in personal actions, the people will have ceased to be their own rulers, having to that extent practically resigned their Government into the hands of the eminent tribunal.

Thus, the major question of judicial power and its reach in the American system, which we saw above had occupied much of Marshall's jurisprudence, remained a real political debate. In a world where the Constitution had recently been revised, and where Congress had repeatedly adjusted the size of the Court (the Court size was increased in 1863 and then decreased in 1866), there was significant reason to think that conflict between the branches would ensue. The Court, knowing it was, as a formal matter, the least powerful branch of government, would likely not escape such a conflict unscathed. These conditions would set the stage for the Court to exercise a degree of self-restraint (see, for example, Vanberg 2005; Carrubba 2009; Staton 2010; Clark 2011). Thus, the real conflict confronting the courts during this era was about the role of the courts in governing society and the extent to which the Court would exercise its power to interfere with the other branches' policy goals. The justices could not escape the reality that, in every case, they were deciding a policy question in the context of significant questions about the role of the courts and the reach of their authority.

Indeed, some systematic data suggest that the Court during this era was cautious. Historically, the Supreme Court has struck down Acts of Congress in about 25% of the cases where they review a law's constitutionality. The Court invalidates a law entirely (that is, strikes the law down "on its face") in roughly 10% of constitutional review cases, and strikes the law down as applied in the remaining 15%. However, between 1877 and 1900, the Court invalidated laws in less than 18% of the cases it reviewed, invalidating laws on their face in only 7% of

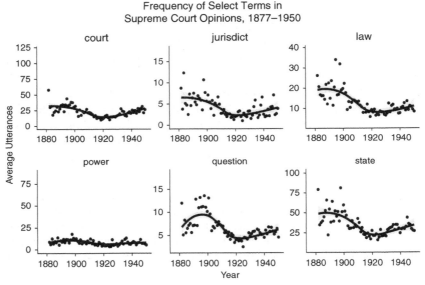

Figure 6.1. *Average number of times select words relating to judicial restraint appear in constitutional law cases, 1877–1950.*

those cases (see Clark and Whittington N.d.). And, as the analysis in Chapter 5 suggests, the language of the justices' opinions suggests a degree of deference by the Court. Figure 6.1 shows the average number of times a handful of words related to judicial restraint appear in constitutional law decisions each year, from 1877 through 1950. These are just a sample of words, but I choose them because they are frequently used in contexts where judges are considering the judicial power; they invoke legal concepts connected to the constraints that courts confront in exercising authority. As these data indicate, these specific words were much more common in judicial opinions during the late nineteenth century than they were a few decades into the twentieth century. We also see, though, an increase in their prevalence during the late 1930s and through the 1940s, another era of particular tension between the elected branches and the Court, also marked by notable judicial restraint (e.g., Clark 2011).

At the same time, though, societal developments – especially in the economy – were shaping the questions the Court addressed as well as the way it resolved them. Consider, for example, the way in which the Court evaluates specific policy questions in light of its preference dimensions. As labor rose as a dominant force in American politics, the conflict between labor and business that started to develop in the mid-nineteenth century became a defining issue by the turn of the twentieth century. Importantly,

Table 6.1. *Relationship between union membership and presence of Business and Economics preference dimension language in Supreme Court opinions, 1881–1930.*

	BLS Estimate	Troy-Sheflin Estimate	Friedman Estimate
Union membership	0.03 (0.01)	0.07 (0.02)	0.02 (0.01)
R^2	0.32	0.37	0.32
N	1610	1227	1610

Numbers are linear regression coefficients, with standard errors in parentheses. Each column shows a different method of calculating union membership. Each model includes fixed effects for the Issue Area variable from the Supreme Court Database associated with each case.

both sides of this conflict were well-organized and benefited from deep resources (relative to other organized interests). As we saw in Chapter 2, research in the law and society tradition often documents how inequalities in resource levels among social groups can have long-run consequences on the direction the law takes.[1]

The Court's docket reflected this change in the nation. Table 6.1 shows the results of a simple regression model of constitutional law cases decided through 1930. The dependent variable is the proportion of each case's opinion text that I estimate to reflect the Economics and Business preference dimension. The key explanatory variable is the number of union members, in the millions, in the United States during the year the case is decided (Rosenbloom 2006, Series Bs4218). Union membership data is incomplete, and different series estimate membership differently and cover different periods of time; each column in the table shows a different estimate of the size of union membership. As a consequence, each model covers a different set of observations. Importantly, I include in each model fixed effects for the Issue Area assigned to the case in the Supreme Court Database (Spaeth et al. 2015). This means that the coefficients show the effect of unionization on the extent to which voting is characterized by the Economics and Business preference dimension, holding constant the general policy area the case implicates.

What we find here is striking. Union membership in the United States is related to the way in which the Supreme Court evaluates cases, holding constant the general issue area that the case implicates. While

---

[1] Olson (1990), for example, shows how even at the level of trial courts, groups who are politically disadvantaged are able to make use of the courts to pursue policy objectives that have comparatively less chance of being advanced in other fora.

Table 6.2. *Relationship between labor strength and presence of Economics and Business preference dimension language in Supreme Court opinions, 1881–1930.*

	(1)	(2)	(3)	(4)
Average annual wages (skilled)	0.12 (0.01)	–	–	–
Average hourly wage	–	0.81 (0.26)	–	–
Number of strikes (1000s)	–	–	0.02 (0.005)	–
Number of employees involved (1000s)	–	–	–	0.03 (0.007)
R^2	0.20	0.32	0.30	0.31
N	2072	931	1493	1349

Numbers are linear regression coefficients, with standard errors in parentheses. Each column shows a model with a different metric of labor strength. Average annual wages is the weighted average salary for a skilled laborer, across all industries, in thousands of dollars. Average hourly wage is the average hourly wage for non-farm hourly employees, weighted across all industries. Number of strikes is the number of strikes, in the thousands, that took place each year. Number of employees involved shows the number of employees (in the thousands) involved each year in striking. Each model includes fixed effects for the Issue Area variable from the Supreme Court Database associated with each case.

the empirical design I use here does not itself demonstrate a *causal* link between the two, it is unlikely that the extent to which the Court's decisions map onto the Business and Economics dimension causes the rate of union membership. In any event, as labor becomes more organized, the tension between labor and business presumably becomes more central to politics, and the Supreme Court reflects that change by shifting the way it writes about legal questions in its constitutional cases. In other words, as society changes, as labor becomes more organized, the content of the Court's opinions change to reflect the increasing significance of labor as a force in American politics. What is more, this relationship is not simply a product of this one proxy for the increasing prominence and power of labor in American society. Table 6.2 shows the relationship between the prevalence of Economics and Business preference dimension language in the Court's opinions and a host of other proxies for the role of labor in society.

The first two columns measure the role of labor using the amount of money one can earn as a laborer. In the first column, I show the relationship between the average annual wage (in thousands of dollars) for a skilled worker and the Court's use of Economics and Business preference dimension language (Morga 2006, Series Ba4290); these data are based on interpolations from the Census. The second column shows the relationship with the average wage for a non-farm hourly employee (Morga 2006, Series Ba4282). The final two columns show alternative metrics of unions, focusing on the exercise of union strength, rather than just the size of its membership. Column (3) shows the relationship between the Court's opinion content and the number of strikes that take place each year (Rosenbloom 2006, Series Ba4954), and Column (4) shows the relationship with the number of workers who participate in strikes (Rosenbloom 2006, Ba4955). Again, we see here evidence that as labor becomes more powerful, and as the conflict between business and labor presumably becomes more acute, the Court's constitutional decision making shifts such that, holding constant the general policy area in which a case is decided, the language shifts in favor of the Economics and Business preference dimension.

Taken together, Tables 6.1 and 6.2 suggest that both structural and contingent factors from outside the Court shaped the way the justices resolve constitutional questions during the late nineteenth and early twentieth century. The growing conflict between labor and business influenced the way the Court interpreted questions that arose in constitutional adjudication, such that the justices made decisions more frequently along the preference dimension associated with "Economics and Business" than it did previously. This is important because it indicates that the way in which constitutional doctrine develops, as we will see in subsequent sections, reflects contemporary political and social events. At the same time, as we will also see in the coming sections, the consequences of the Court's decisions, made in a given social and political context, can be long-lived. The Court during this period was making decisions that were shaped by the labor-business conflict, but they were also establishing precedent that would shape the way it interacts with disparate legal questions for decades to come.

INTERNAL POLITICS AND THE COURT'S CHANGING DOCKET. At the same time as the nature of the Court's docket was being influenced by the changing national economy, a number of other processes internal to the Court were playing out. First, with the massive growth in federal judicial business, the Supreme Court, which had a virtually mandatory jurisdiction, began to suffer from incredible backlogs. Figure 6.2 shows the number of cases decided by the Supreme Court each year, from 1791 through 2015. It also shows the total number of cases filed at the Court each year, from 1880 through 2015. A number of remarkable patterns

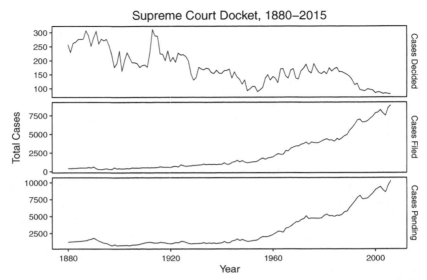

Figure 6.2. *Supreme Court decisions, cases filed and cases pending, 1880–2015.* Reliable data on case filings before 1880 are not available. (Source: Supreme Court Database (Spaeth et al. 2016) and Supreme Court Compendium (Epstein et al. 2007).

stand out. First, while the Court's level of activity increased a bit before the Civil War; after the war there was a fundamental shift in how much work the Court was doing. By the late nineteenth century, the Court was deciding more than 300 cases per year – nearly one per day. In 1891, when Congress created permanent courts of appeals, there was a brief respite in the number of cases decided, as well as a very small decrease in the number of cases filed, but more significant relief did not come until the 1920s, when Congress gave the Court almost total discretion over which cases it would hear. The general point, though, is that the late nineteenth century was a period where the Court was confronting both political and legal challenges, and it was doing so in the context of a structural shift in the quantitative burden of work it confronted.

Interacting with the changing national political and economic environment, the late nineteenth century was an era of fairly rapid turnover on the Court. Between 1877 and 1920, 34 different justices served on the Court. Justices such as Samuel Blatchford, William Woods, LQC Lamar, George Shiras, Stanley Matthews, and Ward Hunt all served during this period and were on the Court for roughly ten years or less each. Justice Howell Jackson served for just two years. Chief Justice Morrison Waite, who was responsible for a number of important decisions, served for only 15 years. The consequence was that during an era of a rapidly changing national

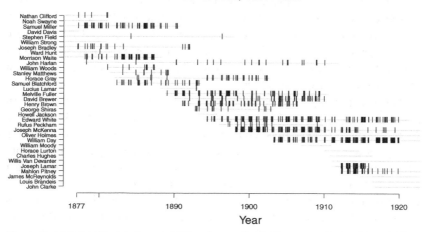

Figure 6.3. *Median justices in constitutional cases decided between 1877 and 1920.* Along the y-axis are the justices who served during the period, organized by the start date of their service (first justices at the top). The x-axis measures time. The grey horizontal lines show the dates during which each justice served. The tick marks indicate individual cases and who was the estimated median justice for that case.

political and economic environment, new justices were being appointed to the Court, meaning that the dynamics and preferences on the Court were rarely stable. Consider Figure 6.3, which shows which justice was estimated to be the pivotal median justice in each case from 1877 through 1920 (setting aside the small handful of cases where fewer than nine justices participated in the case). In this figure, the x-axis represents time, and the y-axis arrays all of the justices who served between 1877 and 1920, with the grey lines showing the time each justice was on the Court. The tick marks represent individual cases and indicate which justice I estimate to have been the pivotal median justice in that case. I calculate the median justice by weighing each justice's ideal point according to the posterior probability of each case being assigned to the case. In other words, if a case has an 80% probability of being about "Crime and Punishment," as estimated in Chapter 5, and a 20% probability of being about "Judicial Power," I calculate a weighted average of each justice's ideal point on those two dimensions, using the posterior probabilities as weights.

As the figure illustrates, quite naturally, some justices are more frequently the median than others. In no case do I estimate Justices Noah Swayne, David Davis, William Strong, Howell Jackson, Oliver Holmes, William Moody, Horace Lurton, Charles Hughes, Willis Van Devanter, James McReynolds, Louis Brandeis, or John Clarke as the median justice.

This finding comports with well-understood features of the Court during this era. For example, Justices Van Devanter and McReynolds were two of the conservative "Four Horsemen" of New Deal notoriety. Others among this group, such as Justices Brandeis, Holmes, and Clarke were very progressive justices who, during their time on the Court, served with generally strong conservative majorities and thus were rarely in a position to be pivotal in any given case.

The top panel in Figure 6.4 shows the conservatism of the median justice each year, from 1877 through 1920, in each of the six dimensions. Notably, there is very little change in the median's location during this time period, except in the Economics and Business preference dimension. The pattern reflects the efforts of Republican presidents, with the support of Republican-controlled Senates, to move the Court to the right on issues of economic regulation. As we will see below, Republican presidents during the late nineteenth century sought to appoint judges who were particularly hostile to state-level economic regulation, and this single issue was something of a litmus test for executive appointments at the time (cf. Gillman 2002).

A second pattern that emerges from the Court, though, is that at different points in time, the Court has been more evenly and consistently divided than during other times. In particular, during the early part of this period, Justice Miller and Chief Justice Waite were most commonly the median justices. That is, the voting coalitions were fairly stable, with a justice or two rather consistently being pivotal. However, as we moved forward in time, and as the turn-of-the-century politics coincide with the high rate of turnover, the politics of the Court become more complex. During the first decade of the twentieth century, as the mix of cases has shifted away from being predominantly about Judicial Power to a mix of cases that involve Economics and Business and Balance of Power in addition to Judicial Power, who serves as the median justice depends increasingly on what a case is about. Chief Justices White and Fuller as well as Justices Day, McKenna, and Brown, and all occupied the pivotal position with frequency during these years, though other justices were often at the center of a case, and there is no clear pattern of a justice or two dominating the Court. However, with a bit more turnover on the Court later that decade, the 1910s saw a consolidation of power in the hands of a few justices – White, Lamar, Pitney, and Day – and the exclusion of other justices from the center. Moreover, the Court was becoming increasingly conservative during this era – most notably on the Economics and Business dimension (recall Figure 5.8 in Chapter 5). Moreover, as Przybyszewski (2005, 147) notes, the justices on the Court during these

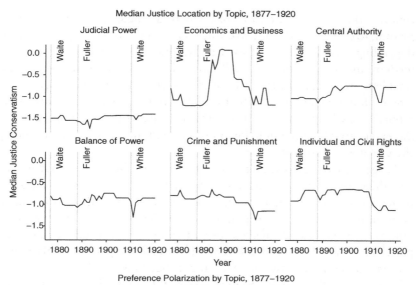

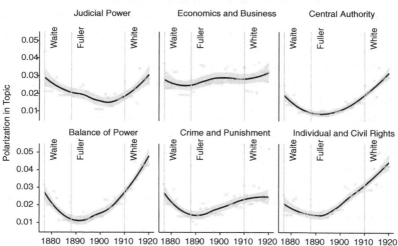

Figure 6.4. *Median justice conservatism in and ideological polarization among the justices in each of the six dimensions, 1877 through 1920.* Polarization is calculated using the method developed by Esteban and Ray (1994) and applied by Clark (2009a) to the Supreme Court.

years came from social backgrounds that particularly predisposed them towards a conservative politics.

So, as the Court's docket shifted away from being simply about the power of the courts to one that dealt increasingly with Economics and Business and then with Balance of Power during the early twentieth century, the Court went from one where a single justice or two was pivotal, to one where the decisive vote could come from nearly any justice, depending on the context of the case, to one where there were multiple median justices, but only a small handful, and many justices would be unable to ever occupy the center of the bench. Consider next Figure 6.4, which shows in greater detail the patterns in preference polarization reported in Chapter 5. Recall that the measure of polarization captures the extent to which the individual justices find themselves "alone" along the preference dimension.

What we can see is that polarization among the justices first wanes and then waxes in both the Judicial Power and the Balance of Power dimensions. In the Economics and Business dimension, there is a similar pattern, though the drop in polarization is sharper, followed by a more intermittent increase during the period from 1890 through 1920. This pattern in polarization reflects what we see with the pattern of pivotality during this period. Between 1880 and 1890, most of the justices were relatively "together" in the political space, but during the following three decades the justices on the Court were increasingly divergent from each other such that by 1920 there was a relatively good deal of political space separating the justices. The Court was more ideologically divided. The implications of this pattern can best be understood by considering two elements of the judicial process discussed in Chapter 1 – political forces both inside and outside of the Court.

Crucially, these changes in the political orientation of the justices are associated with consequential changes in what the Court did in its decisions. Figure 6.5 shows the proportion of the Court's cases where the disposition has a "liberal" orientation, as coded by the Supreme Court Database, for each year from 1877 through 1920. (Each point is scaled to the number of cases decided that term.) Recall from Figure 6.4 that during this period the median's conservatism in five of the six preference dimensions did not move appreciably; only in the Economics and Business preference dimension did the median shift. From 1890 through 1900, the median became more conservative, and it then moved back towards a more liberal orientation over the next decade. In Figure 6.5, we see that from 1880 through 1900, the percent of dispositions coded as liberal decreased, and it then began to increase after 1900. This pattern, then, is consistent with the trends in the ideological orientation of the Court. As the Republicans shifted the Court's composition towards a more conservative one, specifically along the Economics and Business preference dimension, the Court's output became more conservative; as twentieth-century progressives moved the Court back

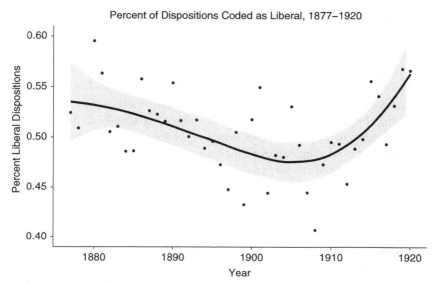

Figure 6.5. *Percent of dispositions in constitutional decisions that have a liberal orientation, 1877–1920*. The figure shows the proportion of case dispositions coded in the Supreme Court Database (Spaeth et al. 2015) as having a liberal disposition, excluding cases whose disposition was not codable as either liberal or conservative. The points are scaled by the number of cases decided each term.

towards a more moderate position, the Court's output became more liberal.

Of course, the case dispositions only tell one part of the story – who wins and who loses. That is an important part of the story, though, because the major struggles of the time often pitted politically powerful forces against each other in the context of constitutional decision making. However, to understand the history of constitutional law, we need to turn from a focus on the macropatterns of constitutional decision making to a more fine-grained examination of the underlying microprocesses that played out in the context of making particular decisions, establishing doctrine along the way.

6.2.2 *Decision Making and the Politics of Ideological Divides*

Let us turn now from those macropatterns to some specific examples that help highlight the microprocesses of constitutional decision making. First, consider the internal dynamics on the Court, both structural and contingent. The primary feature of judicial decision making around which many microtheories are oriented, as we saw in Chapter 2, is that the justices must decide cases one at a time. This means that when a case is presented to the justices, they must negotiate among themselves to determine now just the resolution to the case – who wins, and who loses – but also what the justices will write in their opinion. As we saw in Figure 4.6 in Chapter 4, the typical majority in this era was of fairly stable size – eight justices on average in non-landmark cases, and seven justices on average in landmark cases. Moreover, as Figure 4.7 in Chapter 4 showed, the rate of opinion writing decreased marginally during the final few decades of the nineteenth century (as the justices were becoming less divided) and then began to increase again during the early twentieth century (as the justices were again dividing into sharp voting blocs).

The theories of collegial decision making that have been developed to explain bargaining and opinion writing on the Supreme Court frequently implicate variation in the divisiveness of the Court (Figure 6.3) and the rate of opinion writing (Figure 4.7). Most notably, several models place analytic emphasis on the ideological center of gravity on the Court. Those models are typically designed to explain bargaining in a single case, where the justices know who is the pivotal median justice. The trick is building a coalition to support an outcome and endorse an opinion that holds together at least five justices, so the opinion the Court produces constitutes a majority opinion and therefore carries the weight of law (for a review, see Lax 2011).

In a setting where the pivotal role is shared among many of the justices and polarization is low, the political stakes are lowered. Bargaining is simpler, because the justices share common views about how to decide individual cases; no single justice is the "pivotal" vote who can always exert influence on his colleagues, and as a consequence cooperation among the justices over time is easier to facilitate. However, as disagreement grows, the stakes are heightened. One has to give up more, so to speak, to maintain a coalition with other justices, and power is increasingly concentrated in a small number of justices at the center of the Court. The consequence should be more stable policy content during the era of low polarization and shared pivotality, whereas the working majority coalitions should be more fragile when polarization is heightened and pivotality is concentrated.

Most important for understanding the constitutional politics of the time are two of the preference dimensions uncovered in Chapter 5. Along one dimension – Judicial Power – the justices were in fair agreement behind a strong view of the courts' power to intervene in policy making. As Figure 6.4 shows, polarization on this dimension decreased fairly steadily during the last two decades of the nineteenth century. Along another dimension – Economics and Business – there was quite a deal of volatility in the justices' views. As Presidents Cleveland and Harrison appointed justices such as Lamar, Brewer, Shiras, and Peckham, who were strong supporters of business interests, they at first divided the Court and then, as they developed a critical mass, consolidated the Court around conservative views of industrialism. However, the progressive politics ushered in by Teddy Roosevelt's election as president accompanied a series of departures from the Court that in short order would again shake things up – leading to another increase in polarization and then a consolidation around a return to a more progressive perspective on industry. Most notably, President Roosevelt nominated Justices Holmes and Day to the Court, who were deeply skeptical of corporate power. In many ways, they exemplified the "trust busting" politics that had been so important for Roosevelt's rise to the White House.

Indeed, the Fuller Court was one of "diverse and strong-willed individuals" (Ely 1995, 25). During the 1890s, in particular, the justices often argued intensely among themselves, with Justice Field notoriously argumentative and staunchly supportive of business interests in commerce cases. Fuller had to work hard, then, to maintain collegiality on the Court, which meant developing a substantive due process doctrine that reflected both "[t]he conservative economic view of Democrats Fuller and Peckham...with the Republican policy of defending entrepreneurial liberty" (Ely 1995, 31).

Consider a number of noteworthy decisions during this era. Many of the political and doctrinal implications can best be understood in light of an important case decided slightly before the Fuller Court and the beginning of the period analyzed here, known as *The Slaughter-House Cases* (1873). These cases arose as a challenge to Louisiana's enactment of a statute that created a monopoly on the slaughterhouse business, granting the sole right to operate a slaughterhouse to the Crescent City Stock Landing and Slaughter-House Company, which itself had been established by the state legislature. Butchers in New Orleans objected and brought suit against the state, claiming the statute violated the Thirteenth and Fourteenth Amendments. The Supreme Court concluded that the granting of a monopoly by the state was a legitimate use of the state's police power and did not violate either the Thirteenth or Fourteenth Amendment. The specific questions raised in the case and the doctrinal implications of the decision have been extensively discussed elsewhere. The important part of the decision, for our purposes here, is how the Court, from essentially its first opportunity, interpreted the Fourteenth Amendment's Equal Protection Clause when evaluating limits on state power. The Court held that the history of the Fourteenth Amendment revealed that the Civil War Amendments were intended to end slavery and protect racial minorities from oppression. The Fourteenth Amendment, and the Equal Protection Clause in particular, were not intended to limit a state's power to regulate activity within its own borders. Crucially, the Court limited the application of the Fourteenth Amendment by relying on a long-standing distinction between citizenship of the United Stated and citizenship of a particular state. To quote at length from the majority opinion, the Court writes,

> The first observation we have to make on this clause [All persons born or naturalized in the United States, and subject to the jurisdiction thereof, are citizens of the United States and of the State wherein they reside.] is that it puts at rest both the questions which we stated to have been the subject of differences of opinion. It declares that persons may be citizens of the United States without regard to their citizenship of a particular State, and it overturns the *Dred Scott* decision by making all persons born within the United States and subject to its jurisdiction citizens of the United States. That its main purpose was to establish the citizenship of the negro can admit of no doubt. The phrase, "subject to its jurisdiction" was intended to exclude from its operation children of ministers, consuls, and citizens or subjects of foreign States born within the United States.
>
> The next observation is more important in view of the arguments of counsel in the present case. It is that the distinction between citizenship of the United States and citizenship of a State is clearly recognized and established. Not only may a man be a citizen of the United States without being a citizen of a State, but an important element is necessary to convert the former into the latter. He must reside within the State to make him a citizen of it, but it is only necessary that he should be born or naturalized in the United States to be a citizen of the Union.
>
> It is quite clear, then, that there is a citizenship of the United States, and a citizenship of a State, which are distinct from each other, and which depend upon different characteristics or circumstances in the individual.[2]

Thus, from essentially the beginning, the Court interpreted the Fourteenth Amendment and cases involving industrialization and the unification of the economy in a way that was consistent with pre-war notions of dual sovereignty, where the states and the national governments existed alongside of each other, rather than in a necessarily hierarchical structure. Moreover, the Court in this case did not accept the argument that the Fourteenth Amendment imposed limits on state powers as a consequence of the benefits of citizenship of the United States. Taken in the context of the Reconstruction era, this decision makes sense; as we saw above, the Court at this point was still contending with very real questions about the breadth and depth of its institutional power. The *Slaughter House* decision has the markings of a Court setting out to define judicial power without pushing substantive policy too far. However, as we will see, the decision represents a point from which subsequent debates about the

---

[2] *Slaughter-House Cases*, 83 U.S. 36 (1873), at 73–74.

application of the Bill of Rights to the states will proceed over the next 100 years. The pattern of justices and preference alignment that characterizes the period through roughly 1920 would interact, as we will see below, with this doctrinal foundation laid at the close of Reconstruction.

One of the important, perhaps defining, characteristics of this period was the increasing individuality of Americans (e.g., Novak 1996; Croly 1993; McPherson 1988). The strong commitment to individualism that permeated the American political and economic worlds had led to an exacerbation of income inequality. The doctrine established in *The Slaughter-House Cases* in many ways exacerbated those challenges. The ripple effects of the Court's early Fourteenth Amendment doctrine, particularly its effects on social and political dynamics, would in turn recursively shape the path of law.

In particular, we see the way in which social and legal responses played out when we consider one of the major topics the courts confronted, and which came to be a major part of how the Court interpreted Article I of the Constitution – regulation of transportation, especially commercial railroad transportation. The general trajectory that played out in the wake of the Civil War was that railroads became increasingly important because they enabled businesses to transport their goods across long distances and provided effective means of transportation for people throughout the country. Perhaps most notably, railroads supplanted water transportation – such as via canals or the Mississippi River – as a fast and economical means of commercial transport. That transition had begun prior to the Civil War but consolidated during the closing decades of the nineteenth century. However, at the same time the railroad industry was rife with collusion. As Hilton (1966, 87) observes,

By the mid-1880's the railroad industry was in a mature state of cartelization, the symptoms of which were intolerable to much of the electorate. It was an industry in which the incentives to collusion were enormous. The number of firms serving any given route was small, and in consideration of the heavy investment necessary to build a railroad, there was no prospect that there would ever be so many railroads between major cities that collusion would be obviously unworkable. No pair of cities was served by more than three rival railroads in the early 1870's, and the number between any two major points was never to exceed seven. The industry was confronted by a wide variety of demand conditions, but railroad officers characteristically worked on the presumption that most demands facing them were inelastic.

Hilton further traces the origins of the collusion to 1870, when three railroads connecting Chicago and Omaha were completed and connected. The three companies were of relatively equal power and importance and entered into an agreement to pool the revenues from the three sections of the railroad and began a collusion. According to Hilton, this collusive strategy quickly spread in popularity over the following years.[3]

Indeed, the Court's interpretation of constitutional questions about the unified economy through the primary ideological cleavage that had been in play during the establishment of constitutional law led the Court to strike a markedly pro-business note. In *Pollock v. Farmers' Loan & Trust Co.*, 157 U.S. 429 (1895), the Court infamously held, in a 5-4 decision, that a direct income tax was unconstitutional. The decision was a strong blow to the national government's ability to finance its operations and was particularly vexing in light of the conclusion of the Civil War and growth of the national government's responsibilities and powers, which the dissenters noted. The same year the Court decided *United States v. E.C. Knight Co.*, 156 U.S. 1 (1895), which severely limited the federal government's power to regulate monopolies. (The case did not explicitly strike down the Sherman Antitrust Act, but it circumscribed its applicability so much as to have the practical effect of invalidating the law, at least for a time.) The following year, the Court decided *Plessy v. Ferguson*, 163 U.S. 537 (1896), in which the Court upheld racial segregation laws and established the notorious "separate but equal" doctrine, which held that segregation was constitutional if the regulated entity (in this case, a railroad) provided equal facilities for each race. These are cases where the justices were able to unite around their rather unified (i.e., not polarized) view of strong judicial power and a strong majority's increasingly conservative view of commerce to embolden business interests.

E.C. Knight is a particularly important case, as it provides a window into the way conservative business politics were filtered into constitutional doctrine at the close of the nineteenth century. In that case, the E.C. Knight company had created a monopoly that gave it control of 98% of the production of refined sugar in the United States. However, the Court ruled that even though that constituted a monopoly and was prohibited by the Sherman Antitrust Act, the Act could not be applied to this situation, because while sugar entered and was part of interstate commerce, the monopoly was over production, which is local in nature and therefore not subject to congressional jurisdiction under its power to regulate interstate commerce.

The doctrine that develops during this era, then, can be understood in light of the two underlying microprocesses I highlighted above. First, the Court was confronting a hostile political environment. The Court was

---

[3] Notably, Johnson and Van Metre (1918, 294) cites evidence of railway pooling and collusion in New England, though on a very small scale.

still a relatively weak institution, and the machine politics of the late nineteenth century served to strengthen the influence of business interests. A primary consideration in many decisions was to avoid political reprisal. As Bensel (2000, 324-27) points out, politicians, especially in the states, were particularly antagonistic towards the courts in the area of industrialization. Bensel provides an example of the Indiana state legislature enacting a law that would prohibit out-of-state corporations from doing business in Indiana if they tried at any time to transfer litigation from Indiana state courts into federal courts. Hattam (1993) argues that labor interests similarly opposed judicial intervention in labor-industry disputes. At the same time, this era occurs in the wake of significant efforts by the Republican Party to strengthen the national courts, in the interest of promoting a strong central state, especially with respect to economic regulation (e.g., Gillman 2002). In short, the courts in this period had good reason to beware overstepping the limits of what politicians and powerful interests would tolerate. Limiting the scope of judicial power was one way to avoid repercussions without having to make decisions that they did not like.

Second, the Court comprised a relatively united, conservative group of justices, reflecting electoral politics of the time. Republicans had sought to remake the federal courts, including the Supreme Court, in a conservative fashion. The justices serving at the end of Reconstruction had been appointed by presidents who used opposition to economic regulation as a criterion for appointment (e.g., Gillman 2002, 518). Even later in the decade, when the Democrats were making electoral gains, Republicans continued to hold the Senate and White House, allowing them to control judicial appointments even after Democrats had taken over the House. That would change, though, as we saw above in Figure 6.3, when Teddy Roosevelt came to the White House and was able to make a series of consequential appointments. Once Roosevelt's nominations had transformed the Court, its jurisprudence around industrialism and commerce shifted. In 1911, the Supreme Court decided *Standard Oil v. United States*, which ordered the breakup of Standard Oil under the Sherman Antitrust Act. The same year it decided *United States v. American Tobacco Co.*, which ordered the breakup of American Tobacco, also under the Sherman Antitrust Act. The next year, the government again prevailed at the Court under the Sherman Antitrust Act in its effort to stop Union Pacific Railway's purchase of Southern Pacific Railway. These are decisions that could hardly have been possible with the justices who had served on the Court just ten years earlier.

Crucially, the political swings on the Court gave rise not just to changing law but to a patchwork of doctrine that was difficult to reconcile. In 1895, the Supreme Court held that control of 98% of the sugar production in the country may constitute a monopoly, but because production takes place in a single place (at any given time), Congress could not regulate it as part of interstate commerce. However, just 17 years later the Court held that one railway did not have the right to negotiate a purchase of another on the grounds that the newly created railway would have a monopoly over the industry and therefore could be prohibited by Congress. Those two views of the Congress' role in regulating the economy are in deep tension with each other and would sew the seeds of subsequent legal strife. And, because they dealt with inherently different questions, the later cases did not explicitly repudiate *E.C. Knight*. This is the consequence of piecemeal law making by a Court composed of individuals who change with the politics of the time. It is also the consequence of the interaction between case-by-case policy making on one hand and the changing makeup of the Court driven by electoral politics on the other.

6.2.3 *Politics Beyond the Court*

The cases decided during this time do not just reflect the internal politics of the Court during the late nineteenth and early twentieth century. They also reflect, and are reflected in, political and social events taking place beyond the Court. Thus, the second element of the judicial process that is useful for understanding the implications of the patterns described above concerns the broader political context in which the Court was operating during the time. Two developments, in particular, bear consideration. First, the late nineteenth and early twentieth centuries were periods of significant economic growth. As the national economy unified, manufacturing took hold as a dominant means of employment. By the late nineteenth century, "the railroad, the telegraph, and the telephone were powerful forces unifying the economy...A lot of legal activity, in commercial law and in corporation law, reflected the way business was growing and spilling over borders. The United States had become one big economy; but it was not one big legal system" (Friedman 2002b, 46). That is, the legacy of American law from the nineteenth century, even in the wake of the Civil War, was one in which the states were generally paid a great deal of deference to regulate their own way, within the spheres of their own authority. The economy had been unifying at a rate faster than the law could catch up, and so the courts found themselves bombarded with legal disputes to sort out while working, as we saw above, to decide those individual cases in a way that created a coherent doctrine, or fabric of law.

Because of these challenges, the states began to see the need to coordinate their regulatory efforts (e.g., Stein 2015). During the 1890s, the American Bar Foundation supported the creation of the Conference of State Uniform Law Commissioners, which grew rapidly during that decade. The uniform laws movement had the goal of drafting model laws that could be adopted in many (or all) jurisdictions so as to reduce the difficulties of coordination among the states and facilitate common legal regulatory frameworks. In the last few years of the nineteenth century and first two decades of the twentieth century, the Commissioners on Uniform State Laws produced a number of model statutes, dealing with commerce and corporate regulation, and many of these laws were adopted by the states. However, this development engendered a culture of the states increasingly working to regulate the new industrialized economy in a vacuum of legal infrastructure to guide such regulatory action.

Part and parcel to efforts by the states to coordinate were efforts by the states to get regulations on the books to deal with the quickly spreading challenges presented by the unifying economy. (As noted above, opposition to those regulations was an important characteristic Republican presidents looked for in selecting Supreme Court nominees (e.g., Bensel 2000; Gillman 2002).) Large corporations were taking root across jurisdictional boundaries, giving rise to challenges that were a function of the sheer size of those organizations, such as corruption and questionable practices at the site of actual work. Middle management emerged as a powerful organizational institution to deal with these problems, beginning in railroads, where the very nature of the business made the operation so diffuse as to preclude the possibility that a single person could monitor and supervise the entire thing. States stepped in at various points to provide legal regulation to police what was an uneven bargaining situation, with laborers often finding themselves in deplorable working conditions. It is during this era that Upton Sinclair wrote *The Jungle*, chronicling the extreme working conditions in industrialized American cities (especially in the meatpacking industry). In the language of the case-space model, the Court was confronting a region of the fact space that had never before been the subject of litigation – because the situations that were giving rise to legal disputes were brand new. However, despite these adverse consequences of the unifying economy, there was a bright side – the economy was growing, and the standard of living was on the rise (e.g., Gordon 2017).

Along with the changing economy, Congress set out to reform the country's tax and tariff policies. In 1894, Congress enacted the Wilson-Gorman Tariff Act, which reduced tariff levels on many commodities, and sought to replace the lost revenue with an income tax.

(There had previously been income taxes during times of war, notably during the Civil War.) Charles Pollock sued Farmers' Loan and Trust, of which he owned a small share, when it decided to pay the federal government the tax owed on its profits. The Supreme Court decided the case by holding the Wilson-Gorman law unconstitutional, on the grounds that the income tax constitutes a direct tax and is not apportioned by representation.

The Court's decision in *Pollock v. Farmers' Loan & Trust* is instructive because it represents the way in which politics outside the Court can shape the direction of constitutional law. The issue of tariff reform was a significant one in the late-nineteenth century, finding itself often at the center of presidential platforms and policy debates. Pollock himself was represented by Joseph Hodges Choate, a well-known Wall Street lawyer who was well-connected to the Republican Party. Four years after the Court decided *Pollock*, Choate was appointed ambassador to the United Kingdom by President McKinley. In other words, the *Pollock* case was less about Pollock's concern over Farmers' Loan & Trust paying the tax than it was about the Republican Party's interest in blocking taxes and retaining tariffs (e.g., Irons 2006).

It was in this context that a Court with a volatile orientation along the Business and Economics dimension – that dealing with the regulation of the economy – and one that was also increasingly unified in the view that the courts could and should exercise strong oversight of regulation began to impose limits not just on the federal government but also on states' abilities to regulate the economy. As we saw above, nominations to the Court during the late nineteenth century moved the Court to the right on issues of business and industrialism, but that trajectory was quickly reversed during the first decade of the twentieth century. Reflecting the doctrinal ambivalence created by the pre-war doctrine of federalism and dual sovereignty, the Court decided a number of cases during this period that demonstrated its lack of preparation for dealing with industrialism. In *Lochner v. New York* and *Adair v. United States*, the Court applied the notion of a "liberty of contract" to invalidate both state and federal restrictions on the range of employment agreements into which employees and employers could enter. In the *Employer's Liability Cases*, the Supreme Court invalidated a federal regulation concerning what kind of liability insurance coverage a business must have on the grounds that the regulated industries included employers engaged only in intrastate commerce. These decisions reflect a conclusion that the problems the Court confronted did not have adequate answers in existing legal principles (described above). The Court concluded, in essence, that the blurred distinction between interstate and intrastate commerce meant that no regulatory authority existed, as neither the national nor the state governments were fully competent to regulate.

With this context in hand, we can revisit the macropatterns uncovered in Chapter 5 and in the analysis here. The Court had created for the country, during the Civil War and in its immediate aftermath, a constitutional doctrine that was not well-suited to handle the changing economy. Modern industrialism did not fit neatly into the state versus national framework. The changing economic conditions meant there were issues that existing doctrine did not neatly map into questions of either explicitly national or state competence. And so, when the justices were confronted with a massive stream of issues that implicated constitutional limits on government power and were factually distinct from past situations for which the doctrine had been developed, they found themselves in need of some kind of legal structure to look to. In the language of the case-space model, they needed existing legal rules that could be extended into the new regions of the fact space. To do so, they decided these new cases in light of (1) an increasingly conservative orientation towards business interests, and (2) a unified (i.e., not polarized) ideology of judicial power. Had the Court been more polarized on the issue of judicial power, for example, we might have expected a less consistent doctrine of judicial oversight, and had the Court been less conservative on issues of commerce regulation, we might have expected a more deferential pattern of decisions.

What is more, during this era, a number of early cases implicating racial segregation came to the Court, again in the context of lacking legal infrastructure (read: doctrine) to apply to these cases from new regions of the fact space. The conservative justices used the opportunity to roll back some of the advances progressives had made during the years immediately following the Civil War, most notably in the context of criminal juries. What we saw in Chapter 5, especially in Figure 5.2, was that during this era the Court was not deciding many cases along the Balance of Power preference dimension; rather, there was a small, but steady, collection of cases that implicated the Crime and Punishment dimension. Again, as with the Business and Economics cases, these cases often implicated two preference dimensions – Crime and Punishment and Judicial Power. In *Gibson v. Mississippi* (1896), the Supreme Court walked back efforts to prevent jury discrimination. In that case, the Supreme Court found that an all-white jury did not necessarily constitute an equal protection violation for a black defendant when the formal laws, and judicial interpretations of those laws, in a state do not entail any explicit unequal treatment. In several subsequent cases, the Supreme Court continued to adhere to that principle in refusing to find problems with criminal juries that were clearly stacked against black defendants (Dake 1904, 243–44). Moreover, as Figure 6.4 shows, the justices were not particularly polarized on the issue of Crime and Punishment during this era, and so there was something of a perfect storm of unified opinion on Judicial Power, unified opinion on Crime and Punishment, a relatively conservative ideology, and a political climate in which the Southern states were pushing to regain some of the autonomy they lost during Reconstruction. This spelled disaster for progressives hoping to limit institutionalized racism.

Those decisions by the Supreme Court surely contributed to a number of societal reactions, in turn. The NAACP formed in 1909 and began a pattern of using litigation to pursue its policy objectives. The NAACP was first conceived as the Niagara Movement, which was an effort led by W.E.B. DuBois as a response to what DuBois perceived as a bad political strategy among the groups led by Booker T. Washington.[4] The years leading up to the establishment of the Niagara Movement and then the NAACP had been marked by race riots, most notably the 1908 riot in Springfield, Illinois. In 1909, the Niagara Movement gained the support of many White supporters, notably individuals such as Jane Addams and John Dewey (e.g., Kluger 1975, 93–97). The first president of the NAACP was Moorfield Storey, who was White. Storey, crucially, had a long history of experience in politics and was a successful lawyer. (He was president of the American Bar Association (ABA) during the late nineteenth century.) From nearly the outset, the NAACP set out to use litigation as a means to help Black people, and within a few years it was arguing cases before the Supreme Court.

At the same time as the NAACP was beginning to use litigation to advance causes of racial justice, other special interest groups were adopting a similar strategy. By the 1940s, interest groups – including labor as well as industry groups – were regularly participating in Supreme Court litigation, often as *amicus curiae* – groups not party to a case but with an interest in the outcome. This fundamentally changed the nature of such litigation. As Vose (1958, 27) notes, "The frequent entrance of organizations into Supreme Court cases by means of the *amicus curiae* device has often given litigation the distinct flavor of group combat." Thus, the ripple effects of the Court's doctrine were wide and far. As we will see in the next chapter, the rise of special interest litigation, born of the

---

4 Washington and Booker disagreed about what the right strategy was for Black Americans to improve their social status. Washington thought they should pursue extensive training in vocations that would earn a good living. DuBois perceived that strategy as an admission of Black inferiority and supported more aggressive pursuit of political and educational access.

politics of the early twentieth century, would have pervasive consequences for the development of constitutional law.

6.2.4 *Politics Inside and Outside the Court*

Taken together, this brief history of constitutional law at the turn of the century and the statistical analyses from Chapter 5 reveal an important lesson. Ideological conflicts – both internal among the justices and external between the Court and the other branches of government – as well as social and political developments – both internal changes to the nature of the questions the justices were confronting and those external to the Court as society changed in the wake of industrialization – interacted during the years between 1877 through 1920 in important ways. The Court's docket was being sharply influenced by a new set of policy challenges that the existing legal infrastructure was not set up to handle. Growing tension between labor and business brought challenges to the Court implicating the government's role in regulating the economy. One of the consequences of this change was that the justices began to vote along a distinct ideological cleavage – their voting patterns reflected a preference dimension associated with views about economic regulation and commerce, rather than about the extent and scope of judicial power.

At the same time, the Court was staffed by judges who reflected the deeply divided politics of the antebellum era as well as the culture of industrialism that characterized American society at the close of the nineteenth century. Republican control in the wake of the Civil War had led to a strengthened judiciary, staffed by conservative justices who were skeptical of economic regulation, especially regulations coming from the states. However, by the early twentieth century, Teddy Roosevelt's appointments to the Supreme Court represented something of a progressive interjection, reviving political conflicts that might have otherwise been settled. When Roosevelt left the White House in 1909, his successor, William Howard Taft, set out to remake the courts in a conservative mold. The Republican party had been on the precipice of splitting up when Teddy Roosevelt pushed his progressive political agenda as President, with Taft representing the more conservative wing of the party. During his eight years as president, Taft made six nominations to the Court, who were in general conservative, especially on issues of federalism and to some extent on business and commerce. Most notably, Willis Van Devanter and Mahlon Pitney were Taft appointees who were strongly anti-labor in their political views. However, during the 1913 election, the Republican party's rift exploded. Teddy Roosevelt ran as a third-party candidate, dividing the progressive and conservative wings of the party, and delivering the White House to Woodrow Wilson, a progressive Democrat, who would make three appointments to the Court, including Louis Brandeis and John Clarke, both of whom were particularly progressive on the labor v. business divide. Those changes to the Court's composition resulted in a shift in who was likely to win or lose in constitutional cases and, as a consequence, the types of doctrines developed as the Court moved from deciding cases with respect to the scope of judicial power to establishing substantive law about the constitutionality of economic regulatory schemes.

The shifting content of the Court's docket and ideological orientation of the justices who served on the Court interacted to establish the foundation for a number of constitutional doctrines that would have long-run consequences. In particular, the Court's interpretations of the due process and equal protection clauses of the Fourteenth Amendment would shape important policy battles for decades to come. As we see next, the period spanning from World War I to World War II was one of tumultuous social developments that would be shaped by the constitutional doctrine established during this prior era; moreover, the events of the next few decades would in turn affect not just existing doctrine but an entirely new arena of constitutional decision making.

6.3   FROM WAR TO CRISIS TO POLITICAL REALIGNMENT

As Woodrow Wilson was advancing Progressive goals and shifting the Court somewhat back to the left, the country faced a major shock to its system of governance. World War I broke out in Europe. Wilson was reelected in 1916, in part due to his claim of credit for keeping the country out of the war. However, by 1917, the United States' entry into the war was inevitable, and Congress declared war on April 6 of that year. The war effort entailed a massive expansion of the national government's power. In fact, the national government exerted control over industry and the economy to an extent that might not have been fathomable – and certainly would not have been politically possible – were it not for the war. As Post (1998, 1489) observes, "[t]he federal government took control of the operations of the nation's railroads, its telegraphs and telephones, and its shipping industries. It assumed authority to regulate the production and prices of food and fuel. It actively intervened to shape the priorities of the wartime economy. It instituted sharply progressive income taxes" (see also, Cashman 1988, 493). The first income tax the country had ever had was pushed through by Republicans to finance the Civil War just over fifty years earlier (e.g., McPherson 1988, 443).

When the war ended, much of the national regulatory efforts receded, but there was an air of satisfaction among Progressives and a sense that there had been a major "rupture" in the regulatory ideology of the times (e.g., Post 1998, 1490–91). The possibilities of government regulation of the economy had been expanded, and the notion that constitutional law might have to change to make room for a new regulatory ideology was front-and-center in the presidential election of 1920.

It was in this context that, during the 1920 presidential election, Taft worked hard to make the Supreme Court a central issue, anticipating a great number of vacancies that the next president would be able to fill (Galloway Jr. 1985, 2–4) and sensing the importance of the constitutional battles over the national economy that were to come. Taft threw his political weight behind Warren Harding, who was a very pro-business conservative in the Republican Party, in a bitterly divisive primary for the GOP (Republican Party) nomination for the White House. On the tenth ballot of the 1920 GOP convention, Harding secured the nomination and ultimately won the election in a landslide. After Harding's death in 1923, he was succeeded by his Vice President, Calvin Coolidge, who was also a very pro-business, laissez-faire conservative, and Coolidge was later followed in the White House by Herbert Hoover. These three Republican presidents made a series of appointments to the Supreme Court that resulted in a dramatic move to the right across the board.

At the same time as pro-business interests were dominating presidential politics, the so-called "Roaring Twenties" were under way, which witnessed a massive expansion of the economy. The consequences of the unified economy and Second Industrial Revolution were born out in the spread of technologies previously rare in the common household, such as the telephone, electricity, and radio. There was also a sense of social progression, marked by changes in architecture (for example, the rise of Art Deco) and music (this was the era of an explosion in jazz). Along with the progressive nature of the jazz era, the 1920s were also the period of prohibition in the United States, when alcohol was prohibited by the Eighteenth Amendment as of 1920. Along with prohibition came a rise in organized crime in the country.

Of course, by the close of that decade, the economic conviviality of the Roaring Twenties came to a shattering end, with the crash of 1929 and the ensuing Great Depression. During the four years following the 1929 crash, almost half of the banks in the country failed, which further exacerbated the economic hardships created by the crash and pushed the Depression even deeper. Unemployment peaked around 25% in 1933. And, it was in this climate the Herbert Hoover was resoundingly defeated by Franklin Roosevelt and the Democrats on the promise to give Americans a "New Deal," which became the name for Roosevelt's expansive legislative agenda for rebuilding the American economy. FDR's electoral coalition represented a fundamental shake-up in American politics (e.g., Fraser and Gerstle 1989). He assembled a diverse group of interests who aligned on the central question facing the country at the time – was it time for a new economic model? The details of how this played out occupy the following pages, but to preview, FDR's model for a strong central government empowered to regulate the economy carried the day. By 1940, the country had gone, in just 20 years, from boom to bust to a new understanding of the role of the federal government in daily life. The Supreme Court, and its constitutional jurisprudence, were crucial in this evolution.

6.3.1 Macropatterns in Constitutional Law, 1920–1940

During this era, the Court's docket underwent a dramatic shift in the ideological preference dimensions that characterized the justices' voting. Figure 6.6 shows the representation of each of the ideological preference dimensions on the Court's docket each year from 1877 through 1940. A number of important trends stand out. The centrality of the Judicial Power preference dimension steadily diminished on the Court's docket, continuing the pattern we saw in the previous section. The Economics and Business dimension continued the growth in prominence it had

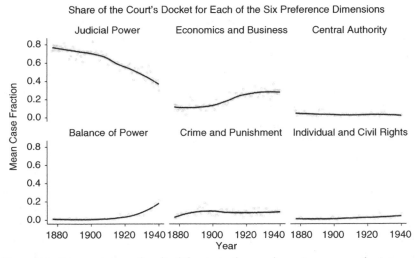

Figure 6.6. *Representation of each of the six preference dimensions among the Supreme Court's constitutional decisions, 1877–1940.* The figure shows, for each year between 1877 and 1940, the average assignment probability among all cases for each of the six preference dimensions.

experienced since the beginning of the Second Industrial Revolution. Meanwhile, the importance of ideological conflict over Balance of Power continued to increase and the Court began to interpret constitutional questions along the Individual and Civil Rights preference dimension. Economic regulation was perhaps the central policy issue at all levels of politics during the Roaring Twenties, and it only continued to be so during the Great Depression, though the ideological preference dimension through which those policy questions were interpreted shifted dramatically away from the traditional Economics and Business dimension. The problems of organized crime, temperance, and other social questions were not yet being decided along preference dimensions that were substantively oriented; rather the Court conceived of those problems, to the extent possible, as issues of Balance of Power. That reflected, to a certain extent, the constitutional legacy of the nineteenth century and the relatively weak jurisprudential infrastructure for dealing with modern regulatory issues the federal government was confronting.

What is more, though, the constitutional jurisprudence the Court developed through the 1920s and 1930s reflects not just the political and social context of times but also the internal politics and institutions of the Court. As noted, the Republican presidents from the 1920s remade the Court in a conservative mold. Figure 6.7 shows each of the justices who served on the Court between 1915 and 1945 and who I estimate

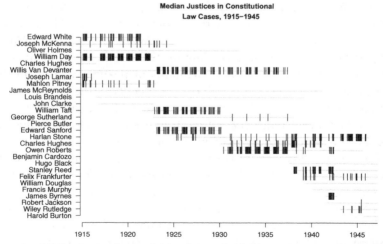

Figure 6.7. *Median justices in constitutional cases decided between 1915 and 1945.* Along the y-axis are the justices who served during the period, organized by the start date of their service (first justices at the top). The x-axis measures time. The grey horizontal lines show the dates during which each justice served. The tick marks indicate individual cases and who was the estimated median justice for that case.

Table 6.3. *Relationship between representation of six preference dimensions and likelihood of each of three justices being the estimated median.*

	Van Devanter	Taft	Sanford
Judicial Power	6.58	1.78	−0.71
	(0.94)	(0.73)	(0.84)
Economics and Business	−1.76	−1.89	1.37
	(0.90)	(0.63)	(0.65)
Central Authority	6.75	1.35	4.33
	(1.76)	(1.69)	(1.70)
Balance of Power	−13.66	−4.03	6.13
	(1.94)	(1.21)	(1.49)
Crime and Punishment	8.52	−0.81	4.02
	(1.66)	(1.90)	(1.66)
Individual and Civil Rights	−8.91	4.03	−2.58
	(3.56)	(1.82)	(2.72)
N	1390		
Residual deviance	4891.5		
Effective degrees of freedom	114		

Cells show estimated multinomial logistic coefficients, with standard errors in parentheses. The dependent variable is the identity of the median justice; results are shown here for only three justices.

to be the median in each case. What we see here is a continuation of the polarization that developed during the first decades of the twentieth century. William Day, a Teddy Roosevelt appointee, was, up until his retirement in 1922, consistently the pivotal justice. After his departure, the median role was served alternatively by Willis Van Devanter, William Taft, or Edward Sanford, depending on the substantive content of the case. Table 6.3 shows the results of a multinomial regression of individual cases, where the dependent variable is the identity of the median justice, and the explanatory variables are the estimated loadings for the case onto each of the six preference dimensions. I show estimates for only the three justices who were frequent medians during this era.

The findings here are instructive. Justice Van Devanter, one of the Four Horsemen who staunchly opposed progressive efforts to regulate the economy, was least likely to be the median justice in cases that implicated the Balance of Power preference dimension, and he was also relatively unlikely to be the median in cases that implicated the Economics and Business or Individual and Civil Rights preference dimensions. Indeed, Van Devanter was particularly conservative on these issues. By contrast, Chief Justice Taft was most likely to be the median in cases that were decided along the Individual and Civil Rights preference dimension. These cases were still rare during his time, but these were the instances in which he found himself at the center of the Court's ideological makeup. Finally, it was Justice Sanford who was most likely to be the median justice in cases involving Balance of Power or the Economics and Business preference dimension. Thus, the frequency with which Van Devanter came to be the median justice during the late-1920s and 1930s is partially associated with the shift in the preference dimensions that the Court's cases activated. Slight increases in cases implicating the Crime and Punishment during this era gave him an opportunity to serve as the median justice, as well as the declining, but still prominent, set of cases decided along the Judicial Power dimension. In the remaining cases during the late 1920s, the median role oscillated between Sanford and Taft, with Sanford having the pivotal vote in cases involving economic regulation, and Taft serving as the median in cases decided along the Individual and Civil Rights dimensions.

Those differences in preferences across the substantive issues reflect a general conservatism along the various ideological preference dimensions. The upper panel in Figure 6.8 replicates a portion of Figure 5.8 in Chapter 5, and the lower panel replicates a portion of Figure 5.10. A number of patterns emerge. First, there was a fairly dramatic move to the right by the median justice in both the Economics and Business and Balance of Power preference dimensions. The justices appointed by Harding, Coolidge, and Hoover more than undid the antitrust progressivism that Roosevelt and Wilson had pushed on the Court with their nominations. Second, there was little change in the median on most of the other preference dimensions, with the exception of the Individual and Civil Rights dimension, where there was some oscillation in the median's conservatism during this period. However, as Figure 6.6 shows, that dimension constituted a very small component of the justices' decision making during this era. At the same time, the conservative move in the median accompanied a drop in polarization during the 1920s and 1930s on the Economics and Business preference dimension, while it led to an increase in polarization on the Balance of Power preference dimension during the same time period. Thus, between 1920 and 1937, we see a Court that is increasingly unified behind a conservative orientation on Economics and Business but more and more divided over questions that implicate the Balance of Power preference dimension.

Making matters worse for progressives, it was not until 1937 that FDR had an opportunity to appoint a justice. However, following the confrontation between FDR and the Supreme Court after the 1936 election, Justice Van Devanter announced his resignation from the Court, and President Roosevelt appointed Hugo Black, an Alabama Democrat

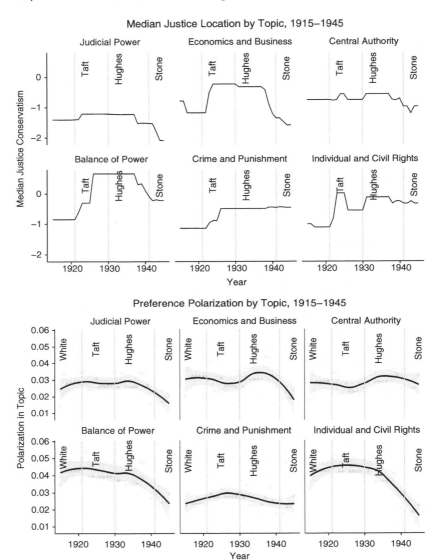

Figure 6.8. *Location of the median justice and ideological polarization among the justices in each of the six dimensions, 1915 through 1945.* Polarization is calculated using the method developed by Esteban and Ray (1994) and applied by Clark (2009a) to the Supreme Court.

and strong supporter of the New Deal, to the Court. Over the next eight years, Roosevelt would completely remake the Court, appointing eight of the justices who were serving on the Court at the time of his death. The Court that Roosevelt left behind was a decidedly more liberal one than the Court he first encountered as President. Moreover, these new, younger

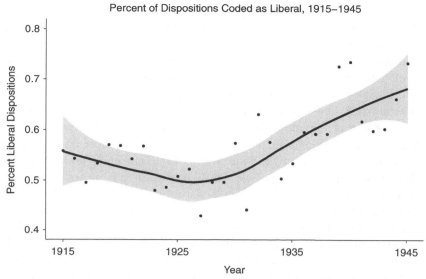

Figure 6.9. *Percent of dispositions in constitutional decisions that have a liberal orientation, 1915–1945.* The figure shows the proportion of case dispositions coded in the Supreme Court Database (Spaeth et al. 2015) as having a liberal disposition, excluding cases whose disposition was not codable as either liberal or conservative.

justices brought to the Court fundamentally different views about the Constitution.

Indeed, as we saw above, the politics of turnover on the Supreme Court had direct consequences for the Court's output. Figure 6.9 shows the percent of case dispositions, among the Court's constitutional decisions, coded as "liberal" each year, according to the Supreme Court Database. The pattern here is distinct. During the period from roughly 1915 through 1930, as Republicans mostly controlled judicial appointments, the Courts were more likely to side with litigants that represented a conservative policy position. However, as FDR remade the Court during his tenure as president, supported by a Democratically controlled Senate, the Court's justices became more liberal (as we saw in Figure 6.7), and the Court's decisions became much more liberal. By the end of World War II, the Court was deciding roughly three-quarters of its cases in a "liberal" direction. Moreover, those case dispositions reflect a sharp change in the Court's jurisprudence, as the justices established doctrine that would fundamentally shift the nature of government power and structure significant policy debates for generations.

Thus, there are three developments taking place during the 1920s and 1930s in the Court's constitutional jurisprudence that the statistical analysis of constitutional decision making helps make evident. First, the Court was continuing the pattern of transitioning from interpreting constitutional questions along the Judicial Power preference dimension and instead was beginning to map the legal and political questions it confronted onto distinct preference dimensions – namely, Economics and Business and Balance of Power. Second, the Court was confronting substantively new questions and challenges. As the unified economy took root and expanded its reach, and the regulatory legacy of the national government's wartime powers loomed large, more diverse issues of regulation, federalism, and the power of the central government made their way to the Court's docket. Those questions came in social context that was unanticipated when the Constitution was written. Third, the electoral politics of the time were erratic, reflecting the major changes the country – and the world – was going through. Progressives triumphed in the context of rising concerns about capitalism, but conservatives took back control for a decade in the wake of World War I, and progressives again took control following the economic crash of 1929. Those erratic electoral politics had implications for the justices. The Republican presidents during the time managed to move the Court considerably to the right, but the intermittently more liberal presidents – Roosevelt and Wilson – had the effect of keeping the Court somewhat more divided, especially on the Balance of Power dimension. Thus, the conservative move on the Court did not mean a consolidation of conservative power but rather the maintenance of a relatively polarized Court, albeit one centered around an increasingly conservative center of gravity.

Between 1920 and 1937, and beyond, changing social conditions, new technological and business problems, and institutional and personnel transitions at the Court set up a collection of external and internal forces that would shape constitutional law. Two areas of law where these forces interacted were regulation of the economy and state power over the individual. The legal doctrines at play in each area were interconnected, in part through the political organization of the law we saw in Chapter 5 and in part through the electoral, social, and legal process that gives rise to constitutional controversy.

6.3.2 Regulating the Economy

The Supreme Court of the 1920s, as it was handling the new onslaught of cases involving Progressive economic regulation and civil liberties claims, was undergoing substantial change itself. As noted above, turnover among the justices was particularly rapid during this time period. And, as Figure 6.8 shows, the consequence was a rapid move to the right, especially on the Economics and Business, Balance of Power, and Individual and Civil Rights preference dimensions. There was also a more gradual, and less pronounced, rightward shift on the Crime and Punishment preference dimension. Taft had made the Supreme Court a major campaign issue in 1920 and, shortly after Harding's election, Taft realized a longtime dream, when he was appointed as Chief Justice, following the death of Edward White. Taft joined a Court that still had two of his own appointees on it and saw four additional changes over the subsequent four years, including the appointment of three Republicans. These political allies and new copartisan justices created the conditions for strong leadership by Taft in the Chief Justice's seat. However, by the end of the decade, financial crisis and a turn in political fortunes meant that the Court would be facing new constitutional questions about economic regulation that would have long-lasting and deep consequences for the structure of American constitutional law.

One of the underlying processes that facilitated the legal developments was a steady move towards mapping economic cases onto the Economics and Business preference dimension, rather than the Judicial Power preference dimension. Figure 6.10 replicates Figure 6.6 from above, but considering only economic cases. (I use the Supreme Court Database Issue Area variable to identify cases where the policy content is primarily one of Economic Activity.) Whereas at the beginning of the period, the typical economic activity case only loaded about 20% into the Economics and Business preference dimension and loaded 75% onto the Judicial Power preference dimension, by the end of the period here, the Economics and Business preference dimension was the dominant dimension for evaluating economic cases. Moreover, as we see, and as becomes crucial at the end of this period and in the next, the Court begins to interpret economic activity cases as matters of federalism as well, especially after 1930.

Of course, the process by which economic activity cases change from implicating the Judicial Power preference dimension, to implicating the Economics and Business preference dimension, to implicating the Balance of Power preference dimension is complex. The justices themselves certainly have the power to interpret substantive policy issues in whatever preference dimension they choose. Moreover, strategic litigants anticipating the justices' views on the various dimensions will have incentives to shape their cases in the most favorable perspective. Moreover, the issues and problems that occur in the world, giving rise to the cases themselves, involve context and circumstances that are prone to activate some dimensions more so than others. This, of course, is one factor the justices might use when sifting through the cases they choose to hear. In four historical examples – the regulatory legacy of World War

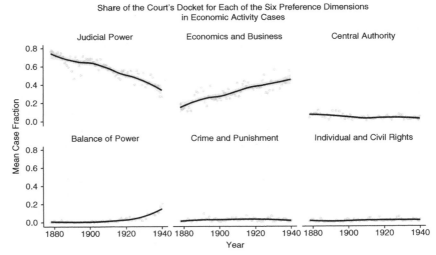

Figure 6.10. *Representation of each of the six preference dimensions among the Supreme Court's constitutional decisions in cases coded as involving economic activity as the major issue area, 1877–1940.* The figure shows, for each year between 1877 and 1940, the average assignment probability among all cases for each of the six preference dimensions.

I; the conflict between labor and business, and the fear of socialism; the push for women's political rights; and the government's response to the Great Depression – we see the way judicial microprocesses and the preference dimensions that characterize constitutional law shaped major components of constitutional law. Specifically, these examples illustrate the interaction among external world events, changing dynamics in American society, and internal political processes at the Court. These examples, then, help illuminate the underlying microprocesses that gave rise to the changing macropatterns we see here.

Regulatory Legacy. World War I had ushered in a period of heavy economic regulation by the national government. Its regulatory reach expanded in ways that were unimaginable beforehand. Even though President Wilson oversaw a rolling back of many of those regulatory schemes at the conclusion of the war, some remained in place. And, as the saying goes, once the genie is let out of the bottle, it cannot be put back in. Progressives had seen during the war a wide range of regulatory possibilities. As Post (1998) describes, the war set up a demand for national economic regulation, and the justification in constitutional law was found in the principle derived from *Munn v. Illinois* that some industries are so "affected with a public interest" that they can justifiably be extensively regulated. In the years before World War I, a number of

Progressive regulatory policies were adopted, often in the states. The leftward shift in the Court on the Economics and Business preference dimension that was effected by the Roosevelt and subsequent Wilson appointments allowed those regulatory policies the opportunity to shift constitutional law.

Despite the Progressive policies that came with the war, Willis (1928), writing contemporaneously, observes that the justices did not fundamentally change the character of constitutional law with that opportunity. In 1914, the justices held, in *German Alliance Insurance Company v. Lewis*,[5] that fire insurance is affected with a public interest and therefore could be regulated. Fire insurance was affected with a public interest, the Court held, because it is indispensable and the provider has a near monopoly on the service. However, eight years later the Supreme Court, in *Wolff Packing Co. v. Court of Industrial Relations*,[6] laid out a more rigorous test for evaluating the propriety of a regulation, identifying three possible ways an industry could be affected with a public interest. The industry should either

"(1) be carried on under a grant of privileges which expressly or impliedly [*sic*] imposes the affirmative duty of rendering a public service, or (2) be an occupation which has survived the period when all trades and callings were regulated, or (3) have a peculiar relation to the public because of the indispensable nature of its service and the exorbitant charges and arbitrary control to which it might subject the public" (Willis 1928, 387–88).

The incomplete progressive transformation in the constitutional law of regulation can be seen in an example from the railroads. The railroads had expanded considerably during the years preceding World War I. However, by 1917, it was apparent they were not adequately prepared to support the country in the war. They had fewer cars than they needed and fuel costs were soaring (Cashman 1988, 4995). In 1916, Congress passed the Adamson Act, a piece of Progressive legislation championed by Woodrow Wilson that created an industry-wide eight-hour workday and required overtime pay. This was the first federal law to regulate work hours in a private business. The Supreme Court upheld that law as constitutional,[7] which had the consequence of further increasing operating costs for the railroads. It was in this context that President Wilson issued a proclamation taking control of the railroad system in December 1917, but soon thereafter secured passage of the Railroad Control Act, which ensured the railroad owners would be adequately

---

[5] 233 U.S. 389.
[6] 262 U.S. 522 (1922).
[7] *Wilson v. New*, 243 U.S. 332 (1917).

compensated, protecting their property rights. The Supreme Court, however, never had an opportunity to rule on the constitutionality of the nationalization of the railroads. In 1920, Congress passed the Esch-Cummins Railroad Act, otherwise known as the Transportation Act of 1920, which returned control of the railroads to their private owners.

However, whereas the Progressives acknowledged that nationalization of the railroads would not be sustained after the end of the war, they had gotten a taste of what they could accomplish by regulating the railroads (as well as other industries). Notably, while the Transportation returned control of the railroads to their owners, it also gave the Interstate Commerce Commission power to push the railroads to consolidate, set minimum shipping rates, and otherwise oversee the railroads' operations. These regulations were aimed, in part, to prevent the kind of industry-wide deterioration that had taken place during the 1910s. Part of that law "authorized the Interstate Commerce Commission to appropriate 'excess' profits from strong railroads in order to create a fund that would benefit financially weak railroads" (Post 1998, 1507). The Supreme Court unanimously upheld that provision.[8] Moreover, other parts of the law were also challenged and upheld by the Supreme Court, including the ICC's power to set minimum fares[9] and to control joint rates between railroads.[10] In the course of these cases, the Court made clear that the railroad system was of sufficient public interest to justify intervention by the federal government.

Whereas Court decisions prior to World War I set some precedent for allowing federal regulation of the railroads, most of the cases it had confronted dealt with the ability to break up or control monopolies or abusive rate collusion. However, the experience of confronting a railway system in disrepair on the eve of great national need for the war changed the national perspective on regulation. Progressives were successful in using the war as a justification for embracing regulation of major national industries, and in the wake of the war, they were able to avoid fully repealing those regulatory regimes and instead simply scale back the depth of the federal government's oversight. The changing national circumstances during the war demonstrated the public interest in industries that might not have been considered to be affected with public interest before the war. Writing for the Court in *Dayton-Goose*, Chief Justice (and former President) Taft observed that under the law that the Court was approving,

---

[8] *Dayton-Goose Creek Railway Co. v. United States*, 263 U.S. 456 (1924).
[9] *Railroad Commission of Wisconsin v. Chicago, B. & Q. R. Co.*, 257 U.S. 563 (1922).
[10] *The New England Divisions Case*, 261 U.S. 184 (1923).

The carrier owning and operating a railroad, however strong financially, however economical in its facilities, or favorably situated as to traffic, is not entitled as of constitutional right to more than a fair net operating income upon the value of its properties which are being devoted to transportation. By investment in a business dedicated to the public service the owner must recognize that, as compared with investment in private business, he cannot expect either high or speculative dividends but that his obligation limits him to only fair or reasonable profit.

This perspective in American law represents a radical transformation from the pro-business, laissez-faire economics that had characterized the previous decades. While the 1920s were certainly not an era of aggressive Progressive regulation, the example of post-war regulation of the railroads shows how the world changing around the Court led to a different understanding of the trade-off between private property and public interest.

Importantly, as Figures 6.8 and 6.10 indicate, the shift to mapping economic activity cases onto the Economics and Business dimension occurs partially during a period when the Court has moved, only temporarily, to the left on the Economics and Business preference dimension. The decisions in *Dayton-Goose Creek Railway*, *Railroad Commission of Wisconsin*, and *The New England Divisions Case* all took place before the Republican presidents from the 1920s had the opportunity to move the Court to the right. Thus, an era of significant changes in the national economy and regulatory development coincided with temporary progressive influence on the Court. However, that coincidence would not last long, as the Court moved to the right on virtually every preference dimension during the coming decade.

Indeed, the regulatory zeal of World War I and conservative reaction in its wake can be seen in a wide host of areas that spread far beyond the kinds of industries one might expect to be swept up in the wartime economy. One notable example comes from the case *Block v. Hirsch*, 256 U.S. 135 (1921). That case dealt with a statute passed by Congress in the aftermath of World War I. The problem was that there was a severe housing shortage, especially in Washington, DC, driven largely by the federal government's employment needs after the war, and Congress created a commission to regulate rent in the capital. The statute also allowed individuals to stay in their rentals, provided they were paying rent, even if the landlord wanted to remove them. In this case, Block was a tenant, and the landlord sold the building to Hirsch. Hirsch wanted to discontinue renting the apartment in the basement of the building, where Block lived, and Block sued to stay. The Supreme Court upheld congressional authority to regulate the rental market, in a 5-4 vote. Writing for the majority in a short opinion, Justice Holmes observed that the demands placed on the country by World War I justified a heightened level of intervention in the economy by the national government. He wrote,

The main point against the law is that tenants are allowed to remain in possession at the same rent that they have been paying, unless modified by the Commission established by the act, and that, thus, the use of the land and the right of the owner to do what he will with his own and to make what contracts he pleases are cut down. But if the public interest be established, the regulation of rates is one of the first forms in which it is asserted, and the validity of such regulation has been settled since *Munn v. Illinois.* It is said that a grain elevator may go out of business, whereas here the use is fastened upon the land. The power to go out of business, when it exists, is an illusory answer to gas companies and waterworks, but we need not stop at that. The regulation is put and justified only as a temporary measure. A limit in time, to tide over a passing trouble, well may justify a law that could not be upheld as a permanent change.

Machinery is provided to secure to the landlord a reasonable rent. It may be assumed that the interpretation of "reasonable" will deprive him in part at least of the power of profiting by the sudden influx of people to Washington caused by the needs of Government and the war, and, thus, of a right usually incident to fortunately situated property – of a part of the value of his property as defined in *International Harvester Co. v. Kentucky.* But while it is unjust to pursue such profits from a national misfortune with sweeping denunciations, the policy of restricting them has been embodied in taxation, and is accepted. It goes little if at all farther than the restriction put upon the rights of the owner of money by the more debatable usury laws. The preference given to the tenant in possession is an almost necessary incident of the policy, and is traditional in English law. If the tenant remained subject to the landlord's power to evict, the attempt to limit the landlord's demands would fail.   256 U.S., at 157–8 (citations omitted)

The following year, Congress reauthorized rent control in Washington, DC. The reauthorization led to more litigation, and the issue again made its way back to the Court, in the case *Chastleton Corp. v. Sinclair*, 264 U.S. 543 (1924). This time, the Court struck down the rent control law, unanimously. Again writing for the majority, Justice Holmes concluded that the decision in *Block* was the right one at the time but that conditions had changed so much in the intervening three years that the law was no longer justified. Justice Holmes wrote,

In our opinion, it is open to inquire whether the exigency still existed upon which the continued operation of the law depended. It is a matter of public knowledge that the government has considerably diminished its demand for employees that was one of the great causes of the sudden influx of people to Washington, and that other causes have lost at least much of their power. It is conceivable that…extensive activity in building has added to the ease of finding an abode. If about all that remains of war conditions is the increased cost of living, that is not, in itself, a justification of the Act   264 U.S, at 548

Certainly forces external to the Court were in part responsible for the change from the Court's decision in *Block* to its decision in *Chastleton*. Justice Holmes makes that evident in his opinion for the Court. However, there are a number of other changes internal to the Court that should be considered. The majority in *Block* comprised Justices Holmes, Brandeis, Clarke, Pitney, and Day. By the time the Court decided *Chastleton*, Justices Day, Clarke, and Pitney had all resigned from the Court. Notably, the two remaining justices from the *Block* majority, then, were Justices Holmes and Brandeis. Justice Holmes wrote the majority opinion in *Chastleton*, and Justice Brandeis wrote a lone concurrence. The three justices from the *Block* majority who left the Court before *Chastleton* were all replaced by justices who were more conservative than they on the Economics and Business and Balance of Power preference dimensions, moving the median of the Court further to the right on those two dimensions.

In addition, the way the justices mapped the dispute in *Chastleton* onto the ideological preference dimensions was markedly different than they did in *Block*. The opinions in *Block* map primarily onto the Judicial Power and Economics and Business preference dimensions. However, the *Chastleton* opinions map more heavily onto the Balance of Power preference dimension in addition to the Judicial Power and Economics and Business dimensions. That shift is consequential, because while the Court had moved to the right on Economics and Business during the intervening years, it had moved more dramatically to the right on Balance of Power. These shifts in the ideological orientation of the justices and the way in which they related the rent control statute to the preference dimensions help account for a fairly stark turnaround in the Court's evaluation of the Washington rent control statute.

At the same time, the post-war economic boom and the successive elections of Harding, Coolidge, and Hoover spelled the end for progressive regulatory efforts at the national level. However, the era witnessed a surge in Progressive economic regulation at the state level. Renstrom (2003, 132–45) provides a thorough overview of the cases in this area. That was particularly true in places where Progressives were politically powerful, such as the Midwest and parts of the Northeast. Thus, landmark cases involved economic regulations from places such as Nebraska, Kansas, and New York. In the *Wolff* case mentioned above, the Court invalidated a Kansas statute that sought to regulate wages in the food preparation industry, finding that the industry is not affected with a public interest. In *Jay Burns Baking Co. v. Bryan* (1924), the Supreme Court invalidated a statute that set a maximum weight for bread loaves. In *Weaver v. Palmer Brothers Co.* (1926), the Court invalidated a Pennsylvania statute that prohibited the use of "shoddy" in the production of quilts and bedding. Shoddy is "any material which has been spun into yarn, knit or woven into fabric, and subsequently cut up, torn up, broken up, or ground up" (*Weaver*, 270 U.S., at 409, quoting the Pennsylvania statute). The Court also invalidated a New Jersey statute regulating employment agency fees in *Ribnik v. McBride* (1928) and a Minnesota statute that regulated prices in industrial cream sales in *Fairmount Creamery Co. v. Minnesota* (1927). To be sure, the Taft Court did not strike down every state economic regulation it confronted, but the general thrust of the 1920s reflects the pro-business, conservative Republicanism that gripped the entire country.

Labor and the Rise of Socialism.   At the same time as the Court was undoing any support for economic regulation that followed World War I, developments at home and abroad in the world of labor were having complementary consequences. Conflict between organized labor and business became a major flash point for legal disputes, and the associated changing social-economic conditions served as a major force on the direction of constitutional law during the early twentieth century. Most immediately, the rise of organized labor shaped the Court's docket. Figure 6.11 shows the relationship between Socialist Party membership in each state in 1910 and the number of cases decided by the Supreme Court involving Economic Activity (Spaeth et al. 2015) between 1910 and 1930 arising out of each state. (Both variables have been logged.) As this figure shows, the larger Socialist Party membership in 1910, the larger the number of cases the Supreme Court decided involving Economic Activity coming out of that state over the next two decades. This suggests that local politics in each state – essentially, the influence of socialist ideology – shaped the kinds of legal and constitutional questions that emerged from the state and made their way to the Court.

Indeed, this pattern is a fairly robust one. Table 6.4 shows a series of regression models in which the dependent variable is the logged number of cases originating in each state during a specified period of time, and the explanatory variables are various metrics of the role of socialism in each state. I consider the number of Economic Activity cases during the entire period from 1910 through 1930 as well as just during the decade from 1920, and I consider the number of Socialist Party members in 1910, as well as the number of Socialist Party members in 1919. These data suggest that constitutional law during this period – especially law made involving cases that implicated Economic Activity – was being made in cases that came to the Court from states with larger contingents of the Socialist Party. Of course, voters participated in other parties as well, including

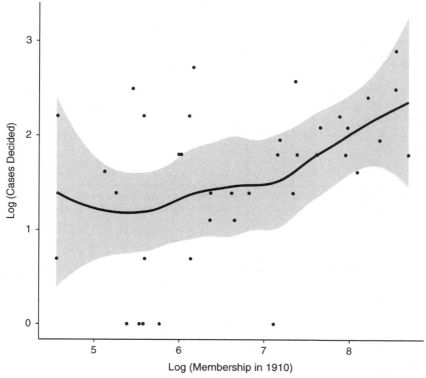

Figure 6.11. *Relationship between Socialist Party membership in each state in 1910 and the number of cases decided by the Supreme Court, arising out of that state, between 1910 and 1930.* Both variables are logged. Data on Supreme Court cases come from the Supreme Court Database. Data on Socialist Party membership come from multiple sources and have been compiled by James Gregory and Rebecca Flores.

single-issue parties. However, membership sizes of the Socialist Party is a close empirical proxy for those other interests as well.

What is more, the context from which disputes arise also shapes the preference dimension to which the Court maps the cases. Table 6.5 shows the results of a fixed effects regression model in which the dependent variable is each case's estimated loading onto the Balance of Power preference dimension. That is, the outcome variable captures the extent to which the Balance of Power preference dimension characterizes the voting cleavage in each case. The key explanatory variable is the metric of Socialist Party strength in each state, measured using either the 1910 or 1919 membership data. Each model includes fixed effects for the Issue Area to which a case is assigned in the Supreme Court Database, capturing the broad policy area implicated by the case. I also show the models

Table 6.4. *Relationship between state-level Socialist Party membership and the number of economic activity cases originating in the state.*

	1910–1930	1920–1930	1910–1930	1920–1930
Log (Membership 1910)	0.31 (0.10)	0.20 (0.10)		
Log (Membership 1919)			0.18 (0.08)	0.15 (0.07)
Intercept	−0.49 (0.70)	−0.59 (0.69)	0.40 (0.52)	−0.24 (0.46)
N	38	38	44	44
R^2	0.20	0.12	0.12	0.11
σ	0.74	0.69	0.81	0.68

Entries are linear regression coefficients with standard errors in parentheses. The dependent variable is the logged number of cases originating in each state during each period.

Table 6.5. *Relationship between Social Party Membership and case loading onto Balance of Power preference dimension.*

	(1)	(2)	(3)	(4)
Log (Membership 1910)	0.01 (0.003)	0.01 (0.003)		
Log (Membership 1919)			0.01 (0.002)	0.01 (0.002)
N	478	478	534	534
R^2	0.19	0.32	0.18	0.30
Issue Area Fixed Effects	✓	✓	✓	✓
Law Fixed Effects		✓		✓
σ	0.07	0.06	0.06	0.06

Coefficients are linear fixed-effects regression estimates, with standard errors in parentheses. The unit of analysis is the constitutional case decided by the Supreme Court, 1910–1930. The dependent variable is the loading of the case onto the Balance of Power preference dimension. Issue Area fixed effects indicate the Issue Area assigned to the case by the Supreme Court Database; Law fixed effects indicate the main law at stake in the case, according to the Supreme Court Database.

including fixed effects for the specific law considered by the Court. (I use the fine-grained "Legal Provision Supplement" variable, which associated each case with one of 206 possible values.) As above, because of missing data from 1910, we have more observations when we use the 1919 membership data.

The findings here are striking, as they indicate that, holding constant the policy and legal areas in which a dispute arises, the political context of the state from which the case comes is associated with variation in which preference cleavage describes the justices' voting patterns. In cases coming from states with a larger Socialist Party, places where the role of the state in regulating labor is more significant, the justices are more likely to decide the case in light of their preferences along the Balance of Power preference dimension. Moreover, there is no relationship between Socialist Party strength at the state level and the loading of a case onto the Economics and Business preference dimension. (There is a slight negative relationship in one specification and virtually zero relationship in all others.) In this way, electoral politics, at least partially responding to changing economic and social circumstances, influenced the content of constitutional law during these years.

What is more, the shifting of voting in these cases onto the Balance of Power preference dimension had particular consequences for the content of the law the Court made in its constitutional decisions. As we have seen, the courts struck a particularly anti-labor tone in their early cases involving unions. For example, in 1908, the Supreme Court decided *Loewe v. Lawlor*, 208 U.S. 274, in which it concluded that union-led boycotts that were part of strikes had the effect of restraining interstate commerce and were therefore illegal under the Sherman Antitrust Act. In response, Progressive Democrats enacted a number of protections for unions, most notably the Clayton Act of 1914. The Clayton Act provided express protections for unions by prohibiting courts from issuing injunctions against union strikes. However, after the triumph of Conservative Republicans in the 1920 election, the courts began to interpret the Clayton Act very narrowly. In 1921, the Supreme Court decided *Duplex Printing Co. v. Deering*, in which a six-justice majority concluded that the Clayton Act

assumes the normal objects of a labor organization to be legitimate, and declares that nothing in the antitrust laws shall be construed to forbid the existence and operation of such organizations or to forbid their members from lawfully carrying out their legitimate objects; and that such an organization shall not be held in itself – merely because of its existence and operation – to be an illegal combination or conspiracy in restraint of trade. But there is nothing in the section to exempt such an organization or its members from accountability where it or they depart from its normal and legitimate objects and engage in an actual combination or conspiracy in restraint of trade. And by no fair or permissible construction can it be taken as authorizing any activity otherwise unlawful, or enabling a normally lawful organization to become a cloak for an illegal combination or conspiracy in restraint of trade as defined by the antitrust laws.   254 U.S., at 469.

In other words, the justices in the majority interpreted the Clayton Act to only protect unions when they were engaged in activity that the courts would otherwise find lawful under the Sherman Antitrust Act. Notably, three of the Progressive justices – Brandeis, Holmes, and Clarke – issued a scathing dissenting opinion, written by Justice Brandeis, in which the justices accuse the majority of ignoring the circumstances that gave rise to the Clayton Act and the clear intent of the legislature that enacted it.

Of course, the broader context was complicated. The rising power of labor unions accompanied a growth in often violent conflict between labor and business. Organized labor was notoriously insular. The goal of most trade-specific unions was the protection of jobs, and union leaders often perceived immigrants as threats to their members. The pan-trade Industrial Workers of the World (IWW) was decidedly less xenophobic and had a global perspective on the labor movement (embodied in its lack of trade-specific membership). Many unions, including the IWW, led strikes that became increasingly large in scale and widespread. These strikes often turned violent – against both the strikers and the non-union workers (often recent immigrants) and corporations. Infamously, the coal miners' strike at the Glendale Gas and Coal Company in West Virginia in 1925 lead to the explosion of a house full of non-union miners. And, when it came time for the Supreme Court to decide how much legal protection to offer unions, the Taft Court typically favored business. It held that labor unions (both the local and national organizations) could be sued for property damage caused during strikes and protests,[11] and that injunctions could be issued against unions whose strikes and boycotts interfered with production by non-union workers[12] (Renstrom 2003).

To be sure, unions were not the only perpetrators of violence and mayhem during this era. The growth in size and power of corporate interests during the preceding decades made business very influential in many localities. One important case that represents the interesting intersection of political and legal issues the Court confronted during the 1920s is *United States v. Wheeler*, 254 U.S. 281 (1920). The case began with a labor strike at a mine in Arizona. The mining company's executives conspired with the local county sheriff to kidnap the strikers, who were then put on a train and dropped off in the desert in New Mexico and warned not to come back to their homes. Ultimately, President Woodrow Wilson intervened, and the Department of Justice brought an indictment against the mining company executives and officials who had committed the kidnapping. When the case reached the Supreme Court,

[11] *United Mine Workers v. Coronado Coal Co.* (1922).
[12] *Coronado Coal Co. v. United Mine Workers* (1925).

the justices held, by a vote of 8-1, that the Constitution prohibits the federal government from bringing charges against the kidnappers. The reasoning was that the Privileges and Immunities Clause of Article IV of the Constitution means that only states can enforce the privileges of citizenship, including the right to free travel. Citing *The Slaughter-House Cases*, Chief Justice White wrote for the Court,

It would be the vainest show of learning to attempt to prove by citations of authority that, up to the adoption of the recent amendments, no claim or pretence [*sic*] was set up that those rights depended on the federal government for their existence or protection, beyond the very few express limitations which the federal Constitution imposed upon the states, such, for instance, as the prohibition against *ex post facto* laws, bills of attainder, and laws impairing the obligation of contracts. But, with the exception of these and a few other restrictions, the entire domain of the privileges and immunities of citizens of the states, as above defined, lay within the constitutional and legislative power.

In an era of increasing tension over labor union rights, the Court was taking a very conservative stance on federalism, prohibiting the federal government from using its authority to protect those who might be the victim of mob rule (both at the hands of corporate interests opposed to unions and at the hands of unions, which were developing in strength and reach throughout society). Notably, the lone dissent in *Wheeler* came from Justice John Clarke, whom I estimate to be the most liberal justice on the Balance of Power preference dimension during the entire period studied in this book.

The *Wheeler* case certainly was neither the beginning nor the end of the Court's involvement in labor organization, and its opinion was not important for the constitutional principles it established. As noted, its logic is firmly rooted in *The Slaugher-House Cases* and the doctrine that underlie that case. However, what is important is that the decision came at a time and in a context where the substantive issues constitutional law would have to contend with were changing. The growth of the labor movement during the early twentieth century and the rising role of organized crime and mob rule meant that these issues, to the extent they were interpreted as matters of federalism, would not come immediately into the sphere of federal regulation. Importantly, because Progressives were more influential in state governments than at the national level, the conflicts between labor and business that gave rise to litigation typically arose out of disputes at the state level rather than the national level. That feature of American politics – an external contingent factor – facilitated, indeed encouraged, the justices' shift from the Economics and Business preference dimension to the Balance of Power preference dimension during the 1920s.

Women and Politics.   A third development taking place during the 1920s is also related to the role of labor. During Reconstruction, a number of previously marginalized political interests began to develop influence. One of the important developments taking place at the time was the women's suffrage movement. The push to secure the right to vote for women had begun well before the Civil War, and there were many important entanglements between the two movements through the mid-nineteenth century. Following the War, women pushed for the right to vote, and the passage of the Fifteenth Amendment, which precludes denial of the right to vote based on race, without a protection for women's right to vote exacerbated what had been a developing rift within the movement between those who were willing to back suffrage for black men before women got the right to vote and those who insisted that women's suffrage and black suffrage be tied together. Of course, the Fifteenth Amendment passed without providing women the right to vote, and the women's suffrage movement continued to grow in strength and expand its political strategies. One strategy was, in essence, civil disobedience, typified, perhaps, by Susan B. Anthony's conviction for voting as a woman. By the turn of the century, the rift in the movement had more-or-less resolved, and the movement began what would culminate in the Nineteenth Amendment, which was ratified by Tennessee in 1920, giving the Amendment the requisite 36 states' approval necessary to enter into force.

When the suffrage movement was working to secure the right to vote during the late nineteenth century, its leaders typically avoided engaging in politically divisive issues, such as prohibition, because they were aiming to build a broad coalition of support and wanted to make the issue about women's political rights, not specific policy issues. However, once women got the right to vote – in essence, once women became part of the electorate in some states, before the Nineteenth Amendment gave them the right to vote in all states – the Progressive Movement sought to push issues that would appeal to women voters. Chief among those issues were policies aimed at what were perceived to be social ills, such as gambling and alcohol. The Woman's Christian Temperance Union, for example, was founded at the tail-end of Reconstruction and linked temperance with Christianity, building a bridge between their political goals and the Christian movements that had fought for the abolition of slavery and gained political strength with the abolitionists' victory in the Civil War. In 1919, the Eighteenth Amendment was ratified, and beginning in 1920 alcohol was prohibited in the United States. At the same time, recall from above that the federal government had been enacting laws to strictly limit immigration, and both World War I and the Red Scare had engendered a degree of xenophobia in the United States, particularly towards Eastern Europeans.

What is more, the labor question increasingly implicated women. With the deteriorating working conditions engendered by the growth of large corporations, women began to enter the workforce, often to supplement their husbands' incomes. However, women were not immune from the dangerous and challenging workplaces that men confronted, as exemplified by infamous atrocities, such as the Triangle Shirtwaist Factory fire in New York in 1911. In that incident, a fire broke out in a garment factory and resulted in roughly 150 deaths of mostly young immigrant women who worked in the garment industry. In the aftermath of that incident, Progressives in New York were successful at achieving a number of policy victories, and the episode had the consequence of uniting issues of women and children's interests with labor protection. However, as noted above, labor interests were notoriously xenophobic and prejudiced, and the significant role that immigrants played in the women labor force complicated matters.

Economic Crash and Regulation. As the 1920s came to a close, the Republican administrations that had controlled the White House for the entire decade along with a Republican Congress and a Supreme Court that had been shaped by consequential appointments throughout the decade realized their policy objectives. Manufacturing and industrial production skyrocketed during the decade, at the same time as government spending was slashed and taxes were cut. The massive growth of the period led to financial speculation, and in 1929 the economy took a turn for the worse. On October 29, 1929, a day known as "Black Tuesday," panic that had been building for more than a month reached a fever pitch, and the ensuing crash, the greatest in American history, set off a ten-year economic downturn, known as the Great Depression.

When Franklin Roosevelt was elected president in 1932, following a landslide election for Democrats in the congressional mid-term election of 1930, he came into office having promised a massive legislative agenda known as the New Deal. FDR's first 100 days in office were marked by a flurry of legislative activity, much of it enacting regulatory and spending provisions aimed at curbing the economic disaster that had spread throughout the country. Two of the most important enactments during the spring 1933 were the Agricultural Adjustment Act (AAA) and the National Industry Recovery Act (NIRA). The former imposed quotas on agricultural production in order to raise crop market prices; the latter created the National Recovery Administration (as well as the

Public Works Administration), which set out to regulate the workplace, prominently banning child labor.

It was not long before the AAA and NIRA were challenged in the judiciary and made their way to the Supreme Court. In 1935, the Supreme Court decided *A.L.A. Schechter Poultry Corp. v. United States*, 295 U.S. 495 (1935), in which it invalidated the NIRA by a unanimous vote. The National Recovery Administration (NRA), created by NIRA, had been involved in negotiating conflicts between industries and labor, with the goal of stabilizing those industries and improving workplace conditions. The primary mechanism the NRA would use was to induce the local companies and unions to agree upon a code for the workplace, which would entail work hours, wages, and preferably a ban on child labor. The NRA would then give those codes the force of law. (The inducement was typically a threat that if the local organizations could not agree upon a code, then the NRA would impose one on them.) The Court held that the NIRA was invalid because it violated the Constitution's nondelegation doctrine by granting to the president authority that was legislative in nature. The Court also concluded that the regulations the NRA imposed were in excess of congressional authority to regulate interstate commerce, because the regulations were operating only at a local level. The Court thus identified a limit to what kinds of activities are part of the stream of interstate commerce. Importantly, the case maps primarily onto the Economics and Business and Balance of Power preference dimensions, and the opinion never mentions the substantive due process doctrine.

An important feature of the NIRA provides some insight into the interaction of the Court's internal forces – the justices' conservatism and its constitutional doctrine – with external forces – the organizational structure of the National Recovery Administration and the interests who brought it to court. As noted, the NRA worked piecemeal, establishing codes in localities one-at-a-time, working industry-by-industry. The reason behind this structure lies in part in the highly organized nature of the industries being regulated. As Skocpol and Finegold (1982, 260) demonstrate, organized industrialists were able to use their political connections and clout to secure for themselves "the relaxation of the antitrust laws and government sponsorship for industry-by-industry cooperation to coordinate prices and regulate production levels and conditions of employment." The highly organized interests, along with the complex implementation of the NIRA, sewed the seeds of discontent that would ultimately force the Court to confront FDR's recovery efforts as a matter of federalism and not just economic regulation.

The year following *Schechter*, the Court struck down the AAA in *United States v. Butler*, by a vote of 6-3. The opinion was written by

Justice Owen Roberts, who by the mid-1930s was the dominant median justice in essentially every case (recall Figure 6.7). The Court held the AAA unconstitutional because it provided farmers with subsidies that were coercive. The majority opinion observes,

> The power to confer or withhold unlimited benefits is the power to coerce or destroy. If the cotton grower elects not to accept the benefits, he will receive less for his crops; those who receive payments will be able to undersell him. The result may well be financial ruin. The coercive purpose and intent of the statute is not obscured by the fact that it has not been perfectly successful. It is pointed out that, because there still remained a minority whom the rental and benefit payments were insufficient to induce to surrender their independence of action, the Congress has gone further and, in the Bankhead Cotton Act, used the taxing power in a more directly minatory fashion to compel submission. This progression only serves more fully to expose the coercive purpose of the so-called tax imposed by the present act. It is clear that the Department of Agriculture has properly described the plan as one to keep a noncooperating minority in line. This is coercion by economic pressure. The asserted power of choice is illusory.
>
> 297 U. S., at 71.

In other words, the government's effort to control the agricultural crop market by inducing farmers to regulate their production was not the kind of regulation of interstate commerce that the Constitution could sanction. Crucially, as in *Schechter*, the Court did not resolve the case as a matter of substantive due process. Rather, the legal doctrine it relied upon concerns Article I and the Tenth Amendment. The votes and opinion in this case, moreover, map most strongly onto the Economics and Business and Balance of Power ideological preference dimensions. That the Court resolves this case along the Economics and Business preference dimension while explicitly declining to resolve a substantive due process claim (the Court rejects the invitation to answer the substantive due process question in footnote 8 of the majority opinion, and the dissent does not mention the issue) is instructive, as it illustrates a political transformation in the Court's approach to interstate commerce.

These cases, among others, exemplify an important development in constitutional law during the 1930s. The Court's approach to interstate commerce was increasingly involving Balance of Power. Recall Figure 6.10, which showed the distribution of the issue dimensions among economic cases. The main trend there is the rise of the Economics and Business dimension over the Judicial Power dimension. However, beginning around 1930, the Balance of Power preference dimension grows in its significance among these cases. This is largely driven by the economic regulations the federal government was pushing in the New Deal. The financial crisis had necessitated intervention into the economy on a scale that had not previously been recognized, and the government was undergoing a fundamental restructuring of the balance of powers between the national and state governments. This struggle is reflected in the Court's docket. This pattern is also evident, though less dramatically, in the other areas of the law.

At the same time as global economic conditions were shifting the kinds of regulatory activities in which the government was engaging, the Court was slow to catch up. In part, this was due to the justices who served on the Court. By the end of his first term in office, FDR had not had a chance to appoint a single justice; the Court was comprised of justices who were appointed in an era when the economic contingencies the country was facing could not have been anticipated. Progressive justices from the early twentieth century thought an expansive reading of the federal government's power entailed regulating monopolistic practices by industries that were affected with a public interest. They could not have imagined extensive regulating of local workplace conditions. Indeed, this was not a point lost on political contemporaries. In the year leading up to his reelection in 1936, in the wake of the Court's decisions in cases like *Schechter* and *Butler*, FDR began plans to stack the Court with new justices who would be more sensitive to the need for the federal government to regulate the economy.

The confrontation between the New Deal Democrats and conservatives on the Court has been well documented. It is one of the momentous events in the history of American separation of powers. Briefly, the Supreme Court's four most conservative justices – those to the right of Justice Roberts: Justices Butler, McReynolds, Sutherland, and Van Devanter – became known as the "Four Horsemen" for their opposition to progressive regulation of the economy. Of course, many of the Court's decisions, such as *Schechter*, were not particularly divided on the Court. After his reelection in 1936, FDR announced his "Court-packing Plan," which would have enabled FDR to appoint additional justices to the Supreme Court, giving him a solid majority. The plan was announced just before the Supreme Court handed down its decision in *West Coast Hotel v. Parrish*, which was a case about the constitutionality of Washington State's minimum wage law. The Supreme Court then announced its decision, upholding the minimum wage law by a vote of 5-4, reversing course from a decision just the prior year in which it decided, also by a 5-4 margin, against a New York State minimum wage law in *Morehead v. New York ex rel. Tipaldo* and overruling its decision from 1923 in *Adkins v. Children's Hospital*, in which it had invalidated a Washington, DC minimum wage law. Famously, Justice Roberts joined the majority, in a decision that went against what many anticipated would have been

Roberts' view on the case, given his vote the previous year in *Morehead*. His decision to vote with the four more liberal members of the Court was dubbed "the switch in time that saved nine."

Scores of studies have recounted the history of these events, some arguing that Roberts' vote was an example of pure politics, with Roberts looking to undermine political support for the Court-packing plan and save the Court's institutional integrity and legitimacy. Others have argued that the decision was actually perfectly predictable as a doctrinal matter and represents the culmination in what had been evolving substantive due process law around the "liberty to contract" and *Lochner*-era jurisprudence. Interestingly, the Court's opinion in *Morehead* maps predominantly onto the Balance of Power preference dimension, with the Economics and Business dimension as the second-most important dimension, and followed by Judicial Power and Individual and Civil Rights. In *West Coast Hotel*, by contrast, the Judicial Power and Business and Economics preference dimensions overtake the Balance of Power dimension as the most important preference dimensions. It is instructive Justice Roberts' estimated ideal point is considerably more liberal on the Economics and Business dimension than on the Balance of Power dimension. This suggests not necessarily that Roberts "switched" his vote but that the Court decided *West Coast Hotel* on a different preference dimension than the one along which it decided *Morehead*, and the consequence was that Justice Roberts found himself preferring a different resolution to the Economics and Business question than to the Balance of Power question.

We can illustrate this difference via the case-space model as in Figure 6.12. Here, I have arrayed the justices in each of the two cases according to the distribution of the preference dimensions in each case and the justices' ideal points in each of those dimensions. (Each justice's location in each case is a weighted average of his ideal point along each of the six dimensions, according to the case's distribution across the six dimensions.) As we can see, the justices line up roughly equivalently in each case, but their precise locations vary considerably as a function of the different representation of the topics between the two cases. The figure also illustrates the estimated location of each case, using the method described in Chapter 3.

What we see here is striking. The estimated locations for the two cases are essentially identical. However, the different loading onto the preference dimensions for the two cases put Justice Roberts to the right of *Morehead* and to the left of *West Coast Hotel*. Of course, the case locations are estimated from the voting data and so should be to the left of Roberts in *Morehead* and to the right in *West Coats Hotel*. However,

Morehead v. New York ex rel. Tipaldo

West Coast Hotel v. Parrish

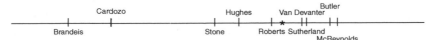

Figure 6.12. *Illustration of justices' ideal points and case locations in* Morehead *and* West Coast Hotel *cases.* The left ends of the dimensions represent more liberal positions; the right ends, more conservative positions. The tick marks indicate the justices' ideal points, and the asterisks indicate the case locations. Justice ideal points are a weighted average of their posterior ideal point estimates on all six of the ideological preference dimensions, according to the posterior estimates of the cases' loadings onto each of the preference dimensions.

that they are at virtually the same location in both cases and the justices are the ones who move around is driven by their different preferences on the different dimensions and the differential loading of the cases onto the dimensions. Of course, the justices choose, to some extent, how they will decide a case – whether they will conceive of the case as more a case that they map onto the Economics and Business dimension or more a case that they map onto the Balance of Power dimension. But, the instructive point is that the change from *Morehead* to *West Coast Hotel* does not seem to be a continuing evolution of the substantive due process doctrine, nor does it seem to be a disingenuous "switch" by Justice Roberts. Rather, it seems the Court interpreted the question of a state-imposed minimum wage differently in the two cases.

Why did the Court conceive of the cases differently? Was the different perspective driven by the litigants bringing the case? Or, did the justices consciously manipulate the frame for the case so as to reach the outcome they thought more prudent? Some history from the case is instructive. In the *Morehead* case, the state of New York argued that the case could be decided without revisiting the *Adkins* precedent from 1923 in which the Supreme Court invalidated the Washington, DC minimum wage law. The New York Court of Appeals (the highest court in New York) had interpreted the statute as an effort to regulate wages, which under the *Adkins* precedent constituted a violating of liberty of contract. Chambers (1969, 52) notes, "Roberts later said that the state's argument that it was unnecessary to overrule *Adkins* to uphold the New York law since the two cases were distinguishable seemed to him 'disingenuous and born of timidity.' He thought the two cases were quite similar."

However, when *West Coast Hotel* came to the Court that fall, Parrish's lawyers specifically asked the Court to overrule *Adkins*. Chambers (1969, 59) quotes Justice Roberts latter comment on why he voted to grant certiorari in *West Coast Hotel*, "in the appeal in the *Parrish* case the authority of *Adkins* was definitely assailed and the Court was asked to reconsider and overrule it. Thus, for the first time, I was confronted with the necessity of facing the soundness of the *Adkins* case." The lawyer for Parrish in the case argued that "the Constitution permitted reasonable regulation for the public welfare and that the statute was within the police power of the state when fixing a minimum wage for women hotel employees" (Chambers 1969, 60). Thus, the argument in favor of the minimum wage law specifically invoked the public welfare as a justification for regulating wages, which casts the question as a matter of federalism, where public welfare is a primary justification for regulation using police powers.

In other words, what transpired in the year between *Morehead* and *West Coast Hotel* was a fundamental transition in how economic regulation was construed from the perspective of the political dimensions of the law. In a maneuver of what Charles Cameron has dubbed "judicial heresthetics,"[13] the minimum wage question was pitched so as to divide the justices differently than it did when it was conceived of merely as a regulation of economic contracting. Whether the different framing of the question was driven by the litigants trying to strategically remake the issue or instead by Roberts seeking a legal frame that would enable him to vote to uphold the law is a matter of debate. However, what the analysis here illustrates is *why* and *how* a slight change from being about the liberty of contract to being about protecting public welfare could consequentially change the outcome in the case and lay the groundwork for a transition in how the Court would interpret New Deal economic regulation.

That transition would have long-run consequences, as we will see below. Moreover, it coincided with a significant period of transition on the Court. Shortly after the Court decided *West Coast Hotel*, Justice Van Devanter announced his retirement, and President Roosevelt finally had an opportunity to appoint a political ally to the Court. By the time he died, eight years later, Roosevelt would appoint a total of eight Supreme Court justices, with Justice Roberts the only justice remaining when FDR died

---

[13] There is no attribution for this term, but rather just a personal account of the coining of the phrase. Epstein and Shvetsova (2002) describe the notion of heresthetical maneuvering in a judicial setting.

who had been on the Court when he was first elected. The consequences were dramatic. As we see in Figure 6.7, Justice Roberts was rarely the pivotal justice after 1937, with that role being played by Justices Stone and Reed over the next few years. Moreover, Figure 6.8 shows that the Court moved dramatically to the left around Roberts, especially on the Balance of Power and Economics and Business preference dimensions. These new justices, in turn, began to turn their attention away from economic regulation and towards new issues that were being brought about by worldwide events, such as World War II and the rise of communism, to which we turn to in the next chapter.

6.3.3 Regulating the Individual

At the same time as the Court was moving from a laissez-faire doctrine of economic regulation at the turn of the century to a fundamental rethinking of the politics of federalism and the power of the central government, it was also being confronted with a new series of social questions that had not been previously part of its constitutional jurisprudence. One can see some of these effects in the increased presence of women and children in the workplace, which we discussed above. However, organized labor and the economic regulation questions that it brought into the national spotlight touched on a related social development of the time – the rise of socialism in Eastern Europe and within the United States. That development starkly shaped the path of substantive due process law, largely through the way legal and policy questions interact in the preference dimensions that characterize constitutional law.

Following the 1917 Bolshevik Revolution in Russia, the "Red Scare" gripped American politics, and the spread of socialist politics spread fear in the American political elite. That fear exacerbated a desire to control labor interests that was a component of the pro-business ideology of the conservative Progressives that dominated national politics during the 1920s. It also gave rise to a desire to control civic and political activities, such as speech and association, and inspired a wave of xenophobia that coincided with a period of increased immigration to the United States from Europe. In 1917, over a veto from President Wilson, Congress enacted the Immigration Act of 1917 (the Asiatic Barred Zone Act), which barred wide classes of immigrants from entering the country. Seven years later, Congress passed, and President Coolidge signed, the Immigration Act of 1924, which imposed very strict quotas on immigration from Eastern Europe and Africa and banned immigration of Asians and Arabs. These statutes created a political and legal climate of discrimination against foreigners, largely out of fear of the socialist political movements both in the United States and abroad. In addition, the Espionage Act of 1917 and the Sedition Act of 1918, enacted to protect against foreign threats during World War I, provided the legal foundation for clamping down on First Amendment rights.

Prior to World War I, there had not been much constitutional jurisprudence concerning civil liberties in general and the First Amendment in particular. However, the clamp down on free speech and other civil liberties that accompanied the labor-business dispute and the fear of socialism and violent revolt began to bring to the Court a series of questions about political freedom. Reflecting these developments in politics, the American Civil Liberties Union was founded in 1920. Much of the ACLU's early work was oriented around free speech, and some of the most prominent early legal cases in which it was involved were about censorship of labor groups. As noted above, the NAACP had been founded a decade earlier, and the two groups often had coinciding interests in civil rights cases, though their interests also conflicted, as in the ACLU's defense of communist groups or the Ku Klux Klan.

Like the Court's general-but-limited conservative doctrine on economic regulation, the Court during the 1920s was also mixed in how it interpreted civil liberties restrictions. Notable instances in this vein include *Gitlow v. New York* (1925), which held that First Amendment free speech rights are not unlimited and that the government could regulate dangerous speech but also began the process of "incorporating" the Bill of Rights. This was the first case in which the Supreme Court explicitly held that the First Amendment imposes restrictions on what the states (rather than only the federal government) can do. Of course, in *Gitlow*, the Court did find that the state could criminalize possession of subversive writings. In *Whitney v. California* (1927), the Court upheld the conviction of a woman for attending and participating in a Communist Party convention, where there was a call to overthrow the United States government. The Taft Court also upheld the federal government's decision to deny naturalization to a Hungarian woman on the grounds that she was a pacifist in *United States v. Schwimmer* (1929). In these, and related, cases, we see the Court developing the early lines of Individual and Civil Rights cases. At the same time, the Court decided cases like *Fiske v. Kansas* (1927), where it upheld a statute that criminalized the participation in radical groups but overturned the conviction of Fiske for trying to recruit members for the Industrial Workers of the World.

A clear trend was taking place. Cases that implicated basic civil liberties, those found in the First Amendment, were increasingly decided along an alternative preference dimension during this period. Consider Figure 6.13 which shows two related trends among First Amendment

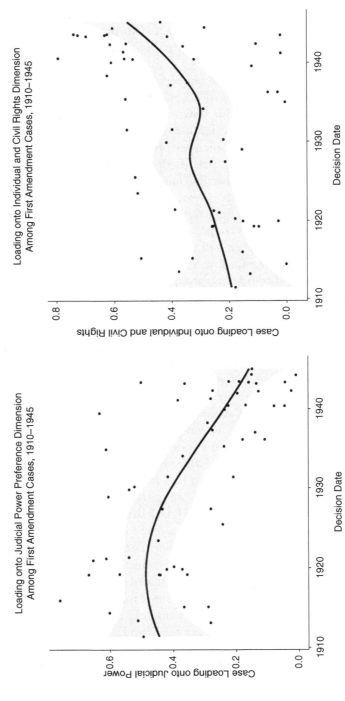

Figure 6.13. *Transition in the political cleavage activated by First Amendment cases, 1910–1945*. The figure shows the extent to which each First Amendment case was mapped onto the Judicial Power preference dimension (left panel) and the Individual and Civil Rights preference dimension (right panel).

cases. The left panel shows each First Amendment case decided between 1910 and 1945 and the extent to which I estimate it was decided along the Judicial Power preference dimension. The right panel shows the extent to which these cases were estimated to be decided along the Individual and Civil Rights preference dimension. As the figure illustrates, these cases were less and less likely to be decided along the Judicial Power preference dimension and increasingly likely to be decided along the Individual and Civil Rights preference dimension. In other words, during the first half of the twentieth century, the politics of constitutional decision making in cases involving First Amendment claims changed – the justices divided along an alternative cleavage.

This shift in the political framing of these cases was consequential. Between 1910 and 1945, the Supreme Court decided 57 cases in which more than half of the opinion loads onto either the Judicial Power or Individual and Civil Rights dimensions. The analytic historical approach allows me to construct a counter-factual scenario to examine how the Court's decision making might have been different. Among those 57 cases, I estimate that 26 would have been decided differently if the justices had not incorporated their preferences along the Individual and Civil Rights dimension.[14]

Notably, as we saw in Chapter 5, these cases did not yet constitute a particularly large proportion of the Court's docket, though many of the justices had particularly conservative views on these dimensions, and they were of great political salience at the time. The infamous Scopes Trial took place in Tennessee in 1925, in which John Scopes was accused of teaching evolution in a public school, in violation of a state law that banned teaching Darwinism. The Supreme Court's existing jurisprudence heavily influenced the way in which it mapped questions of civil liberties and social control onto the ideological preference dimensions. The *Gitlow* opinion, while clearly about First Amendment rights, is mostly about the Individual and Civil Rights preference dimension, though it has a heavy emphasis on Judicial Power, Crime and Punishment, and Balance of Power as well: the *Whitney* case even more so.

---

[14] Specifically, I simulate the vote on each case 1,000 times. I do this by drawing the justices' ideal points and the case parameters from the posterior distribution of the parameters. I then calculate the predicted outcome and then assume there is no weight on the Individual and Civil Rights dimension. I add estimated weight from that dimension to the Judicial Power dimension. For each case, I then calculate the total number of simulations that yield different outcomes under the two weightings. If more than 500 of the simulations yield different predicted outcomes, I code the case as being predicted as having a different outcome without the Individual and Civil Rights dimension.

The political desire to regulate the individual was not limited to activities that could be perceived as explicitly anti-government. One particularly notable example is *Meyer v. Nebraska* (1923). That case concerned a Nebraska statute enacted at the end of World War I that prohibited teaching foreign languages in schools – public, private, or otherwise. The Court invalidated that statute on due process grounds. However, as distinct from the freedom of speech cases in which the Court made the decision along the Individual and Civil Rights and Judicial Power dimensions as well as the Crime and Punishment and Balance of Power dimensions, this case was decided along the Individual and Civil Rights and Judicial Power dimensions alone. A closely related case in *Pierce v. Society of Sisters* (1925), which involved a statute passed in Oregon that mandated students attend public school. As in *Meyer*, the Court invalidated the statute on Fourteenth Amendment grounds. Writing for the unanimous Court, Justice McReynolds argued

Under the doctrine of Meyer v. Nebraska, 262 U. S. 390, we think it entirely plain that the Act of 1922 unreasonably interferes with the liberty of parents and guardians to direct the upbringing and education of children under their control: as often heretofore pointed out, rights guaranteed by the Constitution may not be abridged by legislation which has no reasonable relation to some purpose within the competency of the State. The fundamental theory of liberty upon which all governments in this Union repose excludes any general power of the State to standardize its children by forcing them to accept instruction from public teachers only. The child is not the mere creature of the State; those who nurture him and direct his destiny have the right, coupled with the high duty, to recognize and prepare him for additional obligations.   268 U. S., at 534–5.

Just like *Meyer*, *Pierce* was also decided along the Individual and Civil Rights preference dimension, but the Judicial Power and Business and Economics dimensions are also important in this case. The Economics and Business preference dimension is important in particular because the Court's decision invokes the substantive due process doctrine, specifically as the Court had interpreted that doctrine in *Meyer*.

What the Court is doing in these opinions is important. It is turning the doctrine of substantive due process into a doctrine that recognized not just the protecting of property but of a more nuanced, personal kind of freedom. Substantive due process is being turned from a doctrine developed in the time of industrialization in order to protect private property and capital from regulation into a doctrine that protects individual freedom from regulation. *As the Court is facing new questions about substantive due process, those cases are activating a new preference dimension, and the justices are importing existing doctrine from the Economics and Business preference dimension to establish the law that it applies in this new political context.* It is not necessarily the case that the Taft Court is composed of a group of socially liberal justices. Justice McReynolds, the author of *Pierce*, was a notorious antisemite and would later be a member of the Four Horsemen opposing the New Deal. However, the existing dominant jurisprudence of the time, the legal machinery the Court had to resolve constitutional questions, was all they had to apply to the new social issues arising in the 1920s. Fervor to regulate society in light of the expanding role of women in the economy and politics, the xenophobia that labor disputes and World War I brought about, and increasing concern with social ills meant that the Court confronted types of regulation that had not been contemplated when the substantive due process doctrine had been developed.

Renstrom (2003, 151-55) points out a useful contrast between the decisions in *Meyer* and *Pierce* and the Court's decision in *Buck v. Bell* (1927), which upheld, over a Fourteenth Amendment objection, a Virginia statute that allowed forced sterilization of "persons affected with hereditary insanity, idiocy, imbecility, feeblemindedness, or epilepsy." Part of the rationale for upholding the statute, offered in Justice Holmes' majority opinion, was that the public interest often demands individuals make sacrifices. Holmes wrote,

We have seen more than once that the public welfare may call upon the best citizens for their lives. It would be strange if it could not call upon those who already sap the strength of the State for these lesser sacrifices, often not felt to be such by those concerned, in order to prevent our being swamped with incompetence. It is better for all the world if, instead of waiting to execute degenerate offspring for crime or to let them starve for their imbecility, society can prevent those who are manifestly unfit from continuing their kind. The principle that sustains compulsory vaccination is broad enough to cover cutting the Fallopian tubes. Three generations of imbeciles are enough.[15]

Holmes' reference to sacrifice being required by the public interest is a direct reference to the draft during World War I. However, it is also an indirect reference to the justification for regulation of industries before and during World War I in the name of the public interest, which we saw above. Here, then, we see the Court finding a limit to the protection offered by substantive due process, and we see in that limit direct evidence of the effects of external social factors, such as trust-busting anti-monopoly regulation and the nationalism that swept the nation during World War I.[16]

---

[15] 274 U. S., at 207 (1927) (citations omitted).
[16] Other examples of the effects of the Court's rightward turn on the Balance of Power and Economics and Business dimensions, in particular, can be seen in the Court's incorporation of the Bill of Rights. We already saw above that the Court began the process of incorporating the Bill of Rights, with its decision in *Gitlow*. Indeed,

In my simulation of predicted outcomes, I do not predict the Court would have ruled differently in *Meyer* or *Pierce*, but I do predict a different outcome in *Buck v. Bell*. That the analysis here suggests the first two cases' outcomes do not depend on the presence of the Individual and Civil Rights dimension, whereas the third case's outcome does helps us understand how the path of constitutional law evolved during this era. The justices' relatively stronger views of the courts' power was tempered in *Buck v. Bell* by their conservative views on Individual and Civil Rights. In contrast, the justices' conservatism with respect to individual rights may have tempered their views in the other cases but not enough to sway the outcomes. The upshot is that the systematic differences in the justices' views across these two preference dimensions helps explain why these cases, which presented different questions but activated similar political cleavages, led to different outcomes and what kinds of social and political context might have been able to alter the course of jurisprudence about individual liberty during the early to mid-twentieth century.

Further, whereas the justices were more receptive to liberal interpretations of substantive due process in the context of First Amendment claims, their particular conservatism did not create the conditions for a much more expansive use of incorporation. In particular, as we saw above, crime was a particularly salient political and social issue during the 1920s, and when the Court was confronted with cases involving criminal defendants' rights, the justices' marked conservatism on Crime and Punishment set up consequential limitations on how far incorporation would go under the Taft Court. As Renstrom (2003, 169) observes, the White Court had been somewhat more progressive on issues of criminal defendants' rights. However, as we saw in Figure 6.8, the Court shifted sharply to the right on Crime and Punishment during the first few years of the Taft Court, and the consequences can be seen in how the Court dealt with those White Court precedents.

---

freedom of speech was a subject of important political and social interest during the 1920s. By the 1930s, the Supreme Court began to invalidate some of the restrictive laws and practices that had taken root during the era of morality politics and the Red Scare. The Supreme Court ruled in favor or free speech claims by organized labor who were being blocked from holding public meetings and disseminating allegedly communist literature (*Hague v. Committee for Industrial Organization*, 307 U.S. 496 (1939)) and by communist groups who were prosecuted for flying and saluting red flags (*Stromberg v. California*, 283 U.S. 359 (1931)). Both of these cases rest on claims that substantive due process protects the right to engage in political speech. Moreover, they represent a shift in how substantive due process is used in constitutional law, away from protecting property and economic liberty towards protection of political and civil liberty.

Cases came to the Court regularly during the 1920s involving search and seizure relating to Prohibition. It was in this context that a sharply divided Court decided *Olmstead v. United States* (1928) in which it concluded that wiretapping (in this case, of a bootlegger's phone lines) did not constitute either a search or a seizure and so does not require a warrant. I estimate this case was decided primarily along the Crime and Punishment preference dimension. As distinct from the other civil liberties cases, such as *Meyer,* this case is mostly about Crime and Punishment and not particularly about any other dimension except Judicial Power. The different perspective the justices brought to this case from other civil liberties cases implicated a different set of ideological preferences. And, the justices, who were relatively less polarized at the time than they were on the Individual and Civil Rights preference dimension, split in a curiously divided vote of 5-4, in which each of the dissenting justices wrote his own opinion. Justices Brandeis and Holmes, predictably liberal on Crime and Punishment, wrote dissenting opinions (Holmes' opinion concurred in part with the majority). Holmes argued that the Fourth Amendment might not apply in this particular case but that the government's wiretapping was illegal and so the evidence should not be available as evidence at trial. Brandeis adopted a more hard-line approach, arguing that the Fourth Amendment should apply to wiretapping and claiming that the government's illegal actions undermine its credibility in law enforcement. The other dissenting justices – Stone and Butler – were actually far more conservative on Crime and Punishment, which is part of why the Court demonstrated such low polarization during the era. Justice Butler also wrote that the wiretapping constituted a search but declined to say whether the exclusionary rule – that principle the evidence may not be used as evidence at trial – should apply, claiming that question was not one the Court was asked to resolve. Justice Stone, finally, wrote a very brief opinion saying he concurred with all of the dissenting opinions insofar as they find that the wiretapping was a search and commenting that the Court should be able to address the exclusionary question directly. Of course, *Olmstead* was a case against the federal government and so did not implicate incorporation. But, it was part of a long string of decisions in which the Court held the line on a rather conservative perspective on the limitation on government authority against suspected criminals.

The trajectory of the Court's constitutional decision making in these cases reveals an important development in substantive due process law in particular and constitutional law more generally. During the nineteenth century, and for at least the first decade or so of the twentieth century, constitutional law was primarily concerned with negotiating the balance of power between the state and federal governments and with distinguishing what kinds of economic activity were of a national, rather than a local, character. The conservative politics that dominated the Court shaped substantive due process law into a mechanism for protecting individuals from economic regulation, but by the 1920s and 1930s, changing circumstances in the world had led the government – at all levels – to regulate individual behavior more and more, which brought about new challenges to restrictions on civil liberties. The substantive due process doctrine laid the groundwork for those legal challenges. However, while structural factors may have been in place, there were important contingencies that influenced the path of civil liberties law. The justices on the Supreme Court were of a different time, when restrictions on political and individual freedoms were widely accepted as part of the state's police powers. Anxiety about communism and labor unrest further exacerbated the perceived propriety of those restrictions. Thus, the Court's expropriation of substantive due process from the economic to the individual settings was achieved through an interaction of (1) existing legal structures, (2) the particular perspectives of the Court in the 1920s and 1930s on issues of Individual and Civil Rights, and (3) social conditions that gave rise to efforts to restrain political speech. However, by the 1930s, political anxiety had shifted towards the economy, and the Court began to establish precedents protecting free speech which would later lead to a fuller expansion of civil liberties protections. Seen this way, the revival of substantive due process as a means of protecting individual and political freedom can be understood as a product of forces internal and external to the Court as well as of structural factors and specific contingencies that all coincided.

6.3.4 *Internal and External Forces, Structure, and Contingency*

The period between the World Wars was one of dramatic change in American constitutional law. That change was driven by factors both internal and external to the judiciary. The wartime economy ushered in an era of regulation of the economy that was unfathomable beforehand. In an era where the social ills associated with the unified and industrialized economy, the rise of large corporations and institutions such as middle management, and the quickly changing demographics of the electorate and the workforce interacted with a constitutional doctrine of laissez-faire that disfavored regulation by the federal government and strong conservative political victories. The result was an incomplete progressive makeover of the Court and, as a consequence, a sustained pro-business constitutional doctrine. Substantive due process, during these years, continued to control economic regulation by and large. Industrial interests were well-organized and so could influence legislation. And, when states or the national government did attempt to regulate commerce, the Court generally adopted a standard that was pro-business by presumption. Thus, major developments in the national economy acted as external forces on the Court's due process doctrine and interacted with the particular circumstances of electoral politics as during the 1920s.

At the same time, the country began to confront new political concerns related to the global rise of organized labor interests. Socialism was taking root as a political movement in Eastern Europe and, to a lesser extent, the United States. The result was a degree of social regulation that the substantive due process doctrine was ripe to handle. Increasing efforts to constrain political speech forced the Court to resolve whether the liberty protected under its due process doctrine could incorporate civil liberties enshrined in the Bill of Rights, and the conservative courts of the 1920s and 1930s began to acknowledge some such incorporation, though to a very limited extent. The Court's doctrine thus interacted with a shifting set of problems that implicated different preference dimensions than had the cases that originally established that doctrine. In this way, contingencies, such as the substantive content of the cases coming before the Court, interacted with structural factors, such as the existing legal framework for evaluating liberty claims, and specific forces internal to the Court, such as the ideological preference dimensions that characterize constitutional decision making.

What we see taking place during the 1920s is a growth in the role of labor in national and local politics, which accompanied a broader political and social leftist movement that was causing great fear at home. To the extent these two issues were socially, legally, and politically linked to each other, the Court was able to apply the standards of due process that it developed to protect business to define the early cases involving civil liberties. These cases were cast by the Court as matters of Crime and Punishment, implicating federalism. During the 1920s, the Court similarly saw cases involving organized labor as issues of Crime and Punishment and federalism. The distinction was that the free speech cases also implicated the First Amendment, whereas the organized labor cases implicated the Commerce Clause. But their common links onto the Balance of Power and Crime and Punishment preference dimensions engendered a rather coherent ideological perspective on two otherwise disconnected legal questions. Those social processes therefore implicated the different ideological preference dimensions on the Court when issues of labor and free speech made their way to the Court differently than they would have had the cases come to the Court before World War I and the rise of labor and socialism. The Court handled these cases, as a consequence, differently than it might have otherwise. The foundations of American civil liberties constitutional law, therefore, can only be understood in light of the social and political context that characterized the wise set of issues the Court confronted in the 1920s.

Those joint influences shaped the way the Court handled a number of important developments in constitutional law. The Court during the first half of the twentieth century did not approach these new political and legal challenges by reverting to the standard approach of resolving disputes by reference to their preferences about the scope of judicial power. Neither did they simply apply nineteenth century pro-industry conservatism that was characterized by the Economics and Business preference dimension. Rather, the justices began to differentiate legal problems along competing ideological preference dimensions, largely as a function of the social context from which the new cases arose.

Consider substantive due process – a legal doctrine that developed during the nineteenth century and became synonymous with pro-business Republican courts during the early twentieth century. The doctrine is frequently most directly attributed to the Court's *Dred Scott* decision, but it actually first developed earlier in the mid-nineteenth century "in part to protect the rights of property owners" (Ely Jr. 1999, 319). In essence, the doctrine gives a substantive interpretation to the due process clauses of the Fifth and Fourteenth Amendments, rather than a purely procedural one. Substantive due process was the line of argument the Court invoked to invalidate the limitation on baker's hours in *Lochner v. New York*, where it held that statutes limiting the number of hours a baker could work violated the workers' right to contract. In the 1920s, the Taft Court's interpretation of the cases brought to it about the labor dispute and about social issues involving cultural assimilation and xenophobia was often filtered through the orientation the Court had developed in that earlier era. By the end of the 1930s, though, this transformation was virtually complete. The preference dimensions that characterized the justices voting were much more varied. While the Judicial Power preference dimension still characterized much of the justices' voting, competing preference dimensions were playing a much more significant role. *The Court, in essence, was becoming a more explicitly political institution.* The way justices evaluated legal questions was becoming more complex, and more predictable in light of the substantive policy issues implicated by its cases.

In fact, over the period from 1877 through 1945, we see that the substantive policy content of the dispute in a case becomes more predictive of the distribution of preference dimensions that characterize

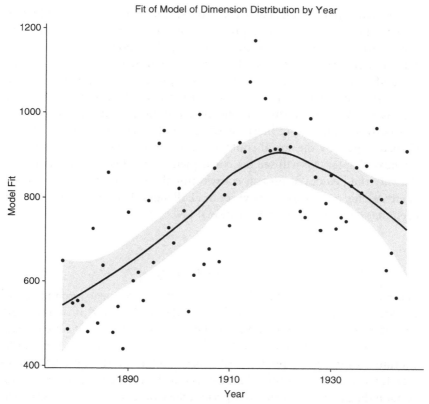

Figure 6.14. *Fit of policy issues to mix of preference dimensions in constitutional cases, 1877–1945.* The figure plots the fit of a Dirichlet regression model of the Supreme Court's constitutional cases, fit separately to each year. The outcome variable is the distribution of the six preference dimensions in each case, and the explanatory variables are 13 dummy variables for the Issue Area assigned to each case in the Supreme Court Database. The figure shows the fit of that model for each year.

the justices' voting in a given case. Consider Figure 6.14. Here, I estimate a Dirichlet regression model in which the dependent variable is the estimated loading of a case onto each preference dimension. Specifically, it is a multivariate model in which for each case there are six dependent variables – the loading onto each of the preference dimensions. The independent variables are just fixed effects for the Issue Area assigned to each case in the Supreme Court Database. I estimate the model separately for each year. In the figure, I show the fit of the fixed effects model for each year, as measured by the log-likelihood. I reverse the values so that values to the right indicate a better fit.

The pattern is immediate. Over time, the policy area in which a case arises becomes a better predictor of which preference dimension characterizes the justices' voting. That is, the voting cleavage that is activated in a case is increasingly well predicted by what the policy issue at hand is. By the end of the era here, the justices' voting is much more *political* than it was in the aftermath of the Civil War. As we have seen, the justices went from dividing mostly along lines about the role of the courts to dividing along lines associated with substantive policy issues, shaped in part by the social context that creates constitutional issues. In the next chapter, we will see the consequences for this transformation in the way the justices approach constitutional decision making when the Court begins to confront a new set of challenges that had not previously been matters of national constitutional law.

6.4   CONCLUSION

In the wake of the Civil War, the Supreme Court's role in governance grew significantly, and it became much more deeply involved in developing constitutional law. The period from the Civil War through the New Deal can be divided into two eras. The first is the period where the Court continues to interpret questions of constitutional interpretation through a preference dimension best characterized as involving the justices' views about judicial power. During this period, the Court is working to establish the meaning of the Civil War Amendments, especially the Fourteenth Amendment's due process and equal protection guarantees.

The analytic history in this chapter establishes a number of patterns. First, the social and political context out of which cases arose between the Civil War and World War II had direct, consequential effects on the way the justices evaluated cases, resolved disputes, and crafted law. We have seen that external politics shaped not just the kinds of cases the Court resolved – the docket – but also the way that disputes were related to the underlying preference dimensions. Second, the politics of judicial turnover have important consequences for the path of constitutional law. As justices depart the Court and are replaced by new ones, the Court's preferences shift differently across the different preference dimensions. Appointments to the Court during the late nineteenth century moved the Court to the right on the Economics and Business preference dimension, but had little effect on the other preference dimensions. The consequence was a conservative shift in the Court's decisions. Later, when FDR was able to make a series of appointments to the Court following the New Deal, the Court moved sharply to the left, as did its decisions.

At the same time as these transformations were taking place, the Court was beginning to confront a new brand of constitutional questions. Linked in many ways to the business-labor conflict, the country was undergoing a period of hostility to civil liberties, especially in the context of political speech by socialists. These new conflicts activated a distinct preference dimension among the justices. First Amendment claims went from dividing the justices along the traditional "Judicial Power" preference dimension to being decided along the "Individual and Civil Rights" preference dimension. At the same time, they still relied on existing doctrinal structures, specifically the substantive due process clauses of the Fifth and Fourteenth Amendments. In this way, then, the evolving social and political context from which cases arose and came to the Court illustrates the path of substantive due process law.

Crucially, what each of the areas of constitutional decision making studied here reveals is that over the period from Reconstruction through the end of World War II, the Supreme Court was beginning to differentiate constitutional questions along ideological preference dimensions. In one sense, the justices were becoming more political, in that the substantive policy questions at hand in a case became more predictive of the voting cleavage. On the other hand, what was transpiring was, at least in part, a move from the justices reflexively evaluating the Court's authority and the limits of its power in matters of constitutional interpretation to instead evaluating the substantive merits of constitutional questions. This alternative way of deciding cases necessarily invoked more, varied dimensions of political preferences than did a simpler prism through which the justices saw virtually all cases.

The data and analysis presented in this chapter, then, illustrates how forces both internal and external to the judiciary shape the path of constitutional law. Moreover, they show how macropatterns in constitutional decision making can be understood in light of microtheories of the judicial process. The decision by the Court to take particular cases for resolution is shaped by the broader social and political context from which legal questions arise. The way in which the justices evaluate a case – the preference cleavages that a dispute activates – is also shaped by that context. At the same time, internal politics and particular contingencies – such as the individuals who serve on the Court at a given point in time – shape the kinds of decisions the Court makes and the path that law follows. We might ask ourselves, as I do in Chapter 8, how today's constitutional law might be different if strategic litigators in the 1930s had not successfully shifted the justices away from voting along the Economics and Business preference dimension to voting along the Balance of Power preference dimension. How might the law have evolved differently if progressives had been more successful at the national level during the 1920s? These are questions that push us to think about counter-factuals that are difficult to imagine. However, an analytic approach to the history of constitutional decision making provides some of the foundation we need to move in that direction.

7

War, Security, and Culture Clash

Following World War II, constitutional law in the United States began to evolve along a path that, in hindsight, might have been somewhat predictable. Though, certainly, there is a great deal of nuance and many developments that were driven by particular events that might now have been foreseen. In this chapter, I continue the analytic history of constitutional law by examining the aggregate patterns in constitutional decision making and their relationships to specific microprocesses taking place both within and outside of the Court. The war's aftermath created a sense of racial tension (among others) in the United States, which gave rise to a number of social problems that influenced the justices' constitutional decision making. The cultural revolution of the 1960s similarly brought the justices and constitutional law into the fray of deeply divisive political issues. The conservative counterrevolution of the 1980s shaped the way constitutional decision making would play out for the remainder of the century.

Those major events, while a broad-brush picture of the details that follow, shaped both *who* served on the Court as well as *what* kinds of questions, and by implication what kinds of ideological preference dimensions, would characterize constitutional decision making for most of the twentieth century. We can see this most easily if we simply examine the composition of the Court's docket since the New Deal. Figure 7.1 shows the distribution of topics on the Court's docket from 1935 through 2012, as measured by the mean proportion of each of the preference dimensions across all cases each term. At least two patterns stand out at first glance. Most dramatic, the Court's docket is activating a mix of preference dimensions at the end of the period that is distinct from the mix of preference dimensions at the beginning of this period. Relative to the transition from Reconstruction through the New Deal, as we saw in Chapter 6, the change in this period is far more dramatic. Second,

Share of the Court's Docket for
Each of the Six Preference Dimensions

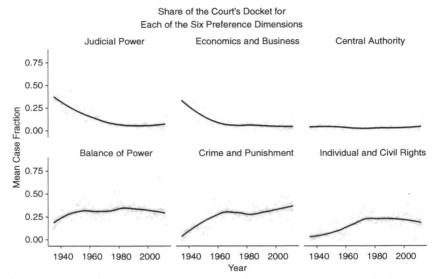

Figure 7.1. *Representation of each of the six preference dimensions among the Supreme Court's constitutional decisions, 1935–2006.* The figure shows, for each year between 1935 and 2012, the average assignment probability among all cases for each of the six preference dimensions.

as contrasted with earlier periods, the Court's cases implicate a greater variety of preference dimensions. Cases involving Crime and Punishment, Balance of Power, and Individual and Political Rights comprise most of the docket. The sharp transition away from deciding cases that implicate the Business and Economics preference dimension is a pattern that has been previously documented. Notably, the Supreme Court went more than half a decade without invalidating a federal law based on the Commerce Clause of the Constitution.

Of course, these empirical patterns only beg the question – where do they come from? Are they exogenously driven by social-political-economic forces? Are they strategically crafted by goal-oriented litigants seeking to use the courts to shape public policy? Are the justices manipulating their cases to act on the preference dimensions they prefer to vote along? Possibly predictably, the answer is that all three of these forces are driving the Court's docket. A handful of microtheories of the judicial process help illuminate certain examples, as we see below, whereas the large macropattern – the Court's shift from arbitrating questions of economic regulation and judicial power to one oriented around criminal law, civil liberties, and civil rights – is itself a force that influences the way in which individual decisions play out.

Finally, the patterns in Figure 7.1 suggest a partitioning of the period into two eras. Through the 1940s and 1950s, we find a period during which the prominence of the Business and Economics and Judicial Power preference dimensions declined, while the docket came to reflect the other preference dimensions to a greater degree than it ever had before. This is in many ways a period of transition on the Court. During the 1960s and 1970s, we see the Court allocating increasing proportions of its docket on cases involving the Crime and Punishment and Individual and Civil Rights preference dimensions. This is an era of cultural revolution and social strife. Finally, since the 1980s, the Court's docket has witnessed a slight increase in the prominence of the Balance of Power preference dimension and a notable increase in the prominence of the Crime and Punishment preference dimension. In the most recent years, the other preference dimensions have been especially marginalized on the Court's docket. Somewhat reminiscent of the late nineteenth century, the late twentieth century is an era of a conservative revolution and has seen a period of constitutional decision making that is mapping changing policy questions onto a stable set of preference dimensions.

In each of the next three sections, I examine these three eras in greater detail. I demonstrate how the mix of case topics interacts with the Court's internal politics to shape how concentrated or diffused power is among the justices. I also demonstrate how the cases coming to the Court reflect developments in society and politics outside of the Court. I show these patterns both in the aggregate but also through an examination of illustrative doctrinal developments and notable Court decisions through the years. In the first of these sections, I examine the period from 1935 through 1953, which is characterized by a fundamental change in the Court's approach to federalism. During these years, the notion of dual federalism was eroded in constitutional law, as the federal government's role expanded into areas of regulation and policy making previously dominated by the states. In the Court's constitutional law, we see this pattern in particular in three areas – civil rights, civil liberties, and criminal law. In the next section, I examine the 1960s and 1970s, which are a period of cultural revolution. This period is characterized by cases that come to the Court in a context of social strife and deep conflict over societal norms and expectations. In the third section, I consider the period from the 1980s through the early 2000s, during which the Court's docket was shaped by a conservative counterrevolution and culture war. As we will see, this period witnessed a return of the states' power in constitutional law and a growing involvement of constitutional law in social policy and regulation.

7.1   THE END OF DUAL FEDERALISM: CIVIL RIGHTS,
       CIVIL LIBERTIES, AND CRIME

By the end of the 1930s, it was clear that the Supreme Court was aligned with Democratic majorities in the elected branches of government concerning the power of the federal government in economic regulation. If the Court's about-face in *West Coast Hotel* was not a strong enough signal of the Court's Commerce Clause views, by the early 1940s, the justices made it crystal clear. In *Wickard* v. *Filburn*, the Court considered a federal law that imposed limits on how much wheat a farmer could grow. The US had just entered World War II when this case came to the justices, and the way they resolved the case was reminiscent of the nationalization of the economy during World War I. Filburn was a farmer who had been growing wheat for his own personal use on his farm; he challenged the limits imposed by the Agricultural Adjustment Act as overreaching congressional authority, because the wheat he was growing was, in his view, entirely divorced from interstate commerce. However, the justices concluded that because every bit of wheat he was growing would be wheat he might have to buy otherwise, potentially through interstate commerce, his growing of wheat did in fact affect interstate commerce. This holding surely would not have been possible without the doctrinal moves the Court made during the 1930s.

At the same time, not only had the Court's legal doctrine shifted during the New Deal, Franklin Roosevelt's eight appointments to the Court fundamentally changed the political conditions within the Court. Though, as we might expect, Roosevelt's appointments had differential effects across the various ideological cleavages, and the changes be brought about on the Court were most profound along the political cleavages about which his policy agenda was most concerned. The top panel in Figure 7.2 shows the estimated conservatism of the median justice in the Court in each of the six preference dimensions, from 1935 through 1953 – covering most of the Hughes Court, as well as the Stone and Vinson Courts.

During the late-1930s and early-1940s, the Court median moved sharply to the left in the Judicial Power, Business and Economics, Central Authority, and Balance of Power preference dimensions. At the same time, though, there was little change in the median's location in the Crime and Punishment and Individual and Civil Rights preference dimensions. Moreover, as we see in the bottom panel of Figure 7.2, in these dimensions, polarization also decreased during these years. The consequence was a Court that was more liberal, and more uniformly so, by the mid-1940s, than it was a decade earlier, at least along four of the ideological preference dimensions.

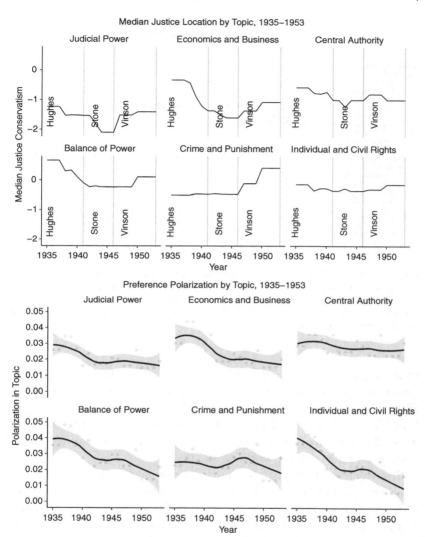

Figure 7.2. *Location of the median justice and ideological polarization among the justices in each of the six dimensions, 1935 through 1953.* Polarization is calculated using the method developed by Esteban and Ray (1994) and applied by Clark (2009a) to the Supreme Court.

As we have seen before, these kinds of changes to the composition of the Court can alter the internal politics in consequential ways. Consider Figure 7.3, which shows the justice I estimate to have been the median in each case between 1935 and 1953. During the early part of this period, the pivotal median role was served by only one or two justices at any given point in time. However, as the Roosevelt appointments brought the Court into a more homogenously liberal orientation, the median role depended

**Median Justices in Constitutional
Law Cases, 1935–1953**

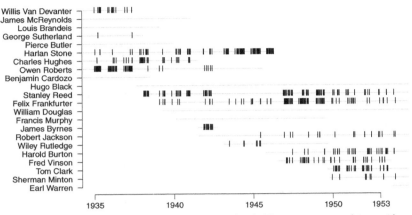

Figure 7.3. *Median justices in constitutional cases decided between 1935 and 1953.* Along the y-axis are the justices who served during the period, organized by the start date of their service (first justices at the top). The x-axis measures time. The grey horizontal lines show the dates during which each justice served. The tick marks indicate individual cases and who was the estimated median justice for that case.

increasingly on the particular mixture of preference dimensions the case activated. The consequence is that whereas for most of the 1940s, Justice Stone was most usually the pivotal median justice, by the early 1950s, Chief Justice Vinson, and Justices Reed, Frankfurter, Burton, and Clark were all potentially pivotal, depending on the relative mix of ideological preference dimensions at work in the case.

To evaluate which justices tend to be the median in which cases, I estimate a multinomial regression model in which the dependent variable is the identity of the median justice. During the period from 1935 through 1953, 13 justices served as the median justice, according to my estimates, in at least one case. Thus, the dependent variable for this empirical model is a categorical, multinomial distribution across those 13 justices for each case. The explanatory variables are the loadings for each case onto each of the six preference dimensions. Formally, let M be the set of 13 justices who served as the median in at least one case between 1935, Y_i indicate the median justice in case i, and λ_i be a vector giving case i's loading onto each of the six ideological preference dimensions. The model I estimate is given by

$$\Pr(Y_i = m) = \frac{\exp\left(f_m\left(\lambda_i\right)\right)}{1 + \sum_{j=2}^{M} \exp\left(f_j\left(\lambda_i\right)\right)} \tag{7.1}$$

where $f_m(\lambda_i) = \beta_{m0} + \beta_{m1}\lambda_{1i} + \beta_{m2}\lambda_{2i} + \cdots + \beta_{m6}\lambda_{6i}$. The result, then, is an estimate of seven coefficients for each justice – the relationship between the loading onto each of the six preference dimensions and the probability of being the median justice, for each of the justices, plus an intercept. The identifying assumption is that there is a baseline median for whom all of the coefficients equal zero. We can interpret the results as metrics of the association between a justice's likelihood of being the estimated median in a case and the extent to which the case maps onto the given preference dimension. I summarize these estimates in Figure 7.4. Here, I show, for each preference dimension, the estimated coefficient, along with a 95% confidence interval, for each justice.

Consider, as an example, Justice Burton, who is shown in the top rows in the panels in Figure 7.4. The more a case loads onto the Balance of Power or Individual and Civil Rights preference dimensions, the more likely he is to be the median justice; however, the more a case loads onto the Crime and Punishment or Judicial Power preference dimensions, the less likely he is to be the median justice. Thus, for a litigant bringing a case to the Court, if the case is likely to activate the Crime and Punishment preference dimension – say, a search and seizure case – the less incentive there is to pitch one's argument towards Justice Burton. Instead, in cases decided along the Crime and Punishment preference dimension, Justices Reed Frankfurter, or Stone are more likely to be the median justice. As we will see later in this chapter, the progression of constitutional law during the mid-twentieth century is characterized by decision making that centers first on the Balance of Power and Crime and Punishment preference dimensions and then later moves onto cases that implicate the Individual and Civil Rights preference dimensions. We should expect, given Figure 7.4, that as the political cleavages implicated by the Court's cases change, so too should the types of arguments the lawyers make along with the justices they identify as pivotal.

The implication is that the voting coalitions will look very different across these different areas of the law. When we think about the process of litigation, there is a further implication that the types of arguments lawyers make and the Court majority embraces will similarly vary across the substantive areas of the law. While many doctrinally oriented histories of constitutional decision making acknowledge this, the mechanism implied by these patterns is that the justices have different views along the different ideological preference dimensions. That variation can induce, in principle, different lines of arguments and produce different voting cleavages. Whereas doctrinally oriented histories of the law take as axiomatic that different areas of the law entail distinct forms of logic and reasoning, the claim I make here is that variation in the Court's decision

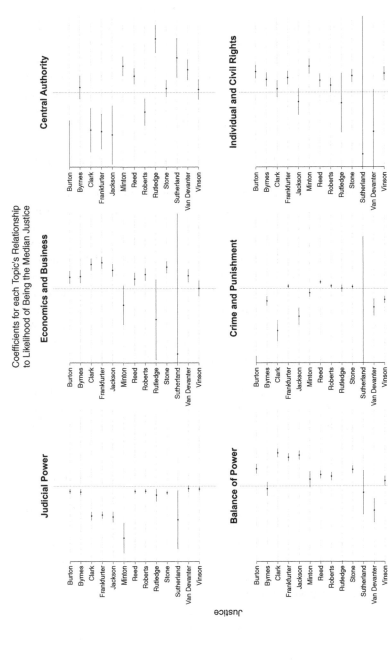

Figure 7.4. *Estimated coefficient from multinomial regression model predicting the estimated median justice from the topic mixture in the case.* The points show point estimates, and the bars show 95% confidence intervals. The vertical dashed line shows the value 0. Positive estimates indicate a higher loading onto the topic is associated with a higher likelihood of being the median justice; negative values indicate a lower likelihood of being the median justice.

making can be attributed to these different voting cleavages that are at least partially associated with substantively defined areas of the law.

However, one common theme during this era is the prominence of federalism questions among the issues that came to the Court. As we saw in Figure 7.1, the Balance of Power preference dimension grew in its prominence on the Court's docket during the 1940s and 1950s. The estimates reported in Figure 7.4 indicate that Justices Frankfurter and, to a lesser extent, Reed were particularly more likely to be the median in cases that activated, to a higher degree, the ideological preference dimension. Indeed, Figure 7.3 shows that Justices Frankfurter and Reed, were particularly frequent medians during those two decades. During the transition period during the 1940s and 1950s, these different voting coalitions would have important implications for constitutional decision making and the future of federalism in American constitutional law. For example, as I show below, the federalizing of criminal law during the mid-20th century would implicate two distinct preference dimensions that pitted the justices differently. The consequence would be that the kinds of cases brought to the Court and the way the lawyers were able to frame them could have sharp effects on the path of constitutional law.

Beyond the changing internal politics at the Court, the doctrinal moves that the justices had made during the 1930s and early 1940s interacted with social and political events taking place beyond the Court's constitutional decision making. That interaction leads in large part to the patterns we see in Figure 7.1. During the 1940s and 1950s, the justices are increasingly voting along a distinct preference dimension – the Balance of Power preference dimension – recognizing the increasing prominence of questions about the boundaries between state and national power. In addition, we see the increasing prominence of two other preference dimensions – the Crime and Punishment and the Individual and Civil Rights preference dimensions. This transition reflects the changing substantive issues that bring to the Court questions about the balance of state and national power. We can see how these politics played out by considering in greater detail two specific areas of the law – civil rights and criminal law – and the microprocesses that underlie the justices' decisions during these years.

7.1.1 Civil Liberties, Civil Rights, and Federalism

In the early twentieth century, the Supreme Court justices began to resolve, with increased frequency, questions about the meaning of the First Amendment's religious liberties clauses. Prominent in the litigation that produced that series of cases were the Jehovah's Witnesses. The religious group participated in myriad cases before the Supreme Court during the first half of the twentieth century, litigating claims about the extent to which government regulations interfered with their right to free exercise of religion. Their experience litigating the First Amendment illuminates a number of important themes in how constitutional decision making evolved over time in conjunction with social and political conditions in the US. One notable example is the Supreme Court's decision in *Minersville* v. *Gobitis* (1940). In that case, the justices held, by a vote of 8-1, that a state could require public school students who were Jehovah's Witnesses to salute the flag during the pledge of allegiance. (They believed it violated their religion's admonition against bearing false witness.) Justice Stone was the lone dissenter.

In the immediate aftermath, a number of events transpired. There were assaults on Jehovah's Witnesses throughout the country (Heller 1943; Peters 2000). Some states modified their statutes concerning religious liberty. West Virginia even adopted language verbatim from Justice Frankfurter's majority opinion in *Gobitis*. Further, the US officially joined World War II the following year, where social and religious conflict was a central issue, making a position of religious intolerance more tenuous. Finally, President Roosevelt, now in his third term in the White House, had the opportunity to appoint two new justices to the Supreme Court and to elevate Justice Stone, the lone dissenter in *Gobitis*, to be Chief Justice.

In response, the Witnesses' organized litigation team set out to find a sympathetic litigant to bring their case back to the Court. Indeed, the Witnesses were engaged during the early and mid-twentieth century in a sustained effort of coordinated litigation, led by Judge Joseph Franklin Rutherford (Henderson 2004). In West Virginia they found the ideal litigant for their case, and by 1942 they were back at the Supreme Court. This time, the majority reversed its decision in *Gobitis*, with two justices switching from their earlier positions to join now-Chief Justice Stone and the two recent appointees to the Court.

The story of the flag salute cases is one of an abrupt about-face that was arguably driven by the impact of the Court's decision in *Gobitis*, changing political and social conditions associated with World War II and personnel turnover on the Court. In this way, it encapsulates many of the related factors I have argued shape the path of constitutional law. However, this example is also important because it is just one manifestation of the growing use of the courts by organized interests to advance political goals. The Witnesses were frequently before the Court, as were other groups who were disadvantaged in the political process, perhaps most notably the NAACP.

In fact, it is not coincidental there was such growth in this form of "impact litigation" at mid-century. America's entrance into World War II exposed a number of challenging social tensions. On one hand, we were fighting against intolerance and fascism abroad; on the other hand, our own society was marked by a number of policies and practices that enshrined racial intolerance. Throughout the country, Jim Crow laws institutionalized segregation in a variety of settings, from public schools to marriage to sports to transportation. The civil rights movement during the 1940s began to grow, partially reflecting the politics of that tension. In 1942, the Congress of Racial Equality was formed and was leading freedom rides throughout the South by the end of the decade. Moreover, racial segregation was not limited to Jim Crow laws in the states. Nearly 1,000,000 black Americans served in the armed forces during World War II, even while they were still segregated and precluded blacks from serving in all capacities.

After the war, the inconsistency between black Americans' service to the country and institutionalized racism became palpable. In February 1946, Isaac Woodward, a World War II combat veteran returning from Camp Gordon in Georgia to his home in North Carolina, was accosted by a fellow bus-rider, who was white, for having taken too much time at a rest stop. The white passenger called the local police, who took Woodward to jail, where he was beaten. In July of that year, another black veteran was dragged from his car and murdered, along with three companions, by 20 white men in Georgia (see Irons 2006, 368–69 for a discussion of these events). Race riots took place in the US, perhaps most notably in Tennessee, growing out of a confrontation between a black Navy veteran, James Stephenson, and a white store owner. It was in this climate that racial tensions began to receive more attention from federal authorities. Attorney General Tom Clark began an investigation into the murders in Georgia, the NAACP spoke out forcefully, and President Truman began to take action.

Truman convened the President's Committee on Civil Rights. He became the first president to address the NAACP in 1947 and in 1948 was the first president to send Congress a Special Message concerning civil rights. In his Special Message, Truman called upon Congress to enact legislation that would create federal authorities to protect civil rights and create federal laws against lynching, employment discrimination, transportation discrimination, and protecting the right to vote. Truman (1948) wrote,

The protection of civil rights begins with the mutual respect for the rights of others which all of us should practice in our daily lives. Through organizations in every community – in all parts of the country – we must continue to develop practical, workable arrangements for achieving greater tolerance and brotherhood.

The protection of civil rights is the duty of every government which derives its powers from the consent of the people. This is equally true of local, state, and national governments. There is much that the states can and should do at this time to extend their protection of civil rights. Wherever the law enforcement measures of state and local governments are inadequate to discharge this primary function of government, these measures should be strengthened and improved.

The Federal Government has a clear duty to see that Constitutional guarantees of individual liberties and of equal protection under the laws are not denied or abridged anywhere in our Union. That duty is shared by all three branches of the Government, but it can be fulfilled only if the Congress enacts modern, comprehensive civil rights laws, adequate to the needs of the day, and demonstrating our continuing faith in the free way of life.

Truman's message is a call to federalize civil rights issues. In his message, he is careful not to accuse the states of failing to protect civil rights – even though he knew they were – and instead argues that civil rights are so important and universal that they need to be the subject of a single national voice. He does not leave room for variation among the states in how civil rights are protected.

The nationalization of civil rights as a political issue was certainly aided by the rapid growth of broadcast television in the 1940s. Especially after World War II, American television networks began to broadcast more extensively and developed a wider range of programming. In 1947, *Meet the Press* debuted on NBC and offered its viewers a 30-minute weekly exploration of contemporary political events. At the same time, popular shows such as *The Ed Sullivan Show* were premiering on national networks. In the following years, television viewership would explode. As Prior (2007, 59) observes, just over 2% of American households owned a television in 1949, but that figure rose to 55% by 1955. As Hall (2005, 1236) notes, during this period,

The mass media, in turn, made the protests "one of the great news stories of the modern era," but they did so very selectively. Journalists' interest waxed and waned along with activists' ability to generate charismatic personalities (who were usually men) and telegenic confrontations, preferably those in which white villains rained down terror on nonviolent demonstrators dressed in their Sunday best.

Thus, three conditions coincided during the mid-twentieth century. The Supreme Court, through its New Deal makeover, had established constitutional legal foundations for breaking down traditional federalism distinctions in matters of public policy; civil rights violations were made especially acute, politically, in the aftermath of World War II; and the changing media environment allowed the entire country to be exposed to egregious racial tensions taking place at any given area in the country, including the powerful visual components that came with broadcast television.

One consequence was an increased role for the courts in civil rights. During the 1940s, the NAACP began an aggressive push to use constitutional litigation to end school desegregation (even at the expense of other civil rights issues, such as labor and economic conditions for African Americans) (e.g., Goluboff 2004). While we do not have detailed data on the presence of civil rights issues on the courts' dockets, there is some evidence to indicate constitutional decision making was influenced by the civil rights movements during the 1940s and 1950s.

It was in this context that the civil rights movement found itself during the late-1940s and early 1950s, when a number of segregationist practices were challenged in court and made their way into the Supreme Court's constitutional decisions. In 1947, the Court decided *Shelley v. Kraemer*, a case about restrictive covenants. Restrictive covenants were agreements by property owners only to sell their property (i.e., houses) to white buyers. That case was brought by the NAACP, which was joined by a large number of *amici curiae*. The justices held that while property owners were free to agree to restrictive covenants among themselves, those agreements could not be enforced in court. Writing for the unanimous case, Chief Justice Vinson said the justices found no

merit in the suggestion that property owners who are parties to these agreements are denied equal protection of the laws if denied access to the courts to enforce the terms of restrictive covenants and to assert property rights which the state courts have held to be created by such agreements. The Constitution confers upon no individual the right to demand action by the State which results in the denial of equal protection of the laws to other individuals. And it would appear beyond question that the power of the State to create and enforce property interests must be exercised within the boundaries defined by the Fourteenth Amendment.

Civil rights movement leaders were also pushing for an end to segregation in education. During these years, the NAACP and other organizations used litigation to challenge segregation at all levels of education. In *Sweatt v. Painter* (1950), the justices held that the University of Texas' separate law school for black students was unequal in both tangible and intangible ways. The justices, obviously keenly aware of what constitutes a properly, effective legal education, noted that not only were the physical facilities unequal across the two schools but that the traditions, alumni networks, faculty, and prestige of the all-white school were qualities that could not be equaled in the separate all-black school. The same day, the Court decided *McLaurin v. Oklahoma State Regents*, a case also brought by the NAACP, in which it declared unconstitutional the segregation of black students at the University of Oklahoma's graduate school of education. In that case, McLaurin had been admitted to the same school as the white students but had been physically separated from them within the school – including in the classroom and library. The justices held that separating racial minorities from others in their education undermined their education and set them at a professional disadvantage later in their careers.

Of course, the campaign to end racial segregation in education came to a head a few years later, when the Court decided *Brown* v. *Board of Education*, in which the justices famously held that separate educational facilities are inherently unequal and found that the Constitution forbids states from maintaining racially segregated public schools. While the Court's decision did not immediately change practice on the ground, and integration was uneven across the country (e.g., Peltason 1971; Giles and Walker 1975; Rosenberg 1991), the decision represents a significant culmination of the nationalization of civil rights law. The Fourteenth Amendment now had implications for how states and localities operate their public schools, insofar as those practices implicate racial discrimination.

7.1.2 Federalizing Criminal Law

At the same time as Americans were experiencing a nationalized civil rights movement, a second substantive policy area was transitioning from a local matter to a question of federal policy making. Decades earlier, in the early part of the century, the federal government began to involve itself more and more in criminal law. In 1910, Congress enacted the Mann Act, which made it a crime to transport women across state lines for reasons related to sexual activity (i.e., prostitution). In 1919, Congress enacted the Dyer Act, which made it a crime to transport stolen motor vehicles across state lines. Just over a decade later, the federal government found itself still expanding its presence in criminal law, passing such statutes as the Lindbergh Law, which criminalized kidnapping across state lines, and the Fugitives from Justice Act, which made it a federal crime for a fugitive to cross state lines.

These statutes and related enactments were driven by the changing nature of crime and law enforcement during the early twentieth century. Advances in transportation made it easier for criminals to cross state lines, and it was challenging for states to coordinate with each other in pursuing criminals and enforcing justice (see, for example, Allen 1958). Crucially, the prohibition era was responsible for the growth of organized crime from being run by locally oriented groups to syndicates with national reach (e.g., Schelling 1971; Reed 1982). Gambling and prostitution, among other crimes, were increasingly run by organizations that reached across state lines. Consider artistic and cultural representations of crime in the 1940s and 1950s, most easily typified by *The Godfather*, which depict the growth of organized crime from its traditional purview to more expansive enterprises. In the 1940s, reflecting this trajectory, Congress amended many of the statutes enacted in the early twentieth century to further integrate the federal government's law-enforcement agencies with state criminal justice efforts.

In addition to the changing nature of crime in the United States, during the early twentieth century, federal law enforcement agencies began to use fingerprint identification to increasingly identify, pursue, and prosecute criminals. However, it was not until the 1940s that fingerprint identification became automated, using computers to match fingerprints with FBI records. With this development, though, the benefits of integrating state law enforcement with federal authority only grew. The result was a push, indeed from both the states and the federal government, to increasingly blur the line between state and national authority in criminal law.

One example of the way in which criminal law came to be federalized concerns how the Supreme Court has handled cases involving forced confessions. Instructively, the first notable case in this line of doctrine involves not just criminal procedure but also the civil rights movement and the NAACP. On December 31, 1939, a married couple and their child were brutally murdered in Oklahoma. The crime shocked the local, rural community. Within two weeks, W.D. Lyons was arrested by the police, who beat and tortured him throughout the next two weeks, demanding a confession. Lyons ultimately confessed, several times to several different officials who beat him.

A few years before, the Supreme Court had, for the first time, invalidated a conviction in a state criminal trial on the basis of an involuntary confession. In *Brown* v. *Mississippi*, several black defendants were accused of murdering a white farmer. The only evidence presented at their one-day trial was their confessions, which had been extracted using whipping by the police (one defendant was hung from a tree while being whipped). Writing for the majority, Chief Justice Hughes declined to specifically extend the Constitution's protection against self-incrimination to the states. Indeed, the Chief Justice observed that the Court's precedents reveal that a state could even eliminate trial by jury, if it so chose. But, the Chief continued, "[b]ecause a State may dispense with a jury trial, it does not follow that it may substitute trial by ordeal. The rack and torture chamber may not be substituted for the witness stand. The State may not permit an accused to be hurried to conviction under mob domination – where the whole proceeding is but a mask – without supplying corrective process" (297 U.S. at 285–86). Thus, the unanimous Court concluded, while the Constitution's specific rights concerning criminal procedure did not apply to the states, the Fourteenth Amendment's Due Process Clause prohibits the states from engaging in torture to extract criminal confessions. Over the following years, the Court heard eight more forced confession cases, expanding the *Brown* ruling in seven of the eight decisions (Blevins 1963, 410).

Returning to Oklahoma case, the NAACP saw in the case the opportunity for a "slam dunk" victory, hoping also to draw enough national press attention to serve as a powerful vehicle for fund-raising and support (e.g., Blevins 1963). However, the justices in this case upheld the conviction. The reason they found the confession admissible was that Lyons made multiple confessions, over a period of time, not just once during the time he was being tortured. The case was Thurgood Marshall's first before the Supreme Court.

Importantly, though, there is a crucial distinction between the fact patterns of the earlier forced confession cases where the Court had overturned the convictions. In the earlier cases, because the confessions were so linked to the abusive behavior on the part of the officials, the justices concluded that the confessions were of questionable veracity, given by the defendant only in order to make the torture stop. In the *Lyons* case, though, the fact that Lyons confessed repeatedly after the abuse suggested that while the police conduct was terrible, the confession was not as questionable. Thus, the rationale for federal involvement in reviewing confessions was logically limited to ensuring that the evidence presented at trial was sound.

However, in the years following *Lyons*, the justices began to consider a second rationale for prohibiting the use of forced confessions – deterring abusive police behavior. On this question, the justices were more divided (e.g., Blevins 1963), and part of that divisiveness has to do with the federalism issues at play. The justices agreed during the 1930s and early 1940s that the federal Constitution prohibits the states from using invalid evidence at a criminal trial – such as questionable confessions obtained through abusive, torturous treatment of defendants. However, the second, newer rationale for excluding forced confessions from trial implies a stronger role for the national government, which pushed the boundaries of contemporary understandings of federalism. This second rational implied the federal courts should be in the business of supervising state and local police authorities. In the mid-1940s, that was a rather novel doctrinal position.

Indeed, the tension between the Constitution's commitment to dual federalism and the direction American constitutional law had taken during the early twentieth century can be seen in a variety of similar cases involving criminal law and the Bill of Rights. And, unlike the forced confessions cases, these rarely implicated racial tension as clearly or sharply. In *Palko* v. *Connecticut*, the defendant had been convicted of murdering a police officer who pursued him following a robbery. The defendant was convicted of second-degree murder, and the State appealed, because it wanted him convicted of first-degree murder. The state supreme court ordered a retrial, at which the defendant was convicted of first-degree murder and sentenced to death. Palko claimed the retrial violated his constitutional protection from double jeopardy, and the case made it to the Supreme Court. The justices sided with the State, declining to incorporate the Fifth Amendment's protection against double jeopardy as a restriction on state action. Writing for the majority, Justice Cardozo argued that only some provisions of the Bill of Rights are applicable to the states. The provisions that are applicable to the states are those that are "of the very essence of a scheme of ordered liberty" (302 U.S., at 325). State practices were only forbidden by the federal Bill of Rights when they "violate those 'fundamental principles of liberty and justice which lie at the base of all our civil and political institutions'" (302 U.S., at 328).

The justices in this case were nearly unanimous. Justice Pierce Butler was the lone dissenter, and he did not even write a dissenting opinion. However, as we saw in Figure 5.6 in Chapter 5, Justice Butler was relatively more liberal in cases involving the Crime and Punishment preference dimension than he was in cases involving the Balance of Power preference dimension. It is instructive, then, to consider that *Palko* came to the Court in 1937, just as the Court was beginning its move in the liberal direction and where, as we saw in Figure 7.2, the justices remained relatively homogenously conservative along the Crime and Punishment preference dimension. However, as we also saw above, the center of gravity and locus of power within the Court would change dramatically over the next decade, altering the internal politics at the Court. At the same time, as we have seen, the social and political conditions outside of the Court were changing rapidly at the same time. The consequences can been seen by considering the cases that came after *Palko*, as the Court began to incorporate elements of the Bill of Rights against the states.

Indeed, just a decade later, the Court decided a string of cases that reveal the balance the justices were walking between a doctrine of incorporation that left some degree of federalism in tact, while recognizing the changing nature of criminal law enforcement and social opinion in the United States. In 1947, the justices decided *Adamson* v. *California*, 332 U.S. 46. In that case, the defendant had been convicted of murder. At trial, he declined to testify in his own behalf, and the prosecution used his refusal to testify, claiming that the refusal could be interpreted by the jury as an admission of guilt by the defendant. The justices, in a 5-4 decision, held that the Fifth Amendment's protection against self-incrimination does not apply to the states. The following year, though, the justices decided *In re Oliver*, 333 U.S. 257 (1948), in which the justices unanimously held that the Sixth Amendment's protection of the right to a public trial is applicable to the states. Justice Black observed that "This nation's accepted practice of guaranteeing a public trial to an accused has its roots in our English common law heritage" (333 U.S., at 266). The thrust of Black's argument was that the view that trials should be public was a matter of *national* opinion – it goes to the core of what American's understand fair, accountable, democratic rule to mean. The sharp division of the justices, along predictable ideological lines, reflects the growing polarization along the Crime and Punishment preference dimension we saw in Figure 7.2.

Just one year later, the Court decided *Wolf* v. *Colorado* 338 U.S. 25 (1949), in which they held that the Fourth Amendment's protection against warrantless search and seizure is applicable to the states. Tellingly, there was no disagreement among the justices about whether the Fourth Amendment is applicable to the states. However, there was sharp disagreement about whether the "exclusionary rule" applies to the states – on this issue, they again split along predicable ideological lines. That rule, which had been developed earlier in the century in the context of federal criminal cases, holds that evidence obtained in violation of the Fourth Amendment is to be excluded from trial. A bare majority of the justices concluded in *Wolf* that while the Amendment's protection applies against the states, the exclusionary rule, as a remedy, does not. In a way reminiscent of *Palko*, Justice Frankfurter, writing for the majority, asserts that because "most of the English-speaking world does not regard as vital to such protection the exclusion of evidence thus obtained, we must hesitate to treat this remedy as an essential ingredient of the right" (338 U.S., at 29).

It is particularly instructive to consider how the competing sides in these cases pitched their arguments to the Court, as it suggests efforts to activate competing ideological preference dimensions. Crucially, the lawyers representing the criminal defendants in these cases were not special-interest lawyers working for large organizations, such as the ACLU. Rather, they were local trial lawyers who took up these cases and made their way to the Supreme Court. However, they were shrewd enough to take note of how the different ways of pitching their cases might alter their chances of winning. In *Adamson*, both sides framed the case as being about criminal procedure in the states. By the time the litigants brought *Wolf* to the Court, the two sides were framing their arguments very differently. In *Wolf*, Phillip Hornbein, Wolf's lawyer, framed his argument as a matter of federal standards for an ordered society. By contrast, the brief for the State of Colorado focuses on the criminal procedure elements of the case. Whereas Wolf's brief presents an argument that begins and ends with questions about what constitutional protections are inherent in a free society, the State's brief starts and ends with questions about how criminal procedures should function. The two sides are intentionally setting out to map the case onto different preference dimensions. Whereas the Court had been becoming increasingly liberal – and, homogenously so – along the Balance of Power preference dimension, there had not been much movement along the Crime and Punishment preference dimension, and these lawyers' efforts to shape the case differently reflects a strategic choice made by advocates who were certainly aware of that difference. In this example, then, we can see how individual choices at the level of lawyers shaping their arguments give rise to the long-run trajectory we see during this era.

More generally, these cases involving criminal law and federalism in the 1940s evince the political and legal challenge that the Court faced in the years following the New Deal era and World War II. Federalism meant that criminal law varied greatly across jurisdictions, and this often gave rise to inequities of justice and practices of questionable constitutionality. In the context of moral outrage at Fascism, racial and religious persecution, and what seemed to be an ever-shrinking world as transportation and media made far corners of the country easily accessible to Americans, the Court had to develop a legal framework for addressing the kinds of practices the Constitution surely intended to prevent.

To be sure, we find evidence of the ideological consequences of federalizing criminal justice when we consider the internal dynamics at the Court during the time. As I have emphasized, the justices' preferences often diverged on these two issues, which meant that when confronted with legal questions that activate both their views on criminal law and their views on federalism, the justices could line up differently than they did in cases that only activated one or the other of those dimensions. Figure 7.5 shows each case coded in the Supreme Court as belonging to the Criminal Procedure Issue Area. For each case, its location in the plot shows its loading onto the Crime and Punishment (x-axis) and Balance of Power (y-axis) preference dimensions. As one can easily see, there are many cases that load heavily, nearly entirely, onto that preference

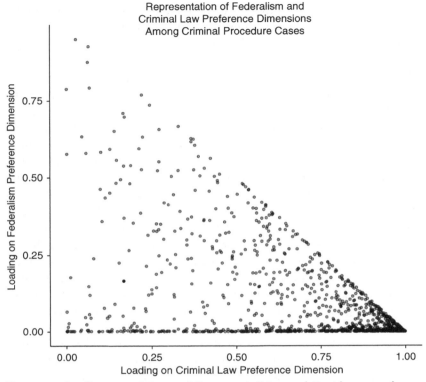

Figure 7.5. *Loading onto Balance of Power and Crime and Punishment preference dimensions among cases in the Criminal Procedure Issue Area in the Supreme Court Database.* Each point shows a single case and the estimated loading (posterior median) onto the Balance of Power and Crime and Punishment preference dimensions.

dimension. These are Criminal Procedure cases where the voting is characterized simply by the justices' preferences along the Crime and Punishment preference dimension. However, the vast majority of cases load at least partially onto another dimension, and for all of the cases with positive values on the y-axis, they load at least partially onto the Balance of Power preference dimension. Some cases, near the top-left corner of the figure, load mostly onto the Balance of Power preference dimension.

Recall in Chapter 6, I illustrate how the switch in time could be explained by a shift in the preference dimensions activated in the case. Here, I perform a similar kind of analysis, considering many cases. In particular, I take each Criminal Procedure case decided between 1950 and 1965, which load at least 25% onto the Crime and Punishment preference dimension and 10% onto the Balance of Power preference dimension. These 122 cases are ones that plausibly are about criminal law and the state-federal relationship. I then calculate the probability of a conservative disposition in each case if the Balance of Power dimension were to go away. Specifically, I take the loading onto the Balance of Power dimension and add it to the Crime and Punishment dimension, and then set the Balance of Power dimension to zero. Using this hypothetical case loading onto the six preference dimensions, I calculate the ideal points for each of the justices who vote in each case. I then calculate the case location, using the method I demonstrate in Chapter 3, and code whether five justices have ideal points to the right of the case location.

Of course, one needs to address the uncertainty in the estimates of the justices preferences, the loading onto each of the preference dimensions, and the case locations. Therefore, I take 1,000 draws from the posterior sample I simulate in Chapter 5 for each of the (1) ideal points, (2) case loadings, and (3) case locations. Thus, for each case, I have 1,000 draws from the posterior, in which I evaluate whether five justices would have voted in a conservative direction had the case not involved the Balance of Power preference dimension. In Figure 7.6, I show the consequences for case dispositions. I first calculate the proportion of draws from the posterior sample in which a majority of the justices voting in the case would have had ideal points to the right of the case location. This quantity can be thought of as the probability that a majority of the justices would have voted conservatively in each case. I then identify the polarity of the actual case disposition from the Supreme Court Database. I report in the figure the proportion of draws in which the median's estimated preference does not correspond to the actual case disposition – i.e., the median is to the right of the case location and the case actually had a liberal outcome, or vice-versa. In other words, then, the figure shows the probability that the case disposition would have been different had the topic mixture been different.

The evidence here is striking. In 44% of the Criminal Procedure cases decided between 1950 and 1965 – 54 cases – the case dispositions hinge on the Balance of Power preference dimension. There are two forces driving this effect. First, the shift in the loading onto the preference dimensions moves the justices. As we saw in Chapter 5, the justices preferences vary across the different preference dimensions, sometimes considerably. This means that, for any given case location, how many justices find themselves to one side or the other depends on how relevant each preference dimension is. Second, the justices' preferences do not all necessarily vary the same way. For example, Hugo Black was more liberal on criminal cases that involved Balance of Power than in criminal cases that did not involve Balance of Power. (This difference is reflected in his views about incorporating the Bill of Rights and is surely related to

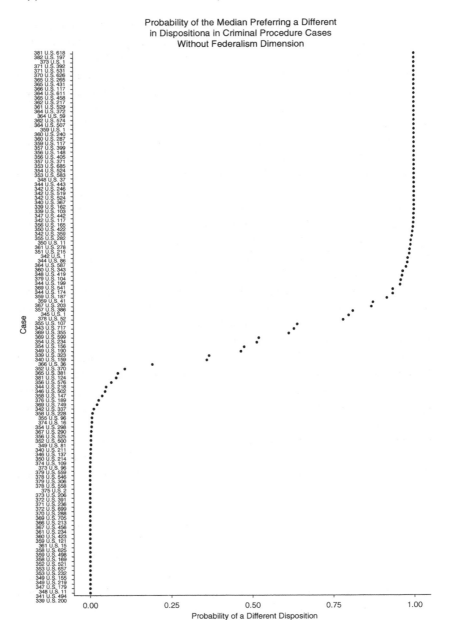

Figure 7.6. *Consequences of changing the case topic mixture for prediction of the case disposition.* The figure reports, for each case, the probability that the median would have preferred a different case disposition under the assumption the case does not activate the Balance of Power preference dimension.

his experience in the New Deal, fighting for national regulatory power.) However, William Brennan, who was also an on-average liberal, was more conservative in criminal cases involving federalism, most likely owed in part to his experience as a state judge in New Jersey.

In sum, then, one feature of constitutional decision making at mid-century is the continued erosion of dual federalism, especially in the context of criminal law. As the nature of crime changed during the 1930s and 1940s, changes in law enforcement practices, such as fingerprint technology and the economic implications of large-scale crime, meant that the consequences of heterogeneous criminal law and procedure around the country became more apparent. At the same time, the consequences of FDR's appointments to the Supreme Court included a rapid move on the Court to a more liberal perspective on federalism, making the Court a hospitable avenue for federalizing criminal procedure. While the justices did not embrace a wholesale incorporation of the Bill of Rights against the states, we see in their decision making an unmistakable pattern of both (1) adopting a more liberal, expansive view of the Bill of Rights' applicability to the states, and (2) expanding the role of the federal government beyond the economic regulation context from which mid-century politics were born.

7.1.3 Federalism and Transition

As has been noted in previous research, the years between 1940 and 1953 were something of a transition period for the Supreme Court (e.g., McCloskey 1972; Urofsky 1997). In one sense, there were internal changes taking place – President Roosevelt had appointed almost an entire Court of justices during the late 1930s and early 1940s, resulting not just in generational turnover but in a fundamental shift in the perspectives brought to bear on federalism among the justices. Coming to the Court during the New Deal and then during World War II, these justices were particularly aware of the upside of federal power and were poised to bring a more liberal orientation to constitutional law. At the same time society was changing in profound ways – the political issues of the day that animated constitutional disputes were fundamentally different from those that were of such heightened importance during the confrontations around the New Deal. Technological changes were making the county smaller, as broadcast television transformed formerly local issues into questions of potential national interest and concern. In a sense, then, this era of transition can be characterized by both internal and external transitions. Those two forces interact to provide a description of constitutional decision making at mid-century.

The new questions coming to the Court meant that distinct ideological preference dimensions were bound to come into play, as we see in Figure 7.1. Moreover, as we saw in Chapter 4, the justices became much more likely to dissent during this era, as the norm of consensus broke down during the 1940s (e.g., Walker, Epstein, and Dixon 1988). In this context, the analysis presented here shows that variation in which preference dimensions are activated in a case is consequential for how the Court decides the case. For example, as Figures 7.4 and 7.6 illustrate, which justice is likely to be pivotal in any given case depends systematically on which preference dimensions the case activates, and the consequences of altering that mix of preference dimensions can change the outcome in a non-trivial number of cases. Some of the examples used here to illustrate these dynamics show how microprocesses, at the level of strategically minded lawyers choosing their cases and crafting their arguments, are linked to those systematic, general patterns.

As we will see in the next section, though, this era of transition was also an era of foundation-laying. The justices' constitutional decision making in the 1940s and early 1950s would further shape responses by special interests setting out to use their courts to achieve policy goals and would have deep consequences of the range of political and social questions that made their way into the body of constitutional law. The country was preparing for a cultural revolution, which would give rise to deep conflicts over the role of American government in regulating individual behavior. The growth of the federal government that took place during the New Deal and in the immediate post-war years was about to be put to new purposes, and the Court would be called upon to make a number of constitutional decisions that touch on a variety of areas never previously contemplated.

7.2   FROM TRANSITION TO CULTURE REVOLUTION

During the decade following World War II, the justices signaled that the Court would be receptive to claims for social progress made by marginalized interests. While doubts remain about the efficacy of judicial remedies for social change (Rosenberg 1992), the preceding analysis indicates the justices were receptive to appeals to expand constitutional law to provide protection for individual and group rights. However, just as the foundation laid by special interests half a century earlier was adapted to the needs of persecuted minorities at mid-century, so too would the advances of the 1940s and 1950s be employed for new purposes during the 1960s and 1970s. As the baby-boomers came of age, the country entered into a period of deep social and cultural conflict. Constitutional law did not escape this transformation in American life. In particular, two forces simultaneously shaped the direction of American constitutional law – the further adaptation of federalism to contemporary notions of national power and the recognition in social regulation of changing social and culture mores.

Those external forces on the law interacted with electoral politics and led to changing internal politics at the Court. Figure 7.7 shows the by-now familiar pair of plots with the median justice's conservatism in each of the six ideological preference dimensions and the degree of preference polarization, for each year, from 1950 through 1975. A number of patterns stand out. First, the Court moved somewhat, though not drastically, to the left along the Balance of Power preference dimension, particularly after the election of President Kennedy in 1960. That move, however, was not associated with an increase in polarization; instead the Court was moving together to the left. At the same time, the Court was becoming increasingly liberal along the Crime and Punishment preference dimension, and increasingly divided. The appointments to the Court during the 1950s and 1960s moved the center of the Court to the left, but the changes were not as monolithic as they were along the Balance of Power preference dimension. Finally, with respect to the Individual and Civil Rights preference dimension, it took a long time until the median justice had moved to the left – it was not until the end of President Johnson's administration that a noticeable change had taken place. However, there was a steady increase in polarization during these decades along that preference dimension.

These differences across those three preference dimensions suggest a complex account of the electoral, appointment, and internal judicial politics of these years. The Court was becoming more homogenously liberal along the Balance of Power preference dimension, more liberal but divided along the Crime and Punishment preference dimension, and more divided but less noticeably liberal along the Individual and Civil Rights preference dimension. These differences would have important consequences for how the justices would resolve the cultural and social constitutional questions that were to come to the justices during these decades, and they would shape the way in which litigants shape their arguments and cases. Consider Figure 7.8, which shows the justices I estimate to have been the median in each case between 1950 and 1975. In the beginning of the era, power was fairly diffused across a number of justices – with Chief Justice Vinson and Justices Reed, Frankfurter, Jackson, Burton, and Clark all having the opportunity to provide the pivotal vote with some regularity. By the mid-1960s, though, the Court

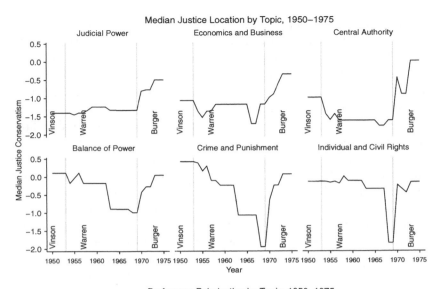

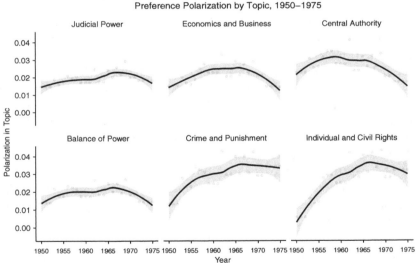

Figure 7.7. *Location of the median justice and ideological polarization among the justices in each of the six dimensions, 1950 through 1975.* Polarization is calculated using the method developed by Esteban and Ray (1994) and applied by Clark (2009a) to the Supreme Court.

was much more deeply divided, with Justices Black and Brennan fairly consistently being in the pivotal role.

That pattern of a divided Court with power concentrated into the hands of one or two justices would continue through the modern era. As we see in the figure, during the early 1970s, Justices Stewart and Blackmun played the pivotal role, along with Justice White, to a lesser

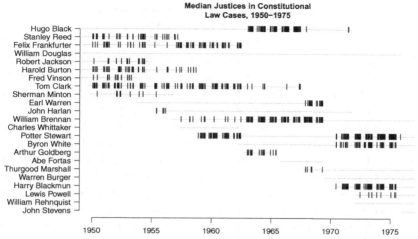

Figure 7.8. *Median justices in constitutional cases decided between 1950 and 1975.* Along the y-axis are the justices who served during the period, organized by the start date of their service (first justices at the top). The x-axis measures time. The grey horizontal lines show the dates during which each justice served. The tick marks indicate individual cases and who was the estimated median justice for that case.

extent. In the next section, we will see this pattern continue in subsequent decades. The point to note here is that as the justices' distribution across the ideological preference dimensions shifted during the 1950s and 1960s, so too did the nature of power on the Court, as the justices settled into a pattern of a more deeply and closely divided Court, with the role of the pivotal justice depending less and less on what the subject matter before the Court was. As before, how these internal political dynamics interacted with the external forces bringing cases and questions to the Court to shape constitutional law can best be seen by examining a few of the particular events in specific substantive areas of the law.

7.2.1 Civil Liberties and Federalism

World War II did not shift only the prominence and acuteness of the interaction between federalism and civil rights violations in the United States – it also shifted the federal balance of civil liberties protections. As we saw in Chapter 6, the Bolshevik Revolution and the ensuing Red Scare in the United States gave rise to a number of governmental practices aimed at restricting the influence of communist political ideology. Those policies in turn led to disputes that shaped substantive due process doctrine in ways that complemented the due process doctrine that was developing in the realm of economic regulation. So too did the onset of the Cold War as Western powers, led by the United States, settled into what was to be a decades-long period of tension with the USSR.

By the late 1940s and early 1950s, a number of events taking place in global politics exacerbated American fear of communism. The Soviets successfully tested a nuclear bomb in 1949, and in 1950 the Korean War broke out. Fear of communism was further stoked by events such as the arrest of Julius and Ethel Rosenberg, the highly publicized work of the House Un-American Activities Committee (HUAC), and persecution efforts led by Senator Joseph McCarthy. Fears of subversion gave rise to practices both inside and outside of government. President Truman began a practice of administering loyalty reviews for federal government employees, while the entertainment industry began the practice of "blacklisting" actors suspected of being communist sympathizers. In 1947, HUAC subpoenaed a number of leading Hollywood figures to testify. Ten of them refused to answer questions, most notably the question whether they were or had been members of the Communist Party. They claimed the First Amendment protected them from having to answer that question. Ultimately, these ten writers and directors, who came to be known as the Hollywood Ten, were convicted of contempt of Congress, and their case made it to the Supreme Court, where the justices denied their request to review the conviction.

Indeed, the Hollywood Ten case was just one example of the intensity with which the American government was pursuing suspected communists at the time. The FBI operated a large-scale data collection and monitoring program in which they tracked communists in the United States. As of 1947, the FBI estimated there were 75,388 members of the Communist Party of the United States of American (CPUSA), according to secret documents. The FBI even tracked members by profession, ethnic or national background, and residence, among other characteristics. These data indicate that membership dropped over the coming years, and by 1952, membership had dropped by two-thirds to 25,497. Figure 7.9 shows the number of CPUSA members in each state as of December 31, 1952. The states range from a minimum of zero in Wyoming to 12,000 in New York. (In the records from 1947, all of the New England states were grouped together as one unit.)

The Supreme Court's docket reflects this geographical variation. Between 1950 and 1960, the justices decided 36 First Amendment cases, according to the Supreme Court Database, and those cases came disproportionately from the states with larger CPUSA memberships. Figure 7.10 shows the relationship between the logged number of First Amendment cases decided from each state between 1950 and 1960 and

Communist Party Membership, 1952

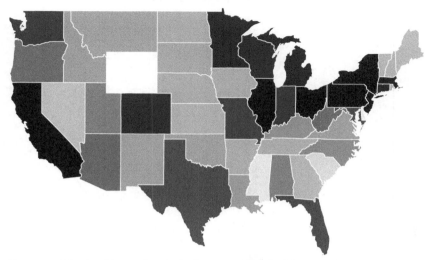

Figure 7.9. *Membership numbers in the Communist Party of the United States of America, as of 1952.* Data come from the FBI New York File # 100-80638, available through the National Archives. Darker shading indicates larger membership.

the logged number of CPUSA members in each state.[1] While there are only 48 datapoints here, there emerges a distinct relationship. The bulk of the cases came from states such as New York, California, Pennsylvania, Ohio, Illinois, and other states with relatively large CPUSA memberships.

In those cases, moreover, the Court made a number of important doctrinal moves. Despite the justices' reluctance to step in to the Hollywood Ten's case, they did engage in active development of First Amendment constitutional law, and their decisions reflect the First Amendment challenges implicated by the times. In 1951, the Court decided *Dennis* v. *United States*. In that case, a number of officials from the Communist Party of the United States of America (CPUSA) had been arrested on charges of conspiring to overthrow the government, in violation of the Smith Act, which had been passed in the years before World War II. The law made it a crime to advocate for the overthrow of the US government. Eugene Dennis and ten other CPUSA leaders were charged by federal officials, who argued that communism, as an ideological movement, advocated for violent revolution and so meeting with a group

[1] Each point is the log of the number of cases, plus one, and the log of the number of CPUSA members, plus one. In many instances, no First Amendment cases came from a given state. And, according to the FBI, there were zero CPUSA members in Wyoming as of 1952.

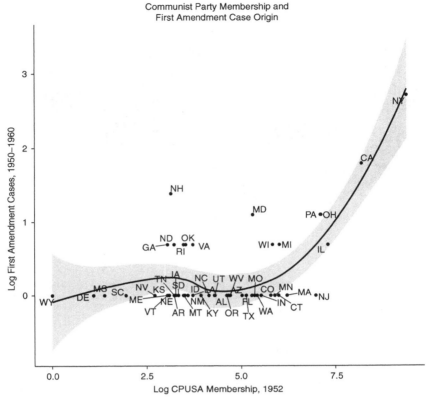

Figure 7.10. *Membership numbers in the Communist Party of the United States of America, as of 1952*. Data come from the FBI New York File # 100-80638, available through the National Archives.

of supporters and advocating communism amounted to a conspiracy to overthrow the US government and so violated the Smith Act.

The Supreme Court upheld Dennis' conviction. The justices, by a 6-2 vote, concluded that the First Amendment did not protect the right to conspire to overthrow the government. Writing for the majority, Chief Justice Vinson reviewed the myriad First Amendment cases decided in the climate of the Red Scare and World War I. He then noted the question in *Dennis* went to the heart of what kinds of activities could constitute "clear and present danger" and therefore fall outside of the scope of First Amendment protection. The Chief Justice argued that the *Dennis* case involved "the development of an apparatus designed and dedicated to the overthrow of the Government, in the context of world crisis after crisis" (341 U.S., at 510) and that certainly neither the First Amendment nor the Court's doctrine could be read to mean that before the Government may act, it must wait until the putsch is about to be executed, the plans have been laid and the signal is awaited. If Government is aware that a group aiming at its overthrow is attempting to indoctrinate its members and to commit them to a course whereby they will strike when the leaders feel the circumstances permit, action by the Government is required

(341 U.S., at 509).

Thus, the majority opinion adopted a more permissive interpretation of the First Amendment, which has come to be known as the "clear and probable danger" test.

During the coming years, however, the justices retreated somewhat from the position staked out in *Dennis*. As Gunther and Sullivan (1997, 1068) note, after *Dennis*, the federal government brought more than 120 cases to court against lower-level Communist Party members. However, as this was taking place, anti-communism fever was subsiding, especially following the death of Senator McCarthy. Among those cases is *Yates* v. *United States* (1957). Though the justices declined to make a constitutional decision about the Smith Act in this case, the Court opinion makes an important distinction between advocacy for an abstract principle and advocacy for action. A few years later, the justices decided *Scales* v. *United States* (1961) in which the majority again whittled away at the Smith Act, arguing that the law only prohibited "active" membership and not "nominal" membership. Finally, in *Noto* v. *United States* (1961), the justices held that there had not been enough evidence presented at the trial that the Communist Party actually advocated overthrowing the government. In just a few short years, then, the Court had gone from treating Communist Party members as having limited First Amendment protections to circumscribing the Smith Act so much as to render it useless. Indeed, in a concurring opinion in *Noto*, Justice Black asserted the Court should have simply held the law unconstitutional. These changes cannot be simply attributed just to internal politics. There had been limited turnover on the Court – between *Dennis* and *Noto*, only Justice Burton had left, being replaced with Justice Stewart, and along most dimensions, but especially the Individual and Civil Rights dimension, those two justices' ideal points were statistically indistinguishable.

However, what had happened was that the Second Red Scare had abated. The country was moving into the 1960s, a period of social and cultural liberation. The cases at the intersection of federalism and civil liberties that decade would reflect those changing social standards and conditions. Take, for example, *New York Times* v. *Sullivan*, which considered the conditions under which the media can be sued for libel and defamation against a public official. In that case, the newspaper had run an advertisement that described efforts being made in the South, including in Alabama, to silence civil rights protesters, including Martin Luther King. Sullivan was a public safety commissioner who sued the New York Times, among others, for libel, arguing that the claims about abuses by the Alabama State Police went beyond the First Amendment's protections for free speech. The justices held, though, that the media benefit from a greater degree of latitude when it comes to public officials and that in order to prevail on a libel claim against the media, the official must show actual malice on the part of the media.

Perhaps better reflecting the changing social and cultural norms of the time, the Court confronted a number of cases that dealt with laws – federal and state – that regulated obscenity and were applied to pornographic publications. In fact, between 1957 and 1970, the Court decided at least 20 cases involving state or federal obscenity laws. This was no coincidence. In 1953, *Playboy* magazine published its first issue, which sold 53,991 copies. Figure 7.11 shows that magazine's average monthly circulation from 1955 through 1971 (though, the years between 1956 and 1960 are missing). By 1955, circulation had increased to more than 310,000 copies, and over the next 15 years, circulation grew exponentially, to more than 6 million in 1971 (Association of National Advertisers 1972). As a point of comparison, the figure also

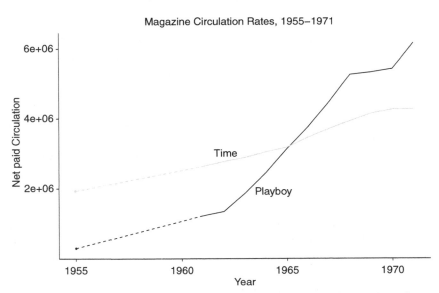

Figure 7.11. *Circulation rates for Playboy and Time magazines, 1955–1971.* Data show average monthly circulation, through all distribution channels, for each year. Years 1956 through 1960 are missing.

shows the average monthly circulation of *Time* magazine during the same period. As we can see, while circulation for that magazine grew during the same time period, it was at nowhere near the same rate as for *Playboy*. Similarly, by 1970, an estimated 22% of movies made in the United States were either rated X or were "sex-oriented unrated" films and accounted for 12.8% of gross receipts (on Obscenity and Pornography 1970, 11, Table 1). Even outside of pornographic movies, sexual content began to appear in movies with increasing frequency, and in 1968, the Motion Picture Association of America introduced a voluntary rating system, which eventually morphed into today's well-known rating system. Beyond obscenity *per se*, social liberalism was taking hold, especially in matters of sexuality, privacy, and expression. Enforcement of anti-sodomy laws began to wane, and in many instances the laws themselves were repealed (Friedman 2005, 570). Some of these, and other, topics made their way onto the Court's docket and shaped constitutional law.

Take, for example, the kinds of free-speech claims that emerged in the context of the Vietnam War, which in many ways served as a flash point for the kinds of disputes that underlie the cultural revolution taking place in the 1960s. In 1965, five public school students from Des Moines decided to wear black armbands to protest the Vietnam War, in violation of a school policy against the practice. Importantly, the students' protest effort was not a one-off, random occurrence. Rather, it came on the heels of a major demonstration in Washington, DC, which was followed by organized efforts to demonstrate opposition to the Vietnam War in Iowa (e.g., Johnson 1997). When the students began their protest by wearing armbands, they were suspended from school, resulting in a lawsuit, which made its way to the Supreme Court. The case, *Tinker* v. *Des Moines* (1969), established a test for evaluating a public school policy or practice that infringes upon a student's right to free speech. The test requires school officials to demonstrate that the policy is not motivated by a desire simply to avoid discussing the subject of the student's speech and that the forbidden conduct, under the policy, would "materially and substantially interfere" with the educational and disciplinary responsibilities of the school. The Court's general posture in 1969 towards opposition to the government reflects a significant change from how the justices viewed such questions in 1951. When the Court decided *Dennis*, Americans were fearful of communism, and the justices who served on the Court had come to the Court during the New Deal era. Society was very much marked by patriotism, and the justices were selected in large part because of their support for a strong national government. By the late 1960s, though, the cultural revolution had turned the patriotic culture of the late 1940s on its head, and the new justices were individuals who had strong commitments to individual civil liberties and a skepticism of efforts to suppress dissent.

What is instructive, though, is that the justices did not seem to be picking their cases in order to rein in the most extreme violations. To see this, let us consider from where the Supreme Court's cases originate. Does the Court take cases from the most conservative places, the most liberal places, or is there some other pattern? Measuring a state's liberalism is a complicated task, both conceptually and empirically. What does it mean for a state to be more or less liberal? Does one have in mind the preferences of the electorate? The voting patterns of the state officials? A state's enacted policies? Political scientists who study state politics as well as measurement theory have worked hard to disentangle these questions and match theoretical concepts to empirical manifestations that can be used to construct measures (e.g., Shor and McCarty 2011; Jenkins 2006; Wright 2004; Berry et al. 1998; Erikson, Wright, and McIver 1993). These approaches variously use data such as roll call votes by state legislators, surveys of state politicians, public opinion polls, or even election results.

Of the various approaches, Berry et al. (1998) provide the necessary temporal coverage to facilitate the kinds of questions I ask here, though their method, like all, is open to criticism about its validity. To measure the ideological orientation of a state, Berry et al. distinguish between the state's citizens and the officials serving in government. They measure the citizens' preferences by weighting the ideal points of each district's representative in Congress and the ideal points of the most recent challenger to that Congressperson, by the share of the vote that each got in that past election. To measure the preferences of the government itself, Berry et al. weight the preferences of each governor and the state congressional delegation. These congressional districts are then combined to create an index of the state's citizenry's aggregate liberalism. In each instance, all of the measures come from interest group ratings of legislators and governors. As such, each measure is essentially a composite of various measures of the voting patterns of elected officials.

With these data, we can examine the Supreme Court's case selection patterns. Figure 7.12 shows two relationships. First, in the left panel, I plot the number of First Amendment cases that came from each state between 1950 and 1970 against the Berry et al. measure of the state's government liberalism. Second, in the right panel, I plot the number of First Amendment cases from each state against the Berry et al. measure of the state's citizenry's liberalism. In each panel, we see there is no association between these two metrics. It does not appear the Court is systematically taking First Amendment cases from the states with the more liberal or conservative politicians or citizenry. To the extent we

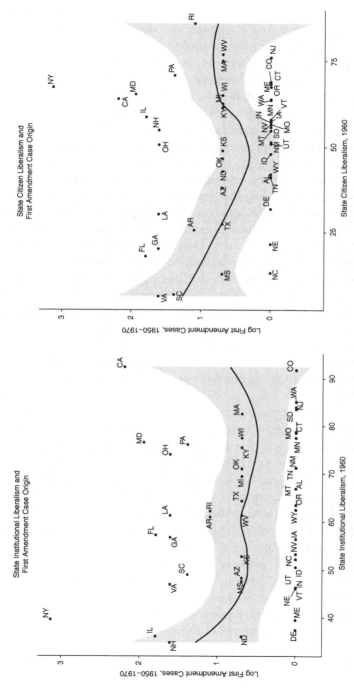

Figure 7.12. *Relationship between the number of First Amendment cases heard by the Supreme Court, 1950–1970, and state liberalism, 1960.*

would expect these states to engage in different practices concerning potential infringement of civil liberties, we might expect to see the Supreme Court focusing its attention on some states more than others. Of course, some states stand out as more frequent subjects of First Amendment constitutional litigation before the Supreme Court – New York, California, Maryland, Illinois, Florida, Georgia, etc. However, there does not seem to be a systematic ideological pattern.

A number of reasons may explain this non-finding, especially when we consider the microprocesses by which the Court takes cases and resolves them in order to craft constitutional law. Recall that during these years, the Court was comprised of justices who were increasingly liberal over time. However, that increased liberalism only began to shift the justices along the Individual and Civil Rights preference dimension during the late 1960s. These justices may have wanted to move First Amendment doctrine to the left. How the justices would select which cases to hear, given that objective, could depend on the underlying process by which the justices craft legal doctrine. There has been no shortage of research examining the bargaining process among the justices that leads to the production of Court opinions (e.g., Murphy 1964; Epstein and Knight 1998; Maltzman, Spriggs and Wahlbeck 2000; Lax and Cameron 2007; Lax 2007; Landa and Lax 2009; Clark and Lauderdale 2010; Lax 2011; Carrubba et al. 2012; Cameron and Kornhauser N.d.), and each of the various arguments suggests different incentives for case selection.

Median-voter-based models of adjudication suggest the case does not matter, because opinion writing is driven entirely by the preferences of the median justice. Other models suggest that the justices in the majority coalition on the disposition (who wins and who loses) have the most influence, and so how the case divides the justices, and in turn what the case facts are (recall the case-space model), can be of great significance for who influences the opinion content, and to what extent. Still other models suggest that the lower court decision sets the agenda, so to speak, for the Court, and so which case the justices take can influence the terms of negotiation among the justices and the content of the opinion. Two of these classes of models – the median-voter models and the lower-court-agenda-setting models – do not make any clear prediction about the pattern of case selection. Thus, one way to understand the findings we see in Figure 7.12 is that doctrinally driven justices do not necessarily exhibit any pattern in case selection, because the particular case facts are not constraining on the justices' ability to pursue their doctrinal goals.

Of course, such an interpretation flies in the face of both contemporary social-scientific models of the judicial process and deeply held axioms of the legal process. The case-space model, among others, strongly suggests that the way the law is constructed is by relating case facts to legal outcomes (e.g., Kornhauser 1992a; Lax 2007, 2011; Callander and Clark 2017). In the legal academy, one frequently hears of the notion of a "good vehicle," which refers to the appropriateness of a case for making a particular decision (e.g., Estrecher and Sexton 1986). Presumably, the notion behind these models and legal conventions is the idea that certain cases are better suited to making various kinds of doctrinal moves than are other cases. If this is so, then a non-pattern in case selection by doctrinally minded justices is difficult to reconcile.

A second issue, which also creates case-selection incentives for the justices is that their choice of cases is constrained by the cases brought to them. We know that the justices do make efforts to direct litigants and signal which kinds of cases they want to hear (e.g., Baird 2007), but what kinds of cases materialize is the product of a complex process. Conflicts need to occur, and in order to make it into court, the parties to the conflict need to not settle their disagreements in the first place. In order to make it to the Supreme Court, multiple layers of the judiciary (state and/or federal) have opportunities to resolve the case. At each of these stages, various cases are whittled away from the Supreme Court's potential docket, and so the set from which the justices select their cases is certainly not a random, representative sample of all of the ones they might have chosen. It could be hard, then, to know what to make of the relationship between the fact patterns in the cases they do hear and the justices' doctrinal moves and objectives (see also Kastellec and Lax 2008).

In particular, we might imagine that if the lower courts and the litigants themselves are strategically anticipating the Supreme Court's oversight, then the cases that are mostly likely to serve as vehicles for Supreme Court doctrinal shifts would be systematically whittled out of the Court's potential docket.[2] If so, then it is unclear whether doctrinal innovation would exhibit any particular pattern of case selection, especially with respect to a measure as rough as the measure of state ideological orientation I have used here. Indeed, one of the challenges that has long faced scholars of law making at the Supreme Court concerns what to make of the relationship between voting patterns and features of the Court's cases, especially given the complicated and poorly understood selection process that goes into creating the Court's docket (e.g., Segal

[2] Westerland et al. (2010) provide evidence that the lower courts strategically anticipate shifts in the Supreme Court justices' preferences.

1984; Richards and Kritzer 2002; Lax and Rader 2010; Pang et al. 2012; Callander and Clark 2017). Below, I return to this example and illustrate the pattern in case selection among First Amendment cases (see Figure 7.23).

7.2.2 *Social Strife and Constitutional Law*

The changing political and social conditions of the 1950s, 60s, and 70s were reflected not just in evolving civil liberties and federalism doctrine. We also see major constitutional developments taking place that are closely linked to a more general increase in social strife and conflict. The cultural revolution of the 1960s has been well documented elsewhere (e.g., Eisen 1969; Brick 2000; Cohen and Zelnik 2002; Marwick 2011), and the conflicts that emerged from the growing civil rights movement during the 1950s and 1960s are perhaps one of the defining features of twentieth-century America. One of the signature events that took place as part of that movement was the political protest. The top panel in Figure 7.13 shows the number of political protests that took place each year from 1940 through 1978 on behalf of racial, religious, ethnic, and gender rights (Burstein 1998). As we see here, there was a slight uptick in demonstrations during the late 1950s, but by the end of the decade and first few years of the 1960s, coinciding with the civil rights sit-ins and Freedom Rides, there was a massive, sudden spike in the number of protests that took place. The protests peaked in 1963 and then steadily declined over the following 15 years.

At the same time, the country was experiencing an unprecedented increase in crime, especially violent crime. The middle panel in Figure 7.13 shows the annual rate of violent crime in the United States for the 40-year period from 1933 through 1979. Just as civil rights protest activity was peaking, the rate at which the crime rate was increasing started to pick up. Between 1960 and 1970, the violent crime rate more than doubled, and the nonviolent crime rate shows a similar pattern. It is not coincidental that the 1968 Democratic Convention, where Hubert Humphrey was selected as the presidential candidate, was marred by violent protests in Chicago. That year, Richard Nixon was elected president in 1968, campaigning in part on a platform of law and order. Finally, while this was taking place, there was a spike in unemployment during the late 1950s and early 1960s. The bottom panel of Figure 7.13 shows unemployment between 1947 and 1979. As the figure shows, during the period between the Korean War and the Vietnam War, unemployment rose from roughly 4% to about 6% – a 50% increase. Then, there was a temporary decrease in unemployment during the last few years of the

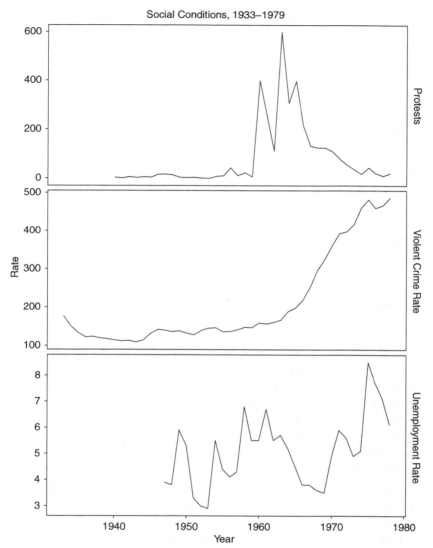

Figure 7.13. *Time series of social conditions during the middle of the twentieth century.* The top panel shows political protests in support of racial, religious, ethnic, and gender rights, 1940–1978. (Source: Burstein 1998). The middle panel shows the violent crime rate in the US, from 1933 through 1979. (Source: of Management et al. 1973; of the Census. U.S. Department of Commerce. 1980). The bottom panel shows the national unemployment rate, from 1947 through 1979. (Source: of Management et al. 1973; of the Census. U.S. Department of Commerce. 1980).

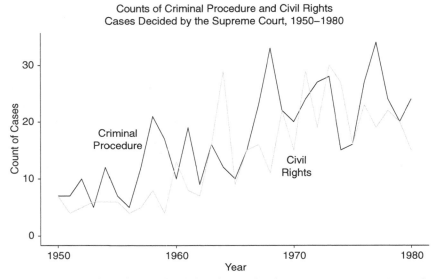

Figure 7.14. *Number of cases decided each year by the Supreme Court in Criminal Procedure and Civil Rights Issue Areas, 1950–1980.* (Source: Spaeth et al. 2015).

1960s before a continuing increase in unemployment during the 1970s. Notably, as the unemployment rate was increasing sharply during the 1970s, the violent crime rate was starting its surge. In short, the country during this era was experiencing a number of deep challenges.

These events had direct effects on American government. A number of pieces of important federal anti-discrimination legislation were enacted during the 1960s, many of which were championed by President Jonson, including the Civil Rights Act of 1964, the Voting Rights Act of 1965, and the Fair Housing Act of 1968, among others. President Nixon, for his part, similarly worked to improve civil rights problems, including pushing efforts to integrate schools, expand affirmative action, and advance women's rights. The Supreme Court was no different. Figure 7.14 shows the number of cases decided by the Supreme Court each year, between 1950 and 1980, that are coded in the Supreme Court Database as falling in each of the Criminal Procedure and Civil Rights Issue Areas. That is, these are cases where the substantive policy question at hand concerns criminal procedure – at the federal or state level – or civil rights. As the data indicate, there is a marked increase in both areas. During the mid-1950s, the Court is deciding roughly ten cases per year in each of these areas. By 1980, that number had doubled.

What is more, the number of Criminal Procedure cases the Court took during this period is related to the crime rate itself. The left-hand panel in Figure 7.15 shows the correlation between the (logged) crime rate each year and the (logged) number of Criminal Procedure cases the Court decided, between 1933 and 1979. Several points are worth noting here. First, there is a positive correlation; in years with higher crime rates, the Supreme Court takes more cases that involve Criminal Procedure. Second, there is something of an upper bound on how many cases the Court decided in this single Issue Area. Once the violent crime rate exceeds 190 violent crimes per 100,000 people (the value 5.25 on the x-axis), the Court is hearing roughly 20 cases per year in the Criminal Procedure Issue Area (the value 3 on the y-axis). That number does not change much as the violent crime rate continues to increase. Here, then, we see evidence consistent with the claim that the Court's docket is changing along with changes in social and political conditions in the United States.

The right-hand panel in Figure 7.15 shows the relationship between the number of cases the Supreme Court decides each year that are coded in the Supreme Court Database as being in the Civil Rights Issue Area and the number of protests that take place in the United States relating to civil rights or similar topics. Again, we see here a positive correlation – the years when there is a greater amount of protesting taking place in the United States motivated by concerns about civil rights and equality are the years when the Supreme Court agrees to decide more cases that have civil rights policy implications. In these substantive areas, as well, we see evidence that the Supreme Court's constitutional docket reflects changes in social and political conditions in the country.

What is more, the broader social and political context is related to which preference dimensions characterize the justices' voting, even conditioning on the broad substantive policy area implicated by a case. That is, holding constant the Issue Area to which a case is assigned – a measure of the policy content of the question before the Court – the crime rate predicts the justices are more likely to evaluate a case – in terms of their voting and opinion writing – as a matter of the Crime and Punishment preference dimension, rather than another preference dimension, such as the Judicial Power preference dimension.

Table 7.1 shows the results of a Dirichlet regression model in which the outcome variable is the distribution across each of the six preference dimensions for each case. The explanatory variables are the log of each year's violent crime rate per 1,000 people as well as fixed effects for the Issue Area to which the case is assigned in the Supreme Court Database. As in previous applications of this regression model in this book, the estimated coefficients tell us the association between the crime rate in a given year and the distribution of a case's opinion text across the six preference dimensions, conditional on the policy issue a case

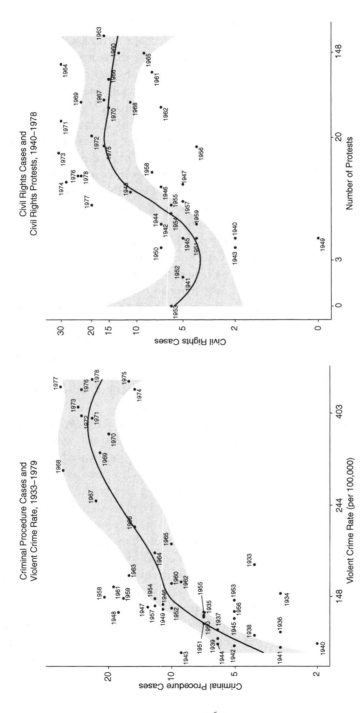

Figure 7.15. *Correlation between number of cases the Supreme Court hears in Criminal Procedure and Civil Rights Issue Areas and social conditions in the United States.* The left panel shows the crime rate and number of Criminal Procedure cases decided, 1933–1979 Sources: (of Management et al. 1973; of the Census. U.S. Department of Commerce. 1980; Spaeth et al. 2015). The right panel shows the amount of civil rights protesting each year and the number of Civil Rights cases decided, 1940–1978 Sources: (Burstein 1998; Spaeth et al. 2015).

Table 7.1. *Relationship between yearly violent crime rate and estimated distribution of preference dimensions in cases,* 1933–1980.

	Judicial Power	Economics and Business	National Power	Balance of Power	Criminal Law	Individual and Civil Rights
Logged Violent Crime Rate	−0.62 (0.04)	−0.18 (0.04)	−0.05 (0.04)	0.21 (0.04)	0.11 (0.04)	0.36 (0.04)
N	2333					
AIC	55608					

Cell estimates are Dirichlet regression coefficients, with standard errors in parentheses. Supreme Court Database Issue Area fixed effects included but not reported.

deals with (as measured by the Issue Area variable). As these estimates illustrate, during the years when the violent crime rate is heightened, the Court's opinions reflect more language associated with the Balance of Power, Crime and Punishment, and Individual and Civil Rights preference dimensions. That is, when the crime rate increases, the justices evaluate cases along the ideological preference dimensions associated with those three topics. Given what we have seen about the nationalizing of criminal law during the mid-twentieth century and the changing cultural and social dynamics at work, these relationships suggest a relationship between external social and political forces and the content of the Supreme Court's constitutional decision making. While this is not evidence that the crime rate is *causing* the justices to evaluate cases in a particular way, it does illustrate that the Court's constitutional decision making is moving in tandem with social conditions in the country.

Moreover, it is not just the way the justices evaluate and describe the constitutional questions that come before them that respond to social and political conditions. The way in which the justices resolve cases is also related to external social and political factors. Figure 7.16 shows the proportion of cases decided in a "liberal" direction each year, as coded by the Supreme Court Database. What we see is that between 1940 and the mid-1960s, the Court increasingly decides cases in a liberal

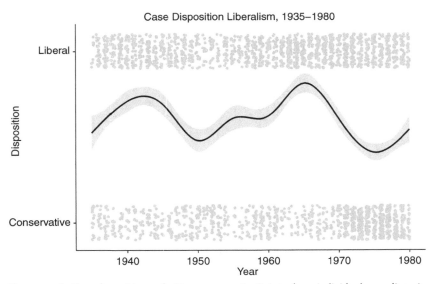

Figure 7.16. *Case disposition polarities, 1935–1980.* Points show individual case disposition polarity, according to Supreme Court Database. (Uncodable cases are excluded.) The line shows a nonlinear scatterplot smoother.

direction. However, by the end of the 1960s, that pattern reverses, as the justices increasingly decide cases in a conservative direction. There are two aspects of this pattern that bear emphasizing. First, the increase in liberalism among the case dispositions accompanies a decrease in unemployment and an increase in civil rights protests during the late 1950s and early 1960s. However, at the same time, as the crime rate began to explode during the late-1960s, and as protest activity exploded, there was a remarkable turnaround as the Court began to issue more and more conservative decisions.

Second, of course, these changes in the Court's output also correspond to high-profile changes in the Court's composition. Between 1950 and 1968, there were nine new appointments to the Supreme Court – for an average of one every other year. Most of these justices were individuals widely perceived either at the time or in history as liberal members of the Court. Even President Eisenhower, the only Republican president between 1932 and 1968, appointed justices with deep liberal legacies, including Chief Justice Earl Warren and Justice William Brennan. Presidents Kennedy and Johnson further cemented the liberal transition that began with FDR's appointments.

Figure 7.17 shows both the median justice's location in each of the preference dimensions between 1950 and 1980, as well as the level of ideal point polarization. A few points bear noting. First, the liberalism that the FDR appointees brought to the Court remained well past their tenure, as the justices remained relatively liberal, and homogenously so, along the Business and Economics preference dimension. The new justices who came to the Court during the 1950s and 1960s shared their predecessors' ideological orientation along this dimension. Second, the liberal transition that was taking place along the Balance of Power preference dimension during the 1940s continued steadily through the 1950s and 1960s, as the median justice became even more liberal along this preference dimension, and the polarization metric indicates the justices steadily coalesced around that more liberal orientation.

Third, the median justice became more liberal along the Crime and Punishment and Individual and Civil Rights preference dimensions, reflecting common historical understandings of this era being one of particular liberalism with respect to these political dimensions. However, less frequently appreciated is the finding here that the transition was uneven between the two preference dimensions. The consequence of the new appointments to the Court was a shift to the left along the Crime and Punishment preference dimension, but an accompanying increase in polarization. The justices were more liberal, on average, but there was an increasing degree of disagreement among them. Along the Individual and

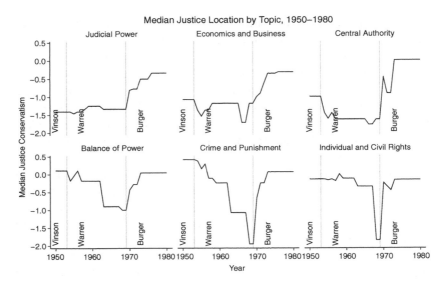

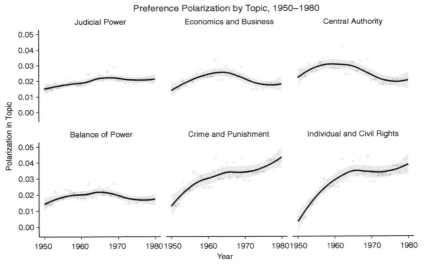

Figure 7.17. *Location of the median justice and ideological polarization among the justices in each of the six dimensions, 1950 through 1980.* Polarization is calculated using the method developed by Esteban and Ray (1994) and applied by Clark (2009a) to the Supreme Court.

Civil Rights preference dimension, there was less change in the median justice's liberalism, but a sharp increase in polarization. Whereas the justices didn't necessarily become more liberal as a whole, the two wings of the Court moved increasingly further apart.

Table 7.2. *Relationship between social conditions and justices' likelihood of voting in a liberal direction.*

	(1)	(2)	(3)
Crime Rate	−0.08	−0.06	−0.11
	(0.02)	(0.01)	(0.01)
Number of Protests	0.04	0.08	
	(0.01)	(0.01)	
Unemployment Rate	−0.002		0.002
	(0.01)		(0.01)
N	37,576	46,191	37,576

The dependent variable is an indicator for whether a justice's vote in a case is coded as liberal in the Supreme Court Database. Entries are logit coefficients with standard errors in parentheses. Each model includes justice-level fixed effects and fixed effects for the Issue Area to which the case is assigned in the Supreme Court Database.

Thus, by the end of the 1960s, the Court was comprised of justices who were on average more liberal than they were 20 years earlier, but the biggest change was that they were more divided along two "hot-button" preference dimensions – Crime and Punishment and Individual and Civil Rights. That divisiveness would have consequences for public perceptions of the Court during this period of social strife and political upheaval. A great deal of public controversy surrounded the Court by the late-1960s. President Johnson's effort to elevate Justice Abe Fortas to be Chief Justice was defeated, in part surrounded by controversy about politically and ethically questionable recusal decisions Fortas had made. Justice Douglas became a lightning rod for conservative criticism, owing to his outspoken views on major cultural and social cleavages. Moreover, in an era where the crime rate was spiking, as we saw in Figure 7.13, Richard Nixon campaigned in part on the Supreme Court's liberalism with respect to criminal defendants. Politicians at all levels of government criticized the Court. As Clark (2011) illustrates, the late 1960s were a period of intense conflict between Congress and the Supreme Court, with members of Congress – especially conservative members – introducing and considering a record number of bills aimed to limit the Court's power in 1968.

Thus, a second feature of the pattern we see in Figure 7.16 is the sharp turn towards more conservative decisions after Nixon's election in 1968. Of course, one of the first things Nixon was able to do was nominate Chief Justice Warren Burger, who oversaw a period of conservative transformation on the Court. However, while the median steadily moved to the right along each of the preference dimensions, with each of Nixon's four appointments during his first four years in office, the Court continued to make a number of decisions that were widely perceived to be liberal, such as its well-known decision in *Roe v. Wade*, holding that the Constitution protects a woman's right to have an abortion.

Assessing, then, the extent to which the Court's increase in liberalism during the 1960s and subsequent conservative shift is attributable to internal or external forces poses something of a challenge, as both social conditions and the Court's membership were changing in tandem. One thing we can do, though, is try to assess whether there is a global relationship between the justices' propensity to vote in a liberal direction and external social conditions. To do this, I estimate a logit regression model in which the dependent variable is the direction of a justice's vote in a case. The explanatory variables are the crime rate in the year the case was decided, the unemployment rate that year, and the number of civil rights protests that year. I include fixed effects for each individual justice and the issue area to which the case is assigned in the Supreme Court Database. Therefore, the estimated coefficients associated with each of the social metrics can be interpreted as the relationship between the metric and the propensity to vote in a liberal direction, net of variation associated with individual justices' propensities to vote in a liberal direction, and systematic variation across substantive policy areas.

The estimates reported here indicate that, holding constant a justice's proclivity to vote in a liberal direction and variation in liberalism associated with the broad substantive policy issues captured by the Issue Area, the justices' votes vary systematically with conditions in society. As the crime rate goes up, the justices are more likely to vote in a conservative direction. As protesting increases, the justices are more likely to vote in a liberal direction. In other words, the justices' votes vary with problems in society. This finding comports with a long line of research that argues the Court relies on public support and is sensitive to the boundaries of what the mass public will support (e.g., Mishler and Sheehan 1993, 1996; Norpoth et al. 1994; Stimson, MacKuen, and Erikson 1995; Flemming and Wood 1997; McGuire and Stimson 2004; Vanberg 2005; Giles, Blackstone and Vining 2008; Carrubba 2009; Friedman 2009; Staton 2010; Epstein and Martin 2010; Clark 2011; Casillas, Enns and Wohlfarth 2011). At the same time, there does not seem to be any relationship between the unemployment rate and the justices' voting patterns. This likely captures the notion that how one responds to concerns about unemployment likely depends on one's underlying ideological orientation, whereas crime and civil unrest have less ambiguous implications for how one responds. During the decades following World War II, then, we see that the Court's decisions reflect changing societal conditions in ways that are consistent with changing political and legal responses to the problems of the day.

Particularly notable are the Court's decisions in the area of criminal procedure. Most Americans know the case *Miranda* v. *Arizona* (1966), if only by way of watching television dramas that depict police officers. In that case, Miranda had been arrested on suspicion of kidnapping. He was interrogated by police and subsequently signed a confession. The case made its way to the Supreme Court, where the justices, by a vote of 5–4, held that an arrested individual must be told of his right to a lawyer before being interrogated. Tellingly, this case came to the Court in the midst of a major movement, shifting the provision of legal aid away from private providers towards government assistance (e.g., Menkel-Meadow 1984). This process included the provision of legal aid to criminal defendants and indigent individuals with civil suits (see Epp 1998, ch. 3, for a discussion of this movement in the United States).

However, *Miranda* was neither the first nor the last case in this era to reflect the changing nature of criminal law and its relationship to social struggles in the country. Earlier in the decade, the justices had famously extended the exclusionary rule to the states, holding, in *Mapp* v. *Ohio* (1961), that evidence seized in violation of the Fourth Amendment could not be used in state court proceedings, applying against the states the doctrine that the Court had developed in *Weeks* v. *United States* (1914) but had declined to require the states adopt in *Wolf* v. *Colorado* (1949) just 12 years earlier. In 1963, the justices decided *Gideon* v. *Wainwright*, holding that the Sixth Amendment requires a state provide counsel for criminal defendants who cannot afford to hire their own. Recall from Figure 7.13 above that these cases are being decided just as the crime rate is beginning its steady rise that would characterize much of the rest of the century. At the same time, these cases are also occurring during an era when the unemployment rate is particularly high, before the temporary drop during the last years of the 1960s. In other words, there is an increasing amount of crime and a relatively high level of poverty in the country. These set the conditions for the justices to hear more and more cases involving disadvantaged criminal defendants. Adding to this set of conditions, as we have seen, the justices who were serving on the Court during this era were particularly liberal. Figure 7.17 shows the justices had become steadily more liberal along the Crime and Punishment preference dimension as well as somewhat more liberal along the Individual and Civil Rights preference dimension.

Consider, for example, the argument made to the justices in *Mapp*, in which the central question was whether to apply the exclusionary rule to the states. In order to make their case, Mapp's attorneys, and the American Civil Liberties Union, which participated as an *amicus curiae*, argued that the states were engaging in regulation that infringed upon individual freedoms. In *Mapp*, the petitioner had been convicted of having obscene material in her possession. During oral argument, Barnard Berkman, representing the ACLU, argued,

We submit that interposing a policeman between a normal adult and his library is not a proper means of accomplishing what might otherwise be a valid legislative purpose. We contend that the statute is arbitrary and excessive. We urge that there are important individual rights which are protected against encroachment by the states by the concept of ordered liberty embodied in the Fourteenth Amendment, and which are substantially and unnecessarily limited by this statute. And we say that the evil sought to be controlled here can be met by less drastic statutory means without limiting the liberties of the citizens of the State of Ohio. Consequently, we feel that the statute is unconstitutional.

Now, our brief has discussed some of the sociological and scientific studies at page 8. In Appendices A and B we have correlated some of the studies which have dealt with the question of whether obscene material results in depravity. We note that, at page 8, the conclusion seems to be that there is no positive study that so holds. We are not saying that this is a necessary consideration to the matter of the First Amendment, clear and present danger. That is not our point. But we are trying to demonstrate that this legislation is not reasonably related to, nor adapted to the accomplishment of any legitimate governmental purpose.

Why must the relationship be shown between the legislative means and the desired result more clearly in this kind of a case? It seems to us that it is because individual rights, such as the right of privacy, the right to which has been substantiated as part of the Fourteenth Amendment in *Wolf versus Colorado* and *Butler versus Michigan*...

And we do not feel it necessary to consider whether the Fourth Amendment is incorporated bodily into the Fourteenth Amendment. We think that certainly the right of privacy is a basic concept of freedom which appears there.

In pushing for a more expansive view of the Fourth Amendment's prohibitions on state power, the advocate rested his argument on the moral and social setting from which the case arose. Surely aware of the justices' increasing liberalism along the Crime and Punishment preference dimension as well as their increasing liberalism along the Individual and Civil Rights preference dimension, he chose to highlight how state laws were having an interactive effect, criminalizing the kinds of behavior that society was finding less and less offensive. The reliance upon "sociological and scientific" evidence, both in the written brief and in oral argument, suggests the importance of changing standards of knowledge and morality in the development of constitutional law.

It is telling, moreover, that the majority opinion in *Mapp* only briefly mentions the fact that the criminal conviction arose because of a statute prohibiting the possession of obscenity. Instead, the majority opinion focuses on the Fourth Amendment argument, overruling *Wolf* and applying the exclusionary rule to the states. In a dissenting opinion, joined by Justices Frankfurter and Whittaker, Justice Harlan accuses the majority of "reaching out" to overrule *Wolf*. The dissenting opinion claims that the real issue at hand was the obscenity statute, which the majority used as cover to make the Fourth Amendment decision at which it wanted to arrive. Though the dissenting justices do not favor reversing the conviction under either scenario, they claim it was inappropriate for the majority to answer the Fourth Amendment question, rather than simply focusing on the obscenity question. In a memorandum, Justice Stewart agrees with the minority that the case should really resolve the question of the obscenity statute's constitutionality, though he believes he would vote to reverse Mapp's conviction even if that were the issue being decided. The claims made in the dissenting opinion, and the vote split in this case, reveal the developing fissures in the Court by the mid-1960s.[3] Indeed, as we saw in Figure 7.17, the justices were considerably more divided along the relevant preference dimensions by the time *Mapp* was decided.

Note the contrast with *Miranda*. In that case, the defendant had been convicted of rape (as well as kidnapping).[4] Even in the progressive era of the mid-1960s, Americans continued to recognize that rape is a vile crime, and so in this case there was little incentive to advance an argument would rest on underlying social forces. Indeed, to the extent societal conditions might affect *Miranda*, they would not be in favor of the defendant. As we saw in Figure 7.13, at the time *Miranda* was decided, the country was at the beginning of what would prove to be a rapidly increasing rate of violent crime. Indeed, the Court's opinion hardly mentions the crime at hand, whereas the dissenting opinion highlights the broader societal impact of the majority decision. Joined by Justices Harlan and Stewart, Justice White wrote,

In some unknown number of cases, the Court's rule will return a killer, a rapist or other criminal to the streets and to the environment which produced him, to repeat his crime whenever it pleases him. As a consequence, there will not be a gain, but a loss, in human dignity. The real concern is not the unfortunate consequences of this new decision on the criminal law as an abstract, disembodied

---

3 Indeed, this example also illustrates the importance of including both majority and non-majority opinions in the analysis, as including only one of these opinions would paint a different picture of the issues at hand than does the consideration of all of the opinions together.
4 The *Miranda* case is actually a consolidation of a set of related cases. In some of the other cases, the defendants had been convicted of rape and murder.

series of authoritative proscriptions, but the impact on those who rely on the public authority for protection, and who, without it, can only engage in violent self-help with guns, knives and the help of their neighbors similarly inclined. There is, of course, a saving factor: the next victims are uncertain, unnamed and unrepresented in this case.

Nor can this decision do other than have a corrosive effect on the criminal law as an effective device to prevent crime. A major component in its effectiveness in this regard is its swift and sure enforcement. The easier it is to get away with rape and murder, the less the deterrent effect on those who are inclined to attempt it. This is still good common sense. If it were not, we should post-haste liquidate the whole law enforcement establishment as a useless, misguided effort to control human conduct.   384 U.S., at 542-3 (Justice White, dissenting)

The invocation of criminals run amok and ineffective criminal law at the very least suggests the consideration of broader social conditions, even if it is only rhetorical and not itself the cause of the justices' votes.

7.2.3 *Social Change and Constitutional Decision Making*

Following a transitional period at mid-century, the Supreme Court entered a period during which its constitutional decision making would be shaped by strong social forces. In particular, during the 1960s, the country was undergoing significant changes, especially with respect to Americans' understanding of social order and individual liberties and privacy. The Second Red Scare abated, and the Court's constitutional decision making in the area of freedom of expression reflected the broader relaxation of fear of subversive political viewpoints. In many ways, these developments reflect well-documented patterns of the courts' sensitivity to national security concerns in their decision making (e.g., Epstein et al. 2005; Clark 2006). At the same time, as the country began to experience increased social unrest and crime, the Court's constitutional decisions reflected the importance of developing a coherent, effective federal criminal law structure. This was particularly crucial in light of the justices' expansion of the federal government's role in criminal law in the preceding decades.

The analysis in this section demonstrates the pattern of interrelated external social dynamics, internal political forces, and constitutional decision making continues even into such a period of unrest. Most instructive, for our purposes here, is how the broader patterns in constitutional decision making can be understood in light of the underlying microprocesses at the Court. Simply put, society was changing, and constitutional law changed with it. What the analysis here lays bare is how social changes and developments drove changes in constitutional law. However, as we see next, the conclusion of the social revolution of the 1960s was not a return to normalcy but rather a social counterrevolution.

Just as in physics where every action is associated with a reaction, progressive movements in politics are typically met with conservative pushback. The closing decades of the twentieth century witnessed precisely this kind of political response to the cultural revolution of mid-century America.

7.3 CULTURE WAR AND CONSERVATIVE REVOLUTION

In 1968, Richard Nixon was elected president, having appealed in particular to social conservatives (the group he would label during his presidency the "silent majority"). The Republicans would control the White House for 20 of the subsequent 24 years, interrupted only by the election of Jimmy Carter in 1976. Even after the Democrats regained the presidency in 1993, Republicans took both chambers of Congress in the 1994 mid-term elections, for the first time in decades. Moreover, with Ronald Reagan's "Southern Strategy" in 1980, many Southern Democrats left the party, becoming Republicans, further undermining progressive politics. One consequence of the conservative shift in electoral politics was a direct effect on the Supreme Court. While some of Nixon's nominees to the Court turned out to be more liberal than he might have hoped, and while George H.W. Bush famously nominated Justice Souter, who greatly disappointed hopeful conservatives, Republican presidents controlled all nominations to the Court for nearly a quarter of a century. Collectively, they appointed ten justices between 1969 and 1992. These new justices would bring very different viewpoints to constitutional decision making and reshape the ideological makeup of the Court along most of the preference dimensions.

Indeed, in Figure 7.18 we see that the median justice became steadily more conservative along each of the six preference dimensions since 1970. What is more, there is a rather consistent pattern with respect to the distribution of preferences on the Court along each of the preference dimensions. Figure 7.18 shows that polarization increased, though to varying degrees, along each preference dimension through the 1970s and 1980s, until the conservative remake of the Court reached an inflection point, after which there was a noticeable drop in polarization. (There were no appointments to the Court between 1994 and 2005, which results in a constant level of polarization through those years.) What these data portend, and what we will see in the remainder of this chapter, is a shift in constitutional decision making from the relatively more progressive perspective that drove constitutional law for nearly a half century, beginning with the Great Depression. The shift would be to a decidedly

Median Justice Location by Topic, 1915–1945

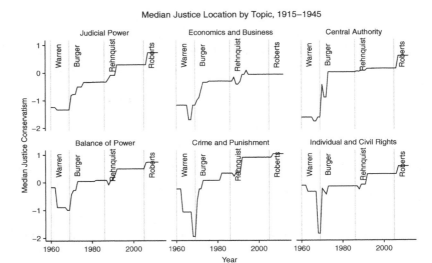

Preference Polarization by Topic, 1960–2012

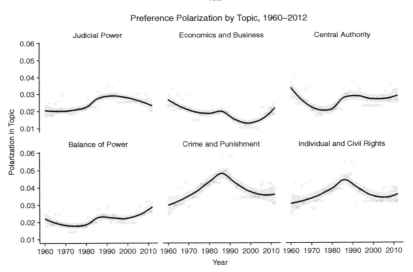

Figure 7.18. *Location of the median justice and ideological polarization among the justices in each of the six dimensions, 1960 through 2012.* Polarization is calculated using the method developed by Esteban and Ray (1994) and applied by Clark (2009a) to the Supreme Court.

more conservative perspective on constitutional meaning, marked in particular by a resurgence of conservative constitutional thought.[5]

---

[5] As I describe below, conservative intellectuals had begun an effort at mid-century to train lawyers and staff the lower courts. This effort is exemplified by the creation

Another consequence for constitutional decision making was more indirect. As the Court entered the final decades of the twentieth century, its docket comprised issues that sharply diverged in substance from those in the first few decades of the century. However, this change in substantive focus did not mean the Court was involved in controversies any less divisive or delicate; rather, the ideological orientation of the new conservative majority meant new legal challenges were brought before the Court. Different policies were put into place by the elected branches of government, as compared to the years before, which meant qualitatively different questions being asked in constitutional decision making. Recall Figure 7.1. There, we saw that through the end of the decade, the justices mapped a smaller and smaller proportion of their constitutional decision making onto their Business and Economics and Judicial Power preference dimensions. Crucially, through the remaining decades of the twentieth century, the justices decided more and more of their constitutional cases along the Crime and Punishment preference dimension. As we saw in the preceding section, this development can have significant consequences for *how* the justices decide cases and, by extension, *what* constitutional law says. Of course, as we will see below, the War on Drugs that began during the Nixon Administration resulted in a skyrocketing amount of federal criminal law and court cases, which raised a host of constitutional questions about criminal procedure and criminal defendants' rights. So, there was a somewhat exogenous, external force driving the Court's agenda.

At the same time, though, as we will see, there was something of a more internal force, as the new conservative justices who arrived at the Court during this era were more inclined to focus on law and order aspects of constitutional questions, thereby implicating the Crime and Punishment preference dimension, than they were to focus on other aspects of cases, such as individual privacy and freedom. The conservative revolution in electoral politics that took place during the 1970s and 1980s focused on a variety of social, cultural, and economic issues. The immediate consequence for constitutional law, though, was borne out in the realm of criminal procedure and criminal defendants' rights. Writing early on during this era, one commentator observed that President Nixon's four appointments had led to a sharp about-face for the Court during which criminal defendants, the poor, and racial minorities no longer benefited from an active Court looking to enforce a strong interpretation of their constitutional rights (Wilkes 1973). Indeed, it was during these years that

and maintenance of the Federalist Society, but the movement was in fact much larger and widespread (e.g., Teles 2008).

the conservative legal movement began to see returns to its investments, as a new generation of legal minds, trained to pursue a conservative political agenda in the courts, came to staff both the bar and the bench (Teles 2008).

One other prominent development in constitutional litigation during the Burger Court was the increased presence of conservative special interest groups. As O'Connor and Epstein (1983) point out, conservative groups began to participate before the Supreme Court as *amici curiae* with increasing frequency through the 1970s. O'Connor and Epstein also note that as those groups began to appear before the Supreme Court, they first focused their efforts in areas of the law related to economic regulation, rather than criminal law or civil liberties. There are several reasons why this strategy would have been attractive. First, as we saw in Figure 7.18, the median justice had moved to the right along the Business and Economics preference dimension (as it had along the other dimensions) by the early 1970s. However, compared with the other dimensions, the justices were much less divided (i.e., the level of preference polarization was relatively low along that dimension). Thus, interest groups looking to move constitutional law to the right would have seen cases that activated that preference dimension as relatively more promising. Still further, it would have been not just the internal politics of the Court but also broader economic conditions that could make economic liberalism a promising area to litigate. The mid-century economic growth had begun to turn for the worse during the late-1960s, as inflation undermined the growth that had come after World War II. The expansion of the welfare state during the 1960s was an easy target for economic conservatives who sought to curtail government power and spending. They would have seen cases about economic regulation a setting in which social conditions would be conducive to their preferred outcomes at the Court.

However, those conservative groups did not have much success in their policy objectives. It was not until later, during the Rehnquist Court, that we began to see conservative special interest groups being more successful in their litigation efforts at the Court. This trend is particularly interesting from the historical perspective of the analysis in this book. The development and ultimate success of conservative litigation groups is a historical force that sits at the intersection of the four types of factors we consider – it is a product of both internal and external conditions, as well as both structural and contingent conditions. As we consider three areas of constitutional decision making in the remainder of this chapter, I will highlight where and how those conservative groups played a particularly notable role.

7.3.1 *Law and Order: From the Cold War to the War on Drugs to the War on Terrorism*

The 1970s were a complicated time in the United States. Coming on the tails of the cultural revolution of the 1960s, the country found itself embroiled in the Vietnam War, experienced difficult and economic conditions, witnessed a conservative move in electoral politics, interrupted by the resignation of a president who had committed felonies in the pursuit of retaining office, and confronted increasing crime and drug use rates. Moreover, congressional activity during this period turned increasingly towards criminal justice. As Lerman and Weaver (2014, 33) show, the late-1960s witnessed a marked increase in the proportion of congressional hearings concerned with criminal justice issues. These various developments in society simultaneously affected both the nature of politics in the United States and the questions that drove constitutional litigation during the final decades of the twentieth century. From the perspective of the twenty-first century, the last few decades have a common theme – politics has been characterized by an on-going concern with security, be it the threat associated with the Cold War or concerns with domestic crime and drug use or contemporary fears about terrorism.

Early in his administration, President Nixon famously declared a war on drugs. Nixon wrote, "America's public enemy number one in the United States is drug abuse. In order to fight and defeat this enemy, it is necessary to wage a new, all-out offensive" (Nixon 1971). Nixon's message was framed in part around the growing level of heroin addiction among veterans of the Vietnam War. Nixon established the Special Action Office for Drug Abuse Prevention, which was a precursor to today's Office of National Drug Control Policy. To head the agency, Nixon tapped Jerome Jaffe, a doctor who had specialized previously in treating opiate addiction. Though Nixon's approach seemed to indicate a perspective on drug abuse that would focus on treatment and prevention, over the coming years, drug policy would come to be oriented more around criminal law enforcement tools than medical ones.[6] That narrative would dovetail with Nixon's broader response to the social and cultural developments of the 1960s. By portraying the country as on the brink of total chaos, Nixon set the stage for a political landscape in which any policy issue could be cast as a matter of maintaining social order. Nowhere was this as true as in the realm of law enforcement and justice. The Supreme Court, as part of that system, quickly found its constitutional

---

[6] By the 1990s, drug control policy would not be handled by doctors, such as Jaffe, but instead by politicians, political actors, and even former military officers.

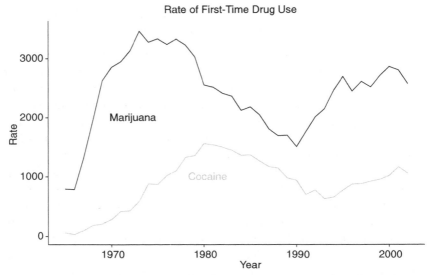

Figure 7.19. *First-time drug use rates, for all ages, 1965–2002.* Data show the number, in thousands, of individuals in the US who first used marijuana (black) and cocaine (grey) each year. (Source: Abuse and Administration 2004.)

docket shifting, due to both external forces shaping the questions that came to the Court and internal politics.

The history of the 1970s, in particular, suggests the former was particularly consequential, as many of the Court's moves in criminal procedure can be understood by reference to the broader social conditions to which I have referenced. For example, as Figure 7.19 shows, the late 1960s and 1970s witnessed a rapid increase in drug use. This trend reversed itself during the 1980s, but then again began to increase during the 1990s. The now-infamous War on Drugs began during this time, escalating notably over the following decades and contributing to the massive explosion of criminal cases on the federal courts' dockets and drug offenders subject to state and federal corrections.

How should we expect these developments to affect constitutional decision making at the Supreme Court? Consider Figure 7.20, which shows, for a hypothetical justice, the benefits associated with any given approach to criminal justice. The x-axis measures conservatism, such that doctrinal orientations further to the right indicate a constitutional order that gives greater power to the government in pursuing criminal cases, whereas doctrinal orientations further to the left indicate a constitutional order that gives the suspect or defendant greater freedom and protection. The y-axis measures both costs and benefits. The solid black line measures the benefits the justice perceives with respect to each policy option,

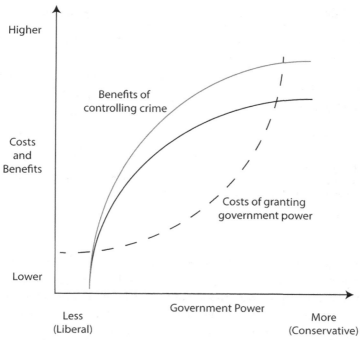

Figure 7.20. *Theoretical cost-benefit analysis for different levels of government power in crime prevention.* The dashed line shows the social costs associated with each level of government control. The solid lines show two potential benefit curves.

particularly in terms of the policy's effectiveness at promoting order and protecting the public from crime. The dashed black line, by contrast, shows the costs associated with each policy, specifically in terms of the threat to defendant rights, due process, and guaranteed constitutional protections. Policies where the solid line is above the dashed line are those where the benefits of a policy outweigh its costs. A justice's *optimal* policy is the one that maximizes the difference between benefits and costs.

Suppose, though, social conditions change, as they did during the 1970s. We know that judges often respond to major social events, such as war, by changing their voting patterns (e.g., Epstein et al. 2005; Clark 2006). What effect might this have on a justice's preferred doctrine? One effect it might have would be to shift the slope of benefits curve upwards, as shown by the solid gray line in Figure 7.20. Under this condition, more conservative policies have relatively more social benefits compared to more liberal policies because the incidence and/or nature of crime has changed. Holding constant a justice's perceived costs associated with each policy, increasing the slope of the benefits curve has the effect of shifting

Table 7.3. *Correlation between rates of drug use and justices'*
voting, 1965–2002.

	All Cases		Criminal Procedure	
	Marijuana Use	Cocaine Use	Marijuana Use	Cocaine Use
Rate of First-Time Use in Year	−0.11 (0.02)	−0.20 (0.03)	−0.11 (0.04)	−0.17 (0.06)
N	42,275	42,275	10,938	10,938

Estimates are coefficients from logit regression models; the dependent variable is whether a justice votes in a liberal direction in a case; the explanatory variables are indicators of first-time drug use in each year and justice-level fixed effects.

the optimal doctrinal position to the right. Thinking about this logic in terms of the case-space model, what a shift in the crime rate would imply is that a justice's preferred threshold would become more conservative. This would mean that he or she would be more likely, ceteris paribus, to vote in a conservative direction in any given case.

Indeed, this is the pattern we observe. As the prevalence of drug use in the United States increased, the justices' voting patterns changed in tandem. Table 7.3 shows the results of a set of empirical models in which the dependent variable is an indicator for whether a justice voted in a liberal direction in a given case. The explanatory variables are the rate of first-time drug use (for all ages) in the year the case was decided, as well as fixed effects for the identity of the justice voting. Thus, the estimated coefficient associated with the rate of drug use tells us how the individual justices' voting patterns changed as the rate of drug use changed. I show four models – measuring drug use with first-time marijuana use and time-time cocaine use, and examining all cases and just criminal procedure cases.

These estimates indicate that as the drug use rate increased, individual justices became less likely to vote in a liberal direction, not just in criminal procedure cases but in all cases. As we have seen in previous analyses, this is consistent with an account of constitutional decision making in which the justices' decisions are related to broader contextual factors driving American society and politics. Of course, though, it is not as though the conservative shift in the Court's constitutional decision making, especially the conservative moves in criminal procedure we saw above, were simply a function of the drug epidemic in the late twentieth century. Rather, these patterns serve simply to highlight how constitutional decision making was moving in tandem with, if not in response to, major social developments at the time.

Despite this broad pattern, the real story of criminal procedure jurisprudence during the 1970s is one of a failed conservative makeover. Most commentators agree that the Nixon appointments amounted to a "counterrevolution that wasn't" (e.g., Blasi 1983; Schwartz 1998). One reason might be that, while Nixon was able to appoint conservatives to the Court, the effect was simply to dilute the liberals' control of the Court while not taking over the entire bench. Figure 7.21 shows the consequences of each of Nixon's appointments for the preference profile along each of the six preference dimensions. The first appointment is the replacement of Chief Justice Warren with Chief Justice Burger in June 1969. The second is the replacement of Justice Fortas with Justice Blackmun. (Justice Blackmun's appointment in June 1970 occurred after Justice Fortas' seat had actually been vacant since his resignation in May 1969.) The third change in the Court's membership was the simultaneous appointment of Justices Powell and Rehnquist to replace Justices Black and Harlan, respectively. In the figure, in each panel, the black arrows connect the exiting justice from the top position with the replacement justice in the lower position. The grey lines, meanwhile, show the change in the location of the median along that preference dimension.

The first thing to notice is that not all of the preference dimensions were affected similarly by each transition. On most of the preference dimensions, Chief Justice Warren was fairly far to the left, while Chief Justice Burger was relatively far to the right, and so his appointment resulted in a significant shift in the preference profile. The replacement of Justice Harlan with Justice Rehnquist has a less dramatic impact, while the replacement of Justice Black with Justice Powell had a different impact across different dimensions. Justice Powell was much further to the right than was Justice Black on the Economics and Business and Balance of Power preference dimensions, whereas they were relatively similar along the Individual and Civil Rights preference dimension. Crucially, though, the Nixon appointments had a mild, if uneven, effect on the location of the median justice. With each successive appointment, Nixon moved the median to the right along the Crime and Punishment preference dimension, while his appointments were not particularly consequential for the Individual and Civil Rights, Economics and Business, or Balance of Power preference dimensions.

Indeed, while the closing decades of the twentieth century witnessed constitutional decision making at the US Supreme Court marked by a conservative effort to curtail the reforms in criminal procedure that had been made by the Stone and Warren Courts, the initial trajectory

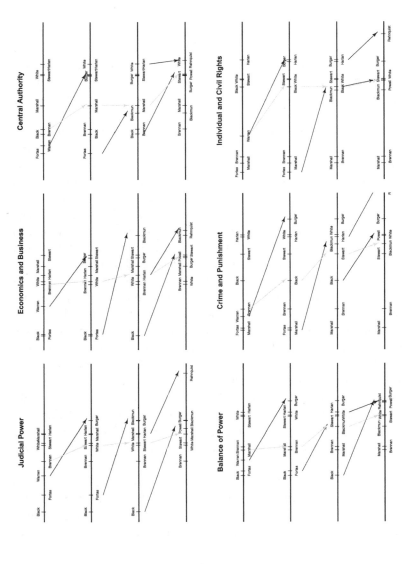

Figure 7.21. *Consequences of Nixon appointments along each of the six preference dimensions.* The black arrows show the change in membership from one natural court to another; the grey lines show the change in the location of the median justice from one natural court to another.

was neither an easy one to pursue or necessarily what conservative politicians had been hoping for in the 1960s. Indeed, it has been observed that the 1970s "were not times for bold moves; it was time for delicate maneuvering" (Decker 1992, 7). That was so because of the social turmoil described above, in conjunction with the conservative criticism that the Warren Court had nakedly ignored precedent and *stare decisis*. The consequence was that those who wished for a conservative revolution in criminal procedure had to look for ways of working within established precedent and to avoid exacerbating major social tensions. Another reason is that, as we see in Figure 7.21, the initial conservative appointments to the Court were not conservative or plentiful enough to overcome the impact that Democratic nominees had had on the Court since the late-1930s. However, by the 1980s, appointments by Presidents Reagan and Bush seem to have finally pushed the Court to the right. As we saw in Figure 7.18, the Rehnquist and Roberts Courts saw a steady move in the location of the median justice further and further to the right, combined with a consolidation of conservative influence, as indicated by the decreasing level of preference polarization along each of the six preference dimensions after about 1990.

What is more, the war on crime was reaching a turning point during the 1990s. The Democrats took back the White House in the election of 1992, but President Clinton was not liberal in the way earlier Democrats had been. Partially in response to the political climate of the 1980s, the Democratic party had shifted to the right. Topics such as criminal justice and welfare reform were embraced by both sides of the aisle. The 1994 Violent Crime Control and Law Enforcement Act in many ways exemplifies the political climate of the time as it pertains to law enforcement. The law had many aspects to it, but the driving force was to raise the penalties for many federal crimes, imposing the infamous "three strikes" rule, which mandated life sentences for violent offenders with two previous convictions (notably, including previous convictions on drug offenses). Two years later, President Clinton also signed the Antiterrorism and Effective Death Penalty Act of 1996 ("AEDPA"). Partly designed to provide tools to combat terrorism (the World Trade Center had been bombed in 1993), the AEDPA strictly limited the resource death row inmates had to habeas corpus relief in the federal courts. In short, what had transpired between the election of President Nixon in 1968 and the election of President Clinton in 1992 was that the courts were no longer in the delicate social context that required careful negotiation of the constitutional posture from the 1960s. The closing years of the century were a time for bold action, spurred on by growing concern about safety and security during the 1980s.

Then, of course, the twenty-first century began with one of the most infamous examples of criminal behavior the world has known – the terrorist attacks of September 11, 2001. The events of that day led to a significant change in Americans' perceptions of the proper limits on government power to protect security. Congress enacted the PATRIOT Act, which, among other things, greatly enhanced government surveillance powers, and the War on Terror resulted in a number of practices that pushed the boundaries between military and law enforcement practices. Notably, the Supreme Court wound up reviewing several of those policies, including the use of indefinite detention of foreign nationals and the denial of the writ of habeas corpus. As we will see, those cases came at a point in time when the conservative makeover of criminal procedure jurisprudence had already reached a point of culmination. Crucially, then, we find at the beginning of the twenty-first century an interaction of structural and contingent forces, driven by external and internal conditions.

Let us consider the beginnings of the conservative counterrevolution where it made one of its most significant impacts – criminal procedure. In particular, the Burger Court's constitutional decision making with respect to criminal defendants' rights curtailed three major prongs of the criminal procedure doctrine established by the Warren Court. The Burger Court made decisions that weakened the rights of the accused, specifically those established in the *Miranda* decision; it made decisions that tilted the balance in favor of the government in the processing of trials, specifically targeting the expansion of defendants' rights typified by *Gideon* v. *Wainwright*; and it limited the breadth and depth of protections afforded by the Fourth Amendment against intrusive searches by authorities, with a notable effort to roll back the protections developed in *Mapp* v. *Ohio* (see, for example Decker 1992; McMahon 2011; Graetz and Greenhouse 2017). Entire books have been written on the conservative doctrinal developments in criminal procedure during the late twentieth century (e.g., Decker 1992), and we could do the same here in order to understand the relationship among internal and external and structural and contingent forces and criminal procedure jurisprudence.

Instead, let us consider but one area of doctrine which, perhaps, best exemplifies how the Burger and Rehnquist Courts pushed back against Warren Court criminal procedure precedents – the rights of criminal suspects embodied in *Miranda*. As the Court moved to the right, and as the events of the late twentieth and early twenty-first century unfolded, the conditions were met for, at first, the creation of minor exceptions to certain rights and, then, the expansion of those rights in order to effectively undermine their very meanings.

In particular, as the War on Drugs expanded, criminal defendants increasingly found themselves in situations where there were opportunities for the government to whittle away at the breadth of the *Miranda* protections. These situations were a function of the increasing prominence of drug trafficking and sales in the US, as well as the simultaneous expansion of police investigative practices. In one example, a defendant had been approached by an undercover police officer in an attempt to purchase heroin. While the sale never took place, the defendant was later brought before a grand jury to testify about the heroin sale network. He was not provided a *Miranda* warning related to his grand jury testimony, and in *U.S.* v. *Mandujano* (1976), the Court had held that individuals subpoenaed to appear before a grand jury do not have the right to *Miranda* warnings.

More significantly, in a pair of cases – *Harris* v. *New York* and *Michigan* v. *Tucker* – the Court held that *Miranda* warnings are not themselves constitutional rights but rather "prophylactic standards" that were designed to help reinforce the constitutional right against self-incrimination. Later, the Court would push this line of logic further to allow for the admissibility of non-coerced confessions (see, for example Belsky 1998, 137). In fact, not only did the Burger Court make incremental steps to de-fang the Warren Court criminal procedure precedents, but so too did the Rehnquist Court over the subsequent 20 years.

However, as Graetz and Greenhouse (2017, 44–45) note, it was particularly telling that the Rehnquist Court did not explicitly overrule the *Miranda* decision. Rather, the conservative majority on the Court incrementally whittled away at the doctrinal breadth and impact of *Miranda*. That was a telling decision because in 1969 when he was an assistant Attorney General, and later as a Supreme Court justice, Rehnquist had been a chief critic of *Miranda*. Indeed, in light of the Courts' decisions during the years since *Miranda* was decided, the precedent had become so weakened that even Rehnquist could come to its defense in 2000, when he authored the majority opinion in *Dickerson* v. *United States* (e.g., Graetz and Greenhouse 2017).

I argue that the increasingly conservative Court did not overturn *Miranda* at any of its opportunities during the 1980s or 1990s is illustrative of the ways in which politics both internal and external to the Court affect the trajectory of Constitutional decision making. At the time *Dickerson* was decided, 94% of Americans supported requiring police to inform arrested individuals of their *Miranda* rights (Gallup Poll, June 22–25, 2000). While Chief Justice Rehnquist did not engage this point in the majority opinion, Justice Scalia's dissent does. Specifically, Justice Scalia noted that the petitioner in the case argued that *Miranda* "should be preserved because the decision occupies a special place in the 'public's consciousness'" (530 U.S., at 464, Scalia, J., dissenting). That Dickerson's advocates thought it important enough to point out in their brief, and that Justice Scalia decided to raise the point in his opinion both suggest that the role of social conditions and culture are a component of constitutional decision making, even in such a high-profile and consequential area of law as this.

It is also important to take note of other factors in the political environment that were playing out during the 1990s. In 1990, Congress enacted the Crime Control Act of 1990, which was a bundle of related statutes aimed at providing law enforcement officials more tools to combat crime. Over the next few years, a series of high-profile violent criminal events took place, including the 1993 bombing of the World Trade Center. Congress subsequently enacted the Violent Crime Control and Law Enforcement Act of 1994. In 1995, Timothy McVeigh and Terry Nichols bombed a federal building in Oklahoma City, and the next year, Congress enacted the Antiterrorisism and Effective Death Penalty Act of 1996. In short, the country was getting tough on crime. The notion that the courts were coddling criminals or undermining the country's safety would have seemed out of place in this context.

Consider Figure 7.22. Here, I show, in the top panel, the total number of prison inmates in the United States each year from 1978 through 2014. The well-documented trend is immediate. During those 36 years, the prison population quadrupled, such that there are nearly 4 million people incarcerated by 2014. What is particularly important, though, is the rate of change during the 1990s. In 1990s, there were just over 2 million people incarcerated. By 2000, that figure had risen to over 3 million – an increase of 50%.

In the right-hand panel, I show the proportion of respondents on the General Social Survey (GSS) who say "we're spending too little halting the rising crime rate."[7] This survey is fielded roughly every other year, though during the early part of the series it was fielded during most years. Up until 1996, the proportion with that view hovers around 70%, reaching its apex in 1994, at 78%. However, thereafter, there was a sharp drop in that view, which seems to potentially have begun to turn around again in 2016. Thus, by the end of the twentieth century, the increasing degree of federal crime-control legislation, conservative judicial doctrine, and large increase in the incarceration rate was also associated with a weakening of public support for increased spending on crime control.

---

[7] Specifically, I use the variable "natcrime" from the GSS series. I exclude all respondents who say they don't know or decline to answer.

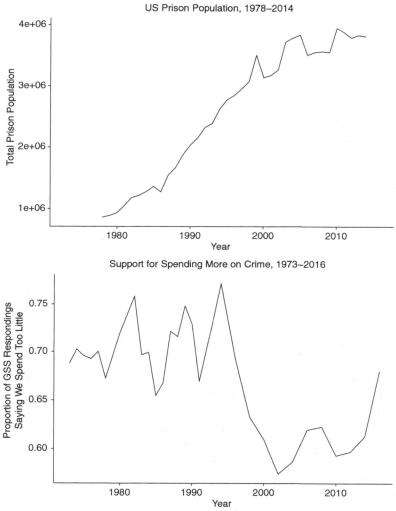

Figure 7.22. *Size of United States prison population and public opinion about spending on crime.* The left-hand panel shows the total number of inmates in US correctional facilities each year from 1978 through 2014. The right-hand panel shows the proportion of respondents on the General Social Survey who express the view that we spend too little on crime control each year the survey was administered from 1973 through 2016.

What is particularly instructive is that individual justices have tended to vote more liberally in criminal procedure cases as the number of prisoners increased. Table 7.4 shows the estimates of an empirical model of individual justices' voting patterns. The outcome variable is whether an individual justice voted in a liberal direction in a case. The explanatory variables are (1) the logged number of prisoners in the United States (in

Table 7.4. *Empirical model of justices' voting in criminal procedure cases, 1978–2012.*

	With Dimension Variables	Without Dimension Variables
Logged Million Prisoners	0.10 (0.04)	0.09 (0.04)
Public Support for More Spending	−0.70 (0.59)	−0.44 (0.58)
N	7427	7427
AIC	9629	9655

Cells show coefficients from logit model, with standard errors in parentheses. Each model includes fixed effects for each justice. The first column also includes an estimate of each case's loading onto each of the preference dimensions.

millions), (2) the proportion of Americans who indicate on the GSS that we spend too little on halting crime, (3) the loading of the case onto each of the six preference dimensions, and (4) fixed effects for each justice. Because I have argued that the internal politics underlying a decision can shape how a case is mapped onto the preference dimensions, one might be concerned that including the loading onto each preference dimension induces post-treatment bias in the estimates of the relationship between the prisoner population and the justices' voting. Thus, I also report the models excluding the preference dimension covariates.

These results are instructive, because they show that among cases about criminal procedure, individual justices vote more liberally as the prisoner population increases. While not meant to be a test of whether the number of people incarcerated causes the justices to vote more liberally, this test does indicate that during the period when the legal infrastructure has led to greater incarceration, the courts have also taken a more progressive approach to criminal procedure. Why that is instructive is that it further documents how the trajectory of social and political conditions and the trajectory of constitutional decision making move in tandem at a broad, systematic level. The illustrative cases discussed above are but particular manifestations of these broad macro patterns.

7.3.2 *Individual Freedom, Privacy, and Culture Clash*

Even while Americans were becoming more concerned about crime and security during the closing decades of the twentieth century, there was a growing level of progressivism with respect to privacy and individual freedom. However, that overall trend masks what might be the more dramatic pattern, which characterizes American politics in the beginning of the twenty-first century – deep polarization.

While electoral politics at the end of the twentieth century reflected a distinctly conservative orientation, there was something subtly progressive about the times. For example, consider the changing role of women in national government. In 1970, there were ten women in the House of Representatives and one woman in the Senate. There were no women on the Supreme Court and only a small handful of women had ever been appointed to lower federal courts. However, during the 1970s, despite cultural pushback represented electorally by Richard Nixon's great silent majority, a great deal of social progress was made. Title IX was enacted in 1972, prohibiting sex discrimination in educational settings. In 1981, Ronald Reagan appointed Sandra Day O'Connor as the first female justice of the Supreme Court, and by 1990, there were 29 women in the House and two in the Senate. In 2016, there were 84 Representatives and 20 Senators serving. Similarly, in 1970, the civilian workforce participation rate for women was just over 45%, whereas it was nearly 58% by 1990 (according to the US Department of Labor). In other words, the role of women in American life was changing rapidly during these years.

Of course, the increasing role of women in political institutions and the private workforce does not mean that the politics of the time were a march towards liberal policies. Rather, it simply stands to show that the conservative shift in criminal procedure jurisprudence did not indicate a retrenchment away from all of the progressive goals of the post-war years. Rather, the Burger and Rehnquist Courts operated in a time of complex, shifting politics. The mid-1970s were marked by a calming of the cultural furor of the 1960s, as progressive advances began to be adopted as part of mainstream American politics.

One of the most notable ways in which the changing politics of the time were reflected in constitutional decision making can be seen in the Court's decisions related to privacy and freedom of expression. Of course, during the 1970s, the Burger Court decided *Roe v. Wade*, which held that the Constitution forbids blanket prohibitions on abortion. The consequence of the Court's decision in *Roe* was, however, a complex progeny involving many different "branches" that dealt with related, but distinct, constitutional questions (see, e.g., Clark and Lauderdale 2012). For example, one line of follow-up questions that the Court addressed in the wake of *Roe* concerned whether minors have a constitutional right to abortion or whether states may require parental consent. In 1979, the Court decided *Belotti v. Baird*, in which it upheld a state's authority to impose parental consent requirements for minors seeking an abortion, provided that the state also allow for a judge to grant an exception upon a minor's request (a so-called judicial bypass).

It was in this political context that, in 1980, Ronald Reagan was elected president in a landslide victory, and the Republican Party gained seats in both the House and the Senate. The 1980 election was largely framed in terms of economic issues, but social conservatives played an important role in the Reagan campaign, and after the election, they found they had gained considerable sway in both the federal government and in state governments around the country. In this climate, states around the country, motivated by social conservatives' political organization, set out throughout the 1980s to craft increasingly contorted restrictions on access to abortion. Those laws led to widespread litigation during the 1980s. In 1983 alone, the Supreme Court decided three major abortion cases. For example, in a case following *Belotti*, *Planned Parenthood* v. *Ashcroft* (1983), the Court was asked to further elaborate on that ruling. In *Ashcroft*, the Court held that a minor's degree of maturity could be a component of a judicial determination about whether to grant a parental notification bypass. Other cases during the early 1980s dealt with other kinds of notification rules, such as whether a doctor can require parental notification even if the state does not (*H.L.* v. *Matheson*) and whether states must allow for judicial bypass when the state only requires parental notice and not parental consent (*Ohio* v. *Akron*). These cases largely represent social and political efforts to regulate abortion subject to the restrictions imposed by *Roe*.[8]

One of the more consequential lines of argumentation in the abortion-related constitutional cases has to do with the interaction of the right to privacy on which *Roe* rests and claims of religious liberty under the First Amendment. The legal roots of this line of legislation, litigation, and argumentation has its roots in the conscientious objector precedents that had come in to particularly sharp relief during the Vietnam War. In the immediate aftermath of *Roe*, Congress enacted the Church Amendment, which provided a conscientious objection to healthcare providers who did not want to participate in abortion or sterilization on the grounds they have religious objections to the practice.

The Church Amendment represents an important development in constitutional thought in the United States. It reflects, in many ways, the growing influence of the religious right in politics and society. A decade earlier, the Supreme Court and Congress had both rejected the notion that personal beliefs could override the Constitution's promise of equal

---

[8] In a related set of cases, the justices had to evaluate restrictions that states adopted that were intended to work around the "viability" standard embraced in *Roe*.

protection in the context of racial discrimination and segregation. In the 1970s, though, the abortion debate would test the reach of that principle as it was applied to religious objections to abortion and birth control.

Importantly, the Supreme Court has yet to resolve this question. Today, many states have used conscientious objection protections to permit pharmacists to refuse to dispense birth control medication, citing religious objections. Other states have enacted statutes that compel pharmacists to fill such prescriptions. In the early-2000s, it was a common conservative strategy to provide individuals and, increasingly, institutions, the right to opt out of public service provision on religious grounds. This legislative debate reflects two related developments in the politics of individual freedom at the end of the twentieth century. First, we see an expanding notion of the reach of civil liberties and individual freedom. Rather than simply reflecting the right to express oneself, the First Amendment was being used increasingly to create exceptions to constitutional or other legal mandates. Second, the tide of civil liberties argumentation was turning from one of advancing progressive policy objectives to a weapon for conservative interests. This was particularly so, again, at the intersection of religious conservatism and free market conservatism.

In fact, one of the major developments in impact litigation during this period illustrates the symbiotic, back-and-forth pattern of constitutional development that I described in Chapter 1. As the Supreme Court became more conservative, its decisions affected, in turn, the kinds of questions that were litigated and the strategies organized interests adopted before the Court (e.g., O'Connor and Epstein 1981, 1985; Burstein 1998). Kobylka (1987) shows, for example, that after the Supreme Court shifted its approach to obscenity in *Miller* v. *California* (1973), conservative interests shifted their approach to First Amendment litigation, and there was a marked shift in the liberal groups who participated in these cases before the Court.

The shift in litigation during the 1970s had particular consequences for principles of individual freedom and liberty. By the end of the twentieth century, the notion that had been at the core of the liberal legal movement during the 1950s and 1960s, was transformed into a bedrock of conservative constitutional thought. However, the consequences of conservative application of that principle were markedly different reflecting, again, many of the powerful social forces acting on the justices and deep transformations in the internal conditions at the Court. One of the areas of law where this transformation was most pronounced was in the Court's approach to government-religion entanglement. Much of this development began with the 1970 decision, authored by Chief Justice Burger, in *Lemon* v. *Kurtzman*. At issue in *Lemon* was a statute in Pennsylvania that allowed the state to reimburse private schools for the salaries of teachers in those schools. Crucially, most of those private schools were Catholic schools. As Graetz and Greenhouse (2017, 218) note, the decision did not at the time seem to be a landmark, but history has shown otherwise. In the majority opinion, Chief Justice Burger articulated what has come to be known as the *Lemon* test, which sets out a standard for evaluating whether a statute violates the Establishment Clause of the First Amendment. The test has three requirements: (1) the statute must have a secular purpose; (2) the statute's primary effect cannot be to advance or inhibit religion; and (3) the statute cannot foster an "excessive entanglement with religion." If a statute fails any of those requirements, it is to be found in violation of the First Amendment.

During the following decades, there were two important developments that had deep consequences for *Lemon*. First, changes in the Court's membership led to both more conservative justices on the bench but also a greater representation of Catholics. We have seen already that the politics of Supreme Court appointments had a profound impact on the Court during the final three decades of the twentieth century. Second, the nature of religious education in the United States changed. Importantly, Protestant and Evangelical Christians abandoned their prior opposition to government support for religious education, building a coalition with conventional conservatives that has led to a broad base of support for public funding of religious education.

According to Jeffries and Ryan (2001), a precipitating event that has led to a change in the public debate about government-funded religious education is the move by Protestants and Evangelicals to stop opposing public funding of religious educational facilities. Previously, those groups opposed public funding because Catholic education was the dominant form of private religious education. However, by the latter half of the twentieth century, private religious schools came to serve as a haven for whites who wanted to avoid racial desegregation in the public schools. White, religious conservatives came to see private educational institutions as opportunities rather than institutions for Catholic indoctrination. In part reflecting that trend, as Jeffries and Ryan (2001) document, the number of non-Catholic Christian academies skyrocketed during the 1970s and 1980s.

One consequence of the growth of non-Catholic Christian education, and the waning opposition of government funding for religious education among Protestants and Evangelicals, was a strong alliance between the Religious Right and more traditional free-market, libertarian conservatives. That political alliance resulted in a number of state laws and policies that ultimately presented the Court with constitutional questions about entanglement between government and religion. It was in this social and political context that the Burger and Rehnquist Courts interpreted and adapted the *Lemon* test over three decades.

Indeed, the conservative justices appointed by presidents Nixon and Reagan held views opposed to strict separation of religion and government. In one early case interpreting *Lemon*, then-Justice Rehnquist wrote for a 5-4 majority in *Mueller* v. *Allen*, upholding a Minnesota income tax deduction that disproportionately affected parents who sent their students to private religious schools. The law in question allowed individuals to deduct expenses for tuition, transportation, and school supplies for parents sending their students to private schools. At the time, nearly all private school enrollment in Minnesota was in religious institutions. The majority held that the statute could pass First Amendment scrutiny, because the benefit that disproportionately affected religiously affiliated individuals was the result of their own private choice – whether to send their students to public or private school – and therefore was not an instance of establishment of religion.

That holding – which introduced the notion of school choice – would turn out to be a bedrock of debate about private education in American politics for years to come. The constitutional move made in *Mueller* represented a binding of religious conservatism and free-market conservatism. It was, in some sense, a point where we see a fundamental shift in how civil liberties, especially a truly libertarian perspective thereof, would play out in American politics after the Cold War. In particular, both Presidents Reagan and George W. Bush included school vouchers in their education policy proposals, representing both the political influence of religious groups and the changing legal landscape around public education. By 2001, the Supreme Court decided *Zelman* v. *Simmons-Harris*, which upheld an Ohio school voucher program. Chief Justice Rehnquist wrote for the five-justice majority, relying on his earlier opinion in *Mueller*, that the program did not violate the First Amendment, even though 82 percent of the beneficiaries were attending religiously affiliated schools. Chief Justice Rehnquist argued that because the voucher system did not encourage individuals to attend religious schools and because private citizens chose religious schools of their own free volition, then the program was sufficiently neutral. (See Graetz and Greenhouse (2017, 222–24) for a discussion of the move from *Mueller* to *Zelman*.)

However, the expansion of individual liberty and personal freedom from traditional progressive causes to more conservative ends was not limited to entanglement between the state and religion. Just as civil libertarians have long embraced content-neutral interpretations of individual freedoms (consider, for example, the ACLU's defense of Nazi protesters in Skokie, Illinois), indeed, one of the areas of conservative civil liberties jurisprudence that complements the Establishment Clause jurisprudence concerns freedom of speech and expression.

Beginning in 1973, the Burger Court came to embrace a more permissive view of the states' power to regulate speech. In a pair of cases, the Court upheld the states' power to regulate obscenity. In *Miller* v. *California*, the Court upheld a statute that regulated obscenity, settling on a three-pronged definition for what constitutes obscene material. In particular, the Court held that something qualifies as obscene and therefore can be restricted, if it (1) appeals to the prurient interest, in the view of a typical person in the community; (2) shows or describes sexual acts, excretory functions, or genitals; and (3) does not have "serious literary, artistic, political, or scientific value." In *Paris Adult Theatre I* v. *Slaton*, the Court upheld a state's authority to prohibit adult movie theaters from showing pornography. These two cases represented an important conservative milestone. The Court made clear the Constitution's protection of free speech is strong but simultaneously took advantage of a subject matter and pair of cases that allowed them to promote conservative policy goals – the restriction of obscene material.

Thinking back to Chapter 5, one of the things we saw was that as the Court became more conservative, its cases tended to involve case locations that were more extreme, suggesting the justices were strategically picking cases they knew would allow them to achieve conservative dispositions, presumably for the purpose of advancing conservative doctrine. Figure 7.23 shows the case locations for all First Amendment cases decided since 1960. (Recall the discussion above about the logic of case selection during this period.) The top panel shows cases that were ultimately decided in a conservative direction, whereas the bottom panel shows cases that were decided in a liberal direction.

There is a distinct contrast between the two patterns. Among the liberal outcomes, the average case location has remained roughly the same over time. However, among the cases with conservative dispositions, there is a trend over time towards cases with locations further to the right. What does this imply? Beginning in the 1960s, cases that had a conservative disposition had locations that were far to the left, so that even relatively moderate justices would prefer the conservative disposition. During the early years of the Burger Court, in order to reach a conservative disposition, the Court would have to confront a case that presented somewhat more extreme case facts, bringing justices to the conservative outcome who might typically be expected to vote in a liberal direction more often.

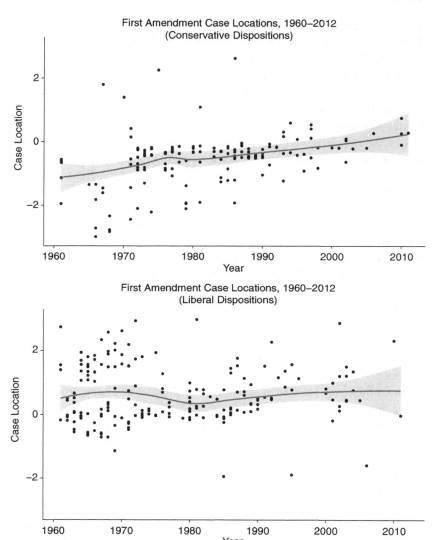

Figure 7.23. *Case locations for First Amendment cases decided between 1960 and 2012.* The top panel shows cases that were decided in a conservative direction; the bottom panel shows cases that were decided in a liberal direction. Points show individual case locations, the line is a nonlinear scatterplot smoother.

Considering the models of bargaining and opinion writing that political scientists have developed and evaluated empirically (e.g., Schwartz 1992; Westerland 2003; Hammond, Bonneau, and Sheehan 2005; Lax and Cameron 2007; Clark and Lauderdale 2010; Carrubba et al. 2012), there are several implications. First, as the majority coalition becomes more ideologically diverse – i.e., when the case location for a conservative disposition is further to the left, then there ought to be more concurring opinions. This follows from an assumption that a justice will be more likely to join an opinion as he or she finds herself closer to the opinion, in a preference dimension. Broader coalitions imply that, all else equal, any given justice is more likely to be further away from the opinion than in a tighter coalition.

Beyond the nature of the coalitions and the content of their opinions, there is a deeper substantive pattern that reflects the conservative direction of First Amendment jurisprudence during the Rehnquist and Roberts Courts. Specifically, we see that the application of principles have been extended to cover interests beyond individuals' civil liberties. In particular, one of the most notable developments in constitutional law during the early twenty-first century has been the extension of individual freedoms to corporations. Consider the landmark decision *Citizens United* v. *FEC* (2010). In that case, the justices invalidated a campaign finance law that imposed regulations on campaign spending by organizations and corporations. The five-justice majority concluded that the law unconstitutionally infringed on corporations' First Amendment protection of freedom of expression. In the empirical model, this case loads primarily (almost entirely) onto the Individual and Civil Rights preference dimension.

Since then, we have seen a number of similar developments in other areas. In *Burwell* v. *Hobby Lobby* (2014), a sharply divided Court held that closely held corporations can benefit from First Amendment protections for religious liberty. In that case, Hobby Lobby, a private corporation, sought to deny contraceptive coverage in its health care insurance. Hobby Lobby's lawyers argued that the corporation's owners held a religious objection to the use of contraception, and so the federal requirement they provide health insurance that includes coverage for contraceptives violates their First Amendment protection for free exercise of religion. The Supreme Court upheld Hobby Lobby's claim that it should be exempt from providing contraceptive coverage. The reason, the five-justice majority claimed, was that the federal contraceptive mandate was not the most narrowly tailored means to achieve the policy goal. While the decision did not answer whether corporations benefit from free-exercise protections under the First Amendment, the ruling does recognize that closely held corporations can hold religious beliefs. Today, debates about the breadth of religious freedom continue in electoral and judicial politics, as conservatives seek to protect businesses that do not want to provide services to gay couples or to provide certain kinds of healthcare.

The trajectory from struggles during the late-1960s and early-1970s to extend civil liberties protections for individuals from traditional interpretations to modern notions of "privacy" provoked a strong conservative counter-movement against judicial activism. One consequence of that conservative movement was a large-scale special interest effort to use the judicial process to advance conservative constitutional doctrine. One indicator of the success of that movement can be found in modern developments in First Amendment law. In particular, the extension of First Amendment protections to individuals seeking to escape federal mandates or prohibitions on discrimination reflect in many ways the same kinds of battles that took place in the mid-twentieth century surrounding debates about racial discrimination. In this way, we are witnessing today the same kind of symbiotic interaction between social conditions, legal context, electoral politics, and judicial process that has driven constitutional decision making throughout American history. These broad, historical patterns, then, can best be understood from a macro-perspective that is grounded in the microprocesses of judicial decision making.

7.4 THE END OF AN ERA?

Constitutional decision making from the mid-twentieth century until the early twenty-first century has been characterized by a delicate but persistent entanglement between the way the Supreme Court addresses questions of constitutional meaning and social and political dynamics. One of the hallmarks of the path of constitutional law through these decades has been the expansion of constitutional decision making beyond a narrow focus on the balance of power between the federal and state governments. Modern constitutional decision making concerns matters ranging from federalism to economic regulation to political and civil rights to privacy and individual freedom.

From the perspective of constitutional decision making in the nineteenth century, the patterns we observe in constitutional decision making at the beginning of the 21st century may seem both foreign and familiar. What might seem foreign is the substance of questions that the Court engages. The incorporation of the Bill of Rights during the twentieth century brought into the world of constitutional law a host of legal issues and disputes that could not have been anticipated at a time when the Bill of Rights was not applied as a restriction on state power. At the same time, the expansion of the federal criminal justice system and the federalization of law enforcement has entangled the national government in a variety of constitutional issues that would not have been possible a century earlier. These developments reflected both broader trends in the social and political organization, especially changes in the nature of the federal government that came on the heels of the Great Depression (see, for example Ackerman 1998).

However, the path constitutional law took during the twentieth century would not have been completely foreign to nineteenth-century observers. What would have been familiar is the connection between the path of law and social forces. What we have seen in this chapter is that many of the broad, systematic patterns documented in the earlier period of constitutional decision making continue to explain patterns we observe today. Constitutional law is a function of the social conditions that give rise to political and legal disputes, as well as the politics of judicial preferences and decision making at the Court. As secular changes in the world have shaped American politics, constitutional law has responded, just as politics has responded to changes in constitutional decision making. For example, the civil rights movement at mid-century was certainly part of a cyclical relationship between law and social movement. As we saw in this chapter, the path that constitutional decision making concerning civil rights took was connected to social and political events at mid-century, including the cultural revolution, the war on drugs, and an increase in violent crime. Similarly, the Republican Revolution in the 1990s was related to patterns in criminal law that had been developing for decades.

While it may always be tempting to perceive oneself as living in times that are historically unique, what this chapter suggests is that what is unique today is the particular questions and context in which judicial decision making takes place. However, the way in which judicial decision making takes place is remarkably consistent with historical patterns. However, it does bear noting that one distinct pattern we observe today is the *decline* in the extent to which the Court has been involved in constitutional interpretation. One of the most widely noted features of Supreme Court decision making generally is the decline in the number of cases the Court decides during the early decades of the twentieth century. So too with constitutional law in particular.

What explains this trajectory and what it means for the future of constitutional decision making is a complex matter. To know what to make of the situation in which Americans find themselves today and the effects contemporary politics and social movements will have on constitutional decision making, it is useful to reflect on the broad patterns we have seen in the preceding two chapters. At the beginning of the twenty-first century, scholars and observers alike are concerned about growing political polarization and economic inequality in the United States. One interpretation of the Court's decreasing volume of constitutional decision making could be that it reflects concerns about the tenuous political environment and a cautiousness on the part of the justices. Another issue at hand in the new century is the growing prominence of security concerns and the primacy of foreign relations in the politics of the day. These are areas where the Constitution is more deferential to executive power and past practice has been for the courts to avoid much involvement. Thus, constitutional decision making in the twenty-first century is likely to be shaped by these social and political conditions as they shape the nature of disputes that come to the courts and frame the dimensions of political conflict that characterize judicial decision making. The question is whether the Supreme Court's retreat from constitutional decision making is merely a temporary phenomenon or instead a symptom of a broader change in how the politics of the twenty-first century are shaping constitutional decision making.

8

Conclusion

The history of constitutional law is a complex matter. What I have tried to accomplish here is to document a set of systematic historical patterns that help illuminate how social-scientific theories of politics can make sense of a unique history. Central to my approach has been the use of a statistical model of judicial decision making designed to use both judges' votes and their opinions to recover the dimensionality of preferences in constitutional decision making. By making use of multiple sources of data to recover different kinds of information, I have argued we can expose otherwise hidden nuance in how judges vote and decide cases.

One of the challenges this approach to analytic history necessarily faces is separating noise from signal. When studying the history of judicial decision making, it can be tempting to be taken in by all the details. After all, it is often the nuance that can be subsequently consequential. Compounding the matter, one might worry that my approach to modeling judicial preferences – one that pushes beyond traditional methods that distill all of politics into a single dimension, or sometimes two – exacerbates this risk. How do we know when we have moved beyond explaining what is systematic to explaining what is just randomness. The data I have used in this book are rich and offer a great deal of potential for the social scientist. However, at the same time, it can be challenging to determine how best to employ multiple kinds of data in conjunction in order to best study politics (for some recent innovations, see Clinton and Meirowitz 2004; Clinton and Lapinksi 2008; Kim, Londregan, and Ratkovic 2015; Bateman, Clinton, and Lapinksi 2016).

I have approached the problem of distilling the systematic from the random components of constitutional history through a blend of qualitative judgment and quantitative analysis. In Chapter 5, we saw that adding additional dimensions to our model of judicial voting yields marked improvements in how well the voting model fits the patterns we observe in judges' votes. However, we also saw that there were a variety of models (i.e., number of dimensions) that yield comparable fits to the data. Here, I have employed my own judgment to assess which additional dimensions are substantively useful. Of course, my decisions will not be without criticism, and it is not likely that scholars will ever settle on the "correct" number of dimensions for modeling judicial decision making.[1] Of course, that is for good reason, all models, including the model I have used here, are simply representations of the world, and the real question to ask is which model is most useful in which setting.

In that sense, the decisions I have made are instructive. *The key point is that constitutional decision making is multidimensional, and that has had consequences for the path of constitutional law in American history.* If we were not to consider the various dimensions that characterize constitutional decision making at the Supreme Court, it would be more difficult to see the patterns in how social forces relate to the path of law. This is because many of the social forces I illustrate are not linked to constitutional law generally but to particular aspects of constitutional decision making. What is more, the analytic history of constitutional decision making illuminates a handful of lessons that past research suggests. Let us consider a few ways in which it does so.

8.1 LESSONS LEARNED

One claim I hope the preceding analyses have substantiated is that an account of the history of constitutional law requires one to focus simultaneously on both internal and external forces that act upon judges. The law evolves in a recursive fashion, whereby judges' decisions in individual cases affect social conditions and the subsequent cases they are asked to resolve, which in turn affect how judges decide those cases. For this reason – that the system of legal evolution is inherently recursive – it is unlikely that any tractable, parsimonious model of legal development will adequately explain most or even many of the interesting phenomena we observe in judicial politics.

This is, of course, not to say that parsimonious theories of the judicial process are without utility. To the contrary! From the beginning, I have outlined a parsimonious model of the judicial process that has guided both the analysis and the interpretation of the data I employ. Using that model, I have shown that, throughout the history of constitutional law,

---

[1] In previous studies, my co-author, Ben Lauderdale, and I have argued for various potential models that consider anywhere from a small number of dimensions, to a modest level of dimensions, to an extremely large number of dimensions (Clark and Lauderdale 2010; Lauderdale and Clark 2012, 2014, 2016).

there emerge patterns in Supreme Court decision making that are best understood in light of well-developed theories of the judicial process. Moreover, existing theoretical models have pointed this analytic history to particular settings from which observations can best be made. In other words, micro-level theory has been important in both the interpretation of empirical patterns and in the discovery of empirical patterns we might have otherwise overlooked or regarded as of little analytic import.

For example, the connection of the LDA+IRT estimator to the case-space model of judicial decision making has facilitated the interpretation of the justices' ideal points and the case parameters. It has also imposed constraints on the kinds of interpretations of the data that we can accept. Further, the analysis of the Court's decision making has been facilitated by existing microtheories of bargaining and opinion writing, which provide the foundations for relating the median justice to the Court's collective output. Other microtheories have pointed the analysis towards the role of litigants in the path of law and informed the kinds of statistical analyses that make sense of broad trends in constitutional decision making. Consider a handful of implications in greater detail.

8.1.1 *Social Organization and the Law*

A vibrant body of research at the intersection of law, sociology, anthropology, psychology, and political science has long emphasized the role that organized social groups play in shaping the law. A number of themes run through this literature, including an emphasis on law as a *functional* instrument (see, for example Galanter 1974; Diver 1979; Neier 1982). The idea is that when individuals with a common interest organize, they can use litigation and the law as a means to achieve their social goals. The NAACP, representing the interests of black Americans who suffered at the hands of discrimination, can develop a litigation strategy to end segregation. Advocacy groups, such as Lambda Legal, representing individuals with minority sexual orientations, can use the courts to advance legal equality.

However, at the same time as existing literature has emphasized the potential for using the law as a means of social change, many studies have suggested that view may be particularly optimistic. There is little evidence, for example, that the NAACP's litigation efforts, culminating in the Supreme Court's decision in *Brown* v. *Board of Education*, had any direct effect on the extent of segregated public education (Rosenberg 1992). Similarly, some scholars have argued that the litigation system is structured so as to favor particular kinds of social interests and litigants – mostly notably, those who are already well-resourced and fortunate (e.g.,

Galanter 1974; Kagan 2009). In this view, we can understand the role of the courts in organized efforts to advance social change only through an appreciation of the structural factors that conditions how and when litigation is an efficacious method for bringing about change.

However, while there might not be much evidence of *particular* decisions having transformative consequences, there is much evidence that the NAACP's litigation success, itself, was more due primarily to the fortuitous combination of individuals, such as Thurgood Marshall, with keen legal acumen and clever approaches to litigation (e.g., Tushnet 1987). In other words, the NAACP's success in Court might be thought of more as a product of contingent factors – that sharp, committed, and clever lawyers were available to the NAACP – rather than structural ones – for example, that the litigation system is designed to be responsive to organized interests, such as the NAACP.

The analyses in Chapters 6 and 7 illustrated, systematically, how organized interests and social movements have influenced the path of constitutional law, both through structural and contextual mechanisms. The empirical patterns documented in those chapters reveals a correspondence between the Court's docket and social movements. We saw, for example, that the Court's cases involving economic activity tended to come from states with larger union membership. We also saw that the Court's involvement with free speech issues reflected the pattern in the strength of the Communist Party. Of course, considerable research in the past has shown that outside actors can have a strong influence on which cases the Court accepts for review (e.g., Caldeira and Wright 1988, 1990a,b; Caldeira, Wright, and Zorn 1999) and that the justices look for particular indicators when choosing among cases (e.g., Perry 1991). The analysis in this book suggests a general trend consistent with those patterns but broader in implication. What these analyses show is that the social conditions in which litigation takes place can affect not just which particular case the Court takes to resolve a dispute but which areas of the law the Court chooses to address in the first place. In the context of the model of judicial decision making I outlined in Chapter 1, the evidence suggests a correspondence between the location of the cases in the case space on which the justices decide, and economic and political conditions in society. That result could result from either a process by which those conditions are linked to the distribution of cases that emerge before the courts or a process by which the justices' choices about *which* cases to decide is connected to those conditions.

Still further, the empirical patterns I have documented show not just that what the Court decides is related to social conditions and organization but so too is *how* the justices vote. We have seen, for example, that crime rates, drug use, and economic conditions all predict which ideological preference dimensions best characterize the justices' votes and the way they describe their decisions. As social, political, and economic conditions change, so too does the ideological cleavage that characterizes the justices' voting patterns. Again, in the context of the model of judicial decision making that I have adopted, this finding indicates a correspondence between conditions in society and which considerations or preference dimensions activate when the justices evaluate a case. What the relevant dimensions of conflict in a case are connected to broader political and economic conditions.

Putting these findings together sheds light on how a number of related microtheories of judicial decision making can jointly account for paths of constitutional law in the United States. By considering how alternative preference dimensions yield different alignments among the justices depending on the substantive context of the case, I have documented the ways in which different interests can advance their goals in constitutional decision making. In the view of constitutional law I have advanced in this book, clever lawyering is not just an idiosyncratic, random component of legal development but instead a structural part of the judicial process. To the extent advocates and special interests understand the substantive nuance in the justices' views, they have an incentive to shape their arguments accordingly. This is very much the story I recounted in Chapter 1 about the switch in time in 1937. Aware of the difference in how the justices line up on matters of federalism and the balance of power, as opposed to commerce and economics, lawyers who wanted to save the minimum wage law were able to successfully recast the question and win the support of the pivotal justice, Owen Roberts.

Thus, by studying the integration of social movements and the path of constitutional law, we can see how institutional processes can be shaped by political and social contexts and how the judicial process reflects and is entangled with the currents of the time. This insight provides a new way of understanding the role of lawyers, activists, and litigants in the long-run path of the law. It also helps us understand the mechanisms by which institutional rules, such as those governing the appeals process, the separation of powers, or elections shape the development of constitutional law.

8.1.2 Electoral Politics and the Path of Constitutional Law

Closely linked to the role of social organization in driving the path of constitutional law is the role of electoral politics in constitutional decision making. However, as contrasted with social organization, the mechanisms by which electoral politics shape constitutional law are more varied. In particular, electoral politics have direct effects on both internal and external forces that shape constitutional decision making. They also affect both structural and contingent conditions.

First, and most directly, electoral politics shape the laws that are written. The Supreme Court is often a topic of debate in the context of political campaigns (e.g., Stephenson 1999). Once in office, elected officials consider the Court's constitutional decisions – especially decisions to invalidate laws on constitutional grounds – when debating policy and crafting new statutes (e.g., Pickerill 2004). Certainly, the evidence from campaign and legislative speech reflect politicians' efforts to advance their goals subject to the shadow of constitutional decision making by the Court.

Indeed, a body of research suggests that changes in the composition of legislatures explains variation in the volume of legislation and *what* subjects legislators address (e.g., Krehbiel 1998; Swers 1998; Binder 1999; Cox and McCubbins 2005). Similarly, there is considerable evidence that the content of public policy moves broadly in tandem with public sentiment (e.g., Stimson, MacKuen, and Erikson 1995; Erikson, MacKuen, and Stimson 2002). For that literature, a primary force that drives elected officials' behavior is a concern about constituent preferences, especially on high-salience issues, and expectations about the degree to which they will be held accountable for legislative outcomes (e.g., Mayhew 1974; Fenno 1978; Arnold 1992). The logic is that democratic accountability creates incentives for elected officials to take positions and advance policies that reflect the issues on the minds of those who sent them to office, lest they be removed from office at the next election (e.g., Canes-Wrone, Brady, and Cogan 2002). Taken in conjunction, the past scholarship brings together a set of microfoundations for the process by which we should expect electoral politics to lead to changes in the cases that comprise constitutional law.

The laws that are "on the books" affect the kinds of constitutional cases that come to the Supreme Court. Laws authorizing or failing to proscribe given police behaviors, for example, can give rise to conflicts that involve constitutional claims under the Fourth, Fifth, Sixth, Seventh, or Fourteenth Amendment with some regularity. Indeed, in the Supreme Court Database, most of the cases coded as being in the "Criminal Procedure" issue area involve interpretations of those four amendments. Other common legislation at hand in those cases includes the Eighth Amendment and statutes such as Omnibus Crime Control, federal criminal procedure rules, and statutes governing habeas corpus.

These last few examples are particularly notable, because they highlight how constitutional cases can be oriented around legislation written in Congress. As elected officials respond to public concerns and salient political issues, new laws and practices are put into place, creating a set of constitutional questions that is potentially different to those that would arise under alternative legal structures.

Importantly, we have seen that the way in which law develops over time depends on the way in which legal controversies activate the different preference dimensions that characterize constitutional decision making. Savvy legislators can take advantage of that regularity by crafting laws in such a way that various kinds of legal disputes will map onto particular preference dimensions. By writing statutes in a given way, Congress can make a criminal law issue into a federalism one, or Congress could turn a matter of question about individual freedom into a matter of judicial power. For example, Pickerill (2004) documents debate in Congress about the proper authority for civil rights legislation in the 1960s. (Specifically, legislators debated whether the matter was properly connected to Congress' power to regulate interstate commerce.) He also shows how the Court, while reviewing the constitutionality of that legislation consulted the debates in Congress in part to discern what members of Congress believed to be the central legal issue at stake. In this way, the content of congressional debate may have helped map questions about civil rights protections onto competing preference dimensions among the justices. That is, just as judges may engage in heresthetical maneuvering to manipulate the dimensions of debate among themselves (Epstein and Shvetsova 2002; Riker 1986), so too might other branches of government engage in efforts to manipulate the way in which the justices approach a case.

The second mechanism by which electoral politics can shape the path of constitutional law is more indirect. Judges in the federal courts hold their jobs "during good behavior," which is essentially a lifetime appointment. The only mechanism for removing them from office is impeachment. One consequence of their tenure is that they are relatively isolated from electoral pressures. Of course, there are tools at the disposal of elected officials to tinker with the courts' power (e.g., Nagel 1965; Rosenberg 1992; Clark 2011) and judges have reasons to worry about their base of public support more generally (e.g., Vanberg 2005; Carrubba 2009; Staton 2010; Clark 2009c, 2011).

However, federal judges, including Supreme Court justices *are* selected by elected officials who themselves face electoral pressures. One way that manifests is through the nomination and confirmation process for federal judges. Presidents have strong incentives to reward their supporters and political base by selecting judges who can advance a particular agenda on the bench. Indeed, during the last century, we witnessed an increasingly partisan nomination and confirmation process (e.g., Epstein et al. 2006). As academics and politicians alike began to recognize the importance of judges' ideological orientations, the political stakes of selecting the right judges became more apparent. The consequence is that who is nominated and confirmed to the Supreme Court in many ways reflects the dominant politics of the time (see, for example Dahl 1957; Abraham 1999; Yalof 2001). Indeed, one of the primary findings in political science studies of Supreme Court nominations and confirmations is that presidents and senators seek to appoint justices who share their own ideological orientations (e.g., Cameron, Cover, and Segal 1990; Segal, Cameron, and Cover 1992; Epstein and Segal 2005; Cameron and Kastellec 2016).[2]

The consequence of these nomination and confirmation politics is that the justices who interpret the constitution largely reflect the patterns in electoral politics during recent years. When elections change the balance of power among competing ideological camps, then, those changes filter into the judiciary through the nomination process and begin to shape how constitutional decision making plays out. There are a handful of ways that the preceding analyses show those changes manifest.

Previous empirical research has consistently illustrated that judges' ideological profiles predict how they vote (for the canonical study, see Segal and Spaeth 2002). Therefore, when the ideological profile of the justices on the Court changes as a consequence of electoral politics, we should expect different decisions by the justices. These different decisions will manifest in myriad ways, as we saw in the preceding chapters. There are ideological incentives that shape the justices' decisions about what issues to engage in in the first place (e.g., Caldeira and Wright 1990b; Perry 1991; Caldeira, Wright, and Zorn 1999; Cameron, Segal, and Songer 2000; Grant, Hendrickson, and Lynch 2012). In the 1940s, as the balance on the Court shifted towards the New Deal Democrats, the Court's focus shifted away from reviewing cases about federal regulation of the economy. By the end of the twentieth century, as conservatives came to control the Court, we saw a shift in the Court's attention towards cases that concerned notions of federalism and deference to the states.

Further, not only does changing the preference profile on the Court lead to changes in what issues with which the Court is involved, it also leads to changes in the kinds of decisions the Court makes. Segal

---

[2] Further, today, these politics are well reflected even in the process of selecting judges for the lower federal courts (e.g., Binder and Maltzman 2004, 2009; Steigerwalt 2010).

and Spaeth (2002) are perhaps most well-known for documenting the relationship between justices' ideological orientations and their votes on the merits of a case. The evidence here suggests that the relationship between justices' preferences and the substantive nature of the cases predicts which ideological cleavages activates. We saw, for example, in Chapter 7 that when judges link criminal law and federalism, they decide cases differently than they do when they consider criminal law in the absence of concerns about federalism. Similarly, Lauderdale and Clark (2014) show that the departure of Justice O'Connor and her replacement by Justice Alito moved the Court to the left on some issues but to the right on others. In other words, as new justices replace former justices, they can have different effects on the Court's perspective on legal questions, depending on how their views across various preference dimensions vary.

That finding implicates not just atomistic models of judging but also models of the collegial nature of judging at the Supreme Court. For example, throughout this book, I have frequently described changes in the Court's composition by reference to the location of the median justice in each of the six preference dimensions. One reason why that has been a useful metric for describing the Court is that most models of collegial decision making on the Court predict that the institutions of collective choice at the Court give great weight to the "center of gravity" on the Court (e.g., Cameron and Kornhauser N.d.; Moraski and Shipan 1999; Westerland 2003; Bonneau et al. 2007; Carrubba et al. 2012). As a consequence, when there is turnover on the Court, the electoral politics of the time will mean that some preference dimensions may be emphasized over others in the selection and confirmation process.

That process will lead to differential impacts on the Court's output across various substantive areas of the law. For example, New Deal Democrats placed a great deal of emphasis on new justices' views about commerce and federalism, but there was much less interest in how the justices would approach issues relating to civil liberties and modern notions of personal freedom. One consequence was that the justices appointed by Franklin Roosevelt found themselves at odds later in their career as the Court's agenda shifted (see, also, Feldman 2010). Similarly, in the political climate of the late twentieth and early twenty-first centuries, potential justices' views on abortion, government regulation, and affirmative action are often focal-points in the nomination and confirmation process. Thus, many of the patterns we have seen in this book can be understood as phenomena inextricably linked to broader political phenomena. In this way, the path of constitutional law can be understood as just one element of the path of American politics.

8.1.3 Path Dependence and Reinforcing Institutions

A third broad lesson we can draw from the analytic history of constitutional law concerns the way in which choices made at one particular time both influence future choices but also are a part of a consistent, systematic pattern of governance. Studies of path dependence in politics typically emphasize the ways in which political actors make choices that set them down a course in which subsequent opportunities for choice reinforce a pattern of behavior (e.g., Pierson 2000; Page et al. 2006; Beim, Clark, and Patty 2017). Particular conditions at a given point in time may create incentives for particular choices that then lead to a situation where it is difficult to change one's behavior. So too with the path of constitutional law.

In the beginning of Chapter 6, I described the political and legal context in which the Supreme Court found itself in the immediate aftermath of the Civil War. Of course, that political and legal context itself was the product of choices that had been made over a long period of time. However, the dramatic change in the Constitution and political order that accompanied the end of the Civil War in many ways provides a convenient and tractable place to consider how "initial conditions" affected the path that constitutional law has since followed. That the country was still working out the nature of federal power, especially the power of the federal courts, meant that at the period of the Second Industrial Revolution, myriad substantive questions in the law implicated the justices' views on the courts' appropriate role in government. Had the debate about the role of the federal courts been as settled then as it is today (not that there remain no questions), we might imagine the justices would have approached economic regulation in the late nineteenth century differently. As we saw in Chapter 6, for example, one way to understand the Court's switch between *Morehead* and *West Coast Hotel* in the late-1930s is through the different ways in which the matter of minimum wage was framed for the justices. Similarly, in Chapter 7 we saw that the connection of a criminal law case to matters of federalism in the twentieth century could affect the way in which the justices ruled. Thus, the overriding lesson here is that the broader context in which a case is decided – what issues have come and been settled before, as well as which issues are currently dominating politics – shapes the way in which legal questions map onto the various dimensions of political disagreement on the Court.

Still further, beyond the role of initial conditions and judges' and politicians' reactions thereto, the extent to which we can understand the law as an equilibrium outcome in a dynamic process is similarly a function of events that are at least partially exogenous to the constitutional order itself. For example, the technological innovations that led to the expansion in railroads facilitated the growth in large corporations. That change in the nature of the US economy gave rise to a host of constitutional questions and problems that had not been contemplated under prior doctrine. Those events then brought to the Court a set of questions, being asked in a particular social context. The decisions the Court made, which were a function of both conditional and structural factors, set the foundation of commerce jurisprudence which would influence not just future constitutional decisions, but electoral politics as well.

Of course, that history can be gleaned from a variety of sources. What the analytic approach here shows is the particular way in which those incentives manifested and how they related to patterns we observe in the Court's response to world events at other points in time through history. For example, in the mid-twentieth century, in the aftermath of World War II, there arose in the US questions about our approach to racial equality and segregation. As I showed in Chapter 7, the Court's docket changed in those years and reflected the trends taking place in electoral politics and social movements.

What is missing from the history I have documented, though, is a theoretical account of why the law emerged and developed in the way it did. I have shown how social conditions and structural factors reinforced each other and contributed to the path of law, but we still do not have a predictive theory of the law that can help us understand how the various levers of politics can be manipulated to shape the way in which constitutional decision making takes place. Under what conditions can institutional choices affect the way in which litigators frame their cases? How *should* legislators anticipate litigation when they write laws? What do we expect to happen when constitutional decision making shifts its focus from one political cleavage to another? I have considered some counter-factual scenarios, but what is missing from the descriptive account in this book is a notion of a general equilibrium in the constitutional order.

However, while the understanding this book contributes to path dependence in the constitutional law is not grounded in a predictive theory, the connection between the analytic description here and normative theories of democratic health is instructive. In particular, what we have seen is that constitutional decision making can be seen from a perspective in which constitutional law is part of the democratic process. This is an important lesson, because it is not obvious that constitutional law necessarily will move in tandem with broader political movements. A school of thought on constitutional interpretation holds that the Constitution should be read as those who originally drafted it would have, and then applied to the problems that arise in contemporary society (e.g., Scalia and

Garner 2012). However, what we observe here is that while the Supreme Court does not respond in a knee-jerk fashion to broader social forces, constitutional decision making is closely linked to politics more broadly. The Court's cases reflect the substantive problems of the day, and the way in which the justices approach those cases – namely, how they relate them to the dominant preference cleavages – is related to the context in which those cases arise. That is, the path our constitutional law takes incorporates, for better or worse, the path our broader politics takes.

8.2 REMAINING PUZZLES

The lessons I draw from the preceding analysis notwithstanding, the claims I make raise some questions which the methods I employ cannot answer. In particular, I consider two such questions in depth. First, what about the other factors that are relevant for understanding the path of constitutional law? How do we situate the story I have presented here into a broader understanding of constitutional law? Second, how do we understand the analysis here as it relates to social science? Is the analysis here social science? What can we do with the methodological approach I advance, beyond studying constitutional decision making at the US Supreme Court?

8.2.1 There's More to Constitutional Law than Politics

As I noted in Chapter 5, one of the interesting features of the preference dimensions I recover is the absence of preference dimensions that correspond to political and social issues we might think are particularly cross-cutting in American life. For example, as I described, it might strike one as curious that there is no distinct dimension that is specifically about racial conflict. We know that many justices have had preferences that are systematically different in cases that implicate race. We might also find it unusual there is no preference dimension that is specifically about national security. Scholars who study inter-branch relations have often noted that the balance of power and degree of deference to the president is shifted when a constitutional or legal question implicates matters of national security (e.g., Wildavsky 1969; Yates and Whitford 1998; Epstein et al. 2005; Clark 2006).

As the analytic history in preceding chapters illustrates, these and other political forces have profound consequences for constitutional decision making. However, the mechanism by which they affect constitutional law is not by constituting a unique, orthogonal preference dimension. Rather, these factors influence constitutional law by changing the nature

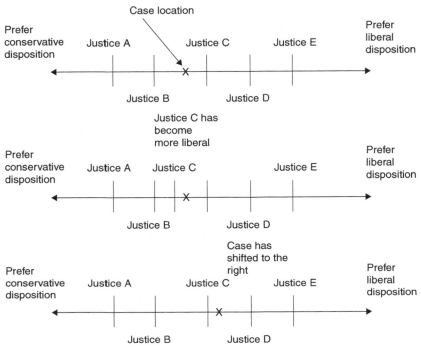

Figure 8.1. *Theoretical representation of a preference profile and two possible ways that a racial element of a case could affect how a justice votes.* In this figure, the top panel shows the preference profile of the five justices in a case. In the middle panel, a new issue is introduced, for example, race. Here, the introduction of race shifts Justice C's ideal point to the left. In the bottom panel, race does not affect the justices' preferences but instead shifts the location of the case, to the right.

of the cases that come to the courts, shaping the social context in which decisions are made and subsequently implemented. Indeed, the observation that some justices seem to be more liberal or conservative on similar questions when they implicate race highlights an important question about what one means when one describes a justice's preferences.

Consider the case-space model. Suppose the preference profile given by Figure 8.1, which shows a dimension related to equal protection claims and civil rights. Consider Justice C, and suppose that it is conventional to describe that justice as "more liberal" on cases involving race than other cases, presumably because he or she is more likely to vote for the liberal outcome in cases that involve a racial issue. Notice there are two observationally equivalent microprocesses that could underlie this empirical pattern. One process, which is what seems to be implied by the claim that the justice is "more liberal" on race cases, could be that Justice C's ideal point shifts to the left because a case involves a racial component. Alternatively, the process could be one where *what is meant to be a case involves all of the elements and issues judges perceive to be relevant to the decision.* Under this latter process, adding a racial element to a case *shifts the case further to the right* so that, depending on where the case falls, some justice or justices may be more or less likely to vote for the liberal outcome when cases involve a racial element.

Notice this latter interpretation of variation in justices' voting patterns is one in which the justice's preferences are stable and do not depend on the content of the case but rather one where the content of the case simply determines how a justice votes. The question, then, is how substantive elements of a case link together to determine where a case is located in the case space. While I have adopted this latter interpretation of what it means for a judge to be more liberal or more conservative on various issues, I have not directly answered the question how cases come to be located where they are in the case space. Rather, I have shown that social conditions are often related to the relevant preference dimensions that characterize judicial voting in cases. To understand why and when a case that implicates race, or really any other substantive issue, may be located differently than a case that does not implicate the particular issue, we need to take a broader perspective on the development of constitutional law than I have in this book.

One of the ways in which understanding the path of law requires us to go beyond the methods I have employed relates to the role that norms and values have in shaping social and legal conflicts. What kinds of disputes that involve race are those in which the racial element is politically or legally relevant? The answer to that question typically requires one to incorporate an understanding of social norms and values and inform our judgment about what kinds of factors rise to a given level of significance. When does a person perceive race to be relevant? Or gender? Or really any other kind of tangible or intangible consideration that might influence *how* someone views a case or controversy.

Another way in which the methods I adopt here provide only a partial window into the path of constitutional law is that they tend to focus on the ways in which social and political forces relate to how the justices approach constitutional law, but I have not focused much on how the justices' decisions in turn influence social and political conditions. In a handful of illustrative examples, I have shown that there are ways in which society responds to Court decisions. One dramatic example, which I described briefly in Chapter 7, is the increased violence against and persecution of Jehovah's Witnesses after the justices sided against them in the 1940 flag salute case and the state legislation that grew directly out of that case. Similarly, in the twenty-first century, we have seen a variety of

attempts to whittle away at marriage equality in the wake of the Supreme
Court's decision prohibiting states from denying marriage licenses to
same-sex couples. However, I have also documented other instances in
which changes to social and political conditions are less specific and more
general, such as the rise in impact litigation that followed from the Court's
early civil liberties decisions.

A more systematic evaluation of how Supreme Court decisions affect
American life would require an explicit analysis of the *content* of the
Court's decisions and then tracing that content through the relevant social
and political indicators. For example, along with my co-authors, I have
argued elsewhere that the Court's decision to step in and resolve a case
in the first instance turns in part on how the justices anticipate their
decision will affect the subsequent flow of cases and legal questions (e.g.,
Beim, Clark, and Patty 2017). As I articulated in Chapter 1, my analysis
stops short of evaluating substantive nuance in the content of the law
the justices articulate. The analysis here is consistent with a wide range
of theoretical models of how the justices write opinions. However, it
goes beyond the scope of what I can do here to trace the second half of
the circular relationship between politics and society and constitutional
decision making. Throughout this book, I have often relied on the median
justice's relative liberalism or conservatism as a way to consider the
ideological valence of the Court's doctrine. I have done this because, as I
noted in Chapter 1, under a wide class of theoretical models, the median
justice's movement over time will be at least correlated with movement in
the Court's output. Nevertheless, there is important nuance among those
theoretical models and in what the justices do, that a more thorough
understanding of the path of law requires systematic documentation of
the content of the Court's opinions over time. I regard it as an endeavor
worthy of a subsequent analysis. One challenge such a study would face,
though, is the need for more coherent theory about the ways in which we
should see social effects from court decisions.

In short, then, there are two important limitations to how well the
analysis here can document the path of constitutional law. The first is that
many of the important factors that influence how the justices approach
a constitutional question involve connecting social values and norms to
the way in which judges draw connections among important factors in
a case to assess what a case means and how they perceive it relative to
their own preferences. Those processes lie beyond the limits of the tools
I use here. The second is that my analyses focus mostly on one half of
the relationship between society and constitutional decision making. I
have neglected much of the path from constitutional decisions to social

conditions. This is not to say that process is unimportant, but rather that it is just beyond the scope of this project.

8.2.2 *Is This Social Science?*

I have attempted to be careful with my use of language as I describe the analyses in this book. As I noted in Chapter 1, my goal has been to strike something of a middle ground between historical description and traditional social-scientific causal inference. I have identified a set of institutional and behavioral mechanisms that I believe can explain the path of constitutional law – or, at least an important component of that path – and I have illustrated patterns in history consistent with those mechanisms. While at times the evidence does not rise to the level of what has come to be known as a "credible" causal estimate, the invocation of an underlying, micro-founded theory of decision making has aided in the interpretation of those patterns. In this sense, the analysis has been at least partially deductive and has been shaped by the structure of social-scientific inquiry.

At the same time, the analytic history of constitutional law underscores a challenge that permeates social science. Social scientists study phenomena in the world with theoretical models with what can be described as an intentional perspective. This is to be contrasted with causal or functional theories (for a brief treatment, see Elster 1983). From an intentional perspective, the research questions usually ask why some individual made a particular decision, considering first and foremost what that individual *wanted* or *intended* to occur. Whether the intended consequence follows is less important than understanding how an actor's beliefs, knowledge, context, and goals interact to drive that individual's decisions. Intentional theories suffer, though, in ways similar to and different from functional accounts. The problem is essentially one of localizing the causal effect. Many intentional theories are characterized by hysteresis – effects that are distant from the suspected causes. For example, many social-scientific theories, especially those in historical investigation, attempt to relate macro-level phenomena at one point in time to macro-level phenomena at another time. However, macro-level phenomena, as we have seen, can only be caused by micro-level action. This year's economic growth does not *cause* next year's economic growth. It may cause particular individual choices this year, which have downstream consequences for next year's economic growth, but by taking those individual choices out of our theoretical (and empirical) account, we have broken the causal chain and introduced a "black box" into our argument. At this point, the logic of causal inference has broken.

Unfortunately, using the standard tools of social science, we are typically limited in our ability to unpack that black box. Because we are studying human beings, pinning down intentions and other latent quantities is often beyond scientific capacity. The best we can hope for is usually a set of circumstantial findings, even if they are rigorously and validly derived. At a minimum, though, I believe the analysis here strikes a useful balance between inference and productive documentation of historical patterns. Where the reader has found the evidence persuasive of a causal claim about the links between social forces or internal politics and constitutional decision making, I hope the evidence proves novel and thought-provoking. Where the claims are less persuasively causal, I hope they can at least provide evidence of empirical regularities that force us to revisit preconceived notions or accepted theoretical claims.

A second aspect of the project that asks whether this analysis constitutes social science is the degree to which the method I employ is limited to studying constitutional, even judicial decision making. For example, could we apply the tools and method of analysis I use to study the history of congressional decision making in the spirit of Poole and Rosenthal (1997). On one hand, I believe the answer is a resounding *yes*. There is nothing particularly limited to judicial decision making about the claim that the content of documents provides information about the substantive dimensions decision makers are considering.

One major difference between Congress and the Supreme Court, though, might be a concern that language in statutes, bills, or debates – the natural sources of substantive information – is more ideologically charged than is the language in Supreme Court opinions. If this is the case, then we might worry about the quality of the measures of the substantive dimensions we would recover from applying LDA to the texts. Would we recover distinct dimensions of political conflict or instead would we recover distinct ideological blocks? While a concern, this is not necessarily a fatal challenge but instead a caution for the analyst. Setting that aside, it is likely the case that by leveraging auxiliary information about what legislators are voting on, we may be able to uncover more dimensionality in their preferences than if we were to simply analyze their voting patterns in isolation.

Of course, the extent to which such an analysis yields consequential new findings in a legislative setting is also an empirical question. However, there are reasons to suspect the shift in how we understand legislative politics could be less dramatic than the shift in how we understand judicial politics. For example, because legislatures tend to have larger memberships than do courts, we should expect it would require more significant perturbations of the preference ordering in order to produce meaningful changes in the preferences of pivotal actors, such as the median of a legislative chamber. Thus, the *practical* consequences of finding higher-dimensional preferences in a larger voting body than in a smaller body (such as a court) could be less significant. At the same time, it remains an empirical question the extent to which the landscape of preferences would appear different were we to employ a voting model that incorporates auxiliary information from the *content* of what legislators are voting on.

In sum, then, there are two main concerns about the relationship between analytic history and social science. With respect to the first, while analytic history is not intended strictly as a method of evaluating causal hypotheses, the integration of microtheories of behavior and the ability to document rigorous empirical regularities allows the method to help adjudicate among competing theoretical models and provides the kind of groundwork necessary for establishing first principles that can guide future theory building. With respect to the second, while it is likely that the marginal gain from studying smaller voting bodies, such as courts, is greater than it is when we study larger bodies, the scientific value of further applications of the method is an empirical model and does not in and of itself pose a threat to the wider intellectual and scientific value of the endeavor.

8.3 AMERICAN POLITICS AND ANALYTIC HISTORY

At the outset of this book, I articulated three goals. The first was to chart an analytic history of constitutional decision making at the US Supreme Court. The second was to understand how both structural and contingent forces shape the path of constitutional law. The third was to establish an approach to studying social-scientific history with a commitment to microtheories of political behavior. At this point, it is appropriate to take stock of how close I have made it to those goals.

The analyses in Chapters 6 and 7 both document large-scale quantitative patterns in constitutional decision making and provide substantive descriptions of illustrative cases. In this way, the analytic history charted there recovers well-understood historical patterns but also uncovers new regularities previously overlooked. In doing so, I am hopeful the analytic history provides new interpretations of past events and outlines empirical patterns for which existing theory cannot readily account.

Concerning the second goal, to reiterate the point above, there are myriad challenges facing our ability to make strong claims about the causal effect of structural and contingent forces on the path of constitutional law. At a minimum, the evidence documented here suggests systematic ways in which social and political conditions move in tandem with constitutional decision making. Moreover, there are some instances in which naturally occurring events provide stronger empirical leverage, and in these instances, we can say more. The theoretical frameworks on which I have relied to interpret the history illustrate how America's government institutions, such as our elections, facilitate the relationship between political contingencies and constitutional decision making. As one considers the various historical events I have documented, it bears keeping in mind the broader insights about how institutional character-istics mitigate or facilitate connections between particular conditions in the world and constitutional decision making.

Finally, regarding the third goal, as I have argued in this chapter, the general approach to studying constitutional law I outline here represents a broader intellectual perspective that can be used to study political decision making more generally. Its power lies not in its ability to help us understand the Constitution, per se, but rather in its ability to help us understand important nuances that are the consequences for an evolving political process, such as constitutional decision making. In that sense, my application to constitutional decision making is intended more to show what we can learn, rather than a defining characteristic of the tools here. In this sense, the ways in which I have shown constitutional decision making to be linked to social and political forces is instructive of a broader phenomenon in American policy making.

At the same time, it is important to note that constitutional law is different from other kinds of law. Private law, for example, governs the interactions among people in society, constitutional law is about the structure of government and balance of power. If one violates private law, there are typically remedies that can be imposed to compensate for the wrong. Individuals can be fined or made to pay restitution. Much public law, which governs the relationship between people and the state, similarly has mechanisms for resolving disputes. Convicted criminals can be fined or imprisoned. What happens, though, when constitutional law is violated? There has been litigation about the question of whether officials can be held liable for violating the Constitution, but these cases do not address the core issue: In what ways should constitutional decision making resemble judicial decision making more generally?

Knowing whether and how we expect constitutional decision making to resemble other kinds of judicial decision making goes to the core of our understanding of what it means to have a constitution. It goes to the heart of deep questions about whether the Supreme Court's claim to have the final say on matters of constitutional interpretation resonates with our understanding of the role of the Constitution in governance. If, for example, the historical patterns I have documented simply conform to what Americans perceive to be the normal pattern of political development, then it is less clear why the courts should have a monopoly on constitutional finality. What is more, if we think it normatively desirable that constitutional meaning and decision making reflect social and political currents of the times, then we must ask what role actors outside the courts should play in giving meaning to the Constitution (see also Tushnet 2000; Eisgruber 2001; Kramer 2004). Resolving these questions is far beyond the scope of this book, and this is not the point to take them up. However, as I conclude, I think it worthwhile to highlight the connections between the analytic history of constitutional decision making I have offered and normative and positive debates in constitutional theory. For, therein lies what I hope to be the main intellectual thrust behind this endeavor – using social scientific theory and empirical evidence to understand the past and inform future choices.

Appendix

Constitutional Law Cases, 1876–2012

- Tameling v. United States Freehold & Emigration Company - 93 U.S. 644 (1876)
- Munn v. Illinois - 94 U.S. 113 (1876)
- Chicago, Burlington & Quincy Railroad Company v. Iowa - 94 U.S. 155 (1876)
- Peik v. Chicago & Northwestern Railway Company - 94 U.S. 164 (1876)
- Chicago, Milwaukee & St. Paul Railroad Company v. Ackley - 94 U.S. 179 (1876)
- Winona & St. Peter Railroad Company v. Blake - 94 U.S. 180 (1876)
- Cammeyer v. Newton - 94 U.S. 225 (1876)
- Inman Steamship Company v. Tinker - 94 U.S. 238 (1876)
- Foster v. Master & Women of Port of New Orleans - 94 U.S. 246 (1876)
- McCready v. Virginia - 94 U.S. 391 (1876)
- Muller v. Dows - 94 U.S. 444 (1876)
- Doyle v. Continental Insurance Company - 94 U.S. 535 (1876)
- New Jersey v. Yard - 95 U.S. 104 (1877)
- Knote v. United States - 95 U.S. 149 (1877)
- Railroad Company v. Hecht - 95 U.S. 168 (1877)
- Bates v. Clark - 95 U.S. 204 (1877)
- Pearson v. Yewdall - 95 U.S. 294 (1877)
- Transportation Line v. Hope - 95 U.S. 297 (1877)
- Shields v. Ohio - 95 U.S. 319 (1877)
- County of Cass v. Johnston - 95 U.S. 360 (1877)
- McMillen v. Anderson - 95 U.S. 37 (1877)
- Railroad Company v. Husen - 95 U.S. 465 (1877)
- Hall v. DeCuir - 95 U.S. 485 (1877)
- Terry v. Anderson - 95 U.S. 628 (1877)
- New Orleans v. Clark - 95 U.S. 644 (1877)
- Farrington v. Tennessee - 95 U.S. 679 (1877)
- Packet Company v. Keokuk - 95 U.S. 80 (1877)
- Pensacola Tel. Co. v. Western Union Tel. Co. - 96 U.S. 1 (1877)
- Williams v. Bruffy - 96 U.S. 176 (1877)
- Conrad v. Waples - 96 U.S. 279 (1877)
- Railroad Company v. Richmond - 96 U.S. 521 (1877)
- Edwards v. Kearzey - 96 U.S. 595 (1877)
- Insurance Company v. Gossler - 96 U.S. 645 (1877)
- Tennessee v. Sneed - 96 U.S. 69 (1877)
- Beer Company v. Massachusetts - 97 U.S. 25 (1877)
- Insurance Company v. Harris - 97 U.S. 331 (1877)
- Young v. United States - 97 U.S. 39 (1877)
- Pennoyer v. Neff - 95 U.S. 714 (1878)
- Davidson v. New Orleans - 96 U.S. 97 (1878)
- Burgess v. Salmon - 97 U.S. 381 (1878)
- Mimmack v. United States - 97 U.S. 426 (1878)
- Keith v. Clark - 97 U.S. 454 (1878)
- Patterson v. Kentucky - 97 U.S. 501 (1878)
- Welch v. Cook - 97 U.S. 541 (1878)
- Cook v. Pennsylvania - 97 U.S. 566 (1878)
- Fertilizing Company v. Hyde Park - 97 U.S. 659 (1878)
- Reynolds v. United States - 98 U.S. 145 (1878)
- Railroad Company v. Georgia - 98 U.S. 359 (1878)
- Railroad Company v. Grant - 98 U.S. 398 (1878)
- Boom Company v. Patterson - 98 U.S. 403 (1878)
- Carr v. United States - 98 U.S. 433 (1878)
- Harkness v. Hyde - 98 U.S. 476 (1878)
- De Treville v. Smalls - 98 U.S. 517 (1878)
- United States v. Union Pacific Railroad Company - 98 U.S. 569 (1878)

- Wilkerson v. Utah - 99 U.S. 130 (1878)
- Transportation Company v. Wheeling - 99 U.S. 273 (1878)
- University v. People - 99 U.S. 309 (1878)
- Transportation Co. v. Chicago - 99 U.S. 635 (1878)
- Dow v. Johnson - 100 U.S. 158 (1879)
- Tennessee v. Davis - 100 U.S. 257 (1879)
- Strauder v. West Virginia - 100 U.S. 303 (1879)
- Packet Company v. St. Louis - 100 U.S. 423 (1879)
- Vicksburg v. Tobin - 100 U.S. 430 (1879)
- Guy v. Baltimore - 100 U.S. 434 (1879)
- Fairfield v. County of Gallatin - 100 U.S. 47 (1879)
- Hauenstein v. Lynham - 100 U.S. 483 (1879)
- Kirtland v. Hotchkiss - 100 U.S. 491 (1879)
- Newton v. Commissioners - 100 U.S. 548 (1879)
- National Bank v. United States - 101 U.S. 1 (1879)
- National Bank v. County of Yanktown - 101 U.S. 129 (1879)
- Cummings v. National Bank - 101 U.S. 153 (1879)
- South Carolina v. Gaillard - 101 U.S. 433 (1879)
- Crampton v. Zabriskie - 101 U.S. 601 (1879)
- Wolsey v. Chapman - 101 U.S. 755 (1879)
- Wright v. Nagle - 101 U.S. 791 (1879)
- Stone v. Mississippi - 101 U.S. 814 (1879)
- Baker v. Selden - 101 U.S. 99 (1879)
- Virginia v. Rives - 100 U.S. 313 (1880)
- Tiernan v. Rinker - 102 U.S. 123 (1880)
- Louisiana v. New Orleans - 102 U.S. 203 (1880)
- Williams v. Bruffy - 102 U.S. 248 (1880)
- People's Bank v. Calhoun - 102 U.S. 256 (1880)
- McElrath v. United States - 102 U.S. 426 (1880)
- Meriwether v. Garrett - 102 U.S. 472 (1880)
- Springer v. United States - 102 U.S. 586 (1880)
- Auffm'ordt v. Rasin - 102 U.S. 620 (1880)
- Hartman v. Greenhow - 102 U.S. 672 (1880)
- Tilghman v. Proctor - 102 U.S. 707 (1880)
- Dennick v. Railroad Company - 103 U.S. 11 (1880)
- Kilbourn v. Thompson - 103 U.S. 168 (1880)
- Blake v. United States - 103 U.S. 227 (1880)
- Miles v. United States - 103 U.S. 304 (1880)
- Webber v. Virginia - 103 U.S. 344 (1880)
- Wolff v. New Orleans - 103 U.S. 358 (1880)
- Neal v. Delaware - 103 U.S. 370 (1880)
- Wilson v. Gaines - 103 U.S. 417 (1880)
- Hall v. Wisconsin - 103 U.S. 5 (1880)
- Railroad Company v. Hamersley - 104 U.S. 1 (1881)

- Barton v. Barbour - 104 U.S. 126 (1881)
- Giles v. Little - 104 U.S. 291 (1881)
- James v. Campbell - 104 U.S. 356 (1881)
- Bonaparte v. Tax Court - 104 U.S. 592 (1881)
- United States v. McBratney - 104 U.S. 621 (1881)
- Kelly v. Pittsburgh - 104 U.S. 78 (1881)
- Ager v. Murray - 105 U.S. 126 (1881)
- Greenwood v. Freight Company - 105 U.S. 13 (1881)
- Louisiana v. Pilsbury - 105 U.S. 278 (1881)
- Asylum v. New Orleans - 105 U.S. 362 (1881)
- Telegraph Company v. Texas - 105 U.S. 460 (1881)
- Bridge Company v. United States - 105 U.S. 470 (1881)
- Packet Company v. Catlettsburg - 105 U.S. 559 (1881)
- Taylor v. Ypsilanti - 105 U.S. 60 (1881)
- United States v. Carll - 105 U.S. 611 (1881)
- Ralls County Court v. United States - 105 U.S. 733 (1881)
- United States v. Lee - 106 U.S. 196 (1882)
- Fink v. O'Neil - 106 U.S. 272 (1882)
- St. Clair v. Cox - 106 U.S. 350 (1882)
- Hodges v. Easton - 106 U.S. 408 (1882)
- Parkersburg v. Brown - 106 U.S. 487 (1883)
- Pace v. Alabama - 106 U.S. 583 (1883)
- Albright v. Teas - 106 U.S. 613 (1883)
- Bush v. Kentucky - 107 U.S. 110 (1883)
- Atlantic Works v. Brady - 107 U.S. 192 (1883)
- Burgess v. Seligman - 107 U.S. 20 (1883)
- Kring v. Missouri - 107 U.S. 221 (1883)
- Embry v. Palmer - 107 U.S. 3 (1883)
- United States v. Phelps - 107 U.S. 320 (1883)
- Wiggins Ferry Co. v. East St. Louis - 107 U.S. 365 (1883)
- Kountze v. Omaha Hotel Co. - 107 U.S. 378 (1883)
- Turner v. Maryland - 107 U.S. 38 (1883)
- People v. Compagnie Generale Transatlantique - 107 U.S. 59 (1883)
- Escanaba Company v. Chicago - 107 U.S. 678 (1883)
- Transportation Company v. Parkersburg - 107 U.S. 691 (1883)
- Louisiana v. Jumel - 107 U.S. 711 (1883)
- Antoni v. Greenhow - 107 U.S. 769 (1883)
- United States v. Britton - 108 U.S. 199 (1883)
- Clark v. Barnard - 108 U.S. 436 (1883)
- Connecticut Mut. Life Ins. Co. v. Cushman - 108 U.S. 51 (1883)
- Vance v. Vance - 108 U.S. 514 (1883)
- New Hampshire v. Louisiana - 108 U.S. 76 (1883)
- United States v. Mitchell - 109 U.S. 146 (1883)
- Snyder v. Marks - 109 U.S. 189 (1883)
- Louisville & Nashville R. Co. v. Palmes - 109 U.S. 244 (1883)
- Louisiana ex Rel. Folsom v. Mayor of New Orleans - 109 U.S. 285 (1883)

- Gilfillan v. Union Canal Co. of Pennsylvania - 109 U.S. 401 (1883)
- Feibelman v. Packard - 109 U.S. 421 (1883)
- Jackson v. Roby - 109 U.S. 440 (1883)
- Cunningham v. Macon & Brunswick R. Co. - 109 U.S. 446 (1883)
- Randall v. Baltimore & Ohio R. Co. - 109 U.S. 478 (1883)
- Providence & N.Y. S.S. Co. v. Hill Mfg. Co. - 109 U.S. 578 (1883)
- Robertson v. Pickrell - 109 U.S. 608 (1883)
- Holland v. Challen - 110 U.S. 15 (1884)
- Legal Tender Cases - 110 U.S. 421 (1884)
- Hurtado v. California - 110 U.S. 516 (1884)
- Killian v. Ebbinghaus - 110 U.S. 568 (1884)
- Hopt v. Utah - 110 U.S. 574 (1884)
- Covell v. Heyman - 111 U.S. 176 (1884)
- Boers v. Preston - 111 U.S. 252 (1884)
- Ames v. Kansas - 111 U.S. 449 (1884)
- Burrow-Giles Lithographic Company v. Sarony - 111 U.S. 53 (1884)
- Hagar v. Reclamation District - 111 U.S. 701 (1884)
- Louisiana ex Rel. Nelson v. Police Jury - 111 U.S. 716 (1884)
- Butchers' Union Co. v. Crescent City Co. - 111 U.S. 746 (1884)
- Foster v. Kansas ex Rel. Johnston - 112 U.S. 201 (1884)
- Reynolds v. Crawfordsville First National Bank - 112 U.S. 405 (1884)
- Butterworth v. United States - 112 U.S. 50 (1884)
- Memphis & L.R. R. Co. v. Railroad Commissioners - 112 U.S. 609 (1884)
- Moran v. New Orleans - 112 U.S. 69 (1884)
- United States v. Waddell - 112 U.S. 76 (1884)
- Elk v. Wilkins - 112 U.S. 94 (1884)
- Cole v. La Grange - 113 U.S. 1 (1885)
- Price v. Pennsylvania Railroad Co. - 113 U.S. 218 (1885)
- Barbier v. Connolly - 113 U.S. 27 (1885)
- Baylis v. Travelers' Insurance Company - 113 U.S. 316 (1885)
- Morgan v. United States - 113 U.S. 476 (1885)
- Erhardt v. Boaro - 113 U.S. 527 (1885)
- Hollister v. Benedict & Burnham Mfg. Co. - 113 U.S. 59 (1885)
- Soon Hing v. Crowley - 113 U.S. 703 (1885)
- Murphy v. Ramsey - 114 U.S. 15 (1885)
- Chapman v. Brewer - 114 U.S. 158 (1885)
- Chesapeake & Ohio Ry. Co. v. Miller - 114 U.S. 176 (1885)
- Gloucester Ferry Company v. Pennsylvania - 114 U.S. 196 (1885)
- Poindexter v. Greenhow - 114 U.S. 269 (1885)
- Poindexter v. Greenhow - 114 U.S. 270 (1885)

- Allen v. Baltimore and Ohio Railroad Co. - 114 U.S. 311 (1885)
- Fort Leavenworth R. Co. v. Lowe - 114 U.S. 525 (1885)
- Chicago, R.I. & P. Ry. Co. v. McGlinn - 114 U.S. 542 (1885)
- United States v. Corson - 114 U.S. 619 (1885)
- Brown v. Houston - 114 U.S. 622 (1885)
- Mayfield v. Richards - 115 U.S. 137 (1885)
- Cincinnati, N.O. & T.P. R. Co. v. Commonwealth - 115 U.S. 321 (1885)
- Gibson v. Lyon - 115 U.S. 439 (1885)
- Kurtz v. Moffitt - 115 U.S. 487 (1885)
- Missouri Pacific Railway Co. v. Humes - 115 U.S. 512 (1885)
- Effinger v. Kenney - 115 U.S. 566 (1885)
- Campbell v. Holt - 115 U.S. 620 (1885)
- New Orleans Gas Co. v. Louisiana Light Co. - 115 U.S. 650 (1885)
- New Orleans Waterworks Co. v. Rivers - 115 U.S. 674 (1885)
- Louisville Gas Co. v. Citizens' Gas Co. - 115 U.S. 683 (1885)
- Hanley v. Donoghue - 116 U.S. 1 (1885)
- Fisk v. Jefferson Police Jury - 116 U.S. 131 (1885)
- United States v. Price - 116 U.S. 43 (1885)
- Roberts v. Reilly - 116 U.S. 80 (1885)
- Smith v. Whitney - 116 U.S. 167 (1886)
- Brown v. Grant - 116 U.S. 207 (1886)
- Presser v. Illinois - 116 U.S. 252 (1886)
- Renaud v. Abbott - 116 U.S. 277 (1886)
- Mobile v. Watson - 116 U.S. 289 (1886)
- Stone v. Farmers' Loan & Trust Co. - 116 U.S. 307 (1886)
- Anderson v. Santa Ana - 116 U.S. 356 (1886)
- Coffey v. United States - 116 U.S. 436 (1886)
- Walling v. Michigan - 116 U.S. 446 (1886)
- United States v. Perkins - 116 U.S. 483 (1886)
- Chaffin v. Taylor - 116 U.S. 567 (1886)
- Royall v. Virginia - 116 U.S. 572 (1886)
- Boyd v. United States - 116 U.S. 616 (1886)
- Vicksburg, S. & P. R. Co. v. Dennis - 116 U.S. 665 (1886)
- Chicago & Northwestern Ry. Co. v. Ohle - 117 U.S. 123 (1886)
- Tennessee v. Whitworth - 117 U.S. 139 (1886)
- Van Brocklin v. Tennessee - 117 U.S. 151 (1886)
- Tua v. Carriere - 117 U.S. 201 (1886)
- Pickard v. Pullman Southern Car Company - 117 U.S. 34 (1886)
- Mackin v. United States - 117 U.S. 348 (1886)
- Turpin v. Burgess - 117 U.S. 504 (1886)
- Hagood v. Southern - 117 U.S. 52 (1886)
- Given v. Wright - 117 U.S. 648 (1886)
- Yick Wo v. Hopkins - 118 U.S. 356 (1886)
- United States v. Kagama - 118 U.S. 375 (1886)
- Santa Clara County v. Southern Pacific R. Co. - 118 U.S. 394 (1886)

- Morgan's Steamship Co. v. Louisiana Board of Health - 118 U.S. 455 (1886)
- Vicksburg & Meridian R. Co. v. Putnam - 118 U.S. 545 (1886)
- Wabash, St. Louis & Pacific Railway Company v. Illinois - 118 U.S. 557 (1886)
- Hart v. United States - 118 U.S. 62 (1886)
- United States v. Landram - 118 U.S. 81 (1886)
- Spraigue v. Thompson - 118 U.S. 90 (1886)
- Philadelphia Fire Ass'n v. New York - 119 U.S. 110 (1886)
- Clark v. Wooster - 119 U.S. 322 (1886)
- Buzard v. Houston - 119 U.S. 347 (1886)
- Johnson v. Chicago & Pac. Elev. Co. - 119 U.S. 388 (1886)
- United States v. Rauscher - 119 U.S. 407 (1886)
- Ker v. Illinois - 119 U.S. 436 (1886)
- Huse v. Glover - 119 U.S. 543 (1886)
- Borer v. Chapman - 119 U.S. 587 (1887)
- Chicago & Alton Railroad v. Wiggins Ferry Company - 119 U.S. 615 (1887)
- United States v. Pacific Railroad - 120 U.S. 227 (1887)
- Rolston v. Missouri Fund Commissioners - 120 U.S. 390 (1887)
- United States v. Arjona - 120 U.S. 479 (1887)
- Robbins v. Shelby County Taxing District - 120 U.S. 489 (1887)
- Corson v. Maryland - 120 U.S. 502 (1887)
- Chicago, B. & K.C. Railroad v. Guffey - 120 U.S. 569 (1887)
- Baldwin v. Franks - 120 U.S. 678 (1887)
- Barron v. Burnside - 121 U.S. 186 (1887)
- Fargo v. Michigan - 121 U.S. 230 (1887)
- Parkinson v. United States - 121 U.S. 281 (1887)
- Ouachita Packet Co. v. Aiken - 121 U.S. 444 (1887)
- Seibert v. Lewis - 122 U.S. 284 (1887)
- Philadelphia & Southern S.S. Co. v. Pennsylvania - 122 U.S. 326 (1887)
- Western Union Telegraph Co. v. Pendleton - 122 U.S. 347 (1887)
- Runkle v. United States - 122 U.S. 543 (1887)
- United States v. Philadelphia & Reading R. Co. - 123 U.S. 113 (1887)
- Spies v. Illinois - 123 U.S. 131 (1887)
- Sands v. Manistee River Improvement Co. - 123 U.S. 288 (1887)
- Mugler v. Kansas - 123 U.S. 623 (1887)
- Murray v. Charleston - 96 U.S. 432 (1887)
- Memphis v. United States - 97 U.S. 293 (1887)
- Gumbel v. Pitkin - 124 U.S. 131 (1888)
- Whitney v. Robertson - 124 U.S. 190 (1888)
- Smith v. Alabama - 124 U.S. 465 (1888)

- Willamette Iron Bridge Co. v. Hatch - 125 U.S. 1 (1888)
- New Orleans Waterworks Co. v. La. Sugar Ref. Co. - 125 U.S. 18 (1888)
- Maynard v. Hill - 125 U.S. 190 (1888)
- Bowman v. Chicago & Northwestern Ry. Co. - 125 U.S. 465 (1888)
- Western Union Tel. Co. v. Attorney General - 125 U.S. 530 (1888)
- Dow v. Beidelman - 125 U.S. 680 (1888)
- California v. Central Pacific R. Co. - 127 U.S. 1 (1888)
- Wisconsin v. Pelican Ins. Co. - 127 U.S. 265 (1888)
- United States v. Beebe - 127 U.S. 338 (1888)
- Ratterman v. Western Union Telegraph Company - 127 U.S. 411 (1888)
- Callan v. Wilson - 127 U.S. 540 (1888)
- Leloup v. Port of Mobile - 127 U.S. 640 (1888)
- Powell v. Pennsylvania - 127 U.S. 678 (1888)
- More v. Steinbach - 127 U.S. 70 (1888)
- Mahon v. Justice - 127 U.S. 700 (1888)
- Kidd v. Pearson - 128 U.S. 1 (1888)
- Asher v. Texas - 128 U.S. 129 (1888)
- Jaehne v. New York - 128 U.S. 189 (1888)
- United States v. Palmer - 128 U.S. 262 (1888)
- United States v. American Bell Telephone Co. - 128 U.S. 315 (1888)
- United States v. DeWalt - 128 U.S. 393 (1888)
- Denny v. Bennett - 128 U.S. 489 (1888)
- Nashville, Chattanooga & St. Louis Ry. v. Alabama - 128 U.S. 96 (1888)
- Dent v. West Virginia - 129 U.S. 114 (1889)
- Stoutenburgh v. Hennick - 129 U.S. 141 (1889)
- Minneapolis & St. Louis Ry. Co. v. Beckwith - 129 U.S. 26 (1889)
- Morris v. Gilmer - 129 U.S. 315 (1889)
- Chapman v. Barney - 129 U.S. 677 (1889)
- Smith v. Adams - 130 U.S. 167 (1889)
- Botiller v. Dominguez - 130 U.S. 238 (1889)
- Friedlander v. Texas & Pacific Ry. Co. - 130 U.S. 416 (1889)
- Butler v. Boston & Savannah Steamship Co. - 130 U.S. 527 (1889)
- Huling v. Kaw Valley Ry. & Improvement Co. - 130 U.S. 559 (1889)
- The Chinese Exclusion Case - 130 U.S. 581 (1889)
- Picard v. East Tennessee, Virginia & Georgia R. Co. - 130 U.S. 637 (1889)
- Arkansas Valley Land & Cattle Co. v. Mann - 130 U.S. 69 (1889)
- Kennon v. Gilmer - 131 U.S. 22 (1889)
- Pennie v. Reis - 132 U.S. 464 (1889)
- Western Union Tel. Co. v. Alabama State Board of Assessment - 132 U.S. 472 (1889)
- Sugg v. Thornton - 132 U.S. 524 (1889)
- Cole v. Cunningham - 133 U.S. 107 (1890)
- Christian v. Atlantic & North Carolina R. Co. - 133 U.S. 233 (1890)
- Geofroy v. Riggs - 133 U.S. 258 (1890)

- Davis v. Beason - 133 U.S. 333 (1890)
- Quebec Steamship Co. v. Merchant - 133 U.S. 375 (1890)
- Lincoln County v. Luning - 133 U.S. 529 (1890)
- Palmer v. McMahon - 133 U.S. 660 (1890)
- Illinois Central R. Co. v. Bosworth - 133 U.S. 92 (1890)
- Hans v. Louisiana - 134 U.S. 1 (1890)
- Medley, Petitioner - 134 U.S. 160 (1890)
- North Carolina v. Temple - 134 U.S. 22 (1890)
- Bell's Gap R. Co. v. Pennsylvania - 134 U.S. 232 (1890)
- Arndt v. Griggs - 134 U.S. 316 (1890)
- Clough v. Curtis - 134 U.S. 361 (1890)
- Chicago, M. & St. P. Ry. Co. v. Minnesota - 134 U.S. 418 (1890)
- Hill v. Merchants' Mut. Ins. Co. - 134 U.S. 515 (1890)
- Home Insurance Co. v. New York - 134 U.S. 594 (1890)
- Crenshaw v. United States - 134 U.S. 99 (1890)
- Leisy v. Hardin - 135 U.S. 100 (1890)
- Lyng v. Michigan - 135 U.S. 161 (1890)
- Detroit v. Osborne - 135 U.S. 492 (1890)
- Cherokee Nation v. Southern Kansas Ry. Co. - 135 U.S. 641 (1890)
- McGahey v. Virginia - 135 U.S. 662 (1890)
- Mormon Church v. United States - 136 U.S. 1 (1890)
- McCall v. California - 136 U.S. 104 (1890)
- Norfolk & Western R. Co. v. Pennsylvania - 136 U.S. 114 (1890)
- United States v. North Carolina - 136 U.S. 211 (1890)
- Minnesota v. Barber - 136 U.S. 313 (1890)
- York v. Texas - 137 U.S. 15 (1890)
- Jones v. United States - 137 U.S. 202 (1890)
- Wheeler v. Jackson - 137 U.S. 245 (1890)
- Grover & Baker Sewing Machine Co. v. Radcliffe - 137 U.S. 287 (1890)
- Auffmordt v. Hedden - 137 U.S. 310 (1890)
- Texas & Pacific Ry. Co. v. Southern Pacific Co. - 137 U.S. 48 (1890)
- Holden v. Minnesota - 137 U.S. 483 (1890)
- Crowley v. Christensen - 137 U.S. 86 (1890)
- Whitehead v. Shattuck - 138 U.S. 146 (1891)
- Cook v. United States - 138 U.S. 157 (1891)
- Alexander v. United States - 138 U.S. 353 (1891)
- Simmons v. Paul - 138 U.S. 439 (1891)
- Brimmer v. Rebman - 138 U.S. 78 (1891)
- Manchester v. Massachusetts - 139 U.S. 240 (1891)
- Natal v. Louisiana - 139 U.S. 621 (1891)
- Pennoyer v. McConnaughy - 140 U.S. 1 (1891)
- Scott v. Neely - 140 U.S. 106 (1891)

- United States v. Van Duzee - 140 U.S. 169 (1891)
- Mullan v. United States - 140 U.S. 240 (1891)
- Reynolds v. Stockton - 140 U.S. 254 (1891)
- Clark Thread Co. v. Willimantic Linen Co. - 140 U.S. 481 (1891)
- McAllister v. United States - 141 U.S. 174 (1891)
- Pullman's Palace Car Co. v. Pennsylvania - 141 U.S. 18 (1891)
- McClain v. Ortmayer - 141 U.S. 419 (1891)
- Crutcher v. Kentucky - 141 U.S. 47 (1891)
- Rogers v. United States - 141 U.S. 548 (1891)
- Voight v. Wright - 141 U.S. 62 (1891)
- Simmons v. United States - 142 U.S. 148 (1891)
- McElvaine v. Brush - 142 U.S. 155 (1891)
- Knight v. United States Land Association - 142 U.S. 161 (1891)
- Maine v. Grand Trunk Ry. Co. - 142 U.S. 217 (1891)
- Kaukauna Water Power Co. v. Green Bay Co. - 142 U.S. 254 (1891)
- New Orleans v. New Orleans Waterworks Co. - 142 U.S. 79 (1891)
- Gulf, Colorado & Santa Fe Ry. Co. v. Ellis - 165 U.S. 150 (1891)
- O'Brien v. Miller - 168 U.S. 287 (1891)
- Boyd v. United States - 142 U.S. 450 (1892)
- Thompson v. United States - 142 U.S. 471 (1892)
- Counselman v. Hitchcock - 142 U.S. 547 (1892)
- Louisville Water Co. v. Clark - 143 U.S. 1 (1892)
- Boyd v. Nebraska ex Rel. Thayer - 143 U.S. 135 (1892)
- Chicago & Grand Trunk Ry. Co. v. Wellman - 143 U.S. 339 (1892)
- Budd v. New York - 143 U.S. 517 (1892)
- United States v. Texas - 143 U.S. 621 (1892)
- Field v. Clark - 143 U.S. 649 (1892)
- United States v. Ballin - 144 U.S. 1 (1892)
- Lacassagne v. Chapuis - 144 U.S. 119 (1892)
- Brenham v. German American Bank - 144 U.S. 173 (1892)
- Logan v. United States - 144 U.S. 263 (1892)
- O'Neil v. Vermont - 144 U.S. 323 (1892)
- Wilson v. Seligman - 144 U.S. 41 (1892)
- United States v. Eaton - 144 U.S. 677 (1892)
- South Spring Hill Gold Mining Co. v. Amador Co. - 145 U.S. 300 (1892)
- Brown v. Smart - 145 U.S. 454 (1892)
- Meehan v. Valentine - 145 U.S. 611 (1892)
- McPherson v. Blacker - 146 U.S. 1 (1892)
- Morley v. Lake Shore & Mich. Sou. Ry. Co. - 146 U.S. 162 (1892)
- Cook v. Hart - 146 U.S. 183 (1892)
- Butler v. Goreley - 146 U.S. 303 (1892)
- Benson v. United States - 146 U.S. 325 (1892)
- Lewis v. United States - 146 U.S. 370 (1892)

- Illinois Central R. Co. v. Illinois - 146 U.S. 387 (1892)
- Huntington v. Attrill - 146 U.S. 657 (1892)
- Lake Shore & Michigan Southern Ry. Co. v. Prentice - 147 U.S. 101 (1893)
- Noble v. Union River Logging R. Co. - 147 U.S. 165 (1893)
- Illinois Central R. Co. v. Decatur - 147 U.S. 190 (1893)
- Shoemaker v. United States - 147 U.S. 282 (1893)
- Glenn v. Garth - 147 U.S. 360 (1893)
- Harmon v. City of Chicago - 147 U.S. 396 (1893)
- Bier v. McGehee - 148 U.S. 137 (1893)
- Indiana v. United States - 148 U.S. 148 (1893)
- Passavant v. United States - 148 U.S. 214 (1893)
- Monongahela Nav. Co. v. United States - 148 U.S. 312 (1893)
- American Constr. Co. v. Jacksonville &c. Co. - 148 U.S. 372 (1893)
- Virginia v. Tennessee - 148 U.S. 503 (1893)
- Chicot County v. Sherwood - 148 U.S. 529 (1893)
- Lascelles v. Georgia - 148 U.S. 537 (1893)
- Giozza v. Tiernan - 148 U.S. 657 (1893)
- Smith v. Whitman Saddle Co. - 148 U.S. 674 (1893)
- St. Louis v. Western Union Telegraph Co. - 148 U.S. 92 (1893)
- Paulsen v. Portland - 149 U.S. 30 (1893)
- California v. San Pablo & Tulare R. Co. - 149 U.S. 308 (1893)
- Minneapolis & St. Louis Ry. Co. v. Emmons - 149 U.S. 364 (1893)
- Wilson v. United States - 149 U.S. 60 (1893)
- Fong Yue Ting v. United States - 149 U.S. 698 (1893)
- Belden v. Chase - 150 U.S. 674 (1893)
- Angle v. Chicago, St. P., M. & Omaha Ry. Co. - 151 U.S. 1 (1894)
- Keystone Mfg. Co. v. Adams - 151 U.S. 139 (1894)
- Hickory v. United States - 151 U.S. 303 (1894)
- Pointer v. United States - 151 U.S. 396 (1894)
- New York & New England R. Co. v. Bristol - 151 U.S. 556 (1894)
- Shively v. Bowlby - 152 U.S. 1 (1894)
- Lawton v. Steele - 152 U.S. 133 (1894)
- Montana Co. v. St. Louis Mining & Milling Co. - 152 U.S. 160 (1894)
- Caha v. United States - 152 U.S. 211 (1894)
- Duncan v. Missouri - 152 U.S. 377 (1894)
- Manuel v. Wulff - 152 U.S. 505 (1894)
- Wharton v. Wise - 153 U.S. 155 (1894)
- Brennan v. Titusville - 153 U.S. 289 (1894)
- Roberts v. Lewis - 153 U.S. 367 (1894)

- Marchant v. Pennsylvania R. Co. - 153 U.S. 380 (1894)
- Brass v. North Dakota ex Rel. Stoeser - 153 U.S. 391 (1894)
- Mobile & Ohio R. Co. v. Tennessee - 153 U.S. 486 (1894)
- Luxton v. North River Bridge Co. - 153 U.S. 525 (1894)
- Miller v. Texas - 153 U.S. 535 (1894)
- New York, L.E. & W. R. Co. v. Pennsylvania - 153 U.S. 628 (1894)
- Lyons v. Woods - 153 U.S. 649 (1894)
- McKane v. Durston - 153 U.S. 684 (1894)
- Northern Pacific R. Co. v. Babcock - 154 U.S. 190 (1894)
- Covington and Cincinnati Bridge Co. v. Kentucky - 154 U.S. 204 (1894)
- Scott v. McNeal - 154 U.S. 34 (1894)
- Reagan v. Farmers' Loan and Trust Co. - 154 U.S. 362 (1894)
- Reagan v. Mercantile Trust Co. - 154 U.S. 413 (1894)
- Pittsburgh, C., C. & St.L. Ry. Co. v. Backus - 154 U.S. 421 (1894)
- Cleveland, C., C. & St.L. Ry. Co. v. Backus - 154 U.S. 439 (1894)
- ICC v. Brimson - 154 U.S. 447 (1894)
- Lloyd v. Matthews - 155 U.S. 222 (1894)
- Thompson v. United States - 155 U.S. 271 (1894)
- Austin v. United States - 155 U.S. 417 (1894)
- Potter v. United States - 155 U.S. 438 (1894)
- Greeley v. Lowe - 155 U.S. 58 (1894)
- United States v. Coe - 155 U.S. 76 (1894)
- South Carolina v. Wesley - 155 U.S. 542 (1895)
- Potts v. Creager - 155 U.S. 597 (1895)
- Hooper v. California - 155 U.S. 648 (1895)
- Postal Telegraph Cable Co. v. Adams - 155 U.S. 688 (1895)
- United States v. E. C. Knight Co. - 156 U.S. 1 (1895)
- Mattox v. United States - 156 U.S. 237 (1895)
- Andrews v. Swartz - 156 U.S. 272 (1895)
- Hudson v. Parker - 156 U.S. 277 (1895)
- Emert v. Missouri - 156 U.S. 296 (1895)
- Coffin v. United States - 156 U.S. 432 (1895)
- Sparf and Hansen v. United States - 156 U.S. 51 (1895)
- Goldey v. Morning News - 156 U.S. 518 (1895)
- Pittsburgh & Southern Coal Co. - 156 U.S. 577 (1895)
- Norfolk & Western R. Co. v. Pendleton - 156 U.S. 667 (1895)
- New Orleans City & Lake R. Co. v. Louisiana - 157 U.S. 219 (1895)
- California v. Southern Pacific Co. - 157 U.S. 229 (1895)
- Pollock v. Farmers' Loan & Trust Co. - 157 U.S. 429 (1895)

- Treat Mfg. Co. v. Standard Steel & Iron Co. - 157 U.S. 674 (1895)
- Johnson v. Sayre - 158 U.S. 109 (1895)
- Pollock v. Farmers' Loan & Trust Company - 158 U.S. 601 (1895)
- Gulf, Colorado & Santa Fe Ry. Co. v. Hefley - 158 U.S. 98 (1895)
- Central Land Co. v. Laidley - 159 U.S. 103 (1895)
- Hilton v. Guyot - 159 U.S. 113 (1895)
- Ritchie v. McMullen - 159 U.S. 235 (1895)
- Sweet v. Rechel - 159 U.S. 380 (1895)
- Winona and St. Peter Land Co. v. Minnesota - 159 U.S. 526 (1895)
- Mills v. Green - 159 U.S. 651 (1895)
- Moore v. Missouri - 159 U.S. 673 (1895)
- Davis v. United States - 160 U.S. 469 (1895)
- Iowa Central Railway Co. v. Iowa - 160 U.S. 389 (1896)
- Chappell v. United States - 160 U.S. 499 (1896)
- Beklnap v. Schild - 161 U.S. 10 (1896)
- Bank of Commerce v. Tennessee - 161 U.S. 134 (1896)
- Phoenix Fire & Marine Ins. Co. v. Tennessee - 161 U.S. 174 (1896)
- Baltzer v. North Carolina - 161 U.S. 240 (1896)
- Hamilton v. Brown - 161 U.S. 256 (1896)
- Davis v. Elmira Savings Bank - 161 U.S. 275 (1896)
- Rosen v. United States - 161 U.S. 29 (1896)
- Spalding v. Vilas - 161 U.S. 483 (1896)
- Geer v. Connecticut - 161 U.S. 519 (1896)
- St. Louis & S.F. Ry. Co. v. James - 161 U.S. 545 (1896)
- Brown v. Walker - 161 U.S. 591 (1896)
- Stanley v. Schwalby - 162 U.S. 255 (1896)
- Great Western Tel. Co. v. Purdy - 162 U.S. 329 (1896)
- Palmer v. Barrett - 162 U.S. 399 (1896)
- Harwood v. Wentworth - 162 U.S. 547 (1896)
- Gibson v. Mississippi - 162 U.S. 565 (1896)
- Charley Smith v. Mississippi - 162 U.S. 592 (1896)
- Wilson v. United States - 162 U.S. 613 (1896)
- Crain v. United States - 162 U.S. 625 (1896)
- Murray v. Louisiana - 163 U.S. 101 (1896)
- Barnitz v. Beverly - 163 U.S. 118 (1896)
- Illinois Central R. Co. v. Illinois - 163 U.S. 142 (1896)
- Bacon v. Texas - 163 U.S. 207 (1896)
- Wong Wing v. United States - 163 U.S. 228 (1896)
- Hanford v. Davies - 163 U.S. 273 (1896)
- Hennington v. Georgia - 163 U.S. 299 (1896)
- United States v. Realty Co. - 163 U.S. 427 (1896)
- Ward v. Race Horse - 163 U.S. 504 (1896)

- Plessy v. Ferguson - 163 U.S. 537 (1896)
- United States v. Ball - 163 U.S. 662 (1896)
- Lowe v. Kansas - 163 U.S. 81 (1896)
- Fallbrook Irrigation Dist. v. Bradley - 164 U.S. 112 (1896)
- Tregea v. Modesto Irrigation Dist. - 164 U.S. 179 (1896)
- Draper v. United States - 164 U.S. 240 (1896)
- Coughran v. Bigelow - 164 U.S. 301 (1896)
- Missouri Pacific Ry. Co. v. Nebraska - 164 U.S. 403 (1896)
- McElroy v. United States - 164 U.S. 76 (1896)
- Ford v. Delta & Pine Land Co. - 164 U.S. 662 (1897)
- Cincinnati, N.O. and Tex. Pac. Ry. Co. v. ICC - 162 U.S. 184 (1897)
- St. Louis & San Francisco Ry. Co. v. Mathews - 165 U.S. 1 (1897)
- Adams Express Co. v. Ohio State Auditor - 165 U.S. 194 (1897)
- Robertson v. Baldwin - 165 U.S. 275 (1897)
- Agnew v. United States - 165 U.S. 36 (1897)
- United States v. McMillan - 165 U.S. 504 (1897)
- Swaim v. United States - 165 U.S. 553 (1897)
- Allgeyer v. Louisiana - 165 U.S. 578 (1897)
- Scott v. Donald - 165 U.S. 58 (1897)
- Walker v. New Mexico & Southern Pacific R. Co. - 165 U.S. 593 (1897)
- New York, N.H. & H. R. Co. v. New York - 165 U.S. 628 (1897)
- The Three Friends - 166 U.S. 1 (1897)
- Grand Lodge F. & A. Masons v. New Orleans - 166 U.S. 143 (1897)
- Chicago, B. & Q. R. Co. v. Chicago - 166 U.S. 226 (1897)
- Gibson v. United States - 166 U.S. 269 (1897)
- United States v. Trans-Missouri Freight Ass'n - 166 U.S. 290 (1897)
- Hooe v. Jamieson - 166 U.S. 395 (1897)
- Martin v. Atchison, T. & S.F. R. Co. - 166 U.S. 399 (1897)
- Gladson v. Minnesota - 166 U.S. 427 (1897)
- American Publishing Co. v. Fisher - 166 U.S. 464 (1897)
- Forsyth v. Hammond - 166 U.S. 506 (1897)
- Long Island Water Supply Co. v. Brooklyn - 166 U.S. 685 (1897)
- Springville v. Thomas - 166 U.S. 707 (1897)
- Twin City Bank v. Nebeker - 167 U.S. 196 (1897)
- Tindal v. Wesley - 167 U.S. 204 (1897)
- Parsons v. United States - 167 U.S. 324 (1897)
- Davis v. Massachusetts - 167 U.S. 43 (1897)
- Merchants' & Manufacturers' Bank v. Pennsylvania - 167 U.S. 461 (1897)
- Camfield v. United States - 167 U.S. 518 (1897)
- Bauman v. Ross - 167 U.S. 548 (1897)
- Wabash Railroad Co. v. Defiance - 167 U.S. 88 (1897)

- ICC v. Alabama Midland Railway Co. - 168 U.S. 144 (1897)
- Underhill v. Hernandez - 168 U.S. 250 (1897)
- Stewart v. Baltimore & Ohio R. Co. - 168 U.S. 445 (1897)
- Douglas v. Kentucky - 168 U.S. 488 (1897)
- Bram v. United States - 168 U.S. 532 (1897)
- Turner v. New York - 168 U.S. 90 (1897)
- Thomas v. Gay - 169 U.S. 264 (1898)
- United States v. Eaton - 169 U.S. 331 (1898)
- Holden v. Hardy - 169 U.S. 366 (1898)
- Savings & Loan Society v. Multnomah County - 169 U.S. 421 (1898)
- Smyth v. Ames - 169 U.S. 466 (1898)
- Backus v. Fort Street Union Depot Co. - 169 U.S. 557 (1898)
- Wilson v. North Carolina - 169 U.S. 586 (1898)
- United States v. Wong Kim Ark - 169 U.S. 649 (1898)
- Hawker v. New York - 170 U.S. 189 (1898)
- Williams v. Mississippi - 170 U.S. 213 (1898)
- Houston & Texas Cent. Ry. Co. v. Texas - 170 U.S. 243 (1898)
- Magoun v. Illinois Trust & Savings Bank - 170 U.S. 283 (1898)
- Thompson v. Utah - 170 U.S. 343 (1898)
- Rhodes v. Iowa - 170 U.S. 412 (1898)
- Plaquemines Tropical Fruit Co. v. Henderson - 170 U.S. 511 (1898)
- Chicago, B. & Q. R. Co. v. Nebraska ex Rel. Omaha - 170 U.S. 57 (1898)
- Wagoner v. Evans - 170 U.S. 588 (1898)
- Schollenberger v. Pennsylvania - 171 U.S. 1 (1898)
- Collins v. New Hampshire - 171 U.S. 30 (1898)
- Patapsco Guano Co. v. North Car. Bd. of Agriculture - 171 U.S. 345 (1898)
- Thompson v. Missouri - 171 U.S. 380 (1898)
- King v. Mullins - 171 U.S. 404 (1898)
- Walla Walla City v. Walla Walla Water Co. - 172 U.S. 1 (1898)
- McCullough v. Virginia - 172 U.S. 102 (1898)
- Blake v. McClung - 172 U.S. 239 (1898)
- Norwood v. Baker - 172 U.S. 269 (1898)
- Pittsburgh &c. Ry. v. Board of Public Works - 172 U.S. 32 (1898)
- Green Bay & Mississippi Canal Co. v. Patten Paper Co. - 172 U.S. 58 (1898)
- Fitts v. McGhee - 172 U.S. 516 (1899)
- United States v. Duell - 172 U.S. 576 (1899)
- Northern Pacific Ry. Co. v. Myers - 172 U.S. 589 (1899)
- Connecticut Mut. Life Ins. Co. v. Spratley - 172 U.S. 602 (1899)
- Meyer v. Richmond - 172 U.S. 82 (1899)
- Dewey v. Des Moines - 173 U.S. 193 (1899)
- Covington v. Kentucky - 173 U.S. 231 (1899)
- Ohio v. Thomas - 173 U.S. 276 (1899)
- Lake Shore & Michigan Southern Ry. Co. v. Ohio - 173 U.S. 285 (1899)
- Wilson v. Eureka City - 173 U.S. 32 (1899)
- Allen v. Smith - 173 U.S. 389 (1899)
- St. Louis, Iron Mountain & St. Paul Ry. Co. v. Paul - 173 U.S. 404 (1899)
- Nicol v. Ames - 173 U.S. 509 (1899)
- Guthrie v. National Bank v. Guthrie - 173 U.S. 528 (1899)
- Cooper v. Newell - 173 U.S. 555 (1899)
- Owensboro National Bank v. Owensboro - 173 U.S. 664 (1899)
- Lake Shore & Michigan Southern Ry. Co. v. Smith - 173 U.S. 684 (1899)
- Capital Traction Co. v. Hof - 174 U.S. 1 (1899)
- Stephens v. Cherokee Nation - 174 U.S. 445 (1899)
- Kirby v. United States - 174 U.S. 47 (1899)
- United States v. Rio Grande Dam & Irrigation Co. - 174 U.S. 690 (1899)
- Chicago, Rock Island & Pacific Ry. Co. v. Sturm - 174 U.S. 710 (1899)
- San Diego Land & Town Co. v. National City - 174 U.S. 739 (1899)
- Holmes v. Hurst - 174 U.S. 82 (1899)
- Atchison, T. & S.F.R. Co. v. Matthews - 174 U.S. 96 (1899)
- Jones v. Meehan - 175 U.S. 1 (1899)
- Simms v. Simms - 175 U.S. 162 (1899)
- Brown v. New Jersey - 175 U.S. 172 (1899)
- Addyston Pipe & Steel Co. v. United States - 175 U.S. 211 (1899)
- Bradfield v. Roberts - 175 U.S. 291 (1899)
- King v. Cross - 175 U.S. 396 (1899)
- La Abra Silver Mining Co. v. United States - 175 U.S. 423 (1899)
- Cumming v. Richmond County Board of Education - 175 U.S. 528 (1899)
- Louisiana v. Texas - 176 U.S. 1 (1900)
- Adirondack Ry. Co. v. New York State - 176 U.S. 335 (1900)
- Thormann v. Frame - 176 U.S. 350 (1900)
- Maxwell v. Dow - 176 U.S. 581 (1900)
- Hancock National Bank v. Farnum - 176 U.S. 640 (1900)
- Bolln v. Nebraska - 176 U.S. 83 (1900)
- Bristol v. Washington County - 177 U.S. 133 (1900)
- Murphy v. Massachusetts - 177 U.S. 155 (1900)
- Petit v. Minnesota - 177 U.S. 164 (1900)
- Gundling v. Chicago - 177 U.S. 183 (1900)
- Ohio Oil Co. v. Indiana - 177 U.S. 190 (1900)
- Quackenbush v. United States - 177 U.S. 20 (1900)
- Louisville & Nashville R. Co. v. Schmidt - 177 U.S. 230 (1900)
- Carter v. Texas - 177 U.S. 442 (1900)

- Great Southern Fire Proof Hotel Co. v. Jones - 177 U.S. 449 (1900)
- Carter v. Roberts - 177 U.S. 496 (1900)
- Shoshone Mining Co. v. Rutter - 177 U.S. 505 (1900)
- Cleveland C., C. & St.L. Ry. Co. v. Illinois - 177 U.S. 514 (1900)
- Los Angeles v. Los Angeles City Water Co. - 177 U.S. 558 (1900)
- L'Hote v. New Orleans - 177 U.S. 587 (1900)
- Knapp, Stout & Co. Company v. McCaffrey - 177 U.S. 638 (1900)
- Houston & Texas Central R. Co. v. Texas - 177 U.S. 66 (1900)
- Plummer v. Coler - 178 U.S. 115 (1900)
- Clarke v. Clarke - 178 U.S. 186 (1900)
- Sully v. American National Bank - 178 U.S. 289 (1900)
- Fitzpatrick v. United States - 178 U.S. 304 (1900)
- New York Life Ins. Co. v. Cravens - 178 U.S. 389 (1900)
- Banholzer v. New York Life Ins. Co. - 178 U.S. 402 (1900)
- Knowlton v. Moore - 178 U.S. 41 (1900)
- Smith v. Reeves - 178 U.S. 436 (1900)
- Motes v. United States - 178 U.S. 458 (1900)
- May v. New Orleans - 178 U.S. 496 (1900)
- Taylor and Marshall v. Beckham - 178 U.S. 548 (1900)
- Scranton v. Wheeler - 179 U.S. 141 (1900)
- Contzen v. United States - 179 U.S. 191 (1900)
- Stearns v. Minnesota - 179 U.S. 223 (1900)
- Williams v. Fears - 179 U.S. 270 (1900)
- Wisconsin, Minnesota & Pacific Railroad v. Jacobson - 179 U.S. 287 (1900)
- Duluth & Iron Range R. Co. v. St. Louis County - 179 U.S. 302 (1900)
- Tyler v. Judges of Court of Registration - 179 U.S. 405 (1900)
- Workman v. New York City - 179 U.S. 552 (1900)
- Wiley v. Sinkler - 179 U.S. 58 (1900)
- American Sugar Refining Co. v. Louisiana - 179 U.S. 89 (1900)
- Neely v. Henkel - 180 U.S. 109 (1901)
- Missouri v. Illinois & Sanitary District of Chicago - 180 U.S. 208 (1901)
- Lampasas v. Bell - 180 U.S. 276 (1901)
- McDonald v. Massachusetts - 180 U.S. 311 (1901)
- New Orleans Debenture Redemption Co. v. Louisiana - 180 U.S. 320 (1901)
- Blythe v. Hinckley - 180 U.S. 333 (1901)
- W. W. Cargill Co. v. Minnesota - 180 U.S. 452 (1901)
- Wilkes County v. Coler - 180 U.S. 506 (1901)
- Rogers Park Water Co. v. Fergus - 180 U.S. 624 (1901)

- Atherton v. Atherton - 181 U.S. 155 (1901)
- Bell v. Bell - 181 U.S. 175 (1901)
- Lynde v. Lynde - 181 U.S. 183 (1901)
- Treat v. White - 181 U.S. 264 (1901)
- Fairbank v. United States - 181 U.S. 283 (1901)
- French v. Barber Asphalt Paving Co. - 181 U.S. 324 (1901)
- Wight v. Davidson - 181 U.S. 371 (1901)
- Tonawanda v. Lyon - 181 U.S. 389 (1901)
- Cass Farm Co. v. Detroit - 181 U.S. 396 (1901)
- Detroit v. Parker - 181 U.S. 399 (1901)
- Red River Valley Bank v. Craig - 181 U.S. 548 (1901)
- Audubon v. Shufeldt - 181 U.S. 575 (1901)
- Mallett v. North Carolina - 181 U.S. 589 (1901)
- DeLima v. Bidwell - 182 U.S. 1 (1901)
- Dooley v. United States - 182 U.S. 222 (1901)
- Downes v. Bidwell - 182 U.S. 244 (1901)
- Homer Ramsdell Trans. Co. v. La Compagnie &c. - 182 U.S. 406 (1901)
- Knoxville Iron Co. v. Harbison - 183 U.S. 13 (1901)
- Dooley v. United States - 183 U.S. 151 (1901)
- Fourteen Diamond Rings v. United States - 183 U.S. 176 (1901)
- Dayton Coal & Iron Co. v. Barton - 183 U.S. 23 (1901)
- District of Columbia v. Eslin - 183 U.S. 62 (1901)
- Cotting v. Kansas City Stock Yards Co. - 183 U.S. 79 (1901)
- Capital City Dairy Co. v. Ohio - 183 U.S. 238 (1902)
- Orr v. Gilman - 183 U.S. 278 (1902)
- Stanton Carter v. McClaughry - 183 U.S. 365 (1902)
- Tucker v. Alexandroff - 183 U.S. 424 (1902)
- Louisville & Nashville R. Co. v. Kentucky - 183 U.S. 503 (1902)
- Nutting v. Massachusetts - 183 U.S. 553 (1902)
- League v. Texas - 184 U.S. 156 (1902)
- Minnesota v. Northern Securities Co. - 184 U.S. 199 (1902)
- Louisville & Nashville R. Co. v. Kentucky - 184 U.S. 27 (1902)
- Terlinden v. Ames - 184 U.S. 270 (1902)
- Skaneateles Waterworks Co. v. Skaneateles - 184 U.S. 354 (1902)
- Detroit v. Detroit Citizens' Street Ry. Co. - 184 U.S. 368 (1902)
- Wilson v. Standefer - 184 U.S. 399 (1902)
- Booth v. Illinois - 184 U.S. 425 (1902)
- Connolly v. Union Sewer Pipe Co. - 184 U.S. 540 (1902)
- Patton v. Brady - 184 U.S. 608 (1902)
- Emblen v. Lincoln Land Co. - 184 U.S. 660 (1902)

- St. Louis Consolidated Coal Co. v. Illinois - 185 U.S. 203 (1902)
- United States v. Lee Yen Tai - 185 U.S. 213 (1902)
- Stockard v. Morgan - 185 U.S. 27 (1902)
- Travelers' Ins. Co. v. Connecticut - 185 U.S. 364 (1902)
- Minnesota v. Hitchcock - 185 U.S. 373 (1902)
- Swafford v. Templeton - 185 U.S. 487 (1902)
- Felsenheld v. United States - 186 U.S. 126 (1902)
- Hanover National Bank v. Moyses - 186 U.S. 181 (1902)
- Reid v. Colorado - 187 U.S. 137 (1902)
- Equitable Life Assur. Soc'y v. Brown - 187 U.S. 308 (1902)
- Fidelity & Deposit Co. of Maryland v. United States - 187 U.S. 315 (1902)
- Turpin v. Lemon - 187 U.S. 51 (1902)
- Dreyer v. Illinois - 187 U.S. 71 (1902)
- Oshkosh Waterworks Co. v. Oshkosh - 187 U.S. 437 (1903)
- Johnson v. New York Life Ins. Co. - 187 U.S. 491 (1903)
- Lone Wolf v. Hitchcock - 187 U.S. 553 (1903)
- Otis v. Parker - 187 U.S. 606 (1903)
- Diamond Glue Co. v. United States Glue Co. - 187 U.S. 611 (1903)
- Hanley v. Kansas City Southern Ry. Co. - 187 U.S. 617 (1903)
- Caldwell v. North Carolina - 187 U.S. 622 (1903)
- Andrews v. Andrews - 188 U.S. 14 (1903)
- Blackstone v. Miller - 188 U.S. 189 (1903)
- Bleistein v. Donaldson Lithographing Co. - 188 U.S. 239 (1903)
- Lottery Case - 188 U.S. 321 (1903)
- Louisville & Jeffersonville Ferry Co. v. Kentucky - 188 U.S. 385 (1903)
- United States v. Lynah - 188 U.S. 445 (1903)
- Reetz v. Michigan - 188 U.S. 505 (1903)
- Waggoner v. Flack - 188 U.S. 595 (1903)
- Helwig v. United States - 188 U.S. 605 (1903)
- Hyatt v. People - 188 U.S. 691 (1903)
- Billings v. Illinois - 188 U.S. 97 (1903)
- Sawyer v. Piper - 189 U.S. 154 (1903)
- Glidden v. Harrington - 189 U.S. 255 (1903)
- Shurtleff v. United States - 189 U.S. 311 (1903)
- Zane v. Hamilton County - 189 U.S. 370 (1903)
- San Diego Land & Town Co. v. Jasper - 189 U.S. 439 (1903)
- Giles v. Harris - 189 U.S. 475 (1903)
- Japanese Immigrant Case - 189 U.S. 86 (1903)
- James v. Bowman - 190 U.S. 127 (1903)
- Hawaii v. Mankichi - 190 U.S. 197 (1903)
- Snyder v. Bettman - 190 U.S. 249 (1903)
- United States v. Michigan - 190 U.S. 379 (1903)

- Conley v. Mathieson Alkali Works - 190 U.S. 406 (1903)
- Howard v. Fleming - 191 U.S. 126 (1903)
- Smith v. Indiana - 191 U.S. 138 (1903)
- Missouri v. Dockery - 191 U.S. 165 (1903)
- Allen v. Pullman's Palace Car Co. - 191 U.S. 171 (1903)
- Atkin v. Kansas - 191 U.S. 207 (1903)
- Hibben v. Smith - 191 U.S. 310 (1903)
- Sharp v. United States - 191 U.S. 341 (1903)
- Anglo-American Provision Co. v. Davis Provision Co. No. 1 - 191 U.S. 373 (1903)
- Wisconsin & Michigan Ry. Co. v. Powers - 191 U.S. 379 (1903)
- Cronin v. Adams - 192 U.S. 108 (1904)
- German Savings & Loan Society v. Dormitzer - 192 U.S. 125 (1904)
- Rogers v. Alabama - 192 U.S. 226 (1904)
- South Dakota v. North Carolina - 192 U.S. 286 (1904)
- Thomas v. United States - 192 U.S. 363 (1904)
- Spreckels Sugar Refining Co. v. McClain - 192 U.S. 397 (1904)
- Cornell v. Coyne - 192 U.S. 418 (1904)
- Buttfield v. Stranahan - 192 U.S. 470 (1904)
- Adams v. New York - 192 U.S. 585 (1904)
- Postal Telegraph-Cable Co. v. Taylor - 192 U.S. 64 (1904)
- Carstairs v. Cochran - 193 U.S. 10 (1904)
- Northern Securities Co. v. United States - 193 U.S. 197 (1904)
- Cincinnati Street Ry. Co. v. Snell - 193 U.S. 30 (1904)
- Barney v. New York - 193 U.S. 430 (1904)
- Gagnon v. United States - 193 U.S. 451 (1904)
- Fargo v. Hart - 193 U.S. 490 (1904)
- Minneapolis & St. L. R. Co. v. Minnesota - 193 U.S. 53 (1904)
- Great Southern Fire Proof Hotel Co. v. Jones - 193 U.S. 532 (1904)
- Newburyport Water Co. v. Newburyport - 193 U.S. 561 (1904)
- Pope v. Williams - 193 U.S. 621 (1904)
- National Mutual Bldg. & Loan Ass'n v. Brahan - 193 U.S. 635 (1904)
- Leigh v. Green - 193 U.S. 79 (1904)
- West v. Louisiana - 194 U.S. 258 (1904)
- Missouri, Kansas & Texas Ry. Co. v. May - 194 U.S. 267 (1904)
- Turner v. Williams - 194 U.S. 279 (1904)
- Bessette v. W. B. Conkey Co. - 194 U.S. 324 (1904)
- Fischer v. St. Louis - 194 U.S. 361 (1904)
- Sun Printing & Publishing Ass'n v. Edwards - 194 U.S. 377 (1904)
- Lloyd v. Dollison - 194 U.S. 445 (1904)
- Binns v. United States - 194 U.S. 486 (1904)
- Public Clearing House v. Coyne - 194 U.S. 497 (1904)
- Cleveland v. Cleveland City Ry. Co. - 194 U.S. 517 (1904)

- Chandler v. Dix - 194 U.S. 590 (1904)
- International Postal Supply Co. v. Bruce - 194 U.S. 601 (1904)
- Beavers v. Henkel - 194 U.S. 73 (1904)
- Bradley v. Lightcap - 195 U.S. 1 (1904)
- Kepner v. United States - 195 U.S. 100 (1904)
- Dorr v. United States - 195 U.S. 138 (1904)
- Stevenson v. Fain - 195 U.S. 165 (1904)
- Aikens v. Wisconsin - 195 U.S. 194 (1904)
- Thomas v. Board of Trustees - 195 U.S. 207 (1904)
- Dobbins v. Los Angeles - 195 U.S. 223 (1904)
- National Exchange Bank v. Wiley - 195 U.S. 257 (1904)
- McCray v. United States - 195 U.S. 27 (1904)
- Olsen v. Smith - 195 U.S. 332 (1904)
- Baltimore Shipbuilding Co. v. Baltimore - 195 U.S. 375 (1904)
- Helena Water Works Co. v. Helena - 195 U.S. 383 (1904)
- Western Union Tel. Co. v. Pennsylvania R. Co. - 195 U.S. 540 (1904)
- Schick v. United States - 195 U.S. 65 (1904)
- Butte City Water Co. v. Baker - 196 U.S. 119 (1905)
- Central of Georgia Ry. Co. v. Murphey - 196 U.S. 194 (1905)
- Cook v. Marshall County - 196 U.S. 261 (1905)
- Hodge v. Muscatine County - 196 U.S. 276 (1905)
- Rooney v. North Dakota - 196 U.S. 319 (1905)
- Munsey v. Clough - 196 U.S. 364 (1905)
- Swift & Co. v. United States - 196 U.S. 375 (1905)
- Smiley v. Kansas - 196 U.S. 447 (1905)
- Allen v. Alleghany Co. - 196 U.S. 458 (1905)
- Corry v. Baltimore - 196 U.S. 466 (1905)
- Coulter v. Louisville & Nashville R. Co. - 196 U.S. 599 (1905)
- Scottish Union Ins. Co. v. Bowland - 196 U.S. 611 (1905)
- Jacobson v. Massachusetts - 197 U.S. 11 (1905)
- National Cotton Oil Co. v. Texas - 197 U.S. 115 (1905)
- Dallemagne v. Moisan - 197 U.S. 169 (1905)
- Clyatt v. United States - 197 U.S. 207 (1905)
- Bishop v. United States - 197 U.S. 334 (1905)
- Louisville & Nashville R. Co. v. Barber Asphalt Co. - 197 U.S. 430 (1905)
- New Orleans Gas Co. v. Drainage Comm'n - 197 U.S. 453 (1905)
- Iron Cliffs Co. v. Negaunee Iron Co. - 197 U.S. 463 (1905)

- Rassmussen v. United States - 197 U.S. 516 (1905)
- Muhlker v. New York & Harlem R. Co. - 197 U.S. 544 (1905)
- Harris v. Balk - 198 U.S. 215 (1905)
- United States v. Ju Toy - 198 U.S. 253 (1905)
- Old Dominion Steamship Co. v. Virginia - 198 U.S. 299 (1905)
- Thompson v. Darden - 198 U.S. 310 (1905)
- Harding v. Harding - 198 U.S. 317 (1905)
- Delaware, L. & W. R. Co. v. Pennsylvania - 198 U.S. 341 (1905)
- Clark v. Nash - 198 U.S. 361 (1905)
- United States v. Winans - 198 U.S. 371 (1905)
- Ah Sin v. Wittman - 198 U.S. 500 (1905)
- Beavers v. Haubert - 198 U.S. 77 (1905)
- Union Refrigerator Transit Co. v. Kentucky - 199 U.S. 194 (1905)
- Marvin v. Trout - 199 U.S. 212 (1905)
- Kies v. Lowrey - 199 U.S. 233 (1905)
- California Reduction Co. v. Sanitary Reduction Works - 199 U.S. 306 (1905)
- Jack v. Kansas - 199 U.S. 372 (1905)
- Carroll v. Greenwich Ins. Co. of New York - 199 U.S. 401 (1905)
- South Carolina v. United States - 199 U.S. 437 (1905)
- Manigault v. Springs - 199 U.S. 473 (1905)
- Trono v. United States - 199 U.S. 521 (1905)
- Jaster v. Currie - 198 U.S. 144 (1906)
- Lochner v. New York - 198 U.S. 45 (1906)
- Louisville & Nashville R. Co. v. Deer - 200 U.S. 176 (1906)
- Knoxville Water Co. v. Knoxville - 200 U.S. 22 (1906)
- Graham v. Folsom - 200 U.S. 248 (1906)
- Gunter v. Atlantic Coast Line R. Co. - 200 U.S. 273 (1906)
- Carfer v. Caldwell - 200 U.S. 293 (1906)
- Hibernia Savings & Loan Society v. San Francisco - 200 U.S. 310 (1906)
- Martin v. Texas - 200 U.S. 316 (1906)
- United States v. Detroit Lumber Co. - 200 U.S. 321 (1906)
- Strickley v. Highland Boy Gold Mining Co. - 200 U.S. 527 (1906)
- Chicago, B. & Q. Ry. Co. v. Drainage Commissioners - 200 U.S. 561 (1906)
- Campbell v. California - 200 U.S. 87 (1906)
- Kentucky v. Powers - 201 U.S. 1 (1906)
- Michigan Central R. Co. v. Powers - 201 U.S. 245 (1906)
- Houston & Texas R. Co. v. Mayes - 201 U.S. 321 (1906)
- Joy v. St. Louis - 201 U.S. 332 (1906)
- Soper v. Lawrence Brothers Co. - 201 U.S. 359 (1906)
- Blair v. Chicago - 201 U.S. 400 (1906)
- Hale v. Henkel - 201 U.S. 43 (1906)
- Cleveland v. Cleveland Elec. Ry. Co. - 201 U.S. 529 (1906)
- Powers v. Detroit, G.H. & M. Ry. Co. - 201 U.S. 543 (1906)

- Haddock v. Haddock - 201 U.S. 562 (1906)
- St. John v. New York - 201 U.S. 633 (1906)
- Burton v. United States - 202 U.S. 344 (1906)
- Ayer & Lord Tie Co. v. Kentucky - 202 U.S. 409 (1906)
- Millard v. Roberts - 202 U.S. 429 (1906)
- Cox v. Texas - 202 U.S. 446 (1906)
- Vicksburg v. Vicksburg Waterworks Co. - 202 U.S. 453 (1906)
- New York Central R. Co. v. Miller - 202 U.S. 584 (1906)
- Oregon v. Hitchcock - 202 U.S. 60 (1906)
- Hodges v. United States - 203 U.S. 1 (1906)
- Northern Assurance Co. v. Grand View Bldg. Assn. - 203 U.S. 106 (1906)
- National Council v. State Council - 203 U.S. 151 (1906)
- Fisher v. Baker - 203 U.S. 174 (1906)
- Pettibone v. Nichols - 203 U.S. 192 (1906)
- Appleyard v. Massachusetts - 203 U.S. 222 (1906)
- Northwestern National Life Ins. Co. v. Riggs - 203 U.S. 243 (1906)
- Martin v. Pittsburgh & Lake Erie R. Co. - 203 U.S. 284 (1906)
- Allen v. Riley - 203 U.S. 347 (1906)
- John Woods & Sons v. Carl - 203 U.S. 358 (1906)
- Fair Haven & Westville R. Co. v. New Haven - 203 U.S. 379 (1906)
- Rearick v. Pennsylvania - 203 U.S. 507 (1906)
- Illinois Central R. Co. v. McKendree - 203 U.S. 514 (1906)
- Cahen v. Brewster - 203 U.S. 543 (1906)
- Board of Education v. Illinois - 203 U.S. 553 (1906)
- Vicksburg v. Vicksburg Waterworks Co. - 206 U.S. 496 (1906)
- American Smelting & Refining Co. v. Lindsley - 204 U.S. 103 (1907)
- Cleveland Elec. Ry. Co. v. Cleveland - 204 U.S. 116 (1907)
- Hatch v. Reardon - 204 U.S. 152 (1907)
- Erie R. Co. v. Erie & Western Transp. Co. - 204 U.S. 220 (1907)
- Ballard v. Hunter - 204 U.S. 241 (1907)
- Bacon v. Walker - 204 U.S. 311 (1907)
- Kansas v. United States - 204 U.S. 331 (1907)
- Western Turf Association v. Greenberg - 204 U.S. 359 (1907)
- Bachtel v. Wilson - 204 U.S. 36 (1907)
- Union Bridge Co. v. United States - 204 U.S. 364 (1907)
- Wallace v. Adams - 204 U.S. 415 (1907)
- Chicago, Burlington & Quincy Ry. Co. v. Babcock - 204 U.S. 585 (1907)
- Coffey v. Harlan County - 204 U.S. 659 (1907)

- Old Wayne Mut. Life Ass'n v. McDonough - 204 U.S. 8 (1907)
- Urquhart v. Brown - 205 U.S. 179 (1907)
- Tinsley v. Treat - 205 U.S. 20 (1907)
- Rochester Ry. Co. v. Rochester - 205 U.S. 236 (1907)
- Johnson v. Browne - 205 U.S. 309 (1907)
- Halter v. Nebraska - 205 U.S. 34 (1907)
- Kawananokoa v. Polyblank - 205 U.S. 349 (1907)
- Metropolitan Life Ins. Co. v. New Orleans - 205 U.S. 395 (1907)
- Patterson v. Colorado - 205 U.S. 454 (1907)
- Whitfield v. Aetna Life Ins. Co. - 205 U.S. 489 (1907)
- Home Savings Bank v. Des Moines - 205 U.S. 503 (1907)
- Green v. Chicago, B. & Q. Ry. Co. - 205 U.S. 530 (1907)
- Wilmington Star Mining Co. v. Fulton - 205 U.S. 60 (1907)
- Atlantic Coast Line R. Co. v. No. Car. Corp. Comm'n - 206 U.S. 1 (1907)
- Adams Express Co. v. Kentucky - 206 U.S. 129 (1907)
- American Express Co. v. Kentucky - 206 U.S. 139 (1907)
- Georgia v. Tennessee Copper Co. - 206 U.S. 230 (1907)
- Grafton v. United States - 206 U.S. 333 (1907)
- Romeu v. Todd - 206 U.S. 358 (1907)
- Buck v. Beach - 206 U.S. 392 (1907)
- Kansas v. Colorado - 206 U.S. 46 (1907)
- Bernheimer v. Converse - 206 U.S. 516 (1907)
- Sauer v. New York - 206 U.S. 536 (1907)
- Taylor v. United States - 207 U.S. 120 (1907)
- Central of Georgia Ry. Co. v. Wright - 207 U.S. 127 (1907)
- Chambers v. Baltimore & Ohio R. Co. - 207 U.S. 142 (1907)
- Hunter v. Pittsburgh - 207 U.S. 161 (1907)
- Raymond v. Chicago Union Traction Co. - 207 U.S. 20 (1907)
- Ozan Lumber Co. v. Union County Nat. Bank - 207 U.S. 251 (1907)
- Polk v. Mutual Reserve Fund Life Ass'n - 207 U.S. 310 (1907)
- Heath & Milligan Mfg. Co. v. Worst - 207 U.S. 338 (1907)
- Tilt v. Kelsey - 207 U.S. 43 (1907)
- Williamson v. United States - 207 U.S. 425 (1908)
- I. M. Darnell & Son Co. v. Memphis - 208 U.S. 113 (1908)
- Adair v. United States - 208 U.S. 161 (1908)
- Braxton County Court v. West Virginia - 208 U.S. 192 (1908)
- Loewe v. Lawlor - 208 U.S. 274 (1908)
- Dick v. United States - 208 U.S. 340 (1908)
- Bassing v. Cady - 208 U.S. 386 (1908)
- United States v. Bitty - 208 U.S. 393 (1908)
- Muller v. Oregon - 208 U.S. 412 (1908)
- Ughbanks v. Armstrong - 208 U.S. 481 (1908)

- Northern Pacific Ry. Co. v. Duluth - 208 U.S. 583 (1908)
- Hairston v. Danville & Western Ry. Co. - 208 U.S. 598 (1908)
- Chin Yow v. United States - 208 U.S. 8 (1908)
- Venner v. Great Northern Ry. Co. - 209 U.S. 24 (1908)
- Hudson County Water Co. v. McCarter - 209 U.S. 349 (1908)
- Battle v. United States - 209 U.S. 36 (1908)
- Longyear v. Toolan - 209 U.S. 414 (1908)
- Scully v. Bird - 209 U.S. 481 (1908)
- Armour Packing Co. v. United States - 209 U.S. 56 (1908)
- Galveston, H. & S.A. Ry. Co. v. Texas - 210 U.S. 217 (1908)
- Fauntleroy v. Lum - 210 U.S. 230 (1908)
- St. Louis, I.M. & S. Ry. Co. v. Taylor - 210 U.S. 281 (1908)
- Western Loan & Savings Co. v. Butte & Boston Min. Co. - 210 U.S. 368 (1908)
- Londoner v. Denver - 210 U.S. 373 (1908)
- Pierce v. Creecy - 210 U.S. 387 (1908)
- Reuben Quick Bear v. Leupp - 210 U.S. 50 (1908)
- Brown v. Fletcher's Estate - 210 U.S. 82 (1908)
- Frasch v. Moore - 211 U.S. 1 (1908)
- Louisville & Nashville R. Co. v. Mottley - 211 U.S. 149 (1908)
- Prentis v. Atlantic Coast Line Co. - 211 U.S. 210 (1908)
- Home Tel. & Tel. Co. v. Los Angeles - 211 U.S. 265 (1908)
- Miller & Lux, Inc. v. East Side Canal & Irrig. Co. - 211 U.S. 293 (1908)
- North American Cold Storage Co. v. Chicago - 211 U.S. 306 (1908)
- New York ex Rel. Silz v. Hesterberg - 211 U.S. 31 (1908)
- Paddell v. New York - 211 U.S. 446 (1908)
- Berea College v. Kentucky - 211 U.S. 45 (1908)
- Louisiana v. Garfield - 211 U.S. 70 (1908)
- Twining v. State - 211 U.S. 78 (1908)
- Kopel v. Bingham - 211 U.S. 468 (1909)
- Lemieux v. Young - 211 U.S. 489 (1909)
- McLean v. Arkansas - 211 U.S. 539 (1909)
- Southern Realty Investment Co. v. Walker - 211 U.S. 603 (1909)
- Knoxville v. Knoxville Water Co. - 212 U.S. 1 (1909)
- Louisville & Nashville R. Co. v. Central Stock Yards Co. - 212 U.S. 132 (1909)
- Ontario Land Co. v. Yordy - 212 U.S. 152 (1909)
- Crawford v. United States - 212 U.S. 183 (1909)

- Willcox v. Consolidated Gas Co. - 212 U.S. 19 (1909)
- American Express Co. v. Mullins - 212 U.S. 311 (1909)
- Nielsen v. California - 212 U.S. 315 (1909)
- Hammond Packing Co. v. Arkansas - 212 U.S. 322 (1909)
- Rakes v. United States - 212 U.S. 55 (1909)
- Moyer v. Peabody - 212 U.S. 78 (1909)
- Waters-Pierce Oil Co. v. Texas - 212 U.S. 86 (1909)
- Hepner v. United States - 213 U.S. 103 (1909)
- Keller v. United States - 213 U.S. 138 (1909)
- Murray v. Wilson Distilling Co. - 213 U.S. 151 (1909)
- Siler v. Louisville & Nashville R. Co. - 213 U.S. 175 (1909)
- Selliger v. Kentucky - 213 U.S. 200 (1909)
- Commercial Mut. Acc. Co. v. Davis - 213 U.S. 245 (1909)
- Maiorano v. Baltimore & Ohio R. Co. - 213 U.S. 268 (1909)
- Leeds & Catlin Co. v. Victor Talking Machine Co. - 213 U.S. 325 (1909)
- American Banana Co. v. United Fruit Co. - 213 U.S. 347 (1909)
- United States v. Delaware & Hudson Co. - 213 U.S. 366 (1909)
- Atchison, Topeka & Santa Fe Ry. Co. v. Sowers - 213 U.S. 55 (1909)
- District of Columbia v. Brooke - 214 U.S. 138 (1909)
- Smithsonian Institution v. St. John - 214 U.S. 19 (1909)
- Adams Express Co. v. Kentucky - 214 U.S. 218 (1909)
- Santiago v. Nogueras - 214 U.S. 260 (1909)
- Western Union Telegraph Co. v. Chiles - 214 U.S. 274 (1909)
- Oceanic Steam Navigation Co. v. Stranahan - 214 U.S. 320 (1909)
- Goodrich v. Ferris - 214 U.S. 71 (1909)
- Welch v. Swasey - 214 U.S. 91 (1909)
- Fall v. Eastin - 215 U.S. 1 (1909)
- Hubert v. New Orleans - 215 U.S. 170 (1909)
- Everett v. Everett - 215 U.S. 203 (1909)
- Marbles v. Creecy - 215 U.S. 63 (1909)
- El Paso & Northeastern Ry. Co. v. Gutierrez - 215 U.S. 87 (1909)
- Kuhn v. Fairmont Coal Co. - 215 U.S. 349 (1910)
- Henley v. Myers - 215 U.S. 373 (1910)
- Minneapolis v. Minneapolis Street Ry. Co. - 215 U.S. 417 (1910)
- ICC v. Illinois Central R. Co. - 215 U.S. 452 (1910)
- Flaherty v. Hanson - 215 U.S. 515 (1910)
- Western Union Telegraph Co. v. Kansas - 216 U.S. 1 (1910)
- Ludwig v. Western Union Telegraph Co. - 216 U.S. 146 (1910)
- Monongahela Bridge Co. v. United States - 216 U.S. 177 (1910)

- Missouri Pacific Ry. Co. v. Kansas - 216 U.S. 262 (1910)
- Hannis Distilling v. Baltimore - 216 U.S. 285 (1910)
- Olmsted v. Olmsted - 216 U.S. 386 (1910)
- Southern Railway Co. v. Greene - 216 U.S. 400 (1910)
- Wright v. Georgia R. & Banking Co. - 216 U.S. 420 (1910)
- Haas v. Henkel - 216 U.S. 462 (1910)
- Orleans Parish v. New York Life Ins. Co. - 216 U.S. 517 (1910)
- Pullman Co. v. Kansas - 216 U.S. 56 (1910)
- Southwestern Oil Co. v. Texas - 217 U.S. 114 (1910)
- St. Louis Southwestern Ry. Co. v. Arkansas - 217 U.S. 136 (1910)
- Missouri Pacific Ry. Co. v. Nebraska - 217 U.S. 196 (1910)
- Brantley v. Georgia - 217 U.S. 284 (1910)
- United States v. Welch - 217 U.S. 333 (1910)
- Weems v. United States - 217 U.S. 349 (1910)
- Standard Oil Co. of Kentucky v. Tennessee - 217 U.S. 413 (1910)
- Grenada Lumber Co. v. Mississippi - 217 U.S. 433 (1910)
- Kidd, Dater & Price Co. v. Musselman Grocer Co. - 217 U.S. 461 (1910)
- Holmgren v. United States - 217 U.S. 509 (1910)
- Brown-Forman Co. v. Kentucky - 217 U.S. 563 (1910)
- Williams v. Arkansas - 217 U.S. 79 (1910)
- International Textbook Co. v. Pigg - 217 U.S. 91 (1910)
- Sistare v. Sistare - 218 U.S. 1 (1910)
- Dozier v. Alabama - 218 U.S. 124 (1910)
- Herndon v. Chicago, R.I. & Pac. Ry. Co. - 218 U.S. 135 (1910)
- Watson v. Maryland - 218 U.S. 173 (1910)
- Holt v. United States - 218 U.S. 245 (1910)
- Ling Su Fan v. United States - 218 U.S. 302 (1910)
- Ladew v. Tennessee Copper Co. - 218 U.S. 357 (1910)
- Moffitt v. Kelly - 218 U.S. 400 (1910)
- Western Union Tel. Co. v. Commercial Milling Co. - 218 U.S. 406 (1910)
- Griffith v. Connecticut - 218 U.S. 563 (1910)
- Calder v. Michigan - 218 U.S. 591 (1910)
- Noble State Bank v. Haskell - 219 U.S. 104 (1911)
- Shallenberger v. First State Bank of Holstein - 219 U.S. 114 (1911)
- Assaria State Bank v. Dolley - 219 U.S. 121 (1911)
- Kentucky Union Co. v. Kentucky - 219 U.S. 140 (1911)
- Bailey v. Alabama - 219 U.S. 219 (1911)
- House v. Mayes - 219 U.S. 270 (1911)
- Brodnax v. Missouri - 219 U.S. 285 (1911)
- Muskrat v. United States - 219 U.S. 346 (1911)
- Southern Pacific Co. v. ICC - 219 U.S. 433 (1911)
- Chicago, Rock Island & Pacific Ry. Co. v. Arkansas - 219 U.S. 453 (1911)
- Louisville & Nashville R. Co. v. Mottley - 219 U.S. 467 (1911)
- American Land Co. v. Zeiss - 219 U.S. 47 (1911)
- Chicago, Burlington & Quincy R. Co. v. McGuire - 219 U.S. 549 (1911)
- Hendrix v. United States - 219 U.S. 79 (1911)
- West Side Belt R. Co. v. Pittsburgh Constr. Co. - 219 U.S. 92 (1911)
- Virginia v. West Virginia - 220 U.S. 1 (1911)
- Flint v. Stone Tracy Co. - 220 U.S. 107 (1911)
- Oklahoma v. Atchison, Topeka & Santa Fe Ry. Co. - 220 U.S. 277 (1911)
- Gavieres v. United States - 220 U.S. 338 (1911)
- Diamond Rubber Co. v. Consolidated Tire Co. - 220 U.S. 428 (1911)
- Light v. United States - 220 U.S. 523 (1911)
- Lindsley v. Natural Carbonic Gas Co. - 220 U.S. 61 (1911)
- West v. Kansas Natural Gas Co. - 221 U.S. 229 (1911)
- Strassheim v. Daily - 221 U.S. 280 (1911)
- Dowdell v. United States - 221 U.S. 325 (1911)
- Liverpool etc. Ins. Co. v. Orleans Assessors - 221 U.S. 346 (1911)
- Wilson v. United States - 221 U.S. 361 (1911)
- Grand Trunk Western Ry. Co. v. Railroad Comm'n - 221 U.S. 400 (1911)
- Texas & New Orleans R. Co. v. Miller - 221 U.S. 408 (1911)
- Gompers v. Bucks Stove & Range Co. - 221 U.S. 418 (1911)
- Fifth Avenue Coach Co. v. New York - 221 U.S. 467 (1911)
- Appleby v. Buffalo - 221 U.S. 524 (1911)
- Coyle v. Smith - 221 U.S. 559 (1911)
- Baltimore & Ohio R. Co. v. ICC - 221 U.S. 612 (1911)
- Hopkins v. Clemson Agricultural College - 221 U.S. 636 (1911)
- Provident Institution for Savings v. Malone - 221 U.S. 660 (1911)
- Blinn v. Nelson - 222 U.S. 1 (1911)
- Southern Railway Co. v. United States - 222 U.S. 20 (1911)
- Mutual Loan Co. v. Martell - 222 U.S. 225 (1911)
- Chicago v. Sturges - 222 U.S. 313 (1911)
- Kalem Co. v. Harper Brothers - 222 U.S. 55 (1911)
- Southern Pacific Co. v. Kentucky - 222 U.S. 63 (1911)
- Berryman v. Whitman College - 222 U.S. 334 (1912)

- Northern Pacific Ry. Co. v. Washington - 222 U.S. 370 (1912)
- Southern Ry. Co. v. Reid - 222 U.S. 424 (1912)
- Southern Ry. Co. v. Reid & Beam - 222 U.S. 444 (1912)
- Soliah v. Heskin - 222 U.S. 522 (1912)
- Keeney v. New York - 222 U.S. 525 (1912)
- ICC v. Union Pacific R. Co. - 222 U.S. 541 (1912)
- Pacific States Tel. & Tel. Co. v. Oregon - 223 U.S. 118 (1912)
- Kiernan v. Portland - 223 U.S. 151 (1912)
- Aetna Life Ins. Co. v. Tremblay - 223 U.S. 185 (1912)
- Jacob v. Roberts - 223 U.S. 261 (1912)
- Atchison, T. & S.F. Ry. Co. v. O'Connor - 223 U.S. 280 (1912)
- Collins v. Texas - 223 U.S. 288 (1912)
- Meyer v. Wells, Fargo & Co. - 223 U.S. 298 (1912)
- Powers v. United States - 223 U.S. 303 (1912)
- Rocca v. Thompson - 223 U.S. 317 (1912)
- Cincinnati v. Louisville & Nashville R. Co. - 223 U.S. 390 (1912)
- Quong Wing v. Kirkendall - 223 U.S. 59 (1912)
- Philadelphia Co. v. Stimson - 223 U.S. 605 (1912)
- Louisville & Nashville R. Co. v. Cook Brewing Co. - 223 U.S. 70 (1912)
- Henry v. A. B. Dick Co. - 224 U.S. 1 (1912)
- Consumers' Company, Ltd. v. Hatch - 224 U.S. 148 (1912)
- Western Union Telegraph Co. v. Richmond - 224 U.S. 160 (1912)
- ICC v. Goodrich Transit Co. - 224 U.S. 194 (1912)
- Haskell v. Kansas Natural Gas Co. - 224 U.S. 217 (1912)
- Converse v. Hamilton - 224 U.S. 243 (1912)
- St. Louis, Iron Mountain etc. Ry. Co. v. Wynn - 224 U.S. 354 (1912)
- ICC v. Humboldt Steamship Co. - 224 U.S. 474 (1912)
- Oregon R. & Navigation Co. v. Fairchild - 224 U.S. 510 (1912)
- Missouri Pacific Ry. Co. v. Castle - 224 U.S. 541 (1912)
- McCaughey v. Lyall - 224 U.S. 558 (1912)
- B. Altman & Co. v. United States - 224 U.S. 583 (1912)
- Graham v. West Virginia - 224 U.S. 616 (1912)
- Gritts v. Fisher - 224 U.S. 640 (1912)
- Choate v. Trapp - 224 U.S. 665 (1912)
- Bigelow v. Old Dominion Copper Mining & Smelting Co. - 225 U.S. 111 (1912)
- Jordan v. Massachusetts - 225 U.S. 167 (1912)
- Johannessen v. United States - 225 U.S. 227 (1912)
- Norfolk & Suburban Turnpike Co. v. Virginia - 225 U.S. 264 (1912)
- Proctor & Gamble Co. v. ICC - 225 U.S. 282 (1912)
- Hyde v. United States - 225 U.S. 347 (1912)
- Brown v. Elliott - 225 U.S. 392 (1912)
- Glasgow v. Moyer - 225 U.S. 420 (1912)
- David Lupton's Sons Co. v. Automobile Club - 225 U.S. 489 (1912)
- Murphy v. California - 225 U.S. 623 (1912)
- Southern Ry. Co. v. Burlington Lumber Co. - 225 U.S. 99 (1912)
- Breese v. United States - 226 U.S. 1 (1912)
- Selover, Bates & Co. v. Walsh - 226 U.S. 112 (1912)
- Eubank v. Richmond - 226 U.S. 137 (1912)
- Central Lumber Co v. South Dakota - 226 U.S. 157 (1912)
- Purity Extract & Tonic Co. v. Lynch - 226 U.S. 192 (1912)
- Buck Stove & Range Co. v. Vickers - 226 U.S. 205 (1912)
- Yazoo & Mississippi Valley R. Co. v. Jackson Vinegar Co. - 226 U.S. 217 (1912)
- Rosenthal v. New York - 226 U.S. 260 (1912)
- Zakonaite v. Wolf - 226 U.S. 272 (1912)
- Darnell v. Indiana - 226 U.S. 390 (1912)
- Williams v. Talladega - 226 U.S. 404 (1912)
- Chicago, R.I. & Pac. Ry. Co. v. Hardwick Elevator Co. - 226 U.S. 426 (1913)
- Adams Express Co. v. Croninger - 226 U.S. 491 (1913)
- Chicago, Burlington & Quincy Ry. Co. v. Miller - 226 U.S. 513 (1913)
- Chicago, St. Paul, M. & O. Ry. Co. v. Latta - 226 U.S. 519 (1913)
- Thompson v. Thompson - 226 U.S. 551 (1913)
- Schmidinger v. Chicago - 226 U.S. 578 (1913)
- De Bary & Co. v. Louisiana - 227 U.S. 108 (1913)
- Heike v. United States - 227 U.S. 131 (1913)
- Ross v. Oregon - 227 U.S. 150 (1913)
- St. Louis Southwestern Ry. Co. v. Alexander - 227 U.S. 218 (1913)
- New York Central & H. R. R. Co. v. Hudson County - 227 U.S. 248 (1913)
- St. Louis, Iron Mountain & Southern Ry. Co. v. Edwards - 227 U.S. 265 (1913)
- Home Tel. & Tel. Co. v. Los Angeles - 227 U.S. 278 (1913)
- Hutchinson v. Valdosta - 227 U.S. 303 (1913)
- Hoke v. United States - 227 U.S. 308 (1913)
- Crenshaw v. Arkansas - 227 U.S. 389 (1913)
- Rogers v. Arkansas - 227 U.S. 401 (1913)
- Bartell v. United States - 227 U.S. 427 (1913)
- Grand Trunk Western Ry. Co. v. South Bend - 227 U.S. 544 (1913)
- Missouri, Kansas & Texas Ry. Co. v. Harriman - 227 U.S. 657 (1913)
- ICC v. Louisville & Nashville R. Co. - 227 U.S. 88 (1913)

- McDermott v. Wisconsin - 228 U.S. 115 (1913)
- Ettor v. Tacoma - 228 U.S. 148 (1913)
- The Fair v. Kohler Die & Specialty Co. - 228 U.S. 22 (1913)
- Michigan Trust Co. v. Ferry - 228 U.S. 346 (1913)
- Slocum v. New York Life Ins. Co. - 228 U.S. 364 (1913)
- Madera Water Works v. Madera - 228 U.S. 454 (1913)
- Adams v. Milwaukee - 228 U.S. 572 (1913)
- Bugajewitz v. Adams - 228 U.S. 585 (1913)
- Metropolis Theatre Co. v. Chicago - 228 U.S. 61 (1913)
- Wood v. Chesborough - 228 U.S. 672 (1913)
- Chicago, Burlington & Quincy R. Co. v. Cram - 228 U.S. 70 (1913)
- City & County of Denver v. New York Trust Co. - 229 U.S. 123 (1913)
- St. Louis, San Francisco & Tex. Ry. Co. v. Seale - 229 U.S. 156 (1913)
- Barrett v. State - 229 U.S. 26 (1913)
- Lewis Publishing Co. v. Morgan - 229 U.S. 288 (1913)
- McGovern v. New York - 229 U.S. 363 (1913)
- Portland Ry. Co. v. Railroad Comm'n - 229 U.S. 397 (1913)
- Charlton v. Kelly - 229 U.S. 447 (1913)
- Chicago, Burlington & Quincy R. Co. v. Hall - 229 U.S. 511 (1913)
- United States v. Chandler-Dunbar Water Power Co. - 229 U.S. 53 (1913)
- Lewis Blue Point Oyster Co. v. Briggs - 229 U.S. 82 (1913)
- Old Colony Trust Co. v. Omaha - 230 U.S. 100 (1913)
- Missouri Pacific Ry. Co. v. Tucker - 230 U.S. 340 (1913)
- Minnesota Rate Case - 230 U.S. 352 (1913)
- Southern Pacific Co. v. Campbell - 230 U.S. 537 (1913)
- Owensboro v. Cumberland Tel. & Tel. Co. - 230 U.S. 58 (1913)
- Boise Artesian Water Co. v. Boise City - 230 U.S. 84 (1913)
- Clement National Bank v. Vermont - 231 U.S. 120 (1913)
- Straus v. Foxworth - 231 U.S. 162 (1913)
- Goldberg v. Daniels - 231 U.S. 218 (1913)
- Marshall v. Dye - 231 U.S. 250 (1913)
- Louisville & Nashville R. Co. v. Garrett - 231 U.S. 298 (1913)
- Sturges & Burn Mfg. Co. v. Beauchamp - 231 U.S. 320 (1913)
- Stratton's Independence, Ltd. v. Howbert - 231 U.S. 399 (1913)
- Peabody v. United States - 231 U.S. 530 (1913)

- John v. Paullin - 231 U.S. 583 (1913)
- Baltic Mining Co. v. Massachusetts - 231 U.S. 68 (1913)
- Luria v. United States - 231 U.S. 9 (1913)
- Wyandotte County Gas Co. v. Kansas - 231 U.S. 622 (1914)
- Hawley v. City of Malden - 232 U.S. 1 (1914)
- Bacon v. Rutland R. Co. - 232 U.S. 134 (1914)
- Patsone v. Pennsylvania - 232 U.S. 138 (1914)
- Adams Express v. New York - 232 U.S. 14 (1914)
- Burbank v. Ernst - 232 U.S. 162 (1914)
- Chicago, Milwaukee & St. Paul Ry. Co. v. Polt - 232 U.S. 165 (1914)
- Billings v. United States - 232 U.S. 261 (1914)
- United States v. Bennett - 232 U.S. 299 (1914)
- Rainey v. United States - 232 U.S. 310 (1914)
- Harrison v. St. Louis & San Francisco R. Co. - 232 U.S. 318 (1914)
- Baccus v. Louisiana - 232 U.S. 334 (1914)
- United States Express Co. v. New York - 232 U.S. 35 (1914)
- United States v. Regan - 232 U.S. 37 (1914)
- Weeks v. United States - 232 U.S. 383 (1914)
- Chicago, Milwaukee & St. Paul Ry. Co. v. Minneapolis - 232 U.S. 430 (1914)
- Swift v. McPherson - 232 U.S. 51 (1914)
- Farmers & Mechanics Savings Bank v. Minnesota - 232 U.S. 516 (1914)
- Plymouth Coal Co. v. Pennsylvania - 232 U.S. 531 (1914)
- Atlantic Coast Line R. Co. v. Goldsboro - 232 U.S. 548 (1914)
- National Safe Deposit Co. v. Stead - 232 U.S. 58 (1914)
- Williamson v. Osenton - 232 U.S. 619 (1914)
- Chicago, Milwaukee & St. Paul Ry. Co. v. Kennedy - 232 U.S. 626 (1914)
- Holt v. Henley - 232 U.S. 637 (1914)
- Garland v. Washington - 232 U.S. 642 (1914)
- Stewart v. Michigan - 232 U.S. 665 (1914)
- Riley v. Massachusetts - 232 U.S. 671 (1914)
- Eberle v. Michigan - 232 U.S. 700 (1914)
- Browning v. Waycross - 233 U.S. 16 (1914)
- Russell v. Sebastian - 233 U.S. 195 (1914)
- Singer Sewing Machine Co. v. Brickell - 233 U.S. 304 (1914)
- Kansas City Southern Ry. Co. v. Anderson - 233 U.S. 325 (1914)
- Hammond Packing Co. v. Montana - 233 U.S. 331 (1914)
- Chicago, Milwaukee & St. P. Ry. Co. v. Iowa - 233 U.S. 334 (1914)
- Tennessee Coal, Iron & R. Co. v. George - 233 U.S. 354 (1914)
- Carondelet Canal & Navigation Co. v. Louisiana - 233 U.S. 362 (1914)
- German Alliance Ins. Co. v. Lewis - 233 U.S. 389 (1914)
- Wheeler v. Sohmer - 233 U.S. 434 (1914)
- Carlesi v. New York - 233 U.S. 51 (1914)

- Richards v. Washington Terminal Co. - 233 U.S. 546 (1914)
- Smith v. Texas - 233 U.S. 630 (1914)
- Missouri, Kansas & Texas Ry. Co. v. Cade - 233 U.S. 642 (1914)
- Erie R. Co. v. New York - 233 U.S. 671 (1914)
- Erie R. Co. v. Williams - 233 U.S. 685 (1914)
- New York Life Ins. Co. v. Head - 234 U.S. 149 (1914)
- International Harvester Co. v. Missouri - 234 U.S. 199 (1914)
- International Harvester Co. v. Kentucky - 234 U.S. 216 (1914)
- Keokee Consolidated Coke Co. v. Taylor - 234 U.S. 224 (1914)
- Atlantic Coast Line R. Co. v. Georgia - 234 U.S. 280 (1914)
- Sault Ste. Marie v. International Transit Co. - 234 U.S. 333 (1914)
- Houston E. & W. Tex. Ry. Co. v. United States - 234 U.S. 342 (1914)
- Grannis v. Ordean - 234 U.S. 385 (1914)
- Missouri Pacific Ry. Co. v. Larabee - 234 U.S. 459 (1914)
- Western Union Telegraph Co. v. Brown - 234 U.S. 542 (1914)
- International Harvester Co. v. Kentucky - 234 U.S. 579 (1914)
- Louisiana v. McAdoo - 234 U.S. 627 (1914)
- Collins v. Kentucky - 234 U.S. 634 (1914)
- Selig v. Hamilton - 234 U.S. 652 (1914)
- Ocampo v. United States - 234 U.S. 91 (1914)
- United States v. Reynolds - 235 U.S. 133 (1914)
- McCabe v. Atchison, T. & S.F. Ry. Co. - 235 U.S. 151 (1914)
- Louisiana Ry. & Nav. Co. v. Behrman - 235 U.S. 164 (1914)
- Sioux Remedy Co. v. Cope - 235 U.S. 197 (1914)
- Pullman Co. v. Knott - 235 U.S. 23 (1914)
- Western Life Indemnity Co. of Illinois v. Rupp - 235 U.S. 261 (1914)
- Choctaw, Oklahoma & Gulf R. Co. v. Harrison - 235 U.S. 292 (1914)
- St Louis Southwestern Ry. Co. v. Kansas - 235 U.S. 350 (1914)
- Drew v. Thaw - 235 U.S. 432 (1914)
- Lankford v. Platte Iron Works Co. - 235 U.S. 461 (1915)
- South Covington & Cincinnati Ry. Co. v. Covington - 235 U.S. 537 (1915)
- Hendrick v. Maryland - 235 U.S. 610 (1915)
- Wadley Southern Ry. Co. v. Georgia - 235 U.S. 651 (1915)
- Coppage v. Kansas - 236 U.S. 1 (1915)
- Simon v. Southern Ry. Co. - 236 U.S. 115 (1915)
- Grant Timber & Mfg. Co. v. Gray - 236 U.S. 133 (1915)
- Heyman v. Hays - 236 U.S. 178 (1915)
- Southern Operating Co. v. Hays - 236 U.S. 188 (1915)
- Brolan v. United States - 236 U.S. 216 (1915)
- Mutual Film Corp. v. Industrial Comm'n of Ohio - 236 U.S. 230 (1915)
- Fox v. Washington - 236 U.S. 273 (1915)
- Globe Bank & Trust Co. v. Martin - 236 U.S. 288 (1915)
- Rail & River Coal Co. v. Yaple - 236 U.S. 338 (1915)
- Miller v. Wilson - 236 U.S. 373 (1915)
- Bosley v. McLaughlin - 236 U.S. 385 (1915)
- Southern Ry. Co. v. Railroad Commission - 236 U.S. 439 (1915)
- United States v. Midwest Oil Co. - 236 U.S. 459 (1915)
- Yost v. Dallas County - 236 U.S. 50 (1915)
- Kirmeyer v. Kansas - 236 U.S. 568 (1915)
- Northern Pacific Ry. Co. v. North Dakota - 236 U.S. 585 (1915)
- Norfolk & Western Ry. Co. v. Conley - 236 U.S. 605 (1915)
- Michigan Central R. Co. v. Michigan R. Comm'n - 236 U.S. 615 (1915)
- American Seeding Machine Co. v. Kentucky - 236 U.S. 660 (1915)
- Wright v. Central of Georgia Ry. Co. - 236 U.S. 674 (1915)
- Wright v. Louisville & Nashville R. Co. - 236 U.S. 687 (1915)
- Davis v. Virginia - 236 U.S. 697 (1915)
- Burdick v. United States - 236 U.S. 79 (1915)
- Chapman v. Zobelein - 237 U.S. 135 (1915)
- Reinman v. Little Rock - 237 U.S. 171 (1915)
- Malloy v. South Carolina - 237 U.S. 180 (1915)
- Riverside and Dan River Cotton Mills v. Menefee - 237 U.S. 189 (1915)
- Thames & Mersey Marine Ins. Co., Ltd. v. United States - 237 U.S. 19 (1915)
- Chicago, Burlington & Quincy R. Co. v. Railroad Comm'n - 237 U.S. 220 (1915)
- Frank v. Mangum - 237 U.S. 309 (1915)
- Booth v. Indiana - 237 U.S. 391 (1915)
- Coe v. Armour Fertilizer Works - 237 U.S. 413 (1915)
- Erie R. Co. v. Solomon - 237 U.S. 427 (1915)
- Spokane & Inland Empire R. Co. v. Whitley - 237 U.S. 487 (1915)
- Collins v. Johnston - 237 U.S. 502 (1915)
- Sligh v. Kirkwood - 237 U.S. 52 (1915)
- Supreme Council of the Royal Arcanum v. Green - 237 U.S. 531 (1915)
- Charleston & Western Carolina Ry. Co. v. Varnville Co. - 237 U.S. 597 (1915)
- Hood v. McGehee - 237 U.S. 611 (1915)
- Morgan v. Devine - 237 U.S. 632 (1915)

- Hartford Life Ins. Co. v. Ibs - 237 U.S. 662 (1915)
- Equitable Life Assur. Soc'y v. Pennsylvania - 238 U.S. 143 (1915)
- Des Moines Gas Co. v. Des Moines - 238 U.S. 153 (1915)
- McDonald v. Pless - 238 U.S. 264 (1915)
- Guinn & Beal v. United States - 238 U.S. 347 (1915)
- Myers v. Anderson - 238 U.S. 368 (1915)
- United States v. Mosley - 238 U.S. 383 (1915)
- Mallinckrodt Chemical Works v. Missouri ex Rel. Jones - 238 U.S. 41 (1915)
- Price v. Illinois - 238 U.S. 446 (1915)
- Southwestern Tel. & Tel. Co. v. Danaher - 238 U.S. 482 (1915)
- Chicago, Milwaukee & St. Paul R. Co. v. Wisconsin - 238 U.S. 491 (1915)
- Wells Fargo & Co. Express v. Ford - 238 U.S. 503 (1915)
- Atchison, Topeka & Santa Fe Ry. Co. v. Vosburg - 238 U.S. 56 (1915)
- Rossi v. Pennsylvania - 238 U.S. 62 (1915)
- Chicago & Alton R. Co. v. Tranbarger - 238 U.S. 67 (1915)
- Provident Savings Life Assur. Soc'y v. Kentucky - 239 U.S. 103 (1915)
- Stewart v. Kansas City - 239 U.S. 14 (1915)
- Heim v. McCall - 239 U.S. 175 (1915)
- Crane v. New York - 239 U.S. 195 (1915)
- Phillip Wagner, Inc. v. Baltimore - 239 U.S. 207 (1915)
- O'Neill v. Leamer - 239 U.S. 244 (1915)
- Houck v. Little River Drainage Dist. - 239 U.S. 254 (1915)
- Mackenzie v. Hare - 239 U.S. 299 (1915)
- Provo Bench Canal & Irrigation Co. v. Tanner - 239 U.S. 323 (1915)
- Weber v. Freed - 239 U.S. 325 (1915)
- Truax v. Raich - 239 U.S. 33 (1915)
- Hadacheck v. Sebastian - 239 U.S. 394 (1915)
- Miller v. Strahl - 239 U.S. 426 (1915)
- Bi-Metallic Investment Co. v. State Board of Equalization - 239 U.S. 441 (1915)
- United States v. Barnow - 239 U.S. 74 (1915)
- Atlantic Coast Line R. Co. v. Glenn - 239 U.S. 388 (1916)
- Myles Salt Co., Ltd v. Iberia Drainage Dist. - 239 U.S. 478 (1916)
- Northwestern Laundry v. City of Des Moines - 239 U.S. 486 (1916)
- Brushaber v. Union Pacific R. Co. - 240 U.S. 1 (1916)
- Stanton v. Baltic Mining Co. - 240 U.S. 103 (1916)
- Tyee Realty Co. v. Anderson - 240 U.S. 115 (1916)
- Dodge v. Osborn - 240 U.S. 118 (1916)
- Dodge v. Brady - 240 U.S. 122 (1916)
- Innes v. Tobin - 240 U.S. 127 (1916)
- Rogers v. Hennepin County - 240 U.S. 184 (1916)
- Kansas City, F.S. & Memphis Ry. Co. v. Botkin - 240 U.S. 227 (1916)
- Embree v. Kansas City & Liberty Blvd. Rd. Dist. - 240 U.S. 242 (1916)
- Mt. Vernon-Woodberry Co. v. Alabama Power Co. - 240 U.S. 30 (1916)
- Seaboard Air Line Ry. Co. v. Railroad Comm'n - 240 U.S. 324 (1916)
- Butler v. Perry - 240 U.S. 328 (1916)
- Rast v. Van Deman & Lewis Co. - 240 U.S. 342 (1916)
- Tanner v. Little - 240 U.S. 369 (1916)
- Pitney v. Washington - 240 U.S. 387 (1916)
- Cuyahoga River Power Co. v. City of Akron - 240 U.S. 462 (1916)
- Armour & Co. v. North Dakota - 240 U.S. 510 (1916)
- St. Louis, Iron Mountain & Southern Ry. Co. v. Arkansas - 240 U.S. 518 (1916)
- Indian Territory Illuminating Oil Co. v. Oklahoma - 240 U.S. 522 (1916)
- Gast Realty & Inv. Co. v. Schneider Granite Co. - 240 U.S. 55 (1916)
- Baltimore & Ohio R. Co. v. United States - 240 U.S. 620 (1916)
- Lamar v. United States - 241 U.S. 103 (1916)
- Minneapolis & St. Louis R. Co. v. Bombolis - 241 U.S. 211 (1916)
- American Well Works Co. v. Layne & Bowler Co. - 241 U.S. 257 (1916)
- Bankers Trust Co. v. Texas & Pacific Ry. Co. - 241 U.S. 295 (1916)
- Donald v. Philadelphia & Reading Coal & Iron Co. - 241 U.S. 329 (1916)
- Texas & Pacific Ry. Co. v. Rigsby - 241 U.S. 33 (1916)
- Southern Ry. Co. v. Gray - 241 U.S. 333 (1916)
- Brazee v. Michigan - 241 U.S. 340 (1916)
- St. Louis & Kansas City Land Co. v. Kansas City - 241 U.S. 419 (1916)
- Rosenberger v. Pacific Express Co. - 241 U.S. 48 (1916)
- New York Life Ins. Co. v. Dunlevy - 241 U.S. 518 (1916)
- Kennedy v. Becker - 241 U.S. 556 (1916)
- Davis v. Hildebrant - 241 U.S. 565 (1916)
- United States v. Nice - 241 U.S. 591 (1916)
- Holmes v. Conway - 241 U.S. 624 (1916)
- McFarland v. American Sugar Refining Co. - 241 U.S. 79 (1916)
- Seton Hall College v. South Orange - 242 U.S. 100 (1916)
- Kansas City, M. & B. R. Co. v. Stiles - 242 U.S. 111 (1916)
- Hutchinson Ice Cream Co. v. Iowa - 242 U.S. 153 (1916)
- Kane v. New Jersey - 242 U.S. 160 (1916)
- Kryger v. Wilson - 242 U.S. 171 (1916)

- Lovato v. New Mexico - 242 U.S. 199 (1916)
- Detroit United Railway v. Michigan - 242 U.S. 238 (1916)
- Long Sault Development Co. v. Call - 242 U.S. 272 (1916)
- Lehon v. City of Atlanta - 242 U.S. 53 (1916)
- United States v. Oppenheimer - 242 U.S. 85 (1916)
- Clark Distilling Co. v. Western Maryland Ry. Co. - 242 U.S. 311 (1917)
- Crane v. Johnson - 242 U.S. 339 (1917)
- McNaughton v. Johnson - 242 U.S. 344 (1917)
- Gasquet v. LaPeyre - 242 U.S. 367 (1917)
- Lake Shore & Michigan Southern Ry. Co. v. Clough - 242 U.S. 375 (1917)
- Baker v. Baker, Eccles & Co. - 242 U.S. 394 (1917)
- Caminetti v. United States - 242 U.S. 470 (1917)
- Thomas Cusack Co. v. City of Chicago - 242 U.S. 526 (1917)
- Hall v. Geiger Jones Co. - 242 U.S. 539 (1917)
- Caldwell v. Sioux Falls Stock Yards Co. - 242 U.S. 559 (1917)
- Merrick v. Halsey & Co. - 242 U.S. 568 (1917)
- Chesapeake & Ohio Ry. Co. v. Public Service Comm'n - 242 U.S. 603 (1917)
- Bond v. Hume - 243 U.S. 15 (1917)
- Enterprise Irrigation Dist. v. Farmers Mut. Canal Co. - 243 U.S. 157 (1917)
- New York Central R. Co. v. White - 243 U.S. 188 (1917)
- Hawkins v. Bleakly - 243 U.S. 210 (1917)
- Mountain Timber Co. v. Washington - 243 U.S. 219 (1917)
- Philadelphia & Reading Ry. Co. v. McKibbin - 243 U.S. 264 (1917)
- Pennington v. Fourth National Bank - 243 U.S. 269 (1917)
- Pease v. Rathbun-Jones Engineering Co. - 243 U.S. 273 (1917)
- Bowersock v. Smith - 243 U.S. 29 (1917)
- United States v. Cress - 243 U.S. 316 (1917)
- Wilson v. New - 243 U.S. 332 (1917)
- Utah Power & Light Co. v. United States - 243 U.S. 389 (1917)
- California v. Deseret Water, Oil & Irrig. Co. - 243 U.S. 415 (1917)
- Bunting v. Oregon - 243 U.S. 426 (1917)
- Selling v. Radford - 243 U.S. 46 (1917)
- Motion Picture Patents Co. v. Universal Film Co. - 243 U.S. 502 (1917)
- New Mexico v. Lane - 243 U.S. 52 (1917)
- Marshall v. Gordon - 243 U.S. 521 (1917)
- McDonald v. Mabee - 243 U.S. 90 (1917)
- Rowland v. Boyle - 244 U.S. 106 (1917)
- New York Central R. Co. v. Winfield - 244 U.S. 147 (1917)

- Erie R. Co. v. Winfield - 244 U.S. 170 (1917)
- Missouri Pacific Ry. Co. v. McGrew Coal Co. - 244 U.S. 191 (1917)
- Southern Pacific Co. v. Jensen - 244 U.S. 205 (1917)
- Clyde Steamship Co. v. Walker - 244 U.S. 255 (1917)
- Seaboard Air Line Railway v. Blackwell - 244 U.S. 310 (1917)
- Saunders v. Shaw - 244 U.S. 317 (1917)
- Western Oil Refining Co. v. Lipscomb - 244 U.S. 346 (1917)
- Mason v. United States - 244 U.S. 362 (1917)
- Mississippi R. Commission v. Mobile & Ohio R. Co. - 244 U.S. 388 (1917)
- Van Dyke v. Geary - 244 U.S. 39 (1917)
- First National Bank of Bay City v. Fellows - 244 U.S. 416 (1917)
- Paine Lumber Co., Ltd. v. Neal - 244 U.S. 459 (1917)
- Greene v. Louisville & Interurban R. Co. - 244 U.S. 499 (1917)
- Louisville & Nashville R. Co. v. Greene - 244 U.S. 522 (1917)
- Puget Sound Traction Co. v. Reynolds - 244 U.S. 574 (1917)
- Adams v. Tanner - 244 U.S. 590 (1917)
- American Express Co. v. Caldwell - 244 U.S. 617 (1917)
- Hendrickson v. Apperson - 245 U.S. 105 (1917)
- Hendrickson v. Creager - 245 U.S. 115 (1917)
- Biddinger v. Commissioner of Police - 245 U.S. 128 (1917)
- St. Louis Southwestern Ry. Co. v. United States - 245 U.S. 136 (1917)
- Hartford Life Ins. Co. v. Barber - 245 U.S. 146 (1917)
- Looney v. Crane Co. - 245 U.S. 178 (1917)
- Contributors to Pennsylvania Hospital v. Philadelphia - 245 U.S. 20 (1917)
- Jones v. City of Portland - 245 U.S. 217 (1917)
- Crew Levick Co. v. Pennsylvania - 245 U.S. 292 (1917)
- Seaboard Air Line Ry. v. North Carolina - 245 U.S. 298 (1917)
- Crane v. Campbell - 245 U.S. 304 (1917)
- New York & Queens Gas Co. v. McCall - 245 U.S. 345 (1917)
- Fidelity & Columbia Trust Co. v. Louisville - 245 U.S. 54 (1917)
- Pennsylvania R. Co. v. Towers - 245 U.S. 6 (1917)
- Buchanan v. Warley - 245 U.S. 60 (1917)
- Selective Draft Law Cases - 245 U.S. 366 (1918)
- Rosen v. United States - 245 U.S. 467 (1918)
- Bates v. Bodie - 245 U.S. 520 (1918)
- Johnson v. Lankford - 245 U.S. 541 (1918)
- Martin v. Lankford - 245 U.S. 547 (1918)

- Northern Ohio Traction & Light Co. v. Ohio - 245 U.S. 574 (1918)
- Stellwager v. Clum - 245 U.S. 605 (1918)
- Armour & Co. v. Virginia - 246 U.S. 1 (1918)
- International Paper Co. v. Massachusetts - 246 U.S. 135 (1918)
- Locomobile Co. v. Massachusetts - 246 U.S. 146 (1918)
- Cheney Bros. Co. v. Massachusetts - 246 U.S. 147 (1918)
- Denver v. Denver Union Water Co. - 246 U.S. 178 (1918)
- United States v. Bathgate - 246 U.S. 220 (1918)
- Oetjen v. Central Leather Co. - 246 U.S. 297 (1918)
- Ricaud v. American Metal Co., Ltd. - 246 U.S. 304 (1918)
- Wells v. Roper - 246 U.S. 335 (1918)
- Omaechevarria v. Idaho - 246 U.S. 343 (1918)
- New York Life Ins. Co. v. Dodge - 246 U.S. 357 (1918)
- Covington v. South Covington & C. Street Ry. Co. - 246 U.S. 413 (1918)
- Great Northern Ry. Co. v. Clara City - 246 U.S. 434 (1918)
- General Railway Signal Co. v. Virginia - 246 U.S. 500 (1918)
- Virginia v. West Virginia - 246 U.S. 565 (1918)
- Waite v. Macy - 246 U.S. 606 (1918)
- Boston Store v. American Graphophone Co. - 246 U.S. 8 (1918)
- Western Union Tel. Co. v. Foster - 247 U.S. 105 (1918)
- Northwestern Mut. Life Ins. Co. v. Wisconsin - 247 U.S. 132 (1918)
- Marin v. Augendahl - 247 U.S. 142 (1918)
- Gasquet v. Fenner - 247 U.S. 16 (1918)
- Peck & Co v. Lowe - 247 U.S. 165 (1918)
- Doyle v. Mitchell Bros. Co. - 247 U.S. 179 (1918)
- York Manufacturing Co. v. Colley - 247 U.S. 21 (1918)
- Lynch v. Turrish - 247 U.S. 221 (1918)
- Hammer v. Dagenhart - 247 U.S. 251 (1918)
- Cox v. Wood - 247 U.S. 3 (1918)
- Southern Pacific Co. v. Lowe - 247 U.S. 330 (1918)
- Lynch v. Hornby - 247 U.S. 339 (1918)
- Peabody v. Eisner - 247 U.S. 347 (1918)
- Sunday Lake Iron Co. v. Wakefield - 247 U.S. 350 (1918)
- McCoy v. Union Elevated R. Co. - 247 U.S. 354 (1918)
- Chelentis v. Luckenbach S.S. Co., Inc. - 247 U.S. 372 (1918)
- Toledo Newspaper Co. v. United States - 247 U.S. 402 (1918)
- Postal Telegraph Cable Co. v. Newport - 247 U.S. 464 (1918)

- Chicago, M. & St.P. Ry. Co. v. Minneapolis Civic Assn. - 247 U.S. 490 (1918)
- Ruddy v. Rossi - 248 U.S. 104 (1918)
- Payne v. Kansas - 248 U.S. 112 (1918)
- Georgia v. Cincinnati Southern Ry. Co. - 248 U.S. 26 (1918)
- Union Pacific R. Co. v. Public Service Comm'n - 248 U.S. 67 (1918)
- Missouri Pacific Ry. Co. v. Kansas - 248 U.S. 276 (1919)
- Flexner v. Farson - 248 U.S. 289 (1919)
- The Hebe Co. v. Shaw - 248 U.S. 297 (1919)
- Merchants Exchange of St. Louis v. Missouri - 248 U.S. 365 (1919)
- Detroit United Ry. v. Detroit - 248 U.S. 429 (1919)
- Cavanaugh v. Looney - 248 U.S. 453 (1919)
- La Tourette v. McMaster - 248 U.S. 465 (1919)
- Pierce Oil Corp. v. City of Hope - 248 U.S. 498 (1919)
- Central of Georgia Ry. Co. v. Wright - 248 U.S. 525 (1919)
- North Pacific Steamship Co. v. Hall Bros Co. - 249 U.S. 119 (1919)
- Arkadelphia Milling Co. v. St. L. S.W. Ry. Co. - 249 U.S. 134 (1919)
- Middleton v. Texas Power & Light Co. - 249 U.S. 152 (1919)
- Missouri & Ark. Co. v. Sebastian County - 249 U.S. 170 (1919)
- Sugarman v. United States - 249 U.S. 182 (1919)
- Seufert Brothers Co. v. United States - 249 U.S. 194 (1919)
- Frohwerk v. United States - 249 U.S. 204 (1919)
- Debs v. United States - 249 U.S. 211 (1919)
- Dominion Hotel, Inc. v. Arizona - 249 U.S. 265 (1919)
- St. Louis Poster Advertising Co. v. St. Louis - 249 U.S. 269 (1919)
- Union Tank Line Co. v. Wright - 249 U.S. 275 (1919)
- Standard Oil Co. v. Graves - 249 U.S. 389 (1919)
- McKinley v. United States - 249 U.S. 397 (1919)
- Lake Erie & Western R. Co. v. Pub. Util. Comm'n - 249 U.S. 422 (1919)
- Corn Products Refining Co. v. Eddy - 249 U.S. 427 (1919)
- Barbour v. Georgia - 249 U.S. 454 (1919)
- Schenck v. United States - 249 U.S. 47 (1919)
- Perley v. North Carolina - 249 U.S. 510 (1919)
- Chalker v. Birmingham & Northwestern Ry. Co. - 249 U.S. 522 (1919)
- New Orleans & Northeastern R. Co. v. Scarlet - 249 U.S. 528 (1919)

- Yazoo & Mississippi Valley R. Co. v. Mullins - 249 U.S. 531 (1919)
- Withnell v. Ruecking Construction Co. - 249 U.S. 63 (1919)
- United States v. Doremus - 249 U.S. 86 (1919)
- Portsmouth Harbor Co. v. United States - 250 U.S. 1 (1919)
- Northern Pacific Ry. Co. v. North Dakota - 250 U.S. 135 (1919)
- American Fire Ins. Co. v. King Lumber & Mfg. Co. - 250 U.S. 2 (1919)
- Parker v. Richard - 250 U.S. 235 (1919)
- Denver, & Rio Grande R. Co. v. Denver - 250 U.S. 241 (1919)
- Blair v. United States - 250 U.S. 273 (1919)
- Commercial Cable Co. v. Burleson - 250 U.S. 360 (1919)
- Pawhuska v. Pawhuska Oil Co. - 250 U.S. 394 (1919)
- Hancock v. Muskogee - 250 U.S. 454 (1919)
- American Mfg. Co. v. St. Louis - 250 U.S. 459 (1919)
- Maxwell v. Bugbee - 250 U.S. 525 (1919)
- Pennsylvania R. Co. v. Public Service Comm'n - 250 U.S. 566 (1919)
- Stilson v. United States - 250 U.S. 583 (1919)
- New York Central R. Co. v. Bianc - 250 U.S. 596 (1919)
- Groesbeck v. Duluth, S.S. & A. Ry. Co. - 250 U.S. 607 (1919)
- Abrams v. United States - 250 U.S. 616 (1919)
- Hamilton v. Kentucky Distilleries & Warehouse Co. - 251 U.S. 146 (1919)
- Stroud v. United States - 251 U.S. 15 (1919)
- Branson v. Bush - 251 U.S. 182 (1919)
- Pacific Gas & Elec. Co. v. Police Court - 251 U.S. 22 (1919)
- Postal Telegraph-Cable Co. v. Warren-Godwin Lumber Co. - 251 U.S. 27 (1919)
- Los Angeles v. Los Angeles Gas & Elec. Corp. - 251 U.S. 32 (1919)
- Chicago, Rock Island & Pacific Ry. Co. v. Cole - 251 U.S. 54 (1919)
- Bragg v. Weaver - 251 U.S. 57 (1919)
- St. Louis, I.M. & Sou. Ry. Co. v. Williams - 251 U.S. 63 (1919)
- Jacob Ruppert v. Caffey - 251 U.S. 264 (1920)
- Western Union Tel. Co. v. Boegli - 251 U.S. 315 (1920)
- Chipman, Ltd. v. Thomas B. Jeffrey Co. - 251 U.S. 373 (1920)
- Silverthorne Lumber Co., Inc. v. United States - 251 U.S. 385 (1920)
- Brooks-Scanlon Co. v. Railroad Commission - 251 U.S. 396 (1920)
- Board of Pub. Util. Comm'rs v. Ynchausti & Co. - 251 U.S. 401 (1920)
- Schaefer v. United States - 251 U.S. 466 (1920)
- McCloskey v. Tobin - 252 U.S. 107 (1920)
- Eisner v. Macomber - 252 U.S. 189 (1920)
- Pennsylvania Gas Co. v. Public Service Comm'n - 252 U.S. 23 (1920)
- Pierce v. United States - 252 U.S. 239 (1920)
- Oklahoma Operating Co. v. Love - 252 U.S. 331 (1920)
- Oklahoma Gin Co. v. Oklahoma - 252 U.S. 339 (1920)
- Shaffer v. Carter - 252 U.S. 37 (1920)
- Kenny v. Supreme Lodge of the World - 252 U.S. 411 (1920)
- State of Missouri v. Holland - 252 U.S. 416 (1920)
- Blumenstock Bros. Advertising Agency v. Curtis Pub. Co. - 252 U.S. 436 (1920)
- Askren v. Continental Oil Co. - 252 U.S. 444 (1920)
- Houston v. Ormes - 252 U.S. 469 (1920)
- Munday v. Wisconsin Trust Co. - 252 U.S. 499 (1920)
- Burnap v. United States - 252 U.S. 512 (1920)
- Canadian Northern Ry. Co. v. Eggen - 252 U.S. 553 (1920)
- Travis v. Yale & Towne Mfg Co. - 252 U.S. 60 (1920)
- Farncomb v. Denver - 252 U.S. 7 (1920)
- United States v. Alaska Steamship Co. - 253 U.S. 113 (1920)
- Maguire v. Trefry - 253 U.S. 12 (1920)
- Knickerbnocker Ice Co. v. Stewart - 253 U.S. 149 (1920)
- Ward v. Love County - 253 U.S. 17 (1920)
- Hawke v. Smith - 253 U.S. 221 (1920)
- Hawke v. Smith - 253 U.S. 231 (1920)
- Green v. Frazier - 253 U.S. 233 (1920)
- Evans v. Gore - 253 U.S. 245 (1920)
- Ohio Valley Water Co. v. Ben Avon Borough - 253 U.S. 287 (1920)
- F. S. Royster Guano v. Virginia - 253 U.S. 412 (1920)
- FTC v. Gratz - 253 U.S. 421 (1920)
- Kwock Jan Fat v. White - 253 U.S. 454 (1920)
- Wallace v. Hines - 253 U.S. 66 (1920)
- Erie Railroad Co. v. Collins - 253 U.S. 77 (1920)
- Erie R. Co. v. Szary - 253 U.S. 86 (1920)
- Underwood Typewriter Co. v. Chamberlain - 254 U.S. 113 (1920)
- International Bridge Co. v. New York - 254 U.S. 126 (1920)
- Western Union Telegraph Co. v. Speight - 254 U.S. 17 (1920)
- Jin Fuey Moy v. United States - 254 U.S. 189 (1920)
- Nicchia v. New York - 254 U.S. 228 (1920)
- United States v. Wheeler - 254 U.S. 281 (1920)
- Walls v. Midland Carbon Co. - 254 U.S. 300 (1920)

- Gilbert v. Minnesota - 254 U.S. 325 (1920)
- Thornton v. Duffy - 254 U.S. 361 (1920)
- Johnson v. Maryland - 254 U.S. 51 (1920)
- Seaboard Air Line Ry. Co. v. United States - 254 U.S. 57 (1920)
- Turner v. Wade - 254 U.S. 64 (1920)
- Arndstein v. McCarthy - 254 U.S. 71 (1920)
- Sullivan v. Kidd - 254 U.S. 433 (1921)
- Duplex Printing Press Co. v. Deering - 254 U.S. 443 (1921)
- St. Louis & San Francisco Ry. Co. v. Public Svc. Comm'n - 254 U.S. 535 (1921)
- Central Union Trust Co. v. Garvan - 254 U.S. 554 (1921)
- Weeds, Inc. v. United States - 255 U.S. 109 (1921)
- Givens v. Zerbst - 255 U.S. 11 (1921)
- Hartford Life Ins. Co. v. Blincoe - 255 U.S. 129 (1921)
- Detroit United Railway v. Detroit - 255 U.S. 171 (1921)
- Smith v. Kansas City Title & Trust Co. - 255 U.S. 180 (1921)
- Baender v. Barnett - 255 U.S. 224 (1921)
- Stoehr v. Wallace - 255 U.S. 239 (1921)
- Gouled v. United States - 255 U.S. 298 (1921)
- Amos v. United States - 255 U.S. 313 (1921)
- Williams v. United States - 255 U.S. 336 (1921)
- Supreme Tribe of Ben-Hur v. Cauble - 255 U.S. 356 (1921)
- Milwaukee Social Democratic Pub. Co. v. Burleson - 255 U.S. 407 (1921)
- Alaska Fish Salting & By-Products Co. v. Smith - 255 U.S. 44 (1921)
- Merchants' Loan & Trust Co. v. Smietanka - 255 U.S. 509 (1921)
- Goodrich v. Edwards - 255 U.S. 527 (1921)
- Walsh v. Brewster - 255 U.S. 536 (1921)
- Southern Iowa Electric Co. v. Chariton - 255 U.S. 539 (1921)
- Port of Seattle v. Oregon & Washington R. Co. - 255 U.S. 56 (1921)
- United States v. L. Cohen Grocery Co. - 255 U.S. 81 (1921)
- Economy Light & Power Co. v. United States - 256 U.S. 113 (1921)
- Bank of Minden v. Clement - 256 U.S. 126 (1921)
- Block v. Hirsch - 256 U.S. 135 (1921)
- Marcus Brown Holding Co., Inc. v. Feldman - 256 U.S. 170 (1921)
- Nickel v. Cole - 256 U.S. 222 (1921)
- St. Louis-S.F. Ry. Co. v. Middlekamp - 256 U.S. 226 (1921)
- Newberry v. United States - 256 U.S. 232 (1921)
- New York v. New Jersey - 256 U.S. 296 (1921)
- New York Trust Co. v. Eisner - 256 U.S. 345 (1921)
- Dillon v. Gloss - 256 U.S. 368 (1921)
- LaBelle Iron Works v. United States - 256 U.S. 377 (1921)
- Minnesota ex Rel. Whipple v. Martinson - 256 U.S. 41 (1921)
- Bethlehem Motors Corp. v. Flynt - 256 U.S. 421 (1921)
- United States v. Yuginovich - 256 U.S. 450 (1921)
- Burdeau v. McDowell - 256 U.S. 465 (1921)
- Dane v. Jackson - 256 U.S. 589 (1921)
- Merchants' Nat'l Bank v. Richmond - 256 U.S. 635 (1921)
- Bowman v. Continental Oil Co. - 256 U.S. 642 (1921)
- Kansas City Sou. Ry. Co. v. Road Improvement Dist. - 256 U.S. 658 (1921)
- Ownbey v. Morgan - 256 U.S. 94 (1921)
- Breiholz v. Board of Supervisors - 257 U.S. 118 (1921)
- United States v. Phellis - 257 U.S. 156 (1921)
- Rockefeller v. United States - 257 U.S. 176 (1921)
- Mitchell Furniture Co. v. Selden Breck Constr. Co. - 257 U.S. 213 (1921)
- Western Fuel Co. v. Garcia - 257 U.S. 233 (1921)
- Eureka Pipe Line Co. v. Hallanan - 257 U.S. 265 (1921)
- United Fuel Gas Co. v. Hallanan - 257 U.S. 277 (1921)
- Danke-Walker Milling Co. v. Bondurant - 257 U.S. 282 (1921)
- Truax v. Corrigan - 257 U.S. 312 (1921)
- Citizens Nat'l Bank v. Durr - 257 U.S. 99 (1921)
- Grant Smith-Porter Ship Co. v. Rohde - 257 U.S. 469 (1922)
- Davis v. Wallace - 257 U.S. 478 (1922)
- Gillespie v. Oklahoma - 257 U.S. 501 (1922)
- Terral v. Burke Construction Co. - 257 U.S. 529 (1922)
- Wallace v. United States - 257 U.S. 541 (1922)
- Railroad Comm'n of Wisconsin v. Chicago, B. & Q. R. Co. - 257 U.S. 563 (1922)
- Hawes v. Georgia - 258 U.S. 1 (1922)
- Fairchild v. Hughes - 258 U.S. 126 (1922)
- Leser v. Garnett - 258 U.S. 130 (1922)
- Crane v. Hahlo - 258 U.S. 142 (1922)
- Texas v. Interstate Commerce Comm'n - 258 U.S. 158 (1922)
- Newton v. Consolidated Gas Co. of New York - 258 U.S. 165 (1922)
- Newton v. New York & Queens Gas Co. - 258 U.S. 178 (1922)
- Newton v. Kings County Lighting Co. - 258 U.S. 180 (1922)
- Irwin v. Wright - 258 U.S. 219 (1922)
- Levy Leasing Co., Inc. v. Siegel - 258 U.S. 242 (1922)
- Balzac v. Porto Rico - 258 U.S. 298 (1922)

- Ferry v. Spokane, P. & S. R. Co. - 258 U.S. 314 (1922)
- Forbes Pioneer Boat Line v. Board of Comm'rs - 258 U.S. 338 (1922)
- First National Bank v. Adams - 258 U.S. 362 (1922)
- Greiner v. Lewellyn - 258 U.S. 384 (1922)
- Galveston Elec. Co. v. Galveston - 258 U.S. 388 (1922)
- United States v. Moreland - 258 U.S. 433 (1922)
- Texas Co. v. Brown - 258 U.S. 466 (1922)
- Stafford v. Wallace - 258 U.S. 495 (1922)
- Lemke v. Farmers Grain Co. - 258 U.S. 50 (1922)
- Sloan Shipyards Corp. v. U.S. Fleet Corp. - 258 U.S. 549 (1922)
- Oklahoma v. Texas - 258 U.S. 574 (1922)
- Lemke v. Homer Farmers Elevator Co. - 258 U.S. 65 (1922)
- New Bedford Dry Dock Co. v. Purdy - 258 U.S. 96 (1922)
- Newton v. New York & Queens Gas Co. - 259 U.S. 101 (1922)
- Heald v. District of Columbia - 259 U.S. 114 (1922)
- Pierce Oil Corp. v. Phoenix Refining Co. - 259 U.S. 125 (1922)
- Atherton Mills v. Johnston - 259 U.S. 13 (1922)
- Bailey v. Drexel Furniture Co. - 259 U.S. 20 (1922)
- Miles v. Safe Deposit & Trust Co. - 259 U.S. 247 (1922)
- Olin v. Kitzmiller - 259 U.S. 260 (1922)
- Industrial Comm'n v. Nordenholt Corp. - 259 U.S. 263 (1922)
- Ng Fung Ho v. White - 259 U.S. 276 (1922)
- Houston v. Southwestern Bell Tel. Co. - 259 U.S. 318 (1922)
- Hill v. Wallace - 259 U.S. 44 (1922)
- Ward & Gow v. Krinsky - 259 U.S. 503 (1922)
- Prudential Ins. Co. v. Cheek - 259 U.S. 530 (1922)
- Chicago, R.I. & P. Ry. Co. v. Perry - 259 U.S. 548 (1922)
- Lipke v. Lederer - 259 U.S. 557 (1922)
- Keokuk & Hamilton Bridge Co. v. United States - 260 U.S. 125 (1922)
- Zucht v. King - 260 U.S. 174 (1922)
- Ozawa v. United States - 260 U.S. 178 (1922)
- Jackman v. Rosenbaum Co. - 260 U.S. 22 (1922)
- Klein v. Burke Construction Co. - 260 U.S. 226 (1922)
- Liberty Oil Co. v. Condon National Bank - 260 U.S. 235 (1922)
- Heisler v. Thomas Colliery Co. - 260 U.S. 245 (1922)

- General Inv. Co. v. Lake Shore & M. Sou. Ry. Co. - 260 U.S. 261 (1922)
- Portsmouth Harbor Land & Hotel Co. v. United States - 260 U.S. 327 (1922)
- St. Louis Cotton Compress Co. v. Arkansas - 260 U.S. 346 (1922)
- Chicago & Northwestern Ry. Co. v. Nye Schneider Fowler Co. - 260 U.S. 35 (1922)
- American Mills Co. v. American Surety Co. - 260 U.S. 360 (1922)
- Champlain Realty Co. v. Brattleboro - 260 U.S. 366 (1922)
- United States v. Lanza - 260 U.S. 377 (1922)
- Pennsylvania Coal Co. v. Mahon - 260 U.S. 393 (1922)
- Wichita R. & Light Co. v. Public Util. Comm'n - 260 U.S. 48 (1922)
- National Union Fire Ins. Co. v. Wanberg - 260 U.S. 71 (1922)
- Charlotte Harbor & Northern Ry. Co. v. Wells - 260 U.S. 8 (1922)
- Sioux City Bridge Co. v. Dakota County - 260 U.S. 441 (1923)
- Rosenberg Bros. & Co., Inc. v. Curtis Brown Co. - 260 U.S. 516 (1923)
- Mason v. United States - 260 U.S. 545 (1923)
- Bankers Trust Co. v. Blodgett - 260 U.S. 647 (1923)
- Lee v. Chesapeake & Ohio Ry. Co. - 260 U.S. 653 (1923)
- Minnesota Commercial Men's Assn. v. Benn - 261 U.S. 140 (1923)
- Douglas v. Noble - 261 U.S. 165 (1923)
- United States v. Bhagat Singh Thind - 261 U.S. 204 (1923)
- Columbia Railway, Gas & Elec. Co. v. South Carolina - 261 U.S. 236 (1923)
- Paducah v. Paducah Railway Co. - 261 U.S. 267 (1923)
- Federal Land Bank of New Orleans v. Crosland - 261 U.S. 374 (1923)
- Keller v. Potomac Elec. Power Co. - 261 U.S. 428 (1923)
- Phipps v. Cleveland Refining Co. - 261 U.S. 449 (1923)
- Thomas v. Kansas City Southern Ry. Co. - 261 U.S. 481 (1923)
- Omnia Commercial Co., Inc. v. United States - 261 U.S. 502 (1923)
- Adkins v. Children's Hosp. - 261 U.S. 525 (1923)
- Hanson Lumber Co., Ltd. v. United States - 261 U.S. 581 (1923)
- Moore v. Dempsey - 261 U.S. 86 (1923)
- Board of Trade v. Olsen - 262 U.S. 1 (1923)
- Cullinan v. Walker - 262 U.S. 134 (1923)
- Bianchi v. Morales - 262 U.S. 170 (1923)
- Oliver Iron Mining Co. v. Lord - 262 U.S. 172 (1923)
- Trenton v. New Jersey - 262 U.S. 182 (1923)
- Newark v. New Jersey - 262 U.S. 192 (1923)

- Southwestern Bell Tel. Co. v. Public Svc. Comm'n - 262 U.S. 276 (1923)
- Davis v. Farmers Cooperative Equity Co. - 262 U.S. 312 (1923)
- Riddle v. Dyche - 262 U.S. 333 (1923)
- L. Vogelstein & Co., Inc. v. United States - 262 U.S. 337 (1923)
- United States v. New River Collieries Co. - 262 U.S. 341 (1923)
- First National Bank of San Jose v. California - 262 U.S. 366 (1923)
- Meyer v. Nebraska - 262 U.S. 390 (1923)
- Bartels v. Iowa - 262 U.S. 404 (1923)
- Collins v. Loisel - 262 U.S. 426 (1923)
- Georgia Railway & Power Co. v. Decatur - 262 U.S. 432 (1923)
- Georgia Ry. & Power Co. v. College Park - 262 U.S. 441 (1923)
- Commonwealth of Massachusetts v. Mellon - 262 U.S. 447 (1923)
- Commercial Trust Co. v. Miller - 262 U.S. 51 (1923)
- Chas. Wolff Packing Co. v. Court of Ind. Relations - 262 U.S. 522 (1923)
- Kentucky Finance Corp. v. Paramount Exchange - 262 U.S. 544 (1923)
- Pennsylvania v. West Virginia - 262 U.S. 553 (1923)
- Georgia Ry. & Power Co. v. Railroad Comm'n - 262 U.S. 625 (1923)
- Farmers & Merchants Bank v. Federal Res. Bank - 262 U.S. 649 (1923)
- A. G. Spalding & Bros. v. Edwards - 262 U.S. 66 (1923)
- Rindge Co. v. Los Angeles - 262 U.S. 700 (1923)
- Milheim v. Moffat Tunnel Improvement Dist. - 262 U.S. 710 (1923)
- Des Moines National Bank v. Fairweather - 263 U.S. 103 (1923)
- Butters v. City of Oakland - 263 U.S. 162 (1923)
- Terrace v. Thompson - 263 U.S. 197 (1923)
- Davis v. Wechsler - 263 U.S. 22 (1923)
- Porterfield v. Webb - 263 U.S. 225 (1923)
- Bunch v. Cole - 263 U.S. 250 (1923)
- Craig v. Hecht - 263 U.S. 255 (1923)
- Security Savings Bank v. California - 263 U.S. 282 (1923)
- Binderup v. Pathe Exchange, Inc. - 263 U.S. 291 (1923)
- Webb v. O'Brien - 263 U.S. 313 (1923)
- Frick v. Webb - 263 U.S. 326 (1923)
- Clallam County v. United States - 263 U.S. 341 (1923)
- North Dakota v. Minnesota - 263 U.S. 365 (1923)
- Lehmann v. State Board of Public Accountancy - 263 U.S. 394 (1923)

- Rooker v. Fidelity Trust Co. - 263 U.S. 413 (1923)
- Brown v. United States - 263 U.S. 78 (1923)
- Schwab v. Richardson - 263 U.S. 88 (1923)
- Tidal Oil Co. v. Flanagan - 263 U.S. 444 (1924)
- Dayton-Goose Creek Ry. Co. v. ICC - 263 U.S. 456 (1924)
- Haavik v. Alaska Packers Assn. - 263 U.S. 510 (1924)
- Delaney v. United States - 263 U.S. 586 (1924)
- Washington-Southern Nav. Co. v. Baltimore Co. - 263 U.S. 629 (1924)
- Pierce Oil Corp. v. Hopkins - 264 U.S. 137 (1924)
- Packard v. Banton - 264 U.S. 140 (1924)
- Texas Transport & Terminal Co., Inc. v. New Orleans - 264 U.S. 150 (1924)
- Jones v. Union Guano Co., Inc. - 264 U.S. 171 (1924)
- Industrial Accid. Comm'n v. James Rolph Co. - 264 U.S. 219 (1924)
- Dorchy v. Kansas - 264 U.S. 286 (1924)
- Radice v. New York - 264 U.S. 292 (1924)
- Mahler v. Eby - 264 U.S. 32 (1924)
- Panama R. Co. v. Johnson - 264 U.S. 375 (1924)
- Rodman v. Pothier - 264 U.S. 399 (1924)
- Sperry Oil & Gas Co. v. Chisholm - 264 U.S. 488 (1924)
- Jay Burns Baking Co. v. Bryan - 264 U.S. 504 (1924)
- Chastleton Corp. v. Sinclair - 264 U.S. 543 (1924)
- Railroad Comm'n v. E. Texas R. Co. - 264 U.S. 79 (1924)
- Atchison, T. & S.F. Ry. Co. v. Wells - 265 U.S. 101 (1924)
- Missouri ex Rel. Burnes National Bank v. Duncan - 265 U.S. 17 (1924)
- Salinger v. Loisel - 265 U.S. 224 (1924)
- Wong Doo v. United States - 265 U.S. 239 (1924)
- Weiss v. Stearn - 265 U.S. 242 (1924)
- United States v. Abilene & Southern Ry. Co. - 265 U.S. 274 (1924)
- Missouri v. Kansas Gas Co. - 265 U.S. 298 (1924)
- Supreme Lodge, Knights of Pythias v. Meyer - 265 U.S. 30 (1924)
- Asakura v. City of Seattle - 265 U.S. 332 (1924)
- R. E. Sheehan Co. v. Shuler - 265 U.S. 371 (1924)
- New York State Railways v. Shuler - 265 U.S. 379 (1924)
- Cook v. Tait - 265 U.S. 47 (1924)
- Walton v. House of Representatives - 265 U.S. 487 (1924)

- Everard's Breweries v. Day - 265 U.S. 545 (1924)
- Hester v. United States - 265 U.S. 57 (1924)
- New York, P. & N. Telegraph Co. v. Dolan - 265 U.S. 96 (1924)
- Ziang Sung Wan v. United States - 266 U.S. 1 (1924)
- Missouri Pacific Ry. Co. v. Road District - 266 U.S. 187 (1924)
- Bass, Ratcliff & Gretton, Ltd. v. State Tax Comm'n - 266 U.S. 271 (1924)
- Endicott Johnson Corp. v. Encyclopedia Press, Inc. - 266 U.S. 285 (1924)
- McCarthy v. Arndstein - 266 U.S. 34 (1924)
- National Paper & Type Co. v. Bowers - 266 U.S. 373 (1924)
- Kansas City Southern Ry. Co. v. Road Dist. - 266 U.S. 379 (1924)
- Aetna Life Ins. Co. v. Dunken - 266 U.S. 389 (1924)
- Michaelson v. United States - 266 U.S. 42 (1924)
- Air-Way Elec. Appliance Corp. v. Day - 266 U.S. 71 (1924)
- Morrison v. Work - 266 U.S. 481 (1925)
- Hygrade Provision Co., Inc. v. Sherman - 266 U.S. 497 (1925)
- Ozark Pipe Line Corp. v. Monier - 266 U.S. 555 (1925)
- Michigan Pub. Util. Comm'n v. Duke - 266 U.S. 570 (1925)
- Merchants Mut. Liab. Ins. Co. v. Smart - 267 U.S. 126 (1925)
- Carroll v. United States - 267 U.S. 132 (1925)
- Samuels v. McCurdy - 267 U.S. 188 (1925)
- Flanagan v. Federal Coal Co. - 267 U.S. 222 (1925)
- Buck v. Kuykendall - 267 U.S. 307 (1925)
- George W. Bush & Sons Co. v. Malloy - 267 U.S. 317 (1925)
- Fort Smith Light & Traction Co. v. Bourland - 267 U.S. 330 (1925)
- Mitchell v. United States - 267 U.S. 341 (1925)
- Missouri Pacific R. Co. v. Stroud - 267 U.S. 404 (1925)
- Lancaster v. McCarty - 267 U.S. 427 (1925)
- Brooks v. United States - 267 U.S. 432 (1925)
- Western & Atlantic R. v. Georgia Pub. Svc. Comm'n - 267 U.S. 493 (1925)
- Steele v. United States No. 1 - 267 U.S. 498 (1925)
- Cooke v. United States - 267 U.S. 517 (1925)
- Yeiser v. Dysart - 267 U.S. 540 (1925)
- Modern Woodmen of America v. Mixer - 267 U.S. 544 (1925)
- Chas. Wolff Packing Co. v. Court of Indus. Rel. - 267 U.S. 552 (1925)
- Stebbins and Hurley v. Riley - 268 U.S. 137 (1925)
- Yee Hem v. United States - 268 U.S. 178 (1925)
- Shafer v. Farmers Grain Co. - 268 U.S. 189 (1925)
- Alpha Portland Cement Co. v. Commonwealth - 268 U.S. 203 (1925)
- Coronado Coal Co. v. United Mine Workers - 268 U.S. 295 (1925)
- Weller v. New York - 268 U.S. 319 (1925)
- Real Silk Hosiery Mills v. Portland - 268 U.S. 325 (1925)
- Toyota v. United States - 268 U.S. 402 (1925)
- Dumbra v. United States - 268 U.S. 435 (1925)
- Frick v. Pennsylvania - 268 U.S. 473 (1925)
- Miles v. Graham - 268 U.S. 501 (1925)
- Pierce v. Society of Sisters - 268 U.S. 510 (1925)
- Marr v. United States - 268 U.S. 536 (1925)
- Edwards v. Cuba Railroad Co. - 268 U.S. 628 (1925)
- William Danzer & Co., Inc. v. Gulf & Ship Island R. Co. - 268 U.S. 633 (1925)
- Davis v. L. L. Cohen & Co., Inc. - 268 U.S. 638 (1925)
- Lee v. Osceola & Little River Road Imp. Dist. - 268 U.S. 643 (1925)
- Gitlow v. People - 268 U.S. 652 (1925)
- Burk-Waggoner Oil Assn. v. Hopkins - 269 U.S. 110 (1925)
- Beazell v. Ohio - 269 U.S. 167 (1925)
- Concrete Appliances Co. v. Gomery - 269 U.S. 177 (1925)
- Agnello v. United States - 269 U.S. 20 (1925)
- New York ex Rel. Woodhaven Co. v. Public Svc. Comm'n - 269 U.S. 244 (1925)
- United States v. New York & Cuba Mail S.S. Co. - 269 U.S. 304 (1925)
- Old Dominion Land Co. v. United States - 269 U.S. 55 (1925)
- New Jersey v. Sargent - 269 U.S. 328 (1926)
- First National Bank v. Anderson - 269 U.S. 341 (1926)
- Connally v. General Construction Co. - 269 U.S. 385 (1926)
- Browning v. Hooper - 269 U.S. 396 (1926)
- United States v. River Rouge Improvement Co. - 269 U.S. 411 (1926)
- Trusler v. Crooks - 269 U.S. 475 (1926)
- Metcalf & Eddy v. Mitchell - 269 U.S. 514 (1926)
- United States v. Minnesota - 270 U.S. 181 (1926)
- Schlesinger v. Wisconsin - 270 U.S. 230 (1926)
- Chicago, I. & L. Ry. Co. v. United States - 270 U.S. 287 (1926)
- Weaver v. Palmer Brothers Co. - 270 U.S. 402 (1926)
- Fidelity & Deposit Co. v. Tafoya - 270 U.S. 426 (1926)

- Liberato v. Royer - 270 U.S. 535 (1926)
- Childers v. Beaver - 270 U.S. 555 (1926)
- Tutun v. United States - 270 U.S. 568 (1926)
- Smith v. Illinois Bell Tel. Co. - 270 U.S. 587 (1926)
- Millers' Indemnity Underwriters v. Braud - 270 U.S. 59 (1926)
- Moore v. New York Cotton Exchange - 270 U.S. 593 (1926)
- Rhode Island Hospital Trust Co. v. Doughton - 270 U.S. 69 (1926)
- Oregon Washington R. & Nav. Co. v. Washington - 270 U.S. 87 (1926)
- Maryland v. Super - 270 U.S. 9 (1926)
- United ex Rel. Hughes v. Gault - 271 U.S. 142 (1926)
- Colorado v. United States - 271 U.S. 153 (1926)
- Bowers v. Kerbaugh-Empire Co. - 271 U.S. 170 (1926)
- Booth Fisheries Co. v. Industrial Relations Comm'n - 271 U.S. 208 (1926)
- General Inv. Co. v. New York Central R. Co. - 271 U.S. 228 (1926)
- Board of Commissioners v. New York Tel. Co. - 271 U.S. 23 (1926)
- Fenner v. Boykin - 271 U.S. 240 (1926)
- Western Paper Makers' Chem. Co. v. United States - 271 U.S. 268 (1926)
- Henkels v. Sutherland - 271 U.S. 298 (1926)
- Corrigan v. Buckley - 271 U.S. 323 (1926)
- Missouri ex Rel. Hurwitz v. North - 271 U.S. 40 (1926)
- Appleby v. Delaney - 271 U.S. 403 (1926)
- Thornton v. United States - 271 U.S. 414 (1926)
- Old Colony Trust Co. v. City of Seattle - 271 U.S. 426 (1926)
- Goltra v. Weeks - 271 U.S. 536 (1926)
- Berizzi Brothers Co. v. Steamship Pesaro - 271 U.S. 562 (1926)
- Frost & Frost Trucking Co. v. Railroad Comm'n - 271 U.S. 583 (1926)
- Jaybird Mining Co v. Weir - 271 U.S. 609 (1926)
- United States v. Chemical Foundation, Inc. - 272 U.S. 1 (1926)
- Palmetto Fire Ins. Co. v. Conn - 272 U.S. 295 (1926)
- Hebert v. Louisiana - 272 U.S. 312 (1926)
- Village of Euclid v. Ambler Realty Co. - 272 U.S. 365 (1926)
- Graves v. Minnesota - 272 U.S. 425 (1926)
- Van Oster v. Kansas - 272 U.S. 465 (1926)
- Hughes Brothers Timber Co. v. Minnesota - 272 U.S. 469 (1926)
- Hanover Fire Ins. Co. v. Harding - 272 U.S. 494 (1926)
- Myers v. United States - 272 U.S. 52 (1926)

- Massachusetts State Grange v. Benton - 272 U.S. 525 (1926)
- Luckenbach Steamship Co. v. United States - 272 U.S. 533 (1926)
- United States v. Brims - 272 U.S. 549 (1926)
- Wachovia Bank & Trust Co. v. Doughton - 272 U.S. 567 (1926)
- Ottinger v. Consolidated Gas Co. - 272 U.S. 576 (1926)
- Ottinger v. Brooklyn Union Gas Co. - 272 U.S. 579 (1926)
- Napier v. Atlantic Coast Line R. Co. - 272 U.S. 605 (1926)
- Uihlein v. State of Wisconsin - 273 U.S. 642 (1926)
- Postum Cereal Co. v. California Fig Nut Co. - 272 U.S. 693 (1927)
- Miller v. Milwaukee - 272 U.S. 713 (1927)
- Albrecht v. United States - 273 U.S. 1 (1927)
- United States ex Rel. Vajtauer v. Commissioner - 273 U.S. 103 (1927)
- James-Dickinson Farm Mortgage Co. v. Harry - 273 U.S. 119 (1927)
- Florida v. Mellon - 273 U.S. 12 (1927)
- McGrain v. Daugherty - 273 U.S. 135 (1927)
- Byars v. United States - 273 U.S. 28 (1927)
- Di Santo v. Pennsylvania - 273 U.S. 34 (1927)
- Missouri Pacific R. Co. v. Porter - 273 U.S. 341 (1927)
- Quon Quon Poy v. Johnson - 273 U.S. 352 (1927)
- Hayman v. City of Galveston - 273 U.S. 414 (1927)
- Tyson & Bro. v. Banton - 273 U.S. 418 (1927)
- Tumey v. Ohio - 273 U.S. 510 (1927)
- Nixon v. Herndon - 273 U.S. 536 (1927)
- Ingenohl v. Olsen & Co. - 273 U.S. 541 (1927)
- First National Bank v. City of Hartford - 273 U.S. 548 (1927)
- Minnesota v. First National Bank of St. Paul - 273 U.S. 561 (1927)
- Liberty Warehouse Co. v. Grannis - 273 U.S. 70 (1927)
- Public Utilities Comm'n v. Attleboro Steam Co. - 273 U.S. 83 (1927)
- McGuire v. United States - 273 U.S. 95 (1927)
- Fairmont Creamery Co. v. Minnesota - 274 U.S. 1 (1927)
- Louis Pizitz Dry Goods Co., Inc. v. Yeldell - 274 U.S. 112 (1927)
- Ohio Public Service Co. v. Ohio ex Rel. Fritz - 274 U.S. 12 (1927)
- Fidelity National Bank v. Swope - 274 U.S. 123 (1927)
- Road Improvement Dist. No. 1 v. Missouri Pac. R. Co. - 274 U.S. 188 (1927)
- Duignan v. United States - 274 U.S. 195 (1927)
- Buck v. Bell - 274 U.S. 200 (1927)
- Zahn v. Board of Public Works - 274 U.S. 325 (1927)
- Phelps v. United States - 274 U.S. 341 (1927)

- Chicago, M. & St.P. Ry. Co. v. Public Util. Comm'n - 274 U.S. 344 (1927)
- Hess v. Pawloski - 274 U.S. 352 (1927)
- Whitney v. California - 274 U.S. 357 (1927)
- Bedford Cut Stone Co. v. Stone Cutters' Assn. - 274 U.S. 37 (1927)
- Fiske v. Kansas - 274 U.S. 380 (1927)
- Fort Smith Light & Traction Co. v. Board of Improvement - 274 U.S. 387 (1927)
- Ohio ex Rel. Clark v. Deckebach - 274 U.S. 392 (1927)
- Cline v. Frink Dairy Co. - 274 U.S. 445 (1927)
- Biddle v. Perovich - 274 U.S. 480 (1927)
- New York v. Illinois & Sanitary District of Chicago - 274 U.S. 488 (1927)
- Power Manufacturing Co. v. Saunders - 274 U.S. 490 (1927)
- Maul v. United States - 274 U.S. 501 (1927)
- Nichols v. Coolidge - 274 U.S. 531 (1927)
- Gorieb v. Fox - 274 U.S. 603 (1927)
- Weedin v. Chin Bow - 274 U.S. 657 (1927)
- Mayor of Vidalia v. McNeely - 274 U.S. 676 (1927)
- Southern Railway Co. v. Kentucky - 274 U.S. 76 (1927)
- Millsaps College v. City of Jackson - 275 U.S. 129 (1927)
- Northwestern Mut. Life Ins. Co. v. Wisconsin - 275 U.S. 136 (1927)
- Blodgett v. Holden - 275 U.S. 142 (1927)
- Marron v. United States - 275 U.S. 192 (1927)
- Gambino v. United States - 275 U.S. 310 (1927)
- Chesapeake & O R. Co. v. Leitch - 275 U.S. 507 (1927)
- Gong Lum v. Rice - 275 U.S. 78 (1927)
- Aetna Ins. Co. v. Hyde - 275 U.S. 440 (1928)
- Roche v. McDonald - 275 U.S. 449 (1928)
- Gulf Fisheries Co. v. MacInerney - 276 U.S. 124 (1928)
- Wuchter v. Pizzutti - 276 U.S. 13 (1928)
- Mississippi ex Rel. Robertson v. Miller - 276 U.S. 174 (1928)
- Delaware, L. & W. R. Co. v. Town of Morristown - 276 U.S. 182 (1928)
- Miller v. Schoene - 276 U.S. 272 (1928)
- Nigro v. United States - 276 U.S. 332 (1928)
- J. W. Hampton, Jr. & Co. v. United States - 276 U.S. 394 (1928)
- Chesapeake & Ohio R. Co. v. Leitch - 276 U.S. 429 (1928)
- Untermyer v. Anderson - 276 U.S. 440 (1928)
- Montana National Bank v. Yellowstone County - 276 U.S. 499 (1928)
- Black & White Cab v. Black & Yellow Cab - 276 U.S. 518 (1928)
- City of New Brunswick v. United States - 276 U.S. 547 (1928)

- Shaw v. Gibson-Zahniser Oil Corp. - 276 U.S. 575 (1928)
- Liberty Warehouse Co. v. Burley Growers' Cooperative - 276 U.S. 71 (1928)
- Blodgett v. Silberman - 277 U.S. 1 (1928)
- Long v. Rockwood - 277 U.S. 142 (1928)
- Plamals v. S.S. "Pinar Del Rio" - 277 U.S. 151 (1928)
- Standard Pipe Line Co. v. Miller County Highway Dist. - 277 U.S. 160 (1928)
- Sprout v. City of South Bend - 277 U.S. 163 (1928)
- Nectow v. City of Cambridge - 277 U.S. 183 (1928)
- Springer v. Government of the Philippine Islands - 277 U.S. 189 (1928)
- Panhandle Oil Co. v. Mississippi ex Rel. Knox - 277 U.S. 218 (1928)
- Brooke v. City of Norfolk - 277 U.S. 27 (1928)
- Willing v. Chicago Auditorium Association - 277 U.S. 274 (1928)
- Coffin Brothers & Co. v. Bennett - 277 U.S. 29 (1928)
- Stipcich v. Metropolitan Life Ins. Co. - 277 U.S. 311 (1928)
- Louisville Gas & Elec. Co. v. Coleman - 277 U.S. 32 (1928)
- Ribnik v. McBride - 277 U.S. 350 (1928)
- Quaker City Cab Co. v. Commonwealth - 277 U.S. 389 (1928)
- Olmstead v. United States - 277 U.S. 438 (1928)
- National Life Ins. Co. v. United States - 277 U.S. 508 (1928)
- Hemphill v. Orloff - 277 U.S. 537 (1928)
- Dugan v. Ohio - 277 U.S. 61 (1928)
- Foster-Fountain Packing Co. v. Haydel - 278 U.S. 1 (1928)
- Louis K. Liggett Co. v. Baldridge - 278 U.S. 105 (1928)
- Washington ex Rel. Seattle Title Trust Co v. Roberge - 278 U.S. 116 (1928)
- Johnson v. Haydel - 278 U.S. 16 (1928)
- Lehigh Valley R. Co. v. Board of Public Utility Comm'rs - 278 U.S. 24 (1928)
- New York ex Rel. Bryant v. Zimmerman - 278 U.S. 63 (1928)
- Hunt v. United States - 278 U.S. 96 (1928)
- Roe v. Kansas ex Rel. Smith - 278 U.S. 191 (1929)
- Williams v. Standard Oil Co. - 278 U.S. 235 (1929)
- International Shoe Co. v. Pinkus - 278 U.S. 261 (1929)
- United Fuel Gas Co. v. Railroad Comm'n - 278 U.S. 300 (1929)
- Chase National Bank v. United States - 278 U.S. 327 (1929)
- Wisconsin v. Illinois - 278 U.S. 367 (1929)
- Arlington Hotel Co. v. Fant - 278 U.S. 439 (1929)

- Nashville, C. & St.L. Ry. v. White - 278 U.S. 456 (1929)
- Cudahy Packing Co. v. Hinkle - 278 U.S. 460 (1929)
- Taft v. Bowers - 278 U.S. 470 (1929)
- Salomon v. State Tax Commission - 278 U.S. 484 (1929)
- Great Northern Ry. Co. v. Minnesota - 278 U.S. 503 (1929)
- Frost v. Corporate Commission of Oklahoma - 278 U.S. 515 (1929)
- Manley v. Georgia - 279 U.S. 1 (1929)
- London Guar. & Acc. Co., Ltd. v. Indus. Accident Co., Ltd. - 279 U.S. 109 (1929)
- Helson and Randolph v. Kentucky - 279 U.S. 245 (1929)
- Sinclair v. United States - 279 U.S. 263 (1929)
- Roschen v. Ward - 279 U.S. 337 (1929)
- Douglas v. New York, N.H. & H. R. Co. - 279 U.S. 377 (1929)
- Nielsen v. Johnson - 279 U.S. 47 (1929)
- Standard Oil Co. v. City of Marysville - 279 U.S. 582 (1929)
- Barry v. United States ex Rel. Cunningham - 279 U.S. 597 (1929)
- Macallan Co. v. Massachusetts - 279 U.S. 620 (1929)
- Western & Atlantic Railroad v. Henderson - 279 U.S. 639 (1929)
- Pocket Veto Case - 279 U.S. 655 (1929)
- Old Colony Trust Co. v. Commissioner - 279 U.S. 716 (1929)
- County of Spokane v. United States - 279 U.S. 80 (1929)
- Carson Petroleum Co. v. Vial - 279 U.S. 95 (1929)
- Gonzalez v. Roman Catholic Archbishop of Manila - 280 U.S. 1 (1929)
- Silver v. Silver - 280 U.S. 117 (1929)
- Bromley v. McCaughn - 280 U.S. 124 (1929)
- Bekins Van Lines, Inc. v. Riley - 280 U.S. 80 (1929)
- Safe Deposit & Trust Co. v. Commonwealth - 280 U.S. 83 (1929)
- Farmers Loan & Trust Co. v. Minnesota - 280 U.S. 204 (1930)
- Corn Exchange Bank v. Coler - 280 U.S. 218 (1930)
- United Rys. & Elec. Co. v. West - 280 U.S. 234 (1930)
- Johnson v. Fleet Corporation - 280 U.S. 320 (1930)
- New Jersey Tel. Co. v. Tax Board - 280 U.S. 338 (1930)
- Carpenter v. Shaw - 280 U.S. 363 (1930)
- Henry Ford & Son, Inc. v. Little Falls Fibre Co. - 280 U.S. 369 (1930)
- Ohio ex Rel. Popovici v. Agler - 280 U.S. 379 (1930)

- United states v. Wurzbach - 280 U.S. 396 (1930)
- Cooper v. United States - 280 U.S. 409 (1930)
- Tagg Bros. & Moorhead v. United States - 280 U.S. 420 (1930)
- United States v. Unzeuta - 281 U.S. 138 (1930)
- Ohio Oil Company v. Conway - 281 U.S. 146 (1930)
- Kentucky v. Indiana - 281 U.S. 163 (1930)
- Moore v. Mitchell - 281 U.S. 18 (1930)
- John Baizley Iron Works v. Span - 281 U.S. 222 (1930)
- Employers' Liability Assurance Corp., Ltd. v. Cook - 281 U.S. 233 (1930)
- May v. Heiner - 281 U.S. 238 (1930)
- Alexander Sprunt & Son, Inc. v. United States - 281 U.S. 249 (1930)
- Miller v. McLaughlin - 281 U.S. 261 (1930)
- Patton v. United States - 281 U.S. 276 (1930)
- Missouri v. Gehner - 281 U.S. 313 (1930)
- Dohany v. Rogers - 281 U.S. 362 (1930)
- Cochran v. Louisiana State Board of Education - 281 U.S. 370 (1930)
- Lindgren v. United States - 281 U.S. 38 (1930)
- Home Insurance Co. v. Dick - 281 U.S. 397 (1930)
- Corporation Commission of Oklahoma v. Lowe - 281 U.S. 431 (1930)
- Cincinnati v. Vester - 281 U.S. 439 (1930)
- Todok v. Union State Bank of Harvard - 281 U.S. 449 (1930)
- FRC v. General Electric Co. - 281 U.S. 464 (1930)
- Tyler v. United States - 281 U.S. 497 (1930)
- Broad River Power Co. v. South Carolina - 281 U.S. 537 (1930)
- Texas & New Orleans R. Co. v. Brotherhood of Ry. Clerks - 281 U.S. 548 (1930)
- Wheeler Lumber Co. v. United States - 281 U.S. 572 (1930)
- Baldwin v. Missouri - 281 U.S. 586 (1930)
- Surplus Trading Co. v. Cook - 281 U.S. 647 (1930)
- Carley & Hamilton, Inc. v. Snook - 281 U.S. 66 (1930)
- Brinkerhoff-Faris Trust & Savings Co. v. Hill - 281 U.S. 673 (1930)
- New Orleans Public Service, Inc. v. City of New Orleans - 281 U.S. 682 (1930)
- Goodell v. Koch - 281 U.S. 704 (1930)
- Ohio v. Akron Metropolitan Part District - 281 U.S. 74 (1930)
- Staten Island Rapid Transit Ry. Co. v. Phoenix Indem. Co. - 281 U.S. 98 (1930)
- Beidler v. South Carolina Tax Commission - 282 U.S. 1 (1930)
- Poe v. Seaborn - 282 U.S. 101 (1930)
- Chicago, St. Paul, Minneapolis & Omaha Ry. Co. v. Holmberg - 282 U.S. 162 (1930)
- District of Columbia v. Colts - 282 U.S. 63 (1930)
- Willcuts v. Bunn - 282 U.S. 216 (1931)

- Memphis & Charleston Ry. Co. v. Pace - 282 U.S. 241 (1931)
- O'Gorman & Young, Inc. v. Hartford Fire Ins. Co. - 282 U.S. 251 (1931)
- United States v. Benz - 282 U.S. 304 (1931)
- Go-Bart Importing Co. v. United States - 282 U.S. 344 (1931)
- Burnet v. Sanford & Brooks Co. - 282 U.S. 359 (1931)
- Educational Films Corp. v. Ward - 282 U.S. 379 (1931)
- International Paper Co. v. United States - 282 U.S. 399 (1931)
- Graham & Foster v. Goodcell - 282 U.S. 409 (1931)
- Russian Volunteer Fleet v. United States - 282 U.S. 481 (1931)
- Furst & Thomas v. Brewster - 282 U.S. 493 (1931)
- Alward v. Johnson - 282 U.S. 509 (1931)
- Various Items of Personal Property v. United States - 282 U.S. 577 (1931)
- Coolidge v. Long - 282 U.S. 582 (1931)
- Alford v. United States - 282 U.S. 687 (1931)
- Husty v. United States - 282 U.S. 694 (1931)
- Abie State Bank v. Bryan - 282 U.S. 765 (1931)
- Hans Rees' Sons, Inc. v. North Carolina - 283 U.S. 123 (1931)
- Milliken v. United States - 283 U.S. 15 (1931)
- Interstate Transit, Inc. v. Lindsey - 283 U.S. 183 (1931)
- Missouri Pacific R. Co. v. Norwood - 283 U.S. 249 (1931)
- Susquehanna Power Co. v. State Tax Comm'n - 283 U.S. 291 (1931)
- Aldridge v. United States - 283 U.S. 308 (1931)
- Stromberg v. California - 283 U.S. 359 (1931)
- Graniteville Mfg. Co. v. Query - 283 U.S. 376 (1931)
- Frank L. Young Co. v. McNeal-Edwards Co. - 283 U.S. 398 (1931)
- Arizona v. California - 283 U.S. 423 (1931)
- East Ohio Gas Co. v. Tax Commission of Ohio - 283 U.S. 465 (1931)
- Gasoline Products Co., Inc. v. Champlin Refining Co. - 283 U.S. 494 (1931)
- Baldwin v. Iowa State Traveling Men's Association - 283 U.S. 522 (1931)
- State Board of Tax Commissioners v. Jackson - 283 U.S. 527 (1931)
- Smith v. Cahoon - 283 U.S. 553 (1931)
- Storaasli v. Minnesota - 283 U.S. 57 (1931)
- Indian Motocycle Co. v. United States - 283 U.S. 570 (1931)
- Phillips v. Commissioner - 283 U.S. 589 (1931)
- United States v. Macintosh - 283 U.S. 605 (1931)
- United States v. Bland - 283 U.S. 636 (1931)

- United States v. Utah - 283 U.S. 64 (1931)
- Near v. Minnesota - 283 U.S. 697 (1931)
- Herron v. Southern Pacific Company - 283 U.S. 91 (1931)
- Columbus & Greenville Ry. Co. v. Miller - 283 U.S. 96 (1931)
- Louisiana Pub. Serv. Comm'n v. Railroad Co. - 284 U.S. 125 (1931)
- United States v. Murdock - 284 U.S. 141 (1931)
- Hardware Dealers Mut. Fire Ins. Co. v. Glidden Co. - 284 U.S. 151 (1931)
- Phillips v. Dime Trust & Safe Deposit Co. - 284 U.S. 160 (1931)
- Mecom v. Fitzsimmons Drilling Co., Inc. - 284 U.S. 183 (1931)
- Hoeper v. Tax Commission of Wisconsin - 284 U.S. 206 (1931)
- Van Huffel v. Harkelrode - 284 U.S. 225 (1931)
- Iowa-Des Moines National Bank v. Bennett - 284 U.S. 239 (1931)
- Santovincenzo v. Egan - 284 U.S. 30 (1931)
- State Tax Commission v. Interstate Nat. Gas. Co., Inc. - 284 U.S. 41 (1931)
- Keating v. Public Nat Bank of New York - 284 U.S. 587 (1931)
- Bandini Petroleum Co. v. Superior Court - 284 U.S. 8 (1931)
- Chicago, Rock Island & Pacific Ry. Co. v. United States - 284 U.S. 80 (1931)
- Chicago & Eastern Illinois R. Co. v. Industrial Comm'n - 284 U.S. 296 (1932)
- Blockburger v. United States - 284 U.S. 299 (1932)
- First National Bank of Boston v. Maine - 284 U.S. 312 (1932)
- Hodge Drive-It-Yourself Co. v. Cincinnati - 284 U.S. 335 (1932)
- Dunn v. United States - 284 U.S. 390 (1932)
- Henkel v. Chicago, St. Paul, Minneapolis & Omaha Ry. Co. - 284 U.S. 444 (1932)
- Packer Corporation of Utah - 285 U.S. 105 (1932)
- Crowell v. Benson - 285 U.S. 22 (1932)
- New State Ice Co. v. Liebmann - 285 U.S. 262 (1932)
- Heiner v. Donnan - 285 U.S. 312 (1932)
- Smiley v. Holm - 285 U.S. 355 (1932)
- Koenig v. Flynn - 285 U.S. 375 (1932)
- Carroll v. Becker - 285 U.S. 380 (1932)
- Burnet v. Coronado Oil & Gas Co. - 285 U.S. 393 (1932)
- Hagner v. United States - 285 U.S. 427 (1932)
- Coombes v. Getz - 285 U.S. 434 (1932)
- United States v. Lefkowitz - 285 U.S. 452 (1932)
- Shriver v. Woodbine Savings Bank - 285 U.S. 467 (1932)
- Taylor v. United States - 286 U.S. 1 (1932)
- Fox Film Corp. v. Doyal - 286 U.S. 123 (1932)

- Bradford Electric Light Co., Inc. v. Clapper - 286 U.S. 145 (1932)
- Utah Power & Light Co. v. Pfost - 286 U.S. 165 (1932)
- Champlin Refining Co. v. Corporation Comm'n of Oklahoma - 286 U.S. 210 (1932)
- McLaughlin v. Alliance Insurance Co. - 286 U.S. 244 (1932)
- Lawrence v. State Tax Commission of Mississippi - 286 U.S. 276 (1932)
- Texas & Pacific Ry. Co. v. United States - 286 U.S. 285 (1932)
- Continental Tie & Lumber Co. v. United States - 286 U.S. 290 (1932)
- Continental Baking Co. v. Woodring - 286 U.S. 352 (1932)
- Sproles v. Binford - 286 U.S. 374 (1932)
- Atlantic Cleaners & Dyers, Inc. v. United States - 286 U.S. 427 (1932)
- Edwards v. United States - 286 U.S. 482 (1932)
- Nixon v. Condon - 286 U.S. 73 (1932)
- Wood v. Broom - 287 U.S. 1 (1932)
- Burnet v. Harmel - 287 U.S. 103 (1932)
- New York Central Securities Corp. v. United States - 287 U.S. 12 (1932)
- American Surety Co. v. Baldwin - 287 U.S. 156 (1932)
- Sgro v. United States - 287 U.S. 206 (1932)
- Stephenson v. Binford - 287 U.S. 251 (1932)
- Advance-Rumely Thresher Co., Inc. v. Jackson - 287 U.S. 283 (1932)
- Sun Oil Co. v. Dalzell Towing Co., Inc. - 287 U.S. 291 (1932)
- Bankers Pocahontas Coal Co. v. Burnet - 287 U.S. 308 (1932)
- Reichelderfer v. Quinn - 287 U.S. 315 (1932)
- Sterling v. Constantin - 287 U.S. 378 (1932)
- Sorrells v. United States - 287 U.S. 435 (1932)
- Powell v. Alabama - 287 U.S. 45 (1932)
- Seaboard Air Line Railway Co. v. Watson - 287 U.S. 86 (1932)
- Schoenthal v. Irving Trust Co. - 287 U.S. 92 (1932)
- Atlantic Coast Line R. Co. v. Ford - 287 U.S. 502 (1933)
- Cook v. United States - 288 U.S. 102 (1933)
- Anglo-Chilean Nitrate Sales Corp v. Alabama - 288 U.S. 218 (1933)
- Nashville, C. & St. Louis Ry. Co. v. Wallace - 288 U.S. 249 (1933)
- New York v. Irving Trust Co. - 288 U.S. 329 (1933)
- Appalachian Coals, Inc. v. United States - 288 U.S. 344 (1933)
- Puerto Rico v. Russell & Co. - 288 U.S. 476 (1933)
- Louis K. Liggett Co. v. Lee - 288 U.S. 517 (1933)
- Hawks v. Hamill - 288 U.S. 52 (1933)

- Levering & Garrigues Co. v. Morrin - 289 U.S. 103 (1933)
- Reinecke v. Smith - 289 U.S. 172 (1933)
- Hurn v. Oursler - 289 U.S. 238 (1933)
- Young v. Masci - 289 U.S. 253 (1933)
- FRC v. Nelson Brothers Bond & Mortgage Co. - 289 U.S. 266 (1933)
- Los Angeles Gas & Elec. Corp. v. Railroad Comm'n - 289 U.S. 287 (1933)
- Williams v. Mayor & City Council of Baltimore - 289 U.S. 36 (1933)
- Washington v. Superior Court - 289 U.S. 361 (1933)
- George Moore Ice Cream Co., Inc. v. Collector - 289 U.S. 373 (1933)
- South Carolina v. Bailey - 289 U.S. 412 (1933)
- Ohio v. Chattanooga Boiler & Tank Co. - 289 U.S. 439 (1933)
- Quercia v. United States - 289 U.S. 466 (1933)
- Board of Trustees of University of Illinois v. United States - 289 U.S. 48 (1933)
- O'Donoghue v. United States - 289 U.S. 516 (1933)
- Williams v. United States - 289 U.S. 553 (1933)
- First National Bank v. Louisiana Tax Commission - 289 U.S. 60 (1933)
- Roberts v. Richland Irrigation District - 289 U.S. 71 (1933)
- Consolidated Textile Corp. v. Gregory - 289 U.S. 85 (1933)
- Bradley v. Public Utilities Commission of Ohio - 289 U.S. 92 (1933)
- Gant v. Oklahoma City - 289 U.S. 98 (1933)
- Minnesota v. Blasius - 290 U.S. 1 (1933)
- Jacobs v. United States - 290 U.S. 13 (1933)
- Johnson Oil Refining Co. v. Oklahoma ex Rel. Mitchell - 290 U.S. 158 (1933)
- Hicklin v. Coney - 290 U.S. 169 (1933)
- Glenn v. Field Packing Co. - 290 U.S. 177 (1933)
- Missouri v. Fiske - 290 U.S. 18 (1933)
- Southern Railway Co. v. Virginia - 290 U.S. 190 (1933)
- Yarborough v. Yarborough - 290 U.S. 202 (1933)
- Gibbes v. Zimmerman - 290 U.S. 326 (1933)
- United States v. Chavez - 290 U.S. 357 (1933)
- Funk v. United States - 290 U.S. 371 (1933)
- Nathanson v. United States - 290 U.S. 41 (1933)
- Home Building & Loan Assn. v. Blaisdell - 290 U.S. 398 (1934)
- Burroughs & Cannon v. United States - 290 U.S. 534 (1934)
- State Corporation Comm'n v. Wichita Gas Co. - 290 U.S. 561 (1934)
- P. F. Petersen Baking Co. v. Bryan - 290 U.S. 570 (1934)
- United States v. Chambers - 291 U.S. 217 (1934)

- City Bank Farmers Trust Co. v. Schnader - 291 U.S. 24 (1934)
- Standard Oil Co. of California v. California - 291 U.S. 242 (1934)
- Alabama v. Arizona - 291 U.S. 286 (1934)
- Local 167, Int'l Brotherhood of Teamsters v. United States - 291 U.S. 293 (1934)
- Murray v. Joe Gerrick & Co. - 291 U.S. 315 (1934)
- Booth v. United States - 291 U.S. 339 (1934)
- Hartford Accident & Indemnity Co. v. Nelson Co. - 291 U.S. 352 (1934)
- Trinityfarm Construction Co. v. Grosjean - 291 U.S. 466 (1934)
- Nebbia v. New York - 291 U.S. 502 (1934)
- Life & Casualty Insurance Co. v. McCray - 291 U.S. 566 (1934)
- Puget Sound Power & Light Co. v. Seattle - 291 U.S. 619 (1934)
- Morrison v. California - 291 U.S. 82 (1934)
- Snyder v. Massachusetts - 291 U.S. 97 (1934)
- Utley v. St. Petersburg - 292 U.S. 106 (1934)
- Clark v. Williard - 292 U.S. 112 (1934)
- Hartford Acc. & Indem. Co. v. Delta & Pine Land Co. - 292 U.S. 143 (1934)
- Sanders v. Armour Fertilizer Works - 292 U.S. 190 (1934)
- Loughran v. Loughran - 292 U.S. 216 (1934)
- McKnett v. St. Louis & San Francisco Ry. Co. - 292 U.S. 230 (1934)
- Principality of Monaco v. Mississippi - 292 U.S. 313 (1934)
- Arizona v. California - 292 U.S. 341 (1934)
- Ohio v. Helvering - 292 U.S. 360 (1934)
- Helvering v. Independent Life Insurance Co. - 292 U.S. 371 (1934)
- Nickey v. Mississippi - 292 U.S. 393 (1934)
- A. Magnano Co. v. Hamilton - 292 U.S. 40 (1934)
- Lee v. Bickell - 292 U.S. 415 (1934)
- W. B. Worthen Co. v. Thomas - 292 U.S. 426 (1934)
- Concordia Fire Insurance Co. v. Illinois - 292 U.S. 535 (1934)
- Lynch v. United States - 292 U.S. 571 (1934)
- City Bank Farmers Trust Co. v. Schnader - 293 U.S. 112 (1934)
- McNally v. Hill - 293 U.S. 131 (1934)
- Mattson v. Department of Labor & Industries - 293 U.S. 151 (1934)
- Detroit Trust Co. v. The Thomas Barlum - 293 U.S. 21 (1934)
- Helvering v. Powers - 293 U.S. 214 (1934)
- United States Mortgage Co. v. Matthews - 293 U.S. 232 (1934)
- Mitchell v. Maurer - 293 U.S. 237 (1934)
- Hamilton v. Regents of University of California - 293 U.S. 245 (1934)
- Mutual Life Insurance Co. v. Johnson - 293 U.S. 335 (1934)
- Schumacher v. Beeler - 293 U.S. 367 (1934)
- Lynch v. New York ex Rel. Pierson - 293 U.S. 52 (1934)
- Long v. Ansell - 293 U.S. 76 (1934)
- Enelow v. New York Life Ins. Co. - 293 U.S. 379 (1935)
- Panama Refining Co. v. Ryan - 293 U.S. 388 (1935)
- Dimick v. Schiedt - 293 U.S. 474 (1935)
- Mooney v. Holohan - 294 U.S. 103 (1935)
- Jurney v. MacCracken - 294 U.S. 125 (1935)
- Jennings v. United States Fidelity & Guaranty Co. - 294 U.S. 216 (1935)
- Old Company's Lehigh, Inc. v. Meeker - 294 U.S. 227 (1935)
- Norman v. Baltimore & Ohio Railroad Co. - 294 U.S. 240 (1935)
- Perry v. United States - 294 U.S. 330 (1935)
- Cooney v. Mountain States Tel. & Tel. Co. - 294 U.S. 384 (1935)
- Nashville, Chattanooga & St. Louis Railway v. Waters - 294 U.S. 405 (1935)
- Alaska Packers Assn. v. Industrial Accident Comm'n - 294 U.S. 532 (1935)
- Stewart Dry Goods Co. v. Lewis - 294 U.S. 550 (1935)
- Metropolitan Cas. Ins. Co. v. Brownell - 294 U.S. 580 (1935)
- Norris v. Alabama - 294 U.S. 587 (1935)
- Semler v. Oregon State Board of Dental Examiners - 294 U.S. 608 (1935)
- Panhandle Eastern Pipe Line Co. v. State Highway Comm'n - 294 U.S. 613 (1935)
- Henry L. Doherty & Co. v. Goodman - 294 U.S. 623 (1935)
- Broderick v. Rosner - 294 U.S. 629 (1935)
- Continental Illinois Nat. Bank v. Chicago, R.I. & P. Ry. Co. - 294 U.S. 648 (1935)
- Fox v. Standard Oil Co. of New Jersey - 294 U.S. 87 (1935)
- United States v. Oregon - 295 U.S. 1 (1935)
- Georgia Railway & Electric Co. v. Decatur - 295 U.S. 165 (1935)
- Federal Land Bank of St. Louis v. Priddy - 295 U.S. 229 (1935)
- Roberts v. New York City - 295 U.S. 264 (1935)
- Aero Mayflower Transit Co. v. Georgia Pub. Svc. Comm'n - 295 U.S. 285 (1935)
- Railroad Retirement Board v. Alton Railroad Co. - 295 U.S. 330 (1935)
- Hollins v. Oklahoma - 295 U.S. 394 (1935)
- Stewart v. Keyes - 295 U.S. 403 (1935)
- Senior v. Braden - 295 U.S. 422 (1935)
- Grovey v. Townsend - 295 U.S. 45 (1935)
- United States v. West Virginia - 295 U.S. 463 (1935)
- United States v. Mack - 295 U.S. 480 (1935)
- Escoe v. Zerbst - 295 U.S. 490 (1935)

- A. L. A. Schechter Poultry Corp. v. United States - 295 U.S. 495 (1935)
- Louisville Joint Stock Land Bank v. Radford - 295 U.S. 555 (1935)
- W. B. Worthen Co. v. Kavanaugh - 295 U.S. 56 (1935)
- Humphrey's Executor v. United States - 295 U.S. 602 (1935)
- Doty v. Love - 295 U.S. 64 (1935)
- Baltimore & Carolina Line, Inc. v. Redman - 295 U.S. 654 (1935)
- Stanley v. Public Utilities Comm'n - 295 U.S. 76 (1935)
- Spielman Motor Sales Co., Inc. v. Dodge - 295 U.S. 89 (1935)
- Schuylkill Trust Co. v. Pennsylvania - 296 U.S. 113 (1935)
- Pacific States Box & Basket Co. v. White - 296 U.S. 176 (1935)
- Fox Film Corp. v. Muller - 296 U.S. 207 (1935)
- Clyde Mallory Lines v. Alabama - 296 U.S. 261 (1935)
- Milwaukee County v. M. E. White Co. - 296 U.S. 268 (1935)
- United States v. Constantine - 296 U.S. 287 (1935)
- Hopkins Federal Savings & Loan Assn. v. Cleary - 296 U.S. 315 (1935)
- Helvering v. St. Louis Union Trust Co. - 296 U.S. 39 (1935)
- Hill v. Martin - 296 U.S. 393 (1935)
- Colgate v. Harvey - 296 U.S. 404 (1935)
- Becker v. St. Louis Union Trust Co. - 296 U.S. 48 (1935)
- Oklahoma v. Barnsdall Refineries, Inc. - 296 U.S. 521 (1936)
- United States v. Butler - 297 U.S. 1 (1936)
- Rickert Rice Mills, Inc. v. Fontenot - 297 U.S. 110 (1936)
- Van der Weyde v. Ocean Transport Co., Ltd. - 297 U.S. 114 (1936)
- Gooch v. United States - 297 U.S. 124 (1936)
- United States v. California - 297 U.S. 175 (1936)
- Treigle v. Acme Homestead Assn. - 297 U.S. 189 (1936)
- Baltimore National Bank v. State Tax Comm'n - 297 U.S. 209 (1936)
- Grosjean v. American Press Co., Inc. - 297 U.S. 233 (1936)
- Borden's Farm Products Co., Inc. v. Ten Eyck - 297 U.S. 251 (1936)
- Mayflower Farms, Inc. v. Ten Eyck - 297 U.S. 266 (1936)
- Brown v. Mississippi - 297 U.S. 278 (1936)
- Ashwander v. Tennessee Valley Auth. - 297 U.S. 288 (1936)
- Pacific Tel. & Tel. Co. v. Tax Commission - 297 U.S. 403 (1936)

- Bayside Fish Flour Co. v. Gentry - 297 U.S. 422 (1936)
- Whitfield v. Ohio - 297 U.S. 431 (1936)
- Matson Navigation Co. v. State Board of Equalization - 297 U.S. 441 (1936)
- Noble v. Oklahoma City - 297 U.S. 481 (1936)
- United States v. Rizzo - 297 U.S. 530 (1936)
- Georgia Railway & Electric Co. v. Decatur - 297 U.S. 620 (1936)
- Bingaman v. Golden Eagle Western Lines, Inc. - 297 U.S. 626 (1936)
- Phillips Petroleum Co. v. Jenkins - 297 U.S. 629 (1936)
- Triplett v. Lowell - 297 U.S. 638 (1936)
- Fisher's Blend Station, Inc. v. State Tax Comm'n - 297 U.S. 650 (1936)
- International Steel & Iron Co. v. National Surety Co. - 297 U.S. 657 (1936)
- Wheeling Steel Corp. v. Fox - 298 U.S. 193 (1936)
- Carter v. Carter Coal Co. - 298 U.S. 238 (1936)
- McCandless v. United States - 298 U.S. 342 (1936)
- St. Joseph Stock Yards Co. v. United States - 298 U.S. 38 (1936)
- Graves v. Texas Co. - 298 U.S. 393 (1936)
- Morf v. Bingaman - 298 U.S. 407 (1936)
- Koshland v. Helvering - 298 U.S. 441 (1936)
- Ashton v. Cameron County Water Imp. Dist. No. 1 - 298 U.S. 513 (1936)
- Morehead v. New York ex rel. Tipaldo - 298 U.S. 587 (1936)
- Gully v. First National Bank - 299 U.S. 109 (1936)
- United States v. Wood - 299 U.S. 123 (1936)
- John Hancock Mut. Life Ins. Co. v. Yates - 299 U.S. 178 (1936)
- Old Dearborn Co. v. Seagram-Distillers Corp. - 299 U.S. 183 (1936)
- Pep Boys v. Pyroil Sales Co., Inc. - 299 U.S. 198 (1936)
- American Tel. & Tel. Co. v. United States - 299 U.S. 232 (1936)
- Binney v. Long - 299 U.S. 280 (1936)
- United States v. Curtiss-Wright Export Corp. - 299 U.S. 304 (1936)
- Valentine v. Great Atlantic & Pacific Tea Co. - 299 U.S. 32 (1936)
- State Board of Equalization v. Young's Market Co. - 299 U.S. 59 (1936)
- Kentucky Whip & Collar Co. v. Illinois Central R. Co. - 299 U.S. 334 (1937)
- DeJonge v. Oregon - 299 U.S. 353 (1937)
- New York ex rel. Whitney v. Graves - 299 U.S. 366 (1937)
- Hauge v. City of Chicago - 299 U.S. 387 (1937)
- New York ex rel. Rogers v. Graves - 299 U.S. 401 (1937)

- Kuehner v. Irving Trust Co. - 299 U.S. 445 (1937)
- Hill v. United States ex rel. Weiner - 300 U.S. 105 (1937)
- Midland Realty Co. v. Kansas City Power & Light Co. - 300 U.S. 109 (1937)
- American Life Ins. Co. v. Stewart - 300 U.S. 203 (1937)
- Aetna Life Ins. Co. v. Haworth - 300 U.S. 227 (1937)
- Henderson Company v. Thompson - 300 U.S. 258 (1937)
- Ingels v. Morf - 300 U.S. 290 (1937)
- New York ex rel. Cohn v. Graves - 300 U.S. 308 (1937)
- Phelps v. Board of Education - 300 U.S. 319 (1937)
- Brush v. Commissioner - 300 U.S. 352 (1937)
- West Coast Hotel Co. v. Parrish - 300 U.S. 379 (1937)
- Wright v. Vinton Branch - 300 U.S. 440 (1937)
- Sonzinsky v. United States - 300 U.S. 506 (1937)
- Virginian Railway Co. v. Railway Employees - 300 U.S. 515 (1937)
- Thompson v. Consolidated Gas Utilities Corp. - 300 U.S. 55 (1937)
- Highland Farms Dairy, Inc. v. Agnew - 300 U.S. 608 (1937)
- District of Columbia v. Clawans - 300 U.S. 617 (1937)
- Ickes v. Fox - 300 U.S. 82 (1937)
- NLRB v. Jones & Laughlin Steel Corp. - 301 U.S. 1 (1937)
- Associated Press v. Labor Board - 301 U.S. 103 (1937)
- National Fertilizer Assn., Inc. v. Bradley - 301 U.S. 178 (1937)
- Bourjois, Inc. v. Chapman - 301 U.S. 183 (1937)
- First Bank Stock Corp. v. Minnesota - 301 U.S. 234 (1937)
- Herndon v. Lowry - 301 U.S. 242 (1937)
- Cincinnati Soap Co. v. United States - 301 U.S. 308 (1937)
- United States v. Belmont - 301 U.S. 324 (1937)
- Anniston Mfg. Co. v. Davis - 301 U.S. 337 (1937)
- Aetna Ins. Co. v. Kennedy to Use of Bogash - 301 U.S. 389 (1937)
- Lindsey v. Washington - 301 U.S. 397 (1937)
- Great Atlantic & Pacific Tea Co. v. Grosjean - 301 U.S. 412 (1937)
- Townsend v. Yeomans - 301 U.S. 441 (1937)
- Hartford Steam Boiler Inspection & Ins. Co. v. Harrison - 301 U.S. 459 (1937)
- Senn v. Tile Layers Protective Union - 301 U.S. 468 (1937)
- Labor Board v. Fruehauf Trailer Co. - 301 U.S. 49 (1937)
- Duke v. United States - 301 U.S. 492 (1937)
- Carmichael v. Southern Coal & Coke Co. - 301 U.S. 495 (1937)
- Mantle Lamp Co. v. Aluminum Products Co. - 301 U.S. 544 (1937)
- Steward Mach. Co. v. Collector - 301 U.S. 548 (1937)
- Labor Board v. Friedman-Harry Marks Clothing Co. - 301 U.S. 58 (1937)
- Helvering v. Davis - 301 U.S. 619 (1937)
- Kelly v. Washington - 302 U.S. 1 (1937)
- Chicago Title & Trust Co. v. Wilcox Bldg. Corp. - 302 U.S. 120 (1937)
- James v. Dravo Contracting Co. - 302 U.S. 134 (1937)
- Silas Mason Co. v. Tax Commission - 302 U.S. 186 (1937)
- Atlantic Refining Co. v. Virginia - 302 U.S. 22 (1937)
- Helvering v. Gowran - 302 U.S. 238 (1937)
- Breedlove v. Suttles - 302 U.S. 277 (1937)
- Worcester County Trust Co. v. Riley - 302 U.S. 292 (1937)
- Palko v. Connecticut - 302 U.S. 319 (1937)
- Honeyman v. Hanan - 302 U.S. 375 (1937)
- United States v. Williams - 302 U.S. 46 (1937)
- Pennsylvania ex rel. Sullivan v. Ashe - 302 U.S. 51 (1937)
- Dodge v. Board of Education of Chicago - 302 U.S. 74 (1937)
- Puget Sound Stevedoring Co. v. State Tax Comm'n - 302 U.S. 90 (1937)
- Hale v. State Board of Assessment & Review - 302 U.S. 95 (1937)
- Railroad Comm'n v. Pacific Gas & Electric Co. - 302 U.S. 388 (1938)
- Alabama Power Co. v. Ickes - 302 U.S. 464 (1938)
- Schuykill Trust Co. v. Pennsylvania - 302 U.S. 506 (1938)
- United States v. McGowan - 302 U.S. 535 (1938)
- Wright v. United States - 302 U.S. 583 (1938)
- S.C. State Highway Dept. v. Barnwell Bros., Inc. - 303 U.S. 177 (1938)
- Atkinson v. State Tax Commission - 303 U.S. 20 (1938)
- Southwestern Bell Tel. Co. v. Oklahoma - 303 U.S. 206 (1938)
- Western Live Stock v. Bureau of Revenue - 303 U.S. 250 (1938)
- Helvering v. Bullard - 303 U.S. 297 (1938)
- Lauf v. E. G. Shinner & Co. - 303 U.S. 323 (1938)
- Lonegran v. United States - 303 U.S. 33 (1938)
- Adair v. Bank of America Assn. - 303 U.S. 350 (1938)

- Helvering v. Mountain Producers Corp. - 303 U.S. 376 (1938)
- Helvering v. Mitchell - 303 U.S. 391 (1938)
- Electric Bond & Share Co. v. SEC - 303 U.S. 419 (1938)
- Lovell v. City of Griffin - 303 U.S. 444 (1938)
- New Negro Alliance v. Sanitary Grocery Co. - 303 U.S. 552 (1938)
- New York Rapid Transit Corp. v. New York - 303 U.S. 573 (1938)
- Adam v. Saenger - 303 U.S. 59 (1938)
- Hale v. Kentucky - 303 U.S. 613 (1938)
- Compania Espanola v. The Navemar - 303 U.S. 68 (1938)
- Connecticut Gen. Life Ins. Co. v. Johnson - 303 U.S. 77 (1938)
- Indiana ex rel. Anderson v. Brand - 303 U.S. 95 (1938)
- Morgan v. United States - 304 U.S. 1 (1938)
- United States v. Klamath & Moadoc Tribes of Indians - 304 U.S. 119 (1938)
- Guaranty Trust Co. v. United States - 304 U.S. 126 (1938)
- United States v. Carolene Products Co. - 304 U.S. 144 (1938)
- Ruhlin v. New York Life Ins. Co. - 304 U.S. 202 (1938)
- United States v. Bekins - 304 U.S. 27 (1938)
- Helvering v. National Grocery Co. - 304 U.S. 282 (1938)
- J. D. Adams Mfg. Co. v. Storen - 304 U.S. 307 (1938)
- Labor Board v. Mackay Radio & Telegraph Co. - 304 U.S. 333 (1938)
- Oklahoma ex rel. Johnson v. Cook - 304 U.S. 387 (1938)
- Mahoney v. Joseph Triner Corp. - 304 U.S. 401 (1938)
- Helvering v. Gerhardt - 304 U.S. 405 (1938)
- Allen v. Regents - 304 U.S. 439 (1938)
- Johnson v. Zerbst - 304 U.S. 458 (1938)
- Denver Union Stock Yard Co. v. United States - 304 U.S. 470 (1938)
- Wright v. Union Central Life Ins. Co. - 304 U.S. 502 (1938)
- Collins v. Yosemite Park & Curry Co. - 304 U.S. 518 (1938)
- Erie Railroad Co. v. Tompkins - 304 U.S. 64 (1938)
- Hinderlider v. La Plata Co. - 304 U.S. 92 (1938)
- Welch v. Henry - 305 U.S. 134 (1938)
- Guaranty Trust Co. v. Virginia - 305 U.S. 19 (1938)
- Consolidated Edison Co. v. Labor Board - 305 U.S. 197 (1938)
- Scher v. United States - 305 U.S. 251 (1938)
- Neblett v. Carpenter - 305 U.S. 297 (1938)
- Davis v. Davis - 305 U.S. 32 (1938)

- Missouri ex rel. Gaines v. Canada - 305 U.S. 337 (1938)
- Sovereign Camp of Woodmen of the World v. Bolin - 305 U.S. 66 (1938)
- Helvering v. Winmill - 305 U.S. 79 (1938)
- Minnesota v. United States - 305 U.S. 382 (1939)
- Indianapolis Brewing Co. v. Liquor Control Comm'n - 305 U.S. 391 (1939)
- Joseph S. Finch Co. v. McKittrich - 305 U.S. 395 (1939)
- Gwin, White & Prince, Inc. v. Henneford - 305 U.S. 434 (1939)
- Princess Lida v. Thompson - 305 U.S. 456 (1939)
- Lyon v. Mutual Benefit Health & Accident Assn. - 305 U.S. 484 (1939)
- Alton R. Co. v. Illinois Commerce Comm'n - 305 U.S. 548 (1939)
- Currin v. Wallace - 306 U.S. 1 (1939)
- Wichita Royalty Co. v. City Nat'l Bank - 306 U.S. 103 (1939)
- Tennessee Elec. Power Co. v. TVA - 306 U.S. 118 (1939)
- Bowen v. Johnston - 306 U.S. 19 (1939)
- Eichholz v. Public Service Comm'n of Missouri - 306 U.S. 268 (1939)
- Titus v. Wallick - 306 U.S. 282 (1939)
- Milk Control Board v. Eisenberg Farm Products - 306 U.S. 346 (1939)
- Pierre v. Louisiana - 306 U.S. 354 (1939)
- Hale v. Bimco Trading, Inc. - 306 U.S. 375 (1939)
- Keifer & Keifer v. RFC Corp. - 306 U.S. 381 (1939)
- Texas v. Florida - 306 U.S. 398 (1939)
- Lanzetta v. New Jersey - 306 U.S. 451 (1939)
- Graves v. New York ex rel. O'Keefe - 306 U.S. 466 (1939)
- Pacific Employers Ins. Co. v. Industrial Accident Comm'n - 306 U.S. 493 (1939)
- State Tax Comm'n v. Van Cott - 306 U.S. 511 (1939)
- Higginbotham v. Baton Rouge - 306 U.S. 535 (1939)
- Honeyman v. Jacobs - 306 U.S. 539 (1939)
- Clark v. Paul Gray, Inc. - 306 U.S. 583 (1939)
- Labor Board v. Fainblatt - 306 U.S. 601 (1939)
- Dixie Ohio Express Co. v. State Revenue Comm'n - 306 U.S. 72 (1939)
- H. P. Welch Co. v. New Hampshire - 306 U.S. 79 (1939)
- Driscoll v. Edison Light & Power Co. - 307 U.S. 104 (1939)
- Rochester Tel. Corp. v. United States - 307 U.S. 125 (1939)
- William Jameson & Co. v. Morgenthau - 307 U.S. 171 (1939)
- United States v. Miller - 307 U.S. 174 (1939)
- United States v. Powers - 307 U.S. 214 (1939)
- Lane v. Wilson - 307 U.S. 268 (1939)
- O'Malley v. Woodrough - 307 U.S. 277 (1939)

- Newark Fire Ins. Co. v. State Board of Tax Appeals - 307 U.S. 313 (1939)
- Perkins v. Elg - 307 U.S. 325 (1939)
- Curry v. McCanless - 307 U.S. 357 (1939)
- Mulford v. Smith - 307 U.S. 38 (1939)
- Graves v. Elliott - 307 U.S. 383 (1939)
- Coleman v. Miller - 307 U.S. 433 (1939)
- American Toll Bridge Co. v. Railroad Comm'n - 307 U.S. 486 (1939)
- Hague v. Committee for Industrial Organization - 307 U.S. 496 (1939)
- United States v. Rock Royal Cooperative, Inc. - 307 U.S. 533 (1939)
- McCrone v. United States - 307 U.S. 61 (1939)
- Massachusetts v. Missouri - 308 U.S. 1 (1939)
- Ziffrin, Inc. v. Reeves - 308 U.S. 132 (1939)
- Valvoline Oil Co. v. United States - 308 U.S. 141 (1939)
- Schneider v. State - 308 U.S. 147 (1939)
- John Hancock Mut. Life Ins. Co. v. Bartels - 308 U.S. 180 (1939)
- Pittman v. Home Owners' Loan Corp. - 308 U.S. 21 (1939)
- United States v. Lowden - 308 U.S. 225 (1939)
- Danforth v. United States - 308 U.S. 271 (1939)
- Bruno v. United States - 308 U.S. 287 (1939)
- Pearson v. McGraw - 308 U.S. 313 (1939)
- Weiss v. United States - 308 U.S. 321 (1939)
- Nardone v. United States - 308 U.S. 338 (1939)
- Treinies v. Sunshine Mining Co. - 308 U.S. 66 (1939)
- Oklahoma Packing Co. v. Oklahoma Gas & Elec. Co. - 309 U.S. 4 (1939)
- Kalb v. Feuerstein - 308 U.S. 433 (1940)
- Helvering v. Hallock - 309 U.S. 106 (1940)
- FCC v. Pottsville Broadcasting Co. - 309 U.S. 134 (1940)
- Illinois Central Ry. Co. v. Minnesota - 309 U.S. 157 (1940)
- McCarroll v. Dixie Greyhound Lines, Inc. - 309 U.S. 176 (1940)
- Chambers v. Florida - 309 U.S. 227 (1940)
- South Chicago Coal & Dock Co. v. Bassett - 309 U.S. 251 (1940)
- Minnesota ex Rel. Pearson v. Probate Court - 309 U.S. 270 (1940)
- McGoldrick v. Berwind-White Coal Mining Co. - 309 U.S. 33 (1940)
- Paramino Lumber Co. v. Marshall - 309 U.S. 370 (1940)
- McGoldrick v. Gulf Oil Corp. - 309 U.S. 414 (1940)
- Helvering v. Bruun - 309 U.S. 461 (1940)
- FCC v. Sanders Brothers Radio Station - 309 U.S. 470 (1940)
- Kersh Lake Drainage Dist. v. Johnson - 309 U.S. 485 (1940)
- United States v. United States Fidelity & Guaranty Co. - 309 U.S. 506 (1940)
- Minnesota v. National Tea Co. - 309 U.S. 551 (1940)
- Maurer v. Hamilton - 309 U.S. 598 (1940)
- Madden v. Commissioner - 309 U.S. 83 (1940)
- James Stewart & Co. v. Sadrakula - 309 U.S. 94 (1940)
- Carlson v. California - 310 U.S. 106 (1940)
- Perkins v. Lukens Steel Co. - 310 U.S. 113 (1940)
- Tigner v. Texas - 310 U.S. 141 (1940)
- United States v. San Francisco - 310 U.S. 16 (1940)
- Cantwell v. Connecticut - 310 U.S. 296 (1940)
- Veix v. Sixth Ward Building & Loan Assn. - 310 U.S. 32 (1940)
- Nashville, Chattanooga & St. Louis Ry. Co. v. Browning - 310 U.S. 362 (1940)
- Sunshine Anthracite Coal Co. v. Adkins - 310 U.S. 381 (1940)
- Colorado Nat'l Bank of Denver v. Bedford - 310 U.S. 41 (1940)
- Osborn v. Ozlin - 310 U.S. 53 (1940)
- White v. Texas - 310 U.S. 530 (1940)
- Railroad Comm'n of Texas v. Rowan & Nichols Oil Co. - 310 U.S. 573 (1940)
- Minersville Sch. Dist. v. Board of Educ. - 310 U.S. 586 (1940)
- Thornhill v. Alabama - 310 U.S. 88 (1940)
- Helvering v. Horst - 311 U.S. 112 (1940)
- Smith v. Texas - 311 U.S. 128 (1940)
- Fidelity Union Trust Co. v. Field - 311 U.S. 169 (1940)
- Six Companies of California v. Highway District - 311 U.S. 180 (1940)
- West v. American Tel. & Tel. Co. - 311 U.S. 223 (1940)
- Wright v. Union Central Life Ins. Co. - 311 U.S. 273 (1940)
- United States v. Appalachian Electric Power Co. - 311 U.S. 377 (1940)
- Wisconsin v. J. C. Penney Co. - 311 U.S. 435 (1940)
- Wisconsin v. Minnesota Mining & Mfg. Co. - 311 U.S. 452 (1940)
- Best & Company, Inc. v. Maxwell - 311 U.S. 454 (1940)
- Milliken v. Meyer - 311 U.S. 457 (1940)
- Helvering v. Northwest Steel Rolling Mills, Inc. - 311 U.S. 46 (1940)
- Stoner v. New York Life Ins. Co. - 311 U.S. 464 (1940)
- Continental Assurance Co. v. Tennessee - 311 U.S. 5 (1940)
- Milk Wagon Drivers' Union v. Lake Valley Co. - 311 U.S. 91 (1940)
- Crane-Johnson Co. v. Helvering - 311 U.S. 54 (1940)

- Southern Steamship Co. v. Labor Board - 316 U.S. 31 (1942)
- Sioux Tribe of Indians v. United States - 316 U.S. 317 (1942)
- Scripps-Howard Radio, Inc. v. FCC - 316 U.S. 4 (1942)
- Hill v. Texas - 316 U.S. 400 (1942)
- Betts v. Brady - 316 U.S. 455 (1942)
- Brillhart v. Excess Ins. Co. - 316 U.S. 491 (1942)
- Faitoute Iron & Steel Co. v. City of Asbury Park - 316 U.S. 502 (1942)
- Kirschbaum Co. v. Walling - 316 U.S. 517 (1942)
- Valentine v. Chrestensen - 316 U.S. 52 (1942)
- Skinner v. Oklahoma ex rel. Williamson - 316 U.S. 535 (1942)
- Ward v. Texas - 316 U.S. 547 (1942)
- Jones v. Opelika - 316 U.S. 584 (1942)
- Wickard v. Filburn - 317 U.S. 111 (1942)
- Ettelson v. Metropolitan Life Ins. Co. - 317 U.S. 188 (1942)
- Pyle v. Kansas - 317 U.S. 213 (1942)
- Garrett v. Moore-McCormack Co, Inc. - 317 U.S. 239 (1942)
- Davis v. Department of Labor and Industries - 317 U.S. 249 (1942)
- Williams v. North Carolina - 317 U.S. 287 (1942)
- Riggs v. Del Drago - 317 U.S. 95 (1942)
- Detroit Bank v. United States - 317 U.S. 329 (1943)
- Parker v. Brown - 317 U.S. 341 (1943)
- United States v. Miller - 317 U.S. 369 (1943)
- United States v. Monia - 317 U.S. 424 (1943)
- Endicott Johnson Corp. v. Perkins - 317 U.S. 501 (1943)
- American Medical Assn. v. United States - 317 U.S. 519 (1943)
- Brady v. Roosevelt Steamship Co. - 317 U.S. 575 (1943)
- Terminal R. Assn. of St. Louis v. Trainmen - 318 U.S. 1 (1943)
- Jerome v. United States - 318 U.S. 101 (1943)
- C. J. Hendry Co. v. Moore - 318 U.S. 133 (1943)
- Penn Dairies, Inc. v. Milk Control Comm'n - 318 U.S. 261 (1943)
- Pacific Coast Dairy, Inc. v. Department of Agriculture - 318 U.S. 285 (1943)
- Hoopeston Canning Co. v. Cullen - 318 U.S. 313 (1943)
- McNabb v. United States - 318 U.S. 332 (1943)
- Anderson v. United States - 318 U.S. 350 (1943)
- Maricopa County v. Valley Nat'l Bank - 318 U.S. 357 (1943)
- O'Donnell v. Great Lakes Dredge & Dock Co. - 318 U.S. 36 (1943)
- Clearfield Trust Co. v. United States - 318 U.S. 363 (1943)
- Helvering v. Griffiths - 318 U.S. 371 (1943)
- Jamison v. Texas - 318 U.S. 413 (1943)
- Largent v. Texas - 318 U.S. 418 (1943)
- Tileston v. Ullman - 318 U.S. 44 (1943)
- Tiller v. Atlantic Coast Line R. Co. - 318 U.S. 54 (1943)
- New York ex rel. Whitman v. Wilson - 318 U.S. 688 (1943)
- Board of County Comm'rs v. Seber - 318 U.S. 705 (1943)
- Jones v. Opelika - 319 U.S. 103 (1943)
- Murdock v. Pennsylvania - 319 U.S. 105 (1943)
- Martin v. City of Struthers - 319 U.S. 141 (1943)
- Douglas v. City of Jeannette - 319 U.S. 157 (1943)
- Lockerty v. Phillips - 319 U.S. 182 (1943)
- National Broadcasting Co., Inc. v. United States - 319 U.S. 190 (1943)
- Great Lakes Dredge & Dock Co. v. Huffman - 319 U.S. 293 (1943)
- Burford v. Sun Oil Co. - 319 U.S. 315 (1943)
- Bailey v. Central Vermont Ry., Inc. - 319 U.S. 350 (1943)
- Altvater v. Freeman - 319 U.S. 359 (1943)
- Galloway v. United States - 319 U.S. 372 (1943)
- St. Pierre v. United States - 319 U.S. 41 (1943)
- Buchalter v. New York - 319 U.S. 427 (1943)
- Mayo v. United States - 319 U.S. 441 (1943)
- Tot v. United States - 319 U.S. 463 (1943)
- Taylor v. Mississippi - 319 U.S. 583 (1943)
- Oklahoma Tax Comm'n v. United States - 319 U.S. 598 (1943)
- West Virginia State Bd. of Educ. v. Barnette - 319 U.S. 624 (1943)
- Central Hanover Bank & Trust Co. v. Kelly - 319 U.S. 94 (1943)
- Marconi Wireless Tel. Co. v. United States - 320 U.S. 1 (1943)
- Meredith v. Winter Haven - 320 U.S. 228 (1943)
- Cafeteria Employees Union v. Angelos - 320 U.S. 293 (1943)
- Magnolia Petroleum Co. v. Hunt - 320 U.S. 430 (1943)
- Hirabayashi v. United States - 320 U.S. 81 (1943)
- Walton v. Southern Package Corp. - 320 U.S. 540 (1944)
- California v. United States - 320 U.S. 577 (1944)
- FPC v. Hope Nat. Gas Co. - 320 U.S. 591 (1944)
- Mercoid Corp. v. Mid-Continent Investment Co. - 320 U.S. 661 (1944)
- City of Yonkers v. United States - 320 U.S. 685 (1944)

- Snowden v. Hughes - 321 U.S. 1 (1944)
- Northwestern Elec. Co. v. FPC - 321 U.S. 119 (1944)
- Carter v. Virginia - 321 U.S. 131 (1944)
- Prince v. Massachusetts - 321 U.S. 158 (1944)
- Anderson Nat'l Bank v. Luckett - 321 U.S. 233 (1944)
- Tennant v. Peoria & Pekin Union Ry. Co. - 321 U.S. 29 (1944)
- Demorest v. City Bank Farmers Trust Co. - 321 U.S. 36 (1944)
- Johnson v. Yellow Cab Transit Co. - 321 U.S. 383 (1944)
- Yakus v. United States - 321 U.S. 414 (1944)
- Bowles v. Willingham - 321 U.S. 503 (1944)
- Follett v. Town of McCormick - 321 U.S. 573 (1944)
- Cornell Steamboat Co. v. United States - 321 U.S. 634 (1944)
- Smith v. Allwright - 321 U.S. 649 (1944)
- McLean Trucking Co. v. United States - 321 U.S. 67 (1944)
- Mahnich v. Southern Steamship Co. - 321 U.S. 96 (1944)
- Ashcraft v. Tennessee - 322 U.S. 143 (1944)
- United States v. County of Allegheny - 322 U.S. 174 (1944)
- Union Brokerage Co. v. Jensen - 322 U.S. 202 (1944)
- Huddleston v. Dwyer - 322 U.S. 232 (1944)
- Northwest Airlines, Inc. v. Minnesota - 322 U.S. 292 (1944)
- McLeod v. J. E. Dilworth Co. - 322 U.S. 327 (1944)
- International Harvester v. Department of Treasury - 322 U.S. 340 (1944)
- Keefe v. Clark - 322 U.S. 393 (1944)
- L. P. Steuart & Bro., Inc. v. Bowles - 322 U.S. 398 (1944)
- Pollock v. Williams - 322 U.S. 4 (1944)
- International Harvester Co. v. Department of Taxation - 322 U.S. 435 (1944)
- Great Northern Life Ins. Co. v. Read - 322 U.S. 47 (1944)
- Feldman v. United States - 322 U.S. 487 (1944)
- Wisconsin Gas & Electric Co. v. United States - 322 U.S. 526 (1944)
- Lyons v. Oklahoma - 322 U.S. 596 (1944)
- United States v. Mitchell - 322 U.S. 65 (1944)
- United States v. White - 322 U.S. 694 (1944)
- United States v. Ballard - 322 U.S. 78 (1944)
- Pope v. United States - 323 U.S. 1 (1944)
- Spector Motor Co. v. McLaughlin - 323 U.S. 101 (1944)
- Smith v. Davis - 323 U.S. 111 (1944)
- Armour & Co. v. Wantock - 323 U.S. 126 (1944)

- Carolene Products Co. v. United States - 323 U.S. 18 (1944)
- Steele v. Louisville & N. R. Co. - 323 U.S. 192 (1944)
- Korematsu v. United States - 323 U.S. 214 (1944)
- Sage Stores Co. v. Kansas - 323 U.S. 32 (1944)
- Walling v. Helmerich & Payne, Inc. - 323 U.S. 37 (1944)
- Barber v. Barber - 323 U.S. 77 (1944)
- Coffman v. Breeze Corporations, Inc. - 323 U.S. 316 (1945)
- City of Cleveland v. United States - 323 U.S. 329 (1945)
- National Metropolitan Bank v. United States - 323 U.S. 454 (1945)
- Ford Motor Co. v. Department of Treasury - 323 U.S. 459 (1945)
- Williams v. Kaiser - 323 U.S. 471 (1945)
- Tomkins v. Missouri - 323 U.S. 485 (1945)
- Thomas v. Collins - 323 U.S. 516 (1945)
- United States v. Pennsylvania R. Co. - 323 U.S. 612 (1945)
- Herb v. Pitcairn - 324 U.S. 117 (1945)
- State Farm Mut. Automobile Ins. Co. v. Duel - 324 U.S. 154 (1945)
- Charleston Federal Savings & Loan Assn. v. Alderson - 324 U.S. 182 (1945)
- Dow Chemical Co. v. Halliburton Oil Well Cementing Co. - 324 U.S. 320 (1945)
- United States v. Commodore Park, Inc. - 324 U.S. 386 (1945)
- Malinski v. New York - 324 U.S. 401 (1945)
- House v. Mayo - 324 U.S. 42 (1945)
- Georgia v. Pennsylvania Railroad Co. - 324 U.S. 439 (1945)
- United States v. Willow River Power Co. - 324 U.S. 499 (1945)
- Market Street R. Co. v. Railroad Commission - 324 U.S. 548 (1945)
- Colorado-Wyoming Gas Co. v. FPC - 324 U.S. 626 (1945)
- Hooven & Allison Co. v. Evatt - 324 U.S. 652 (1945)
- White v. Ragen - 324 U.S. 760 (1945)
- Rice v. Olson - 324 U.S. 786 (1945)
- Cramer v. United States - 325 U.S. 1 (1945)
- Williams v. North Carolina - 325 U.S. 226 (1945)
- Esenwein v. Commonwealth - 325 U.S. 279 (1945)
- Chase Securities Corp. v. Donaldson - 325 U.S. 304 (1945)
- Sinclair & Carroll Co., Inc. v. Interchemical Corp. - 325 U.S. 327 (1945)
- Federation of Labor v. McAdory - 325 U.S. 450 (1945)
- North Carolina v. United States - 325 U.S. 507 (1945)
- Hill v. Florida - 325 U.S. 538 (1945)
- Nebraska v. Wyoming - 325 U.S. 589 (1945)

- Lincoln Nat'l Life Ins. Co. v. Read - 325 U.S. 673 (1945)
- Borden Co. v. Borella - 325 U.S. 679 (1945)
- Inland Empire Council v. Millis - 325 U.S. 697 (1945)
- Southern Pacific Co. v. Arizona - 325 U.S. 761 (1945)
- Allen Bradley Co. v. Electrical Workers - 325 U.S. 797 (1945)
- Screws v. United States - 325 U.S. 91 (1945)
- Associated Press v. United States - 326 U.S. 1 (1945)
- Radio Station WOW, Inc. v. Johnson - 326 U.S. 120 (1945)
- Bridges v. Wixon - 326 U.S. 135 (1945)
- East New York Savings Bank v. Hahn - 326 U.S. 230 (1945)
- Hawk v. Olson - 326 U.S. 271 (1945)
- Gange Lumber Co. v. Rowley - 326 U.S. 295 (1945)
- International Shoe v. State of Washington - 326 U.S. 310 (1945)
- Fernandez v. Wiener - 326 U.S. 340 (1945)
- Mine Safety Appliances Co. v. Forrestal - 326 U.S. 371 (1945)
- Railway Mail Assn. v. Corsi - 326 U.S. 88 (1945)
- Guaranty Trust Co. v. York - 326 U.S. 99 (1945)
- Mississippi Publishing Corp. v. Murphree - 326 U.S. 438 (1946)
- Railroad Retirement Bd. v. Duquesne Warehouse Co. - 326 U.S. 446 (1946)
- Marsh v. Alabama - 326 U.S. 501 (1946)
- Tucker v. Texas - 326 U.S. 517 (1946)
- New York v. United States - 326 U.S. 572 (1946)
- Township of Hillsborough v. Cromwell - 326 U.S. 620 (1946)
- United States v. New York Telephone Co. - 326 U.S. 638 (1946)
- Hulbert v. Twin Falls County - 327 U.S. 103 (1946)
- Estep v. United States - 327 U.S. 114 (1946)
- Hannegan v. Esquire, Inc. - 327 U.S. 146 (1946)
- Martino v. Michigan Window Cleaning Co. - 327 U.S. 173 (1946)
- Oklahoma Press Publishing Co. v. Walling - 327 U.S. 186 (1946)
- Griffin v. Griffin - 327 U.S. 220 (1946)
- Duncan v. Kahanamoku - 327 U.S. 304 (1946)
- United States v. Petty Motor Co. - 327 U.S. 372 (1946)
- Commissioner v. Wilcox - 327 U.S. 404 (1946)
- Nippert v. Richmond - 327 U.S. 416 (1946)
- Wilson v. Cook - 327 U.S. 474 (1946)

- S.R.A., Inc. v. Minnesota - 327 U.S. 558 (1946)
- Kennecott Copper Corp. v. State Tax Commission - 327 U.S. 573 (1946)
- M. Kraus & Bros., Inc. v. United States - 327 U.S. 614 (1946)
- Bell v. Hood - 327 U.S. 678 (1946)
- North American Co. v. SEC - 327 U.S. 686 (1946)
- Canizio v. New York - 327 U.S. 82 (1946)
- Case v. Bowles - 327 U.S. 92 (1946)
- Swanson v. Marra Brothers, Inc. - 328 U.S. 1 (1946)
- First Iowa Hydro-Electric Cooperative v. FPC - 328 U.S. 152 (1946)
- Thiel v. Southern Pacific Co. - 328 U.S. 217 (1946)
- Porter v. Lee - 328 U.S. 246 (1946)
- United States v. Causby - 328 U.S. 256 (1946)
- United States v. Lovett - 328 U.S. 303 (1946)
- Pennekamp v. Florida - 328 U.S. 331 (1946)
- Morgan v. Virginia - 328 U.S. 373 (1946)
- Prudential Ins. Co. v. Benjamin - 328 U.S. 408 (1946)
- Robertson v. California - 328 U.S. 440 (1946)
- Colegrove v. Green - 328 U.S. 549 (1946)
- Davis v. United States - 328 U.S. 582 (1946)
- Girouard v. United States - 328 U.S. 61 (1946)
- Zap v. United States - 328 U.S. 624 (1946)
- Pinkerton v. United States - 328 U.S. 640 (1946)
- Knauer v. United States - 328 U.S. 654 (1946)
- Hust v. Moore-McCormack Lines, Inc. - 328 U.S. 707 (1946)
- Kotteakos v. United States - 328 U.S. 750 (1946)
- American Tobacco Co. v. United States - 328 U.S. 781 (1946)
- Queenside Hills Realty Co., Inc. v. Saxl - 328 U.S. 80 (1946)
- Seas Shipping Co., Inc. v. Sieracki - 328 U.S. 85 (1946)
- Halliburton Oil Well Cementing Co. v. Walker - 329 U.S. 1 (1946)
- Alma Motor Co. v. Timken-Detroit Axle Co. - 329 U.S. 129 (1946)
- Cleveland v. United States - 329 U.S. 14 (1946)
- Carter v. Illinois - 329 U.S. 173 (1946)
- Ballard v. United States - 329 U.S. 187 (1946)
- Fiswick v. United States - 329 U.S. 211 (1946)
- United States v. Carmack - 329 U.S. 230 (1946)
- Freeman v. Hewitt - 329 U.S. 249 (1946)
- Champlin Refining Co. v. United States - 329 U.S. 29 (1946)
- Eagles v. Samuels - 329 U.S. 304 (1946)
- United States v. Alcea Band of Tillamooks - 329 U.S. 40 (1946)
- Cook v. Fortson - 329 U.S. 675 (1946)
- Richfield Oil Corp. v. State Bd. of Equalization - 329 U.S. 69 (1946)

- American Power & Light Co. v. SEC - 329 U.S. 90 (1946)
- MacGregor v. Westinghouse Elec. & Mfg. Co. - 329 U.S. 402 (1947)
- International Harvester Co. v. Evatt - 329 U.S. 416 (1947)
- Board of Governors v. Agnew - 329 U.S. 441 (1947)
- Louisiana ex rel. Francis v. Resweber - 329 U.S. 459 (1947)
- Morris v. Jones - 329 U.S. 545 (1947)
- Albrecht v. United States - 329 U.S. 599 (1947)
- United States v. N.Y. Rayon Importing Co., Inc. - 329 U.S. 654 (1947)
- DeMeerleer v. Michigan - 329 U.S. 663 (1947)
- Everson v. Board of Education - 330 U.S. 1 (1947)
- Oklahoma v. United States Civil Service Comm'n - 330 U.S. 127 (1947)
- Bozza v. United States - 330 U.S. 160 (1947)
- Angel v. Bullington - 330 U.S. 183 (1947)
- United States v. United Mine Workers - 330 U.S. 258 (1947)
- Testa v. Katt - 330 U.S. 386 (1947)
- Joseph v. Carter & Weeks Stevedoring Co. - 330 U.S. 422 (1947)
- Cardillo v. Liberty Mut. Ins. Co. - 330 U.S. 469 (1947)
- Kotch v. Board of River Port Pilot Comm'rs - 330 U.S. 552 (1947)
- Penfield Co. v. SEC - 330 U.S. 585 (1947)
- New York ex rel. Halvey v. Halvey - 330 U.S. 610 (1947)
- Industrial Comm'n of Wisconsin v. McCartin - 330 U.S. 622 (1947)
- Haupt v. United States - 330 U.S. 631 (1947)
- Land v. Dollar - 330 U.S. 731 (1947)
- United Public Workers v. Mitchell - 330 U.S. 75 (1947)
- Bethlehem Steel Co. v. State Labor Relations Board - 330 U.S. 767 (1947)
- Crane v. Commissioner - 331 U.S. 1 (1947)
- Fleming v. Rhodes - 331 U.S. 100 (1947)
- Fleming v. Mohawk Wrecking & Lumber Co. - 331 U.S. 111 (1947)
- Harris v. United States - 331 U.S. 145 (1947)
- Rice v. Santa Fe Elevator Corp. - 331 U.S. 218 (1947)
- Craig v. Harney - 331 U.S. 367 (1947)
- United States v. Walsh - 331 U.S. 432 (1947)
- Greenough v. Tax Assessors - 331 U.S. 486 (1947)
- Clark v. Allen - 331 U.S. 503 (1947)
- United States v. Bayer - 331 U.S. 532 (1947)
- Rescue Army v. Municipal Court of Los Angeles - 331 U.S. 549 (1947)
- Order of United Commercial Travelers of America v. Wolfe - 331 U.S. 586 (1947)
- Williams v. Austrian - 331 U.S. 642 (1947)
- Independent Warehouses, Inc. v. Scheele - 331 U.S. 70 (1947)
- United States v. Dickinson - 331 U.S. 745 (1947)
- United States v. Petrillo - 332 U.S. 1 (1947)
- Foster v. Illinois - 332 U.S. 134 (1947)
- Gayes v. New York - 332 U.S. 145 (1947)
- Atlantic Coast Line R. Co. v. Phillips - 332 U.S. 168 (1947)
- United States v. California - 332 U.S. 19 (1947)
- United States v. Yellow Cab Co. - 332 U.S. 218 (1947)
- Fahey v. Mallonee - 332 U.S. 245 (1947)
- Fay v. New York - 332 U.S. 261 (1947)
- Delgadillo v. Carmichael - 332 U.S. 388 (1947)
- Adamson v. California - 332 U.S. 46 (1947)
- Patton v. Mississippi - 332 U.S. 463 (1947)
- Silesian-American Corp v. Clark - 332 U.S. 469 (1947)
- Marino v. Ragen - 332 U.S. 561 (1947)
- Sealfon v. United States - 332 U.S. 575 (1948)
- United States v. Di Re - 332 U.S. 581 (1948)
- Haley v. Ohio - 332 U.S. 596 (1948)
- Sipuel v. Board of Regents - 332 U.S. 631 (1948)
- Oyama v. California - 332 U.S. 633 (1948)
- United States v. Sullivan - 332 U.S. 689 (1948)
- Von Moltke v. Gillies - 332 U.S. 708 (1948)
- Johnson v. United States - 333 U.S. 10 (1948)
- C. & S. Air Lines, Inc. v. Waterman S.S. Corp. - 333 U.S. 103 (1948)
- Seaboard Air Line R. Co. v. Daniel - 333 U.S. 118 (1948)
- Funk Brothers Seed Co. v. Kalo Inoculant Co. - 333 U.S. 127 (1948)
- Woods v. Cloyd W. Miller Co. - 333 U.S. 138 (1948)
- Fisher v. Hurst - 333 U.S. 147 (1948)
- King v. Order of United Commercial Travelers - 333 U.S. 153 (1948)
- Donaldson v. Read Magazine, Inc. - 333 U.S. 178 (1948)
- Cole v. Arkansas - 333 U.S. 196 (1948)
- McCollum v. Board of Education - 333 U.S. 203 (1948)
- Bob-Lo Excursion Co. v. Michigan - 333 U.S. 28 (1948)
- United States v. Line Material Co. - 333 U.S. 287 (1948)
- Eccles v. Peoples Bank - 333 U.S. 426 (1948)
- Woods v. Stone - 333 U.S. 472 (1948)
- Winters v. New York - 333 U.S. 507 (1948)
- Connecticut Mut. Life Ins. Co. v. Moore - 333 U.S. 541 (1948)
- Moore v. New York - 333 U.S. 565 (1948)
- Bute v. Illinois - 333 U.S. 640 (1948)
- Andres v. United States - 333 U.S. 740 (1948)
- Musser v. Utah - 333 U.S. 95 (1948)
- United States v. Paramount Pictures, Inc. - 334 U.S. 131 (1948)

- Mandeville Island Farms v. American Crystal Sugar - 334 U.S. 219 (1948)
- Hurd v. Hodge - 334 U.S. 24 (1948)
- Price v. Johnston - 334 U.S. 266 (1948)
- Sherrer v. Sherrer - 334 U.S. 343 (1948)
- Coe v. Coe - 334 U.S. 378 (1948)
- Toomer v. Witsell - 334 U.S. 385 (1948)
- Takahashi v. Fish & Game Comm'n - 334 U.S. 410 (1948)
- Estin v. Estin - 334 U.S. 541 (1948)
- Kreiger v. Kreiger - 334 U.S. 555 (1948)
- Saia v. New York - 334 U.S. 558 (1948)
- Republic Nat. Gas Co. v. Oklahoma - 334 U.S. 62 (1948)
- Central Greyhound Lines, Inc. v. Mealey - 334 U.S. 653 (1948)
- Wade v. Mayo - 334 U.S. 672 (1948)
- Trupiano v. United States - 334 U.S. 699 (1948)
- Gryger v. Burke - 334 U.S. 728 (1948)
- Townsend v. Burke - 334 U.S. 736 (1948)
- Lichter v. United States - 334 U.S. 742 (1948)
- Shapiro v. United States - 335 U.S. 1 (1948)
- United States v. CIO - 335 U.S. 106 (1948)
- Ludecke v. Watkins - 335 U.S. 160 (1948)
- Ahrens v. Clark - 335 U.S. 188 (1948)
- MacDougall v. Green - 335 U.S. 281 (1948)
- Upshaw v. United States - 335 U.S. 410 (1948)
- Uveges v. Pennsylvania - 335 U.S. 437 (1948)
- McDonald v. United States - 335 U.S. 451 (1948)
- Goesaert v. Cleary - 335 U.S. 464 (1948)
- Michelson v. United States - 335 U.S. 469 (1948)
- Frazier v. United States - 335 U.S. 497 (1948)
- Memphis Nat. Gas Co. v. Stone - 335 U.S. 80 (1948)
- Hirota v. MacArthur - 338 U.S. 197 (1948)
- Lincoln Union v. Northwestern Co. - 335 U.S. 525 (1949)
- AFL v. American Sash & Door Co. - 335 U.S. 538 (1949)
- Jungersen v. Ostby & Barton Co. - 335 U.S. 560 (1949)
- Commissioner v. Estate of Church - 335 U.S. 632 (1949)
- Railway Express Agency, Inc. v. New York - 336 U.S. 106 (1949)
- Ott v. Mississippi Valley Barge Line Co. - 336 U.S. 169 (1949)
- La Crosse Telephone Corp. v. Wisconsin Board - 336 U.S. 18 (1949)
- Daniel v. Family Security Life Ins. Co. - 336 U.S. 220 (1949)
- Labor Board v. Stowe Spinning Co. - 336 U.S. 226 (1949)
- Automobile Workers v. Wisconsin Board - 336 U.S. 245 (1949)
- Algoma Plywood v. Wisconsin Board - 336 U.S. 301 (1949)
- Oklahoma Tax Comm'n v. Texas Company - 336 U.S. 342 (1949)
- Krulewitch v. United States - 336 U.S. 440 (1949)
- Giboney v. Empire Storage & Ice Co. - 336 U.S. 490 (1949)
- H. P. Hood & Sons, Inc. v. Du Mond - 336 U.S. 525 (1949)
- Wilkerson v. McCarthy - 336 U.S. 53 (1949)
- Rice v. Rice - 336 U.S. 674 (1949)
- Wade v. Hunter - 336 U.S. 684 (1949)
- California v. Zook - 336 U.S. 725 (1949)
- Kovacs v. Cooper - 336 U.S. 77 (1949)
- Terminiello v. Chicago - 337 U.S. 1 (1949)
- Smith v. United States - 337 U.S. 137 (1949)
- Empresa Siderurgica, S.A. v. County of Merced - 337 U.S. 154 (1949)
- Young v. Ragen - 337 U.S. 235 (1949)
- Williams v. New York - 337 U.S. 241 (1949)
- FCC v. WJR, The Goodwill Station, Inc. - 337 U.S. 265 (1949)
- United States v. Cors - 337 U.S. 325 (1949)
- Union National Bank v. Lamb - 337 U.S. 38 (1949)
- Ragan v. Merchants Transfer & Warehouse Co. - 337 U.S. 530 (1949)
- Woods v. Interstate Realty Co. - 337 U.S. 535 (1949)
- Cohen v. Beneficial Indus. Loan Corp. - 337 U.S. 541 (1949)
- Wheeling Steel Corp. v. Glander - 337 U.S. 562 (1949)
- National Mut. Ins. Co. v. Tidewater Transfer Co., Inc. - 337 U.S. 582 (1949)
- Larson v. Domestic & Foreign Commerce Corp. - 337 U.S. 682 (1949)
- Cosmopolitan Shipping Co. v. McAllister - 337 U.S. 783 (1949)
- Kimball Laundry Co. v. United States - 338 U.S. 1 (1949)
- Brinegar v. United States - 338 U.S. 160 (1949)
- Wolf v. Colorado - 338 U.S. 25 (1949)
- Treichler v. Wisconsin - 338 U.S. 251 (1949)
- Brown v. Western Railway of Alabama - 338 U.S. 294 (1949)
- United States v. Toronto Nav. Co. - 338 U.S. 396 (1949)
- Wilmette Park Dist. v. Campbell - 338 U.S. 411 (1949)
- Watts v. Indiana - 338 U.S. 49 (1949)
- Turner v. Pennsylvania - 338 U.S. 62 (1949)
- Harris v. South Carolina - 338 U.S. 68 (1949)
- Lustig v. United States - 338 U.S. 74 (1949)
- Christoffel v. United States - 338 U.S. 84 (1949)
- FPC v. East Ohio Gas Co. - 338 U.S. 464 (1950)
- Savorgnan v. United States - 338 U.S. 491 (1950)

- Knauff v. Shaughnessy - 338 U.S. 537 (1950)
- Bryan v. United States - 338 U.S. 552 (1950)
- Wissner v. Wissner - 338 U.S. 655 (1950)
- New Jersey Ins. Co. v. Division of Tax Appeals - 338 U.S. 665 (1950)
- Hiatt v. Brown - 339 U.S. 103 (1950)
- United States v. Commodities Trading Corp. - 339 U.S. 121 (1950)
- Dennis v. United States - 339 U.S. 162 (1950)
- Darr v. Burford - 339 U.S. 200 (1950)
- South v. Peters - 339 U.S. 276 (1950)
- Cassell v. Texas - 339 U.S. 282 (1950)
- Mullane v. Central Hanover Bank & Trust Co. - 339 U.S. 306 (1950)
- United States v. Bryan - 339 U.S. 323 (1950)
- Wong Yang Sung v. McGrath - 339 U.S. 33 (1950)
- American Communications Assn. v. Douds - 339 U.S. 382 (1950)
- Automobile Workers v. O'Brien - 339 U.S. 454 (1950)
- Hughes v. Superior Court - 339 U.S. 460 (1950)
- Teamsters Union v. Hanke - 339 U.S. 470 (1950)
- Building Service Union v. Gazzam - 339 U.S. 532 (1950)
- United States v. Rabinowitz - 339 U.S. 56 (1950)
- Ewing v. Mytinger & Casselberry, Inc. - 339 U.S. 594 (1950)
- Sweatt v. Painter - 339 U.S. 629 (1950)
- McLaurin v. Oklahoma State Regents - 339 U.S. 637 (1950)
- Travelers Health Assn. v. Virginia - 339 U.S. 643 (1950)
- Quicksall v. Michigan - 339 U.S. 660 (1950)
- Skelly Oil Co. v. Phillips Petroleum Co. - 339 U.S. 667 (1950)
- Swift & Co. v. Compania Caribe - 339 U.S. 684 (1950)
- United States v. Louisiana - 339 U.S. 699 (1950)
- United States v. Texas - 339 U.S. 707 (1950)
- Johnson v. Eisentrager - 339 U.S. 763 (1950)
- United States v. Kansas City Life Ins. Co. - 339 U.S. 799 (1950)
- Henderson v. United States - 339 U.S. 816 (1950)
- Osman v. Douds - 339 U.S. 846 (1950)
- Solesbee v. Balcom - 339 U.S. 9 (1950)
- Southern Railway Co. v. Mayfield - 340 U.S. 1 (1950)
- Feres v. United States - 340 U.S. 135 (1950)
- A. & P. Tea Co. v. Supermarket Corp. - 340 U.S. 147 (1950)
- Blau v. United States - 340 U.S. 159 (1950)
- McGrath v. Kristensen - 340 U.S. 162 (1950)
- Cities Service Co. v. Peerless Co. - 340 U.S. 179 (1950)
- Phillips Petroleum Co. v. Oklahoma - 340 U.S. 190 (1950)
- United States v. Munsingwear, Inc. - 340 U.S. 36 (1950)
- Kiefer-Stewart Co. v. Seagram & Sons, Inc. - 340 U.S. 211 (1951)
- Niemotko v. Maryland - 340 U.S. 268 (1951)
- Kunz v. New York - 340 U.S. 290 (1951)
- Feiner v. New York - 340 U.S. 315 (1951)
- Blau v. United States - 340 U.S. 332 (1951)
- Dean Milk Co. v. City of Madison - 340 U.S. 349 (1951)
- Rogers v. United States - 340 U.S. 367 (1951)
- Bus Employees v. Wisconsin Board - 340 U.S. 383 (1951)
- Canton Railroad Co. v. Rogan - 340 U.S. 511 (1951)
- Norton Co. v. Department of Revenue - 340 U.S. 534 (1951)
- Johnson v. Muelberger - 340 U.S. 581 (1951)
- Spector Motor Service, Inc. v. O'Connor - 340 U.S. 602 (1951)
- California Auto. Assn. v. Maloney - 341 U.S. 105 (1951)
- United States v. Pewee Coal Co., Inc. - 341 U.S. 114 (1951)
- Joint Anti-Fascist Refugee Committee v. McGrath - 341 U.S. 123 (1951)
- West Virginia ex rel. Dyer v. Sims - 341 U.S. 22 (1951)
- Alabama Comm'n v. Southern R. Co. - 341 U.S. 341 (1951)
- Tenney v. Brandhove - 341 U.S. 367 (1951)
- Schwegmann Bros. v. Calvert Distillers Corp. - 341 U.S. 384 (1951)
- Standard Oil Co. v. New Jersey - 341 U.S. 428 (1951)
- Hoffman v. United States - 341 U.S. 479 (1951)
- Dennis v. United States - 341 U.S. 494 (1951)
- Gerende v. Election Board - 341 U.S. 56 (1951)
- Hughes v. Fetter - 341 U.S. 609 (1951)
- Breard v. Alexandria - 341 U.S. 622 (1951)
- Collins v. Hardyman - 341 U.S. 651 (1951)
- United States v. Williams - 341 U.S. 70 (1951)
- Garner v. Los Angeles Board - 341 U.S. 716 (1951)
- Williams v. United States - 341 U.S. 97 (1951)
- Stack v. Boyle - 342 U.S. 1 (1951)
- Stefanelli v. Minard - 342 U.S. 117 (1951)
- Cook v. Cook - 342 U.S. 126 (1951)
- Palmer v. Asche - 342 U.S. 134 (1951)
- Lorain Journal Co. v. United States - 342 U.S. 143 (1951)
- United States v. Carignan - 342 U.S. 36 (1951)
- Gallegos v. Nebraska - 342 U.S. 55 (1951)
- Rochin v. California - 342 U.S. 165 (1952)

- Carson v. Roane-Anderson Co. - 342 U.S. 232 (1952)
- Morissette v. United States - 342 U.S. 246 (1952)
- Halcyon Lines v. Haen Ship. & Refitting Corp. - 342 U.S. 282 (1952)
- Georgia R. & Banking Co. v. Redwine - 342 U.S. 299 (1952)
- Guessefeldt v. McGrath - 342 U.S. 308 (1952)
- Cities Service Co. v. McGrath - 342 U.S. 330 (1952)
- Boyce Motor Lines, Inc. v. United States - 342 U.S. 337 (1952)
- Dice v. Akron, Canton & Youngstown R. Co. - 342 U.S. 359 (1952)
- United States v. New Wrinkle, Inc. - 342 U.S. 371 (1952)
- Standard Oil Co. v. Peck - 342 U.S. 382 (1952)
- Memphis Steam Laundry Cleaner, Inc. v. Stone - 342 U.S. 389 (1952)
- First Nat'l Bank v. United Air Lines, Inc. - 342 U.S. 396 (1952)
- Sutton v. Leib - 342 U.S. 402 (1952)
- Mullaney v. Anderson - 342 U.S. 415 (1952)
- Day-Brite Lighting, Inc. v. Missouri - 342 U.S. 421 (1952)
- Doremus v. Board of Education - 342 U.S. 429 (1952)
- Perkins v. Benguet Consolidated Mining Co. - 342 U.S. 437 (1952)
- Adler v. Board of Educ. of City of New York - 342 U.S. 485 (1952)
- Frisbie v. Collins - 342 U.S. 519 (1952)
- Carlson v. Landon - 342 U.S. 524 (1952)
- Harisiades v. Shaughnessy - 342 U.S. 580 (1952)
- Sacher v. United States - 343 U.S. 1 (1952)
- Bruner v. United States - 343 U.S. 112 (1952)
- Rutkin v. United States - 343 U.S. 130 (1952)
- Ray v. Blair - 343 U.S. 154 (1952)
- Stroble v. California - 343 U.S. 181 (1952)
- Beauharnais v. Illinois - 343 U.S. 250 (1952)
- Zorach v. Clauson - 343 U.S. 306 (1952)
- United States v. Oregon State Med. Soc'y - 343 U.S. 326 (1952)
- Madsen v. Kinsella - 343 U.S. 341 (1952)
- Pennsylvania Power Co. v. FPC - 343 U.S. 414 (1952)
- Joseph Burstyn, Inc. v. Wilson - 343 U.S. 495 (1952)
- Youngstown Sheet & Tube Co. v. Sawyer - 343 U.S. 579 (1952)
- Kawakita v. United States - 343 U.S. 717 (1952)
- On Lee v. United States - 343 U.S. 747 (1952)
- Railroad Trainmen v. Howard - 343 U.S. 768 (1952)
- Leland v. Oregon - 343 U.S. 790 (1952)
- Casey v. United States - 343 U.S. 808 (1952)
- Gelling v. Texas - 343 U.S. 960 (1952)
- Brown v. Board of Education - 344 U.S. 1 (1952)
- Mandoli v. Acheson - 344 U.S. 133 (1952)
- Brown v. Board of Education - 344 U.S. 141 (1952)
- United States v. Caltex, Inc. - 344 U.S. 149 (1952)
- United States v. Cardiff - 344 U.S. 174 (1952)
- Building Union v. Ledbetter Erection Co., Inc. - 344 U.S. 178 (1952)
- Wieman v. Updegraff - 344 U.S. 183 (1952)
- Schwartz v. Texas - 344 U.S. 199 (1952)
- United States v. Universal C.I.T. Credit Corp. - 344 U.S. 218 (1952)
- Public Service Comm'n v. Wycoff Co., Inc. - 344 U.S. 237 (1952)
- Sweeney v. Woodall - 344 U.S. 86 (1952)
- Kedroff v. Saint Nicholas Cathedral - 344 U.S. 94 (1952)
- Edelman v. California - 344 U.S. 357 (1953)
- De La Rama Steamship Co., Inc. v. United States - 344 U.S. 386 (1953)
- Brown v. Allen - 344 U.S. 443 (1953)
- Kwong Hai Chew v. Colding - 344 U.S. 590 (1953)
- Lutwak v. United States - 344 U.S. 604 (1953)
- Howard v. Commissioners - 344 U.S. 624 (1953)
- United States v. Reynolds - 345 U.S. 1 (1953)
- Baltimore & Ohio R. Co. v. United States - 345 U.S. 146 (1953)
- Plumbers Union v. Graham - 345 U.S. 192 (1953)
- Shaughnessy v. Mezei - 345 U.S. 206 (1953)
- United States v. Kahriger - 345 U.S. 22 (1953)
- Heikkila v. Barber - 345 U.S. 229 (1953)
- Dameron v. Brodhead - 345 U.S. 322 (1953)
- Poulos v. New Hampshire - 345 U.S. 395 (1953)
- United States v. Rumely - 345 U.S. 41 (1953)
- Terry v. Adams - 345 U.S. 461 (1953)
- Wells v. Simonds Abrasive Co. - 345 U.S. 514 (1953)
- May v. Anderson - 345 U.S. 528 (1953)
- Avery v. Georgia - 345 U.S. 559 (1953)
- United States v. W. T. Grant Co. - 345 U.S. 629 (1953)
- Levinson v. Deupree - 345 U.S. 648 (1953)
- Fowler v. Rhode Island - 345 U.S. 67 (1953)
- Orloff v. Willoughby - 345 U.S. 83 (1953)
- United States v. Nugent - 346 U.S. 1 (1953)
- District of Columbia v. John R. Thompson Co., Inc. - 346 U.S. 100 (1953)
- New York, N.H. & H. R. Co. v. Nothnagle - 346 U.S. 128 (1953)
- Burns v. Wilson - 346 U.S. 137 (1953)
- Stein v. New York - 346 U.S. 156 (1953)
- Barrows v. Jackson - 346 U.S. 249 (1953)
- Olberding v. Illinois Central R. Co., Inc. - 346 U.S. 338 (1953)

- Atchison, T. & S.F. Ry. Co. v. Pub. Util. Comm'n - 346 U.S. 346 (1953)
- Toolson v. New York Yankees, Inc. - 346 U.S. 356 (1953)
- Arkansas v. Texas - 346 U.S. 368 (1953)
- Pope & Talbot, Inc. v. Hawn - 346 U.S. 406 (1953)
- Wilko v. Swan - 346 U.S. 427 (1953)
- Howell Chevrolet Co. v. Labor Board - 346 U.S. 482 (1953)
- Garner v. Teamsters Union - 346 U.S. 485 (1953)
- United States v. Morgan - 346 U.S. 502 (1954)
- Salsburg v. Maryland - 346 U.S. 545 (1954)
- Madruga v. Superior Court - 346 U.S. 556 (1954)
- Superior Films, Inc. v. Department of Education - 346 U.S. 587 (1954)
- Pereira v. United States - 347 U.S. 1 (1954)
- Kern Limerick, Inc. v. Scurlock - 347 U.S. 110 (1954)
- Irvine v. California - 347 U.S. 128 (1954)
- Michigan-Wisconsin Pipe Line Co. v. Calvert - 347 U.S. 157 (1954)
- Adams v. Maryland - 347 U.S. 179 (1954)
- United States v. Employing Plasterers Assn. - 347 U.S. 186 (1954)
- Longshoremen's Union v. Boyd - 347 U.S. 222 (1954)
- Remmer v. United States - 347 U.S. 227 (1954)
- Walters v. City of St. Louis - 347 U.S. 231 (1954)
- Accardi v. Shaughnessy - 347 U.S. 260 (1954)
- Alabama v. Texas - 347 U.S. 272 (1954)
- FCC v. American Broadcasting Co., Inc. - 347 U.S. 284 (1954)
- Miller Brothers Co. v. Maryland - 347 U.S. 340 (1954)
- Railway Express Agency, Inc. v. Virginia - 347 U.S. 359 (1954)
- Franklin Nat'l Bank v. New York - 347 U.S. 373 (1954)
- Alaska Steamship Co., Inc. v. Petterson - 347 U.S. 396 (1954)
- Brownell v. Singer - 347 U.S. 403 (1954)
- Maryland Casualty Co. v. Cushing - 347 U.S. 409 (1954)
- Barsky v. Board of Regents - 347 U.S. 442 (1954)
- Hernandez v. Texas - 347 U.S. 475 (1954)
- Brown v. Board of Education of Topeka - 347 U.S. 483 (1954)
- Bolling v. Sharpe - 347 U.S. 497 (1954)
- Capital Service, Inc. v. Labor Board - 347 U.S. 501 (1954)
- Galvan v. Press - 347 U.S. 522 (1954)
- Leyra v. Denno - 347 U.S. 556 (1954)
- Walder v. United States - 347 U.S. 62 (1954)
- United Workers v. Laburnum Corp. - 347 U.S. 656 (1954)
- Phillips Petroleum Co. v. Wisconsin - 347 U.S. 672 (1954)
- Massey v. Moore - 348 U.S. 105 (1954)
- Offutt v. United States - 348 U.S. 11 (1954)
- Berman v. Parker - 348 U.S. 26 (1954)
- Chandler v. Fretag - 348 U.S. 3 (1954)
- National Union v. Arnold - 348 U.S. 37 (1954)
- Castle v. Hayes Freight Lines, Inc. - 348 U.S. 61 (1954)
- Watson v. Employers Liab. Assur. Corp., Ltd. - 348 U.S. 66 (1954)
- United States v. Acri - 348 U.S. 211 (1955)
- Wilburn Boat Co. v. Fireman's Fund Ins. Co. - 348 U.S. 310 (1955)
- National City Bank of New York v. Republic of China - 348 U.S. 356 (1955)
- Sapir v. United States - 348 U.S. 373 (1955)
- Gonzales v. United States - 348 U.S. 407 (1955)
- Lewis v. United States - 348 U.S. 419 (1955)
- Commissioner v. Glenshaw Glass Co. - 348 U.S. 426 (1955)
- General American Investors Co., Inc. v. Commissioner - 348 U.S. 434 (1955)
- Employees v. Westinghouse Elec. Co. - 348 U.S. 437 (1955)
- Weber v. Anheuser-Busch, Inc. - 348 U.S. 468 (1955)
- Williamson v. Lee Optical, Inc. - 348 U.S. 483 (1955)
- United States v. Bramblett - 348 U.S. 503 (1955)
- Clothing Workers v. Richman Brothers Co. - 348 U.S. 511 (1955)
- Boston Metals Co. v. The Winding Gulf - 349 U.S. 122 (1955)
- United States v. Nielson - 349 U.S. 129 (1955)
- Society for Savings v. Bowers - 349 U.S. 143 (1955)
- Quinn v. United States - 349 U.S. 155 (1955)
- Emspak v. United States - 349 U.S. 190 (1955)
- Bart v. United States - 349 U.S. 219 (1955)
- Brown v. Board of Education of Topeka - 349 U.S. 294 (1955)
- Marcello v. INS - 349 U.S. 302 (1955)
- Peters v. Hobby - 349 U.S. 331 (1955)
- Williams v. Georgia - 349 U.S. 375 (1955)
- Carroll v. Lanza - 349 U.S. 408 (1955)
- Shaughnessy v. Pedreiro - 349 U.S. 48 (1955)
- Bell v. United States - 349 U.S. 81 (1955)
- Bisso v. Inland Waterways Corp. - 349 U.S. 85 (1955)
- United States ex rel. Toth v. Quarles - 350 U.S. 11 (1955)
- Indian Towing Co., Inc. v. United States - 350 U.S. 61 (1955)
- Reece v. Georgia - 350 U.S. 85 (1955)
- Pennsylvania ex Rel. Herman v. Claudy - 350 U.S. 116 (1956)

- Bernhardt v. Polygraphic Co. of America, Inc. - 350 U.S. 198 (1956)
- Rea v. United States - 350 U.S. 214 (1956)
- United States v. Twin City Power Co. - 350 U.S. 222 (1956)
- Costello v. United States - 350 U.S. 359 (1956)
- Remmer v. United States - 350 U.S. 377 (1956)
- Ullmann v. United States - 350 U.S. 422 (1956)
- Millinery Center Building Corp. v. Commissioner - 350 U.S. 456 (1956)
- Werner Machine Co., Inc. v. Director of Taxation - 350 U.S. 492 (1956)
- Pennsylvania v. Nelson - 350 U.S. 497 (1956)
- Schulz v. Pennsylvania R. Co. - 350 U.S. 523 (1956)
- Archawski v. Hanioti - 350 U.S. 532 (1956)
- International Harvester Credit Corp. v. Goodrich - 350 U.S. 537 (1956)
- Slochower v. Board of Education - 350 U.S. 551 (1956)
- Armstrong v. Armstrong - 350 U.S. 568 (1956)
- Griffin v. Illinois - 351 U.S. 12 (1956)
- Covey v. Town of Somers - 351 U.S. 141 (1956)
- Johnston v. United States - 351 U.S. 215 (1956)
- Railway Employees' Dept. v. Hanson - 351 U.S. 225 (1956)
- Offutt Housing Co. v. County of Sarpy - 351 U.S. 253 (1956)
- Durley v. Mayo - 351 U.S. 277 (1956)
- Black v. Cutter Laboratories - 351 U.S. 292 (1956)
- Jay v. Boyd - 351 U.S. 345 (1956)
- Kinsella v. Kreuger - 351 U.S. 470 (1956)
- Reid v. Covert - 351 U.S. 487 (1956)
- Cole v. Young - 351 U.S. 536 (1956)
- Mine Workers v. Arkansas Oak Floorings Co. - 351 U.S. 62 (1956)
- Nelson v. City of New York - 352 U.S. 103 (1956)
- Walker v. City of Hutchinson - 352 U.S. 112 (1956)
- Leslie Miller, Inc. v. Arkansas - 352 U.S. 187 (1956)
- Bank of America v. Parnell - 352 U.S. 29 (1956)
- Reid v. Covert - 354 U.S. 1 (1956)
- Fikes v. Alabama - 352 U.S. 191 (1957)
- Leiter Minerals, Inc. v. United States - 352 U.S. 220 (1957)
- Delli Paoli v. United States - 352 U.S. 232 (1957)
- Pollard v. United States - 352 U.S. 354 (1957)
- Senko v. LaCrosse Dredging Corp. - 352 U.S. 370 (1957)
- Butler v. Michigan - 352 U.S. 380 (1957)
- Breithaupt v. Abram - 352 U.S. 432 (1957)
- Radovich v. National Football League - 352 U.S. 445 (1957)
- Rogers v. Missouri Pac. R. Co. - 352 U.S. 500 (1957)
- Ferguson v. Moore-McCormack Lines, Inc. - 352 U.S. 521 (1957)
- United States v. Auto Workers - 352 U.S. 567 (1957)
- Guss v. Utah Labor Relations Bd. - 353 U.S. 1 (1957)
- Meat Cutters v. Fairlawn Meats, Inc. - 353 U.S. 20 (1957)
- Pennsylvania v. Board of Trusts - 353 U.S. 230 (1957)
- Schware v. Board of Bar Examiners - 353 U.S. 232 (1957)
- San Diego Building Trades Council v. Garmon - 353 U.S. 26 (1957)
- Trainmen v. Chicago R. & I. R. Co. - 353 U.S. 30 (1957)
- Kremen v. United States - 353 U.S. 346 (1957)
- Textile Workers v. Lincoln Mills - 353 U.S. 448 (1957)
- California v. Taylor - 353 U.S. 553 (1957)
- Fowler v. Wilkinson - 353 U.S. 583 (1957)
- Jencks v. United States - 353 U.S. 657 (1957)
- Lehmann v. Carson - 353 U.S. 685 (1957)
- Chessman v. Teets - 354 U.S. 156 (1957)
- Watkins v. United States - 354 U.S. 178 (1957)
- Sweezy v. New Hampshire - 354 U.S. 234 (1957)
- Theard v. United States - 354 U.S. 278 (1957)
- Teamsters Union v. Vogt, Inc. - 354 U.S. 284 (1957)
- Yates v. United States - 354 U.S. 298 (1957)
- Service v. Dulles - 354 U.S. 363 (1957)
- West Point Wholesale Grocery Co. v. Opelika - 354 U.S. 390 (1957)
- Vanderbilt v. Vanderbilt - 354 U.S. 416 (1957)
- Kingsley Books, Inc. v. Brown - 354 U.S. 436 (1957)
- Mallory v. United States - 354 U.S. 449 (1957)
- Morey v. Doud - 354 U.S. 457 (1957)
- Roth v. United States - 354 U.S. 476 (1957)
- Wilson v. Girard - 354 U.S. 524 (1957)
- Rathbun v. United States - 355 U.S. 107 (1957)
- Rowoldt v. Perfetto - 355 U.S. 115 (1957)
- Youngdahl v. Rainfair - 355 U.S. 131 (1957)
- Moore v. Michigan - 355 U.S. 155 (1957)
- Green v. United States - 355 U.S. 184 (1957)
- McGee v. International Life Ins. Co. - 355 U.S. 220 (1957)
- Lambert v. California - 355 U.S. 225 (1957)
- Alcorta v. Texas - 355 U.S. 28 (1957)
- Benanti v. United States - 355 U.S. 96 (1957)
- Ladner v. United States - 355 U.S. 282 (1958)
- Staub v. City of Baxley - 355 U.S. 313 (1958)
- Lawn v. United States - 355 U.S. 339 (1958)
- Gordon v. Texas - 355 U.S. 369 (1958)
- United States v. City of Detroit - 355 U.S. 466 (1958)

- Devries v. Baumgartner's Electric Construction Co. - 359 U.S. 498 (1959)
- Beacon Theatres, Inc. v. Westover - 359 U.S. 500 (1959)
- Bibb v. Navajo Freight Lines, Inc. - 359 U.S. 520 (1959)
- State Athletic Commission v. Dorsey - 359 U.S. 533 (1959)
- Vitarelli v. Seaton - 359 U.S. 535 (1959)
- Barenblatt v. United States - 360 U.S. 109 (1959)
- Harrison v. NAACP - 360 U.S. 167 (1959)
- County of Allegheny v. Frank Mashuda Co. - 360 U.S. 185 (1959)
- Martin v. Creasy - 360 U.S. 219 (1959)
- Mills v. Louisiana - 360 U.S. 230 (1959)
- NAACP v. Alabama - 360 U.S. 240 (1959)
- Louisiana Power & Light Co. v. Thibodaux - 360 U.S. 25 (1959)
- Burns v. Ohio - 360 U.S. 252 (1959)
- Napue v. Illinois - 360 U.S. 264 (1959)
- Anonymous Nos. 6 and 7 v. Baker - 360 U.S. 287 (1959)
- Marshall v. United States - 360 U.S. 310 (1959)
- Spano v. New York - 360 U.S. 315 (1959)
- Safeway Stores, Inc. v. Oklahoma Grocers - 360 U.S. 334 (1959)
- Palermo v. United States - 360 U.S. 343 (1959)
- Pittsburgh Plate Glass Co. v. United States - 360 U.S. 395 (1959)
- Southwestern Sugar Co. v. River Terminals - 360 U.S. 411 (1959)
- Raley v. Ohio - 360 U.S. 423 (1959)
- Lassiter v. Northampton County Bd. of Elections - 360 U.S. 45 (1959)
- Greene v. McElroy - 360 U.S. 474 (1959)
- Farmers Educ. & Co-op. Union v. WDAY, Inc. - 360 U.S. 525 (1959)
- Barr v. Matteo - 360 U.S. 564 (1959)
- Howard v. Lyons - 360 U.S. 593 (1959)
- Kingsley Int'l Pictures Corp. v. Regents - 360 U.S. 684 (1959)
- Uphaus v. Wyman - 360 U.S. 72 (1959)
- Smith v. California - 361 U.S. 147 (1959)
- Harris v. Pennsylvania R. Co. - 361 U.S. 15 (1959)
- Faubus, v. Aaron - 361 U.S. 197 (1959)
- Steelworkers v. United States - 361 U.S. 39 (1959)
- Henry v. United States - 361 U.S. 98 (1959)
- Blackburn v. Alabama - 361 U.S. 199 (1960)
- Stirone v. United States - 361 U.S. 212 (1960)
- Kinsella v. Singleton - 361 U.S. 234 (1960)
- Grisham v. Hagan - 361 U.S. 278 (1960)
- McElroy v. Guagliardo - 361 U.S. 281 (1960)
- Hess v. United States - 361 U.S. 314 (1960)
- Oil Workers Unions v. Missouri - 361 U.S. 363 (1960)

- Superior Court v. Yellow Cab - 361 U.S. 373 (1960)
- Phillips Chem. Co. v. Dumas ISD - 361 U.S. 376 (1960)
- Forman v. United States - 361 U.S. 416 (1960)
- Bates v. Little Rock - 361 U.S. 516 (1960)
- Petite v. United States - 361 U.S. 529 (1960)
- Nelson v. Los Angeles County - 362 U.S. 1 (1960)
- United States v. Raines - 362 U.S. 17 (1960)
- Thompson v. City of Louisville - 362 U.S. 199 (1960)
- Scripto, Inc. v. Carson - 362 U.S. 207 (1960)
- Abel v. United States - 362 U.S. 217 (1960)
- Jones v. United States - 362 U.S. 257 (1960)
- Mitchell v. H. B. Zachry Co. - 362 U.S. 310 (1960)
- Burlington-Chicago Cartage v. United States - 362 U.S. 401 (1960)
- Dusky v. United States - 362 U.S. 402 (1960)
- Huron Portland Cement Co. v. City of Detroit - 362 U.S. 440 (1960)
- United States v. Republic Steel Corp. - 362 U.S. 482 (1960)
- Mitchell v. Trawler Racer, Inc. - 362 U.S. 539 (1960)
- Parker v. Ellis - 362 U.S. 574 (1960)
- United States v. Thomas - 362 U.S. 58 (1960)
- Talley v. California - 362 U.S. 60 (1960)
- United States v. Alabama - 362 U.S. 602 (1960)
- Levine v. United States - 362 U.S. 610 (1960)
- Rohr Aircraft Corp. v. County of San Diego - 362 U.S. 628 (1960)
- DeVeau v. Braisted - 363 U.S. 144 (1960)
- Kreshik v. Saint Nicholas Cathedral - 363 U.S. 190 (1960)
- Douglas v. Green - 363 U.S. 192 (1960)
- United States v. Manufacturers Nat'l Bank - 363 U.S. 194 (1960)
- Clay v. Sun Ins. Office, Ltd. - 363 U.S. 207 (1960)
- Kimm v. Rosenberg - 363 U.S. 405 (1960)
- Hannah v. Larche - 363 U.S. 420 (1960)
- Metlakatla Indian Community v. Egan - 363 U.S. 555 (1960)
- Flemming v. Nestor - 363 U.S. 603 (1960)
- Miner v. Atlass - 363 U.S. 641 (1960)
- Hudson v. North Carolina - 363 U.S. 697 (1960)
- Commissioner v. Gillette Motor Transport, Inc. - 364 U.S. 130 (1960)
- Wolfe v. North Carolina - 364 U.S. 177 (1960)
- Elkins v. United States - 364 U.S. 206 (1960)
- Michalic v. Cleveland Tankers, Inc. - 364 U.S. 325 (1960)
- Gomillion v. Lightfoot - 364 U.S. 339 (1960)
- McPhaul v. United States - 364 U.S. 372 (1960)
- Armstrong v. United States - 364 U.S. 40 (1960)
- Polites v. United States - 364 U.S. 426 (1960)

- Boynton v. Virginia - 364 U.S. 454 (1960)
- Shelton v. Tucker - 364 U.S. 479 (1960)
- Bush v. Orleans Parish School Board - 364 U.S. 500 (1960)
- Reina v. United States - 364 U.S. 507 (1960)
- Gonzales v. United States - 364 U.S. 59 (1960)
- Callanan v. United States - 364 U.S. 587 (1961)
- Carbo v. United States - 364 U.S. 611 (1961)
- McNeal v. Culver - 365 U.S. 109 (1961)
- Eastern R. Conference v. Noerr Motors - 365 U.S. 127 (1961)
- Monroe v. Pape - 365 U.S. 167 (1961)
- Costello v. United States - 365 U.S. 265 (1961)
- Nolan v. Transocean Air Lines - 365 U.S. 293 (1961)
- Wilson v. Schnettler - 365 U.S. 381 (1961)
- Wilkinson v. United States - 365 U.S. 399 (1961)
- Times Film Corp. v. City of Chicago - 365 U.S. 43 (1961)
- Braden v. United States - 365 U.S. 431 (1961)
- Pugach v. Dollinger - 365 U.S. 458 (1961)
- Michigan Nat'l Bank v. Michigan - 365 U.S. 467 (1961)
- Silverman v. United States - 365 U.S. 505 (1961)
- Reynolds v. Cochran - 365 U.S. 525 (1961)
- Rogers v. Richmond - 365 U.S. 534 (1961)
- ORLEANS PARISH SCHOOL BOARD v. BUSH - 365 U.S. 569 (1961)
- Ferguson v. Georgia - 365 U.S. 570 (1961)
- Chapman v. United States - 365 U.S. 610 (1961)
- United States v. Virginia Elec. & Pwr. Co. - 365 U.S. 624 (1961)
- Smith v. Bennett - 365 U.S. 708 (1961)
- Burton v. Wilmington Parking Authority - 365 U.S. 715 (1961)
- Kossick v. United Fruit - 365 U.S. 731 (1961)
- Moses Lake Homes, Inc. v. Grant County - 365 U.S. 744 (1961)
- Cohen v. Hurley - 366 U.S. 117 (1961)
- Kolovrat v. Oregon - 366 U.S. 187 (1961)
- James v. United States - 366 U.S. 213 (1961)
- Eli Lilly & Co. v. Sav-on-Drugs, Inc. - 366 U.S. 276 (1961)
- Louisiana ex rel. Gremillion v. NCAAP - 366 U.S. 293 (1961)
- Montana v. Kennedy - 366 U.S. 308 (1961)
- Konigsberg v. State Bar of California - 366 U.S. 36 (1961)
- McGowan v. Maryland - 366 U.S. 420 (1961)
- Two Guys v. McGinley - 366 U.S. 582 (1961)
- Braunfeld v. Brown - 366 U.S. 599 (1961)
- Gallagher v. Crown Kosher Super Market - 366 U.S. 617 (1961)
- United States v. Oregon - 366 U.S. 643 (1961)
- Irvin v. Dowd - 366 U.S. 717 (1961)

- Communist Party v. SACB - 367 U.S. 1 (1961)
- Scales v. United States - 367 U.S. 203 (1961)
- Noto v. United States - 367 U.S. 290 (1961)
- Gori v. United States - 367 U.S. 364 (1961)
- Reck v. Pate - 367 U.S. 433 (1961)
- Deutch v. United States - 367 U.S. 456 (1961)
- Torcaso v. Watkins - 367 U.S. 488 (1961)
- Poe v. Ullman - 367 U.S. 497 (1961)
- Culombe v. Connecticut - 367 U.S. 568 (1961)
- Mapp v. Ohio - 367 U.S. 643 (1961)
- Marcus v. Search Warrant - 367 U.S. 717 (1961)
- Machinists v. Street - 367 U.S. 740 (1961)
- Cafeteria Workers v. McElroy - 367 U.S. 886 (1961)
- Federal Land Bank v. Kiowa County - 368 U.S. 146 (1961)
- Garner v. Louisiana - 368 U.S. 157 (1961)
- Martin v. Walton - 368 U.S. 25 (1961)
- Cramp v. Board of Public Instruction - 368 U.S. 278 (1961)
- United States v. Union Central Life Ins. Co. - 368 U.S. 291 (1961)
- Campbell v. Hussey - 368 U.S. 297 (1961)
- A. L. Mechling Barge Lines, Inc. v. United States - 368 U.S. 324 (1961)
- Hamilton v. Alabama - 368 U.S. 52 (1961)
- Hoyt v. Florida - 368 U.S. 57 (1961)
- McMahon v. Milam Manufacturing Co. - 368 U.S. 7 (1961)
- Western Union Telegraph Co. v. Pennsylvania - 368 U.S. 71 (1961)
- Chewning v. Cunningham - 368 U.S. 443 (1962)
- Oyler v. Boles - 368 U.S. 448 (1962)
- Charles Dowd Box Co., Inc. v. Courtney - 368 U.S. 502 (1962)
- St. Helena Parish School Board v. Hall - 368 U.S. 515 (1962)
- Public Affairs Associates, Inc. v. Rickover - 369 U.S. 111 (1962)
- Fong Foo v. United States - 369 U.S. 141 (1962)
- Kesler v. Department of Public Safety - 369 U.S. 153 (1962)
- Baker v. Carr - 369 U.S. 186 (1962)
- Bailey v. Patterson - 369 U.S. 31 (1962)
- Turner v. City of Memphis - 369 U.S. 350 (1962)
- A. & Gulf Stevedores v. Ellerman Lines, Ltd. - 369 U.S. 355 (1962)
- Metlakatla Indian Community v. Egan - 369 U.S. 45 (1962)
- Dairy Queen, Inc. v. Wood - 369 U.S. 469 (1962)
- Carnley v. Cochran - 369 U.S. 506 (1962)
- Beck v. Washington - 369 U.S. 541 (1962)
- Hutcheson v. United States - 369 U.S. 599 (1962)
- Organized Village of Kake v. Egan - 369 U.S. 60 (1962)
- Malone v. Bowdin - 369 U.S. 643 (1962)

- Free v. Bland - 369 U.S. 663 (1962)
- Lynch v. Overholser - 369 U.S. 705 (1962)
- Russell v. United States - 369 U.S. 749 (1962)
- Griggs v. Allegheny County - 369 U.S. 84 (1962)
- Teamsters v. Lucas Flour Co. - 369 U.S. 95 (1962)
- Calbeck v. Travelers Ins. Co. - 370 U.S. 114 (1962)
- Taylor v. Louisiana - 370 U.S. 154 (1962)
- Porter v. Aetna Cas. & Sur. Co. - 370 U.S. 159 (1962)
- Marine Engineers v. Interlake Co. - 370 U.S. 173 (1962)
- Sinclair Refining Co. v. Atkinson - 370 U.S. 195 (1962)
- Grumman v. United States - 370 U.S. 288 (1962)
- Wood v. Georgia - 370 U.S. 375 (1962)
- Beard v. Stahr - 370 U.S. 41 (1962)
- Engel v. Vitale - 370 U.S. 421 (1962)
- State Board of Ins. v. Todd Shipyards Corp. - 370 U.S. 451 (1962)
- Manual Enterprises, Inc. v. Day - 370 U.S. 478 (1962)
- Gallegos v. Colorado - 370 U.S. 49 (1962)
- Glidden Co. v. Zdanok - 370 U.S. 530 (1962)
- Central R. Co. v. Pennsylvania - 370 U.S. 607 (1962)
- Link v. Wabash R. Co. - 370 U.S. 626 (1962)
- United States v. Davis - 370 U.S. 65 (1962)
- Robinson v. California - 370 U.S. 660 (1962)
- Silber v. United States - 370 U.S. 717 (1962)
- Lassiter v. United States - 371 U.S. 10 (1962)
- Ford v. Ford - 371 U.S. 187 (1962)
- Smith v. Evening News Association - 371 U.S. 195 (1962)
- Schroeder v. City of New York - 371 U.S. 208 (1962)
- Alabama v. United States - 371 U.S. 37 (1962)
- Cannata v. City of New York - 371 U.S. 4 (1962)
- Labor Board v. Reliance Fuel Oil Corp. - 371 U.S. 224 (1963)
- United States v. Buffalo Savings Bank - 371 U.S. 228 (1963)
- Jones v. Cunningham - 371 U.S. 236 (1963)
- Paul v. United States - 371 U.S. 245 (1963)
- Cleary v. Bolger - 371 U.S. 392 (1963)
- NAACP v. Button - 371 U.S. 415 (1963)
- Wong Sun v. United States - 371 U.S. 471 (1963)
- Williams v. Zuckert - 371 U.S. 531 (1963)
- Construction Laborers v. Curry - 371 U.S. 542 (1963)
- Mercantile Nat'l Bank v. Langdeau - 371 U.S. 555 (1963)
- Kennedy v. Mendoza-Martinez - 372 U.S. 144 (1963)
- Edwards v. South Carolina - 372 U.S. 229 (1963)
- Harrison v. Missouri Pacific R. Co. - 372 U.S. 248 (1963)
- United States v. National Dairy Products Corp. - 372 U.S. 29 (1963)
- Townsend v. Sain - 372 U.S. 293 (1963)
- Gideon v. Wainwright - 372 U.S. 335 (1963)
- Douglas v. California - 372 U.S. 353 (1963)
- Gray v. Sanders - 372 U.S. 368 (1963)
- Fay v. Noia - 372 U.S. 391 (1963)
- Lane v. Brown - 372 U.S. 477 (1963)
- Draper v. Washington - 372 U.S. 487 (1963)
- Lynumn v. Illinois - 372 U.S. 528 (1963)
- Gibson v. Florida Legislative Investigation Comm. - 372 U.S. 539 (1963)
- Bantam Books, Inc. v. Sullivan - 372 U.S. 58 (1963)
- Michigan Nat'l Bank v. Robertson - 372 U.S. 591 (1963)
- Dugan v. Rank - 372 U.S. 609 (1963)
- Dixilyn Drilling Corp. v. Crescent Co. - 372 U.S. 697 (1963)
- Basham v. Pennsylvania R. Co. - 372 U.S. 699 (1963)
- Ferguson v. Skrupa - 372 U.S. 726 (1963)
- Downum v. United States - 372 U.S. 734 (1963)
- Sanders v. United States - 373 U.S. 1 (1963)
- Florida Avocado Growers v. Paul - 373 U.S. 132 (1963)
- Gutierrez v. Waterman Steamship Corp. - 373 U.S. 206 (1963)
- Peterson v. City of Greenville - 373 U.S. 244 (1963)
- Lombard v. Louisiana - 373 U.S. 267 (1963)
- Wright v. Georgia - 373 U.S. 284 (1963)
- Wisconsin v. FPC - 373 U.S. 294 (1963)
- Gober v. City of Birmingham - 373 U.S. 374 (1963)
- Sperry v. Florida - 373 U.S. 379 (1963)
- Lopez v. United States - 373 U.S. 427 (1963)
- Haynes v. Washington - 373 U.S. 503 (1963)
- Watson v. City of Memphis - 373 U.S. 526 (1963)
- Cepero v. United States Congress - 373 U.S. 545 (1963)
- Arizona v. California - 373 U.S. 546 (1963)
- Hawaii v. Gordon - 373 U.S. 57 (1963)
- White v. Maryland - 373 U.S. 59 (1963)
- Johnson v. Virginia - 373 U.S. 61 (1963)
- Halliburton Oil Well Cementing Co. v. Reilly - 373 U.S. 64 (1963)
- Wheeldin v. Wheeler - 373 U.S. 647 (1963)
- McNeese v. Board of Educ. - 373 U.S. 668 (1963)
- Goss v. Board of Education - 373 U.S. 683 (1963)
- Plumbers' Union v. Borden - 373 U.S. 690 (1963)

- Iron Workers v. Perko - 373 U.S. 701 (1963)
- Rideau v. Louisiana - 373 U.S. 723 (1963)
- Brady v. Maryland - 373 U.S. 83 (1963)
- Willner v. Committee on Character - 373 U.S. 96 (1963)
- Yellin v. United States - 374 U.S. 109 (1963)
- Fitzgerald v. United States Lines Co. - 374 U.S. 16 (1963)
- School Dist. of Abington Tp. v. Schempp - 374 U.S. 203 (1963)
- Ker v. California - 374 U.S. 23 (1963)
- Sherbert v. Verner - 374 U.S. 398 (1963)
- Rosenberg v. Fleuti - 374 U.S. 449 (1963)
- Gastelum-Quinones v. Kennedy - 374 U.S. 469 (1963)
- Bus Employees v. Missouri - 374 U.S. 74 (1963)
- United States v. Pioneer American Ins. Co. - 374 U.S. 84 (1963)
- Durfee v. Duke - 375 U.S. 106 (1963)
- Pickelsimer v. Wainwright - 375 U.S. 2 (1963)
- Retail Clerks v. Schermerhorn - 375 U.S. 96 (1963)
- Cade v. Louisiana - 375 U.S. 44 (1963)
- Fahy v. Connecticut - 375 U.S. 85 (1963)
- Liner v. Jafco, Inc. - 375 U.S. 301 (1964)
- Humphrey v. Moore - 375 U.S. 335 (1964)
- Polar Ice Cream Co. v. Andrews - 375 U.S. 361 (1964)
- Schiro, Mayor of New Orleans v. Bynum - 375 U.S. 395 (1964)
- Anderson v. Martin - 375 U.S. 399 (1964)
- England v. Medical Examiners - 375 U.S. 411 (1964)
- Wesberry v. Sanders - 376 U.S. 1 (1964)
- City of New Orleans v. Barthe - 376 U.S. 189 (1964)
- Neill v. Cook - 376 U.S. 202 (1964)
- Honeywood v. Rockefeller - 376 U.S. 222 (1964)
- Sears, Roebuck & Co. v. Stiffel Co. - 376 U.S. 225 (1964)
- Compco Corp. v. Day-Brite Lighting, Inc. - 376 U.S. 234 (1964)
- Yiatchos v. Yiatchos - 376 U.S. 306 (1964)
- Preston v. United States - 376 U.S. 364 (1964)
- Banco Nacional de Cuba v. Sabbatino - 376 U.S. 398 (1964)
- Wright v. Rockefeller - 376 U.S. 52 (1964)
- Ungar v. Sarafite - 376 U.S. 575 (1964)
- Hamilton v. Alabama - 376 U.S. 650 (1964)
- United States v. Barnett - 376 U.S. 681 (1964)
- Arnold v. North Carolina - 376 U.S. 773 (1964)
- Henry v. City of Rock Hill - 376 U.S. 776 (1964)
- Railroad Trainmen v. Virginia Bar - 377 U.S. 1 (1964)

- Hattiesburg Unions v. Broome Co. - 377 U.S. 126 (1964)
- Coleman v. Alabama - 377 U.S. 129 (1964)
- Simpson v. Union Oil Co. of California - 377 U.S. 13 (1964)
- Clinton v. Virginia - 377 U.S. 158 (1964)
- Schneider v. Rusk - 377 U.S. 163 (1964)
- Clay v. Sun Ins. Office, Ltd. - 377 U.S. 179 (1964)
- Parden v. Terminal R. Co. - 377 U.S. 184 (1964)
- Massiah v. United States - 377 U.S. 201 (1964)
- Griffin v. School Board - 377 U.S. 218 (1964)
- Calhoun v. Latimer - 377 U.S. 263 (1964)
- NAACP v. Alabama ex rel. Flowers - 377 U.S. 288 (1964)
- Hostetter v. Idlewild Bon Voyage Liquor Corp. - 377 U.S. 324 (1964)
- Department of Revenue v. James B. Beam Co. - 377 U.S. 341 (1964)
- Baggett v. Bullitt - 377 U.S. 360 (1964)
- Chamberlin v. Dade County Board - 377 U.S. 402 (1964)
- Donovan v. City of Dallas - 377 U.S. 408 (1964)
- J. I Case Co. v. Borak - 377 U.S. 426 (1964)
- General Motors Corp. v. Washington - 377 U.S. 436 (1964)
- United States v. Tateo - 377 U.S. 463 (1964)
- Reynolds v. Sims - 377 U.S. 533 (1964)
- Labor Board v. Fruit Packers - 377 U.S. 58 (1964)
- WMCA, Inc. v. Lomenzo - 377 U.S. 633 (1964)
- Maryland Committee v. Tawes - 377 U.S. 656 (1964)
- Davis v. Mann - 377 U.S. 678 (1964)
- Roman v. Sincock - 377 U.S. 695 (1964)
- Lucas v. Forty-Fourth Gen. Assembly of Colorado - 377 U.S. 713 (1964)
- Malloy v. Hogan - 378 U.S. 1 (1964)
- Aguilar v. Texas - 378 U.S. 108 (1964)
- Department of Alcoholic Beverage Control v. Ammex Ware. - 378 U.S. 124 (1964)
- Griffin v. Maryland - 378 U.S. 130 (1964)
- Barr v. City of Columbia - 378 U.S. 146 (1964)
- Robinson v. Florida - 378 U.S. 153 (1964)
- Jacobellis v. Ohio - 378 U.S. 184 (1964)
- Quantity of Books v. Kansas - 378 U.S. 205 (1964)
- Bell v. Maryland - 378 U.S. 226 (1964)
- Bouie v. City of Columbia - 378 U.S. 347 (1964)
- Jackson v. Denno - 378 U.S. 368 (1964)
- United States v. Boyd - 378 U.S. 39 (1964)
- Escobedo v. Illinois - 378 U.S. 478 (1964)
- Aptheker v. Secretary of State - 378 U.S. 500 (1964)
- Murphy v. Waterfront Comm'n - 378 U.S. 52 (1964)
- Cooper v. Pate - 378 U.S. 546 (1964)
- Meyers v. Thigpen - 378 U.S. 554 (1964)

- Glass v. Hancock County Election Commission - 378 U.S. 558 (1964)
- Pinney v. Butterworth - 378 U.S. 564 (1964)
- Hill v. Davis - 378 U.S. 565 (1964)
- Grove Press v. Gerstein - 378 U.S. 577 (1964)
- Schlagenhauf v. Holder - 379 U.S. 104 (1964)
- Gillespie v. United States Steel Corp. - 379 U.S. 148 (1964)
- McLaughlin v. Florida - 379 U.S. 184 (1964)
- Tancil v. Woolls - 379 U.S. 19 (1964)
- Heart of Atlanta Motel, Inc. v. United States - 379 U.S. 241 (1964)
- Katzenbach v. McClung - 379 U.S. 294 (1964)
- Hamm v. City of Rock Hill - 379 U.S. 306 (1964)
- Scranton v. Drew - 379 U.S. 40 (1964)
- Garrison v. Louisiana - 379 U.S. 64 (1964)
- California v. Lo-Vaca Gathering Co. - 379 U.S. 366 (1965)
- Fortson v. Dorsey - 379 U.S. 433 (1965)
- Henry v. Mississippi - 379 U.S. 443 (1965)
- Turner v. Louisiana - 379 U.S. 466 (1965)
- Stanford v. Texas - 379 U.S. 476 (1965)
- City of El Paso v. Simmons - 379 U.S. 497 (1965)
- Cox v. Louisiana - 379 U.S. 536 (1965)
- Cox v. Louisiana - 379 U.S. 559 (1965)
- Texas v. New Jersey - 379 U.S. 674 (1965)
- United States v. Ventresca - 380 U.S. 102 (1965)
- United States v. Mississippi - 380 U.S. 128 (1965)
- Louisiana v. United States - 380 U.S. 145 (1965)
- Department of Mental Hygiene v. Kirchner - 380 U.S. 194 (1965)
- Swain v. Alabama - 380 U.S. 202 (1965)
- Singer v. United States - 380 U.S. 24 (1965)
- Radio Union v. Broadcast Svc. of Mobile, Inc. - 380 U.S. 255 (1965)
- Reserve Life Insurance Co. v. Bowers - 380 U.S. 258 (1965)
- Henry v. Collins - 380 U.S. 356 (1965)
- Crider v. Zurich Ins. Co. - 380 U.S. 39 (1965)
- Pointer v. Texas - 380 U.S. 400 (1965)
- Douglas v. Alabama - 380 U.S. 415 (1965)
- American Oil Co. v. Neill - 380 U.S. 451 (1965)
- Hanna v. Plumer - 380 U.S. 460 (1965)
- Dombrowski v. Pfister - 380 U.S. 479 (1965)
- Freedman v. Maryland - 380 U.S. 51 (1965)
- Corpora v. New York - 380 U.S. 520 (1965)
- Harman v. Forssenius - 380 U.S. 528 (1965)
- Armstrong v. Manzo - 380 U.S. 545 (1965)
- Griffin v. California - 380 U.S. 609 (1965)
- Carrington v. Rash - 380 U.S. 89 (1965)
- Zemel v. Rusk - 381 U.S. 1 (1965)
- Corbett v. Stergios - 381 U.S. 124 (1965)
- Holt v. Virginia - 381 U.S. 131 (1965)

- Lamont v. Postmaster General - 381 U.S. 301 (1965)
- Case v. Nebraska - 381 U.S. 336 (1965)
- McLeod v. Ohio - 381 U.S. 356 (1965)
- Scott v. Germano - 381 U.S. 407 (1965)
- Maryland v. United States - 381 U.S. 41 (1965)
- Jordan v. Silver - 381 U.S. 415 (1965)
- United States v. Brown - 381 U.S. 437 (1965)
- Griswold v. Connecticut - 381 U.S. 479 (1965)
- Estes v. Texas - 381 U.S. 532 (1965)
- Linkletter v. Walker - 381 U.S. 618 (1965)
- United Mine Workers v. Pennington - 381 U.S. 657 (1965)
- Cameron v. Johnson - 381 U.S. 741 (1965)
- Simons v. Miami Beach First Nat'l Bank - 381 U.S. 81 (1965)
- Bradley v. School Board of City of Richmond - 382 U.S. 103 (1965)
- Swift & Co. v. Wickham - 382 U.S. 111 (1965)
- United States v. Romano - 382 U.S. 136 (1965)
- Steelworkers v. R. H. Bouligny, Inc. - 382 U.S. 145 (1965)
- Harris v. United States - 382 U.S. 162 (1965)
- Walker Process Eqpt., Inc. v. Food Machinery Corp. - 382 U.S. 172 (1965)
- United States v. Huck Manufacturing Co. - 382 U.S. 197 (1965)
- Albertson v. SACB - 382 U.S. 70 (1965)
- Shuttlesworth v. City of Birmingham - 382 U.S. 87 (1965)
- Evans v. Newton - 382 U.S. 296 (1966)
- Katchen v. Landy - 382 U.S. 323 (1966)
- United States v. Yazell - 382 U.S. 341 (1966)
- California v. Buzard - 382 U.S. 386 (1966)
- Giaccio v. Pennsylvania - 382 U.S. 399 (1966)
- Tehan v. Shott - 382 U.S. 406 (1966)
- Engineers v. Chicago, R.I. & Pac. R. Co. - 382 U.S. 423 (1966)
- Graham v. John Deere Co. - 383 U.S. 1 (1966)
- Baxstrom v. Herold - 383 U.S. 107 (1966)
- Brown v. Louisiana - 383 U.S. 131 (1966)
- Hicks v. District of Columbia - 383 U.S. 252 (1966)
- South Carolina v. Katzenbach - 383 U.S. 301 (1966)
- Pate v. Robinson - 383 U.S. 375 (1966)
- Perry v. Commerce Loan Co. - 383 U.S. 392 (1966)
- Memoirs v. Massachusetts - 383 U.S. 413 (1966)
- Ginzburg v. United States - 383 U.S. 463 (1966)
- Mishkin v. New York - 383 U.S. 502 (1966)
- Linn v. United Plant Guard Workers - 383 U.S. 53 (1966)
- Kent v. United States - 383 U.S. 541 (1966)
- Harper v. Virginia Bd. of Elections - 383 U.S. 663 (1966)
- United Mine Workers v. Gibbs - 383 U.S. 715 (1966)
- Rosenblatt v. Baer - 383 U.S. 75 (1966)

- United States v. Price - 383 U.S. 787 (1966)
- Brookhart v. Janis - 384 U.S. 1 (1966)
- Elfbrandt v. Russell - 384 U.S. 11 (1966)
- TEXAS v. UNITED STATES - 384 U.S. 155 (1966)
- Amell v. United States - 384 U.S. 158 (1966)
- Ashton v. Kentucky - 384 U.S. 195 (1966)
- Mills v. Alabama - 384 U.S. 214 (1966)
- United States v. Blue - 384 U.S. 251 (1966)
- Rinaldi v. Yeager - 384 U.S. 305 (1966)
- TILLMAN v. CITY OF PORT ARTHUR - 384 U.S. 315 (1966)
- Sheppard v. Maxwell - 384 U.S. 333 (1966)
- Seagram & Sons v. Hostetter - 384 U.S. 35 (1966)
- Shillitani v. United States - 384 U.S. 364 (1966)
- Cheff v. Schnackenberg - 384 U.S. 373 (1966)
- Miranda v. Arizona - 384 U.S. 436 (1966)
- Katzenbach v. Morgan - 384 U.S. 641 (1966)
- Nicolas v. United States - 384 U.S. 678 (1966)
- Gojack v. United States - 384 U.S. 702 (1966)
- Johnson v. New Jersey - 384 U.S. 719 (1966)
- Burns v. Richardson - 384 U.S. 73 (1966)
- Davis v. North Carolina - 384 U.S. 737 (1966)
- Schmerber v. California - 384 U.S. 757 (1966)
- Georgia v. Rachel - 384 U.S. 780 (1966)
- City of Greenwood v. Peacock - 384 U.S. 808 (1966)
- Dennis v. United States - 384 U.S. 855 (1966)
- Bond v. Floyd - 385 U.S. 116 (1966)
- Canada Packers, Ltd. v. Atchison, T. & S.F. Ry. So. - 385 U.S. 182 (1966)
- Watkins v. Conway - 385 U.S. 188 (1966)
- Long v. District Court - 385 U.S. 192 (1966)
- Lewis v. United States - 385 U.S. 206 (1966)
- INS v. Errico - 385 U.S. 214 (1966)
- Fortson v. Morris - 385 U.S. 231 (1966)
- Woodby v. INS - 385 U.S. 276 (1966)
- Hoffa v. United States - 385 U.S. 293 (1966)
- Osborn v. United States - 385 U.S. 323 (1966)
- Kelsey v. Corbett - 385 U.S. 35 (1966)
- Parker v. Gladden - 385 U.S. 363 (1966)
- Adderly v. Florida - 385 U.S. 39 (1966)
- Bank of Marin v. England - 385 U.S. 99 (1966)
- Time, Inc. v. Hill - 385 U.S. 374 (1967)
- Swann v. Adams - 385 U.S. 440 (1967)
- Nave v. City of Seattle - 385 U.S. 450 (1967)
- Duddleston v. Grills - 385 U.S. 455 (1967)
- United States v. Laub - 385 U.S. 475 (1967)
- Garrity v. New Jersey - 385 U.S. 493 (1967)
- Spevack v. Klein - 385 U.S. 511 (1967)
- Short v. Ness Produce Co. - 385 U.S. 537 (1967)
- Sims v. Georgia - 385 U.S. 538 (1967)
- Whitus v. Georgia - 385 U.S. 545 (1967)
- Spencer v. Texas - 385 U.S. 554 (1967)
- Keyishian v. Board of Regents - 385 U.S. 589 (1967)

- Berenyi v. Immigration Director - 385 U.S. 630 (1967)
- Miller v. Pate - 386 U.S. 1 (1967)
- Kilgarlin v. Hill - 386 U.S. 120 (1967)
- Vaca v. Sipes - 386 U.S. 171 (1967)
- Chapman v. California - 386 U.S. 18 (1967)
- Klopfer v. North Carolina - 386 U.S. 213 (1967)
- Swenson v. Bosler - 386 U.S. 258 (1967)
- McCray v. Illinois - 386 U.S. 300 (1967)
- Neely v. Martin K. Eby Construction Co., Inc. - 386 U.S. 317 (1967)
- Honda v. Clark - 386 U.S. 484 (1967)
- State Farm Fire & Cas. Co. v. Tashire - 386 U.S. 523 (1967)
- Pierson v. Ray - 386 U.S. 547 (1967)
- Cooper v. California - 386 U.S. 58 (1967)
- Specht v. Patterson - 386 U.S. 605 (1967)
- Giles v. Maryland - 386 U.S. 66 (1967)
- Waldron v. Moore-McCormack Lines, Inc. - 386 U.S. 724 (1967)
- Anders v. California - 386 U.S. 738 (1967)
- Entsminger v. Iowa - 386 U.S. 748 (1967)
- National Bellas Hess v. Department of Revenue - 386 U.S. 753 (1967)
- Redrup v. New York - 386 U.S. 767 (1967)
- Sailors v. Board of Educ. of Kent County - 387 U.S. 105 (1967)
- Boutilier v. INS - 387 U.S. 118 (1967)
- Abbott Laboratories v. Gardner - 387 U.S. 136 (1967)
- Toilet Goods Assn., Inc. v. Gardner - 387 U.S. 158 (1967)
- Gardner v. Toilet Goods Assn., Inc. - 387 U.S. 167 (1967)
- Afroyim v. Rusk - 387 U.S. 253 (1967)
- Warden v. Hayden - 387 U.S. 294 (1967)
- Chicago & N.W. R. Co. v. A., T & S.F. R. Co. - 387 U.S. 326 (1967)
- Reitman v. Mulkey - 387 U.S. 369 (1967)
- American Trucking Assns. v. A., T. & S.F. R. Co. - 387 U.S. 397 (1967)
- Commissioner v. Estate of Bosch - 387 U.S. 456 (1967)
- Camara v. Municipal Court - 387 U.S. 523 (1967)
- See v. City of Seattle - 387 U.S. 541 (1967)
- Dombrowski v. Eastland - 387 U.S. 82 (1967)
- Holding v. Blankenship - 387 U.S. 94 (1967)
- Loving v. Virginia - 388 U.S. 1 (1967)
- Curtis Pub. Co. v. Butts - 388 U.S. 130 (1967)
- Washington v. Texas - 388 U.S. 14 (1967)
- United States v. Wade - 388 U.S. 218 (1967)
- Gilbert v. California - 388 U.S. 263 (1967)
- Stovall v. Denno - 388 U.S. 293 (1967)
- Walker v. City of Birmingham - 388 U.S. 307 (1967)
- United States v. Arnold, Schwinn & Co. - 388 U.S. 365 (1967)
- Berger v. New York - 388 U.S. 41 (1967)
- Burgett v. Texas - 389 U.S. 109 (1967)
- United States v. Rands - 389 U.S. 121 (1967)
- Mempa v. Rhay - 389 U.S. 128 (1967)

- Wyandotte Transportation Co. v. United States - 389 U.S. 191 (1967)
- Lucas v. Rhodes - 389 U.S. 212 (1967)
- Mine Workers v. Illinois Bar Assn. - 389 U.S. 217 (1967)
- Nash v. Florida Industrial Comm'n - 389 U.S. 235 (1967)
- Jones v. Georgia - 389 U.S. 24 (1967)
- Zwickler v. Koota - 389 U.S. 241 (1967)
- United States v. Robel - 389 U.S. 258 (1967)
- Newton Trucking Co. v. United States - 389 U.S. 30 (1967)
- Burke v. Ford - 389 U.S. 320 (1967)
- Katz v. United States - 389 U.S. 347 (1967)
- Rockefeller v. Wells - 389 U.S. 421 (1967)
- Whitehill v. Elkins - 389 U.S. 54 (1967)
- Beckley Newspapers v. Hanks - 389 U.S. 81 (1967)
- Zschernig v. Miller - 389 U.S. 429 (1968)
- Randolph v. United States - 389 U.S. 570 (1968)
- Louisiana Financial Assistance Comm. v. Poindexter - 389 U.S. 571 (1968)
- James v. Gilmore - 389 U.S. 572 (1968)
- Strickland Transportation Co., Inc. v. United States - 389 U.S. 574 (1968)
- Hardin v. Kentucky Utilities Co. - 390 U.S. 1 (1968)
- Smith v. Illinois - 390 U.S. 129 (1968)
- Teitel Film Corp. v. Cusack - 390 U.S. 139 (1968)
- Albrecht v. Herald Co. - 390 U.S. 145 (1968)
- Schneider v. Smith - 390 U.S. 17 (1968)
- Harris v. United States - 390 U.S. 234 (1968)
- Lee v. Washington - 390 U.S. 333 (1968)
- Walker v. Wainwright - 390 U.S. 335 (1968)
- Poafpybitty v. Skelly Oil Co. - 390 U.S. 365 (1968)
- Simmons v. United States - 390 U.S. 377 (1968)
- Marchetti v. United States - 390 U.S. 39 (1968)
- Avery v. Midland County - 390 U.S. 474 (1968)
- Greenwald v. Wisconsin - 390 U.S. 519 (1968)
- United States v. Jackson - 390 U.S. 570 (1968)
- Cameron v. Johnson - 390 U.S. 611 (1968)
- Grosso v. United States - 390 U.S. 62 (1968)
- Ginsberg v. New York - 390 U.S. 629 (1968)
- Interstate Circuit, Inc. v. City of Dallas - 390 U.S. 676 (1968)
- Scafati v. Greenfield - 390 U.S. 713 (1968)
- Barber v. Page - 390 U.S. 719 (1968)
- St. Amant v. Thompson - 390 U.S. 727 (1968)
- Permian Basin Area Rate Cases - 390 U.S. 747 (1968)
- Haynes v. United States - 390 U.S. 85 (1968)
- Mathis v. United States - 391 U.S. 1 (1968)
- Bruton v. United States - 391 U.S. 123 (1968)
- Duncan v. Louisiana - 391 U.S. 145 (1968)
- Bloom v. Illinois - 391 U.S. 194 (1968)
- Dyke v. Taylor Implement Mfg. Co., Inc. - 391 U.S. 216 (1968)
- Joint Industry Board v. United States - 391 U.S. 224 (1968)
- Carafas v. LaVallee - 391 U.S. 234 (1968)
- Food Employees v. Logan Valley Plaza, Inc. - 391 U.S. 308 (1968)
- Darwin v. Connecticut - 391 U.S. 346 (1968)
- United States v. O'Brien - 391 U.S. 367 (1968)
- Green v. County Sch. Bd. of New Kent County - 391 U.S. 430 (1968)
- Raney v. Board of Education - 391 U.S. 443 (1968)
- Monroe v. Board of Comm'rs of City of Jackson - 391 U.S. 450 (1968)
- Rabeck v. New York - 391 U.S. 462 (1968)
- Reading Co. v. Brown - 391 U.S. 471 (1968)
- Witherspoon v. Illinois - 391 U.S. 510 (1968)
- Peyton v. Rowe - 391 U.S. 54 (1968)
- Bumper v. North Carolina - 391 U.S. 543 (1968)
- Pickering v. Board of Education - 391 U.S. 563 (1968)
- Johnson v. Florida - 391 U.S. 596 (1968)
- Levy v. Louisiana - 391 U.S. 68 (1968)
- Glona v. American Guar. & Liab. Ins. Co. - 391 U.S. 73 (1968)
- Terry v. Ohio - 392 U.S. 1 (1968)
- Maryland v. Wirtz - 392 U.S. 183 (1968)
- Harrison v. United States - 392 U.S. 219 (1968)
- Board of Education v. Allen - 392 U.S. 236 (1968)
- Gardner v. Broderick - 392 U.S. 273 (1968)
- Sanitation Men v. Commissioner of Sanitation - 392 U.S. 280 (1968)
- Campbell Painting Corp. v. Reid - 392 U.S. 286 (1968)
- Roberts v. Russell - 392 U.S. 293 (1968)
- King v. Smith - 392 U.S. 309 (1968)
- Mancusi v. DeForte - 392 U.S. 364 (1968)
- Lee v. Florida - 392 U.S. 378 (1968)
- Fortnightly Corp. v. United Artists Television, Inc. - 392 U.S. 390 (1968)
- Sibron v. New York - 392 U.S. 40 (1968)
- Jones v. Alfred H. Mayer Co. - 392 U.S. 409 (1968)
- Hanover Shoe, Inc. v. United Shoe Machinery Corp. - 392 U.S. 481 (1968)
- Powell v. Texas - 392 U.S. 514 (1968)
- DeStefano v. Woods - 392 U.S. 631 (1968)
- Lee Art Theatre, Inc. v. Virginia - 392 U.S. 636 (1968)
- Flast v. Cohen - 392 U.S. 83 (1968)
- WHYY, Inc. v. Borough of Glassboro - 393 U.S. 117 (1968)
- Locomotive Firemen v. Chicago R. I. & Pac. R. Co. - 393 U.S. 129 (1968)
- Louisiana Educ. Comm. for Needy Children v. Poindexter - 393 U.S. 17 (1968)

- Carroll v. Princess Anne - 393 U.S. 175 (1968)
- United States v. Phosphate Export Assn. - 393 U.S. 199 (1968)
- McConnell v. Rhay - 393 U.S. 2 (1968)
- South Carolina State Board of Education v. Brown - 393 U.S. 222 (1968)
- Williams v. Rhodes - 393 U.S. 23 (1968)
- Alderman v. United States - 394 U.S. 165 (1968)
- Arsenault v. Massachusetts - 393 U.S. 5 (1968)
- Epperson v. Arkansas - 393 U.S. 97 (1968)
- Goldblatt v. Town of Hempstead - 369 U.S. 590 (1969)
- Thorpe v. Housing Auth. - 393 U.S. 268 (1969)
- Stoner v. California - 376 U.S. 483 (1969)
- United States v. Augenblick - 393 U.S. 348 (1969)
- Gardner v. California - 393 U.S. 367 (1969)
- Smith v. Hooey - 393 U.S. 374 (1969)
- Hunter v. Erickson - 393 U.S. 385 (1969)
- Spinelli v. United States - 393 U.S. 410 (1969)
- Presbyterian Church v. Hull Church - 393 U.S. 440 (1969)
- Johnson v. Avery - 393 U.S. 483 (1969)
- Tinker v. Des Moines Sch. Dist. - 393 U.S. 503 (1969)
- Allen v. State Bd. of Elections - 393 U.S. 544 (1969)
- Golden v. Zwickler - 394 U.S. 103 (1969)
- Gregory v. City of Chicago - 394 U.S. 111 (1969)
- Citizen Publishing Co. v. United States - 394 U.S. 131 (1969)
- Shuttlesworth v. City of Birmingham - 394 U.S. 147 (1969)
- Kaufman v. United States - 394 U.S. 217 (1969)
- Desist v. United States - 394 U.S. 244 (1969)
- Harris v. Nelson - 394 U.S. 286 (1969)
- Orozco v. Texas - 394 U.S. 324 (1969)
- Snyder v. Harris - 394 U.S. 332 (1969)
- Hadnott v. Amos - 394 U.S. 358 (1969)
- Railroad Trainmen v. Terminal Co. - 394 U.S. 369 (1969)
- Foster v. California - 394 U.S. 440 (1969)
- McCarthy v. United States - 394 U.S. 459 (1969)
- Kirkpatrick v. Preisler - 394 U.S. 526 (1969)
- Wells v. Rockefeller - 394 U.S. 542 (1969)
- Stanley v. Georgia - 394 U.S. 557 (1969)
- Street v. New York - 394 U.S. 576 (1969)
- Shapiro v. Thompson - 394 U.S. 618 (1969)
- Watts v. United States - 394 U.S. 705 (1969)
- Davis v. Mississippi - 394 U.S. 721 (1969)
- Frazier v. Cupp - 394 U.S. 731 (1969)
- NLRB v. Wyman-Gordon Co. - 394 U.S. 759 (1969)
- McDonald v. Board of Election Comm'rs - 394 U.S. 802 (1969)
- Kramer v. Caribbean Mills, Inc. - 394 U.S. 823 (1969)
- Utah v. United States - 394 U.S. 89 (1969)
- Frank v. United States - 395 U.S. 147 (1969)
- Sullivan v. United States - 395 U.S. 169 (1969)
- United States v. Montgomery County Bd. of Educ. - 395 U.S. 225 (1969)
- Boykin v. Alabama - 395 U.S. 238 (1969)
- Harrington v. California - 395 U.S. 250 (1969)
- O'Callahan v. Parker - 395 U.S. 258 (1969)
- Gaston County v. United States - 395 U.S. 285 (1969)
- Daniel v. Paul - 395 U.S. 298 (1969)
- Sniadach v. Family Finance Corp. - 395 U.S. 337 (1969)
- Rodrigue v. Aetna Cas. & Sur. Co. - 395 U.S. 352 (1969)
- Red Lion Broadcasting Co., Inc. v. FCC - 395 U.S. 367 (1969)
- Willingham v. Morgan - 395 U.S. 402 (1969)
- Jenkins v. McKeithen - 395 U.S. 411 (1969)
- Brandenburg v. Ohio - 395 U.S. 444 (1969)
- Williams v. Oklahoma City - 395 U.S. 458 (1969)
- Powell v. McCormack - 395 U.S. 486 (1969)
- United States v. Covington - 395 U.S. 57 (1969)
- NLRB v. Gissel Packing Co., Inc. - 395 U.S. 575 (1969)
- Leary v. United States - 395 U.S. 6 (1969)
- Kramer v. Union Free Sch. Dist. No. 15 - 395 U.S. 621 (1969)
- Cipriano v. City of Houma - 395 U.S. 701 (1969)
- North Carolina v. Pearce - 395 U.S. 711 (1969)
- Chimel v. California - 395 U.S. 752 (1969)
- Benton v. Maryland - 395 U.S. 784 (1969)
- Von Cleef v. New Jersey - 395 U.S. 814 (1969)
- Shipley v. California - 395 U.S. 818 (1969)
- Alexander v. Holmes County Bd. of Ed. - 396 U.S. 19 (1969)
- Nacirema Operating Co., Inc. v. Johnson - 396 U.S. 212 (1969)
- Sullivan v. Little Hunting Park, Inc. - 396 U.S. 229 (1969)
- Dowell v. Board of Education - 396 U.S. 269 (1969)
- Hall v. Beals - 396 U.S. 45 (1969)
- Anderson's Black Rock, Inc. v. Pavement Co. - 396 U.S. 57 (1969)
- Minor v. United States - 396 U.S. 87 (1969)
- Carter v. West Feliciana Parish Sch. Bd. - 396 U.S. 290 (1970)
- Carter v. Jury Commission of Greene County - 396 U.S. 320 (1970)
- Turner v. Fouche - 396 U.S. 346 (1970)
- Maryland & Va. Churches v. Sharpsburg Church - 396 U.S. 367 (1970)

- Turner v. United States - 396 U.S. 398 (1970)
- Evans v. Abney - 396 U.S. 435 (1970)
- Ross v. Bernhard - 396 U.S. 531 (1970)
- Toussie v. United States - 397 U.S. 112 (1970)
- Pike v. Bruce Church, Inc. - 397 U.S. 137 (1970)
- United States v. Reynolds - 397 U.S. 14 (1970)
- Data Processing Svc. Orgs. v. Camp - 397 U.S. 150 (1970)
- Barlow v. Collins - 397 U.S. 159 (1970)
- Longshoremen v. Ariadne Shipping Co., Ltd. - 397 U.S. 195 (1970)
- Northcross v. Board of Education - 397 U.S. 232 (1970)
- United States v. Van Leeuwen - 397 U.S. 249 (1970)
- Goldberg v. Kelly - 397 U.S. 254 (1970)
- Illinois v. Allen - 397 U.S. 337 (1970)
- Waller v. Florida - 397 U.S. 387 (1970)
- Rosado v. Wyman - 397 U.S. 397 (1970)
- Ashe v. Swenson - 397 U.S. 436 (1970)
- Dandridge v. Williams - 397 U.S. 471 (1970)
- Wyman v. Bowens - 397 U.S. 49 (1970)
- Hadley v. Junior Coll. Dist. - 397 U.S. 50 (1970)
- Lewis v. Martin - 397 U.S. 552 (1970)
- Bachellar v. Maryland - 397 U.S. 564 (1970)
- Walz v. Tax Comm'n of City of New York - 397 U.S. 664 (1970)
- Colonnade Catering Corp. v. United States - 397 U.S. 72 (1970)
- Rowan v. Post Office Dept. - 397 U.S. 728 (1970)
- Brady v. United States - 397 U.S. 742 (1970)
- McMann v. Richardson - 397 U.S. 759 (1970)
- Parker v. North Carolina - 397 U.S. 790 (1970)
- Reetz v. Bozanich - 397 U.S. 82 (1970)
- Adickes v. S. H. Kress & Co. - 398 U.S. 144 (1970)
- Boys Markets, Inc. v. Retail Clerks Union - 398 U.S. 235 (1970)
- Atlantic Coast L. R. Co. v. Engineers - 398 U.S. 281 (1970)
- Hellenic Lines Ltd. v. Rhoditis - 398 U.S. 306 (1970)
- Price v. Georgia - 398 U.S. 323 (1970)
- Welsh v. United States - 398 U.S. 333 (1970)
- Moragne v. States Marine Lines, Inc. - 398 U.S. 375 (1970)
- Evans v. Cornman - 398 U.S. 419 (1970)
- Schacht v. United States - 398 U.S. 58 (1970)
- Greenbelt Co-Op. Publ. Assn., Inc. v. Bresler - 398 U.S. 6 (1970)
- Chandler v. Judicial Council - 398 U.S. 74 (1970)
- Coleman v. Alabama - 399 U.S. 1 (1970)
- California v. Green - 399 U.S. 149 (1970)
- City of Phoenix v. Kolodziejski - 399 U.S. 204 (1970)
- Nelson v. George - 399 U.S. 224 (1970)
- Williams v. Illinois - 399 U.S. 235 (1970)
- Vale v. Louisiana - 399 U.S. 30 (1970)
- Chambers v. Maroney - 399 U.S. 42 (1970)
- Baldwin v. New York - 399 U.S. 66 (1970)
- Williams v. Florida - 399 U.S. 78 (1970)
- Oregon v. Mitchell - 400 U.S. 112 (1970)
- North Carolina v. Alford - 400 U.S. 25 (1970)
- United States v. Maryland Savings-Share Ins. Corp. - 400 U.S. 4 (1970)
- Arnold Tours, Inc. v. Camp - 400 U.S. 45 (1970)
- Dutton v. Evans - 400 U.S. 74 (1970)
- Wyman v. James - 400 U.S. 309 (1971)
- Perkins v. Matthews - 400 U.S. 379 (1971)
- Blount v. Rizzi - 400 U.S. 410 (1971)
- Wisconsin v. Constantineau - 400 U.S. 433 (1971)
- Mayberry v. Pennsylvania - 400 U.S. 455 (1971)
- United States v. Jorn - 400 U.S. 470 (1971)
- Usner v. Luckenbach Overseas Corp. - 400 U.S. 494 (1971)
- Groppi v. Wisconsin - 400 U.S. 505 (1971)
- Phillips v. Martin Marietta Corp. - 400 U.S. 542 (1971)
- Piccirillo v. New York - 400 U.S. 548 (1971)
- Baird v. State Bar of Arizona - 401 U.S. 1 (1971)
- Sanks v. Georgia - 401 U.S. 144 (1971)
- Law Students Research Council v. Wadmond - 401 U.S. 154 (1971)
- Dyson v. Stein - 401 U.S. 200 (1971)
- Byrne v. Karalexis - 401 U.S. 216 (1971)
- Harris v. New York - 401 U.S. 222 (1971)
- Monitor Patriot Co. v. Roy - 401 U.S. 265 (1971)
- Time, Inc. v. Pape - 401 U.S. 279 (1971)
- Ocala Star-Banner Co. v. Damron - 401 U.S. 295 (1971)
- Relford v. Commandant - 401 U.S. 355 (1971)
- Younger v. Harris - 401 U.S. 37 (1971)
- Boddie v. Connecticut - 401 U.S. 371 (1971)
- Tate v. Short - 401 U.S. 395 (1971)
- Griggs v. Duke Power Co. - 401 U.S. 424 (1971)
- Gillette v. United States - 401 U.S. 437 (1971)
- Grove Press, v. Maryland State Board of Censors - 401 U.S. 480 (1971)
- Durham v. United States - 401 U.S. 481 (1971)
- Ohio v. Wyandotte Chemicals Corp. - 401 U.S. 493 (1971)
- Radich v. New York - 401 U.S. 531 (1971)
- Labine v. Vincent - 401 U.S. 532 (1971)
- Whiteley v. Warden - 401 U.S. 560 (1971)
- United Transp. Union v. State Bar of Michigan - 401 U.S. 576 (1971)
- Investment Co. Inst. v. Camp - 401 U.S. 617 (1971)
- Williams v. United States - 401 U.S. 646 (1971)

- Samuels v. Mackell - 401 U.S. 66 (1971)
- Mackey v. United States - 401 U.S. 667 (1971)
- United States v. U.S. Coin & Currency - 401 U.S. 715 (1971)
- United States v. White - 401 U.S. 745 (1971)
- Boyle v. Landry - 401 U.S. 77 (1971)
- Hill v. California - 401 U.S. 797 (1971)
- Rewis v. United States - 401 U.S. 808 (1971)
- Rogers v. Bellei - 401 U.S. 815 (1971)
- Perez v. Ledesma - 401 U.S. 82 (1971)
- Kitchens v. Smith - 401 U.S. 847 (1971)
- Swann v. Charlotte-Mecklenburg Bd. of Educ. - 402 U.S. 1 (1971)
- California Dept. of Human Resources v. Java - 402 U.S. 121 (1971)
- James v. Valtierra - 402 U.S. 137 (1971)
- Perez v. United States - 402 U.S. 146 (1971)
- McGautha v. California - 402 U.S. 183 (1971)
- Blonder Tongue v. University of Illinois Found. - 402 U.S. 313 (1971)
- Davis v. Board of Sch. Comm'rs of Mobile County - 402 U.S. 33 (1971)
- United States v. Reidel - 402 U.S. 351 (1971)
- United States v. Thirty-Seven Photographs - 402 U.S. 363 (1971)
- Richardson v. Perales - 402 U.S. 389 (1971)
- McDaniel v. Barresi - 402 U.S. 39 (1971)
- Organization for a Better Austin v. Keefe - 402 U.S. 415 (1971)
- California v. Byers - 402 U.S. 424 (1971)
- North Carolina State Bd. of Educ. v. Swann - 402 U.S. 43 (1971)
- Moore v. Charlotte-Mecklenburg Bd. of Educ. - 402 U.S. 47 (1971)
- Bell v. Burson - 402 U.S. 535 (1971)
- Palmer v. City of Euclid - 402 U.S. 544 (1971)
- Coates v. City of Cincinnati - 402 U.S. 611 (1971)
- United States v. Vuitch - 402 U.S. 62 (1971)
- Nelson v. O'Neil - 402 U.S. 622 (1971)
- Perez v. Campbell - 402 U.S. 637 (1971)
- Connor v. Johnson - 402 U.S. 690 (1971)
- Gordon v. Lance - 403 U.S. 1 (1971)
- Whitcomb v. Chavis - 403 U.S. 124 (1971)
- Cohen v. California - 403 U.S. 15 (1971)
- Abate v. Mundt - 403 U.S. 182 (1971)
- Connell v. Higginbotham - 403 U.S. 207 (1971)
- Johnson v. Mississippi - 403 U.S. 212 (1971)
- Palmer v. Thompson - 403 U.S. 217 (1971)
- Motor Coach Employees v. Lockridge - 403 U.S. 274 (1971)
- Rosenbloom v. Metromedia - 403 U.S. 29 (1971)
- Graham v. Department of Pub. Welfare - 403 U.S. 365 (1971)
- Bivens v. Six Unknown Fed. Narcotics Agents - 403 U.S. 388 (1971)
- Jenness v. Fortson - 403 U.S. 431 (1971)
- Coolidge v. New Hampshire - 403 U.S. 443 (1971)
- McKeiver v. Pennsylvania - 403 U.S. 528 (1971)
- Lemon v. Kurtzman - 403 U.S. 602 (1971)
- Tilton v. Richardson - 403 U.S. 672 (1971)
- New York Times Co. v. United States - 403 U.S. 713 (1971)
- Griffin v. Breckenridge - 403 U.S. 88 (1971)
- NLRB v. Nash-Finch Co. - 404 U.S. 138 (1971)
- Younger v. Gilmore - 404 U.S. 15 (1971)
- May v. City of Chicago - 404 U.S. 189 (1971)
- Victory Carriers, Inc. v. Law - 404 U.S. 202 (1971)
- Santobello v. New York - 404 U.S. 257 (1971)
- Picard v. Connor - 404 U.S. 270 (1971)
- Townsend v. Swank - 404 U.S. 282 (1971)
- United States v. Marion - 404 U.S. 307 (1971)
- United States v. Bass - 404 U.S. 336 (1971)
- Schilb v. Kuebel - 404 U.S. 357 (1971)
- Harris v. Washington - 404 U.S. 55 (1971)
- Pease v. Hansen - 404 U.S. 70 (1971)
- Reed v. Reed - 404 U.S. 71 (1971)
- Richardson v. Belcher - 404 U.S. 78 (1971)
- Chevron Oil Co. v. Huson - 404 U.S. 97 (1971)
- SEC v. Medical Committee for Human Rights - 404 U.S. 403 (1972)
- Diffenderfer v. Central Baptist Church - 404 U.S. 412 (1972)
- United States v. Tucker - 404 U.S. 443 (1972)
- Lego v. Twomey - 404 U.S. 477 (1972)
- Groppi v. Leslie - 404 U.S. 496 (1972)
- California Motor Transp. Co. v. Trucking Unlimited - 404 U.S. 508 (1972)
- Haines v. Kerner - 404 U.S. 519 (1972)
- Love v. Pullman Co. - 404 U.S. 522 (1972)
- Connor v. Williams - 404 U.S. 549 (1972)
- Bullock v. Carter - 405 U.S. 134 (1972)
- Roudebush v. Hartke - 405 U.S. 15 (1972)
- Giglio v. United States - 405 U.S. 150 (1972)
- Papachristou v. City of Jacksonville - 405 U.S. 156 (1972)
- D. H. Overmyer Co., Inc. v. Frick - 405 U.S. 174 (1972)
- Richardson v. Wright - 405 U.S. 208 (1972)
- Hawaii v. Standard Oil Co. of California - 405 U.S. 251 (1972)
- Adams v. Illinois - 405 U.S. 278 (1972)
- Rabe v. Washington - 405 U.S. 313 (1972)
- Cruz v. Beto - 405 U.S. 319 (1972)
- Dunn v. Blumstein - 405 U.S. 330 (1972)
- Schneble v. Florida - 405 U.S. 427 (1972)
- Eisenstadt v. Baird - 405 U.S. 438 (1972)
- Loper v. Beto - 405 U.S. 473 (1972)
- Humphrey v. Cady - 405 U.S. 504 (1972)
- Gooding v. Wilson - 405 U.S. 518 (1972)
- Lynch v. Household Finance Corp. - 405 U.S. 538 (1972)
- Lindsey v. Normet - 405 U.S. 56 (1972)
- Alexander v. Louisiana - 405 U.S. 625 (1972)
- Stanley v. Illinois - 405 U.S. 645 (1972)

- Cole v. Richardson - 405 U.S. 676 (1972)
- Sierra Club v. Morton - 405 U.S. 727 (1972)
- Colombo v. New York - 405 U.S. 9 (1972)
- Washington v. General Motors Corp. - 406 U.S. 109 (1972)
- Weber v. Aetna Cas. & Sur. Co. - 406 U.S. 164 (1972)
- Minnesota State Senate v. Beens - 406 U.S. 187 (1972)
- Wisconsin v. Yoder - 406 U.S. 205 (1972)
- United States v. Biswell - 406 U.S. 311 (1972)
- Andrews v. Louisville & Nashville R. Co. - 406 U.S. 320 (1972)
- Johnson v. Louisiana - 406 U.S. 356 (1972)
- Apodaca v. Oregon - 406 U.S. 404 (1972)
- Kastigar v. United States - 406 U.S. 441 (1972)
- Zicarelli v. New Jersey Investigation Comm'n - 406 U.S. 472 (1972)
- Deepsouth Packing Co., Inc. v. Laitram Corp. - 406 U.S. 518 (1972)
- Jefferson v. Hackney - 406 U.S. 535 (1972)
- Socialist Labor Party v. Gilligan - 406 U.S. 583 (1972)
- Brooks v. Tennessee - 406 U.S. 605 (1972)
- United States v. Midwest Video Corp. - 406 U.S. 649 (1972)
- Kirby v. Illinois - 406 U.S. 682 (1972)
- Jackson v. Indiana - 406 U.S. 715 (1972)
- First Nat'l City Bank v. Banco Nacional de Cuba - 406 U.S. 759 (1972)
- Illinois v. City of Milwaukee - 406 U.S. 91 (1972)
- Colten v. Kentucky - 407 U.S. 104 (1972)
- James v. Strange - 407 U.S. 128 (1972)
- Adams v. Williams - 407 U.S. 143 (1972)
- Moose Lodge No. 107 v. Irvis - 407 U.S. 163 (1972)
- Flower v. United States - 407 U.S. 197 (1972)
- Mitchum v. Foster - 407 U.S. 225 (1972)
- McNeil v. Patuxent Institution - 407 U.S. 245 (1972)
- Argersinger v. Hamlin - 407 U.S. 25 (1972)
- Flood v. Kuhn - 407 U.S. 258 (1972)
- United States v. United States Dist. Ct. - 407 U.S. 297 (1972)
- Shadwick v. City of Tampa - 407 U.S. 345 (1972)
- Murel v. Baltimore City Crim. Ct. - 407 U.S. 355 (1972)
- Turner v. Arkansas - 407 U.S. 366 (1972)
- Milton v. Wainwright - 407 U.S. 371 (1972)
- Pipefitters v. United States - 407 U.S. 385 (1972)
- Wright v. Council of City of Emporia - 407 U.S. 451 (1972)
- Peters v. Kiff - 407 U.S. 493 (1972)
- Barker v. Wingo - 407 U.S. 514 (1972)
- Lloyd Corp., Ltd. v. Tanner - 407 U.S. 551 (1972)
- Fuentes v. Shevin - 407 U.S. 67 (1972)
- Laird v. Tatum - 408 U.S. 1 (1972)
- Grayned v. City of Rockford - 408 U.S. 104 (1972)
- Healy v. James - 408 U.S. 169 (1972)
- Mancusi v. Stubbs - 408 U.S. 204 (1972)
- Furman v. Georgia - 408 U.S. 238 (1972)
- Gelbard v. United States - 408 U.S. 41 (1972)
- Morrissey v. Brewer - 408 U.S. 471 (1972)
- United States v. Brewster - 408 U.S. 501 (1972)
- Board of Regents of State Colleges v. Roth - 408 U.S. 564 (1972)
- Perry v. Sindermann - 408 U.S. 593 (1972)
- Gravel v. United States - 408 U.S. 606 (1972)
- Branzburg v. Hayes - 408 U.S. 665 (1972)
- Kleindienst v. Mandel - 408 U.S. 753 (1972)
- Moore v. Illinois - 408 U.S. 786 (1972)
- Police Dept. of City of Chicago v. Mosley - 408 U.S. 92 (1972)
- O'Brien v. Brown - 409 U.S. 1 (1972)
- California v. LaRue - 409 U.S. 109 (1972)
- Neil v. Biggers - 409 U.S. 188 (1972)
- Trafficante v. Metropolitan Life Ins. Co. - 409 U.S. 205 (1972)
- Swenson v. Stidham - 409 U.S. 224 (1972)
- Executive Jet Aviation v. City of Cleveland - 409 U.S. 249 (1972)
- Heublein, Inc. v. South Carolina Tax Comm'n - 409 U.S. 275 (1972)
- California v. Krivda - 409 U.S. 33 (1972)
- Robinson v. Hanrahan - 409 U.S. 38 (1972)
- Ward v. Village of Monroeville - 409 U.S. 57 (1972)
- Gottschalk v. Benson - 409 U.S. 63 (1972)
- Evco v. Jones - 409 U.S. 91 (1972)
- Philpott v. Essex County Welfare Bd. - 409 U.S. 413 (1973)
- United States v. Kras - 409 U.S. 434 (1973)
- American Trial Lawyers v. N.J. Supreme Court - 409 U.S. 467 (1973)
- Almota Farmers Elev. & Whse. Co. v. United States - 409 U.S. 470 (1973)
- Robinson v. Neil - 409 U.S. 505 (1973)
- Goosby v. Osser - 409 U.S. 512 (1973)
- Ham v. South Carolina - 409 U.S. 524 (1973)
- Gomez v. Perez - 409 U.S. 535 (1973)
- United States v. Dionisio - 410 U.S. 1 (1973)
- Roe v. Wade - 410 U.S. 113 (1973)
- Doe v. Bolton - 410 U.S. 179 (1973)
- United States v. Mara - 410 U.S. 19 (1973)
- McGinnis v. Royster - 410 U.S. 263 (1973)
- Chambers v. Mississippi - 410 U.S. 284 (1973)
- Mahan v. Howell - 410 U.S. 315 (1973)
- Lehnhausen v. Lake Shore Auto Parts Co. - 410 U.S. 356 (1973)
- Department of Motor Vehicles v. Rios - 410 U.S. 425 (1973)
- Tillman v. Wheaton-Haven Recreation Assn., Inc. - 410 U.S. 431 (1973)
- Illinois v. Somerville - 410 U.S. 458 (1973)
- Braden v. 30th Judicial Circuit Court of Kentucky - 410 U.S. 484 (1973)

- Hurtado v. United States - 410 U.S. 578 (1973)
- Linda R. S. v. Richard D. - 410 U.S. 614 (1973)
- United Air Lines, Inc. v. Mahin - 410 U.S. 623 (1973)
- Ortwein v. Schwab - 410 U.S. 656 (1973)
- Papish v. Board of Curators - 410 U.S. 667 (1973)
- Marston v. Lewis - 410 U.S. 679 (1973)
- Burns v. Fortson - 410 U.S. 686 (1973)
- LaVallee v. Delle Rose - 410 U.S. 690 (1973)
- Salyer Land Co. v. Tulare Water Dist. - 410 U.S. 719 (1973)
- EPA v. Mink - 410 U.S. 73 (1973)
- Associated Enterprises v. Toltec Dist. - 410 U.S. 743 (1973)
- Rosario v. Rockefeller - 410 U.S. 752 (1973)
- San Antonio Indep. Sch. Dist. v. Rodriguez - 411 U.S. 1 (1973)
- Mescalero Apache Tribe v. Jones - 411 U.S. 145 (1973)
- McClanahan v. Arizona State Tax Comm'n - 411 U.S. 164 (1973)
- Lemon v. Kurtzman - 411 U.S. 192 (1973)
- Davis v. United States - 411 U.S. 233 (1973)
- Tollett v. Henderson - 411 U.S. 258 (1973)
- Employees v. Missouri Pub. Health Dept. - 411 U.S. 279 (1973)
- Askew v. American Waterways Operators, Inc. - 411 U.S. 325 (1973)
- Hensley v. Municipal Court - 411 U.S. 345 (1973)
- Palmore v. United States - 411 U.S. 389 (1973)
- United States v. Russell - 411 U.S. 423 (1973)
- Preiser v. Rodriguez - 411 U.S. 475 (1973)
- Georgia v. United States - 411 U.S. 526 (1973)
- Gibson v. Berryhill - 411 U.S. 564 (1973)
- New Jersey Welfare Rights Org. v. Cahill - 411 U.S. 619 (1973)
- City of Burbank v. Lockheed Air Terminal, Inc. - 411 U.S. 624 (1973)
- Frontiero v. Richardson - 411 U.S. 677 (1973)
- Moor v. County of Alameda - 411 U.S. 693 (1973)
- Gagnon v. Scarpelli - 411 U.S. 778 (1973)
- Chaffin v. Stynchcombe - 412 U.S. 17 (1973)
- Schneckloth v. Bustamonte - 412 U.S. 218 (1973)
- Cupp v. Murphy - 412 U.S. 291 (1973)
- Doe v. McMillan - 412 U.S. 306 (1973)
- United States v. United States Tax Comm'n - 412 U.S. 363 (1973)
- Strunk v. United States - 412 U.S. 434 (1973)
- Vlandis v. Kline - 412 U.S. 441 (1973)
- Michigan v. Payne - 412 U.S. 47 (1973)
- Wardius v. Oregon - 412 U.S. 470 (1973)
- City of Kenosha v. Bruno - 412 U.S. 507 (1973)

- United States v. Nevada - 412 U.S. 534 (1973)
- Dean v. Gadsden Times Publishing Corp. - 412 U.S. 543 (1973)
- Goldstein v. California - 412 U.S. 546 (1973)
- Gaffney v. Cummings - 412 U.S. 735 (1973)
- White v. Regester - 412 U.S. 755 (1973)
- White v. Weiser - 412 U.S. 783 (1973)
- Barnes v. United States - 412 U.S. 837 (1973)
- CBS v. Democratic Nat'l Committee - 412 U.S. 94 (1973)
- Gilligan v. Morgan - 413 U.S. 1 (1973)
- Kaplan v. California - 413 U.S. 115 (1973)
- United States v. 12 200-Ft. Reels of Film - 413 U.S. 123 (1973)
- United States v. Orito - 413 U.S. 139 (1973)
- Colgrove v. Battin - 413 U.S. 149 (1973)
- Miller v. California - 413 U.S. 15 (1973)
- Keyes v. School Dist. No. 1 - 413 U.S. 189 (1973)
- Almeida-Sanchez v. United States - 413 U.S. 266 (1973)
- United States v. Ash - 413 U.S. 300 (1973)
- Pittsburgh Press Co. v. Human Rel. Comm'n - 413 U.S. 376 (1973)
- Cady v. Dombrowski - 413 U.S. 433 (1973)
- Norwood v. Harrison - 413 U.S. 455 (1973)
- Levitt v. Committee for Public Ed. - 413 U.S. 472 (1973)
- Heller v. New York - 413 U.S. 483 (1973)
- Paris Adult Theatre I v. Slaton - 413 U.S. 49 (1973)
- Roaden v. Kentucky - 413 U.S. 496 (1973)
- United States Dept. of Agriculture v. Murry - 413 U.S. 508 (1973)
- United States Dept. of Agriculture v. Moreno - 413 U.S. 528 (1973)
- CSC v. Letter Carriers - 413 U.S. 548 (1973)
- Broadrick v. Oklahoma - 413 U.S. 601 (1973)
- Sugarman v. Dougall - 413 U.S. 634 (1973)
- Gosa v. Mayden - 413 U.S. 665 (1973)
- Hunt v. McNair - 413 U.S. 734 (1973)
- Committee for Public Education v. Nyquist - 413 U.S. 756 (1973)
- Sloan v. Lemon - 413 U.S. 825 (1973)
- Alexander v. Virginia - 413 U.S. 836 (1973)
- Hess v. Indiana - 414 U.S. 105 (1973)
- Cupp v. Naughten - 414 U.S. 141 (1973)
- Board of Pharmacy v. Snyder's Drug Stores - 414 U.S. 156 (1973)
- United States v. Robinson - 414 U.S. 218 (1973)
- Gustafson v. Florida - 414 U.S. 260 (1973)
- Zahn v. International Paper Co. - 414 U.S. 291 (1973)
- Bonelli Cattle Co. v. Arizona - 414 U.S. 313 (1973)
- Department of Game v. Puyallup Tribe - 414 U.S. 44 (1973)
- Kusper v. Pontikes - 414 U.S. 51 (1973)
- Lefkowitz v. Turley - 414 U.S. 70 (1973)
- United States v. Calandra - 414 U.S. 338 (1974)

- Marshall v. United States - 414 U.S. 417 (1974)
- Communist Party of Indiana v. Whitcomb - 414 U.S. 441 (1974)
- O'Shea v. Littleton - 414 U.S. 488 (1974)
- Spomer v. Littleton - 414 U.S. 514 (1974)
- O'Brien v. Skinner - 414 U.S. 524 (1974)
- Lau v. Nichols - 414 U.S. 563 (1974)
- Sea-Land Svcs., Inc. v. Gaudet - 414 U.S. 573 (1974)
- Cleveland Bd. of Educ. v. LaFleur - 414 U.S. 632 (1974)
- Phillips Petroleum Co. v. Texaco Inc. - 415 U.S. 125 (1974)
- Lewis v. City of New Orleans - 415 U.S. 130 (1974)
- United States v. Kahn - 415 U.S. 143 (1974)
- United States v. Matlock - 415 U.S. 164 (1974)
- Curtis v. Loether - 415 U.S. 189 (1974)
- Memorial Hosp. v. Maricopa County - 415 U.S. 250 (1974)
- Davis v. Alaska - 415 U.S. 308 (1974)
- National Cable Television Assn. v. United States - 415 U.S. 336 (1974)
- FPC v. New England Power Co. - 415 U.S. 345 (1974)
- Johnson v. Robison - 415 U.S. 361 (1974)
- Steffel v. Thompson - 415 U.S. 452 (1974)
- Hagans v. Lavine - 415 U.S. 528 (1974)
- Smith v. Goguen - 415 U.S. 566 (1974)
- Mayor v. Educational Equality League - 415 U.S. 605 (1974)
- Edelman v. Jordan - 415 U.S. 651 (1974)
- Lubin v. Panish - 415 U.S. 709 (1974)
- Storer v. Brown - 415 U.S. 724 (1974)
- American Party of Texas v. White - 415 U.S. 767 (1974)
- United States v. Edwards - 415 U.S. 800 (1974)
- Village of Belle Terre v. Boraas - 416 U.S. 1 (1974)
- Super Tire Engineering Co. v. McCorkle - 416 U.S. 115 (1974)
- Arnett v. Kennedy - 416 U.S. 134 (1974)
- California Bankers Assn. v. Shultz - 416 U.S. 21 (1974)
- Scheuer v. Rhodes - 416 U.S. 232 (1974)
- DeFunis v. Odegaard - 416 U.S. 312 (1974)
- Kahn v. Shevin - 416 U.S. 351 (1974)
- Pernell v. Southall Realty - 416 U.S. 363 (1974)
- Lehman Brothers v. Schein - 416 U.S. 386 (1974)
- Procunier v. Martinez - 416 U.S. 396 (1974)
- Gooding v. United States - 416 U.S. 430 (1974)
- Kewanee Oil Co. v. Bicron Corp. - 416 U.S. 470 (1974)
- United States v. Chavez - 416 U.S. 562 (1974)
- Mitchell v. W. T. Grant Co. - 416 U.S. 600 (1974)
- Beasley v. Food Fair of North Carolina, Inc. - 416 U.S. 653 (1974)
- Calero-Toledo v. Pearson Yacht Leasing Co. - 416 U.S. 663 (1974)
- Corning Glass Works v. Brennan - 417 U.S. 188 (1974)
- Blackledge v. Perry - 417 U.S. 21 (1974)
- City of Pittsburgh v. Alco Parking Corp. - 417 U.S. 369 (1974)
- Fuller v. Oregon - 417 U.S. 40 (1974)
- Wheeler v. Barrera - 417 U.S. 402 (1974)
- Michigan v. Tucker - 417 U.S. 433 (1974)
- Geduldig v. Aiello - 417 U.S. 484 (1974)
- Morton v. Mancari - 417 U.S. 535 (1974)
- Gilmore v. City of Montgomery - 417 U.S. 556 (1974)
- Cardwell v. Lewis - 417 U.S. 583 (1974)
- Ross v. Moffitt - 417 U.S. 600 (1974)
- Kosydar v. National Cash Register Co. - 417 U.S. 62 (1974)
- Jimenez v. Weinberger - 417 U.S. 628 (1974)
- Parker v. Levy - 417 U.S. 733 (1974)
- Pell v. Procunier - 417 U.S. 817 (1974)
- Saxbe v. Washington Post Co. - 417 U.S. 843 (1974)
- Jenkins v. Georgia - 418 U.S. 153 (1974)
- United States v. Richardson - 418 U.S. 166 (1974)
- Schlesinger v. Reservists Committee - 418 U.S. 208 (1974)
- Richardson v. Ramirez - 418 U.S. 24 (1974)
- Miami Herald Pub. Co. v. Tornillo - 418 U.S. 241 (1974)
- Letter Carriers v. Austin - 418 U.S. 264 (1974)
- Lehman v. City of Shaker Heights - 418 U.S. 298 (1974)
- Gertz v. Robert Welch, Inc. - 418 U.S. 323 (1974)
- Spence v. Washington - 418 U.S. 405 (1974)
- Taylor v. Hayes - 418 U.S. 488 (1974)
- Codispoti v. Pennsylvania - 418 U.S. 506 (1974)
- Wolff v. McDonnell - 418 U.S. 539 (1974)
- Secretary of the Navy v. Avrech - 418 U.S. 676 (1974)
- United States v. Nixon - 418 U.S. 683 (1974)
- Milliken v. Bradley - 418 U.S. 717 (1974)
- Hamling v. United States - 418 U.S. 87 (1974)
- Gulf Oil Corp. v. Copp Paving Co., Inc. - 419 U.S. 186 (1974)
- Allenberg Cotton Co., Inc. v. Pittman - 419 U.S. 20 (1974)
- American Radio Assn. v. Mobile S.S. Assn. - 419 U.S. 215 (1974)
- Cantrell v. Forest City Publishing Co. - 419 U.S. 245 (1974)
- Schick v. Reed - 419 U.S. 256 (1974)
- Jackson v. Metropolitan Edison Co. - 419 U.S. 345 (1974)
- Sosna v. Iowa - 419 U.S. 393 (1975)
- Cousins v. Wigoda - 419 U.S. 477 (1975)
- Schlesinger v. Ballard - 419 U.S. 498 (1975)

- Taylor v. Louisiana - 419 U.S. 522 (1975)
- United States v. Mazurie - 419 U.S. 544 (1975)
- Standard Pressed Steel Co. v. Department of Revenue - 419 U.S. 560 (1975)
- Goss v. Lopez - 419 U.S. 565 (1975)
- North Georgia Finishing, Inc. v. Di-Chem, Inc. - 419 U.S. 601 (1975)
- Chapman v. Meier - 420 U.S. 1 (1975)
- Gerstein v. Pugh - 420 U.S. 103 (1975)
- Board of Sch. Comm'rs of Indianapolis v. Jacobs - 420 U.S. 128 (1975)
- Train v. Campaign Clean Water, Inc. - 420 U.S. 136 (1975)
- United States v. Bisceglia - 420 U.S. 141 (1975)
- Drope v. Missouri - 420 U.S. 162 (1975)
- Lefkowitz v. Newsome - 420 U.S. 283 (1975)
- Wood v. Strickland - 420 U.S. 308 (1975)
- United States v. Wilson - 420 U.S. 332 (1975)
- Train v. City of New York - 420 U.S. 35 (1975)
- Serfass v. United States - 420 U.S. 377 (1975)
- Cox Broadcasting Corp. v. Cohn - 420 U.S. 469 (1975)
- United States v. Maine - 420 U.S. 515 (1975)
- Southeastern Promotions, Ltd. v. Conrad - 420 U.S. 546 (1975)
- Huffman v. Pursue, Ltd. - 420 U.S. 592 (1975)
- Weinberger v. Wiesenfeld - 420 U.S. 636 (1975)
- Austin v. New Hampshire - 420 U.S. 656 (1975)
- Oregon v. Hass - 420 U.S. 714 (1975)
- Schlesinger v. Councilman - 420 U.S. 738 (1975)
- Harris County Comm'rs v. Moore - 420 U.S. 77 (1975)
- Iannelli v. United States - 420 U.S. 770 (1975)
- Colonial Pipeline Co. v. Traigle - 421 U.S. 100 (1975)
- Johnson v. Mississippi - 421 U.S. 213 (1975)
- Hill v. Stone - 421 U.S. 289 (1975)
- Meek v. Pittenger - 421 U.S. 349 (1975)
- Withrow v. Larkin - 421 U.S. 35 (1975)
- United States v. Reliable Transfer Co., Inc. - 421 U.S. 397 (1975)
- Johnson v. Railway Express Agency, Inc. - 421 U.S. 454 (1975)
- Eastland v. United States Servicemen's Fund - 421 U.S. 491 (1975)
- Breed v. Jones - 421 U.S. 519 (1975)
- Fry v. United States - 421 U.S. 542 (1975)
- United States v. Tax Comm'n of Mississippi - 421 U.S. 599 (1975)
- Mullaney v. Wilbur - 421 U.S. 684 (1975)
- Stanton v. Stanton - 421 U.S. 7 (1975)
- Murphy v. Florida - 421 U.S. 794 (1975)
- Erznoznik v. City of Jacksonville - 422 U.S. 205 (1975)
- Hicks v. Miranda - 422 U.S. 332 (1975)
- Preiser v. Newkirk - 422 U.S. 395 (1975)

- Albemarle Paper Co. v. Moody - 422 U.S. 405 (1975)
- Muniz v. Hoffman - 422 U.S. 454 (1975)
- Warth v. Seldin - 422 U.S. 490 (1975)
- United States v. Peltier - 422 U.S. 531 (1975)
- O'Connor v. Donaldson - 422 U.S. 563 (1975)
- Brown v. Illinois - 422 U.S. 590 (1975)
- Cort v. Ash - 422 U.S. 66 (1975)
- Weinberger v. Salfi - 422 U.S. 749 (1975)
- Faretta v. California - 422 U.S. 806 (1975)
- Herring v. New York - 422 U.S. 853 (1975)
- United States v. Brignoni-Ponce - 422 U.S. 873 (1975)
- United States v. Ortiz - 422 U.S. 891 (1975)
- Doran v. Salem Inn, Inc. - 422 U.S. 922 (1975)
- Weinstein v. Bradford - 423 U.S. 147 (1975)
- Turner v. Department of Emplt. Security - 423 U.S. 44 (1975)
- Texas v. White - 423 U.S. 67 (1975)
- Connecticut v. Menillo - 423 U.S. 9 (1975)
- Michigan v. Moseley - 423 U.S. 96 (1975)
- Barrett v. United States - 423 U.S. 212 (1976)
- Mathews v. Weber - 423 U.S. 261 (1976)
- Michelin Tire Corp. v. Wages - 423 U.S. 276 (1976)
- DOVE v. UNITED STATES - 423 U.S. 325 (1976)
- Rizzo v. Goode - 423 U.S. 362 (1976)
- United States v. Watson - 423 U.S. 411 (1976)
- Buckley v. Valeo - 424 U.S. 1 (1976)
- Mathews v. Eldridge - 424 U.S. 319 (1976)
- De Canas v. Bica - 424 U.S. 351 (1976)
- Great A&P Tea Co., Inc. v. Cottrell - 424 U.S. 366 (1976)
- Time, Inc. v. Firestone - 424 U.S. 448 (1976)
- Hudgens v. NLRB - 424 U.S. 507 (1976)
- Ristaino v. Ross - 424 U.S. 589 (1976)
- United States v. Dinitz - 424 U.S. 600 (1976)
- East Carroll Parish Sch. Bd. v. Marshall - 424 U.S. 636 (1976)
- McCarthy v. Philadelphia Civil Svc. Comm'n - 424 U.S. 645 (1976)
- Garner v. United States - 424 U.S. 648 (1976)
- McKinney v. Alabama - 424 U.S. 669 (1976)
- Paul v. Davis - 424 U.S. 693 (1976)
- Franks v. Bowman Transportation Co., Inc. - 424 U.S. 747 (1976)
- Colorado River Water Conserv. Dist. v. United States - 424 U.S. 800 (1976)
- Greer v. Spock - 424 U.S. 828 (1976)
- Beer v. United States - 425 U.S. 130 (1976)
- Middendorf v. Henry - 425 U.S. 25 (1976)
- Hills v. Gautreaux - 425 U.S. 284 (1976)
- Baxter v. Palmigiano - 425 U.S. 308 (1976)
- Beckwith v. United States - 425 U.S. 341 (1976)
- Fisher v. United States - 425 U.S. 391 (1976)
- United States v. Miller - 425 U.S. 435 (1976)
- Moe v. Salish & Kootenai Tribes - 425 U.S. 463 (1976)

- Hampton v. United States - 425 U.S. 484 (1976)
- Estelle v. Williams - 425 U.S. 501 (1976)
- Francis v. Henderson - 425 U.S. 536 (1976)
- United States v. Mandujano - 425 U.S. 564 (1976)
- Hynes v. Mayor of Oradell - 425 U.S. 610 (1976)
- Alfred Dunhill of London, Inc. v. Republic of Cuba - 425 U.S. 682 (1976)
- Hospital Bldg. Co. v. Trustees of Rex Hosp. - 425 U.S. 738 (1976)
- Va. Pharmacy Bd. v. Va. Consumer Council - 425 U.S. 748 (1976)
- Arizona v. New Mexico - 425 U.S. 794 (1976)
- Geders v. United States - 425 U.S. 80 (1976)
- Washington v. Davis - 426 U.S. 229 (1976)
- Simon v. Eastern Kentucky Welf. Rights. Org. - 426 U.S. 26 (1976)
- City of Charlotte v. Firefighters - 426 U.S. 283 (1976)
- United States v. MacCollom - 426 U.S. 317 (1976)
- Bishop v. Wood - 426 U.S. 341 (1976)
- New Hampshire v. Maine - 426 U.S. 363 (1976)
- Bryan v. Itasca County - 426 U.S. 373 (1976)
- Hortonville Dist. v. Hortonville Educ. Assn. - 426 U.S. 482 (1976)
- Kleppe v. New Mexico - 426 U.S. 529 (1976)
- FEA v. Algonquin SNG, Inc. - 426 U.S. 548 (1976)
- Examining Bd. v. Flores de Otero - 426 U.S. 572 (1976)
- Doyle v. Ohio - 426 U.S. 610 (1976)
- Henderson v. Morgan - 426 U.S. 637 (1976)
- Pennsylvania v. New Jersey - 426 U.S. 660 (1976)
- City of Eastlake v. Forest City Enterprises, Inc. - 426 U.S. 668 (1976)
- Mathews v. Diaz - 426 U.S. 67 (1976)
- Roemer v. Board of Public Works of Maryland - 426 U.S. 736 (1976)
- Hughes v. Alexandria Scrap Corp. - 426 U.S. 794 (1976)
- National League of Cities v. Usery - 426 U.S. 833 (1976)
- Hampton v. Mow Sun Wong - 426 U.S. 88 (1976)
- Aldinger v. Howard - 427 U.S. 1 (1976)
- Machinists v. Wisconsin Employment Rel. Comm'n - 427 U.S. 132 (1976)
- Runyon v. McCrary - 427 U.S. 160 (1976)
- Meachum v. Fano - 427 U.S. 215 (1976)
- Montanye v. Haymes - 427 U.S. 236 (1976)
- McDonald v. Santa Fe Trail Transp. Co. - 427 U.S. 273 (1976)
- City of New Orleans v. Dukes - 427 U.S. 297 (1976)
- Massachusetts Bd. of Retirement v. Murgia - 427 U.S. 307 (1976)
- North v. Russell - 427 U.S. 328 (1976)
- Elrod v. Burns - 427 U.S. 347 (1976)
- Pasadena City Bd. of Educ. v. Spangler - 427 U.S. 424 (1976)
- Fitzpatrick v. Bitzer - 427 U.S. 445 (1976)
- Andresen v. Maryland - 427 U.S. 463 (1976)
- Mathews v. Lucas - 427 U.S. 495 (1976)
- Young v. American Mini Theatres, Inc. - 427 U.S. 50 (1976)
- Nebraska Press Assn. v. Stuart - 427 U.S. 539 (1976)
- Ludwig v. Massachusetts - 427 U.S. 618 (1976)
- United States v. Agurs - 427 U.S. 97 (1976)
- Usery v. Turner Elkhorn Mining Co. - 428 U.S. 1 (1976)
- Singleton v. Wulff - 428 U.S. 106 (1976)
- Bellotti v. Baird - 428 U.S. 132 (1976)
- Gregg v. Georgia - 428 U.S. 153 (1976)
- Proffitt v. Florida - 428 U.S. 242 (1976)
- Jurek v. Texas - 428 U.S. 262 (1976)
- Woodson v. North Carolina - 428 U.S. 280 (1976)
- Roberts v. Louisiana - 428 U.S. 325 (1976)
- South Dakota v. Opperman - 428 U.S. 364 (1976)
- Stone v. Powell - 428 U.S. 465 (1976)
- Planned Parenthood v. Danforth - 428 U.S. 52 (1976)
- United States v. Martinez-Fuerte - 428 U.S. 543 (1976)
- Cantor v. Detroit Edison Co. - 428 U.S. 579 (1976)
- General Elec. Co. v. Gilbert - 429 U.S. 125 (1976)
- Madison Sch. Dist. v. Wisconsin Empl. Rel. Comm'n - 429 U.S. 167 (1976)
- Mathews v. De Castro - 429 U.S. 181 (1976)
- Craig v. Boren - 429 U.S. 190 (1976)
- Estelle v. Gamble - 429 U.S. 97 (1976)
- Connally v. Georgia - 429 U.S. 245 (1977)
- Arlington Heights v. Metropolitan Housing Dev. Corp. - 429 U.S. 252 (1977)
- Mt. Healthy City Sch. Dist. v. Doyle - 429 U.S. 274 (1977)
- Boston Stock Exchange v. State Tax Comm'n - 429 U.S. 318 (1977)
- G. M. Leasing Corp. v. United States - 429 U.S. 338 (1977)
- State Land Bd. v. Corvallis Sand & Gravel Co. - 429 U.S. 363 (1977)
- United States v. Donovan - 429 U.S. 413 (1977)
- United States v. County of Fresno - 429 U.S. 452 (1977)
- Oregon v. Mathiason - 429 U.S. 492 (1977)
- Stanton v. Stanton - 429 U.S. 501 (1977)
- Weatherford v. Bursey - 429 U.S. 545 (1977)
- Whalen v. Roe - 429 U.S. 589 (1977)

- Codd v. Velger - 429 U.S. 624 (1977)
- United Jewish Organizations v. Carey - 430 U.S. 144 (1977)
- Marks v. United States - 430 U.S. 188 (1977)
- Califano v. Goldfarb - 430 U.S. 199 (1977)
- Complete Auto Transit, Inc. v. Brady - 430 U.S. 274 (1977)
- Farmer v. Carpenters - 430 U.S. 290 (1977)
- Oklahoma Pub. Co. v. District Court - 430 U.S. 308 (1977)
- Califano v. Webster - 430 U.S. 313 (1977)
- Juidice v. Vail - 430 U.S. 327 (1977)
- Gardner v. Florida - 430 U.S. 349 (1977)
- Swain v. Pressley - 430 U.S. 372 (1977)
- Brewer v. Williams - 430 U.S. 387 (1977)
- Atlas Roofing Co., Inc. v. Occupational Safety Comm'n - 430 U.S. 442 (1977)
- Castaneda v. Partida - 430 U.S. 482 (1977)
- Jones v. Rath Packing - 430 U.S. 519 (1977)
- National Geographic Soc'y v. Board of Equal. - 430 U.S. 551 (1977)
- United States v. Martin Linen Supply Co. - 430 U.S. 564 (1977)
- Ingraham v. Wright - 430 U.S. 651 (1977)
- Wooley v. Maynard - 430 U.S. 705 (1977)
- Delaware Tribal Business Committee v. Weeks - 430 U.S. 73 (1977)
- Trimble v. Gordon - 430 U.S. 762 (1977)
- Fiallo v. Bell - 430 U.S. 787 (1977)
- Bounds v. Smith - 430 U.S. 817 (1977)
- United States Trust Co. v. New Jersey - 431 U.S. 1 (1977)
- Dixon v. Love - 431 U.S. 105 (1977)
- Kremens v. Bartley - 431 U.S. 119 (1977)
- Henderson v. Kibbe - 431 U.S. 145 (1977)
- Chappelle v. Greater Baton Rouge Airport Dist. - 431 U.S. 159 (1977)
- United States v. Wong - 431 U.S. 174 (1977)
- United States v. Washington - 431 U.S. 181 (1977)
- Territory of Guam v. Olsen - 431 U.S. 195 (1977)
- Abood v. Detroit Bd. of Educ. - 431 U.S. 209 (1977)
- Douglas v. Seacoast Products, Inc. - 431 U.S. 265 (1977)
- Smith v. United States - 431 U.S. 291 (1977)
- Connor v. Finch - 431 U.S. 407 (1977)
- Trainor v. Hernandez - 431 U.S. 434 (1977)
- Ohio Bureau of Employment Svcs. v. Hodory - 431 U.S. 471 (1977)
- Moore v. City of East Cleveland - 431 U.S. 494 (1977)
- Scarborough v. United States - 431 U.S. 563 (1977)
- Splawn v. California - 431 U.S. 595 (1977)
- United States v. Ramsey - 431 U.S. 606 (1977)
- Blackledge v. Allison - 431 U.S. 63 (1977)
- Roberts v. Louisiana - 431 U.S. 633 (1977)

- Abney v. United States - 431 U.S. 651 (1977)
- Carey v. Population Svcs. Int'l - 431 U.S. 678 (1977)
- Illinois Brick Co. v. Illinois - 431 U.S. 720 (1977)
- Ward v. Illinois - 431 U.S. 767 (1977)
- United States v. Lovasco - 431 U.S. 783 (1977)
- Lefkowitz v. Cunningham - 431 U.S. 801 (1977)
- Smith v. Organization of Foster Families - 431 U.S. 816 (1977)
- Linmark Assocs., Inc. v. Township of Willingboro - 431 U.S. 85 (1977)
- Nyquist v. Mauclet - 432 U.S. 1 (1977)
- Jeffers v. United States - 432 U.S. 137 (1977)
- Brown v. Ohio - 432 U.S. 161 (1977)
- Patterson v. New York - 432 U.S. 197 (1977)
- Lee v. United States - 432 U.S. 23 (1977)
- Hankerson v. North Carolina - 432 U.S. 233 (1977)
- Northeast Marine Terminal Co., Inc. v. Caputo - 432 U.S. 249 (1977)
- Dobbert v. Florida - 432 U.S. 282 (1977)
- Hunt v. Washington State Apple Advertising Comm'n - 432 U.S. 333 (1977)
- National Socialist Party of America v. Village of Skokie - 432 U.S. 43 (1977)
- Beal v. Doe - 432 U.S. 438 (1977)
- Maher v. Roe - 432 U.S. 464 (1977)
- Poelker v. Doe - 432 U.S. 519 (1977)
- Manson v. Brathwaite - 432 U.S. 98 (1977)
- United States v. Chadwick - 433 U.S. 1 (1977)
- Jones v. North Carolina Prisoners' Labor Union, Inc. - 433 U.S. 119 (1977)
- Puyallup Tribe, Inc. v. Department of Game - 433 U.S. 165 (1977)
- Shaffer v. Heitner - 433 U.S. 186 (1977)
- Wolman v. Walters - 433 U.S. 229 (1977)
- Milliken v. Bradley - 433 U.S. 267 (1977)
- Dothard v. Rawlinson - 433 U.S. 321 (1977)
- Bates v. State Bar of Arizona - 433 U.S. 350 (1977)
- Continental T.V., Inc. v. GTE Sylvania, Inc. - 433 U.S. 36 (1977)
- Dayton Bd. of Educ. v. Brinkman - 433 U.S. 406 (1977)
- Nixon v. Administrator of General Services - 433 U.S. 425 (1977)
- Zacchini v. Scripps-Howard Broadcasting Co. - 433 U.S. 562 (1977)
- Coker v. Georgia - 433 U.S. 584 (1977)
- Vendo Co. v. Lektro-Vend Corp. - 433 U.S. 623 (1977)
- Finch v. United States - 433 U.S. 676 (1977)
- Harris v. Oklahoma - 433 U.S. 682 (1977)
- Wainwright v. Sykes - 433 U.S. 72 (1977)
- Pennsylvania v. Mimms - 434 U.S. 106 (1977)
- New York v. Cathedral Academy - 434 U.S. 125 (1977)
- Nashville Gas Co. v. Satty - 434 U.S. 136 (1977)

- United States v. New York Telephone Co. - 434 U.S. 159 (1977)
- Rinaldi v. United States - 434 U.S. 22 (1977)
- Califano v. Jobst - 434 U.S. 47 (1977)
- County Bd. of Arlington County, Virginia v. Richards - 434 U.S. 5 (1977)
- Key v. Doyle - 434 U.S. 59 (1977)
- Philadelphia Newspapers, Inc. v. Jerome - 434 U.S. 241 (1978)
- Quilloin v. Walcott - 434 U.S. 246 (1978)
- Adamo Wrecking Co. v. United States - 434 U.S. 275 (1978)
- Carter v. Miller - 434 U.S. 356 (1978)
- Bordenkircher v. Hayes - 434 U.S. 357 (1978)
- Zablocki v. Redhail - 434 U.S. 374 (1978)
- Raymond Motor Transportation, Inc. v. Rice - 434 U.S. 429 (1978)
- United States Steel Corp. v. Multistate Tax Comm'n - 434 U.S. 452 (1978)
- Arizona v. Washington - 434 U.S. 497 (1978)
- United States v. Board of Comm'rs of Sheffield - 435 U.S. 110 (1978)
- Ray v. Atlantic Richfield Co. - 435 U.S. 151 (1978)
- Oliphant v. Suquamish Indian Tribe - 435 U.S. 191 (1978)
- Ballew v. Georgia - 435 U.S. 223 (1978)
- Carey v. Piphus - 435 U.S. 247 (1978)
- United States v. Ceccolini - 435 U.S. 268 (1978)
- Foley v. Connelie - 435 U.S. 291 (1978)
- United States v. Wheeler - 435 U.S. 313 (1978)
- Lakeside v. Oregon - 435 U.S. 333 (1978)
- Massachusetts v. United States - 435 U.S. 444 (1978)
- Holloway v. Arkansas - 435 U.S. 475 (1978)
- Nixon v. Warner Communications, Inc. - 435 U.S. 589 (1978)
- Simpson v. United States - 435 U.S. 6 (1978)
- McDaniel v. Paty - 435 U.S. 618 (1978)
- Elkins v. Moreno - 435 U.S. 647 (1978)
- City of Los Angeles v. Manhart - 435 U.S. 702 (1978)
- Department of Revenue v. Stevedoring Assn. - 435 U.S. 734 (1978)
- First Nat'l Bank of Boston v. Bellotti - 435 U.S. 765 (1978)
- Board of Curators, Univ. of Missouri v. Horowitz - 435 U.S. 78 (1978)
- Landmark Communications, Inc. v. Virginia - 435 U.S. 829 (1978)
- United States v. MacDonald - 435 U.S. 850 (1978)
- Memphis Light, Gas & Water Div. v. Craft - 436 U.S. 1 (1978)
- Scott v. United States - 436 U.S. 128 (1978)
- Flagg Bros., Inc. v. Brooks - 436 U.S. 149 (1978)
- Sears, Roebuck & Co. v. Carpenters - 436 U.S. 180 (1978)
- Pinkus v. United States - 436 U.S. 293 (1978)
- Marshall v. Barlow's, Inc. - 436 U.S. 307 (1978)
- Baldwin v. Fish & Game Comm'n of Montana - 436 U.S. 371 (1978)
- Ohralik v. Ohio State Bar Assn. - 436 U.S. 447 (1978)
- Taylor v. Kentucky - 436 U.S. 478 (1978)
- Santa Clara Pueblo v. Martinez - 436 U.S. 49 (1978)
- General Atomic Co. v. Felter - 436 U.S. 493 (1978)
- Michigan v. Tyler - 436 U.S. 499 (1978)
- Zurcher v. Stanford Daily - 436 U.S. 547 (1978)
- Monell v. Department of Soc. Svcs. - 436 U.S. 658 (1978)
- Agosto v. INS - 436 U.S. 748 (1978)
- FCC v. National Citizens Committee - 436 U.S. 775 (1978)
- Kulko v. Superior Ct. - 436 U.S. 84 (1978)
- Burks v. United States - 437 U.S. 1 (1978)
- Exxon Corp. v. Governor of Maryland - 437 U.S. 117 (1978)
- Greene v. Massey - 437 U.S. 19 (1978)
- Moorman Mfg. Co. v. Bair - 437 U.S. 267 (1978)
- Crist v. Bretz - 437 U.S. 28 (1978)
- Mincey v. Arizona - 437 U.S. 385 (1978)
- Hicklin v. Orbeck - 437 U.S. 518 (1978)
- Wise v. Lipscomb - 437 U.S. 535 (1978)
- Sanabria v. United States - 437 U.S. 54 (1978)
- California v. Texas - 437 U.S. 601 (1978)
- City of Philadelphia v. New Jersey - 437 U.S. 617 (1978)
- Will v. Calvert Fire Ins. Co. - 437 U.S. 655 (1978)
- Hutto v. Finney - 437 U.S. 678 (1978)
- Houchins v. KQED, Inc. - 438 U.S. 1 (1978)
- Penn Central Transportation Co. v. New York City - 438 U.S. 104 (1978)
- Franks v. Delaware - 438 U.S. 154 (1978)
- McAdams v. McSurely - 438 U.S. 189 (1978)
- Swisher v. Brady - 438 U.S. 204 (1978)
- Allied Structural Steel Co. v. Spannaus - 438 U.S. 234 (1978)
- Regents of Univ. of California v. Bakke - 438 U.S. 265 (1978)
- Butz v. Economou - 438 U.S. 478 (1978)
- Furnco Constr. Corp. v. Waters - 438 U.S. 567 (1978)
- Lockett v. Ohio - 438 U.S. 586 (1978)
- Duke Power Co. v. Carolina Env. Study Group - 438 U.S. 59 (1978)
- FCC v. Pacifica Foundation - 438 U.S. 726 (1978)
- Alabama v. Pugh - 438 U.S. 781 (1978)
- Rakas v. Illinois - 439 U.S. 128 (1978)
- Corbitt v. New Jersey - 439 U.S. 212 (1978)
- Lalli v. Lalli - 439 U.S. 259 (1978)

- Michigan v. Doran - 439 U.S. 282 (1978)
- Dougherty County Bd. of Educ. v. White - 439 U.S. 32 (1978)
- Holt Civic Club v. City of Tuscaloosa - 439 U.S. 60 (1978)
- New Motor Vehicle Bd. v. Orrin W. Fox Co. - 439 U.S. 96 (1978)
- Duren v. Missouri - 439 U.S. 357 (1979)
- Colautti v. Franklin - 439 U.S. 379 (1979)
- Givhan v. Western Line Cons. Sch. Dist. - 439 U.S. 410 (1979)
- Leis v. Flynt - 439 U.S. 438 (1979)
- Hisquierdo v. Hisquierdo - 439 U.S. 572 (1979)
- Friedman et al. v. Rogers et al. - 440 U.S. 1 (1979)
- Miller v. Youakim - 440 U.S. 125 (1979)
- Illinois State Bd. of Elections v. Socialist Workers Party - 440 U.S. 173 (1979)
- Aronson v. Quick Point Pencil Co. - 440 U.S. 257 (1979)
- Orr v. Orr - 440 U.S. 268 (1979)
- Quern v. Jordan - 440 U.S. 332 (1979)
- Scott v. Illinois - 440 U.S. 367 (1979)
- Lake County Estates v. Tahoe Reg. Planning Agency - 440 U.S. 391 (1979)
- Nevada v. Hall - 440 U.S. 410 (1979)
- NLRB v. Catholic Bishop of Chicago - 440 U.S. 490 (1979)
- New York Tel. Co. v. New York Dept. of Labor - 440 U.S. 519 (1979)
- New York City Transit Auth. v. Beazer - 440 U.S. 568 (1979)
- County of Los Angeles v. Davis - 440 U.S. 625 (1979)
- Delaware v. Prouse - 440 U.S. 648 (1979)
- United States v. Caceres - 440 U.S. 741 (1979)
- Vance v. Bradley - 440 U.S. 93 (1979)
- Burch v. Louisiana - 441 U.S. 130 (1979)
- Arizona Pub. Svc. Co. v. Snead - 441 U.S. 141 (1979)
- Herber v. Lando - 441 U.S. 153 (1979)
- Dalia v. United States - 441 U.S. 238 (1979)
- Chrysler Corp. v. Brown - 441 U.S. 281 (1979)
- Hughes v. Oklahoma - 441 U.S. 322 (1979)
- Parham v. Hughes - 441 U.S. 347 (1979)
- North Carolina v. Butler - 441 U.S. 369 (1979)
- Caban v. Mohammed - 441 U.S. 380 (1979)
- Addington v. Texas - 441 U.S. 418 (1979)
- Japan Line, Ltd. v. County of Los Angeles - 441 U.S. 434 (1979)
- Smith v. Arkansas State Hwy. Employees Local - 441 U.S. 463 (1979)
- United States v. 564.54 Acres of Land - 441 U.S. 506 (1979)
- Bell v. Wolfish - 441 U.S. 520 (1979)
- Chapman v. Houston Welfare Rights Organization - 441 U.S. 600 (1979)
- Cannon v. University of Chicago - 441 U.S. 677 (1979)
- Ambach v. Norwick - 441 U.S. 68 (1979)
- Kentucky v. Whorton - 441 U.S. 786 (1979)
- Gladstone, Realtors v. Village of Bellwood - 441 U.S. 91 (1979)
- Greenholtz v. Inmates of Nebraska Penal Complex - 442 U.S. 1 (1979)
- County Court of Ulster County v. Allen - 442 U.S. 140 (1979)
- Dunaway v. New York - 442 U.S. 200 (1979)
- Davis v. Passman - 442 U.S. 228 (1979)
- Personnel Adm'r of Massachusetts v. Feeney - 442 U.S. 256 (1979)
- Babbitt v. United Farm Workers Nat'l Union - 442 U.S. 289 (1979)
- Lo-Ji Sales, Inc. v. New York - 442 U.S. 319 (1979)
- Moore v. Sims - 442 U.S. 415 (1979)
- Torres v. Puerto Rico - 442 U.S. 465 (1979)
- United States v. Helstoski - 442 U.S. 500 (1979)
- Sandstrom v. Montana - 442 U.S. 510 (1979)
- Parham v. J.R. - 442 U.S. 584 (1979)
- Parker v. Randolph - 442 U.S. 62 (1979)
- Secretary of Pub. Welfare v. Institutionalized Juveniles - 442 U.S. 640 (1979)
- Fare v. Michael C. - 442 U.S. 707 (1979)
- Smith v. Maryland - 442 U.S. 735 (1979)
- Mackey v. Montrym - 443 U.S. 1 (1979)
- Hutchinson v. Proxmire - 443 U.S. 111 (1979)
- Wolston v. Reader's Digest Assn., Inc. - 443 U.S. 157 (1979)
- Steelworkers v. Weber - 443 U.S. 193 (1979)
- Califano v. Boles - 443 U.S. 282 (1979)
- Jackson v. Virginia - 443 U.S. 307 (1979)
- Michigan v. DeFillippo - 443 U.S. 31 (1979)
- Gannett Co., Inc. v. DePasquale - 443 U.S. 368 (1979)
- Columbus Bd. of Educ. v. Penick - 443 U.S. 449 (1979)
- Brown v. Texas - 443 U.S. 47 (1979)
- Dayton Bd. of Educ. v. Brinkman - 443 U.S. 526 (1979)
- Rose v. Mitchell - 443 U.S. 545 (1979)
- Barry v. Barchi - 443 U.S. 55 (1979)
- Jones v. Wolf - 443 U.S. 595 (1979)
- Bellotti v. Baird - 443 U.S. 622 (1979)
- Morland v. Sprecher - 443 U.S. 709 (1979)
- Califano v. Westcott - 443 U.S. 76 (1979)
- Smith v. Daily Mail Pub. Co. - 443 U.S. 97 (1979)
- Kaiser Aetna v. United States - 444 U.S. 164 (1979)
- Vaughn v. Vermilion Corp. - 444 U.S. 206 (1979)
- Andrus v. Allard - 444 U.S. 51 (1979)
- Ybarra v. Illinois - 444 U.S. 85 (1979)
- McLain v. Real Estate Board of New Orleans, Inc. - 444 U.S. 232 (1980)
- Vance v. Terrazas - 444 U.S. 252 (1980)
- Martinez v. California - 444 U.S. 277 (1980)

- World-Wide Volkwagen Corp. v. Woodson - 444 U.S. 286 (1980)
- Rush v. Savchuk - 444 U.S. 320 (1980)
- Brown v. Glines - 444 U.S. 348 (1980)
- Idaho ex rel. Evans v. Oregon - 444 U.S. 380 (1980)
- Secretary of Navy v. Huff - 444 U.S. 453 (1980)
- Tague v. Louisiana - 444 U.S. 469 (1980)
- Snepp v. United States - 444 U.S. 507 (1980)
- Schaumburg v. Citizens for Better Environment - 444 U.S. 620 (1980)
- Committee for Pub. Educ. v. Regan - 444 U.S. 646 (1980)
- NLRB v. Yeshiva Univ. - 444 U.S. 672 (1980)
- United States v. Apfelbaum - 445 U.S. 115 (1980)
- United States v. Clarke - 445 U.S. 253 (1980)
- Rummel v. Estelle - 445 U.S. 263 (1980)
- Vance v. Universal Amusement Co., Inc. - 445 U.S. 308 (1980)
- Deposit Guar. Nat'l Bank of Jackson v. Roper - 445 U.S. 326 (1980)
- United States Parole Comm'n v. Geraghty - 445 U.S. 388 (1980)
- Trammel v. United States - 445 U.S. 40 (1980)
- Mobil Oil Corp. v. Commissioner of Taxes - 445 U.S. 425 (1980)
- United States v. Crews - 445 U.S. 463 (1980)
- Vitek v. Jones - 445 U.S. 480 (1980)
- Branti v. Finkel - 445 U.S. 507 (1980)
- Lewis v. United States - 445 U.S. 55 (1980)
- Payton v. New York - 445 U.S. 573 (1980)
- Whalen v. United States - 445 U.S. 684 (1980)
- Cal. Liquor Dealers v. Midcal Aluminum, Inc. - 445 U.S. 97 (1980)
- Carlson v. Green - 446 U.S. 14 (1980)
- Wengler v. Druggists Mut. Ins. Co. - 446 U.S. 142 (1980)
- City of Rome v. United States - 446 U.S. 156 (1980)
- Baldasar v. Illinois - 446 U.S. 222 (1980)
- Rhode Island v. Innis - 446 U.S. 291 (1980)
- Cuyler v. Sullivan - 446 U.S. 335 (1980)
- Godfrey v. Georgia - 446 U.S. 420 (1980)
- Navarro Savings Assn. v. Lee - 446 U.S. 458 (1980)
- United States v. Mendenhall - 446 U.S. 544 (1980)
- City of Mobile v. Bolden - 446 U.S. 55 (1980)
- Harrison v. PPG Industries, Inc. - 446 U.S. 578 (1980)
- Harris v. Rosario - 446 U.S. 651 (1980)
- Supreme Court of Virginia v. Consumers Union - 446 U.S. 719 (1980)
- Washington v. Confederated Tribes - 447 U.S. 134 (1980)
- Exxon Corp. v. Department of Rev. of Wisconsin - 447 U.S. 207 (1980)
- Jenkins v. Anderson - 447 U.S. 231 (1980)
- Agins v. City of Tiburon - 447 U.S. 255 (1980)
- Lewis v. BT Investment Managers, Inc. - 447 U.S. 27 (1980)
- Brown v. Louisiana - 447 U.S. 323 (1980)
- Hicks v. Oklahoma - 447 U.S. 343 (1980)
- Bryant v. Yellen - 447 U.S. 352 (1980)
- Illinois v. Vitale - 447 U.S. 410 (1980)
- Reeves, Inc. v. Stake - 447 U.S. 429 (1980)
- Carey v. Brown - 447 U.S. 455 (1980)
- Consolidated Edison Co. v. Public Svc. Comm'n - 447 U.S. 530 (1980)
- New York Gaslight Club, Inc. v. Carey - 447 U.S. 54 (1980)
- Central Hudson Gas & Elec. v. Public Svc. Comm'n - 447 U.S. 557 (1980)
- NLRB v. Retail Store Employees Union - 447 U.S. 607 (1980)
- Beck v. Alabama - 447 U.S. 625 (1980)
- Walter v. United States - 447 U.S. 649 (1980)
- United States v. Raddatz - 447 U.S. 667 (1980)
- Sun Ship, Inc. v. Pennsylvania - 447 U.S. 715 (1980)
- United States v. Payner - 447 U.S. 727 (1980)
- Pruneyard Shopping Ctr. v. Robins - 447 U.S. 74 (1980)
- Roadway Express, Inc. v. Piper - 447 U.S. 752 (1980)
- O'Bannon v. Town Court Nursing Ctr. - 447 U.S. 773 (1980)
- Maine v. Thiboutot - 448 U.S. 1 (1980)
- Maher v. Gagne - 448 U.S. 122 (1980)
- White Mountain Apache Tribe v. Bracker - 448 U.S. 136 (1980)
- Central Machinery Co. v. Tax Commission - 448 U.S. 160 (1980)
- Thomas v. Washington Gas Light Co. - 448 U.S. 261 (1980)
- Harris v. McRae - 448 U.S. 297 (1980)
- Adams v. Texas - 448 U.S. 38 (1980)
- Reid v. Georgia - 448 U.S. 438 (1980)
- Fullilove v. Klutznick - 448 U.S. 448 (1980)
- Richmond Newspapers, Inc. v. Virginia - 448 U.S. 555 (1980)
- Ohio v. Roberts - 448 U.S. 56 (1980)
- Indus. Union Dept. v. Amer. Petroleum Inst. - 448 U.S. 607 (1980)
- Rawlings v. Kentucky - 448 U.S. 98 (1980)
- Colorado v. Bannister - 449 U.S. 1 (1980)
- United States v. DiFrancesco - 449 U.S. 117 (1980)
- Webb's Fabulous Pharmacies, Inc. v. Beckwith - 449 U.S. 155 (1980)
- United States. R. Retirement Bd. v. Fritz - 449 U.S. 166 (1980)
- United States v. Will - 449 U.S. 200 (1980)
- Stone v. Graham - 449 U.S. 39 (1980)
- Allen v. McCurry - 449 U.S. 90 (1980)
- United States v. Darusmont - 449 U.S. 292 (1981)
- Allstate Ins. Co. v. Hague - 449 U.S. 302 (1981)

- Watkins v. Sowders - 449 U.S. 341 (1981)
- United States v. Morrison - 449 U.S. 361 (1981)
- United States v. Cortez - 449 U.S. 411 (1981)
- Minnesota v. Clover Leaf Creamery Co. - 449 U.S. 456 (1981)
- Fedorenko v. United States - 449 U.S. 490 (1981)
- Sumner v. Mata - 449 U.S. 539 (1981)
- Chandler v. Florida - 449 U.S. 560 (1981)
- Democratic Party v. Wisconsin ex rel. La Follette - 450 U.S. 107 (1981)
- Florida DHRS v. Florida Nursing Home Assn. - 450 U.S. 147 (1981)
- Diamond v. Diehr - 450 U.S. 175 (1981)
- Schweiker v. Wilson - 450 U.S. 221 (1981)
- Weaver v. Graham - 450 U.S. 24 (1981)
- Wood v. Georgia - 450 U.S. 261 (1981)
- Carter v. Kentucky - 450 U.S. 288 (1981)
- Chicago & N.W. Transp. Co. v. Kalo Brick - 450 U.S. 311 (1981)
- Albernaz v. United States - 450 U.S. 333 (1981)
- H. L. v. Matheson - 450 U.S. 398 (1981)
- Hudson v. Louisiana - 450 U.S. 40 (1981)
- Kirchberg v. Feenstra - 450 U.S. 455 (1981)
- Michael M. v. Superior Ct. - 450 U.S. 464 (1981)
- Rosewell v. LaSalle Nat'l Bank - 450 U.S. 503 (1981)
- Montana v. United States - 450 U.S. 544 (1981)
- San Diego Gas & Elec. Co. v. City of San Diego - 450 U.S. 621 (1981)
- Kassel v. Consolidated Freightways Corp. - 450 U.S. 662 (1981)
- Thomas v. Review Bd., Ind. Empl. Sec. Div. - 450 U.S. 707 (1981)
- Pennhurst State Sch. & Hosp. v. Halderman - 451 U.S. 1 (1981)
- City of Memphis v. Greene - 451 U.S. 100 (1981)
- Scindia Steam Nav. Co., Ltd. v. Santos - 451 U.S. 156 (1981)
- Rosales-Lopez v. United States - 451 U.S. 182 (1981)
- Steagald v. United States - 451 U.S. 204 (1981)
- California v. Sierra Club - 451 U.S. 287 (1981)
- City of Milwaukee v. Illinois - 451 U.S. 304 (1981)
- Ball v. James - 451 U.S. 355 (1981)
- Bullington v. Missouri - 451 U.S. 430 (1981)
- Estelle v. Smith - 451 U.S. 454 (1981)
- Edwards v. Arizona - 451 U.S. 477 (1981)
- Webb v. Webb - 451 U.S. 493 (1981)
- Alessi v. Raybestos-Manhattan, Inc. - 451 U.S. 504 (1981)
- Parratt v. Taylor - 451 U.S. 527 (1981)
- Flynt v. Ohio - 451 U.S. 619 (1981)

- Texas Indus., Inc. v. Radcliff Materials, Inc. - 451 U.S. 630 (1981)
- W. & S. Life Ins. Co. v. Board of Equalization - 451 U.S. 648 (1981)
- Maryland v. Louisiana - 451 U.S. 725 (1981)
- Little v. Streater - 452 U.S. 1 (1981)
- Minnick v. California Dept. of Corrections - 452 U.S. 105 (1981)
- County of Washington v. Gunther - 452 U.S. 161 (1981)
- Lassiter v. Department of Social Svcs. - 452 U.S. 18 (1981)
- Hodel v. Virginia Surface Mining - 452 U.S. 264 (1981)
- Hodel v. Indiana - 452 U.S. 314 (1981)
- Rhodes v. Chapman - 452 U.S. 337 (1981)
- Jones v. Helms - 452 U.S. 412 (1981)
- Connecticut Bd. of Pardons v. Dumschat - 452 U.S. 458 (1981)
- American Textile Mfrs. Inst., Inc. v. Donovan - 452 U.S. 490 (1981)
- Donovan v. Dewey - 452 U.S. 594 (1981)
- Schad v. Borough of Mount Ephraim - 452 U.S. 61 (1981)
- Heffron v. Soc'y for Krishna Consciousness - 452 U.S. 640 (1981)
- Michigan v. Summers - 452 U.S. 692 (1981)
- New York State Liquor Auth. v. Bellanca - 452 U.S. 714 (1981)
- Middlesex County Sewerage Auth. v. Sea Clammers - 453 U.S. 1 (1981)
- USPS v. Council of Greenburgh Civic Assns. - 453 U.S. 114 (1981)
- California Med. Assn. v. FEC - 453 U.S. 182 (1981)
- McCarty v. McCarty - 453 U.S. 210 (1981)
- Haig v. Agee - 453 U.S. 280 (1981)
- California v. Prysock - 453 U.S. 355 (1981)
- CBS, Inc. v. FCC - 453 U.S. 367 (1981)
- Robbins v. California - 453 U.S. 420 (1981)
- New York v. Belton - 453 U.S. 454 (1981)
- Gulf Offshore Co. v. Mobil Oil Corp. - 453 U.S. 473 (1981)
- Metromedia, Inc. v. City of San Diego - 453 U.S. 490 (1981)
- Rostker v. Goldberg - 453 U.S. 57 (1981)
- Commonwealth Edison Co. v. Montana - 453 U.S. 609 (1981)
- Dames & Moore v. Regan - 453 U.S. 654 (1981)
- Fair Assessment in Real Estate Assn. v. McNary - 454 U.S. 100 (1981)
- Jago v. Van Curen - 454 U.S. 14 (1981)
- Watt v. Energy Action Educ. Foundation - 454 U.S. 151 (1981)
- Widmar v. Vincent - 454 U.S. 263 (1981)
- Citizens Against Rent Control v. City of Berkeley - 454 U.S. 290 (1981)
- Ridgway v. Ridgway - 454 U.S. 46 (1981)
- Hutto v. Davis - 454 U.S. 370 (1982)
- Cabell v. Chavez-Salido - 454 U.S. 432 (1982)

- Valley Forge Coll. v. Americans United - 454 U.S. 464 (1982)
- Texaco, Inc. v. Short - 454 U.S. 516 (1982)
- Washington v. Chrisman - 455 U.S. 1 (1982)
- Princeton Univ. v. Schmid - 455 U.S. 100 (1982)
- Eddings v. Oklahoma - 455 U.S. 104 (1982)
- Merrion v. Jicarilla Apache Tribe - 455 U.S. 130 (1982)
- Smith v. Phillips - 455 U.S. 209 (1982)
- United States v. Lee - 455 U.S. 252 (1982)
- City of Mesquite v. Aladdin's Castle, Inc. - 455 U.S. 283 (1982)
- New England Power Co. v. New Hampshire - 455 U.S. 331 (1982)
- Havens Realty Corp. v. Coleman - 455 U.S. 363 (1982)
- G. D. Searle & Co. v. Cohn - 455 U.S. 404 (1982)
- Logan v. Zimmerman Brush Co. - 455 U.S. 422 (1982)
- Railway Labor Executives' Assn. v. Gibbons - 455 U.S. 457 (1982)
- Murphy v. Hunt - 455 U.S. 478 (1982)
- Hoffman Estates v. The Flipside, Hoffman Estates - 455 U.S. 489 (1982)
- Rose v. Lundy - 455 U.S. 509 (1982)
- Wainright v. Torna - 455 U.S. 586 (1982)
- Sumner v. Mata - 455 U.S. 591 (1982)
- Lane v. Williams - 455 U.S. 624 (1982)
- McElroy v. United States - 455 U.S. 642 (1982)
- United Transp. Union v. Long Island R. Co. - 455 U.S. 678 (1982)
- Underwriters Nat'l Assur. v. N.C. Life & Acc. - 455 U.S. 691 (1982)
- United States v. New Mexico - 455 U.S. 720 (1982)
- Santosky v. Kramer - 455 U.S. 745 (1982)
- United States v. MacDonald - 456 U.S. 1 (1982)
- Engle v. Isaac - 456 U.S. 107 (1982)
- Schweiker v. McClure - 456 U.S. 188 (1982)
- Longshoremen v. Allied Int'l, Inc. - 456 U.S. 212 (1982)
- Larson v. Valente - 456 U.S. 228 (1982)
- Weinberger v. Rossi - 456 U.S. 25 (1982)
- Merrill Lynch v. Curran - 456 U.S. 353 (1982)
- Greene v. Lindsey - 456 U.S. 444 (1982)
- Brown v. Hartlage - 456 U.S. 45 (1982)
- Kremer v. Chemical Constr. Corp. - 456 U.S. 461 (1982)
- American Soc'y of Mech. Eng'rs v. Hydrolevel - 456 U.S. 556 (1982)
- Hopper v. Evans - 456 U.S. 605 (1982)
- Oregon v. Kennedy - 456 U.S. 667 (1982)
- FERC v. Mississippi - 456 U.S. 742 (1982)
- United States v. Ross - 456 U.S. 798 (1982)
- Mills v. Habluetzel - 456 U.S. 91 (1982)

- Rodriguez v. Popular Democratic Party - 457 U.S. 1 (1982)
- Blum v. Bacon - 457 U.S. 132 (1982)
- California v. Texas - 457 U.S. 164 (1982)
- Plyler v. Doe - 457 U.S. 202 (1982)
- Mills v. Rogers - 457 U.S. 291 (1982)
- Youngberg v. Romeo - 457 U.S. 307 (1982)
- Tibbs v. Florida - 457 U.S. 31 (1982)
- California v. Grace Brethren Church - 457 U.S. 393 (1982)
- Middlesex County Ethics Comm. v. Bar Assn. - 457 U.S. 423 (1982)
- Patsy v. Board of Regents of State of Florida - 457 U.S. 496 (1982)
- Zobel v. Williams - 457 U.S. 55 (1982)
- Schmidt v. Oakland Unif. Sch. Dist. - 457 U.S. 594 (1982)
- Globe Newspaper Co. v. Superior Ct. - 457 U.S. 596 (1982)
- Edgar v. MITE Corp. - 457 U.S. 624 (1982)
- Foremost Ins. Co. v. Richardson - 457 U.S. 668 (1982)
- Taylor v. Alabama - 457 U.S. 687 (1982)
- Nixon v. Fitzgerald - 457 U.S. 731 (1982)
- Harlow v. Fitzgerald - 457 U.S. 800 (1982)
- Rendell-Baker v. Kohn - 457 U.S. 830 (1982)
- Cory v. White - 457 U.S. 85 (1982)
- Lugar v. Edmondson Oil Co., Inc. - 457 U.S. 922 (1982)
- Clements v. Fashing - 457 U.S. 957 (1982)
- Blum v. Yaretsky - 457 U.S. 991 (1982)
- Toll v. Moreno - 458 U.S. 1 (1982)
- Fidelity Fed. S. & L. v. De la Cuesta - 458 U.S. 141 (1982)
- Michigan v. Thomas - 458 U.S. 259 (1982)
- Asarco Inc. v. Idaho State Tax Comm'n - 458 U.S. 307 (1982)
- Woolworth Co. v. Taxation Dept. - 458 U.S. 354 (1982)
- General Bldg. Contractors Assn., Inc. v. Pennsylvania - 458 U.S. 375 (1982)
- Loretto v. Teleprompter Manhattan CATV Corp. - 458 U.S. 419 (1982)
- Washington v. Seattle Sch. Dist. No. 1 - 458 U.S. 457 (1982)
- Northern Pipeline v. Marathon Pipe Line - 458 U.S. 50 (1982)
- Crawford v. Los Angeles Board of Educ. - 458 U.S. 527 (1982)
- Snapp & Son, Inc. v. Puerto Rico ex rel. Barez - 458 U.S. 592 (1982)
- Rogers v. Lodge - 458 U.S. 613 (1982)
- Florida Dept. of State v. Treasure Salvors, Inc. - 458 U.S. 670 (1982)
- Mississippi Univ. for Women v. Hogan - 458 U.S. 718 (1982)
- New York v. Ferber - 458 U.S. 747 (1982)
- Enmund v. Florida - 458 U.S. 782 (1982)
- Ramah Navajo Sch. Bd., Inc. v. Bureau of Rev. - 458 U.S. 832 (1982)
- United States v. Valenzuela-Bernal - 458 U.S. 858 (1982)

- NAACP v. Claiborne Hardware Co. - 458 U.S. 886 (1982)
- Sporhase v. Nebraska ex rel. Douglas - 458 U.S. 941 (1982)
- Larkin v. Grendel's Den, Inc. - 459 U.S. 116 (1982)
- Xerox Corp. v. County of Harris - 459 U.S. 145 (1982)
- FEC v. National Right to Work Comm. - 459 U.S. 197 (1982)
- Brown v. Socialist Workers Comm. - 459 U.S. 87 (1982)
- Pillsbury Co. v. Conboy - 459 U.S. 248 (1983)
- Director, OWCP v. Perini North River Assocs. - 459 U.S. 297 (1983)
- Missouri v. Hunter - 459 U.S. 359 (1983)
- Memphis Bank & Trust Co. v. Garner - 459 U.S. 392 (1983)
- Marshall v. Lonberger - 459 U.S. 422 (1983)
- South Dakota v. Neville - 459 U.S. 553 (1983)
- Cone Mem. Hosp. v. Mercury Constr. Corp. - 460 U.S. 1 (1983)
- White v. Mass. Council of Constr. Employers - 460 U.S. 204 (1983)
- EEOC v. Wyoming - 460 U.S. 226 (1983)
- United States v. Knotts - 460 U.S. 276 (1983)
- Perry Educ. Ass'n v. Perry Educators' Ass'n - 460 U.S. 37 (1983)
- District of Columbia Ct. of Appeals v. Feldman - 460 U.S. 462 (1983)
- Florida v. Royer - 460 U.S. 491 (1983)
- Minneapolis Star v. Minnesota Comm'r - 460 U.S. 575 (1983)
- Operating Engineers v. Jones - 460 U.S. 669 (1983)
- Texas v. Brown - 460 U.S. 730 (1983)
- United States v. Rylander - 460 U.S. 752 (1983)
- Anderson v. Celebrezze - 460 U.S. 780 (1983)
- Morris v. Slappy - 461 U.S. 1 (1983)
- Connick v. Myers - 461 U.S. 138 (1983)
- PG & E v. State Energy Comm'n - 461 U.S. 190 (1983)
- Olim v. Wakinekona - 461 U.S. 238 (1983)
- Block v. Board of School Lands - 461 U.S. 273 (1983)
- Martinez v. Bynum - 461 U.S. 321 (1983)
- Kolender v. Lawson - 461 U.S. 352 (1983)
- Verlinden B.V. v. Central Bank of Nigeria - 461 U.S. 480 (1983)
- Regan v. Taxation With Representation - 461 U.S. 540 (1983)
- Bob Jones Univ. v. United States - 461 U.S. 574 (1983)
- Bearden v. Georgia - 461 U.S. 660 (1983)
- Bell v. New Jersey - 461 U.S. 773 (1983)
- City of Los Angeles v. Lyons - 461 U.S. 95 (1983)

- Pickett v. Brown - 462 U.S. 1 (1983)
- Idaho v. Evans - 462 U.S. 1017 (1983)
- Exxon Corp. v. Eagerton - 462 U.S. 176 (1983)
- FTC v. Grolier, Inc. - 462 U.S. 19 (1983)
- Illinois v. Gates - 462 U.S. 213 (1983)
- Chappell v. Wallace - 462 U.S. 296 (1983)
- New Mexico v. Mescalero Apache Tribe - 462 U.S. 324 (1983)
- Bush v. Lucas - 462 U.S. 367 (1983)
- Philko Aviation, Inc. v. Shacket - 462 U.S. 406 (1983)
- Akron v. Akron Ctr. for Reprod. Health - 462 U.S. 416 (1983)
- Planned Parenthood Assn. v. Ashcroft - 462 U.S. 476 (1983)
- Simopoulos v. Virginia - 462 U.S. 506 (1983)
- Texas v. New Mexico - 462 U.S. 554 (1983)
- United States v. Villamonte-Marquez - 462 U.S. 579 (1983)
- FNC Bank v. Banco Para el Comercio - 462 U.S. 611 (1983)
- Illinois v. Lafayette - 462 U.S. 640 (1983)
- United States v. Place - 462 U.S. 696 (1983)
- Karcher v. Daggett - 462 U.S. 725 (1983)
- United States v. Ptasynski - 462 U.S. 74 (1983)
- Mennonite Bd. of Missions v. Adams - 462 U.S. 791 (1983)
- Brown v. Thomson - 462 U.S. 835 (1983)
- Zant v. Stephens - 462 U.S. 862 (1983)
- INS v. Chadha - 462 U.S. 919 (1983)
- Franchise Tax Bd. v. Construction Laborers - 463 U.S. 1 (1983)
- Michigan v. Long - 463 U.S. 1032 (1983)
- Arizona Governing Comm. v. Norris - 463 U.S. 1073 (1983)
- Nevada v. United States - 463 U.S. 110 (1983)
- Container Corp. v. Franchise Tax Bd. - 463 U.S. 159 (1983)
- United States v. Mitchell - 463 U.S. 206 (1983)
- Lehr v. Robertson - 463 U.S. 248 (1983)
- Solem v. Helm - 463 U.S. 277 (1983)
- Motor Veh. Mfrs. Ass'n v. State Farm Ins. - 463 U.S. 29 (1983)
- Jones v. United States - 463 U.S. 354 (1983)
- Mueller v. Allen - 463 U.S. 388 (1983)
- Belknap, Inc. v. Hale - 463 U.S. 491 (1983)
- Arizona v. San Carlos Apache Tribe - 463 U.S. 545 (1983)
- Bolger v. Youngs Drug Products Corp. - 463 U.S. 60 (1983)
- Rice v. Rehner - 463 U.S. 713 (1983)
- Jones v. Barnes - 463 U.S. 745 (1983)
- Illinois v. Andreas - 463 U.S. 765 (1983)
- Marsh v. Chambers - 463 U.S. 783 (1983)
- Shaw v. Delta Air Lines, Inc. - 463 U.S. 85 (1983)
- American B. & T. v. Dallas County - 463 U.S. 855 (1983)
- Barefoot v. Estelle - 463 U.S. 880 (1983)
- California v. Ramos - 463 U.S. 992 (1983)

- Ohio v. Kovacs - 469 U.S. 274 (1985)
- New Jersey v. T.L.O. - 469 U.S. 325 (1985)
- Evitts v. Lucey - 469 U.S. 387 (1985)
- Wainwright v. Witt - 469 U.S. 412 (1985)
- United States v. Maine - 469 U.S. 504 (1985)
- Garcia v. San Antonio Transit Auth. - 469 U.S. 528 (1985)
- United States v. Young - 470 U.S. 1 (1985)
- Oneida County v. Oneida Ind. Nation - 470 U.S. 226 (1985)
- Supreme Court of N.H. v. Piper - 470 U.S. 274 (1985)
- Oregon v. Elstad - 470 U.S. 298 (1985)
- FEC v. NCPAC - 470 U.S. 480 (1985)
- Shea v. Louisiana - 470 U.S. 51 (1985)
- Cleveland Bd. of Educ. v. Loudermill - 470 U.S. 532 (1985)
- FNB Atlanta v. County Tax Assessors - 470 U.S. 583 (1985)
- Wayte v. United States - 470 U.S. 598 (1985)
- Bennett v. New Jersey - 470 U.S. 632 (1985)
- Bennett v. Kentucky DOE - 470 U.S. 656 (1985)
- Winston v. Lee - 470 U.S. 753 (1985)
- Hayes v. Florida - 470 U.S. 811 (1985)
- Metropolitan Life Ins. Co. v. Ward - 470 U.S. 869 (1985)
- Tennessee v. Garner - 471 U.S. 1 (1985)
- United States v. Miller - 471 U.S. 130 (1985)
- CIA v. Sims - 471 U.S. 159 (1985)
- Allis-Chalmers Corp. v. Lueck - 471 U.S. 202 (1985)
- Hunter v. Underwood - 471 U.S. 222 (1985)
- Alamo Found'n v. Secy. of Labor - 471 U.S. 290 (1985)
- Francis v. Franklin - 471 U.S. 307 (1985)
- California v. Carney - 471 U.S. 386 (1985)
- Tennessee v. Street - 471 U.S. 409 (1985)
- Burger King Corp. v. Rudzewicz - 471 U.S. 462 (1985)
- Ponte v. Real - 471 U.S. 491 (1985)
- Harper & Row v. Nation Enterprises - 471 U.S. 539 (1985)
- Black v. Romano - 471 U.S. 606 (1985)
- Zauderer v. Office of Disc. Counsel - 471 U.S. 626 (1985)
- Hillsborough County v. Auto. Med. Labs. - 471 U.S. 707 (1985)
- Metropolitan Life v. Massachusetts - 471 U.S. 724 (1985)
- Montana v. Blackfeet Tribe - 471 U.S. 759 (1985)
- Garrett v. United States - 471 U.S. 773 (1985)
- United States v. Locke - 471 U.S. 84 (1985)
- NFU Ins. Cos. v. Crow Tribe - 471 U.S. 845 (1985)
- Russell v. United States - 471 U.S. 858 (1985)
- Williams v. Vermont - 472 U.S. 14 (1985)

- Caldwell v. Mississippi - 472 U.S. 320 (1985)
- Baldwin v. Alabama - 472 U.S. 372 (1985)
- Wallace v. Jaffree - 472 U.S. 38 (1985)
- Superintendent v. Hill - 472 U.S. 445 (1985)
- Maryland v. Macon - 472 U.S. 463 (1985)
- Jensen, v. Quaring - 472 U.S. 478 (1985)
- McDonald v. Smith - 472 U.S. 479 (1985)
- Brockett v. Spokane Arcades, Inc. - 472 U.S. 491 (1985)
- Mitchell v. Forsyth - 472 U.S. 511 (1985)
- Hooper v. Bernalillo County Assessor - 472 U.S. 612 (1985)
- United States v. Albertini - 472 U.S. 675 (1985)
- Estate of Thornton v. Caldor, Inc. - 472 U.S. 703 (1985)
- Dun & Bradstreet, Inc. v. Greenmoss Builders - 472 U.S. 749 (1985)
- Phillips Petroleum Co. v. Shutts - 472 U.S. 797 (1985)
- Jean v. Nelson - 472 U.S. 846 (1985)
- Williamson Cty. Planning v. Hamilton Bank - 473 U.S. 172 (1985)
- Walters v. Radiation Survivors - 473 U.S. 305 (1985)
- Grand Rapids Sch. Dist. v. Ball - 473 U.S. 373 (1985)
- Aguilar v. Felton - 473 U.S. 402 (1985)
- Cleburne v. Cleburne Living Ctr. - 473 U.S. 432 (1985)
- United States v. Montoya de Hernandez - 473 U.S. 531 (1985)
- Thomas v. Union Carbide - 473 U.S. 568 (1985)
- United States v. Bagley - 473 U.S. 667 (1985)
- Cornelius v. NAACP Leg. Def. Fund - 473 U.S. 788 (1985)
- Miller v. Fenton - 474 U.S. 104 (1985)
- United States v. Riverside Bayview - 474 U.S. 121 (1985)
- Thomas v. Arn - 474 U.S. 140 (1985)
- Delaware v. Fensterer - 474 U.S. 15 (1985)
- Univ. of Michigan v. Ewing - 474 U.S. 214 (1985)
- Pa. Bur. of Corr. v. Marshals Svc. - 474 U.S. 34 (1985)
- Hill v. Lockhart - 474 U.S. 52 (1985)
- Green v. Mansour - 474 U.S. 64 (1985)
- Heath v. Alabama - 474 U.S. 82 (1985)
- Ake v. Oklahoma - 470 U.S. 68 (1986)
- Vasquez v. Hillery - 474 U.S. 254 (1986)
- Wainwright v. Greenfield - 474 U.S. 284 (1986)
- United States v. Loud Hawk - 474 U.S. 302 (1986)
- Daniels v. Williams - 474 U.S. 327 (1986)
- Davidson v. Cannon - 474 U.S. 344 (1986)
- Cabana v. Bullock - 474 U.S. 376 (1986)
- Transcontinental Gas v. State Oil Bd. - 474 U.S. 409 (1986)
- United States v. Lane - 474 U.S. 438 (1986)

- Witters v. Svcs. for the Blind - 474 U.S. 481 (1986)
- PG&E v. Public Utilities Comm'n - 475 U.S. 1 (1986)
- New York v. Class - 475 U.S. 106 (1986)
- Texas v. McCullough - 475 U.S. 134 (1986)
- Nix v. Whiteside - 475 U.S. 157 (1986)
- Connolly v. PBGC - 475 U.S. 211 (1986)
- Morris v. Mathews - 475 U.S. 237 (1986)
- Wis. Dept. of Indus. v. Gould, Inc. - 475 U.S. 282 (1986)
- Chicago Teachers Union v. Hudson - 475 U.S. 292 (1986)
- Whitley v. Albers - 475 U.S. 312 (1986)
- Malley v. Briggs - 475 U.S. 335 (1986)
- Exxon Corp. v. Hunt - 475 U.S. 355 (1986)
- City of Renton v. Playtime Theatres - 475 U.S. 41 (1986)
- Moran v. Burbine - 475 U.S. 412 (1986)
- Goldman v. Weinberger - 475 U.S. 503 (1986)
- Bender v. Williamsport Area Sch. Dist. - 475 U.S. 534 (1986)
- Holbrook v. Flynn - 475 U.S. 560 (1986)
- Golden State Transit Corp. v. Los Angeles - 475 U.S. 608 (1986)
- Michigan v. Jackson - 475 U.S. 625 (1986)
- Philadelphia Newspapers v. Hepps - 475 U.S. 767 (1986)
- Aetna Life Ins. Co. v. Lavoie - 475 U.S. 813 (1986)
- New York v. P. J. Video, Inc. - 475 U.S. 868 (1986)
- United States v. Maine - 475 U.S. 89 (1986)
- Skipper v. South Carolina - 476 U.S. 1 (1986)
- Smalis v. Pennsylvania - 476 U.S. 140 (1986)
- Lockhart v. McCree - 476 U.S. 162 (1986)
- California v. Ciraolo - 476 U.S. 207 (1986)
- Dow Chemical Co. v. United States - 476 U.S. 227 (1986)
- Wygant v. Jackson Bd. of Educ. - 476 U.S. 267 (1986)
- Turner v. Murray - 476 U.S. 28 (1986)
- La. Pub. Svc. Comm'n v. FCC - 476 U.S. 355 (1986)
- ILA v. Davis - 476 U.S. 380 (1986)
- Los Angeles v. Preferred Communications - 476 U.S. 488 (1986)
- Lee v. Illinois - 476 U.S. 530 (1986)
- Brown-Forman v. N.Y. State Liq. Auth. - 476 U.S. 573 (1986)
- Bowen v. Academy of Family Physicians - 476 U.S. 667 (1986)
- Crane v. Kentucky - 476 U.S. 683 (1986)
- Bowen v. Roy - 476 U.S. 693 (1986)
- Thornburgh v. Amer. Coll. of Obstetricians - 476 U.S. 747 (1986)
- Batson v. Kentucky - 476 U.S. 79 (1986)
- Reed v. Campbell - 476 U.S. 852 (1986)

- East River S.S. Corp. v. Transamerica - 476 U.S. 858 (1986)
- Affiliated Tribes v. Wold Engineering - 476 U.S. 877 (1986)
- Nantahala P. & L. v. Thornburg - 476 U.S. 953 (1986)
- Wardair Canada v. Fla. Dept. of Rev. - 477 U.S. 1 (1986)
- Maine v. Taylor - 477 U.S. 131 (1986)
- Darden v. Wainwright - 477 U.S. 168 (1986)
- Offshore Logistics, Inc. v. Tallentire - 477 U.S. 207 (1986)
- Anderson v. Liberty Lobby, Inc. - 477 U.S. 242 (1986)
- International Union v. Brock - 477 U.S. 274 (1986)
- Memphis Comm. Sch. Dist. v. Stachura - 477 U.S. 299 (1986)
- MacDonald et al. v. County of Yolo - 477 U.S. 340 (1986)
- Kimmelman v. Morrison - 477 U.S. 365 (1986)
- Ford v. Wainwright - 477 U.S. 399 (1986)
- Bowen v. PAOSSE - 477 U.S. 41 (1986)
- Kuhlmann v. Wilson - 477 U.S. 436 (1986)
- Murray v. Carrier - 477 U.S. 478 (1986)
- Smith v. Murray - 477 U.S. 527 (1986)
- Meritor Savings Bank v. Vinson - 477 U.S. 57 (1986)
- Ohio Civ. Rgts. Comm'n v. Dayton Chr. Pub. Schs. - 477 U.S. 619 (1986)
- Lyng v. Castillo - 477 U.S. 635 (1986)
- McMillan v. Pennsylvania - 477 U.S. 79 (1986)
- Press-Enterprise Co. v. Superior Ct. - 478 U.S. 1 (1986)
- Davis v. Bandemer - 478 U.S. 109 (1986)
- Bowers v. Hardwick - 478 U.S. 186 (1986)
- Japan Whaling Ass'n v. Cetacean Soc'y - 478 U.S. 221 (1986)
- Allen v. Hardy - 478 U.S. 255 (1986)
- Papasan v. Allain - 478 U.S. 265 (1986)
- Thornburg v. Gingles - 478 U.S. 30 (1986)
- Posadas de P.R. Assocs. v. Tourism Co. - 478 U.S. 328 (1986)
- Allen v. Illinois - 478 U.S. 364 (1986)
- Bazemore v. Friday - 478 U.S. 385 (1986)
- Sheet Metal Workers v. EEOC - 478 U.S. 421 (1986)
- Firefighters v. City of Cleveland - 478 U.S. 501 (1986)
- Rose v. Clark - 478 U.S. 570 (1986)
- Baker v. General Motors Corp. - 478 U.S. 621 (1986)
- Bethel Sch. Dist. v. Fraser - 478 U.S. 675 (1986)
- Arcara v. Cloud Books, Inc. - 478 U.S. 697 (1986)
- Bowsher v. Synar - 478 U.S. 714 (1986)
- Merrell Dow Pharmaceuticals v. Thompson - 478 U.S. 804 (1986)
- CFTC v. Schor - 478 U.S. 833 (1986)

- Rose v. Arkansas State Police - 479 U.S. 1 (1986)
- R. J. Reynolds Tob. v. Durham County - 479 U.S. 130 (1986)
- Colorado v. Connelly - 479 U.S. 157 (1986)
- Munro v. Socialist Workers - 479 U.S. 189 (1986)
- Tashjian v. Republican Party - 479 U.S. 208 (1986)
- FEC v. Mass. Cit. for Life - 479 U.S. 238 (1986)
- City of Newport v. Iacobucci - 479 U.S. 92 (1986)
- Kelly v. Robinson - 479 U.S. 36 (1986)
- Preseault v. ICC - 494 U.S. 1 (1986)
- California Fed. S & L v. Guerra - 479 U.S. 272 (1987)
- Griffith v. Kentucky - 479 U.S. 314 (1987)
- 324 Liquor Corp. v. Duffy - 479 U.S. 335 (1987)
- Burke v. Barnes - 479 U.S. 361 (1987)
- Colorado v. Bertine - 479 U.S. 367 (1987)
- Clarke v. Securities Indus. Ass'n - 479 U.S. 388 (1987)
- Wright v. Roanoke Redevelopment Auth. - 479 U.S. 418 (1987)
- Int'l Paper Co. v. Ouellette - 479 U.S. 481 (1987)
- Connecticut v. Barrett - 479 U.S. 523 (1987)
- California v. Brown - 479 U.S. 538 (1987)
- Colorado v. Spring - 479 U.S. 564 (1987)
- Asahi Metal Indus. v. Superior Court - 480 U.S. 102 (1987)
- Hobbie v. Unemplt. Appeals Comm'n - 480 U.S. 136 (1987)
- United States v. Paradise - 480 U.S. 149 (1987)
- California v. Cabazon Band of Indians - 480 U.S. 202 (1987)
- Martin v. Ohio - 480 U.S. 228 (1987)
- FCC v. Florida Power Corp. - 480 U.S. 245 (1987)
- United States v. Dunn - 480 U.S. 294 (1987)
- Arizona v. Hicks - 480 U.S. 321 (1987)
- Illinois v. Krull - 480 U.S. 340 (1987)
- Town of Newton v. Rumery - 480 U.S. 386 (1987)
- Pennsylvania v. Ritchie - 480 U.S. 39 (1987)
- Keystone Bituminous v. DeBenedictis - 480 U.S. 470 (1987)
- Cal. Coastal Comm'n v. Granite Rock Co. - 480 U.S. 572 (1987)
- Johnson v. Transportation Agency - 480 U.S. 616 (1987)
- Alaska Airlines, Inc. v. Brock - 480 U.S. 678 (1987)
- O'Connor v. Ortega - 480 U.S. 709 (1987)
- Maryland v. Garrison - 480 U.S. 79 (1987)
- Pennzoil v. Texaco, Inc. - 481 U.S. 1 (1987)

- Tison v. Arizona - 481 U.S. 137 (1987)
- Cruz v. New York - 481 U.S. 186 (1987)
- Richardson v. Marsh - 481 U.S. 200 (1987)
- Ark. Writers' Project v. Ragland - 481 U.S. 221 (1987)
- Brock v. Roadway Express, Inc. - 481 U.S. 252 (1987)
- McCleskey v. Kemp - 481 U.S. 279 (1987)
- Hitchcock v. Dugger - 481 U.S. 393 (1987)
- Tull v. United States - 481 U.S. 412 (1987)
- Meese v. Keene - 481 U.S. 465 (1987)
- Pope v. Illinois - 481 U.S. 497 (1987)
- Arizona v. Mauro - 481 U.S. 520 (1987)
- Rotary Int'l v. Rotary Club of Duarte - 481 U.S. 537 (1987)
- Pennsylvania v. Finley - 481 U.S. 551 (1987)
- Rose v. Rose - 481 U.S. 619 (1987)
- Gray v. Mississippi - 481 U.S. 648 (1987)
- CTS Corp. v. Dynamics Corp. of America - 481 U.S. 69 (1987)
- Hodel v. Irving - 481 U.S. 704 (1987)
- Young v. U.S. ex rel. Vuitton et Fils - 481 U.S. 787 (1987)
- United States v. Mendoza-Lopez - 481 U.S. 828 (1987)
- IBEW v. Hechler - 481 U.S. 851 (1987)
- Fort Halifax Packing v. Coyne - 482 U.S. 1 (1987)
- Texas v. New Mexico - 482 U.S. 124 (1987)
- Rockford Life Ins. v. Dept. of Revenue - 482 U.S. 182 (1987)
- Utah Div. of State Lands v. United States - 482 U.S. 193 (1987)
- Lutheran Church v. County of Los Angeles - 482 U.S. 304 (1987)
- O'Lone v. Estate of Shabazz - 482 U.S. 342 (1987)
- Board of Pardons v. Allen - 482 U.S. 369 (1987)
- California v. Superior Court - 482 U.S. 400 (1987)
- Miller v. Florida - 482 U.S. 423 (1987)
- City of Houston v. Hill - 482 U.S. 451 (1987)
- Perry v. Thomas - 482 U.S. 483 (1987)
- Booth v. Maryland - 482 U.S. 496 (1987)
- Airport Comm'rs v. Jews for Jesus - 482 U.S. 569 (1987)
- Edwards v. Aguillard - 482 U.S. 578 (1987)
- Frazier v. Heebe - 482 U.S. 641 (1987)
- New York v. Burger - 482 U.S. 691 (1987)
- Kentucky v. Stincer - 482 U.S. 730 (1987)
- Turner v. Safley - 482 U.S. 78 (1987)
- South Dakota v. Dole - 483 U.S. 203 (1987)
- Puerto Rico v. Branstad - 483 U.S. 219 (1987)
- Tyler Pipe v. Wash. Dept. of Rev. - 483 U.S. 232 (1987)
- Amer. Trucking Assns. v. Scheiner - 483 U.S. 266 (1987)
- Corp. of Presiding Bishop v. Amos - 483 U.S. 327 (1987)
- McNally v. United States - 483 U.S. 350 (1987)
- Rankin v. McPherson - 483 U.S. 378 (1987)

- Buchanan v. Kentucky - 483 U.S. 402 (1987)
- Solorio v. United States - 483 U.S. 435 (1987)
- Rock v. Arkansas - 483 U.S. 44 (1987)
- Welch v. Texas Dept. of Highways - 483 U.S. 468 (1987)
- S.F. Arts & Athletics, Inc. v. USOC - 483 U.S. 522 (1987)
- Rivera v. Minnich - 483 U.S. 574 (1987)
- Bowen v. Gilliard - 483 U.S. 587 (1987)
- Anderson v. Creighton - 483 U.S. 635 (1987)
- Sumner v. Nevada Dept. of Prisons - 483 U.S. 66 (1987)
- Nollan v. California Coastal Comm'n - 483 U.S. 825 (1987)
- Griffin v. Wisconsin - 483 U.S. 868 (1987)
- REAGAN v. ABOUREZK - 484 U.S. 1 (1987)
- HARTIGAN v. ZBARAZ - 484 U.S. 171 (1987)
- Karcher v. May - 484 U.S. 72 (1987)
- Omni Capital v. Rudolf Wolff & Co. - 484 U.S. 97 (1987)
- Thompson v. Thompson - 484 U.S. 174 (1988)
- Lowenfield v. Phelps - 484 U.S. 231 (1988)
- Hazelwood Sch. Dist. v. Kuhlmeier - 484 U.S. 260 (1988)
- Westfall v. Erwin - 484 U.S. 292 (1988)
- Honig v. Doe - 484 U.S. 305 (1988)
- Virginia v. Amer. Booksellers Ass'n - 484 U.S. 383 (1988)
- Taylor v. Illinois - 484 U.S. 400 (1988)
- Phillips Petroleum Co. v. Mississippi - 484 U.S. 469 (1988)
- Department of the Navy v. Egan - 484 U.S. 518 (1988)
- United States v. Owens - 484 U.S. 554 (1988)
- Pennell v. City of San Jose - 485 U.S. 1 (1988)
- United States v. Robinson - 485 U.S. 25 (1988)
- Gulfstream Aerospace v. Mayacamas - 485 U.S. 271 (1988)
- Schneidewind v. ANR Pipeline Co. - 485 U.S. 293 (1988)
- Boos v. Barry - 485 U.S. 312 (1988)
- Bennett v. Arkansas - 485 U.S. 395 (1988)
- Lyng v. Northwest Indian Cemetery - 485 U.S. 439 (1988)
- Hustler Magazine, Inc. v. Falwell - 485 U.S. 46 (1988)
- Tulsa Prof. Collection Svcs. v. Pope - 485 U.S. 478 (1988)
- P. R. Consumer Affairs v. Isla Petroleum - 485 U.S. 495 (1988)
- South Carolina v. Baker - 485 U.S. 505 (1988)
- Mathews v. United States - 485 U.S. 58 (1988)
- Hicks v. Feiock - 485 U.S. 624 (1988)
- United States v. Providence Journal Co. - 485 U.S. 693 (1988)
- Kungys v. United States - 485 U.S. 759 (1988)
- Chick Kam Choo v. Exxon Corp. - 486 U.S. 140 (1988)

- Wheat v. United States - 486 U.S. 153 (1988)
- FDIC v. Mallen - 486 U.S. 230 (1988)
- D. H. Holmes Co., Ltd. v. McNamara - 486 U.S. 24 (1988)
- Satterwhite v. Texas - 486 U.S. 249 (1988)
- New Energy Co. v. Limbach - 486 U.S. 269 (1988)
- California v. Greenwood - 486 U.S. 35 (1988)
- Maynard v. Cartwright - 486 U.S. 356 (1988)
- Mills v. Maryland - 486 U.S. 367 (1988)
- Lingle v. Norge Div., Magic Chef, Inc. - 486 U.S. 399 (1988)
- Meyer v. Grant - 486 U.S. 414 (1988)
- McCoy v. Court of appeals of Wisconsin - 486 U.S. 429 (1988)
- Clark v. Jeter - 486 U.S. 456 (1988)
- Shapero v. Kentucky Bar Assn. - 486 U.S. 466 (1988)
- Michigan v. Chesternut - 486 U.S. 567 (1988)
- City of New York v. FCC - 486 U.S. 57 (1988)
- Johnson v. Mississippi - 486 U.S. 578 (1988)
- Webster v. Doe - 486 U.S. 592 (1988)
- Arizona v. Roberson - 486 U.S. 675 (1988)
- Bankers Life & Cas. Co. v. Crenshaw - 486 U.S. 71 (1988)
- Sun Oil Co. v. Wortman - 486 U.S. 717 (1988)
- Lakewood v. Plain Dealer Publ. Co. - 486 U.S. 750 (1988)
- Mackey v. Lanier Collection Agcy. - 486 U.S. 825 (1988)
- Bendix Autolite v. Midwesco Enterprises - 486 U.S. 888 (1988)
- New York Club Ass'n v. City of New York - 487 U.S. 1 (1988)
- Coy v. Iowa - 487 U.S. 1012 (1988)
- Felder v. Casey - 487 U.S. 131 (1988)
- Franklin v. Lynaugh - 487 U.S. 164 (1988)
- Doe v. United States - 487 U.S. 201 (1988)
- Patterson v. Illinois - 487 U.S. 285 (1988)
- Schweiker v. Chilicky - 487 U.S. 412 (1988)
- Kadrmas v. Dickinson Pub. Schs. - 487 U.S. 450 (1988)
- Frisby v. Schultz - 487 U.S. 474 (1988)
- Boyle v. United Technologies Corp. - 487 U.S. 500 (1988)
- Murray v. United States - 487 U.S. 533 (1988)
- Bowen v. Kendrick - 487 U.S. 589 (1988)
- Supreme Court of Virginia v. Friedman - 487 U.S. 59 (1988)
- Morrison v. Olson - 487 U.S. 654 (1988)
- Riley v. Nat'l Fed'n of the Blind - 487 U.S. 781 (1988)
- Ross v. Oklahoma - 487 U.S. 81 (1988)
- United States v. Kozminski - 487 U.S. 931 (1988)
- Braswell v. United States - 487 U.S. 99 (1988)
- NCAA v. Tarkanian - 488 U.S. 179 (1988)
- Smith v. Spisak - 08-724 (1988)
- Lockhart v. Nelson - 488 U.S. 33 (1988)
- Arizona v. Youngblood - 488 U.S. 51 (1988)
- Penson v. Ohio - 488 U.S. 75 (1988)
- Goldberg v. Sweet - 488 U.S. 252 (1989)

- Perry v. Leeke - 488 U.S. 272 (1989)
- Duquesne Light Co. v. Barasch - 488 U.S. 299 (1989)
- Allegheny-Pittsburgh Coal Co. v. County Comm'n - 488 U.S. 336 (1989)
- Mistretta v. United States - 488 U.S. 361 (1989)
- Argentine Rep. v. Amerada Hess - 488 U.S. 428 (1989)
- Florida v. Riley - 488 U.S. 445 (1989)
- City of Richmond v. J. A. Croson Co. - 488 U.S. 469 (1989)
- United States v. Broce - 488 U.S. 563 (1989)
- Texas Monthly, Inc. v. Bullock - 489 U.S. 1 (1989)
- Mesa v. California - 489 U.S. 121 (1989)
- Bonito Boats v. Thunder Craft Boats - 489 U.S. 141 (1989)
- DeShaney v. Winnebago Cty. DSS - 489 U.S. 189 (1989)
- Eu v. S.F. Cty. Democratic Cent. Comm. - 489 U.S. 214 (1989)
- Harris v. Reed - 489 U.S. 255 (1989)
- Teague v. Lane - 489 U.S. 288 (1989)
- Castille v. Peoples - 489 U.S. 346 (1989)
- Fort Wayne Books, Inc. v. Indiana - 489 U.S. 46 (1989)
- NW Cent. Pipeline v. Kans. Corp. Comm'n - 489 U.S. 493 (1989)
- Karahalios v. Nat'l Fed'n of Fed. Employees - 489 U.S. 527 (1989)
- Blanton v. City of No. Las Vegas - 489 U.S. 538 (1989)
- Barnard v. Thorstenn - 489 U.S. 546 (1989)
- Brower v. County of Inyo - 489 U.S. 593 (1989)
- Skinner v. Railway Lab. Execs. Ass'n - 489 U.S. 602 (1989)
- Nat'l Treas. Emp. Union v. Von Raab - 489 U.S. 656 (1989)
- Board of Estimate of NYC v. Morris - 489 U.S. 688 (1989)
- Davis v. Michigan Dept. of Treasury - 489 U.S. 803 (1989)
- Frazee v. Ill. Dept. of Empl. Secur. - 489 U.S. 829 (1989)
- American Foreign Svc. Ass'n v. Garfinkel - 490 U.S. 153 (1989)
- Cotton Petroleum Corp. v. New Mexico - 490 U.S. 163 (1989)
- City of Dallas v. Stanglin - 490 U.S. 19 (1989)
- Skinner v. Mid-America Pipeline Co. - 490 U.S. 212 (1989)
- Graham v. Connor - 490 U.S. 386 (1989)
- Thornburgh v. Abbott - 490 U.S. 401 (1989)
- Ky. Dept. of Corrections v. Thompson - 490 U.S. 454 (1989)
- R. de Quijas v. Shearson/Am. Exp. - 490 U.S. 477 (1989)
- Maleng v. Cook - 490 U.S. 488 (1989)
- Finley v. United States - 490 U.S. 545 (1989)
- ASARCO v. Kadish - 490 U.S. 605 (1989)
- Hildwin v. Florida - 490 U.S. 638 (1989)
- Amerada Hess v. Div. of Taxation - 490 U.S. 66 (1989)
- Hernandez v. Commissioner - 490 U.S. 680 (1989)
- Alabama v. Smith - 490 U.S. 794 (1989)
- South Carolina v. Gathers - 490 U.S. 805 (1989)
- Cal. Equalization Bd. v. Sierra Summit - 490 U.S. 844 (1989)
- Gomez v. United States - 490 U.S. 858 (1989)
- California v. ARC America Corp. - 490 U.S. 93 (1989)
- Pennsylvania v. Union Gas Co. - 491 U.S. 1 (1989)
- Michael H. v. Gerald D. - 491 U.S. 110 (1989)
- Patterson v. McLean Credit Union - 491 U.S. 164 (1989)
- Dellmuth v. Muth - 491 U.S. 223 (1989)
- Carella v. California - 491 U.S. 263 (1989)
- Healy v. Beer Institute, Inc. - 491 U.S. 324 (1989)
- New Orleans Pub. Svc. v. City Council - 491 U.S. 350 (1989)
- Jones v. Thomas - 491 U.S. 376 (1989)
- Texas v. Johnson - 491 U.S. 397 (1989)
- Public Citizen v. Department of Justice - 491 U.S. 440 (1989)
- Florida Star v. B.J.F. - 491 U.S. 524 (1989)
- Massachusetts v. Oakes - 491 U.S. 576 (1989)
- Will v. Michigan Dept. of State Police - 491 U.S. 58 (1989)
- United States v. Monsanto - 491 U.S. 600 (1989)
- Caplin & Drysdale v. United States - 491 U.S. 617 (1989)
- Harte-Hanks Communs. v. Connaughton - 491 U.S. 657 (1989)
- Ward v. Rock Against Racism - 491 U.S. 781 (1989)
- Quinn v. Millsap - 491 U.S. 95 (1989)
- Murray v. Giarratano - 492 U.S. 1 (1989)
- Sable Communications v. FCC - 492 U.S. 115 (1989)
- Duckworth v. Eagan - 492 U.S. 195 (1989)
- BFI, Inc. v. Kelco Disposal, Inc. - 492 U.S. 257 (1989)
- Penry v. Lynaugh - 492 U.S. 302 (1989)
- Granfinanciera, S.A. v. Nordberg - 492 U.S. 33 (1989)
- Stanford v. Kentucky - 492 U.S. 361 (1989)
- Brendale v. Confederated Tribes - 492 U.S. 408 (1989)
- State Univ. of New York v. Fox - 492 U.S. 469 (1989)
- Webster v. Reproductive Health Svcs. - 492 U.S. 490 (1989)

- County of Allegheny v. ACLU - 492 U.S. 573 (1989)
- Hoffman v. Conn. Dept. of Inc. Maint. - 492 U.S. 96 (1989)
- John Doe Agcy. v. John Doe Corp. - 493 U.S. 146 (1989)
- Univ. of Pa. v. EEOC - 493 U.S. 182 (1990)
- FW/PBS v. City of Dallas - 493 U.S. 215 (1990)
- Spallone v. U.S. - 493 U.S. 265 (1990)
- James v. Illinois - 493 U.S. 307 (1990)
- Dowling v. U.S. - 493 U.S. 342 (1990)
- Swaggart Ministries v. Board of Equalization - 493 U.S. 378 (1990)
- Kirkpatrick & Co. v. Evtl. Tectonics - 493 U.S. 400 (1990)
- FTC v. Superior Ct. TLA - 493 U.S. 411 (1990)
- Tafflin v. Levitt - 493 U.S. 455 (1990)
- Holland v. Illinois - 493 U.S. 474 (1990)
- Baltimore City DSS v. Bouknight - 493 U.S. 549 (1990)
- Zinermon v. Burch - 494 U.S. 113 (1990)
- Carden v. Arkoma Assocs. - 494 U.S. 185 (1990)
- Washington v. Harper - 494 U.S. 210 (1990)
- United States v. Verdugo-Urquidez - 494 U.S. 259 (1990)
- Blystone v. Pennsylvania - 494 U.S. 299 (1990)
- Maryland v. Buie - 494 U.S. 325 (1990)
- Michigan v. Harvey - 494 U.S. 344 (1990)
- Boyde v. California - 494 U.S. 370 (1990)
- Butler v. McKellar - 494 U.S. 407 (1990)
- McKoy v. North Carolina - 494 U.S. 433 (1990)
- Lewis v. Continental Bank Corp. - 494 U.S. 472 (1990)
- Saffle v. Parks - 494 U.S. 484 (1990)
- Lytle v. Household Mfg., Inc. - 494 U.S. 545 (1990)
- Chauffeurs Local 391 v. Terry - 494 U.S. 558 (1990)
- Butterworth v. Smith - 494 U.S. 624 (1990)
- Austin v. Mich. Chamber of Comm. - 494 U.S. 652 (1990)
- U.S. Department of Labor v. Triplett - 494 U.S. 715 (1990)
- Clemons v. Mississippi - 494 U.S. 738 (1990)
- Yellow Freight Syst. v. Donnelly - 494 U.S. 820 (1990)
- Employment Div. v. Smith. - 494 U.S. 872 (1990)
- Florida v. Wells - 495 U.S. 1 (1990)
- Osborne v. Ohio - 495 U.S. 103 (1990)
- New York v. Harris - 495 U.S. 14 (1990)
- Whitmore v. Arkansas - 495 U.S. 149 (1990)
- Missouri v. Jenkins - 495 U.S. 33 (1990)
- United Steelworkers v. Rawson - 495 U.S. 362 (1990)

- United States v. Munoz-Flores - 495 U.S. 385 (1990)
- North Dakota v. United States - 495 U.S. 423 (1990)
- California v. FERC - 495 U.S. 490 (1990)
- Grady v. Corbin - 495 U.S. 508 (1990)
- Pennsylvania DPW v. Davenport - 495 U.S. 552 (1990)
- Burnham v. Superior Court - 495 U.S. 604 (1990)
- Duro v. Reina - 495 U.S. 676 (1990)
- Minnesota v. Olson - 495 U.S. 91 (1990)
- Keller v. State Bar of California - 496 U.S. 1 (1990)
- Horton v. California - 496 U.S. 128 (1990)
- American Trucking Ass'ns v. Smith - 496 U.S. 167 (1990)
- McKesson Corp. v. Div. of AB & T - 496 U.S. 18 (1990)
- Board of Educ. v. Mergens - 496 U.S. 226 (1990)
- Illinois v. Perkins - 496 U.S. 292 (1990)
- United States v. Eichman - 496 U.S. 310 (1990)
- Alabama v. White - 496 U.S. 325 (1990)
- Howlett v. Rose - 496 U.S. 356 (1990)
- OPM v. Richmond - 496 U.S. 414 (1990)
- Michigan State Police v. Sitz - 496 U.S. 444 (1990)
- Pennsylvania v. Muniz - 496 U.S. 582 (1990)
- English v. General Elec. Co. - 496 U.S. 72 (1990)
- Peel v. Attorney Disc. Comm'n - 496 U.S. 91 (1990)
- Milkovich v. Lorain Journal - 497 U.S. 1 (1990)
- Illinois v. Rodriguez - 497 U.S. 177 (1990)
- Sawyer v. Smith - 497 U.S. 227 (1990)
- Cruzan v. Director, MDH - 497 U.S. 261 (1990)
- Sisson v. Ruby - 497 U.S. 358 (1990)
- Collins v. Youngblood - 497 U.S. 37 (1990)
- Hodgson v. Minnesota - 497 U.S. 417 (1990)
- Ohio v. Akron Center - 497 U.S. 502 (1990)
- Metro Broadcasting v. FCC - 497 U.S. 547 (1990)
- Rutan v. Republican Party - 497 U.S. 62 (1990)
- Walton v. Arizona - 497 U.S. 639 (1990)
- United States v. Kokinda - 497 U.S. 720 (1990)
- Lewis v. Jeffers - 497 U.S. 764 (1990)
- Idaho v. Wright - 497 U.S. 805 (1990)
- Maryland v. Craig - 497 U.S. 836 (1990)
- Lujan v. Nat'l Wildlife Fed'n - 497 U.S. 871 (1990)
- Ingersoll-Rand Co. v. McClendon - 498 U.S. 133 (1990)
- Minnick v. Mississippi - 498 U.S. 146 (1990)
- Miles v. Apex Marine Corp. - 498 U.S. 19 (1990)
- Cage v. Louisiana - 498 U.S. 39 (1990)
- Langenkamp v. Culp - 498 U.S. 42 (1990)
- FMC Corp. v. Holliday - 498 U.S. 52 (1990)

- Morales v. Trans World Airlines, Inc. - 504 U.S. 374 (1992)
- Sochor v. Florida - 504 U.S. 527 (1992)
- Lujan v. Defenders of Wildlife - 504 U.S. 555 (1992)
- Ankenbrandt v. Richards - 504 U.S. 689 (1992)
- Foucha v. Louisiana - 504 U.S. 71 (1992)
- Morgan v. Illinois - 504 U.S. 719 (1992)
- Allied-Signal, Inc. v. Director, Div. of Taxation - 504 U.S. 768 (1992)
- Nordlinger v. Hahn - 505 U.S. 1 (1992)
- Lucas v. South Carolina Coastal Council - 505 U.S. 1003 (1992)
- Forsyth County v. Nationalist Movement - 505 U.S. 123 (1992)
- New York v. United States - 505 U.S. 144 (1992)
- American Nat. Red Cross v. S. G. - 505 U.S. 247 (1992)
- Wright v. West - 505 U.S. 277 (1992)
- Sawyer v. Whitley - 505 U.S. 333 (1992)
- Georgia v. McCollum - 505 U.S. 42 (1992)
- Medina v. California - 505 U.S. 437 (1992)
- Cipollone v. Liggett Group, Inc. - 505 U.S. 504 (1992)
- Lee v. Weisman - 505 U.S. 577 (1992)
- International Soc. for Krishna Consciousness, Inc. v. Lee - 505 U.S. 672 (1992)
- Kraft Gen. Foods, Inc. v. Iowa Dept. of Revenue and Finance - 505 U.S. 71 (1992)
- Franklin v. Massachusetts - 505 U.S. 788 (1992)
- Lee v. International Soc. for Krishna Consciousness, Inc. - 505 U.S. 830 (1992)
- Planned Parenthood of Southeastern Pa. v. Casey - 505 U.S. 833 (1992)
- Gade v. National Solid Wastes Management Assn. - 505 U.S. 88 (1992)
- District of Columbia v. Greater Washington Bd. of Trade - 506 U.S. 125 (1992)
- Parke v. Raley - 506 U.S. 20 (1992)
- Lockhart v. Fretwell - 506 U.S. 364 (1992)
- Herrera v. Collins - 506 U.S. 390 (1992)
- Richmond v. Lewis - 506 U.S. 40 (1992)
- Soldal v. Cook County - 506 U.S. 56 (1992)
- Mississippi v. Louisiana - 506 U.S. 73 (1992)
- Voinovich v. Quilter - 507 U.S. 146 (1992)
- Reno v. Flores - 507 U.S. 292 (1992)
- Arave v. Creech - 507 U.S. 463 (1992)
- United States v. Dixon - 509 U.S. 688 (1992)
- Nixon v. United States - 506 U.S. 224 (1993)
- Cincinnati v. Discovery Network, Inc. - 507 U.S. 410 (1993)
- Itel Containers Int'l Corp. v. Huddleston - 507 U.S. 60 (1993)
- Brecht v. Abrahamson - 507 U.S. 619 (1993)
- CSX Transp., Inc. v. Easterwood - 507 U.S. 658 (1993)
- Withrow v. Williams - 507 U.S. 680 (1993)
- Edenfield v. Fane - 507 U.S. 761 (1993)
- Oklahoma Tax Comm'n v. Sac and Fox Nation - 508 U.S. 114 (1993)
- Sullivan v. Louisiana - 508 U.S. 275 (1993)
- FCC v. Beach Communications, Inc. - 508 U.S. 307 (1993)
- Minnesota v. Dickerson - 508 U.S. 366 (1993)
- Lamb's Chapel v. Center Moriches Union Free School Dist. - 508 U.S. 384 (1993)
- Wisconsin v. Mitchell - 508 U.S. 476 (1993)
- Department of Treasury v. Fabe - 508 U.S. 491 (1993)
- Church of Lukumi Babalu Aye, Inc. v. Hialeah - 508 U.S. 520 (1993)
- Concrete Pipe & Products of Cal., Inc. v. Construction Laborers Pension Trust for Southern Cal. - 508 U.S. 602 (1993)
- South Dakota v. Bourland - 508 U.S. 679 (1993)
- United States v. Padilla - 508 U.S. 77 (1993)
- Cardinal Chemical Co. v. Morton Int'l, Inc. - 508 U.S. 83 (1993)
- Zobrest v. Catalina Foothills School Dist. - 509 U.S. 1 (1993)
- Sale v. Haitian Centers Council, Inc. - 509 U.S. 155 (1993)
- Helling v. McKinney - 509 U.S. 25 (1993)
- Johnson v. Texas - 509 U.S. 350 (1993)
- Godinez v. Moran - 509 U.S. 389 (1993)
- United States v. Edge Broadcasting Co. - 509 U.S. 418 (1993)
- Reno v. Catholic Social Services, Inc. - 509 U.S. 43 (1993)
- TXO Production Corp. v. Alliance Resources Corp. - 509 U.S. 443 (1993)
- Alexander v. United States - 509 U.S. 544 (1993)
- Austin v. United States - 509 U.S. 602 (1993)
- Shaw v. Reno - 509 U.S. 630 (1993)
- Harper v. Virginia Dept. of Taxation - 509 U.S. 86 (1993)
- Albright v. Oliver - 510 U.S. 266 (1993)
- Hagen v. Utah - 510 U.S. 399 (1993)
- FDIC v. Meyer - 510 U.S. 471 (1993)
- John Hancock Mut. Life Ins. Co. v. Harris Trust and Sav. Bank - 510 U.S. 86 (1993)
- Mine Workers v. Bagwell - 512 U.S. 821 (1993)
- Weiss v. United States - 510 U.S. 163 (1994)
- Schiro v. Farley - 510 U.S. 222 (1994)
- Victor v. Nebraska - 511 U.S. 1 (1994)
- J. E. B. v. Alabama ex rel. T. B. - 511 U.S. 127 (1994)
- Stansbury v. California - 511 U.S. 318 (1994)
- Kokkonen v. Guardian Life Ins. Co. of America - 511 U.S. 375 (1994)
- C & A Carbone, Inc. v. Clarkstown - 511 U.S. 383 (1994)
- Dalton v. Specter - 511 U.S. 462 (1994)

- Associated Industries of Mo. v. Lohman - 511 U.S. 641 (1994)
- Waters v. Churchill - 511 U.S. 661 (1994)
- Nichols v. United States - 511 U.S. 738 (1994)
- Department of Revenue of Mont. v. Kurth Ranch - 511 U.S. 767 (1994)
- Farmer v. Brennan - 511 U.S. 825 (1994)
- Oregon Waste Systems, Inc. v. Department of Environmental Quality of Ore. - 511 U.S. 93 (1994)
- Romano v. Oklahoma - 512 U.S. 1 (1994)
- Livadas v. Bradshaw - 512 U.S. 107 (1994)
- Ibanez v. Florida Dept. of Business and Professional Regulation, Bd. of Accountancy - 512 U.S. 136 (1994)
- Simmons v. South Carolina - 512 U.S. 154 (1994)
- West Lynn Creamery, Inc. v. Healy - 512 U.S. 186 (1994)
- United States v. Carlton - 512 U.S. 26 (1994)
- Barclays Bank PLC v. Franchise Tax Bd. of Cal. - 512 U.S. 298 (1994)
- Dolan v. City of Tigard - 512 U.S. 374 (1994)
- Honda Motor Co. v. Oberg - 512 U.S. 415 (1994)
- City of Ladue v. Gilleo - 512 U.S. 43 (1994)
- Davis v. United States - 512 U.S. 452 (1994)
- Department of Taxation and Finance of N. Y. v. Milhelm Attea & Bros. - 512 U.S. 61 (1994)
- Turner Broadcasting System, Inc. v. FCC - 512 U.S. 622 (1994)
- Board of Ed. of Kiryas Joel Village School Dist. v. Grumet - 512 U.S. 687 (1994)
- Madsen v. Women's Health Center, Inc. - 512 U.S. 753 (1994)
- O'Melveny & Myers v. FDIC - 512 U.S. 79 (1994)
- Tuilaepa v. California - 512 U.S. 967 (1994)
- Reich v. Collins - 513 U.S. 106 (1994)
- U.S. Bancorp Mortgage Co. v. Bonner Mall Partnership - 513 U.S. 18 (1994)
- Schlup v. Delo - 513 U.S. 298 (1994)
- United States v. Treasury Employees - 513 U.S. 454 (1994)
- Harris v. Alabama - 513 U.S. 504 (1994)
- Jerome B. Grubart, Inc. v. Great Lakes Dredge & Dock Co. - 513 U.S. 527 (1994)
- United States v. X-Citement Video, Inc. - 513 U.S. 64 (1994)
- U.S. Term Limits, Inc. v. Thornton - 514 U.S. 779 (1994)
- Lebron v. National Railroad Passenger Corporation - 513 U.S. 374 (1995)
- American Airlines, Inc. v. Wolens - 513 U.S. 219 (1995)
- Allied-Bruce Terminix Cos. v. Dobson - 513 U.S. 265 (1995)
- Arizona v. Evans - 514 U.S. 1 (1995)

- Oklahoma Tax Comm'n v. Jefferson Lines, Inc. - 514 U.S. 175 (1995)
- Plaut v. Spendthrift Farm, Inc. - 514 U.S. 211 (1995)
- Freightliner Corp. v. Myrick - 514 U.S. 280 (1995)
- McIntyre v. Ohio Elections Comm'n - 514 U.S. 334 (1995)
- Kyles v. Whitley - 514 U.S. 419 (1995)
- Rubin v. Coors Brewing Co. - 514 U.S. 476 (1995)
- California Dept. of Corrections v. Morales - 514 U.S. 499 (1995)
- United States v. Lopez - 514 U.S. 549 (1995)
- Hubbard v. United States - 514 U.S. 695 (1995)
- Reynoldsville Casket Co. v. Hyde - 514 U.S. 749 (1995)
- Wilson v. Arkansas - 514 U.S. 927 (1995)
- Ryder v. United States - 515 U.S. 177 (1995)
- Adarand Constructors, Inc. v. Peña - 515 U.S. 200 (1995)
- Wilton v. Seven Falls Co. - 515 U.S. 277 (1995)
- Witte v. United States - 515 U.S. 389 (1995)
- Gutierrez de Martinez v. Lamagno - 515 U.S. 417 (1995)
- Oklahoma Tax Comm'n v. Chickasaw Nation - 515 U.S. 450 (1995)
- Sandin v. Conner - 515 U.S. 472 (1995)
- Hurley v. Irish-American Gay, Lesbian and Bisexual Group of Boston, Inc. - 515 U.S. 557 (1995)
- Florida Bar v. Went For It, Inc. - 515 U.S. 618 (1995)
- Vernonia School Dist. 47J v. Acton - 515 U.S. 646 (1995)
- Capitol Square Review and Advisory Bd. v. Pinette - 515 U.S. 753 (1995)
- Rosenberger v. Rector and Visitors of Univ. of Va. - 515 U.S. 819 (1995)
- Miller v. Johnson - 515 U.S. 900 (1995)
- Wood v. Bartholomew - 516 U.S. 1 (1995)
- Tuggle v. Netherland - 516 U.S. 10 (1995)
- Fulton Corp. v. Faulkner - 516 U.S. 325 (1995)
- Bennis v. Michigan - 516 U.S. 442 (1995)
- Seminole Tribe of Fla. v. Florida - 517 U.S. 44 (1995)
- BMW of North America, Inc. v. Gore - 517 U.S. 559 (1995)
- Board of Comm'rs, Wabaunsee Cty. v. Umbehr - 518 U.S. 668 (1995)
- Yamaha Motor Corp., U.S. A. v. Calhoun - 516 U.S. 199 (1996)
- Peacock v. Thomas - 516 U.S. 349 (1996)
- Wisconsin v. City of New York - 517 U.S. 1 (1996)

- Barnett Bank of Marion Cty., N. A. v. Nelson - 517 U.S. 25 (1996)
- Rutledge v. United States - 517 U.S. 292 (1996)
- Cooper v. Oklahoma - 517 U.S. 348 (1996)
- 44 Liquormart, Inc. v. Rhode Island - 517 U.S. 484 (1996)
- Romer v. Evans - 517 U.S. 620 (1996)
- Doctor's Associates, Inc. v. Casarotto - 517 U.S. 681 (1996)
- Ornelas v. United States - 517 U.S. 690 (1996)
- Quackenbush v. Allstate Ins. Co. - 517 U.S. 706 (1996)
- Smiley v. Citibank (South Dakota), N. A. - 517 U.S. 735 (1996)
- Loving v. United States - 517 U.S. 748 (1996)
- Richards v. Jefferson County - 517 U.S. 793 (1996)
- Whren v. United States - 517 U.S. 806 (1996)
- Shaw v. Hunt - 517 U.S. 899 (1996)
- Gray v. Netherland - 518 U.S. 152 (1996)
- United States v. Ursery - 518 U.S. 267 (1996)
- Lewis v. United States - 518 U.S. 322 (1996)
- Lewis v. Casey - 518 U.S. 343 (1996)
- Montana v. Egelhoff - 518 U.S. 37 (1996)
- Gasperini v. Center for Humanities, Inc. - 518 U.S. 415 (1996)
- Medtronic, Inc. v. Lohr - 518 U.S. 470 (1996)
- United States v. Virginia - 518 U.S. 515 (1996)
- Colorado Republican Federal Campaign Comm. v. Federal Election Comm'n - 518 U.S. 604 (1996)
- Felker v. Turpin - 518 U.S. 651 (1996)
- O'Hare Truck Service, Inc. v. City of Northlake - 518 U.S. 712 (1996)
- Denver Area Ed. Telecommunications Consortium, Inc. v. FCC - 518 U.S. 727 (1996)
- Pennsylvania v. Labron - 518 U.S. 938 (1996)
- M. L. B. v. S. L. J. - 519 U.S. 102 (1996)
- Babbitt v. Youpee - 519 U.S. 234 (1996)
- Ohio v. Robinette - 519 U.S. 33 (1996)
- United States v. Wells - 519 U.S. 482 (1996)
- Arizonans for Official English v. Arizona - 520 U.S. 43 (1996)
- Kansas v. Hendricks - 521 U.S. 346 (1996)
- Glickman v. Wileman Brothers & Elliott, Inc. - 521 U.S. 457 (1996)
- Printz v. United States - 521 U.S. 898 (1996)
- General Motors Corp. v. Tracy - 519 U.S. 278 (1997)
- United States v. Watts - 519 U.S. 148 (1997)
- Schenck v. Pro-Choice Network of Western N. Y. - 519 U.S. 357 (1997)
- Maryland v. Wilson - 519 U.S. 408 (1997)
- Regents of Univ. of Cal. v. Doe - 519 U.S. 425 (1997)
- Lynce v. Mathis - 519 U.S. 433 (1997)
- Bennett v. Spear - 520 U.S. 154 (1997)

- Turner Broadcasting System, Inc. v. FCC - 520 U.S. 180 (1997)
- United States v. Lanier - 520 U.S. 259 (1997)
- Chandler v. Miller - 520 U.S. 305 (1997)
- Timmons v. Twin Cities Area New Party - 520 U.S. 351 (1997)
- Richards v. Wisconsin - 520 U.S. 385 (1997)
- Camps Newfound/Owatonna, Inc. v. Town of Harrison - 520 U.S. 564 (1997)
- Edmond v. United States - 520 U.S. 651 (1997)
- Clinton v. Jones - 520 U.S. 681 (1997)
- Suitum v. Tahoe Regional Planning Agency - 520 U.S. 725 (1997)
- De Buono v. NYSA-ILA Medical and Clinical Services Fund - 520 U.S. 806 (1997)
- Boggs v. Boggs - 520 U.S. 833 (1997)
- Gilbert v. Homar - 520 U.S. 924 (1997)
- O'Dell v. Netherland - 521 U.S. 151 (1997)
- Agostini v. Felton - 521 U.S. 203 (1997)
- Idaho v. Coeur d'Alene Tribe of Idaho - 521 U.S. 261 (1997)
- City of Boerne v. Flores - 521 U.S. 507 (1997)
- Washington v. Glucksberg - 521 U.S. 702 (1997)
- Vacco v. Quill - 521 U.S. 793 (1997)
- Raines v. Byrd - 521 U.S. 811 (1997)
- Reno v. American Civil Liberties Union - 521 U.S. 844 (1997)
- Chicago v. International College of Surgeons - 522 U.S. 156 (1997)
- State Oil Co. v. Khan - 522 U.S. 3 (1997)
- National Credit Union Admin. v. First Nat. Bank & Trust Co. - 522 U.S. 479 (1997)
- Foster v. Love - 522 U.S. 67 (1997)
- Hudson v. United States - 522 U.S. 93 (1997)
- Spencer v. Kemna - 523 U.S. 1 (1997)
- Almendarez-Torres v. United States - 523 U.S. 224 (1997)
- Baker v. General Motors Corp. - 522 U.S. 222 (1998)
- Lunding v. New York Tax Appeals Tribunal - 522 U.S. 287 (1998)
- Ohio Adult Parole Authority v. Woodard - 523 U.S. 272 (1997)
- County of Sacramento v. Lewis - 523 U.S. 833 (1997)
- United States v. Bajakajian - 524 U.S. 321 (1997)
- Quality King Distributors, Inc. v. L'anza Research Int'l, Inc. - 523 U.S. 135 (1998)
- Gray v. Maryland - 523 U.S. 185 (1998)
- Hetzel v. Prince William County - 523 U.S. 208 (1998)
- Texas v. United States - 523 U.S. 296 (1998)
- Feltner v. Columbia Pictures Television, Inc. - 523 U.S. 340 (1998)
- United States v. United States Shoe Corp. - 523 U.S. 360 (1998)
- Breard v. Greene - 523 U.S. 371 (1998)
- Campbell v. Louisiana - 523 U.S. 392 (1998)
- Miller v. Albright - 523 U.S. 420 (1998)

- California v. Deep Sea Research, Inc. - 523 U.S. 491 (1998)
- Bousley v. United States - 523 U.S. 614 (1998)
- United States v. Ramirez - 523 U.S. 65 (1998)
- Arkansas Ed. Television Comm'n v. Forbes - 523 U.S. 666 (1998)
- Ohio Forestry Assn., Inc. v. Sierra Club - 523 U.S. 726 (1998)
- Steel Co. v. Citizens for Better Environment - 523 U.S. 83 (1998)
- United States v. Cabrales - 524 U.S. 1 (1998)
- Federal Election Comm'n v. Akins - 524 U.S. 11 (1998)
- Phillips v. Washington Legal Foundation - 524 U.S. 156 (1998)
- Hohn v. United States - 524 U.S. 236 (1998)
- Pennsylvania Bd. of Probation and Parole v. Scott - 524 U.S. 357 (1998)
- Wisconsin Dept. of Corrections v. Schacht - 524 U.S. 381 (1998)
- Clinton v. City of New York - 524 U.S. 417 (1998)
- Eastern Enterprises v. Apfel - 524 U.S. 498 (1998)
- National Endowment for Arts v. Finley - 524 U.S. 569 (1998)
- United States v. Balsys - 524 U.S. 666 (1998)
- Monge v. California - 524 U.S. 721 (1998)
- Hopkins v. Reeves - 524 U.S. 88 (1998)
- Knowles v. Iowa - 525 U.S. 113 (1998)
- Calderon v. Coleman - 525 U.S. 141 (1998)
- Lopez v. Monterey County - 525 U.S. 266 (1998)
- Department of Commerce v. United States House of Representatives - 525 U.S. 316 (1998)
- Reno v. American-Arab Anti-Discrimination Comm. - 525 U.S. 471 (1998)
- Minnesota v. Carter - 525 U.S. 83 (1998)
- Minnesota v. Mille Lacs Band of Chippewa Indians - 526 U.S. 172 (1998)
- Arizona Dept. of Revenue v. Blaze Constr. Co. - 526 U.S. 32 (1998)
- Monterey v. Del Monte Dunes at Monterey, Ltd. - 526 U.S. 687 (1998)
- Buckley v. American Constitutional Law Foundation, Inc. - 525 U.S. 182 (1999)
- West Covina v. Perkins - 525 U.S. 234 (1999)
- Central State Univ. v. American Assn. of Univ. Professors, Central State Univ. Chapter - 526 U.S. 124 (1999)
- South Central Bell Telephone Co. v. Alabama - 526 U.S. 160 (1999)
- Conn v. Gabbert - 526 U.S. 286 (1999)
- Wyoming v. Houghton - 526 U.S. 295 (1999)
- Mitchell v. United States - 526 U.S. 314 (1999)
- American Mfrs. Mut. Ins. Co. v. Sullivan - 526 U.S. 40 (1999)
- Saenz v. Roe - 526 U.S. 489 (1999)

- Hunt v. Cromartie - 526 U.S. 541 (1999)
- Florida v. White - 526 U.S. 559 (1999)
- Wilson v. Layne - 526 U.S. 603 (1999)
- Hanlon v. Berger - 526 U.S. 808 (1999)
- Neder v. United States - 527 U.S. 1 (1999)
- Lilly v. Virginia - 527 U.S. 116 (1999)
- Greater New Orleans Broadcasting Assn., Inc. v. United States - 527 U.S. 173 (1999)
- Strickler v. Greene - 527 U.S. 263 (1999)
- Jones v. United States - 527 U.S. 373 (1999)
- Chicago v. Morales - 527 U.S. 41 (1999)
- Jefferson County v. Acker - 527 U.S. 423 (1999)
- Maryland v. Dyson on Petition for Writ of Certiorari to the Court of Special Appeals of Maryland - 527 U.S. 465 (1999)
- Florida Prepaid Postsecondary Ed. Expense Bd. v. College Savings Bank - 527 U.S. 627 (1999)
- College Savings Bank v. Florida Prepaid Postsecondary Ed. Expense Bd. - 527 U.S. 666 (1999)
- Alden v. Maine - 527 U.S. 706 (1999)
- Flippo v. West Virginia âŁ" 528 U.S. 11 (1999)
- Illinois v. Wardlow - 528 U.S. 119 (1999)
- Reno v. Condon - 528 U.S. 141 (1999)
- Martinez v. Court of Appeal of Cal., Fourth Appellate Dist. - 528 U.S. 152 (1999)
- Friends of Earth, Inc. v. Laidlaw Environmental Services (TOC), Inc. - 528 U.S. 167 (1999)
- Weeks v. Angelone - 528 U.S. 225 (1999)
- Fiore v. White - 528 U.S. 23 (1999)
- Smith v. Robbins - 528 U.S. 259 (1999)
- United States v. Martinez-Salazar - 528 U.S. 304 (1999)
- Kimel v. Florida Bd. of Regents - 528 U.S. 62 (1999)
- Carmell v. Texas - 529 U.S. 513 (1999)
- Hunt-Wesson, Inc. v. Franchise Tax Bd. of Cal. - 528 U.S. 458 (2000)
- Roe v. Flores-Ortega - 528 U.S. 470 (2000)
- Rice v. Cayetano - 528 U.S. 495 (2000)
- Village of Willowbrook v. Olech - 528 U.S. 562 (2000)
- Board of Regents of Univ. of Wis. System v. Southworth - 529 U.S. 217 (2000)
- Garner v. Jones - 529 U.S. 244 (2000)
- Florida v. J.L. - 529 U.S. 266 (2000)
- Bond v. United States - 529 U.S. 334 (2000)
- Norfolk Southern R.Co. v. Shanklin - 529 U.S. 344 (2000)
- Williams v. Taylor, Warden - 529 U.S. 362 (2000)
- Nelson v. Adams USA, Inc. - 529 U.S. 460 (2000)
- United States v. Morrison - 529 U.S. 598 (2000)
- Portuondo v. Agard - 529 U.S. 61 (2000)

- Vermont Agency of Natural Resources v. United States ex rel. Stevens - 529 U.S. 765 (2000)
- United States v. Playboy Entertainment Group, Inc. - 529 U.S. 803 (2000)
- Jones v. United States - 529 U.S. 848 (2000)
- United States v. Locke - 529 U.S. 89 (2000)
- Ramdass v. Angelone - 530 U.S. 156 (2000)
- SantaFe Independent School Dist. v. Doe - 530 U.S. 290 (2000)
- Miller v. French - 530 U.S. 327 (2000)
- Crosby v. National Foreign Trade Council - 530 U.S. 363 (2000)
- Dickerson v. United States - 530 U.S. 428 (2000)
- Apprendi v. New Jersey - 530 U.S. 466 (2000)
- California Democratic Party v. Jones - 530 U.S. 567 (2000)
- Troxel v. Granville - 530 U.S. 57 (2000)
- Boy Scouts of America v. Dale - 530 U.S. 640 (2000)
- Mitchell v. Helms - 530 U.S. 793 (2000)
- Stenberg v. Carhart - 530 U.S. 914 (2000)
- Seling v. Young - 531 U.S. 250 (2000)
- Bush v. Palm Beach County Canvassing Bd. - 531 U.S. 70 (2000)
- Bush v. Gore - 531 U.S. 98 (2000)
- Rogers v. Tennessee - 532 U.S. 451 (2000)
- Indianapolis v. Edmond - 531 U.S. 32 (2000)
- Brentwood Academy v. Tennessee Secondary School Athletic Assn. - 531 U.S. 288 (2001)
- Illinois v. McArthur - 531 U.S. 326 (2001)
- Board of Trustees of Univ. of Ala. v. Garrett - 531 U.S. 356 (2001)
- Whitman v. American Trucking Assns., Inc. - 531 U.S. 457 (2001)
- Cook v. Gralike - 531 U.S. 510 (2001)
- Legal Services Corp. v. Velazquez - 531 U.S. 533 (2001)
- Texas v. Cobb - 532 U.S. 162 (2001)
- Ohio v. Reiner - 532 U.S. 17 (2001)
- Easley v. Cromartie - 532 U.S. 234 (2001)
- Atwater v. Lago Vista - 532 U.S. 318 (2001)
- Shafer v. South Carolina - 532 U.S. 36 (2001)
- Bartnicki v. Vopper - 532 U.S. 514 (2001)
- Ferguson v. Charleston - 532 U.S. 67 (2001)
- Arkansas v. Sullivan - 532 U.S. 769 (2001)
- Florida v. Thomas - 532 U.S. 774 (2001)
- Norfolk Shipbuilding & Drydock Corp. v. Garris - 532 U.S. 811 (2001)
- Kansas v. Colorado - 533 U.S. 1 (2001)
- Saucier v. Katz - 533 U.S. 194 (2001)
- Idaho v. United States - 533 U.S. 262 (2001)
- Kyllo v. United States - 533 U.S. 27 (2001)
- INS v. St. Cyr - 533 U.S. 289 (2001)
- United States v. United Foods, Inc. - 533 U.S. 405 (2001)
- Lorillard Tobacco Co. v. Reilly - 533 U.S. 525 (2001)

- Tuan Anh Nguyen v. INS - 533 U.S. 53 (2001)
- Palazzolo v. Rhode Island - 533 U.S. 606 (2001)
- Zadvydas v. Davis - 533 U.S. 678 (2001)
- Good News Club v. Milford Central School - 533 U.S. 98 (2001)
- United States v. Knights - 534 U.S. 112 (2001)
- Correctional Services Corp. v. Malesko - 534 U.S. 61 (2001)
- McKune v. Lile - 536 U.S. 24 (2001)
- Dusenbery v. United States - 534 U.S. 161 (2002)
- Kelly v. South Carolina - 534 U.S. 246 (2002)
- United States v. Arvizu - 534 U.S. 266 (2002)
- Thomas v. Chicago Park Dist. - 534 U.S. 316 (2002)
- Porter v. Nussle - 534 U.S. 516 (2002)
- Raygor v. Regents of Univ. of Minn. - 534 U.S. 533 (2002)
- Mickens v. Taylor - 535 U.S. 162 (2002)
- Ashcroft v. Free Speech Coalition - 535 U.S. 234 (2002)
- Tahoe-Sierra Preservation Council, Inc. v. Tahoe Regional Planning Agency - 535 U.S. 302 (2002)
- Thompson v. Western States Medical Center - 535 U.S. 357 (2002)
- Los Angeles v. Alameda Books, Inc. - 535 U.S. 425 (2002)
- Ashcroft v. American Civil Liberties Union - 535 U.S. 564 (2002)
- Lapides v. Board of Regents of Univ. System of Ga. - 535 U.S. 613 (2002)
- United States v. Cotton - 535 U.S. 625 (2002)
- Verizon Md. Inc. v. Public Serv. Comm'n of Md. - 535 U.S. 635 (2002)
- Alabama v. Shelton - 535 U.S. 654 (2002)
- Bell v. Cone - 535 U.S. 685 (2002)
- Federal Maritime Comm'n v. South Carolina Ports Authority - 535 U.S. 743 (2002)
- Watchtower Bible & Tract Soc. of N. Y., Inc. v. Village of Stratton - 536 U.S. 150 (2002)
- Barnes v. Gorman - 536 U.S. 181 (2002)
- United States v. Drayton - 536 U.S. 194 (2002)
- Gonzaga Univ. v. Doe - 536 U.S. 273 (2002)
- Atkins v. Virginia - 536 U.S. 304 (2002)
- Columbus v. Ours Garage & Wrecker Service, Inc. - 536 U.S. 424 (2002)
- Utah v. Evans - 536 U.S. 452 (2002)
- BE&K Constr. Co. v. NLRB - 536 U.S. 516 (2002)
- Harris v. United States - 536 U.S. 545 (2002)
- Ring v. Arizona - 536 U.S. 584 (2002)
- United States v. Ruiz - 536 U.S. 622 (2002)
- Kirk v. Louisiana âŁ" 536 U.S. 635 (2002)
- Zelman v. Simmons-Harris - 536 U.S. 639 (2002)
- Hope v. Pelzer - 536 U.S. 730 (2002)
- Republican Party of Minn. v. White - 536 U.S. 765 (2002)

- Board of Ed. of Independent School Dist. No. 92 of Pottawatomie Cty. v. Earls - 536 U.S. 822 (2002)
- Sattazahn v. Pennsylvania - 537 U.S. 101 (2002)
- Pierce County v. Guillen - 537 U.S. 129 (2002)
- Eldred v. Ashcroft - 537 U.S. 186 (2002)
- Woodford v. Visciotti - 537 U.S. 19 (2002)
- Sprietsma v. Mercury Marine - 537 U.S. 51 (2002)
- Connecticut Dept. of Public Safety v. Doe - 538 U.S. 1 (2003)
- Ewing v. California - 538 U.S. 11 (2003)
- Cuyahoga Falls v. Buckeye Community Hope Foundation - 538 U.S. 188 (2003)
- Brown v. Legal Foundation of Wash. - 538 U.S. 216 (2003)
- Virginia v. Black - 538 U.S. 343 (2003)
- State Farm Mut. Automobile Ins. Co. v. Campbell - 538 U.S. 408 (2003)
- Jinks v. Richland County - 538 U.S. 456 (2003)
- Franchise Tax Bd. of Cal. v. Hyatt - 538 U.S. 488 (2003)
- Demore v. Kim - 538 U.S. 510 (2003)
- Illinois ex rel. Madigan v. Telemarketing Associates, Inc. - 538 U.S. 600 (2003)
- Kaupp v. Texas - 538 U.S. 626 (2003)
- Lockyer v. Andrade - 538 U.S. 63 (2003)
- Pharmaceutical Research and Mfrs. of America v. Walsh - 538 U.S. 644 (2003)
- Los Angeles v. David - 538 U.S. 715 (2003)
- Nevada Dept. of Human Resources v. Hibbs - 538 U.S. 721 (2003)
- Chavez v. Martinez - 538 U.S. 760 (2003)
- Bunkley v. Florida - 538 U.S. 835 (2003)
- Smith v. Doe - 538 U.S. 84 (2003)
- Beneficial Nat. Bank v. Anderson - 539 U.S. 1 (2003)
- Fitzgerald v. Racing Assn. of Central Iowa - 539 U.S. 103 (2003)
- Virginia v. Hicks - 539 U.S. 113 (2003)
- Overton v. Bazzetta - 539 U.S. 126 (2003)
- Federal Election Comm'n v. Beaumont - 539 U.S. 146 (2003)
- Sell v. United States - 539 U.S. 166 (2003)
- United States v. American Library Assn., Inc. - 539 U.S. 194 (2003)
- Gratz v. Bollinger - 539 U.S. 244 (2003)
- Grutter v. Bollinger - 539 U.S. 306 (2003)
- American Ins. Assn. v. Garamendi - 539 U.S. 396 (2003)
- Wiggins v. Smith - 539 U.S. 510 (2003)
- Citizens Bank v. Alafabco, Inc. - 539 U.S. 52 (2003)
- Lawrence v. Texas - 539 U.S. 558 (2003)
- Hillside Dairy Inc. v. Lyons - 539 U.S. 59 (2003)

- Stogner v. California - 539 U.S. 607 (2003)
- McConnell v. Federal Election Comm'n - 02-1674 (2003)
- McConnell v. Federal Election Comm'n - 02-1674 (2003)
- McConnell v. Federal Election Comm'n - 02-1674 (2003)
- Maryland v. Pringle - 02-809 (2003)
- Illinois v. Lidster - 02-1060 (2004)
- Locke v. Davey - 02-1315 (2004)
- United States v. Banks - 02-473 (2004)
- Frew v. Hawkins - 02-628 (2004)
- Fellers v. United States - 02-6320 (2004)
- Groh v. Ramirez - 02-811 (2004)
- Banks v. Dretke - 02-8286 (2004)
- Iowa v. Tovar - 02-1541 (2004)
- Tennessee Student Assistance Corporation v. Hood - 02-1606 (2004)
- City of Littleton v. Z. J. Gifts D-4, L. L. C. - 02-1609 (2004)
- Tennessee v. Lane - 02-1667 (2004)
- Yarborough v. Alvarado - 02-1684 (2004)
- Crawford v. Washington - 02-9410 (2004)
- United States v. Lara - 03-107 (2004)
- Sabri v. United States - 03-44 (2004)
- Thornton v. United States - 03-5165 (2004)
- Elk Grove Unified School Dist. v. Newdow - 02-1624 (2004)
- Blakely v. Washington - 02-1632 (2004)
- Aetna Health Inc. v. Davila - 02-1845 (2004)
- Rumsfeld v. Padilla - 03-1027 (2004)
- Ashcroft v. American Civil Liberties Union - 03-218 (2004)
- Rasul v. Bush - 03-334 (2004)
- Cheney v. United States Dist. Court for D. C. - 03-475 (2004)
- Schriro v. Summerlin - 03-526 (2004)
- Hiibel v. Sixth Judicial Dist. Court of Nev., Humboldt Cty. - 03-5554 (2004)
- Devenpeck v. Alford - 03-710 (2004)
- Florida v. Nixon - 03-931 (2004)
- Roper v. Simmons - 03-633 (2005)
- Johnson v. California - 03-636 (2005)
- Smith v. Massachusetts - 03-8661 (2005)
- Illinois v. Caballes - 03-923 (2005)
- United States v. Booker - 04-104 (2005)
- United States v. Booker - 04-104 (2005)
- Granholm v. Heald - 03-1116 (2005)
- Johanns v. Livestock Marketing Assn. - 03-1164 (2005)
- Tenet v. Doe - 03-1395 (2005)
- Muehler v. Mena - 03-1423 (2005)
- Exxon Mobil Corp. v. Saudi Basic Industries Corp. - 03-1696 (2005)
- Bates v. Dow Agrosciences LLC - 03-388 (2005)
- Cutter v. Wilkinson - 03-9877 (2005)
- Lingle v. Chevron U. S. A. Inc. - 04-163 (2005)
- Clingman v. Beaver - 04-37 (2005)
- Deck v. Missouri - 04-5293 (2005)

- American Trucking Assns., Inc. v. Michigan Pub. Serv. Comm'n - 03-1230 (2005)
- Gonzales v. Raich - 03-1454 (2005)
- McCreary County v. American Civil Liberties Union of Ky. - 03-1693 (2005)
- Miller-El v. Dretke - 03-9659 (2005)
- Kelo v. New London - 04-108 (2005)
- Castle Rock v. Gonzales - 04-278 (2005)
- San Remo Hotel, L. P. v. City and County of San Francisco - 04-340 (2005)
- Metro-Goldwyn-Mayer Studios Inc. v. Grokster, Ltd. - 04-480 (2005)
- Wilkinson v. Austin - 04-495 (2005)
- Rompilla v. Beard - 04-5462 (2005)
- Bradshaw v. Stumpf - 04-637 (2005)
- Gonzales v. O Centro Esp rita Beneficente Uni o do Vegetal - 04-1084 (2006)
- Ayotte v. Planned Parenthood of Northern New Eng. - 04-1144 (2006)
- Central Va. Community College v. Katz - 04-885 (2006)
- Oregon v. Guzek - 04-928 (2006)
- Brown v. Sanders - 04-980 (2006)
- Georgia v. Randolph - 04-1067 (2006)
- Rumsfeld v. Forum for Academic and Institutional Rights, Inc. - 04-1152 (2006)
- Holmes v. South Carolina - 04-1327 (2006)
- Jones v. Flowers - 04-1477 (2006)
- Arkansas Dept. of Health and Human Servs. v. Ahlborn - 04-1506 (2006)
- Northern Ins. Co. of N. Y. v. Chatham County - 04-1618 (2006)
- DaimlerChrysler Corp. v. Cuno - 04-1704 (2006)
- Garcetti v. Ceballos - 04-473 (2006)
- Samson v. California - 04-9728 (2006)
- Brigham City v. Stuart - 05-502 (2006)
- Davis v. Washington - 05-5224 (2006)
- Kansas v. Marsh - 04-1170 (2006)
- Arlington Central School Dist. Bd. of Ed. v. Murphy - 05-18 (2006)
- Clark v. Arizona - 05-5966 (2006)
- Dixon v. United States - 05-7053 (2006)
- Washington v. Recuenco - 05-83 (2006)
- Ayers v. Belmontes - 05-493 (2006)
- Carey v. Musladin - 05-785 (2006)
- Massachusetts v. EPA - 05-1120 (2007)
- Philip Morris USA v. Williams - 05-1256 (2007)
- Whorton v. Bockting - 05-595 (2007)
- MedImmune, Inc. v. Genentech, Inc. - 05-608 (2007)
- Cunningham v. California - 05-6551 (2007)
- Lance v. Coffman - 06-641 (2007)
- Microsoft Corp. v. AT&T Corp. - 05-1056 (2007)
- Watters v. Wachovia Bank, N. A. - 05-1342 (2007)
- Schriro v. Landrigan - 05-1575 (2007)
- Scott v. Harris - 05-1631 (2007)
- Gonzales v. Carhart - 05-380 (2007)
- James v. United States - 05-9264 (2007)
- Davenport v. Washington Ed. Assn. - 05-1589 (2007)
- Wilkie v. Robbins - 06-219 (2007)
- Uttecht v. Brown - 06-413 (2007)
- Tellabs, Inc. v. Makor Issues & Rights, Ltd. - 06-484 (2007)
- Fry v. Pliler - 06-5247 (2007)
- Rita v. United States - 06-5754 (2007)
- Brendlin v. California - 06-8120 (2007)
- Danforth v. Minnesota - 06-8273 (2008)
- Boumediene v. Bush - 06-1195 (2008)
- Taylor v. Sturgell - 07-371 (2008)
- Kennedy v. Louisiana - 07-343 (2008)
- Wyeth v. Levine - 06-1249 (2009)
- Summers v. Earth Island Institute - 07-463 (2009)
- Herring v. United States - 07-513 (2009)
- Pearson v. Callahan - 07-751 (2009)
- Haywood v. Drown - 07-10374 (2009)
- Corley v. United States - 07-10441 (2009)
- Kansas v. Ventris - 07-1356 (2009)
- Montejo v. Louisiana - 07-1529 (2009)
- Arizona v. Gant - 07-542 (2009)
- FCC v. Fox Television Stations, Inc. - 07-582 (2009)
- Caperton v. A. T. Massey Coal Co. - 08-22 (2009)
- Bobby v. Bies - 08-598 (2009)
- Melendez-Diaz v. Massachusetts - 07-591 (2009)
- Northwest Austin Municipal Util. Dist. No. One v. Holder - 08-322 (2009)
- Safford Unified School Dist. #1 v. Redding - 08-479 (2009)
- Yeager v. United States - 08-67 (2009)
- Alvarez v. Smith - 08-351 (2009)
- Beard v. Kindler - 08-992 (2009)
- Citizens United v. Federal Election Comm'n - 08-205 (2010)
- Florida v. Powell - 08-1175 (2010)
- Berghuis v. Smith - 08-1402 (2010)
- Padilla v. Kentucky - 08-651 (2010)
- Maryland v. Shatzer - 08-680 (2010)
- United States v. Stevens - 08-769 (2010)
- Thaler v. Haynes - 09-273 (2010)
- Renico v. Lett - 09-338 (2010)
- United States v. Comstock - 08-1224 (2010)
- Ontario v. Quon - 08-1332 (2010)
- Berghuis v. Thompkins - 08-1470 (2010)
- Graham v. Florida - 08-7412 (2010)
- Levin v. Commerce Energy, Inc. - 09-223 (2010)
- Dillon v. United States - 09-6338 (2010)
- Christian Legal Soc. Chapter of Univ. of Cal., Hastings College of Law v. Martinez - 08-1371 (2010)
- Skilling v. United States - 08-1394 (2010)
- Holder v. Humanitarian Law Project - 08-1498 (2010)

- Free Enterprise Fund v. Public Company Accounting Oversight Bd. - 08-861 (2010)
- Bilski v. Kappos - 08-964 (2010)
- Monsanto Co. v. Geertson Seed Farms - 09-475 (2010)
- Doe v. Reed - 09-559 (2010)
- Williamson v. Mazda Motor of America, Inc. - 08-1314 (2011)
- Michigan v. Bryant - 09-150 (2011)
- NASA v. Nelson - 09-530 (2011)
- Harrington v. Richter - 09-587 (2011)
- Premo v. Moore - 09-658 (2011)
- Pepper v. United States - 09-6822 (2011)
- Felkner v. Jackson - 10-797 (2011)
- Sossamon v. Texas - 08-1438 (2011)
- Cullen v. Pinholster - 09-1088 (2011)
- Chamber of Commerce of United States of America v. Whiting - 09-115 (2011)
- Kentucky v. King - 09-1272 (2011)
- Virginia Office for Protection and Advocacy v. Stewart - 09-529 (2011)
- AT&T Mobility LLC v. Concepcion - 09-893 (2011)
- Brown v. Entertainment Merchants Assn. - 08-1448 (2011)
- Bullcoming v. New Mexico - 09-10876 (2011)
- J. D. B. v. North Carolina - 09-11121 (2011)
- Davis v. United States - 09-11328 (2011)
- Bond v. United States - 09-1227 (2011)
- Borough of Duryea v. Guarnieri - 09-1476 (2011)
- PLIVA, Inc. v. Mensing - 09-993 (2011)
- Turner v. Rogers - 10-10 (2011)
- Stern v. Marshall - 10-179 (2011)
- Arizona Free Enterprise Club s Freedom Club PAC v. Bennett - 10-238 (2011)

- Nevada Comm n on Ethics v. Carrigan - 10-568 (2011)
- Goodyear Dunlop Tires Operations, S. A. v. Brown - 10-76 (2011)
- Sorrell v. IMS Health Inc. - 10-779 (2011)
- Minneci v. Pollard - 10-1104 (2012)
- United States v. Jones - 10-1259 (2012)
- PPL Montana, LLC v. Montana - 10-218 (2012)
- National Meat Assn. v. Harris - 10-224 (2012)
- Golan v. Holder - 10-545 (2012)
- Hosanna-Tabor Evangelical Lutheran Church and School v. EEOC - 10-553 (2012)
- Howes v. Fields - 10-680 (2012)
- Smith v. Cain - 10-8145 (2012)
- Kurns v. Railroad Friction Products Corp. - 10-879 (2012)
- Perry v. New Hampshire - 10-8974 (2012)
- Mayo Collaborative Services v. Prometheus Laboratories, Inc. - 10-1150 (2012)
- Blueford v. Arkansas - 10-1320 (2012)
- Lafler v. Cooper - 10-209 (2012)
- Missouri v. Frye - 10-444 (2012)
- Zivotofsky v. Clinton - 10-699 (2012)
- Florence v. Board of Chosen Freeholders of County of Burlington - 10-945 (2012)
- Armour v. Indianapolis - 11-161 (2012)
- FCC v. Fox Television Stations, Inc. - 10-1293 (2012)
- Miller v. Alabama - 10-9646 (2012)
- Arizona v. United States - 11-182 (2012)
- Match-E-Be-Nash-She-Wish Band of Pottawatomi Indians v. Patchak - 11-246 (2012)
- Southern Union Co. v. United States - 11-94 (2012)

Bibliography

Abraham, Henry J. 1999. *Justices, Presidents and Senators: A History of the U.S. Supreme Court Appointments from Washington to Clinton.* Lanham, MD: Rowman & Littlefield Publishers, Inc.

Abuse, Substace and Mental Health Services Administration. 2004. "Results from the 2003 National Survey on Drug Use and Health: National Findings."

Ackerman, Bruce. 1991. *We the People 1: Foundations.* Cambridge, MA: Belknap Press of Harvard University Press.

1998. *We the People 2: Transformations.* Cambridge, MA: Belknap.

Adams, John Quincy. 1839. "The Jubilee of the Constitution: A Discourse." Delivered at the request of The New York Historical Society, New York: City of New York, Tuesday, the 30th of April.

Allen, Francis A. 1958. "The Supreme Court, Federalism, and State Systems of Criminal Justice." *DePaul L. Rev.* 8:213.

Ansolabehere, Stephen, James M. Snyder Jr., and Charles Stewart III. 2001. "The Effects of Party and Preferences on Congressional Roll-Call Voting." *Legislative Studies Quarterly*: 533–572.

Ansolabehere, Stephen and Shanto Iyengar. 1995. *Going Negative: How Political Advertising Shrinks and Polarises the Electorate.* New York: Free Press.

Arnold, R Douglas. 1992. *The Logic of Congressional Action.* New Haven, CT: Yale University Press.

Association of National Advertisers, Inc. 1972. "Magazine Circulation and Rate Trends, 1940-1971."

Bailey, Michael A. 2007. "Comparable Preference Estimates across Time and Institutions for the Court, Congress, and Presidency." *American Journal of Political Science* 51(3):433–448.

Baird, Vanessa A. 2004. "The Effect of Politically Salient Decisions on the US Supreme Court's Agenda." *Journal of Politics* 66(3):755–772.

2007. *Answering the Call of the Court: How Justices and Litigants Set the Supreme Court Agenda.* Charlottesville: University of Virginia Press.

Baker, Scott and Claudio Mezetti. 2012. "A Theory of Rational Jurisprudence." *Journal of Political Economy* 120(3):513–551.

Bateman, David A., Joshua D. Clinton, and John S. Lapinksi. 2016. "A House Divided? Roll Calls, Polarization, and Policy Differences in the U.S. House, 1877-2011." *American Journal of Political Science* 61(3):698–714.

Beim, Deborah. 2017. "Learning in the Judicial Hierarchy." *Journal of Politics* 79(2):591–604.

Beim, Deborah, Alexander V. Hirsch, and Jonathan P. Kastellec. 2014. "Whistleblowing and Compliance in the Judicial Hierarchy." *American Journal of Political Science* 58(4):904–918.

Beim, Deborah, Tom S. Clark, and John W. Patty. 2017. "Why Do Courts Delay?" *Journal of Law & Courts* 5(2):199–241.

Belsky, Martin H. 1998. The Burger Court and Criminal Justice: A Counter-Revolution in Expectations. In *The Burger Court: Counter-Revolution or Confirmation*, ed. Bernard Schwartz. New York: Oxford University Press.

Benedict, Michael Les. 2011. "New Perspectives on the Waite Court." *Tulsa Law Review* 47:109.

Bensel, Richard F. 2000. *The Political Economy of American Industrialization, 1877-1900*. New York: Cambridge University Press.

Berry, William, Evan Ringquist, Richard Fording, and Russell Hanson. 1998. "Measuring Citizen and Government Ideology in the American States, 1960-1993." *American Journal of Political Science* 42(1):327–348.

Binder, Sarah A. 1999. "The Dynamics of Legislative Gridlock, 1947–96." *American Political Science Review* 93(3):519–533.

Binder, Sarah A. and Forrest Maltzman. 2004. "The Limits of Senatorial Courtesy." *Legislative Studies Quarterly* 39:5–22.

2009. *Advice and Dissent: The Struggle to Shape the Federal Judiciary*. Washington, DC: Brookings Institution Press.

Blackstone, Bethany. 2013. "An Analysis of Policy-Based Congressional Responses to the US Supreme Court's Constitutional Decisions." *Law & Society Review* 47(1):199–228.

Blasi, Vincent, ed. 1983. *The Burger Court: The Counter-Revolution That Wasn't*. New Haven, CT: Yale University Press.

Blei, David M., Andrew Y. Ng and Michael I. Jordan. 2003. "Latent dirichlet allocation." *Journal of Machine Learning Research* 3:993–1022.

Blevins, John F. 1963. "Lyons v. Oklahoma, the NAACP, and Coerced Confessions under the Hughes, Stone, and Vinson Courts, 1936-1949." *Virginia Law Review* 90:387–464.

Bonneau, Chris W., Thomas H. Hammond, Forrest Maltzman, and Paul J. Wahlbeck. 2007. "Agenda Control, the Median Justice, and the Majority Opinion on the U.S. Supreme Court." *American Journal of Political Science* 51(4):890–905.

Brandwein, Pamela. 2011. *Rethinking the Judicial Settlement of Reconstruction*. New York: Cambridge University Press.

Brick, Howard. 2000. *Age of Contradiction: American Thought and Culture in the 1960s*. Ithaca, NY: Cornell University Press.

Brudney, James J. and Corey Ditslear. 2008. "Liberal Justices' Reliance on Legislative History: Principle, Strategy, and the Scalia Effect." *Berkeley Journal of Employment and Labor Law* 29(3):117–173.

Bueno de Mesquita, Ethan and Matthew Stephenson. 2002. "Informative Precedent and Intrajudicial Communication." *American Political Science Review* 96(4):1–12.

Burstein, Paul. 1998. *Discrimination, Jobs and Politics: The Struggle for Equal Employment Opportunity in the United States since the New Deal.* Chicago, IL: University of Chicago Press.

Caldeira, Greg A., John R. Wright, and Christopher J. W. Zorn. 1999. "Sophisticated Voting and Gate-Keeping in the Supreme Court." *Journal of Law Economics and Organization* 15:549–572.

Caldeira, Gregory A. and John R. Wright. 1988. "Organized Interests and Agenda Setting in the U.S. Supreme Court." *American Political Science Review* 82(4):1109–1127.

1990*a*. "Amici Curiae before the Supreme Court: Who Participates, When, and How Much?" *The Journal of Politics* 52(3):782–806.

1990*b*. "The Discuss List: Agenda Building in the Supreme Court." *Law and Society Review* 24(3):807–836.

Callander, Steven and Tom S. Clark. 2017. "Precedent and Doctrine in a Complicated World." *American Political Science Review* 111(1): 184–203.

Cameron, Charles M. 1993. "New Avenues for Modeling Judicial Politics." Prepared for delivery at the Conference on the Political Economy of Public Law, Rochester, N.Y.

Cameron, Charles M., Albert D. Cover, and Jeffrey A. Segal. 1990. "Senate Voting on Supreme Court Nominees: A Neoinstitutional Model." *The American Political Science Review* 84(2):525–534.

Cameron, Charles M., Jeffrey A. Segal, and Donald R. Songer. 2000. "Strategic Auditing in a Political Hierarchy: An Informational Model of the Supreme Court's Certiorari Decisions." *American Political Science Review* 94:101–116.

Cameron, Charles M. and Jonathan P. Kastellec. 2016. "Are Supreme Court Nominations a Move-the-Median Game?" *American Political Science Review* 110(4):778–797.

Cameron, Charles M. and Lewis A. Kornhauser. N.d. "Modeling Colegial Courts (3): Adjudication Equilibria." New York University School of Law working paper.

Campbell, Angus, Philip E. Converse, Warren E. Miller, and Donald E. Stokes. 1966. *The American Voter.* New York: Wiley.

Canes-Wrone, Brandice, David W. Brady and John F. Cogan. 2002. "Out of Step, Out of Office: Electoral Accountability and House Members Voting." *American Political Science Review* 96(1):127–140.

Carrubba, Cliff, Barry Friedman, Andrew Martin, and Georg Vanberg. 2012. "Who Controls the Content of Supreme Court Opinions?" *American Journal of Political Science* 56(2):400–412.

Carrubba, Clifford J. 2009. "A Model of the Endogenous Development of Judicial Institutions in Federal and International Systems." *Journal of Politics* 71(1):55–69.

Carrubba, Clifford J. and Tom S. Clark. 2012. "Rule Creation in a Political Hierarchy." *American Political Science Review* 106(3):622–643.

Cashman, Sean Dennis. 1988. *America in the Age of the Titans: The Progressive Era and World War I.* New York: Press.

Casillas, Christopher J., Peter K. Enns, and Patrick. C Wohlfarth. 2011. "How Public Opinion Constrains the US Supreme Court." *American Journal of Political Science* 55(1):74–88.

Chambers, John W. 1969. "The Big Switch: Justice Roberts and the Minimum-Wage Cases, 10LAB." *Labor History* 44(57):71–73.

Clark, Tom S. 2006. "Judicial Decision-Making During Wartime." *Journal of Empirical Legal Studies* 3(3):397–419.

2009a. "Measuring Ideological Polarization on the U.S. Supreme Court." *Political Research Quarterly* 62(1):146–157.

2009b. "A Principal-Agent Model of En Banc Review." *Journal of Law, Economics & Organization* 25(1):55–79.

2009c. "The Separation of Powers, Court-curbing and Judicial Legitimacy." *American Journal of Political Science* 53(4):971–989.

2011. *The Limits of Judicial Independence.* New York: Cambridge University Press.

2016. "Scope and Precedent: Judicial Rule-Making Under Uncertainty." *Journal of Theoretical Politics* 28(3):353–384.

Clark, Tom S. and Benjamin E. Lauderdale. 2012. "The Genealogy of Law." *Political Analysis* 20(3):329–350.

2010. "Locating Supreme Court Opinions in Doctrine Space." *American Journal of Political Science* 54(4):871–890.

Clark, Tom S. and Clifford J. Carrubba. 2012. "A Theory of Opinion Writing in the Judicial Hierarchy." *Journal of Politics* 74(2):584–603.

Clark, Tom S. and Jonathan P. Kastellec. 2013. "The Supreme Court and Percolation in the Lower Courts: An Optimal Stopping Model." *Journal of Politics* 75(1):150–168.

Clark, Tom S. and Keith E. Whittington. N.d. "Judicial Review of Acts of Congress, 1790-2006." Emory University working paper.

Clinton, Joshua and Adam Meirowitz. 2004. "Testing Explanations of Strategic Voting in Legislatures: A Reexamination of the Compromise of 1790." *American Journal of Political Science* 48(4):821–835.

Clinton, Joshua D. and John Lapinksi. 2008. "Laws and Roll Calls in the U.S. Congress, 1891–1994." *Legislative Studies Quarterly* 33(4):511–542.

Clinton, Joshua D., Simon Jackman, and Douglas Rivers. 2004. "The Statistical Analysis of Roll Call Data." *American Political Science Review* 98(2):355–370.

Clinton, Robert Lowry. 1994. "Game Theory, Legal History, and the Origins of Judicial Review: A Revisionist Anaylsis of Marbury v. Madison." *American Journal of Political Science* 38:285–302.

Cohen, Robert and Reginald E Zelnik. 2002. *The Free Speech Movement: Reflections on Berkeley in the 1960s.* California: Univ of California Press.

Cooley, Thomas McIntyre. 1898. *The General Principles of Constitutional Law in the United States of America.* Boston, MA: Little, Brown.

Corwin, Edward S. 1929. "The 'Higher Law' Background of American Constitutional Law." *Harvard Law Review* 42(3):365–409.

Cox, Gary W. and Mathew D. McCubbins. 2005. *Setting the Agenda: Responsible Party Government in the US House of Representatives.* Cambridge University Press.

Croly, Herbert. 1993. *The Promise of American Life.* New York: Transaction Books.

Cushman, Barry. 1998. *Rethinking the New Deal Court.* New York: Oxford University Press.

Dahl, Robert. 1957. "Decision-Making in a Democracy: The Supreme Court as National Policy-Maker." *Journal of Public Law* 6(2):279–295.

Dake, B. Frank. 1904. "The Negro Before the Supreme Court." *Albany Law Journal* LXVI(8):238–248.

Daughety, Andrew F. and Jennifer F. Reinganum. 2006. "Speaking up: A Model of Judicial Dissent and Discretionary Review." *Supreme Court Economic Review* pp. 1–41.

Decker, John F. 1992. *Revolution to the Right: Criminal Procedure Jurisprudence during the Burger-Rehnquist Court era.* New York: Garland Pub.

Devins, Neal and Louis Fisher. 2015. *The Democratic Constitution.* New York: Oxford University Press.

Diver, Colin S. 1979. "The Judge as Political Powerbroker: Superintending Structural Change in Public Institutions." *Virginia Law Review* 1979:43–106.

Duer, William Alexander. 1956. *A Course of Lectures on the Constitutional Jurisprudence of the United States Delivered Annually in Columbia College, New York.* The Lawbook Exchange, Ltd.

Eisen, Jonathan. 1969. *The Age of Rock, Sounds of the American Cultural Revolution: A Reader.* Vol. 1 New York: Random House.

Eisgruber, Christopher L. 2001. *Constitutional Self-Government.* Cambridge, MA: Harvard University Press.

Ellison, Glenn and Richard Holden. 2014. "A Theory of Rule Development." *Journal of Law, Economics, and Organizations* 30(4):649–682.

Elster, Jon. 1983. *Explaining Technical Change: A Case Study in the Philosophy of Science.* New York: Cambridge University Press.

Ely, James W., Jr. 1995. *The Chief Justiceship of Melville W. Fuller, 1888-1910.* Columbia, SC: University of South Carolina Press.

  1999. "Oxymoron Reconsidered: Myth and Reality in the Origins of Substantive Due Process." *Constitutional Commentary* 16:315.

Epp, Charles R. 1998. *The Rights Revolution: Lawyers, Activists, and Supreme Courts in Comparative Perspective.* New York: Cambridge Univ Press.

  2010. *Making Rights Real: Activists, Bureaucrats, and the Creation of the Legalistic State.* Chicago, IL: University of Chicago Press.

Epstein, Lee and Andrew D. Martin. 2010. "Does Public Opinion Influence the Supreme Court? Possibly Yes (But We're Not Sure Why)." *University of Pennsylvania Journal of Constitutional Law* 13:263.

Epstein, Lee, Daniel E. Ho, Gary King, and Jeffrey A. Segal. 2005. "Supreme Court During Crisis." *New York University Law Review* 80:1–116.

Epstein, Lee and Jack Knight. 1998. *The Choices Justices Make.* Washington, D.C.: C.Q. Press.

Epstein, Lee and Jeffrey A. Segal. 2005. *Advice and Consent: The Politics of Judicial Appointments.* New York: Oxford University Press.

Epstein, Lee, Jeffrey A. Segal, Harold J. Spaeth, and Thomas G. Walker. 2007. *The Supreme Court Compendium: Data, Decisions and Developments.* 4 ed. Washington, D.C.: Congressional Quarterly Inc.

Epstein, Lee and Olga Shvetsova. 2002. "Heresthetical Maneuvering on the US Supreme Court." *Journal of Theoretical Politics* 14(1):93–122.

Epstein, Lee, René Lindstädt, Jeffrey A Segal, and Chad Westerland. 2006. "The Changing Dynamics of Senate Voting on Supreme Court Nominees." *Journal of Politics* 68(2):296–307.

Erikson, Robert S., Gerald C. Wright, and John P. McIver. 1993. *Statehouse Democracy: Public Opinion and Policy in the American States*. New York: Cambridge University Press.

Erikson, Robert S., Michael B. MacKuen, and James A. Stimson. 2002. *The Macro Polity*. New York: Cambridge University Press.

Eskridge, Jr., William N. 1991. "Reneging on History? Playing the Court/Congress/President Civil Rights Game." *California Law Review* 79(2):613–684.

Esteban, Joan-Maria and Debraj Ray. 1994. "On the Measurement of Polarization." *Econometrica: Journal of the Econometric Society*: 819–851.

Estrecher, Samuel and John Sexton. 1986. *Redefining the Supreme Court's Role: A Theory of Managing the Federal Judicial Process*. New Haven: Yale University Press.

Fehrenbacher, Don Edward. 2001. *The Dred Scott Case: Its Significance in American Law and Politics*. New York: Oxford University Press.

Feldman, Noah. 2010. *Scorpions: The Battles and Triumphs of FDR's Great Supreme Court Justices*. New York: Twelve.

Fenno, Jr., Richard F. 1978. *Home Style: House Members in Their Districts*. New York: Longman.

Ferejohn, John and Charles Shipan. 1990. "Congressional Influence on Bureaucracy." *Journal of Law, Economics & Organization* 6(Special Issue):1–20.

Flemming, Roy B. and B. Dan Wood. 1997. "The Public and the Supreme Court: Individual Justice Responsiveness to American Policy Moods." *American Journal of Political Science* 41(2):468–498.

Fowler, James H. and Sangick Jeon. 2008. "The Authority of Supreme Court Precedent: A Network Analysis." *Social Networks* 30(1):16–30.

Fowler, James H., Timothy R. Johnston, James F. Spriggs, II, Sangick Jeon, and Paul J. Wahlbeck. 2007. "Network Analysis and the Law: Measuring the Legal Importance of Precedents at the U.S. Supreme Court." *Political Analysis* 15(3):324–346.

Fox, Justin and Georg Vanberg. 2014. "Narrow versus Broad Judicial Decisions." *Journal of Theoretical Politics* 26(3):355–383.

Fraser, Steve and Gary Gerstle. 1989. *The Rise and Fall of the New Deal Order, 1930-1980*. Princeton, NJ: Princeton University Press.

Friedman, Barry. 2002a. "The Birth of an Academic Obsession: The History of the Countermajoritarian Difficulty, Part Five." *Yale Law Journal* 112(2):153–259.

2005. "The Politics of Judicial Review." *Texas Law Review* 84:257–337.

2009. *The Will of the People: How Public Opinion Has Influenced the Supreme Court and Shaped the Meaning of the Constitution*. New York: Farrar, Straus and Giroux.

Friedman, Lawrence M. 2002b. *American Law in the 20th Century*. Yale University Press.

Fritz, Christian G. 2007. *American Sovereigns: The People and America's Constitutional Tradition before the Civil War.* New York: Cambridge University Press.

Galanter, Marc. 1974. "Why the 'haves' come out ahead: Speculations on the limits of legal change." *Law & Society Review* 9(1):95–160.

Galloway Jr., Russell W. 1985. "The Taft Court (1921-29)" *Santa Clara Law Review* 25:1.

Gely, Rafael and Pablo T. Spiller. 1990. "A Rational Choice Theory of Supreme Court Statutory Decisions with Applications to the State Farm and Grove City Cases." *Journal of Law, Economics, and Organization* 6:263–300.

Gennaioli, Nicola and Andrei Shleifer. 2007. "The Evolution of Common Law." *Journal of Political Economy* 115(1):43–68.

Giles, Micheal W., Bethany Blackstone, and Rich Vining. 2008. "The Supreme Court in American Democracy: Unraveling the Linkages between Public Opinion and Judicial Decision-making." *Journal of Politics* 70(2):293–306.

Giles, Micheal W. and Thomas G. Walker. 1975. "Judicial Policy-Making and Southern School Segregation." *The Journal of Politics* 37(04):917–936.

Giles, Micheal W., Thomas G. Walker and Christopher Zorn. 2006. "Setting Judicial Agenda: The Decision to Grant en banc Review in the US Courts of Appeals." *Journal of Politics* 68(4):852–866.

Giles, Micheal W., Virginia A. Hettinger, Christopher Zorn, and Todd C. Peppers. 2007. "The Etiology of the Occurrence of En Banc Review in the U.S. Court of Appeals." *American Journal of Political Science* 51(3):449–63.

Gillman, Howard. 2002. "How Political Parties Can Use the Courts to Advance Their Agendas: Federal Courts in the United States, 1875-1891." *American Political Science Review* 96(3):511–524.

Gillman, Howard, Mark Graber, and Keith E. Whittington. 2012a. *American Constitutionalism I: Structures of Government.* New York: Oxford University Press.

Gillman, Howard, Mark Graber, and Keith E. Whittington. 2012b. *American Constitutionalism II: Rights and Liberties.* New York: Oxford University Press.

Goebel, Jr., Julius. 1938. "Constitutional History and Constitutional Law." *Columbia Law Review* 38(4):555–577.

Goluboff, Risa Lauren. 2004. "Let Economic Equality Take Care of Itself: The NAACP, Labor Litigation, and the Making of Civil Rights in the 1940s." *UCLA L. Rev.* 52:1393.

Gordon, Robert J. 2017. *The Rise and Fall of American Growth: The US Standard of Living since the Civil War.* Princeton, NJ: Princeton University Press.

Graber, Mark A. 2006. *Dred Scott and the Problem of Constitutional Evil.* New York: Cambridge University Press.

Graetz, Michael J. and Linda Greenhouse. 2017. *The Burger Court and the Rise of the Judicial Right.* New York: Simon & Schuster.

Graham, Howard Jay. 1950. "The Early Antislavery Backgrounds of the Fourteenth Amendment." *Wisconsin Law Review* 1950(4):610–661.

Grant, Emily, Scott A. Hendrickson, and Michael S. Lynch. 2012. "The Ideological Divide: Conflict and the Supreme Court's Certiorari Decision." *Clev. St. L. Rev.* 60:559.

Greif, Avner. 2006. *Institutions and the Path to the Modern Economy: Lessons from Medieval Trade.* New York: Cambridge University Press.

Gronlund, Mimi Clark. 2010. *Supreme Court Justice Tom C. Clark: A Life of Service.* Houston, TX: University of Texas Press.

Gunther, Gerald. 1970. *Constitutional Law: Cases and Materials.* Westbury, NY: Foundation Press.

Gunther, Gerald and Kathleen M. Sullivan. 1997. *Constitutional Law.* 13th ed. Westbury, NY: Foundation Press.

Guthrie, William Dameron. 1898. *Lectures on the Fourteenth Article of Amendment to the Constitution of the United States: Delivered Before the Dwight Alumni Association, New York, April-May, 1898.* Boston, MA: Little, Brown.

Gutmann, Amy and Dennis Thompson. 2009. *Democracy and Disagreement.* Cambridge, MA: Harvard University Press.

Hall, Jacquelyn Dowd. 2005. "The Long Civil Rights Movement and the Political Uses of the Past." *The Journal of American History* 91(4):1233–1263.

Hall, Kermit L. 1999. *The Oxford Guide to United States Supreme Court Decisions.* 2 ed. New York: Oxford University Press.

Hammond, Thomas H., Chris W. Bonneau, and Reginald S. Sheehan. 2005. *Strategic Behavior and Policy Choice on the U.S. Supreme Court.* Palo Alto, CA: Stanford University Press.

Harvey, Anna and Michael J. Woodruff. 2013. "Confirmation Bias in the United States Supreme Court Judicial Database." *Journal of Law, Economics, & Organization* 29(2):414–460.

Hattam, Victoria C. 1993. *Labor Visions and State Power: The Origins of Business Unionism in the United States.* Princeton, NJ: Princeton University Press.

Heller, Francis H. 1943. "A Turning Point for Religious Liberty." *Virginia Law Review* 29(4):440–459.

Henderson, Jennifer Jacobs. 2004. "The Jehovah's Witnesses and Their Plan to Expand First Amendment Freedoms." *Journal of Church & State* 46:811.

Hentoff, Nat. 1990. "The Constitutionalist." *The New Yorker* March 12:45–70.

Hettinger, Virginia A., Stephanie A. Lindquist, and Wendy L. Martinek. 2004. "Comparing Attitudinal and Strategic Accounts of Dissenting Behavior on the U.S. Courts of Appeals." *American Journal of Political Science* 48:123–137.

Hilton, George W. 1966. "The Consistency of the Interstate Commerce Act." *Journal of Law & Economics* 9:87–113.

Ho, Daniel E. and Kevin M. Quinn. 2010. "How Not to Lie with Judicial Votes: Misconceptions, Measurement, and Models." *California Law Review* 98(3):813–876.

Holmes, Jr., Oliver Wendell. 1897. "The Path of the Law." *Harvard Law Review* 10:457–478.

Horwitz, Morton J. 1992. *The Transformation of American Law, 1870–1960: The Crisis of Legal Orthodoxy.* New York: Oxford University Press.

Iaryczower, Matias and Matthew Shum. 2012. "The Value of Information in the court: Get it Right, Keep it Tight." *American Economic Review* 102(1):202–237.

Irons, Peter. 2006. *A People's History of the Supreme Court: The Men and Women Whose Cases and Decisions Have Shaped Our Constitution: Revised Edition.* New York: Penguin.

Jackman, Simon. 2001. "Multidimensional Analysis of Roll Call Data via Bayesian Simulation: Identification, Estimation, Inference and Model Checking." *Political Analysis* 9(3):227–241.

Jacobi, Tonja and Emerson H. Tiller. 2007. "Legal Doctrine and Political Control." *Journal of Law, Economics, & Organization* 23(2):326–345.

Jeffries, John C., Jr. and James E. Ryan. 2001. "A Political History of the Establishment Clause." *Michigan Law Review* 100(2):279–370.

Jenkins, Shannon. 2006. "The Impact of Party and Ideology on Roll-Call Voting in State Legislatures." *Legislative Studies Quarterly* 31(2):235–257.

Johnson, Emory R. and Thurman W. Van Metre. 1918. *Principles of Railroad Transportation.* New York: D. Appleton.

Johnson, John W. 1997. *The Struggle for Students Rights:* Tinker v. Des Moines *and the 1960s.* Kansas: University of Kansas Press.

Kaczorowski, Robert J. 1987. "To Begin the Nation Anew: Congress, Citizenship, and Civil Rights after the Civil War." *American Historical Review* 92(1):45–68.

Kagan, Robert A. 2009. *Adversarial Legalism: The American Way of Law.* Cambridge, MA: Harvard University Press.

Kastellec, Jonathan P. 2007. "Panel Composition and Judicial Compliance on the United States Courts of Appeals." *Journal of Law, Economics & Organization* 23(2):421–441.

Kastellec, Jonathan P. and Jeffrey R. Lax. 2008. "Case Selection and the Study of Judicial Politics." *Journal of Empirical Legal Studies* 53(3):407–446.

Kim, In Song, John Londregan, and Marc Ratkovic. 2015. "Voting, Speechmaking, and the Dimensions of Conflict in the US Senate." Princeton University working paper.

Klarman, Michael. 2004. *From Jim Crow to Civil Rights.* New York: Oxford University Press.

Kluger, Richard. 1975. *Simple Justice.* New York: Vintage Books.

Knight, Jack. 2009. "Are Empiricists Asking the Right Questions about Judicial Decisionmaking?" *Duke Law Journal* 58:1531–1556.

Knight, Jack and James Johnson. 1997. "What sort of political equality does deliberative democracy In James Bohman and William Rehg," *Deliberative Democracy: Essays on Reason and Politics,* Cambridge, MA: MIT Press, pp. 279–319.

Knight, Jack and Lee Epstein. 1996. "On the Struggle for Judicial Supremacy." *Law & Society Review* 30(1):87–130.

Kobylka, Joseph F. 1987. "A Court-created Context for Group Litigation: Libertarian Groups and Obscenity." *The Journal of Politics* 49(4):1061–1078.

Kornhauser, Lewis. A. 1992a. "Modeling Collegial Courts *I*: Path Dependence." *International Review of Law and Economics* 12:169–185.

    1992b. "Modeling Collegial Courts *II*: Legal Doctrine." *Journal of Law Economics & Organization* 8:441–470.

Kramer, Larry D. 2004. *The People Themselves.* New York: Oxford University Press.

Krehbiel, Keith. 1998. *Pivotal Politics: A Theory of U.S. Lawmaking*. Chicago, IL: University of Chicago Press.

2007. "Supreme Court Appointments as a Move-the-Median Game." *American Journal of Political Science* 51(2):231–240.

Landa, Dimitri and Jeffrey R Lax. 2009. "Legal Doctrine in Collegial Courts." *Journal of Politics* (Forthcoming).

Lauderdale, Benjamin E. 2010. "Unpredictable Voters in Ideal Point Estimation." *Political Analysis* 18(2):151–171.

Lauderdale, Benjamin E. and Tom S. Clark. 2014. "Scaling Politically Meaningful Dimensions Using Texts and Votes." *American Journal of Political Science* 58(3):754–771.

2016. "Estimating Vote-specific Preferences from Roll Call Data Using Conditional Autoregressive Priors." *The Journal of Politics* 78(4):1153–1169.

2012. "The Supreme Court's Many Median Justices." *American Political Science Review* 106(4):847–866.

Lax, Jeffrey R. 2007. "Constructing Legal Rules on Appellate Courts." *American Political Science Review* 101(3):591–604.

2011. "The New Judicial Politics of Legal Doctrine." *Annual Review of Political Science* 14:131–157.

2012. "Political Constraints on Legal Doctrine: How Hierarchy Shapes the Law." *Journal of Politics* 74(3):765–781.

Lax, Jeffrey R. and Charles M. Cameron. 2007. "Bargaining and Opinion Assignment on the U.S. Supreme Court." *Journal of Law, Economics, and Organization* 23(2):276–302.

Lax, Jeffrey R. and Kelly T. Rader. 2010. "Legal Constraints on Supreme Court Decision Making: Do Jurisprudential Regimes Exist?" *The Journal of Politics* 72(02):273–284.

Lerman, Amy E. and Vesla M. Weaver. 2014. *Arresting Citizenship: The Democratic Consequences of American Crime Control*. Chicago, IL: University of Chicago Press.

Levi, Edward. 1949. *An Introduction to Legal Reasoning*. Chicago, IL: University of Chicago Press.

Maltzman, Forrest, James F. Spriggs, II, and Paul J. Wahlbeck. 2000. *Crafting Law on the Supreme Court: The Collegial Game*. New York: Cambridge University Press.

Martin, Andrew D. and Kevin M. Quinn. 2002. "Dynamic Ideal Point Estimation Via Markov Chain Monte Carlo for the U.S. Supreme Court, 1953-1999." *Political Analysis* 10(2):134–153.

Marwick, Arthur. 2011. *The Sixties: Cultural Revolution in Britain, France, Italy, and the United States, c. 1958-c. 1974*. New York: A&C Black.

Mayhew, David E. 1974. *Congress: The Electoral Connection*. New Haven, CT: Yale University Press.

McCloskey, Robert G. 1972. *The Modern Supreme Court*. Cambridge, MA: Harvard University Press.

McGuire, Kevin T. and Georg Vanberg. 2005. "Mapping the Policies of the U.S. Supreme Court: Data, Opinions, and Constitutional Law." Paper presented at the Annual Meeting of the American Political Science Association, Washington, D.C., September 1-5.

McGuire, Kevin T. and James A. Stimson. 2004. "The Least Dangerous Branch Revisited: New Evidence on Supreme Court Responsiveness to Public Preferences." *Journal of Politics* 66(4):1018–1035.

McMahon, Kevin J. 2011. *Nixon's Court*. Chicago, IL: University of Chicago Press.

McPherson, James M. 1988. *Battle Cry of freedom: The Civil War Era*. New York: Oxford University Press.

Meernik, James and Joseph Ignagni. 1997. "Judicial Review and Coordinate Construction of the Constitution." *American Journal of Political Science* 41(2):447–467.

Menkel-Meadow, Carrie. 1984. "Legal Aid in the United States: The Professionalization and Politicization of Legal Services in the 1980's." *Osgoode Hall Law Journal* 22:29.

Mishler, William and Reginald S. Sheehan. 1993. "The Supreme Court as a Countermajoritarian Institution? The Impact of Public Opinion on Supreme Court Decisions." *American Political Science Review* 87(1):87–101.

Mishler, William and Reginald S. Sheehan. 1996. "Public Opinion, the Attitudinal Model, and Supreme Court Decision Making: A Micro-Analytic Perspective." *Journal of Politics* 58(1):169–200.

Moraski, Bryon J. and Charles R. Shipan. 1999. "The Politics of Supreme Court Nominations: A Theory of Institutional Constraints and Choices." *American Journal of Political Science* 43(4):1069–1095.

Morga, Robert A. 2006. Wages and Wage Inequality. In *Historical Statistics of the United States, Earliest Times to the Present: Millennial Edition*, eds. Douglas Eckberg, Susan B. Carter, Scott Sigmund Gartner, Michael R. Haines, Alan L. Olmstead, Richard Sutch and Gavin Wright. New York: Cambridge University Press.

Murphy, Walter F. 1964. *Elements of Judicial Strategy*. Chicago, IL: University of Chicago Press.

Nagel, Stuart S. 1965. "Court-Curbing Periods in American History." *Vanderbilt Law Review* 18(3):925–944.

Neier, Aryeh. 1982. *Only Judgment: The Limits of Litigation in Social Change*. Middletown, CT: Wesleyan University Press, pp. 127–140.

Nixon, Richard. 1971. "Remarks about an intensified program for drug abuse prevention and control." *June* 17, 1971. Archived by Gerhard Peters and John T. Woolley." The American Presidency Project.

Noel, Hans. 2013. *Political Parties and Political Ideologies in America*. New York: Cambridge University Press.

Norpoth, Helmut, Jeffrey A. Segal, William Mishler and Reginald S. Sheehan. 1994. "Popular Influence on Supreme Court Decisions." *American Political Science Review* 88(03):711–724.

Novak, William J. 1996. *The People's Welfare: Law & Regulation in Nineteenth-Century America*. Chapel Hill, NC: University of North Carolina Press.

Novkov, Julie. 2015. "Understanding Law as a Democratic Institution Through US Constitutional Development." *Law & Social Inquiry* 40(3):811–832.

O'Connor, Karen and Lee Epstein. 1981. "Amicus Curiae Participation in U.S. Supreme Court Litigation: AnAppraisal of Hakman's 'Folklore'." *Law and Society Review* 16(2):311–320.

1983. "The Rise of Conservative Interest Group Litigations." *The Journal of Politics* 45(2):479–489.

1985. "Bridging the Gap between Congress and the Supreme Court: Interest Groups and the Erosion of the American Rule Governing Awards of Attorneys' Fees." *The Western Political Quarterly* 38(2):238–249.

of Management, United States. Office, Budget. Statistical Policy Division, United States. Social and Economic Statistics Administration. 1973. *Social Indicators, 1973: Selected Statistics on Social Conditions and Trends in the United States*. US Government Printing Office.

of the Census. U.S. Department of Commerce., United States. Bureau. 1980. *Social Indicators III: Selected Data on Social Conditions and Trends in the United States*. US Government Printing Office.

Olson, Susan M. 1990. "Interest-group Litigation in Federal District Court: Beyond the Political Disadvantage Theory." *The Journal of Politics* 52(3):854–882.

on Obscenity, United States. Commission and Pornography. 1970. *Report of the Commission on Obscenity and Pornography, September 1970*. Vol. 7 Government Press.

Page, Scott E. et al. 2006. "Path Dependence." *Quarterly Journal of Political Science* 1(1):87–115.

Pang, Xun, Barry Friedman, Andrew D. Martin, and Kevin M. Quinn. 2012. "Endogenous Jurisprudential Regimes." *Political Analysis* 20(4): 417–436.

Peltason, Jack Walter. 1971. *Fifty-eight Lonely Men: Southern Federal Judges and School Desegregation*. Vol. 74 Champaign, IL: University of Illinois Press.

Perry, Jr., H.W. 1991. *Deciding to Decide: Agenda Setting in the United States Supreme Court*. Cambridge, MA: Harvard University Press.

Peters, Shawn Francis. 2000. *Judging Jehovah's Witnesses*. Lawrence, KS: University Press of Kansas.

Phillips, Wendell and Andrew Jackson Graham. 1862. *The War for the Union: A Lecture*. Vol. 25 New York: EE Barker.

Pickerill, J. Mitchell. 2004. *Constitutional Deliberation in Congress: The Impact of Judicial Review in a Separated System*. Durham, NC: Duke University Press.

Pierson, Paul. 2000. "Increasing Returns, Path Dependence, and the Study of Politics." *American Political Science Review* 94(2):251–267.

Poole, Keith T. and Howard Rosenthal. 1997. *Congress: A Political-Economic History of Roll Call Voting*. Oxford: Oxford University Press.

Popkin, Samuel L. 1994. *The reasoning Voter: Communication and Persuasion in Presidential Campaigns*. Chicago, IL: University of Chicago Press.

Posner, Richard A. 2008. *How Judges Think*. Cambridge, MA: Harvard University Press.

Post, Robert C. 1998. "Defending the Lifeworld: Substantive Due Process in the Taft Court Era." *Boston University Law Review* 78:1489.

Pound, Roscoe. 1905. "Do We Need a Philosophy of Law?" *Columbia Law Review* 5(5):339–353.

Prior, Markus. 2007. *Post-broadcast Democracy: How Media Choice Increases Inequality in Political Involvement and Polarizes Elections*. New York: Cambridge University Press.

Pritchett, C. Herman. 1948. *The Roosevelt Court; A Study in Judicial Politics and Values, 1937-1947*. New York: Macmillan Co.

Przybyszewski, Linda. 2005. The Fuller Court (1888-1910): Property and Liberty. In *The United States Supreme Court: The Pursuit of Justice*, ed. Christopher Tomlins. Boston, MA: Houghton Mifflin.

Reed, Thomas J. 1982. "The Development of the Propensity Rule in Federal Criminal Causes 1840-1975." *University of Cincinnati Law Review* 51:299.

Renstrom, Peter G. 2003. *The Taft Court: Justices, Rulings, and Legacy*. Santa Barbara, CA: ABC-CLIO.

Rice, Douglas. 2017. "Issue Divisions and U.S. Supreme Court Decision Making." *Journal of Politics* 79(1):201–222.

Richards, Mark J. and Herbert M. Kritzer. 2002. "Jurisprudential Regimes in Supreme Court Decision Making." *American Political Science Review* 96(2):305–320.

Riker, William H. 1982. *Political Theory and the Art of Heresthetics*. Publisher not identified.

    1986. *The Art of Political Manipulation*. Vol. 587 New Haven, CT: Yale University Press.

Rivers, Douglas. 2003. "Identification of Multidimensional Spatial Voting Models." Stanford University working paper.

Rogers, James R. 2001. "Information and Judicial Review: A Signaling Game of Legislative-Judicial Interaction." *American Journal of Political Science* 45(1):84–99.

Rogers, James R. and Georg Vanberg. 2007. "Resurrecting Lochner: A Defense of Unprincipled Judicial Activism." *Journal of Law, Economics & Organization* 23(2):442–468.

Rosenberg, Gerald N. 1991. *The Hollow Hope: Can Courts Bring About Social Change?* Chicago, IL: University of Chicago Press.

    1992. "Judicial Independence and the Reality of Political Power." *Review of Politics* 54(3):369–388.

Rosenbloom, Joshua L. 2006. Union Membership: 1880–1999. In *Historical Statistics of the United States, Earliest Times to the Present: Millennial Edition*, eds. Douglas Eckberg, Susan B. Carter, Scott Sigmund Gartner, Michael R. Haines, Alan L. Olmstead, Richard Sutch and Gavin Wright. New York: Cambridge University Press.

Scalia, Antonin and Bryan A. Garner. 2012. *Reading Law*. St. Paul, MN: Thomson/West.

Schanzenbach, Max M. and Emerson H. Tiller. 2006. "Strategic Judging under the US Sentencing Guidelines: Positive Political Theory and Evidence." *The Journal of Law, Economics, & Organization* 23(1):24–56.

Schelling, Thomas C. 1971. "What is the business of organized crime?" *The American Scholar* 40(4):643–652.

Schubert, Glendon. 1958. "The Study of Judicial Decision Making as an Aspect of Political Behavior." *American Political Science Review* 52(4):1007–1025.

Schwartz, Bernard, ed. 1998. *The Burger Court: Counter-Revolution or Confirmation?* New York: Oxford University Press.

Schwartz, Edward P. 1992. "Policy, Precedent, and Power: A Positive Theory of Supreme Court Decision-Making." *Journal of Law, Economics, & Organization* 8(2):219–252.

Scott, Kevin M. 2006. "Understanding Judicial Hierarchy: Reversals and Behaviour of Intermediate Appellate Judges." *Law & Society Review* 40(1):163–192.

Segal, Jeffrey A. 1984. "Predicting Supreme Court Cases Probabilistically: The Search and Seizure Cases, 1962-1981." *American Political Science Review* 78(4):891–900.

Segal, Jeffrey A., Charles M. Cameron and Albert D. Cover. 1992. "A Spatial Model of Roll Call Voting: Senators, Constituents, Presidents,and Interest Groups in Supreme Court Confirmations." *American Journal of Political Science* 36(1):96–121.

Segal, Jeffrey. A. and Harold J. Spaeth. 1993. *The Supreme Court and the Attitudinal Model*. New York: Cambridge University Press.

   2002. *The Supreme Court and the Attitudinal Model Revisited*. New York: Cambridge University Press.

Sergeant, John. 1832. *Select Speeches of John Sergeant, of Pennsylvania, 1818-1828*. Philadelphia, PA: EL Carey & A. Hart.

Shor, Boris and Nolan McCarty. 2011. "The Ideological Mapping of American Legislatures." *American Political Science Review* 105(03):530–551.

Skocpol, Theda and Kenneth Finegold. 1982. "State Capacity and Economic Intervention in the Early New Deal." *Political Science Quarterly* 97(2):255–278.

Spaeth, Harold J. and David J. Peterson. 1971. "The Analysis and Interpretation of Dimensionality: The Case of Civil Liberties Decision Making." *Midwest Journal of Political Science* 15(3):415–441.

Spaeth, Harold J., Lee Epstein, Theodore W. Ruger, Keith E. Whittington, Jeffrey A. Segal and Andrew D. Martin. 2015. "The Supreme Court Database." http://supremecourtdatabase.org.

Spiegelhalter, D. J., N. G. Best, B. P. Carlin, and A. Van der Linde. 2002. "Bayesian Measures of Model Complexity and Fit (with Discussion)." *Journal of the Royal Statistical Society (Series B)* 64(4):583–616.

Spriggs, II, James F. and Thomas G. Hansford. 2001. "Explaining the Overruling of U.S. Supreme Court Precedent." *Journal of Politics* 63(63):1091–1111.

Staton, Jeffrey K. 2010. *Judicial Power and Strategic Communication in Mexico*. New York: Cambridge University Press.

Staton, Jeffrey K. and Georg Vanberg. 2008. "The Value of Vagueness: Delegation, Defiance, and Judicial Opinions." *American Journal of Political Science* 52(3):504–519.

Steigerwalt, Amy. 2010. *Battle Over the Bench: Senators, Interest Groups, and Lower Court Confirmations*. Charlottesville: University of Virginia Press.

Stein, Robert A. 2015. "Strengthening Federalism: The Uniform State Law Movement in the United States." *Minnesota Law Review* 99: 2253–2272.

Stephens, Alexander Hamilton. 1868. *A Constitutional View of the Late War Between the States*. Vol. 1 National Publishing Company.

Stephenson, Jr., Donald Grier. 1999. *Campaigns & the Court*. New York: Columbia University Press.

Stimson, James A., Michael B. MacKuen and Robert S. Erikson. 1995. "Dynamic Representation." *American Political Science Review* 89(3): 543–565.

Story, Joseph. 1833. "Story's Commentaries." *American Jurist & Law Magazine* 9:241.

Swers, Michele L. 1998. "Are women more likely to vote for women's issue bills than their male colleagues?" *Legislative Studies Quarterly* 23(3):435–448.

Tahk, Alexander. 2015. "Properties of Ideal-Point Estimators." Paper presented at the Conference on Ideal Point Models, Massachusetts Institute of Technology, Cambridge, MA.

Taylor, John. 1920. *Cinstruction Construed, and Constitutional Vindicated*. Richmond, VA: The Lawbook Exchange, Ltd.

Teles, Steven M. 2008. *The Rise of the Conservative Legal Movement*. Princeton: Princeton University Press.

TenBroek, Jacobus. 1965. *Equal Under Law*. New York: Collier Books.

Thomas, Kenneth R. 2014. *The Constitution of the United States: Analysis and Interpretation*. Congressional Research Service: Government Printing Office.

Truman, Harry S. 1948. "Special Message to the Congress on Civil Rights." Online by Gerhard Peters and John T. Woolley, The American Presidency Project. www.presidency.ucsb.edu/ws/?pid=13006.

Tushnet, Mark. 2000. *Taking the Constitution Away from the Courts*. Princeton, NJ: Princeton University Press.

Tushnet, Mark V. 1987. *The NAACP's Legal Strategy against Segregated Education, 1925-1950*. Chapel Hill: University of North Carolina Press.

Urofsky, Melvin I. 1997. *Division and Discord: The Supreme Court under Stone and Vinson, 1941–1953*. Columbia: University of South Carolina Press.

van Deemter, Kees. 2010. *Not Exactly: In Praise of Vagueness*. New York: Oxford University Press.

Vanberg, Georg. 2005. *The Politics of Constitutional Review in Germany*. New York: Cambridge University Press.

Vose, Clement E. 1958. "Litigation as a Form of Pressure Group Activity." *The Annals of the American Academy of Political and Social Science* 319(1):20–31.

Wahlbeck, Paul J. 1997. "The Life of the Law: Judicial Politics and Legal Change." *Journal of Politics* 59(3):778–802.

Walker, Thomas G., Lee Epstein and William J. Dixon. 1988. "On the Mysterious Demise of Consensual Norms in the United States Supreme Court." *The Journal of Politics* 50(2):361–389.

Weingast, Barry R. 2005. Persuasion, Preference Change, and Critical Junctures: The Microfoundations of a Macroscopic Concept. In *Preferences and Situations: Points of Intersection Between Historical and Rational Choice In*, edited by Barry R. Weingast and Ira Katznelson. New York: Russell Sage Foundation.

Westerland, Chad. 2003. "Who Owns the Majority Opinion? An Examination of Policymaking on the U.S. Supreme Court." Presented at the Annual Meeting of the American Political Science Association.

Westerland, Chad, Jeffrey A. Segal, Lee Epstein, Charles M. Cameron and Scott Comparato. 2010. "Strategic Defiance and Compliance in the U.S. Courts of Appeals." *American Journal of Political Science* 54(4):891–905.

Wildavsky, Aaron. 1969. "The two presidencies." *Trans-Action* 4:230–243.

Wilkes, Donald E., Jr. 1973. "The New Federalism in Criminal Procedure: State Court Evasion of the Burger Court." *Kentucky Law Journal* 62:421.

Willis, Hugh Evander. 1928. "When is a Business Affected by a Public Interest?" *Indiana Law Journal* 3(5):3.

Wilson, John Laird. 1878. *Battles of America by Sea and Land with Biographies of Naval and Military Commanders. Vol. III: The Great Civil War James S. Virtue. New York: Patterson & Neilson.*

Wright, Gerald. 2004. "Representation in America's Legislatures." *Indiana University: National Science Foundation Grant 9.*

Yalof, David Alistair. 2001. *Pursuit of Justices: Presidential Politics and the Selection of Supreme Court Nominees.* University of Chicago Press.

Yates, Jeff and Andrew Whitford. 1998. "Presidential Power and the United States Supreme Court." *Political Research Quarterly* 51(2):539–550. Research Note.

Index